IN THE LANDS OF THE ROMANOVS

In the Lands of the Romanovs

An Annotated Bibliography of First-hand
English-language Accounts
of the Russian Empire (1613-1917)

Anthony Cross

http://www.openbookpublishers.com

© 2014 Anthony Cross

The text of this book is licensed under a Creative Commons Attribution 4.0 International license (CC BY 4.0). This license allows you to share, copy, distribute and transmit the text; to adapt it and to make commercial use of it providing that attribution is made to the author (but not in any way that suggests that he endorses you or your use of the work). Attribution should include the following information:

Cross, Anthony, *In the Land of the Romanovs: An Annotated Bibliography of First-hand English-language Accounts of the Russian Empire (1613-1917)*, Cambridge, UK: Open Book Publishers, 2014. http://dx.doi.org/10.11647/OBP.0042

Please see the list of illustrations for attribution relating to individual images. Every effort has been made to identify and contact copyright holders and any omissions or errors will be corrected if notification is made to the publisher. As for the rights of the images from Wikimedia Commons, please refer to the Wikimedia website (for each image, the link to the relevant page can be found in the list of illustrations).

In order to access detailed and updated information on the license, please visit: http://www.openbookpublishers.com/product/268#copyrighttab

Further details about CC BY licenses are available at: http://creativecommons.org/licenses/by/4.0

ISBN Paperback: 978-1-78374-057-4
ISBN Hardback: 978-1-78374-058-1
ISBN Digital (PDF): 978-1-78374-059-8
ISBN Digital ebook (epub version): 978-1-78374-060-4
ISBN Digital ebook (mobi version): 978-1-78374-061-1
DOI: 10.11647/OBP.0042

Cover image: Johnson's Europe, in A.J. Johnson, *Johnson's New Illustrated (Steel Plate) Family Atlas* (New York: Johnson and Ward, 1864), Wikimedia http://commons.wikimedia.org/wiki/File:Johnson,_A.J._Europe._1864.jpg

All paper used by Open Book Publishers is SFI (Sustainable Forestry Initiative), and PEFC (Programme for the Endorsement of Forest Certification Schemes) Certified.

Printed in the United Kingdom and United States by Lightning Source for Open Book Publishers

Contents

List of Illustrations	vii
Preface	xiii
Introduction	1
1. Reigns of the First Romanovs: Mikhail Fedorovich (1613-1645), Aleksei Mikhailovich (1645-1676), and Fedor Alekseevich (1676-1682)	63
2. Reigns of Peter I (1682-1725), including joint reign with Ivan V (1682-1696) and regency of Sophia (1686-1689), and Catherine I (1725-1727)	71
3. Reigns of Peter II (1727-1730), Anna Ivanovna (1730-1740), Ivan VI (1740-1741), and Elizabeth (1741-1762)	81
4. Reigns of Peter III (1762) and Catherine II (1762-1796)	91
5. Reign of Paul I (1796-1801)	115
6. Reign of Alexander I (1801-1825)	119
7. Reign of Nicholas I (1825-1855)	149
8. The Crimean War (28 March 1854-27 April 1856)	185
9. Reign of Alexander II (1855-1881)	227
10. Reign of Alexander III (1881-1894)	273
11. Reign of Nicholas II (1894-1917)	311
Bibliography of Bibliographies	405
Index of Authors	407

Digital Resources

A free, socially enhanced version of this book is available via our website. We encourage you to help develop this collaborative edition by adding new entries and creating links to existing resources.
You can access this online version via:

>http://www.openbookpublishers.com/isbn/9781783740574

List of Illustrations

1	Portrait of Aleksei Mikhailovich, in Samuel Collins, *The Present State of Russia* (London: J. Winter for D. Newman, 1671). Wellcome Trust, London: http://wellcomeimages.org/indexplus/obf_images/52/6c/5505fbbb60e719803d9da656fffc.jpg	3
2	Peter I in Russian dress during the Grand Embassy (n.d.), artist unknown. Wikimedia Commons: http://commons.wikimedia.org/wiki/File:Peter_I_in_russian_dress_during_Grand_Embassy.jpg	4
3	Portrait of William Tooke (1820), engraving by Joseph Collyer the Younger, after Martin Archer Shee. National Portrait Gallery, London. Wikimedia Commons: http://commons.wikimedia.org/wiki/File:William_Tooke.jpg	7
4	Portrait of Claire Clairmont (1819) by Amelia Curran. Oil on canvas. Reproduced in Robert Gittings and Jo Manton, *Claire Clairmont and the Shelleys* (Oxford: Oxford University Press, 1992). Wikimedia Commons: http://commons.wikimedia.org/wiki/File:Claire_Clairmont,_by_Amelia_Curran.jpg	9
5	St Petersburg, Senate Square, 14 December, 1825 (1825-26), by Karl Kolman. Reproduced in *Literaturnye mesta Rossii* (Moskva: Sovetskaia Rossiia, 1987). Wikimedia Commons: http://commons.wikimedia.org/wiki/File:Peterburg,_Senate_Square,_1825,_dec._14.jpg	10
6	Portrait of Elizabeth, Countess of Craven, later Margravine of Anspach (1778), by George Romney. Oil on canvas. Wikimedia Commons: http://commons.wikimedia.org/wiki/File:ElizabethCraven.jpg	11
7	Count Francesco Algarotti (1745), by Jean-Étienne Liotard. Pastel on parchment. Rijksmuseum, Amsterdam. Wikimedia Commons: http://commons.wikimedia.org/wiki/File:Jean-%C3%89tienne_Liotard_-_Portret_van_Graaf_Francesco_Algarotti.jpg	12
8	John Henniker-Major, 2nd Baron Henniker (1780s-90s), by Henry Hudson, after George Romney. Mezzotint. National Portrait Gallery, London. Wikimedia Commons: http://commons.wikimedia.org/wiki/File:2ndLordHenniker.jpg	13

9	William Coxe, Russian edition of his *Travels into Poland, Russia, Sweden and Denmark* (Moscow: I. Smirnov, 1837). Wikimedia Commons: http://bit.ly/1kJGgwN	14
10 a	Title page of the 1799 German edition of Peter Simon Pallas, *Bemerkungen auf einer Reise in die südlichen Statthalterschaften des Russischen Reichs in den Jahren 1793 und 1794* (Leipzig: Gottfried Martini, 1799). Stadtgeschichtliches Museum, Leipzig. Wikimedia Commons: http://commons.wikimedia.org/wiki/File:Travels_through_the_southern_Provinces_of_the_Russian_Empire-deutsch.jpg	16
10 b	Title page of the 1812 English edition of Peter Simon Pallas, *Travels through the southern Provinces of the Russian Empire, in the years 1793 and 1794* (London: John Stockdale, 1812). Stadtgeschichtliches Museum, Leipzig. Wikimedia Commons: http://commons.wikimedia.org/wiki/File:Travels_through_the_southern_Provinces_of_the_Russian_Empire-english.jpg	16
11	*A map of Kamtschatka engraved from the russian map by Tho. Jefferys*, in Stepan Petrovich Krasheninnikov: *The history of Kamtschatka and the Kurilski Islands with the countries adjacent; Illustrated with maps and cuts. Published at Petersbourg in the Russian language by order of her Imperial Majesty and translated into English by James Grieve* (Glocester: printed by R. Raikes for T. Jefferys, 1764). Wikimedia Commons: http://commons.wikimedia.org/wiki/File:A_map_of_Kamtschatka_engraved_from_the_russian_map_by_Tho_Jefferys.jpg	17
12	Edmund Spencer, *Travels in Circassia, Krim-tartary, &c: including a steam voyage down the Danube, from Vienna to Constantinople, and round the Black Sea* (London: H. Colburn, 1839). Wikimedia Commons: http://commons.wikimedia.org/wiki/File:Circassian._Travels_in_Circassia,_Krim-tartary,_%26c.jpg	23
13	British bombardment of the fortress Bomarsund (Aland Islands) during the Crimean war (1854), artist unknown. Wikimedia Commons: http://commons.wikimedia.org/wiki/File:Bombardment_of_Bomarsund.jpg	28
14	Only known photograph of Mary Seacole (1805-1881), taken c.1873 by Maull & Company in London, photographer unknown. Wikimedia Commons: http://commons.wikimedia.org/wiki/File:Seacole_photo.jpg	31
15	Sketch of Mary Seacole's "British Hotel" in the Crimea (n.d.), by Lady Alicia Blackwood. Wikimedia Commons: http://commons.wikimedia.org/wiki/File:Blackwood_Seacole_sketch.png	31
16	William Simpson photographed by Roger Fenton on Cathcart Hill before Sevastopol, Crimea, 1855. Adrian Lipscomb collection. Wikimedia Commons: http://commons.wikimedia.org/wiki/File:William_Simpson_in_the_Crimea.jpg	32

List of Illustrations ix

17	Balaklava harbour (Crimea) [1855], photograph by Roger Fenton. Wikimedia Commons: http://commons.wikimedia.org/wiki/File:Cossack_bay.Balaklava_1855.3a06075r.jpg	32
18	Portrait of Donald Mackenzie Wallace (no later than 1905), photographer unknown. Wikimedia Commons: http://commons.wikimedia.org/wiki/File:Portrait_of_Donald_Mackenzie_Wallace.jpg	34
19 a-b	Title page and photograph of a first edition of Florence Crauford Grove, *The Frosty Caucasus* (1875). Wikimedia Commons: http://commons.wikimedia.org/wiki/File:The_Frosty_Caucasus,_front_page.jpg and http://en.wikipedia.org/wiki/File:The_Frosty_Caucasus_%281875%29.jpg	35
20	"The Great Game: the Afghan Emir Sher Ali Khan with his 'friends' Russia and Great Britain" (30 November, 1878), cartoon by Sir John Tenniel. Wikimedia Commons: http://commons.wikimedia.org/wiki/File:Great_Game_cartoon_from_1878.jpg	37
21	Portrait of Moses Montefiore (n.d.), artist unknown. Wikimedia Commons: http://commons.wikimedia.org/wiki/File:Moses_Montefiore.jpg	41
22	Tolstoi organising famine relief in Samara (1891), photographer unknown. Wikimedia Commons: http://commons.wikimedia.org/wiki/File:Tolstoy_organising_famine_relief_in_Samara,_1891.jpg	43
23	Thomas Stevens on his penny-farthing bicycle. Image from his *Around the world on a bicycle* (London: Sampson Low, Marston, Searle and Rivington, 1887). Cornell University Library. Wikimedia Commons: http://commons.wikimedia.org/wiki/File:Thomas_Stevens_bicycle.jpg	44
24	Harry de Windt (no image credit). Photograph published in his *From Paris to New York by land* (Thomas Nelson & Sons: London, Edinburgh, Dublin and New York, 1903). Projects Gutenberg: http://www.gutenberg.org/files/26007/26007-h/26007-h.htm. Wikimedia Commons: http://commons.wikimedia.org/wiki/File:Harry_de_Windt.jpg	46
25	The Governor-General of India George Curzon with his wife Mary in Delhi (29 December 1902), photographer unknown. Published in Joachim K. Bautze, *Das koloniale Indien. Photographien von 1855 bis 1910* (Köln: Fackelträger Verlag, 2007), p. 211. Wikimedia Commons: http://commons.wikimedia.org/wiki/File:George_Curzon_and_Mary_Curzon_on_the_elephant_Lakshman_Prasad_1902-12-29_in_Delhi.jpg	48
26	Portrait of Mandell Creighton (1902) by Hubert von Herkomer. Oil on canvas. National Portrait Gallery, London. Wikimedia Commons: http://commons.wikimedia.org/wiki/File:Mandell_Creighton_by_Sir_Hubert_von_Herkomer.jpg	49

27   A Christmas dinner on the heights before Sevastopol (Capt Burnaby   54
     is the fifth figure from the left), by J.A. Vinter. Tinted lithograph.
     Published in *The Seat of War in the East* (London: Paul & Dominic
     Colnaghi & Co., 13 & 14 Pall Mall East; Paris: Goupil & Cie, 1855).
     Wikimedia Commons: http://commons.wikimedia.org/wiki/File:
     A_Christmas_dinner_on_the_heights_before_Sebastopol.jpg

28   Pen portrait of Stephen Graham, by Vernon Hill. Published in   55
     Stephen Graham, *Changing Russia* (London: John Lane, 1913),
     frontispiece.

29   Mikhail Fedorovich, first tsar of the house of Romanov (n.d.), artist   62
     unknown. Wikimedia Commons: http://commons.wikimedia.org/
     wiki/File:Michael_titularnik.jpg

30   Aleksei Mikhailovich (n.d.), artist unknown. Hermitage Museum,   62
     St Petersburg. Wikimedia Commons: http://commons.wikimedia.
     org/wiki/File:Alexis_I_of_Russia.jpg

31   Fedor Alekseevich (1685), by Ivan Saltanov, Erofei Elin and   62
     Luka Smolianov. The Moscow Kremlin. Wikimedia Commons:
     http://commons.wikimedia.org/wiki/File:Feodor_III_by_Ivan_
     Saltanov_-_detail.JPG

32   Peter the Great (1698), by Godfrey Kneller. Oil on canvas. Royal   70
     Collection. Wikimedia Commons: http://upload.wikimedia.org/
     wikipedia/commons/9/9b/Peter_I_by_Kneller.jpg

33   Catherine I (1717), by Jean-Marc Nattier. Oil on canvas. Hermitage 70
     Museum, St Petersburg. Wikimedia Commons: http://commons.
     wikimedia.org/wiki/File:Catherine_I_of_Russia_by_Nattier.jpg

34   Peter II of Russia (circa 1730), by Ioann Vedekind. Wikimedia   80
     Commons: http://commons.wikimedia.org/wiki/File:Peter_II_of_
     Russia_by_Vedekind.jpg

35   Anna Ivanovna (circa 1730), artist unknown. Moscow State Historical 80
     Museum. Wikimedia Commons: http://commons.wikimedia.org/
     wiki/File:Anna_of_Russia_by_anonymous_%281730s,_GIM%29.jpg

36   Empress Elizabeth (n.d.), by Ivan Argunov. Tretyakov Gallery,   80
     Moscow. Wikimedia Commons: http://commons.wikimedia.org/
     wiki/File:Ivan_Argunov_02.jpeg

37   Great Duke Peter Fedorovich, later Peter III (1758), by Fedor   90
     Rokotov. Oil on canvas. Tretyakov Gallery, Moscow. Wikimedia
     Commons: http://commons.wikimedia.org/wiki/File:Peter_III_of_
     Russia_by_Rokotov.jpg

38   Catherine II the Legislatress in the Temple of the Goddess of Justice   90
     (1783), by Dmitrii Levitskii. Oil on canvas. Russian Museum, St
     Petersburg. Wikimedia Commons: http://commons.wikimedia.
     org/wiki/File:Dmitry_Levitsky_-_Portrait_of_Catherine_II_
     the_Legislatress_in_the_Temple_of_the_Goddess_of_Justice_-_
     Google_Art_Project.jpg

List of Illustrations xi

39   Paul I, Emperor of Russia (n.d.), by Vladimir Borovikovskii. Oil on canvas. Wikimedia Commons: http://commons.wikimedia.org/wiki/File:Borovikovsky_Pavel_I.jpg?uselang=en-gb   114

40   Alexander I (c.1814/1815), by François de Gérard. Reproduced in Matti Klinge (ed.), *Helsingin yliopisto 1640–1990: Keisarillinen Aleksanterin yliopisto 1808–1917* (Helsinki: Otava, 1989), p. 15. Wikimedia Commons: http://commons.wikimedia.org/wiki/File:Alexander_I_by_Gerard.jpg   118

41   Nicholas I (1856), by Vladimir Dmitrievich Sverchkov. Oil on canvas. Hermitage Museum, St Petersburg. Wikimedia Commons: http://commons.wikimedia.org/wiki/File:Au_service_des_Tsars_-_Nicolas_1er_-_01.jpg   148

42   Charge of the Light Cavalry Brigade, 25th Oct. 1854, under Major General the Earl of Cardigan, print by William Simpson (1 March 1855). Published by Goupil & Cie, Paris, and Day & Son, London. The Library of Congress. Wikimedia Commons: http://commons.wikimedia.org/wiki/File:William_Simpson_-_Charge_of_the_light_cavalry_brigade,_25th_Oct._1854,_under_Major_General_the_Earl_of_Cardigan.png   184

43   Alexander II (n.d.), photographer unknown. Wikimedia Commons: http://commons.wikimedia.org/wiki/File:Alexander_II_of_Russia_photo.jpg   226

44   Alexander III (n.d.), photograph by Félix Nadar. Wikimedia Commons: http://commons.wikimedia.org/wiki/File:Alexander_III._Czar_Of_Russia_Nadar.jpg   272

45   Nicholas II (1898), photograph by A. A. Pasetti. Wikimedia Commons: http://commons.wikimedia.org/wiki/File:Tsar_Nicholas_II_-1898.jpg   310

Preface

The compilation of bibliographies is a long and exacting business. To hurry is inevitably to invite numerous omissions, although slowness is obviously not in itself a virtue, but it allows more generously for serendipity, the fortuitous discovery of unsuspected relevant material. This bibliography has been decades in its maturation. Its origins can be traced as far back as the late 1960s, when I was invited to become the General Editor of a reprint series for Frank Cass Publishers, entitled "Russia through European Eyes" and producing eleven titles by 1972. It was a period when I began to collect travel accounts of Russia, initially desultorily but soon assiduously, and also completed the anthology *Russia under western eyes, 1517-1825* (1971) that reflected early travellers' reactions to the Muscovy/Russia they visited not only in words but in drawings and paintings. Some years later I compiled for IDC Publishers of Leiden a finding list of some 400 accounts, 250 of which were made available on microfiche and described in *Russia through the eyes of foreigners: travel and personal accounts from the sixteenth century to the October Revolution 1917*.

My intention to produce a bibliography of personal accounts of Russia had stalled, however, with the appearance of Harry W. Nerhood's *To Russia and return: an annotated bibliography of travelers' English-language accounts of Russia from the ninth century to the present*, published in 1968 by Ohio State University Press. If it had even approached its compiler's intention to "bring together in one place the pertinent information on all available reports of journeys to Russia that have been published in the English language", my work would have been unnecessary. Although frequently cited as comprehensive and authoritative, Nerhood's bibliography fails on almost every count and is an unreliable guide for any researcher or, indeed, collector. Leaving aside the inaccuracies in describing editions, dating journeys, and annotating contents, suffice it to say that for the three centuries or so during which the Romanovs occupied the Russian throne it registers some 630 accounts, which is just over half the total included and described in the present work.

Fortunately, there are a number of bibliographies and other sources, published both earlier and later, that supplement and correct Nerhood and they are listed in my "Bibliography of bibliographies". Nonetheless, there is none that shares the same aims and objectives of the present work.

I have registered 1243 personal accounts, ranging from a few letters or diary entries to mighty tomes, that have appeared in book form – I exclude journal publications and manuscript sources which in an ideal world and with generous assistance would be collected. The bibliography is not simply or only one of travel accounts, although travellers, be they tourists or explorers, dominate. The emphasis is on the personal account, be the author diplomat or merchant, engineer or craftsman, physician or clergyman, gardener or artist, governess or tutor, or much else, of a residence in or visit to Russia, a Russia widely understood and in keeping with the historical moment.

Many of the books did not of course appear in the lifetimes of the writers and the transition from archive to printed book continues apace. Nevertheless, the bibliography is arranged chronologically in accord with the date of the writer's arrival in Russia or the beginning of an account, and is subdivided, with the exception of the Crimean War, according to the reigns of the various Romanovs. It provides a clear impression of the significant quantitative increase from the seventeenth century through the eighteenth and nineteenth centuries and ending with the twenty-two-year reign of Nicholas II, abruptly truncated, but witnessing a veritable flood of works during years that encompassed wars and revolutions on an unprecedented scale and attracted for many and varied reasons the eyes and minds of the world.

It is the first English edition of a work that is registered and subsequent editions are only noted if they introduce significant changes or additions. Numerous accounts that were written by Americans and many more that have been translated into English, principally from German and French, are of course included. However, the first edition of a work as originally published in America is given only if there was no subsequent English edition. The original titles of translated works are provided where appropriate.

The award of a Leverhulme Emeritus Fellowship in 2008 was the catalyst that allowed a mass of handwritten cards and notebooks to be brought into initial order with the secretarial assistance of Teresa Jones. I am truly grateful to the Leverhulme Trust for the award that also enabled me to visit St Petersburg and inspect rare editions in the incomparable collection of Rossica in the State Public Library. It also, most importantly, allowed me to enlist as my research assistant Robin Mills, whose input has been invaluable, particularly for the Crimean War and Nicholas II sections. When my work on the entries was complete I was fortunate to have my Author Index expertly prepared by Charlotte Simpson.

All the books listed have been examined *de visu* with a few exceptions or, in the case of rare American editions, from digitalized versions. The vast majority of the books are held in the British Library and in the Cambridge University Library, where I am particularly indebted to the staff in the Rare Books Room for their expertise and unfailing patience in dealing with a seemingly unending flow of requests. I am grateful to Julie Curtis in Oxford and Angela Byrne in Dublin for tracking down particularly elusive items.

The following details have been registered: name of author (anonymous authors subsequently identified are in square brackets), title, place of publication, publisher and year, number of pages or of volumes. Each entry is annotated with brief details of author, including dates of birth and death whenever possible, the itinerary and specific dates of journey/residence in Russia (with pages indicated). The five items from the reign of Catherine II marked with an asterisk are the products of armchair travellers and are included as a warning to those who might regard them as authentic. Three later accounts, the authenticity of which is open to doubt, are also similarly indicated. Dates are according to the New Style, but the designations of the two 1917 revolutions as the February and the October have been retained.

Finally, it is a privilege to acknowledge the generous financial contribution that the Cambridge University Library has made towards the publication of this bibliography and to express my gratitude to Open Book Publishers of Cambridge and its managing director Dr Alessandra Tosi for their willingness to take on the project and bring it to a rapid and successful conclusion.

Cambridge, January 2014

Introduction

I

When in 1613, following the Time of Troubles, the first Romanov came to the throne of Muscovy, sixty years had elapsed since, in the words of Richard Hakluyt, "the strange and wonderful Discoverie of Russia" by the English. It was Hakluyt who gathered together in his *Principal navigations, voiages, [traffiques,] and discoueries of the English nation* (first published in 1589 and again in expanded form in 1598-1600) the corpus of writing left by the first English explorers, traders and diplomats for, as he further remarked, "I meddle in this worke with the Navigations onely of our owne nation".[1] The accounts, beginning with that of Richard Chancellor, who survived the ill-fated expedition led by Sir Hugh Willoughby to make his way from the White Sea to Moscow for a momentous audience with Ivan IV in 1553, also include the several journeys that took Anthony Jenkinson down the Volga to Astrakhan and into Persia from 1557, as well as later embassies sent by Queen Elizabeth that produced the poetic epistles of George Turbervile, accompanying ambassador Thomas Randolph in 1568, with their characterization of the Muscovites as "a people passing rude, to vice vile inclin'd", and the no less damning appraisal by Giles Fletcher in his *Of the Russe commonwealth* (1591) that the Muscovy Company, fearing it would harm the all important trading privileges, scrambled to suppress and Hakluyt was careful to edit (as he had also done with Turbervile).[2]

---

1 Richard Hakluyt, *The principal navigations voyages traffiques & discoveries of the English nation, made by sea or overland to the remote & farthest distant quarters of the earth at any time within the compasse of these 1600 yeares*, vol. I (London: J.M. Dent, 1907), pp. 6-7.
2 For an excellent commentary and anthology, see Lloyd E. Berry and Robert O. Crummey (eds.), *Rude & barbarous kingdom: Russia in the accounts of sixteenth-century English voyagers* (Madison, Milwaukee and London: University of Wisconsin Press, 1968).

http://dx.doi.org/10.11647/OBP.0042.12

It was to a non-English source, however, that Turbervile had reverently referred at the end of his third epistle, advising his addressee Parker "if thou list to know the Russes well,/ To Sigismundus book repair, who all the trueth can tell". The renowned Austrian diplomat and scholar Freiherr Sigmund von Herberstein's *Rerum moscoviticarum commentarii*, published in Vienna in 1549 and pre-dating the English "discovery", informed Turbervile and Fletcher and many others who knew it in its Latin original (for only in the mid-nineteenth century was an English version available). It was nevertheless the diversity and quality of the English contribution that were more widely appreciated in Elizabethan England, and later. John Milton, for instance, in his *Brief history of Muscovia* paid tribute to the "many things not unprofitable to the knowledge of Nature, and other Observations" that had been a consequence of the early voyages, if perturbed by what he considered "the excessive love of Gain and Traffick [that] had animated the design".[3]

Milton's work, in which his narrative had finished with the accession of Mikhail Fedorovich, was written probably in the 1650s but published posthumously only in 1682, a year momentous in Russian history as marking the beginning of the joint rule of Peter I and his half-brother Ivan V under the regency of their sister Sophia. The previous seventy years of Romanov rule had not, however, witnessed a comparable wealth of English writings on Russia and Anglo-Russian relations deteriorated steadily during the first decades and were broken off following the execution of Charles I in 1649. The sixteenth century had provided examples of authors who inevitably were to loom large down the reigns, voyager/explorer, diplomat, merchant, and under the first Romanovs we find, for instance, among the relatively few English accounts that of William Gourdon, a Hull pilot in the service of the Muscovy Company exploring the northern rivers of Siberia and also describing life among the native Samoeds in 1614-15 (A1); and of the famous botanist John Tradescant the Elder, detailing in his diary the specimens he was collecting near Archangel in 1618 (A2). It was from the White Sea and Archangel that embassies had made their way to Moscow since the middle of the sixteenth century and the 1663-64 embassy of Charles Howard, the Earl of Carlisle found its chronicler not in the earl's private secretary, the poet Andrew Marvell, but in a Swiss-born attendant in his suite (A9).

---

3 John Milton, *A brief history of Moscovia and other less-known countries lying eastward of Russia as far as Cathay. Gathered from the writings of several eye-witnesses* (London: printed by M. Flesher for Brabazon Aylmer, 1682), p. 69.

The embassy would encounter in the capital two men pursuing professions that would loom large among authors on Russia at least down the eighteenth century – the foreign doctor in Russian service, represented by Samuel Collins, body physician to Tsar Aleksei Mikhailovich (fig. 1) from 1660 to 1669, and author of *The present state of Russia*, based on letters he had sent from Moscow to the eminent scientist Robert Boyle and posthumously published in 1671 (A6); and the mercenary or soldier of fortune, exemplified at his most successful in the Scot Patrick Gordon, whose diaries of his long years in Russian service from 1661 to his death in 1699, during which he rose to the rank of general and confidant of the young Tsar Peter, were partially published in 1859 and only now are in the process of appearing in full (A7-8).

Fig. 1. Portrait of Aleksei Mikhailovich, in Samuel Collins, *The Present State of Russia* (London: J. Winter for D. Newman, 1671). Wellcome Trust, London.

Of these accounts only those of Gourdon, Collins and Carlisle were published in the seventeenth century, when the meagre original English offerings were augmented by foreign accounts, among which Adam Olearius's *Voyages & travels,* published in English translation in 1662 (A4), rivalled Herberstein's in its influence on contemporary readers. However, after the excitement aroused by the Elizabethan accounts and the arrival of the first Muscovite embassies in London, English interest in, and knowledge of, Russia stagnated, as England lost its trading advantages to Holland.

II

It was an interest that was to quicken once more, when it became known that Peter I, reigning alone since 1696, intended to travel to the West. After a period of some fifteen years from the beginning of his joint rule to the departure in 1697 of the Great Embassy, during which the translation of a French Jesuit's account of extensive travels that took him through Muscovy to the frontiers of China was the sole offering to the English public (B1), a flurry of publications between 1698 and c.1705 reflected something of the excitement that preceded the Tsar's arrival, continued during his stay, and never really abated, despite the deterioration of relations in the last decade of his reign.[4]

Fig. 2 Peter I in Russian dress during the Grand Embassy (n.d.), artist unknown.

---

4 For the continuing impact of Peter on the British consciousness, see Anthony Cross, *Peter the Great through British eyes: perceptions and representations of the tsar since 1698* (Cambridge: Cambridge University Press, 2000).

Many of these publications obviously do not fall within the parameters of this bibliography, but of the seven publications that do, three are by English authors, the first, the log of a ship's captain (B8), while the second, a single folio sheet published in 1699 (B9), signals the arrival in Russian service of the English master shipwright, a category of immense importance in the creation of Peter's navy, but not figuring otherwise among memoirists of the period. It is, however, the third work that deserves perhaps special mention, although it is never included in discussions of "travel" literature. The anonymous "English gentleman" of the title page, who signs his preface as "T.C.", might claim to be the first of British "Grand Tourists" to visit Russia: *The new atlas, or, travels and voyages in Europe, Asia, Africa and America* (1698) is an account of nine years' travel, beginning in 1684, that eventually took the author to Moscow, travelling up the Volga from Astrakhan, and further sightseeing in Novgorod, Vologda and other towns before his departure for Poland (B2).

The eighteenth century, when Muscovy became Russia and its window on the West opened wide with the founding of St Petersburg, was soon to bring a greater number of accounts and also new categories of authors.

As a result of Peter the Great's recruitment drive in London during his visit in 1698 there was an influx of specialists into Russian service, particularly, as has already been suggested, those skilled in all aspects of shipbuilding and things maritime. Among them was Captain John Perry, recruited on a ten-year contract as a hydraulic engineer and working on various canal projects to link the Volga and the Don and Petersburg and the Volga. In 1716 he published *The state of Russia under the present Czar*, which proved one of the most influential works on Peter's "new" Russia, detailing the vicissitudes of working for the Russians while offering a sympathetic picture of the young Tsar attempting to reform a backward and recalcitrant nation (B10). The tradition of British specialists and craftsmen was very strong in the last decades of the century and included architects and landscape gardeners, stonemasons and smiths, instrument-makers and engineers, but few published accounts of their activities and experiences. The later nineteenth century in contrast presents a rich array of accounts by men who, for instance, were managers of factories and industrial enterprises in places far removed from the capital.

The status of the diplomat changed during Peter's reign when Anglo-Russian diplomatic relations were put on a firmer footing and the first permanent ambassadors were appointed (fig. 2). Charles Whitworth, appointed envoy-extraordinary in 1704 and to full ambassadorial rank in 1709, spent ten years in Russia and wrote on his return to London *An account of Russia as it was in the year 1710* (B16).

Distributed as a government briefing document on his return, it only found its way into print when published by Horace Walpole at his Strawberry Hill press in 1758. Even at that late date it may nonetheless be considered as the first such publication by a British diplomat under the Romanovs. Whitworth's example was followed without such a time-gap by *An account of Russia, 1767* by Sir George Macartney, printed soon after his return from his ambassadorship and again destined for a restricted circle of readers (D5). Whitworth and Macartney in common with all the British diplomatic representatives down the eighteenth century (and beyond) sent their regular dispatches and reports to the British government. These were eventually published, in not in their entirety, at the end of the following century through the efforts of the Imperial Russian Historical Society and with their mixture of court gossip, politics, military affairs and social events occupy an important and distinctive place in the bibliography (e.g. B15, C2, C20-23, D14). It was, however, the work of a German rather than British diplomat that had contemporary resonance, appearing in English translation as *The present state of Russia* in the last years of Peter's reign: the Hanoverian Resident in St Petersburg Friedrich Weber, also serving British interests after George I came to the throne in August 1714, edited his diary of the five years he was in Russia to produce an account that was particularly informative about the growth of the Tsar's new capital, "a wonder of the world" (B22).

Although the Muscovy Company had been established soon after the English first-footed in Russia, it was revitalised during the reign of Peter the Great as the Russia Company and began an era of unprecedented growth and prosperity down the eighteenth century. Known within Russia as the British Factory, it moved its headquarters from Archangel to St Petersburg in 1723 and its members provided the core of a rapidly growing British community in the new Russian capital that numbered more than 1500 residents by the end of Catherine II's reign. From the merchants of the Factory came two of the few accounts written and published by British authors in the first half of the eighteenth century. James Spilman's *A journey through Russia into*

Persia, published in 1742 (D11), was followed in 1754 by Jonas Hanway's far more substantial *Historical account of the British trade over the Caspian Sea: with the author's journal of travels from England through Russia into Persia* (D19). However, as the influence of the Russia Company waned during Alexander I's reign, only one or two further accounts of little significance emerged from the merchant milieu.

Far more productive were the Anglican clergymen, appointed by the Russia Company to tend to the well-being of the British community in St Petersburg, where the English church stands in the middle of what became known as the English Embankment, and soon thereafter in Cronstadt, and later in the nineteenth century in such places as Moscow, Archangel and Odessa. Many of the clergy combined care for their flock with scholarly pursuits. During Peter I's reign, Rev. Thomas Consett and during Catherine II's, Revs John Glen King and William Tooke (fig. 3) published works illuminating Russian Orthodoxy and Russian history as well as the contemporary scene.

Fig. 3 William Tooke (1820), engraving by Joseph Collyer the Younger, after Martin Archer Shee. National Portrait Gallery, London.

One of Tooke's notable publications after his return from Russia was a translation rather than an original work: Henry Storch's *Picture of Petersburgh* (1801) provided a comprehensive update on the flourishing state of the Russian capital nearly a hundred years after Weber's work (D64).

Doctors remained prominent, serving at the Russian court and in state institutions and educational establishments as well as in aristocratic households. Two Scots doctors, John Bell and John Cook, not only wrote but saw published in their lifetimes wide-ranging books that also qualify as travel accounts with their descriptions of their adventures as physicians attached to Russian embassies sent through Siberia to China and to Astrakhan and onto Persia respectively. Bell's *Travels from St. Petersburg in Russia, to diverse parts of Asia* (1763) earned the rare commendation of Dr Johnson and in emphasizing "the observations, which then appeared to me worth remarking, without attempting to embellish them, by taking any of the liberties of exaggeration, or invention, frequently imputed to travellers" (B23), Bell laid down a marker that many future travellers continued to ignore. Dr Thomas Dimsdale, perhaps the most widely known of British doctors in eighteenth-century Russia, was not in Russian service but was invited to St Petersburg on two occasions for a specific reason, the first most famously to inoculate Catherine II and her son the Tsarevich Pavel Petrovich against smallpox in 1768, a journey he subsequently described in his *Tracts on inoculation, written and published at St Petersburg in the year 1768* (1781) (D17). For the most part the British doctors in Russian service in the eighteenth century were non-publishing, the outstanding exception being Dr Matthew Guthrie, physician to the Noble Cadet Corps in St Petersburg during Catherine II's reign and making endless but anonymous contributions about Russian life to the Edinburgh journal *The Bee* in the 1790s, but notable as the "editor" of his wife's travels, published in London in 1802 as *A tour, performed in the years 1795-6, through the Taurida, or Crimea* and much read by British travellers journeying south from Moscow to the Crimea (D70).

The French-born Mrs Guthrie was but the last in a series of women whose impressions of Russia, invariably conveyed in the form of letters, were published during the eighteenth century. The British governess is perhaps more usually associated with the mid-nineteenth century, in fact and in fiction, but she makes her appearance at a very early stage as a published author on Russia. Elizabeth Justice spent three years as a governess in the family of a prosperous English merchant in the Russian capital during the reign of the Empress Anna Ivanovna, and after her return published in 1739 *Voyage to Russia*, and a second edition with additions in 1746, revealing her far from favourable reaction to many aspects of Russian life (C8). British governesses were to be much in demand among families of the Russian aristocracy, a consequence of the growth of Anglophilia towards the close of Catherine II's reign, but none followed Mrs Justice's lead – it is only of recent times that we have seen published the diaries of the Irish Wilmot sisters, who were companions to the famous Princess Dashkova in the early years of the nineteenth century (F3), and the fascinating if incomplete *Journals* of Claire Clairmont (fig. 4), Byron's mistress and mother of his daughter Augusta, who spent more than three years as a governess in Moscow from late 1823 (F93-94).

Fig. 4 Portrait of Claire Clairmont (1819) by Amelia Curran. Oil on canvas. Reproduced in Robert Gittings and Jo Manton, *Claire Clairmont and the Shelleys* (Oxford: Oxford University Press, 1992).

It was in the eighteenth century in accord with a widespread convention to preserve the anonymity of a female author that "a lady" was first used in a book's title in a specifically Anglo-Russian context. *Letters from a lady, who resided some years in Russia* was published in 1779, when the lady in question was known as Mrs Jane Vigor, although she had arrived in Russia in 1728 during the reign of Peter II as wife of the British Consul-General Thomas Ward and became after his death in 1731 the wife of the British Resident Claudius Rondeau (C3). It is as Lady Rondeau that she is often erroneously known, although she was plain Mrs, as she was when she married for a third time William Vigor, a Russian Company merchant, under which name in the year after her death were published *Eleven additional letters from Russia, in the reign of Peter II. By the late Mrs Vigor. Never before published* (1784) (C4). Mrs Ward-Rondeau-Vigor might be said to have initiated another significant tradition, that of the account, most frequently the letters, of a diplomat's wife, which describe court and social life and provide the intimate and gossipy details absent from the dispatches of their husbands. An outstanding later example are the letters of Mrs Anne Disbrowe, wife of the British minister plenipotentiary at the end of the reign of Alexander I who recounts events connected with the failed uprising of 14 December 1825 (F104; fig. 5).

Fig. 5 St Petersburg, Senate Square, 14 December, 1825 (1825-26), by Karl Kolman. Reproduced in *Literaturnye mesta Rossii* (Moskva: Sovetskaia Rossiia, 1987).

A lady to whom the title belonged by birth and marriage rather than by convention was Elizabeth Craven (née Berkeley), who included her encounters at the court of Catherine the Great in her adventurous *Journey through the Crimea to Constantinople* (1789) (D48). Lady Craven (fig. 6) was the first female British tourist to publish her letters at a time when for a number of reasons Russia appeared with increasing frequency in the itineraries of travellers.

The Grand Tour enjoyed its heyday in the eighteenth century and although Dr Johnson might assert that "the grand object of travelling is to see the shores of the Mediterranean",[5] the northern lands increasingly

---

5   James Boswell, *Life of Johnson* (Oxford: Oxford University Press, 1970), p. 742.

beckoned the more intrepid travellers, several of whom travelled, pen in hand and with an eye on possible publication.

Fig. 6 Portrait of Elizabeth, Countess of Craven, later Margravine of Anspach (1778), by George Romney. Oil on canvas.

Although the otherwise unidentified C.T. has been suggested as the first English publishing tourist in Russia from the first years of Peter I's reign, it was St Petersburg, founded in 1703, that was to prove the great tourist attraction, fulfilling the hopes of its first Governor-General Prince Alexander Menshikov that it "should become another Venice, to see which Foreigners would travel thither purely out of curiosity".[6] One of the first Englishmen to be so attracted was Sir Francis Dashwood of Hell-Fire Club notoriety, who as a young man of twenty-five took the opportunity to accompany the British envoy-extraordinary Baron Forbes to St Petersburg, where he spent three weeks in June 1733, recording in his diary that "I am well contented with my journey, and think it very much, worth any curious man's while, going to See, and to Stay there three weeks or a month, but after Curiosity is Satisfied, I think one could amuse oneself better, in more Southern Climates".[7] Dashwood's diary remained unpublished for two hundred years, but the letters of the Italian scholar Francesco Algarotti (fig. 7)

---

6 Quoted in [F.C. Weber], *The present state of Russia,* vol. I (London: printed for W. Taylor, W. and J. Innys, and J. Osborn, 1723), p. 4.
7 Dashwood's account has not appeared in book form and is not registered in the bibliography. See Sir Francis Dashwood, 'Diary of a visit to St Petersburg in 1733', ed. Betty Kemp, *Slavonic and East European Review,* XXXVIII (1959), p. 206.

to his English friend Lord Hervey, dating from 1738, might be considered the first published tourist's reaction to Peter's capital, appearing in English translation in 1769, already in the reign of the great Catherine (C15).

Fig. 7 Count Francesco Algarotti (1745), by Jean-Étienne Liotard. Pastel on parchment. Rijksmuseum, Amsterdam.

The first real example of an English Grand Tourist's account of St Petersburg, published soon after a visit, was the twenty-three-year old Sir Nathaniel Wraxall's *Cursory remarks made in a tour through some of the northern parts of Europe* (1775) that enjoyed three further editions, emphazing in its changing titles the "tour" (D25). A decade or so later, another traveller, the Scot Andrew Swinton, declared that "Russia begins now to make a part of the grand tour, and not the least curious or useful part of it" (D59), while the specific designation in a title of a "Northern tour" seems to have been used for the first time in 1775 on John Henniker's (fig. 8) manuscript diary, extracts from which have only recently been published (D26).

Fig. 8 John Henniker-Major, 2nd Baron Henniker (1780s-90s), by Henry Hudson, after George Romney. Mezzotint. National Portrait Gallery, London.

Russian "tours" began to appear with some regularity as the century drew to a close, but it is an indication of how little Russia was known, or perhaps books about it were read, that at least four accounts by "armchair travellers" were readily accepted as genuine – and sadly, continue to be so (and are therefore included in the bibliography as D18, D19, D58, D60 to alert readers to the mystification). In 1792 the *Critical Review* attacked "persons, who during the time of their supposed peregrinations, were scarcely ever out of their closets", and who, in the opinion of the reviewer, included poor Swinton, whose description of his visit to Petersburg and its environs in 1788-89 is in fact one of the more original and interesting accounts.[8] Ironically, two years later, the same journal heaped praise on the English translation of a work by the notorious plagiarist Pierre Nicholas Chantreau (D58).[9]

It was not only the tourists themselves who described their exploits in print but also the tutors, ironically known as "bear-leaders", who accompanied many of the young aristocrats. Two of their number, both Cambridge dons, gained particular renown in the late eighteenth and early nineteenth centuries: Rev. William Coxe's *Travels into Poland, Russia,*

---

8 *Critical Review*, V (1792), p. 294.
9 *Ibid.*, ns X (1794), p. 497. See A.G. Cross, 'The armchair traveller "in" Catherine II's Russia', in *Rossiia, Zapad, Vostok: vstrechnye techeniia*, ed. V.E. Bagno (St Petersburg: Nauka, 1996), pp. 313-21. More generally, Percy G. Adams, *Travellers and travel liars 1660-1800)* (Berkeley and Los Angeles: University of California Press, 1962).

Sweden and Denmark (fig. 9) enjoyed no less than six, ever expanding, editions between 1784 and 1803 and became, despite its size, a sort of Murray or Baedeker of its age (D28), while Rev. Edward Clarke's *Travels in various countries of Europe, Asia and Africa,* recording his hostile reaction to the Russia of Paul I, only appeared in 1810 (E4), but was much reprinted thereafter, perhaps in harmony with the increasing Russophobia of the reign of Nicholas I.

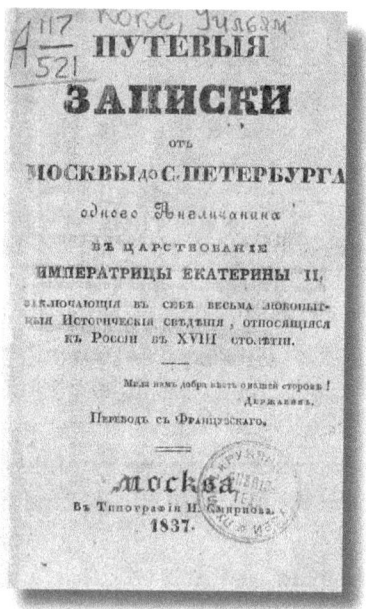

Fig. 9 William Coxe, Russian edition of his *Travels into Poland, Russia, Sweden and Denmark* (Moscow: I. Smirnov, 1837).

Coxe travelled by a much-used northern route from Poland into Russia and out via Finland to Sweden. Clarke went south from Moscow to the Crimea and the Sea of Azov and then on to Constantinople. This was a route that had been used since Russia's annexation of the Crimea in 1783 and increasingly so in the aftermath of the French Revolution. In the year before Catherine II made her famous journey to her newly acquired territories, Lady Craven had been entranced by the beauty of the region and the forty pages she devoted to the Crimea remained the only description to appear in book form in the eighteenth century, although in 1786 there had appeared in *Gentleman's Magazine* a much more informed essay by an anonymous British officer who had visited the area and advertised as "the only account of the Krimea ever given to the publick.¹⁰ Many British travellers followed Lady Craven to the Crimea particularly in the 1790s (after the end of the Russo-Turkish War of 1787-91) and the early years of the nineteenth century, but few were intent on publishing their impressions.¹¹ The remarkable and voluminous diaries of an Oxford don, John Parkinson, remained unpublished until 1971 (D66). Originally planning to travel across Russia to China, he and his charge, the future 1st Lord Skelmersdale, settled for a round trip that would take them to Siberia as far as Tobolsk and then south to the Caspian and the edge of the Caucasus before crossing to the Crimea and returning through Ukraine to Moscow and St Petersburg, in 1792-94.

It was on his way to the Crimea, at Sarepta on the Volga, that Parkinson met the eminent German naturalist and member of the Russian Academy of Sciences, Professor Peter Pallas. Pallas was leading an Academy expedition to the south of Russia which he described in a work first published in German but was widely known among British travellers in the first of several English versions, *Travels through the southern provinces of the Russian Empire, in the years 1793 and 1794* (1802-03) (D67; figs. 10a and b).

Pallas had entered Russian service in 1767 and was soon dispatched with a six-year expedition that took him deep to Siberia. A partial English translation under the title *Travels into Siberia and Tartary, provinces of the Russian empire* appeared in 1788-89 in John Trusler's *The habitable world described* (D11). It represents but one of a number of descriptions of scientific expeditions and voyages of exploration to appear in English with increasing frequency during Catherine's reign. Other examples include the French astronomer Jean-Baptiste Chappe d'Auteroche's *A journey into Siberia* (1770) that so infuriated the Empress by its negative portrayal of Russian civilization (C27), *Travels in Kamtschatka, during the years 1787 and 1788* (1790) by Jean-Baptiste-Barthélemy de Lesseps, a translator attached to the La Pérouse circumnavigation that had reached the Sea of Okhotsk in July 1786 (D53), and *An account of a geographical and astronomical expedition to the northern parts of Russia*, the so-called Joseph Billings's expedition of 1785-94, written by Martin Sauer, its secretary, and published in England in 1802 (D44).

---

10 *Gentleman's Magazine*, LVI, pt 2 (1786), pp. 644-48, 847-51.
11 See Anthony Cross, 'From the assassination of Paul I to Tilsit: the British in Russia and their travel writings (1801-1807)', *Journal of European Studies*, XLII (2012), no. 1, pp. 5- 21. http://dx.doi.org/10.1177/0047244111428842

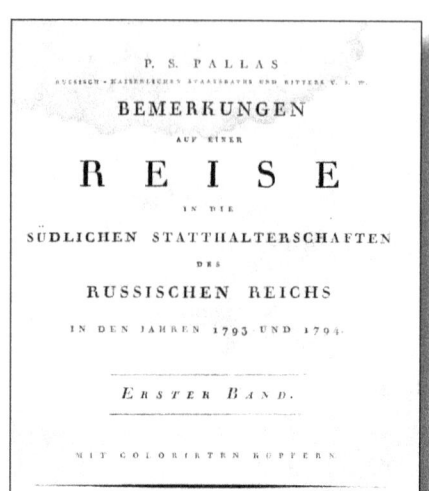 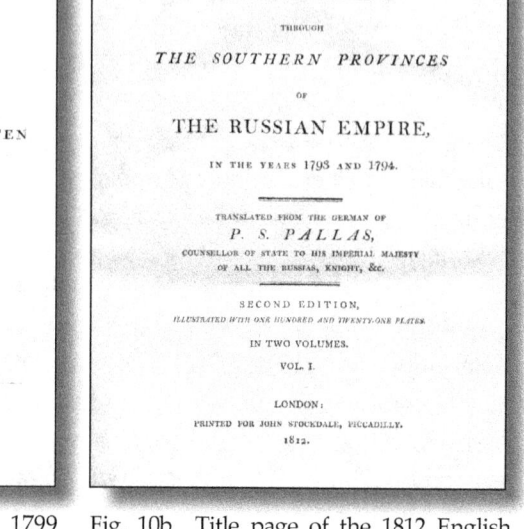

Fig. 10a Title page of the 1799 German edition of Peter Simon Pallas, *Bemerkungen auf einer Reise in die südlichen Statthalterschaften des Russischen Reichs in den Jahren 1793 und 1794* (Leipzig: Gottfried Martini, 1799), Stadtgeschichtliches Museum, Leipzig.

Fig. 10b Title page of the 1812 English edition of Peter Simon Pallas, *Travels through the southern Provinces of the Russian Empire, in the years 1793 and 1794* (London: John Stockdale, 1812), Stadtgeschichtliches Museum, Leipzig.

Such publications obviously belong to a tradition that had begun for English readers with Hakluyt and many works, admittedly mainly translations from foreign originals in Latin, German or French, had subsequently also appeared in England. Siberia had a particular attraction and fascination for writers and public alike. In the first half of the century an influential publication was *An historico-geographical description of the north and eastern parts of Europe and Asia; but more particularly of Russia, Siberia, and Great Tartary* (1738), written by the Swede Philipp von Strahlenberg, who was captured at the battle of Poltava in 1709 and spent thirteen years as a captive in Siberia (B17). The interest was equally fed by English translations of Russian works of exploration such as Stepan Krasheninnikov's *History of Kamtschatka, and the Kurilski islands* (1764; fig. 11) and *Account of a voyage of discovery to the north east of Siberia, the frozen ocean and the north-east sea* (1806) by Gavriil Sarychev, who had been on the Billings expedition.

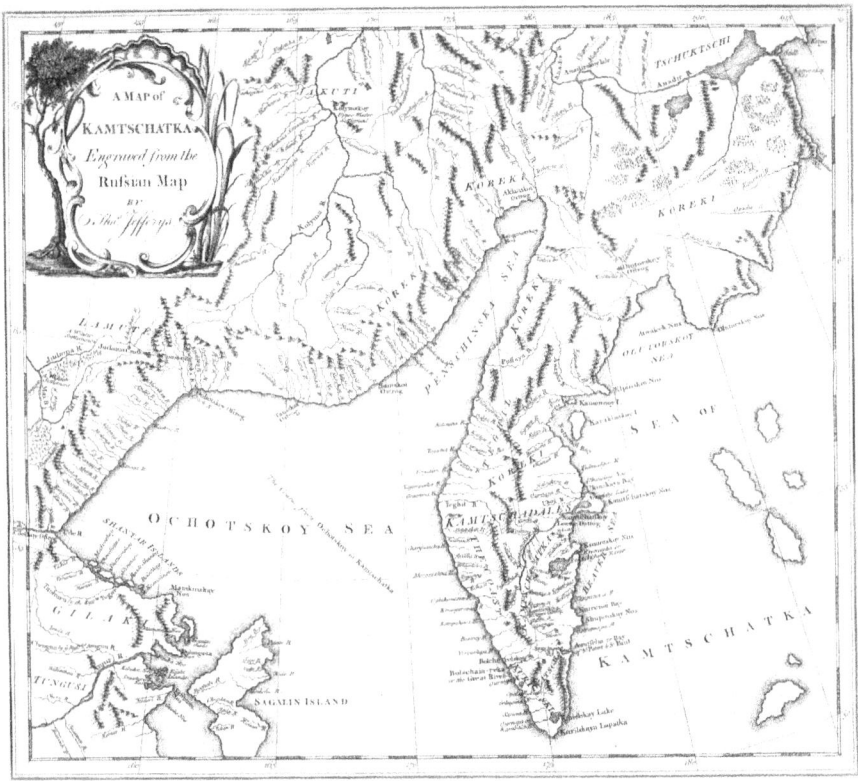

Fig. 11 *A map of Kamtschatka engraved from the russian map by Tho. Jefferys*, in Stepan Petrovich Krasheninnikov, *The history of Kamtschatka and the Kurilski Islands with the countries adjacent; Illustrated with maps and cuts. Published at Petersbourg in the Russian language by order of her Imperial Majesty and translated into English by James Grieve* (Glocester: printed by R.Raikes for T. Jefferys, 1764).

III

The interplay between accounts of "tours" and of serious scientific expeditions continues into the reigns of Alexander I and his brother Nicholas I, which cover the whole of the first half of the nineteenth century up to the Crimean War. Russia was firmly embarked on further expansion of its empire, opening up ever new fields to explore.

Long before the Romanovs Muscovy had seen considerable territorial expansion in the fifteenth and sixteenth centuries during the reigns of Ivan III, Vasilii III and Ivan IV: Ivan IV with his capture of Kazan and Astrakhan achieved control of the Volga and the north-western shores of the Caspian, but a secure outlet to the Baltic or access to the Black Sea eluded him. However, there was important expansion in the east, beyond the Urals, initially by Cossack bands under Ermak penetrating into Siberia in 1582. Towns founded during this period in both the Volga territories and Siberia included Orel in 1564, Voronezh and Ufa in 1586 and Tobolsk in 1587. In the seventeenth century, particularly after the Time of Troubles and with the accession of the first Romanov, Siberia was rapidly colonized and the eastern seaboard reached by 1639. Again the establishment of now famous towns and settlements mark the Russian advance: Tomsk (1604) on the Tom River, Eniseisk (1619) and Krasnoiarsk (1628) on the Enisei, Iakutsk on the Lena, Verkhoiansk (1638) on the Iana, Irkutsk (1652) on the Angara near Lake Baikal, Okhotsk (1649) on the Sea of Okhotsk, and Bolsheretsk (1704) near the tip of Kamchatka. The late seventeenth century was also important for the gaining or in some cases, the re-gaining of lands in the south west, particularly in Ukraine and White Russia during the reign of Aleksei Mikhailovich, but it was only at the beginning of the eighteenth century that Peter I succeeded in restoring to Russia its vital outlet on the Baltic.

Russian expansion under Peter might seem relatively insignificant when seen on a map of the period: an area to the west and north of Novgorod, a narrow strip of land along the southern and western shores of the Caspian, the peninsular of Kamchatka. It represented nonetheless the consolidation of a wide landmass, stretching from the Baltic to the Pacific with encroachment to the south into the Ottoman empire. The stage was set for Catherine II's drive for expansion, inevitably to the south and south-west, resulting in the acquisition of a large swathe of Polish territory after the final partition of 1795 and the wresting of the Black Sea steppes and the Crimea from the Turks. Peter had founded St Petersburg in 1703, asserting as it were Russia's rightful place by the Baltic; Catherine, whose desire to follow her great predecessor's lead was writ in stone on the statue of the Bronze Horseman, created the port of Odessa in 1794, determined to exploit the commercial and military advantages of the Black Sea.

Under Alexander I Napoleon's Grand Duchy of Poland came under Russian control in 1812 and was followed by the Grand Duchy of Finland in 1815, extending Russian control of the Baltic. Highly significant gains were made in the south with the acquisition of Georgia over the period 1801-10 and Bessarabia in 1812, which brought Russia to the borders of the Austrian empire, and further areas of the Caucasus were added by the end of his reign. It was in the same area that Nicholas extended his empire, pushing his frontiers into Armenia and embracing more of the Black Sea littoral, consolidated by the Treaty of Adrianople in 1829.

Of the 108 entries in the bibliography for the reign of Alexander and of the 131 for Nicholas's, just over half were published before 1855. Of the remaining, many were letters or diaries that were included in autobiographies written in the twilight of the author's life or in posthumous biographies, while yet others saw the light of day only of recent times, testifying to the continuing interest in accounts of Russia and of travel literature in general and as often as not accompanied with scholarly introductions and annotation. The works published before the Crimean War nevertheless provide important evidence not only of the popularity of existing genres and of author categories but also of the evolving state of Anglo-Russian diplomatic and cultural relations and the changing focus of public attention.

The brief period of Anglo-Russian harmony between the end of the reign of "Crazy Paul" in March 1801 and the Russo-French Treaty at Tilsit in July 1807 which saw publication of the travels of Mrs Guthrie and of Professor Pallas from the previous decade brought an influx of British tourists visiting not only St Petersburg and Moscow but drawn to the "new" Russia of the Crimea and the Black Sea littoral. The antiquities and archaeological sites of the Crimea inevitably evoked associations with the classical world, particularly for the young Oxbridge tourists, some of whom, fired by the emergent Hellenism of the age, proceeded to Constantinople and on to Greece itself. However, in almost every case, their letters or diaries were not published for a number of years (see Heber (F11), Royston (F17) and Kelsall (F20), and, of course, from Paul's reign, Clarke (E4), whom they all knew, and Tweddell (E3)) and therefore were not so much setting as sharing a trend, manifest in the other publications of the time (F9, F12). Reuilly's *Travels in the Crimea* (F4) was translated for Richard Phillips's *Collection of Modern and Contemporary Voyages and Travels* that also provided the public with translations of foreign travelogues along the more usual northern tourist routes (F7, F8). The presence of the British tourist in Alexander's pre-Tilsit Russia was more loudly announced, however, with Sir John Carr's *A northern summer; or, travels round the Baltic, through Denmark, Sweden, Russia, Prussia, and part of Germany, in the year 1804,* also (F6) and Sir Robert Ker Porter's *Travelling sketches in Russia and Sweden, during the years 1805, 1806, 1807, 1808* (F13), both also printed for Phillips in 1805 and 1809 respectively. It was to the same period that the merchant George

Green's travels belong but it was only in 1813 that he published what was in many ways the first modest attempt at a English-language guide-book for travellers to St Petersburg and Moscow, as its sub-title clearly reveals: *with a description of the post towns, and every thing interesting, in the Russian and Prussian capitals, &c.; to which are added, the names, distances, and price, of every post; and a vocabulary of the most useful terms in English and Russian* (F14). It was the desire to see a burnt-out Moscow that brought tourists again to Russia in the wake of the Napoleonic invasion of June-December 1812 and the subsequent Allied advance on Paris (F54, F56).

A unique British insight into these momentous events was provided by Robert, later General Sir Robert, Wilson, who had first visited Russia before Tilsit and subsequently published his *Brief remarks on the character and composition of the Russian army* (1810) (F19). Returning in 1812, Wilson was attached to Kutuzov's staff and was with the Russian army as it advanced through Europe, but it was only a decade after his death in 1847 that his diaries and letters were eventually published (F18, F48, F49). It was, of course, the French tragedy in Russia that was best reflected in the eye-witness accounts of participants that were published in the immediate aftermath and for many years thereafter. Of the fifteen accounts translated from French originals, only three, however, appeared during Alexander's reign and one from the first year of Nicholas's (F32, F33, F35, F41).

In June 1814, soon after the Allies had entered Paris, Alexander I paid a triumphant visit to England. It was during that visit that the Tsar met the noted Quaker William Allen and other Friends as well as representatives of the British and Foreign Bible Society. The Russia of the strongly religious Tsar, where the Russian Bible Society had been founded the previous year, was to become a magnet for missionaries from England and Scotland. Allen and Stephen Grellet carried out missionary work in southern Russia in 1818-19 (F78, F79), by which time Daniel Wheeler, invited by Alexander to undertake the draining of the marshes near the Russian capital, had brought out a party of Quakers, twenty assistants and family members, to begin the work that was to keep them in Russia until the early 1830s (F70, F71). Missionaries of the BFBS had been in St Petersburg since the summer of 1812 when Rev. John Patterson arrived and for the next fifteen years travelled throughout the Russian empire furthering the aims of the Russian Bible Society. His memoirs (F59) appeared only in the year of his death, 1858, but extracts from his letters and those of his colleagues, Rev. Ebenezer Henderson and Rev. Robert Pinkerton, were published as early as 1817 (F62,

F65). All travelled extensively in the Crimea and the Caucasus, where the Edinburgh Missionary Society had established as early as 1802 a mission at Karass that was visited also by Rev. William Glen in the 1820s (F86). Representatives of other societies, such as Rev. Joseph Wolff of the London Society for Promoting Christianity among the Jews (F107) and Heinrich Zwick of the Moravian Brotherhood, working for the Russian Bible Society among the Kalmyk tribes (F92), were also active in southern Russia. During Nicholas's reign the BFBS remained prominent: in 1833 there arrived in the Russian capital its agent George Borrow to supervise the translation of the New Testament into Manchu (F33), although he is perhaps better known in a Russian context for the translations from Pushkin he published during his two-year sojourn. Twenty years later, it was in many ways fitting that in what was to be the last year of Nicholas's reign a deputation of three Quakers should be sent from London in a noble but vain attempt to avert the outbreak of war (G129-31).

A substantial, distinctive, and in some instances controversial contribution was made by British doctors, particularly at the juncture of the two reigns. They were no longer in the service of the court as in earlier reigns but predominantly in the employ of noble families. Between 1824 and 1829 a succession of four doctors served for varying lengths of time in the household of the Anglophile Count, later Prince, Mikhail Vorontsov, son of the long-serving Russian ambassador in London and appointed governor-general of New Russia in 1823. Three of them produced books, in the most interesting of which Robert Lee described in detail the death in Taganrog of Alexander I and also the ensuing Decembrist uprising (F106). Dr Lee's account appeared only in 1854, but his successors, Augustus Bozzi Granville and Edward Morton, were not slow to publish: Granville's monumental *St Petersburgh* (1828), based on a mere few weeks' residence in the Russian capital in the autumn of 1827, proved very popular and went into a third edition in 1835 (G5), by which time Morton had published his own book that includes not only a detailed description of Odessa, where he had lived with the Vorontsovs for two years, but was also *"intended to give some account of Russia as it is, and not as it is represented to be"*, not least by Granville (G9). Other doctors also produced interesting accounts during this period: George Lefevre, who was knighted in 1832 for his service as physician to the British embassy in St Petersburg, spent no less than fifteen years in Russia up to 1842 and produced rather vague memoirs in the year after his return (G10), but the impact made by the work of Dr

Robert Lyall was considerably greater. Lyall, initially house physician to a Moscow aristocratic family, produced soon after his return to England in 1823, following some eight years in Russia, his monumental *The Character of the Russians, and a detailed history of Moscow* (1823) (F61) that despite its (unauthorized) dedication to the Tsar, was, according to the Russian embassy in London, "written against his government, and the entire Russian nation".[12] The good doctor also laid claim to be included in the category of travellers, publishing in 1825 his *Travels in Russia, the Krimea, the Caucasus, and Georgia* (F90).

The books by Granville and Morton were also to be titled or sub-titled "travels", as indeed were a score or more of other works from the same decade and countless ones before and after, but perhaps more indicative of a new trend was the title Granville gave to his third edition of 1835: *Guide to St Petersburgh: a journal of travels*. As the Grand Tour gave way to middle-class tourism, an indication that Russia was beginning to appeal to a wider public was the appearance of the "tourist guide". In the late 1830s there was published Francis Coghlan's *Guide to St. Petersburg & Moscow, by Hamburg, Lubeck, Travemunde, and by steam-packet, across the Baltic to Cronstadt; fully detailing every form and expense from London-Bridge to St. Petersburg* (G37) and the anonymous *Guide to Moscow, containing a description of the public edifices, historical notices, useful statistics, and an itinerary of the road from St. Petersburgh, to which is added a vocabulary of useful words and phrases* (G38) that were soon followed by the first "Murray" for Russia in 1839 (G62), which was several times updated.

It was Lyall's itinerary that distinguished his travels from those of his doctor colleagues. His was an account of a journey to the south of Russia, but just one of a swelling number. It has already been remarked how the Crimea began to attract tourists after the annexation of 1783, especially the young Hellenists at the beginning of Alexander's reign. Russia's further territorial acquisitions in the Caucasus and Bessarabia were soon reflected in the titles of works, beginning with the translations from the German of Baron Campenhausen in 1808 (F12), Klaproth in 1814 (F22), and the Freygangs in 1823 (F27). The first British traveller to use "Georgia" in his title would seem to be Colonel John Johnson, travelling from India through the Caucasus and Ukraine in 1817 (F75), followed by Sir Robert Ker Porter, travelling the same year from St Petersburg to Georgia and through the

---

12 Quoted by Lyall himself in an appendix to his following book, *Travels in Russia, the Krimea, the Caucasus, and Georgia*, vol. II (London, 1825), p. 519.

Caucasus to Persia (F76), while the two missionaries, Rev. Glen and Rev. Henderson, publishing in 1823 and 1826 respectively, were to introduce the word "Caucasus" (F86, F63). What was essentially a trickle in Alexander's reign became a veritable stream in Nicholas' as travellers travelled north and south through Georgia, the Caucasus, Bessarabia and Circassia, as well visiting the Crimea and New Russia, particularly Odessa. Some forty accounts, differing greatly in their detail and focus, written by a whole range of travellers, including numerous military men with an interest in Russia's continuing struggles with Turkey (G11, G12, G14, G15, G19), and intent on inspecting her new territories brought the Russian south very much to the attention of the public. It was Circassia – whose peoples were locked in armed struggle against the Russians for decades until their final subjugation in 1864 – that was thrust into the limelight in 1836, when the British schooner *Vixen* was seized by a Russian warship in the Black Sea for illicit trade with the tribesmen. The ship's supercargo, James Stanislaus Bell, who was released from detention in Sevastopol a month later, was to publish an account of his subsequent travels as *Journal of a residence in Circassia during the years 1837, 1838 and 1839* (G48) and initiate a steady stream of books about the region in the 1840s (fig. 12), often hostile to Russia (G65, G67, G68, G119).

Fig. 12 Edmund Spencer, *Travels in Circassia, Krim-tartary, &c: including a steam voyage down the Danube, from Vienna to Constantinople, and round the Black Sea* (London: H. Colburn, 1839).

The challenges of distance and climate seemed to have deterred many from undertaking journeys into Siberia. Few accounts appeared before the mid-1820s, although in some cases they reflected journeys made a decade or so earlier. Pre-eminent among the authors were "pedestrian" John Dundas Cochrane, a Royal Navy captain who travelled as far as Kamchatka in 1820-21 mainly on foot (F82) and who on his return through Moscow met "blind" James Holman, a former naval lieutenant about to journey through Siberia in 1823 but who was later accused of being a spy by the Russian authorities and was escorted under guard out of the country (F89). Doubts were raised about what the travellers indeed accomplished, not least by Peter Dobell, who had spent many years in Siberia from 1812 before eventually publishing his *Travels in Kamtchatka and Siberia; with a narrative of a residence in China* (F30) in 1830 and two years later, under the pseudonym "a friend to truth", published his polemic entitled *Russia as it is, and not as it has been represented*. During Nicholas's reign, perhaps the most reliable information on Siberia was supplied by the German scientist Georg Erman (G4), but of particular note was Sir George Simpson's pioneering circumnavigation of the world by land begun in London that took him from Okhotsk to St Petersburg in 1842 (G80). George Cottrell (G73), travelling as far as Irkutsk in 1840 and taking to task all his predecessors, including not only Holman but also Dobell, offers his own considered views on the exile system and Siberia's natural resources.

The nineteenth-century variant of the Grand Tourist, now travelling without the guidance of a tutor, was still to be found in the salons of the new and old capitals and publishing his journals for the delectation but, more often, the ridicule of readers and critics alike (e.g. G21, G24, G25). It was in the mid-1830s that a certain Rayford Ramble decided it was opportune to publish his *Travelling opinions and sketches, in Russia and Poland* (F80), dating back to a journey of 1819, and could still assert that "as for Russia, no one knows any thing about it. That is the very reason why I wish to go thither, in preference to any other place". It was the Rambles of the time who elicited a broadside from the alleged Russian interlocutor of Leitch Ritchie, author of a volume on the two capitals for Heath's *Picturesque Annual for 1836* (F36):

> It seems strange to me that you English should travel to Russia for the avowed purpose of making yourselves acquainted with the manners and character of the people, yet without comprehending a single word of their language. You come here with the greatest prejudices against us as a nation. You see every thing different from what you have been accustomed to at home, except the manners of some dozen families whom you visit.

You make no inquiries, no reflections, no allowances. You examine this rude but mighty colossus through your opera glass, or from the windows of your travelling chariot. In the towns your valet de place is your prime authority; in the country you wander about in utter darkness, unable to understand a single object, and unable to ask a single question. You then return home satisfied with having attained the object of your tour; and sit down, without a single malevolent feeling in your breast, but out of pure ignorance, to add to the mass of falsehoods and absurdities with which Europe is already inundated.[13]

Ritchie felt obliged to acknowledge that his Russian acquaintance had a point.

Ignorance of the Russian language was a constant reproach, but it was only the long-time residents who had any realistic hope of acquiring at least a working knowledge. The continual objection to the descriptions of the tourist is against the superficiality of what is supposedly observed and recorded, although there was a growing interest in the life of Russians outside aristocratic circles and outside the capitals. In 1839 two books appeared that seemed to emphasize in their titles the change of focus. If it was only deep into his second volume that Robert Bremner left the delights of St Petersburg and Moscow for the promised *Excursions in the interior of Russia* (G47), Richard Venables's *Domestic scenes in Russia: in a series of letters describing a year's residence in that country, chiefly in the interior* (G53) did not disappoint. Venables, Cambridge graduate and country parson, accompanied his Russian wife on a visit to her relations in Tambov province, where he became much interested in the problems of serfdom and the rhythms and patterns of provincial life. He was of course not alone, many authors, British and foreign, had attempted over previous decades to describe Russian mores in city and country, but Venables was indicative of a trend, perhaps most tellingly embodied in the writings of a number of women, who lived and worked in Russia at this period.

It is in the books of Elizabeth Rigby (later Lady Eastlake) (G63), Rebecca McCoy (G88), Charlotte Bourne (G98), and Mary Smith (G113), all living in Russia in the 1840s, that with varying success the flavour of life in provincial Russia is captured. It was Revel where Elizabeth Rigby stayed with her sister, who was married to an Estonian nobleman, although she

---

13 A similar note was struck by Thomas Shaw, a long-time tutor in Russia and translator of Pushkin, writing a few years later (Thomas B. Shaw, *Blackwood's Edinburgh Magazine*, vol. LIII, no. 329 (March 1843), p. 282).

also spent much time in St Petersburg: keenly aware of the differences between Estonians and Russians, she was drawn to both Russian traditions and the Russian language, which she began immediately to learn and praised it as "at once florid and concise – pliable and vigorous, tender and stern; – redundant in imagery, laconic in axiom, graceful in courtesy, strong in argument, soothing in feeling, and tremendous in denunciation, the latent energies of the language are a prophetic guarantee of the destinies of the nation". Rebecca McCoy, who spent eleven years in Russia as a domestic teacher of English and companion, offered her far from uncritical *The Englishwoman in Russia: impressions of the society and manners of the Russians at home* as "a simple account of the manners, customs, and *genre de vie chez eux* of a people whose domestic habits are comparatively but little known to the English nation". It was as a governess in the noble Dolgorukii family in Moscow and on their Tula estate that Charlotte Bourne spent three years, learning the language well enough to produce an English verse translation of a stanza from Pushkin's *Evgenii Onegin* and recording fascinating glimpses of some of the literary and intellectual lions of the time. Mary Smith, on the other hand, emphasizes her "travels" during the six years she spent in Russia up to the very end of Nicholas's reign, seemingly also as a companion and governess, but her observations remain disappointingly general.

Remembering the role of the "lady" author in eighteenth-century accounts, it perhaps occasions no surprise that all four books were published anonymously, three bearing the designation "by a lady", and only Elizabeth Rigby robustly refusing a similar suggestion from her publisher John Murray. It is in fact only of very recent times that the identities of two of the authors (McCoy and Bourne) have been established. Another former governess who did put her name to her book when it was eventually published in 1863 was Lucy Finlay, who had spent some eight years in Russia as a governess before she married in St Petersburg the artist and architect Thomas Witlam Atkinson. Atkinson was to earn fame for the descriptions and drawings of his travels through Siberia and Central Asia that he published in 1858 and 1860 (G107-08), in which, however, he made no mention that he had been accompanied throughout by his wife and baby son. It was two years after his death in 1861 that his wife put the record straight with her moving book entitled *Recollections of Tartar steppes and their inhabitants* and signed simply "Mrs Atkinson" (G109).

Venables brought out a second edition of his book in 1856 at the end of the Crimean War, thinking, rightly, that what he had observed, would be helpful in "understanding the Russians". Apart from Rigby's book, published in 1841 and again in 1842, the works by Bourne, McCoy and Smith also appeared during or soon after the Crimean War, in 1855, 1856 and 1859, already in the reign of a new Russian ruler, soon to be hailed as the "Tsar-liberator".

However, during the previous reign there had been more than enough authors willing to encourage Russophobia among the British public, following the example on the British domestic scene of the pro-Turkish David Urquhart, outspoken defender of Circassian independence against Russian aggression, and the Marquis de Custine, author of the highly influential denunciation of Nicholas's Russia, *La Russie en 1839*, which appeared in English translation in 1843 as *Empire of the czars* (G66). Broadsides against Nicholas's Russia were fired by William Jesse, an army officer on half pay, who left in the summer of 1840 "without regret, glad to escape from "a land of tyrants and a den of slaves", and Charles Henningsen (G93-94), hiding under a pseudonym but ever ready to approve of Custine's strictures, and fulminating against that "dark arena, where corruption and oppression in the most revolting forms are still daily running riot, battening on the sufferings of millions, and the brutalizing abasement of whole races".[14]

IV

The Crimean War was in so many respects a watershed in Anglo-Russian relations. Since the reign of Peter I there had been several occasions when diplomatic relations were strained and broken and the two countries made belligerent noises. Indeed, during the Ochakov Crisis towards the end of Catherine II's reign, at the time of Paul I's rapprochement with Napoleon, and subsequent to the Russo-French agreement at Tilsit in 1807, war seemed if not imminent, then possible. It was, however, only on 14 September 1854

---

14 The classic study remains J.H. Gleason, *The genesis of Russophobia in Great Britain: a study of the interaction of policy and opinion* (Cambridge, Mass.: Harvard University Press, 1950). On the many fluctuations in Anglo-Russian relations at this period, nevertheless see Harold N. Ingle, *Nesselrode and the Russian rapprochement with Britain, 1836-1844* (Berkeley, Los Angeles and London: University of California Press, 1976).

that for the first time British soldiers set foot on Russian soil to fight the Russian army in a bloody, protracted, heroic, but ultimately militarily pointless conflict.

Fig. 13 British bombardment of the fortress Bomarsund (Aland Islands) during the Crimean war (1854), artist unknown.

It was a conflict that spawned a mighty literature in Britain and continues to do so. No genre escaped: poets penned odes and sonnets and dirges and found triumph in defeat for the valiant 600; writers of fiction, particularly that aimed for boys, spun their tales of British heroism; preachers fulminated from the pulpits, claiming God for the British; newspapers and journals packed their columns with all manner of newsworthy items and sensational reports; and the readers of *Punch* delighted in the cartoons directed not only against the shambling bear that was Russia and its Tsar but increasingly against the bungling British generals and incompetent administrators.[15]

The first contributions by combatants to the literature of the Crimean War came from two navy men who never set foot in the Crimea as such but were captured when HMS *Tiger* went aground after taking part in the bombardment of Odessa and it was to Odessa, pride of New Russia, that they were taken. Both 1st Lieutenant Royer and Midshipman Barker were quick to produce books that were not, however, harrowing tales of imprisonment and deprivation but veritable paeans to the hospitality and

---

15 See Anthony Cross, *The Russian theme in English literature from the sixteenth century to 1980: an introductory survey and a bibliography* (Oxford: Willem A. Meeuws, 1985); Patrick Waddington, *"Theirs but to do and die": the poetry of the charge of the Light Brigade at Balaklava 25 October 1854* (Cotgrave: Astra Press, 1995); Anthony Cross, 'The Crimean War and the Caricature War', *Slavonic and East European Review*, LXXXIV (2006), pp. 460-80.

grace of their captor hosts (H1, H2). Back in England on 9 July 1854, Royer wrote in his preface dated September, that he offered his work "with no political object, but simply with a view to record the Author's impressions of a country which he has recently visited, under circumstances of no little interest at the present moment, and to satisfy in some measure the curiosity naturally felt by the British Public, with regard to all events connected with the scenes of the War in the East". He was right – no less than six editions appeared before the end of the year.

The role of the navy in the Black Sea and the Baltic, and indeed in the Sea of Okhotsk is often overlooked in the context of the struggle on the peninsula itself, although it receives due emphasis in the subsequent accounts of combatants from senior admirals to junior officers (e.g. H3-7, H9-10, H127), if not from ratings. The ordinary soldiers in contrast find their voice in numerous accounts which may not have been published in their lifetime but which posterity has been zealous to recover from the obscurity of family and regimental archives. The Crimean War section of the bibliography lists 145 accounts, of which fifty-two were published between 1854 and 1859, a further forty-three by the end of the nineteenth century, twenty in the first half of the twentieth century, and no less than thirty more since 1950. Within the overall total there are only eight foreign accounts, four, possibly five, translated from French (H24, H25, H107, H117, H125) and one from German (H118), and two written by Americans, one of whom was the skipper of a troop ship on loan to the French and the other, a reporter (H89, H99): one of the French accounts (H125), by the French chef Alexis Soyer, who was responsible for reforming the diets of the Allied troops and installing new ovens, offers a unique insight into the complexities of provisioning an invading force. The British accounts form an imposing, diverse, and frequently moving record of an epic struggle, in which life in the trenches before Sevastopol or in tents at Balaklava and elsewhere, cavalry charges, hails of shells and bullets, shortages of supplies and food, omnipresent death and disease, extremes of weather, all play their part. To some extent they parallel the often harrowing French accounts of Napoleon's invasion in 1812 and anticipate some of the accounts of the horrors of WWI on the Russian front. They include accounts by soldiers and officers who spent some time in Russian captivity: the cavalryman, for instance, who took part in the Charge of the Light Brigade, was captured by Cossacks, and was marched off into the interior to Voronezh, and describes Russian towns and families with whom he was billeted as well as the often bad treatment he received (H33); captured officers, who were generally well treated and moved with freedom in the towns where they were held (H106, H141). After the armistice many officers fraternized with the Russians, became tourists and described, often in detail, excursions to the caves of Inkerman, the sultan's palace at Bakhchiserai and other parts of the Crimean peninsular (H31, H49, H66, H67, H95, H112).

While such touristic activities are perhaps understandable in the aftermath of the conflict, tourism during the war is not, but there were more than a few people who made the journey from England precisely to see the sites of recent battles and, if they were "fortunate", to witness action. Such was Henry Bushby, who described an "enjoyable" month's visit early in the campaign (H83), or the self-styled "travelling gentlemen", the two Money brothers (H131), while the antics and adventures of Rev. Wickenden beggar belief (H72). The phenomenon of "war tourism" aroused only consternation in a French pastor offering solace to the wounded (H117). Virtually in the same category are the wives of serving officers who watched from the hilltops while their menfolk waged war: Frances Duberly, wife of a regimental paymaster and a great horsewoman, not only witnessed the charge of the Light Brigade but managed to get her journal published in London even before her return to England (H29), while Ellen Palmer undeniably showed a lot of pluck during her visit to see her officer brother, one of the survivors of the 600 (H102).

There were, however, women whose presence in the Crimea was dictated by their wish to offer help to the sick and the wounded. There is little doubt that the Crimean War is associated with the name of Florence Nightingale before that of any military participant in the conflict. It was not from her pen at that time or, indeed, later, at least in book form, that the contribution that nurses, serving both in Turkey at the military hospital at Scutari and across the Black Sea in the hospital at Balaklava, could be appreciated. One of the Sisters of Mercy who accompanied Miss Nightingale published her memoir some years after the events (H108), but it was a voice highly critical of the lady of the lamp that made itself heard already in 1857 (H111), the year that there also appeared the *Wonderful adventures of Mrs Seacole in many lands* with an introduction by the influential correspondent of *The Times*, William Russell: Mary Seacole (fig. 14), of mixed Scottish-Creole descent, who, rejected as a nurse, nevertheless went to the Crimea, setting up a British Hotel (fig. 15) near Sevastopol and nursing the wounded (H116).

More positive assessments of Nightingale's achievements came from the civil doctors, who worked with her at Scutari (H122), but there are also several accounts by the military surgeons and doctors attached to units heavily involved in the fighting (e.g. H20, H43, H53, H62, H112).

Fig. 14 Only known photo of Mary Seacole (1805-1881), taken c.1873, photographer unknown.

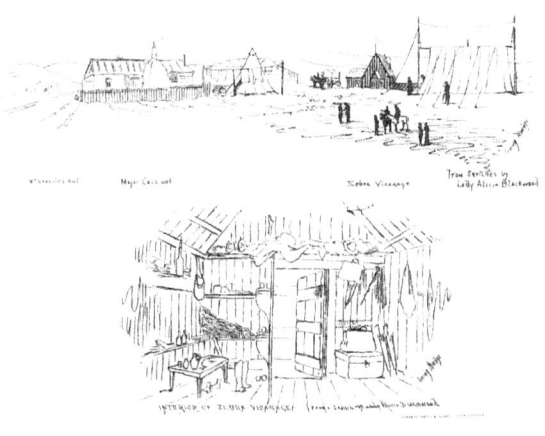

Fig. 15 Sketch of Mary Seacole's "British Hotel" in the Crimea (n.d.), by Lady Alicia Blackwood.

William Russell, who had written of Seacole, "I trust that England will not forget one who nursed her sick, who sought out her wounded to aid and succour them, and who performed the last offices for some of her illustrious dead", enjoyed much longer fame than she. On the monument erected to his memory in St Paul's he is described as "the first and greatest of war correspondents". He was with the troops that left Southampton in March 1854, witnessed the landing at Kalamita Bay on 14 September and covered all the subsequent events of the war. His dispatches to *The Times* alerted the British public to the true horrors of the war, the vast mismanagement and above all to the heroism of the private soldier. His dispatches were collected as yearly accounts and many times reprinted (H63). His example was to be followed thereafter in every major conflict in which Russia (and not only Russia, of course) was involved and we have literally dozens of books emanating from correspondents following, for instance, the Russo-Japanese War and the Russian participation in WWI, as well as reporting the 1905 and 1917 revolutions.

The Crimean War was also the war of drawings and sketchbooks, bringing fame to William "Crimean" Simpson (fig. 16), hailed as the "earliest of war artists" and producing numerous sketches from the war zone, including one of Balaklava at the behest of Queen Victoria, which were later sold as albums (H87-88).

Fig. 16 William Simpson photographed by Roger Fenton on Cathcart Hill before Sevastopol, Crimea, 1855. Adrian Lipscomb collection.

There were other artists such as Constantin Guys, whom *The Illustrated London News* sent out as its roving artist (H37), as well as amateur artists among the military (H15, H26, H109). It was also, even more importantly, the war when Roger Fenton with his "photographic van", sponsored by Thomas Agnew & Sons (as Simpson had been by Colnaghi), photographed military commanders, local figures, and studies of camp life (fig. 17), and ushered in, unbeknowingly, the era of the travel and other accounts, illustrated with photographs (H114).

Fig. 17 Balaklava harbour (Crimea) [1855], photograph by Roger Fenton.

V

Alexander II came to the throne when the Crimean War was at its height and reigned for twenty-six years before a terrorist's bomb ended his life. For all his liberal impulses and reforms, his was a reign marked by much bloodshed and warfare, but in the early years, the signing of the Treaty of Paris of 30 March 1856 that brought the Crimean conflict to an end and discussions within Russia about the imminent emancipation of the serfs seemed to promise better things.

Inevitably, in the aftermath of the war the Crimea attracted tourists who visited the battlefields and then moved off to other attractions (e.g. I3, I4, I9, I18), but of considerable more interest were the memoirs of combatants who felt drawn to revisit the region at later stages of their lives (see H14, H48, H81, H87). Tourists were soon returning in numbers, many still drawn to St Petersburg and Moscow, arriving by train through Poland or by steamer to Cronstadt. Designed as a tourist's guide to the northern ports to which the North of Europe Steam Company's steamers sailed and to the towns reached by the connecting railway routes, was James Mahony's *The book of the Baltic* (1857) (I7).

Early in the reign other momentous, if very different events engaged the attention of visitors. The signing of the emancipation act of 3 March 1861 evoked new interest in the lives of the peasantry and in the consequences of "freedom". Henry Sutherland Edwards's *The Russians at home*, published in the year of the Emancipation, examined both the support for, and opposition to it (I34), and a few years later, the title of Robert Anderson's *Sketches of Russian life before and during the emancipation of the serfs* reflected the author's main focus (I35). Both authors had spent long years in Russia, as had Herbert Barry, a manager of ironworks in Tambov and Nizhnii Novgorod, who was particular attentive to changes that emancipation had brought, contending that for the two classes, nobles and serfs, that had existed pre-1861, now four – nobles, merchants, shopkeepers and peasants – were evident (I87-88). The study of post-Emancipation Russia was taken to a new level by the publication in 1877 of *Russia*, the result of Donald Mackenzie Wallace's, five years of extensive travels through European Russia (I90; fig. 18).

Fig. 18 Portrait of Donald Mackenzie Wallace (no later than 1905), photographer unknown.

Russia was attracting ever more British travellers and explorers, intent on reaching the furthest parts of the empire, be it Siberia and Kamchatka or the newly acquired territories of the south east. A striking number were members of the Royal Geographical Society, founded in 1830 and receiving its royal charter in 1859. In the early 1840s Sir Roderick Murchison, who was soon to become the Society's long-serving president, had travelled extensively through the Urals, producing a work of lasting value on the geology of the region (G70). His achievement was matched by another future president, the geographer and mountaineer Douglas Freshfield, who first climbed in the Caucasus in 1868 (I80), returned on two further occasions during Alexander III's reign, and produced by the end of the century the monumental account of *The exploration of the Caucasus* (J142). Other members travelling through the Caucasus included Viscount Pollington in 1865 (I61) and August Mounsey in 1866 (I62), while Major Herbert Wood was invited to join the Russian Geographical Society's expedition to the Aral Sea in 1874 (I122). Commodore John Buchan Telfer, travelling extensively with his Russian wife through Transcaucasia in the early 1870s, projected his book on the region as a well-informed guide-book for tourists undertaking a 92-day round trip from Odessa (I119). It was, however, through Siberia to Mongolia that William Whyte journeyed in 1869 (I86), and Edward Rae studied the lives of the Samoeds in 1874 (I127) and returned in 1880 to explore the White Sea coast and the Kola peninsula (I178). It was the Russian North, known in part to British readers via the first reports in Hakluyt, that also attracted Captain Joseph Wiggins, one of the most renowned of Victorian Arctic explorers, pioneering the route via the Kara Sea to the River Enisei from 1874 (I121).

The Caucasus had become a magnet for followers of mountaineering, which had gained increasing popularity in Britain following the establishing of the Alpine Club of London in 1857. One of the club's early presidents and a most experienced climber was Florence Crauford Grove, author of *The Frosty Caucasus* (fig. 19), who recounted his tramps through the Caucasus in 1874 (I124) and who conquered Mt Elbruz, following Freshfield, who had also made the first ascent of Mt Kazbek.

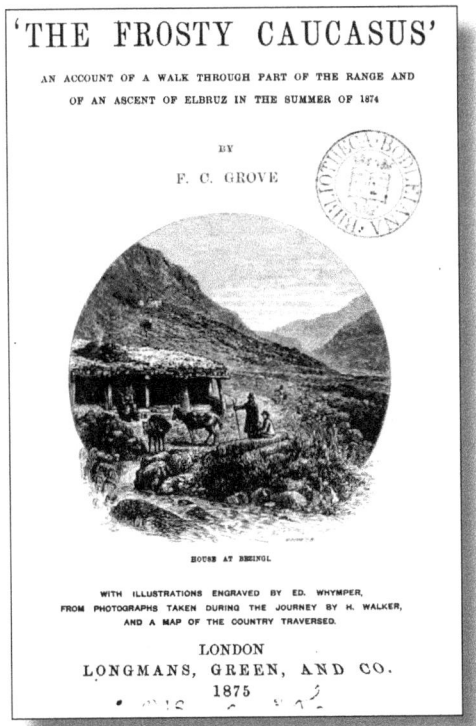

Fig. 19 Title page and photograph of a first edition of Florence Crauford Grove, *The Frosty Caucasus* (1875).

A decade later, one of the most famous of early British mountaineers, Alfred Mummery, scaled Dych Tau for the first time and was promptly elected to the Alpine Club (J84). Climbing was just one of the energetic forms of sport enjoyed by the British and of course many were drawn to hunt and shoot on country estates as well as in the mountains. "Sport" seems to have been used for the first time in a title in Ferdinand St John's *Rambles in Germany, France, Italy and Russia, in search of sport*, published in 1853 (G59), but referring to a visit in 1838. It appeared thereafter with increasing frequency, in, for example, Clive Phillips-Wolley's *Sport in the Crimea and Caucasus* (I133) and John Baddeley's *Russia in the 'eighties': sport and politics* (I170). But of course, hunting, shooting and fishing were staple pursuits for members of the British colony in St Petersburg, as evidenced by books such as James Whishaw's memoirs (I146) and his relative Fred Whishaw's *Out of doors in Tsarland* and *The romance of the woods* (I147-48). Although shooting was not excluded, observing birds was the nobler pursuit of the Scottish naturalist John Harvie-Brown, who first went to the White Sea in 1872 (I99), but on his second visit in 1876 to the Pechora was accompanied by the noted amateur ornithologist Henry Seebohm (I129). Seebohm penetrated further into Siberia two years later, sailing with Captain Wiggins along the Enesei (I145).

Possibly for a number of officers with the Indian Army and for many civilians far removed from the realities the "Great Game" was yet another sporting event, albeit one protracted over a century or more and with a vast playing field of many countries.[16] Coined by Arthur Conolly, who as a young twenty-two year old lieutenant had left London in August 1829 to join his regiment in India, travelling through Russia to Persia (G17) and who in 1842 was to be brutally executed by the emir of Bokhara, it had its origins in the reign of Catherine II and of her son Paul, who sent off an army to capture India, was fanned into flame by Napoleon's attempt to convince Alexander I to do the same, and erupted particularly after the Crimean War. There was a steady stream of officers who had journeyed through Russia since the reign of Alexander I, watching Russia's relentless military advance. Colonel Valentine Baker and two other officers travelled through Central Asia in 1873 with the specific aim of gathering "political, geographical, and strategical information that might be valuable" (I114). It was, however, the larger-than-life, Russian-speaking Captain Fred

---

16 See Peter Hopkirk, *The Great Game: on secret service in High Asia* (London: John Murray, 1990).

Burnaby of the Royal Horse Guards who stirred up the Russophobic fears of the British public with the publication in 1876 of his best-seller, *A ride to Khiva*, in which he described his mid-winter journey through Russia, with the surprising agreement of the Russian minister of war, to the khanate of Khiva, "protected" by Russia since 1873 (I132). Burnaby rode off again the following winter to eastern Turkey to assess the increasing tense situation developing between Turkey and Russia and the threat to British interests and even as he penned his second book (I142), war broke out and the Russian army moved towards Constantinople.

It was to be a conflict extensively covered by reporters from British and American newspapers, ever more in evidence since the Crimean War. David Ker, the future well-known author of boys' fiction, had covered events leading to the Russian appropriation of Khiva for the *Daily Telegraph* (I108) and Januarius MacGahan of the *New York Herald* witnessed its fall on 9 June 1873 (I115). MacGahan was to be one of seventeen international correspondents reporting the Russo-Turkish war of 1877-78 whose dispatches for the *Daily News* were collected in two annual volumes (I149). Other American and British accounts appeared over the next few years (I148-52, I155), but of especial interest for illuminating the other, Turkish, side of the war and in particular the stubborn Turkish defence of the fortress of Plevna, which fell finally in December 1877 and led to the peace treaty of San Stefano on 3 March 1878 (fig. 20), were two books written by British subjects serving with the Turks (I153-54), while the most idiosyncratic addition were undoubtedly the five poetic cantos the Scottish doctor, John McCosh devoted to "the war of the czar" (I156).

Fig. 20 "The Great Game: the afghan Emir Sher Ali Khan with his 'friends' Russia and Great Britain" (30 November, 1878), cartoon by Sir John Tenniel.

Alexander II's reign was also the reign of the Americans. Americans of course were no strangers to Russia.[17] When Catherine II was on the throne, John Ledyard, who had been on Captain Cook's last voyage, published his account that included a description of Kamchatka in 1783 (D32), four years before he returned to undertake a journey across Siberia that led only to his arrest and expulsion from Russia in 1788 (D56). This was a year before John Paul Jones, regarded as a traitor by the British, was also expelled after his ill-fated service in the Russian navy. His memoirs (D55), like Ledyard's diary (D56), were published only decades after the events. Similar delays, often attributable to the discretion of diplomats, occurred during the reigns of both Alexander I (F16, F24-25, F50-51) and Nicholas I (G22-23, G32, G54, G78-79). Some eighteen accounts in the bibliography refer to Nicholas's reign, but only six of which, all by tourists, appeared within it. What seems to have been the first American tourist account to be published in England was the lawyer John Stephens's *Incidents of travel, in Greece, Turkey, Russia and Poland* (1838), utterly conventional but enjoying several editions (G41). Another lawyer, George Ditson, stayed in the south, claiming in his *Circassia*, published in 1850 (G109), to be the first American to visit and describe the region. John Maxwell (G103) travelled in the same year as Ditson (1847) but his tour took him only as far as Kazan from St Petersburg. He was particularly alive to the presence of American engineers in Russian service. Russian expansion of the railway system had led to the recruitment of foreign specialists and the purchase of machinery and locomotives (for British counterparts, see G89, G102). Prominent among the Americans were Major George Whistler, who worked on the Petersburg-Moscow railway link from 1842 until his death in 1849 (G87), and Joseph Harrison, who sold rolling stock and locomotives for the same railway (G88). In 1857, already in the reign of Alexander II, the firm of Winans, Harrison and Winans won a contract to remount the railway (I21).

During the Crimean War American sympathies, particularly following the fall of Sevastopol, were decidedly pro-Russia and in the years following Alexander II's accession the rapprochement was much in evidence and is

---

[17] There is a considerable literature on American presence in Russia. See Anna M. Babey, *Americans in Russia 1776-1917: a study of the American travelers in Russia from the American Revolution to the Russian Revolution* (New York: Comet Press, 1938); Max M Laserson, *The American impact on Russia 1784-1917* (New York: Macmillan, 1950); Thomas A. Bailey, *America faces Russia: Russian-American relations from early times to our day* (Gloucester, Mass.: Peter Smith, 1964). Of the leading Russian authority Nikolai Bolkhovitinov's many relevant works, only *The beginnings of Russian-American relations 1775-1815* (Cambridge, Mass. and London: Harvard University Press, 1975) and not the subsequent volumes has appeared in English.

seen by many as the golden period of Russo-American relations, despite the fact that during the long years of the American Civil War, there seemed many a paradox in the relative positions of the Union and the Confederacy vis-à-vis Russia and Britain. The emancipation of the serfs in 1861 could not but engage the interest of Americans in the context of their own difficult path to the 13th Amendment and the abolition of slavery in 1865 (I65). A year later, in 1866, Congress sent Gustavus Fox to congratulate the Tsar on his surviving the first of several attempts to assassinate him and Russian society went to excess in its pro-American raptures (I64). The willingness of the Tsar to sell Alaska to America for a relative pittance in 1867 might also be seen as further evidence of his benevolence, although other factors were obviously at play: it was a change of ownership noted already in an account of the following year: *Travel and adventure in the territory of Alaska, formerly Russian America – now ceded to the United States – and in various other parts of the north Pacific.* (I60). Virtually a quarter of the 180 entries for Alexander's reign were written by Americans and they provide not only an indication of the rapidly increasing presence of Americans throughout all parts of the Russian empire but also of a variety of activities and roles that rival but do not equal those of the British.

They included in their ranks two diplomats who were outstanding scholars: Jeremiah Curtin (I51, K66) and Eugene Schuyler (I78, I113) were both linguists, translators, and much else, and travelled extensively in Russia, particularly in central Asia. They were eclipsed as an influential contemporary voice by George Kennan, who first came to Russia as a young member of a Russo-American telegraph surveying expedition that spent three years in Siberia and on Kamchatka in the late 1860s and published some years later in 1871 his *Tent life in Siberia* (I59). It was, however, the book that resulted from his fourth visit to Siberia in 1885 that was to be decisive in alerting the American and British publics to the abuses within the Russian penal system and provoked much controversy (J36).

It would be remiss not to mention that among American visitors during this reign was none other than Samuel Langhorne Clemens, already using his pseudonym Mark Twain but not yet author of *The adventures of Tom Sawyer* and its sequel, *Adventures of Huckleberry Finn*. He was briefly in the Crimea and Odessa with a group of American tourists in the summer of 1867 and met the Tsar in Yalta, finding him well-disposed to Americans, possibly not unconnected with his having just sold them Alaska for $7.2 million (I71). It was merely a happy coincidence that precisely at the time that Twain was visiting the south of Russia and paying his compliments to the Tsar at Yalta there arrived in St Petersburg a famous English humourist, Lewis Carroll, but in his more modest everyday guise as Rev. Charles Dodgson, an Oxford don, accompanied by his colleague Rev. Henry Liddon (I73). While Twain's travels "in pursuit of recreation" was published in its first English edition in 1871 (I71), Carroll's journal, first appearing in America in 1928, was to wait until 1965 (I72). Carroll subsequently had little to say about Russia; Twain in contrast had much to say and write, suggesting for example in 1886 that

> Power, when lodged in the hands of man, means oppression – insures oppression: it means oppression always: [...] give it to the high priest of the Christian Church in Russia, the Emperor, and with a wave of his hand he will brush a multitude of young men, nursing mothers, gray headed patriarchs, gently young girls, like so many unconsidered flies, into the unimaginable hells of his Siberia, and go blandly to his breakfast, unconscious that he has committed a barbarity.[18]

Like many of his fellow-countrymen, Twain had been much influenced by reading Kennan and his attitude to Russia and to its ruler, who was now Alexander III, had changed fundamentally.

VI

The shortest by more than a decade of reigns beginning in the nineteenth century, Alexander III's was marked by ultra conservatism and internal repression but was free from the wars that had been virtually ever present before and certainly after and earned the Tsar the unlikely title of "the Peacemaker". The first years of the new Tsar's reign was marked by events of very different character and import that were nevertheless strongly reflected in English-language accounts.

The first was a tragedy far away from Moscow that commanded the attention of the British and in particular the American publics. On 12 June 1881 the USS *Jeannette*, originally a Royal Navy vessel, which had set out on 8 July 1879 on an expedition to the North Pole via the Bering Strait, was crushed by ice and sank off the Siberian coast. The commander, George De Long, and his men were obliged to try to make their way across the ice and then by three small boats towards the delta of the Lena. Two boats with twenty-five men reached different points on the mainland and only

---

18 'The New Dynasty', in *Mark Twain: collected tales, sketches, speeches, & essays 1852-1890*, edited by Louis J. Budd (New York: Library of America, 1992), p. 883.

thirteen were to survive. Diaries of both some who perished and others who survived were published over the next few years (J3-7), as were the accounts of those who were sent to find them (J8-9, J12).

The incredible hardships suffered by De Long's crew were of a different order from the horrors of the pogroms that swept through the south-west of Russia, in towns such as Odessa and Kiev, in 1881-83, triggered in part by the assassination of Alexander II, the responsibility for which was placed by some on the Jews. The Jews had suffered persecution since the mid-eighteenth century but were increasingly subjected to restrictions on their movements both within and outside the Pale of Settlement. In 1846 the banker and philanthropist Moses Montefiore (fig. 21) in his capacity as president of the Board of Deputies of British Jews had visited Russia to plead the Jewish cause in an audience with Nicholas I; in July 1872 he repeated the visit, ostensibly to offer Alexander II congratulations on the 200th anniversary of the birth of Peter the Great, and reported back on the improved lot of Russian Jews over the past two decades (G99, I106).

Fig. 21 Portrait of Moses Montefiore (n.d.), artist unknown.

Already in his hundred and first year in 1885, he had lived, however, to hear of the horrors of the new pogroms. Although the British press and pamphleteers with such publications as the *Times*'s *Persecution of the Jews, 1881* (1882) responded to the events in Russia, the bibliography registers no first-hand accounts from British observers. It was an American, James Buel, travelling in Russia in 1882, who published the following year his indictment of Russia's treatment of the Jews (J19), which, a decade later, was taken up by the American novelist Harold Frederic in a series of articles for the *New York Times* in September 1891 (published in book form only in 1904 (J109)), but which were contested by the London-based American artist Joseph Pennell in articles for the *Illustrated London News* in December and appearing as a book the following year (J111).

Buel was one of the few travel writers to use the word "nihilism" in his title but far from the only one to discuss the burning issues of nihilism and terrorism, only accentuated by the assassination of Alexander II after a series of similar attempts. Nihilism was "the controlling cause of my visit to Russia", asserted the American clergyman James Buckley in his *The midnight sun: the tsar and the nihilist* (J34), while for the correspondent of the Chicago *Daily News* Russia was simply *The land of the nihilist* (J69). All three examples are American: British travellers seemed more reluctant to use the word, at least in titles. Not so in fiction. Nihilism brought to the English novel a string of novels with such stirring titles as *A nihilist princess* or *Narka the nihilist*, and, indeed, a play, Oscar Wilde's *Vera: or the nihilists*, so much so that as late as 1899 a speaker at the Anglo-Russian Society complained that "five novels out of six will have a Nihilistic plot. [...] all this may serve to make an exciting story, but it does not give a true picture of Russian life as I have learnt to know it during a residence of many years in that country".[19] Formed in 1893, the Anglo-Russian Literary Society's brand of conservative Russophilia was in essence designed to combat, unsuccessfully, the anti-Russian governmental stance of the powerful Society of Friends of Russian Freedom and its organ *Free Russia*, established three years earlier in 1890 on the initiative of Sergei Stepniak-Kravchinskii, one of a group of influential Russian political émigrés in London. To a greater degree than ever before British Russophobia was underpinned by a sympathy for the oppressed and for those factions, including nihilists, struggling to curb the excesses of autocratic power.

The winter of 1891 saw Russia caught in further tragic events as famine spread along the Volga and gradually further afield to the Urals and the Black Sea, claiming an estimated half-million victims by the end of the following year. The Russian governmental response was slow, begrudging and fudging, help from outside, particularly from Britain and the USA, was immediate and generous. Two Englishmen, who knew Russia well, James Steveni and Edward Hodgetts, toured the area and reported on the

---

19 F. Toulmin Smith, 'That the representation of Russian life in English novels is mislleading', *Anglo-Russian Literary Society Proceedings*, no. 25 (1899), pp. 88-110.

conditions for the *Daily Chronicle* and Reuters respectively, publishing books the following year (J112-13), while detailed accounts of the extensive American relief operation that involved bringing ships from America with food supplies were also soon to appear (J115-17).

Prominent among Russians volunteering to aid the starving peasantry was Leo Tolstoi (fig. 22), trenchant in his criticism of Tsar and Orthodox church for their seeming reluctance to help, and it was in Riazan, some hundred miles southeast of Moscow on the river Oka, that the Swede Jonas Stadling, working to alleviate the suffering, met him in March 1892 (J114), a few months before Francis Reeves, who had arrived with supplies from America (J116).

Fig. 22 Tolstoi organising famine relief in Samara (1891), photographer unknown.

Visits to Tolstoi, whether he was involved in famine relief or at home in Moscow or on his estate at Iasnaia Poliana, had become virtually *de rigueur* for foreign travellers, particularly British and American enthusiasts for his fiction or social, moral and religious works.[20] The diplomat and scholar, Eugene Schuyler, during his stint at the American embassy in St Petersburg, seems to have initiated the trend as early as 1868 (I78), but it was in the 80s and 90s that a trickle of "pilgrims" threatened to become a flood. During Alexander III's reign, some thirteen such visits are registered and the visitors include some remarkable figures, both British and American. In March 1888 Tolstoi was visited by Rev. Lansdell, who was on his way to Chinese Mongolia (J75), a few weeks later, by William Stead, the editor

---

20 See R.F. Christian, 'The road to Yasnaya Polyana: some pilgrims from Britain and their reminiscences', *Slavonic and East European Review*, LXVI (1988), pp. 526-52; Robert Whittaker, 'Tolstoy's American visitors: memories of personal encounters, 1868-1909', *TriQuarterly*, nos. 110-11 (Fall 2001), pp. 213-73.

of *Pall Mall* (J78), and then, for the first of many visits, by Aylmer Maude, the noted translator of Tolstoi's works (J87). In late 1892 two Quakers, John Neave and John Bellows, discussed the plight of the Stundists and of religious minorities whom they were to visit in the Causcasus region (J121-22), before they were followed in the following February by an even more renowned English translator, Constance Garnett (J125). Her American counterpart as translator and writer on Russian literature, Isabel Hapgood, paid many visits to Tolstoi in 1887-89 (J67), and from among her fellow countrymen, mention might be made of the educational reformer Ernest Crosby, closely observing the "Tolstoyan" methods of instruction in the village school at Iasnaia Poliana (J139), and the eccentric Thomas Stevens, who in June 1886 had abandoned his penny farthing on the Russian stage of his attempt to go *Around the world on a bicycle* (J58; fig. 23) and opted for a circus mustang when visiting Tolstoi in the summer of 1890 (J99).

Fig. 23 Thomas Stevens on his penny-farthing bicycle. Image from his *Around the world on a bicycle* (London: Sampson Low, Marston, Searle and Rivington, 1887). Cornell University Library.

During the following reign of Nicholas II the pilgrimages continued unabated. A further fifteen visits, a far from exhaustive total, are mentioned in the bibliography and only in the last few years up to his death in 1910 is there a noticeable decrease.

The American presence during Alexander III's reign was even more marked than during his father's, despite the deterioration of Russo-American relations. Sixty-three of the 142 accounts registered, some 44%, relate to American experiences of Russia. For the most part, Russia was but part of round-the-world tours, reflected in titles such as *Arctic sunbeams: or from Broadway to the Bosphorus by way of the North Cape* (J1), *A tour round the world, being a brief sketch of the most interesting sights seen in Europe, Africa, Asia, and America, while on a two years' ramble* (J29) or *People and countries visited in a winding journey around the world* (J52), but it was also the specific destination for individuals and groups, intent, like the Indiana publisher, to relate "in a natural way, what I saw in a summer's travel, through a remarkable country, among a strange and interesting people" (J71). There were, as noted elsewhere, travellers with very different agenda and objectives.

There are nineteen accounts by women, twelve American and predominantly tourists of varying degrees of perceptiveness ("Russia impressed me as too vast to comprehend" (J83)), the rest, British. Of the latter, Jane Harrison (J61) and Constance Garnett (J125) have left only disappointingly brief and fragmentary evidence of their visits in 1886 and 1893 respectively, but Bettina Walker's memories of her studies as a young pianist in St Petersburg from 1886 are considerably more interesting (J63). In the summer of 1887, Elizabeth Brown, director of the solar section of the Liverpool Astronomical Society, travelled to Kineshma on the Volga to observe the solar eclipse, although with disappointing results (J72), while Nellie Peel, a year after her curtsey as a debutante in the 1892 London season, decided to travel to Siberia on a yacht, on which one of her companions was none other than Captain Wiggins, and sailed as far as the mouth of the Enesei, exhibiting, in the words of Lord Dufferin, the former ambassador to Russia, "the audacity of our modern maidens" (J130). It was, however, a nurse who had served during the Russo-Turkish War in 1878, Kate Marsden, who was to steal the headlines. In 1891 she left Moscow for Siberia to visit the leper colony at Viliusk in Iakutia and to search for a herb that was said to check the disease (J102). On her return to London after her epic journey, much of it on horseback, she became one of the first women to be elected a Fellow of the Royal Geographical Society but her story was widely doubted.

Marsden's heroics were but one of many accounts of Siberia by British and American travellers during this period, almost all of whom had something to contribute to the burning issue of the day, the Russian penal system and the fate of exiles in Siberia. Siberia, eternal snows and exile had formed an unavoidable triangle in the minds of Europeans at least since the time of Peter the Great and down the decades many travellers recorded meetings with exiles and prisoners: during Catherine II's reign, for example, John Parkinson devoted fascinating pages to his encounters with exiles in Tobolsk in 1793 (D66) and under Nicholas I several encounters with exiled Decembrists are described by Charles Cottrell (G73), Samuel Hill (G104) and particularly by the Atkinsons (G107, G108). In 1866 the American journalist and author Thomas Knox wrote much about the exile system (I63), but it was Rev. Henry Lansdell's *Through Siberia* (I171), recounting his first travels of 1879, when he distributed bibles and religious tracts wherever he found hands to take them and visited many of the places of exile and penal colonies, that was to fuel a controversy that was to rage for at least another decade. Lansdell's work, in which he made generally conciliatory remarks about the operation of the system, was published only in 1882, following the assassination of Alexander II and in a context of much wider condemnation of Russian oppression. It did, however, receive support in *Siberia as it is*, published in 1892 by Harry de Windt (fig. 24), in which he describes a journey in the summer of 1890 specifically to inspect prisons and to show that Siberia "was not so black as it is painted" (J98).

Fig. 24 Harry de Windt (no image credit). Photograph published in his *From Paris to New York by land* (Thomas Nelson & Sons: London, Edinburgh, Dublin and New York, 1903).

A few years later De Windt published the text of a lecture he had delivered in London to the Foreign Press Association, defending his views of Russian prisons not only in Siberia but also on Sakhalin (J134), which he had also visited in 1894, publishing in 1896 his *The new Siberia: being an account of a visit to the penal island of Sakhalin, and political prison and mines of the Trans-Baikal district, eastern Siberia* (J135). In all these works De Windt was openly crossing swords with the American George Kennan. Kennan had visited Russia for the fourth time in May 1885 and embarked on extensive travels through Siberia, accompanied by the photographer George Frost. What he saw made him a committed opponent of the Russian penal system and on his return to America, the critical articles he wrote for the *Century* magazine that had sponsored his visit and his extensive lecturing were highly influential even before the appearance of his book in 1891 (J36). In England, their influence was acknowledged by, for instance, Lionel Gowing, crossing Siberia in the winter of 1886-87 (J64) and by Dr Emile Dillon, the Russian-based correspondent of the *Daily Telegraph*, who under the pseudonym E. B. Lanin published in the *Fortnightly Review* in July 1890 "Russian prisons: the simple truth", attacking Lansdell and De Windt and moving the poet Algernon Swinburne to write his apologia for tyrannicide in the same journal, "Russia: an ode". Lanin's collected articles appeared in 1892 under the title *Russian characteristics* (J89).

Siberia, however, during Alexander III's reign invited discussion not only of exile but also of railways. In the spring of 1893 Dr Charles Wenyon travelled *Across Siberia on the great post-road*, claiming to be one of the last Englishmen to go "in the old fashioned way" by tarantas, steamer and rail from Vladivostok to the Urals (J126). It was three years earlier that the future Nicholas II, then Tsarevich, had inaugurated the construction of the far eastern section of the great Trans-Siberian railway and in the same year, 1890, a bridge was constructed across the Ural River, allowing the single-track railway which was being constructed simultaneously from Moscow to enter Siberia from the west. The completion and the glory of the railway was, however, in reality an event of the following reign.

Several years before the Trans-Siberian, however, another major railway project had been launched. In the spring of 1888 George Dobson sent letters to *The Times*, later re-issued as a book (J79), describing the opening of the Transcaspian railway. Begun in 1879 and originally from Uzun-Ada on the Caspian, it followed from its new terminus at the harbour of Krasnovodsk the route of the Silk Road, reaching via Bokhara Samarkand, which had become part of the Russian empire in 1868. The title of Dobson's book, *Russia's railway advance into Central Asia,* clearly indicates British fears of Russian expansionism. It came on the heels of the work of the Afghan Boundary Commission, described in 1887 by Lt. Arthur Yate in an equally eloquently entitled book, *England and Russia face to face in Asia* (J41), based on articles for the *Daily Telegraph*. Originally conceived as a military railway to assist actions against local tribes, the Transcaspian soon showed its great economic potential as well as its threat to British interests, well understood by George Curzon (fig. 25), the future viceroy of India, whose *Russia in Central Asia* (J86), records his "journey, taken under circumstances of exceptional ease and advantage" along the line in 1889.

Fig. 25 The Governor-General of India George Curzon with his wife Mary in Delhi (29 December 1902), photographer unknown. Published in Joachim K. Bautze, *Das koloniale Indien. Photographien von 1855 bis 1910* (Köln: Fackelträger Verlag, 2007), p. 211.

A decade later, the railway was extended to Tashkent, which soon after its seizure in 1865 had become the capital of Russian Turkestan.

VII

The coronation of the Tsars in Moscow presented a spectacle that foreign diplomats and dignitaries and visiting travellers witnessed and described with varying degrees of fascination and boredom. A number of young English aristocrats descended on Moscow in September 1801 to witness the installation of Alexander I (F2), while the Duke of Devonshire headed a special embassy to attend the coronation of Nicholas I in September 1826, as described in the letters of Mrs Disbrowe (F104). The *Daily News* sent a special correspondent, John Murphy, to cover Alexander II's coronation in September 1856 (I12), an event also described in *Russia after the war* by the prolific author Selina Bunbury (I11). Not unexpectedly, Queen Victoria sent her son the Duke of Edinburgh and his Russian wife, the former Grand Duchess Maria Aleksandrovna, to attend the coronation of Alexander III in May 1883, a ceremony described in letters to his wife by Viscount Wolseley, who accompanied them (J25).

The interest in the coronation of Nicholas II was, however, unprecedented, and only increased by the tragic events that followed it. Nine accounts, two of which are by American observers, describe the coronation. The majority were written by members of the official British party accompanying Queen Victoria's representatives, on this occasion the Duke and Duchess of Connaught, and included Bishop Mandell Creighton (K22; fig. 26) and W.J. Birkbeck (J82), the acknowledged authority on the Russian church, and Lieutenant-General Grenfell (K20), as well as by a journalist Richard Davis (K24) and the translator and writer Arthur Sykes, who was a member of a tourist group (K23).

Fig. 26 Portrait of Mandell Creighton (1902), by Hubert von Herkomer.
Oil on canvas. National Portrait Gallery, London.

Both Davis and Sykes were apparently not in Moscow when four days after the coronation, on 26 May 1896, there occurred the stampede and death of some 1300 people at Khodynskoe pole, a large open space in the north west of Moscow which had been used without mishap for festive events after the coronation of Alexander III. Completely different reactions to the events were recorded by an American visitor and a long-time British resident. John Logan's revealingly entitled book, *In joyful Russia* (K19), is an account of "a thoroughly delightful trip" to a country "in holiday attire" and certainly not to be spoilt by tragic events for "it is not best to let the unthinking brood too deeply over the irretrievable", but the Tolstoyan Aylmer Maude attacked "the conventional, superficial laudations of a spectacle which enlightened conscience and sober reason must see in a wholly different light" (K26).

The Tsar's decision to attend the gala ball at the French embassy in the evening of the tragedy earned him the sobriquet of "the bloody" from his critics; some eight and a half years later, his retiring to Tsarskoe selo on the day before the events of Bloody Sunday, 22 January 1905, brought him even greater dishonour. The Russia over which he ruled witnessed in the early years of the new century widespread and growing internal unrest and protest but also a disastrous war against Japan and all at a time of Anglo-Russian hostility.

The Russo-Japanese War of 1904-06, when British sympathies were for the Japanese, officially at least, attracted much attention and was covered in great detail by correspondents sent by American and European newspapers and journals and their reports were often subsequently gathered together, re-edited and published in book form. As tension mounted in 1903 Bertram Simpson, writing under his pseudonym Bertram Weale, was dispatched to Manchuria and, highly critical of Russian presence in the area, dedicated his book *Manchu and Muscovite* to the "gallant Japanese nation" (K114). When hostilities broke out in February 1904 Frederick McKenzie, the Canadian correspondent of the *Daily Mail*, was soon reporting from the Japanese side (K129), while the experienced Scottish journalist Douglas Story on his arrival at Mukden became the first foreign correspondent formally accredited to the Russian army on 24 April 1904 (J133). Maurice Baring, appointed by the *Morning Post* (K134), and Guy Brooke, the Reuter's correspondent (K135), travelled out together on the Trans-Siberian to Kharbin in May to report the war, while Oliver Greener, "a secret agent in Port Arthur", sent reports to both *The Times* and the *China Times* (K136). The experiences of the Irish journalist Francis McCullagh were even more fraught: he was with the

Russian forces at Mukden in March 1905 when he was captured by the Japanese and sent off to Japan as a POW (K126).

The war was played out against a backcloth of social unrest and riots, giving rise for the first time to ominous titles that were not all the result of hindsight. Even before Bloody Sunday, George Perris, who wrote for various English newspapers, entitled his book *Russia in revolution* (K4), while Henry Nevinson witnessed *The dawn in Russia or scenes in the Russian revolution* (K149), once again re-arranged articles previously published in the *Daily Chronicle*, and under the intriguing title *The cable game: the adventures of an American press-boat in Turkish waters during the Russian revolution* (K154) Stanley Washburn followed, as had Nevinson, revolutionary events in the Russian south, notably in Odessa. Karl Joubert, an Englishman of Huguenot descent, reeled off three books in 1904 with each title more doom-laden than the previous: *Russia as it really is* (K13), *The truth about the tsar and the present state of Russia* (K122), where Nicholas II is dubbed "the last of the Romanoffs", and *The fall of tsardom* (K138). Russia was already "red" for Kellog Durland (K157) and John Foster Fraser (K161). It was a time of turmoil and feverish expectation, such that the Virginia lawyer William Edwards, on honeymoon and only briefly in St Petersburg and Moscow in September 1902, felt able to predict "a saturnalia of blood and tears, a squaring of ten centuries' accounts, more fraught with human anguish and human joy than ever dreamed a Marat and a Robespierre" (K97)

One of the great themes of the period was inevitably travel on the Trans-Siberian, begun in 1890 but only completed in 1916. It was the great "ribbon of iron" along which towards Vladivostok the anthropologist and translator Annette Meakin travelled with her mother in 1900, the first Englishwomen to accomplish that journey (K73), whilst in the opposite direction Dr Francis Clark with his wife and son claimed in the same year to be the first Americans "to go around the world by the new route" (K70). In 1900 the journey still involved a ferry ride across Lake Baikal from the temporary terminus at Port Baikal to Mysovsk, and two new steel-hulled ice-breaking boats that had been built in Newcastle-upon-Tyne, the huge train-ferry the *Baikal* and the smaller *Angara*, came into service that year. It was only in 1904 after horrendous difficulties in construction that the Circum-Baikal railway was completed and it became possible to travel the whole route by rail.

It was precisely in 1900, however, that the Russian Ministry of Ways of Communication published an English-language *Guide to the Great Siberian*

Railway that in exhaustive detail described not only the main railway but all its connecting lines and provided over 350 photographs of the railways and also of the towns and villages and their inhabitants.[21] If its aim was to entice Anglo-American tourists to journey along the whole length of the railway and possibly along its connecting lines then it would seem to have succeeded. There are literally dozens of accounts from the first two decades of Nicholas's reign about journeys on the Trans-Siberian in full and in part, some naming the railway in titles such as Michael Shoemaker's *The great Siberian railway from St. Petersburg to Pekin* (K94), Clarence Cary's *The Trans-Siberian route or notes of a journey from Pekin to New York in 1902* (K95) and Emil Fischer's *Overland via the Trans-Siberian railway: description of a trip from the Far East to Europe and the United States of America* (K169), while others simply refer to travel through Siberia itself. Often well illustrated with photographs, the books offer on the one hand their authors' pronouncements on the comforts or lack of them in the dining cars and sleeping compartments, in the inadequate unisex washrooms, and on the other, more serious lucubrations on the railway's implications for immigration, for the exploitation of Siberia's natural resources and for its military importance, soon to be put to the test with the outbreak of the Russo-Japanese War.

The comforts, relatively speaking, of travelling by train notwithstanding, Siberia and the border lands and far reaches of the Russian empire continued to offer formidable challenges to explorers and sportsmen. In 1895-96 the wealthy expatriate Elim Demidov, Prince of San Donato, was accompanied by prominent British sportsmen on three shooting expeditions in the Caucasus (K9) and followed these with further expeditions to the Altai in 1897 (K31) and to Kamchatka in 1900 (K69). The Earl of Ronaldshay, although he did much of his travelling by the Transcaspian and Trans-Siberian, nevertheless also shot wild sheep in the Altai in 1903 (K106), as did Major Harold Swayne during his furlough from the army in India

---

21 *Guide to the Great Siberian Railway.* Edited by A.I. Dmitriev-Mamanov and A.F. Zdziarski. English translation by Miss L. Kukol-Yasnopolsky, revised by John Marshall (St Petersburg: Typography of the Artitstic Printing Society, 1900). For a comprehensive history that makes wide use of some of the travellers' accounts listed in this bibliography, see Harmon Tupper, *To the great ocean: the taming of Siberia and the building of the Trans-Siberian Railway* (London: Secker & Warburg, 1965). See also Christian Wolmar, *To the edge of the world: the story of the Trans-Siberian express, the world's greatest railway* (London: Atlantic Books, 2013).

(K108). The region seemingly exerted a particular fascination for officers in the Indian army: Captain John Wood's *Travel & sport in Turkestan* (K178) was soon followed by, for example, Lt. Percy Etherton's *Across the roof of the world: a record of sport and travel through Kashmir, Gilgit, Hunza, the Pamirs, Chinese Turkistan, Mongolia and Siberia* (K206). The Altai attracted the expert climber Samuel Turner, who climbed Mount Belukha in 1903 (K102-03), while the Pamirs saw increasing numbers of travellers and hunters, including Ralph Cobbold, bagging his first tiger (K46). It was a region that was the destination of serious scientific expeditions, such as undertaken and described by Lt. Axel Olufsen of the Danish army (K14-15), but was also "opened up" for the everyday traveller by the Transcaspian. Many travellers might be named, but let that of one remarkable lady suffice: Ella Christie, the distinguished Scottish traveller and gardener, took part as the sole female in expeditions through Turkestan in 1910 and 1912, during the latter becoming the first British woman ever to enter Khiva (K215). In the north of Russia, the bear and the wolf, traditional victims of the hunting classes, continued to offer "sport" (K158), but it was the birds that drew the Nottingham ornithologist Henry Pearson and his friends on several cruises through northern waters in the late 1890s (K8, K65).

Rail, boat, sled, carriage, horse (K16), even camel (J14) all took travellers on their various routes through Russia. Thomas Stevens had wisely abandoned his penny-farthing for the Russian leg of his journey in 1886 (J58), but cyclists on much more reliable models were soon pedalling their way through Russia. In November 1890 two American students travelled *Across Asia on a bicycle* and were briefly in Russian territory, reaching Samarkand before proceeding to China (J106). It was in the south of Russia, from Odessa through the Crimea and the Caucasus, that Sir John Foster Fraser and friends cycled also as part of a world tour that occupied no less than 774 days in the second half of the decade (K29). In purely Russian terms it was the British cycling enthusiast Robert Jefferson who was the real star. He claimed a record for his round trip from Warsaw to Moscow in fifty days in the early summer of 1895 (K30) and returned three years later intent on replicating Colonel Burnaby's (fig. 27) famous ride to Khiva. He entered Russia from Galicia and then from Moscow, accompanied by Russian cycling friends, he followed the Volga and crossing the Kirghiz steppe, was eventually was received by the khan of Khiva (K48).

Fig. 27 A Christmas dinner on the heights before Sevastopol (Capt Burnaby is the fifth figure from the left), by J.A. Vinter. Tinted lithograph. Published in *The Seat of War in the East* (London: Paul & Dominic Colnaghi & Co., 13 & 14 Pall Mall East; Paris: Goupil & Cie, 1855).

Jefferson soon switched his loyalties to the new fangled motor car but did not enter Russia on his trip to Constantinople. The first account in the bibliography is Claude Anet's *Through Persia in a motor-car by Russia and the Caucasus* (K141), recording a trip in the spring of 1905, but it was in the summer of 1907 that Prince Scipione Borghese won an international race from Pekin to Paris, racing through Siberia to St Petersburg in his Itala, accompanied by Luigi Barzini, whose account includes some wonderful photographs of their encounters and mishaps in Russia (K166).

Of all the ways of travelling it was the most natural and reliable of them all, on foot, that obviously took explorers to the summits in the Caucasus and the Pamirs and across difficult terrain, but walking under a new name and with new connotations became a fashion towards the end of the nineteenth century: it was the era of the tramp, the vagabond, the wanderer, who restlessly moved from place to place, country to country, living simply, avoiding cities, roaming the countryside. Tramping, generically different from the more genteel ramble (as exemplified in the titles of Isabel Hapgood's *Russian rambles* (J67) or David McConaughy's *Rambles through Russia and in Norway and Sweden* (J85)), first appears in the bibliography in the title of the American Lee Meriwether's *A tramp trip: how to see Europe on fifty cents a day* (1886, J46), in which "desirous of seeing something of low life", he made his way from Odessa to St Petersburg, as did a decade later Josiah Flint, including a Russian episode in his *Tramping with tramps: studies and sketches of vagabond life* (K42). Variations on titles are offered by John Patterson's *My vagabondage, being the intimate autobiography of a nature's nomad* (K10) and Max Müller's *Reminiscences of a roving life* (K64), which he further explains as "a life of a wanderer – a vagabond – and nothing more". While Carl Joubert claimed to have spent many years as a tramp (*brodiaga*) exploring Russia (K13), the "tramp" in both title and lifestyle is firmly linked with the name of Stephen Graham (fig. 28), who described his Russian adventures from 1906 to 1917 in a steady stream of books, beginning with *A vagabond in the Caucasus* (K232) and *A tramp's sketches* (K233) that took him to every corner of *Undiscovered Russia* (K234). It was entirely in keeping with the image of the Russia he loved that he eschewed St Petersburg, until the outbreak of war in 1914 obliged him to visit the city for the first time on his way back to England.

Fig. 28 Pen portrait of Stephen Graham, by Vernon Hill. Published in Stephen Graham, *Changing Russia* (London: John Lane, 1913), frontispiece.

Graham is just one of a number of figures from Nicholas II's reign whose links with Russia through their often frequent visits and range of acquaintances, their work as journalists, their lecturing, and constant publications that ranged beyond travel accounts into plays and novels with Russian settings, essays in periodicals and separate collections, and articles in newspapers and magazines brought them reputations as Russia buffs. Another is Bernard, later Sir Bernard, Pares, the pioneer of Russian studies in British universities, who paid his first visit to Russia several years before Graham and became deeply involved in the working of the Duma, convened for the first time in 1906 (K123). At the outbreak of war he was appointed

British military observer to the Russian army and remained at the front for three years (K309). The multi-talented Maurice Baring was introduced to Russia in 1901, was a correspondent during the Russo-Japanese War, and became literally enamoured of many aspects of the Russian land, culture and people that were subsequently reflected in his work in many genres, including novels, plays and poetry. Sharing with Pares and Baring a public school and Cambridge background, Morgan Philips Price, who was to become a prominent Labour politician, came somewhat later to the Russian scene, visiting Siberia in the spring of 1910 (K219) and returning as a correspondent for the *Manchester Guardian* to report the war in the Caucasus (K322) and to observe first the February Revolution, then the October for which he had initially much sympathy (K379-81). In their later years Graham (K193), Pares (K58-59), Baring (K79), and Price (K380) all produced memoirs that emphasize the major role that Russia played in their lives. Pares had his American equivalent in Samuel Harper, who made numerous trips to Russia between 1904 and 1939, studied like Pares at Moscow University, and devoted his career to the study of Russia at the University of Chicago from 1912 (K119).

Graham was in the Altai mountains when in July 1914 news reached him of the outbreak of WWI (K290). It was a war that inevitably was to dominate and colour all subsequent accounts of Russia, not least when Russian participation collapsed into revolution. It was also a war in which the British were neither the foe as in the Crimea nor the outsider observer as in the case of Russia's conflicts with the Ottoman empire, but the ally, the active participant, the involved reporter and observer. Of the 390 accounts listed in the bibliography for Nicholas's reign, about 100 date from its last three years and many more, begun in earlier times, extend into the period of war and revolution. Predominantly and expectedly British and American, they nonetheless include key works translated from French and German, and they reflect the diplomatic, military, political and social issues of the time.

Pares, as we have seen, was appointed as a British military observer with the Russian army and it was in this or a similar capacity that other British military personnel were involved. Major-General Sir Alfred Knox, who had been had been military attaché at the Petersburg embassy since 1911, was appointed liaison officer to the Russian army in 1914, visiting the eastern front on several occasions (K311), while in March 1916 Samuel Hoare, later Lord Templeton, was sent by British intelligence to Russia to work with the Russian general staff (K352). Chief of the British Military Mission and attached to the G.H.Q. of the Russian armies at Mogilev from August 1914 to April 1917 was Major-General Sir John Hanbury-Williams (K310). At a more humble level, John Morse fought as "an Englishman in the Russian ranks" (K300) for nine months in Russian Poland until his capture by, and escape from, the Germans in 1914-15. The Canadian William Gibson volunteered in 1914 (K304) and Richard Boleslavski was in a Polish volunteer lancer regiment with the Russian army on the eastern front in 1916 (K363), although the American pilot Bert Hall, serving with the French, arrived too late in January 1917 to aid the Russian air service (K377).

It was, however, as nurses and medical orderlies in hospitals or in the field that British presence during the war was most marked and effective. The once highly popular novelist Hugh Walpole used his experiences with a Russian Red Cross unit in the Carpathians (K315) for the first of his two novels on Russian themes, *The Dark Forest* (1916), while in the space of little more than two years (1916-17) Robert Scotland Liddell published an impressive trilogy about his Red Cross service with the Russian army in Poland and in Georgia and the Caucasus (K335-37), introducing in his last volume a series of vignettes of nurses whom he had met at the front. Violetta Thurstan joined the Russian Red Cross after service in Belgium and was soon wounded by shrapnel, from which she convalesced in Petrograd (K317). Although she entitled her book *A British nurse in Bolshevik Russia* (K356) Margaret Barber had arrived in Petrograd in 1916 and worked in hospitals in a number of Russia towns up to the end of 1919, whereas Florence Farmborough left her post as a governess in Moscow to train as a nurse with the outbreak of war and served at the front until 1917 (K185), as did Mary Britnieva, born in Russia to Anglo-Russian parents (K314). Dr Elsie Inglis headed a seventy-six-strong nursing unit of the Scottish Women's Hospitals for Russia that was in the south of Russia and Roumania in 1916-17 (K364-66). It was her work as a nurse for the Swedish Red Cross that brought Elsa Brändström her fame as the "Angel of Siberia", where since 1915 she had cared for countless German and Austrian POWs (K303).

The accounts of German nationals who became prisoners of war indeed occupy a small but distinctive place in the bibliography. Edward Dwinger (K334) and Hans Kohn (K341), who both later earned considerable reputations as authors, if in very different fields, endured long years of captivity in Siberian camps from 1915, as did Hereward Price, the title of whose book, *Boche and Bolshevik: experiences of an Englishman in the German army and in Russian prisons* (K327), reveals something of his unique fate. Price, who was eventually was to become a professor in an American university, as did Kohn, was drafted into the German army while he was a lecturer at Bonn. Two German nationals, who were not in the German army, were among those arrested within Russia and sent to camps: Theodor Kroeger, born and educated in Russia, tried unsuccessfully to escape to Germany in 1914, but, suspected of being a spy, spent two years in Siberian camps (K298), while Johann Dietrich, a hypnotist, was detained while on a professional visit to Petrograd (K307). Finally, an Austrian POW, Gustav Krist, captured in November 1914, endured long years of captivity not in Siberia but in Turkestan before his repatriation in 1921 (K321).

Russian participation in the war was described by the international corps of journalists on an unprecedented scale. If the Crimean War witnessed the birth of war journalism and subsequent conflicts were covered by an ever growing number of correspondents, WWI saw legions of journalists reporting from the capital and provincial cities and from the battlefields and behind the lines. Newspapers recruited people on the spot to contribute regular pieces or sent out their special correspondents and, as the bibliography clearly shows, many of the journalists subsequently gathered together their reports and published them and other materials as books.

The American lawyer-turned-journalist Stanley Washburn, one of the most seasoned of Russia reporters, having covered the Russo-Japanese War and the 1905 Revolution (K154), was the special war correspondent of *The Times* from September 1914 and his articles were quickly collected and re-edited to form a trilogy under the general title of *Field notes from the Russian front* and published in 1915-17 (K313, K340, K362). The first volume is notable for the photographs by George Mewes of the *Daily Mirror*, the only "official" English photographer with the Russian armies. During the same Polish campaign in 1914-15 a colleague reporting for the *Daily Telegraph* was Granville Fortescue, who had been the military attaché at the American embassy during the Russo-Japanese war (K299). Among the first British reporters were Hugh Walpole, already mentioned for his work with the Russian Red Cross but initially sent to report the war for the *Daily Mail* and *Saturday Review* (K315), and

Morgan Price, reporting for the *Manchester Guardian* (K322). Walpole's last role in these years was as head of the British Propaganda Unit, to which Denis Garstin, who earlier contributed articles to the *Morning Post* and the *Daily News*, was also attached (K218). In 1916 Henry Fyfe, who was to be the first journalist to report the murder of Rasputin at the end of that year, was previously at the Galician front, writing for *The War Illustrated* and other publications, but his reports, which were often heavily censored, never subsequently appeared in book form (K328). John Pollock, who spent four years in Russia between 1915 and 1919, also working for the Russian Red Cross, published in 1919 his *War and revolution in Russia* which comprised articles he had sent to the *Manchester Guardian* and other English newspapers. Robert Liddell was yet another who combined service with the Red Cross with reporting for the *Sphere* as its special correspondent. Further American reporters of note were Arno Dosch-Fleurot for the New York *World* (K369) and Richard Child for *Collier's Weekly* (K358). Florence Harper, who was the staff war correspondent of *Leslie's Weekly* but later served at the front as a nurse at a Red Cross hospital, worked with the photographer Donald Thompson to produce an album of extraordinary photographs of Russia at war and in revolution in addition to a narrative of her experiences (K370-72).

From the seat of government rather than from the front, the dispatches sent by the various foreign ambassadors and members of their embassies informed their governments of what they could glean from ministers and officials, of the substance of new decrees and orders, of the mood of the people in the capital and, where possible, elsewhere. Collections of dispatches and reports, diaries and letters included in autobiographies and biographies, as well as books on the country were a staple of British publications on Russia almost from the very beginning of contacts and in the nineteenth century were swelled by their American equivalents. They emerge as a particularly invaluable source for the events of the first two decades of the twentieth century.

Sir Cecil Spring-Rice was in the British embassy during the Russo-Japanese war and the 1905 revolution. His letters to Mrs Roosevelt, wife of the American president, occupy a special place in his correspondence during this period (K113) and are complemented by the memoirs of Earl Onslow, then Viscount Cranley, who was personal secretary to three ambassadors over the same period (K116). They were briefly colleagues of Sir Nevile Henderson, whose first stint at the embassy was from December 1905 to April 1909, and he returned in 1912 to serve under Sir George Buchanan (K153). Buchanan was in post some eight momentous years from 1910 to 1918, recorded in his memoirs published in 1923 as *My Mission to Russia* (K225). Another notable member of the embassy staff was H.J. Bruce, who was Head of Chancery from 1913 to 1918 and was to marry the ballerina Tamara Karsavina (K263-64). Two British consuls provide important commentaries on events away from the capital: Thomas Preston was consul in Ekaterinburg between 1913 and 1917 and still in post at the time of the murder of the imperial family (K155); and Bruce Lockhart, Consul-General in Moscow from 1914 to 1917, was to achieve greater notoriety in Bolshevik Russia for his involvement in the so-called "Lockhart plot" (K242-44). Although obviously occupying no official position other than that of "family" it is pertinent to note in this context the string of books produced from the 1920s until shortly before her death in 1959, by Buchanan's daughter, Meriel, which become increasingly repetitive, when not strident in the defence of her father's actions (K226-30), but her first book, published in 1918, is a detailed description of life in *Petrograd the city of trouble, 1914-1918* (K305). The two American ambassadors during these years, George Marye (K316) and his successor David Francis (K353-54), have both left their memoirs, as has the respected French ambassador, Maurice Paléologue, who charted his four-year sojourn in the Russian capital in meticulous detail (K297). Attachés in the American and French embassies, James Houghteling (K378) and comte Louis de Robien (K387), also published diaries that covered the February Revolution. Finally, the memoirs of the experienced and fluent Russian speaking Dutch diplomat William Oudenyk describe his many visits and stays in Russia from 1898 to the end of 1918, when he was acting minister of the Dutch legation (K56).

The war was still raging, at least on the western front, when the reign of the Romanovs came to an end with the abdication on 15 March 1917 of Nicholas II following the February Revolution. Ahead were the critical months up to the October Revolution, when the Provisional Government, headed first by Prince Lvov and then by Aleksandr Kerenskii, attempted to keep Russia in the war. It is a period described not only in many of the accounts registered in the bibliography but in at least twenty more, written by people who arrived after the Tsar's abdication; it is nonetheless a period outside the scope of this bibliography, which is dedicated to descriptions of Russia under the Romanovs. This Introduction, despite its length, is an attempt precisely to introduce themes, trends and events during and across reigns, to highlight the richness and variety of English-language first-hand accounts of the Russian empire, to encourage research and reading, rather than offer exhaustive treatment of any specific topic. It is the gateway, nothing more, to the bibliography itself.

Fig. 29 Mikhail Fedorovich, first tsar of the house of Romanov (n.d.), artist unknown.

Fig. 30 Aleksei Mikhailovich (n.d.), artist unknown. Hermitage Museum, St Petersburg.

Fig. 31 Fedor Alekseevich (1685), by Ivan Saltanov, Erofei Elin and Luka Smolianov. The Moscow Kremlin.

1. REIGNS OF THE FIRST ROMANOVS: MIKHAIL FEDOROVICH (1613-1645), ALEKSEI MIKHAILOVICH (1645-1676), and FEDOR ALEKSEEVICH (1676-1682)

A1) Gourdon, William, 'Later observations of William Gourdon, in his wintering at Pustozera, in the yeares 1614, and 1615, with a description of the Samoyeds life'. In Samuel Purchas, *Hakluytus posthumus or Purchas his pilgrimes, contayning a history of the world, in sea voyages & lande trauells, by Englishmen & others*. London: for Henry Fetherston, 1625. 4 vols.

> The notes by a Hull pilot in the service of the Muscovy Company on a journey to the Pechora and Ob rivers in 1611 (also published in Purchas) pre-date the accession of the first Romanov, but between 20 November 1614 and 21 August 1615, when he set sail for Holland, Gourdon was again in the area (vol. III, pp. 255-65).

A2) Tradescant, John, 'A viage of ambassod, undertaken by the right honorable Dudlie Diggs in the year 1618'. In Joseph Hamel, *England and Russia comprising the voyages of John Tradescant the elder, Sir Hugh Willoughby, Richard Chancellor, Nelson, and others to the White Sea*. Translated by John Studdy Leigh. London: Richard Bentley, 1854. xii+422pp.

> Extracts, with interpolated commentary by Hamel, from the manuscript diary of the gardener and botanist Tradescant the elder (d. 1638), who joined Sir Dudley Digges's embassy which reached the Dvina and Archangel in July 1618. Tradescant stayed in the area, collecting and describing wildlife and botanical specimens, until setting out again for England on 5 August (pp. 258-81).

A3) Beauplan, Guillaume Le Vasseur, de, 'A description of Ukraine, containing several provinces of the kingdom of Poland, lying between the confines of Muscovy, and the borders of Transylvania. Together with their customs, manner of life, and how they manage their wars'. Written in French by the sieur de Beauplan. In *A collection of voyages and travels, some now first printed from original manuscripts. Others translated out of foreign languages, and now first publish'd in English*. London: for Awnsham and John Churchill, 1704. 4 vols. [See also Guillaume Le Vasseur, sieur de Beauplan, *A description of Ukraine*. Introduction, translation, and notes by Andrew B. Pernal and Dennis F. Essar. Cambridge, Mass.: Harvard University Press, 1993. cxiv+242pp.]

> The fruit of a seventeen-year residence in the Polish-Lithuanian commonwealth from 1630 by the French engineer and cartographer Beauplan (1600?-75) and the first comprehensive account of Ukraine, first published in Rouen in 1651 but translated from the 1660 edition (vol. I, pp. 571-610).

A4) Olearius, Adam, *The voyages & travels of the ambassadors sent by Frederick Duke of Holstein, to the Great Duke of Muscovy, and the King of Persia, begun in the year M.DC.XXXIII and finish'd in M.DC.XXXIX; containing a compleat history of Muscovy, Tartary, Persia, and other adjacent countries, with several publick transactions reaching neer the present times.* Faithfully rendered into English [from the German] by John Davies. London: Thomas Dring and John Starkey, 1662. xxii+424pp. [See also *The travels of Olearius in seventeenth-century Russia*. Translated and edited by Samuel H. Baron. Stanford: Stanford University Press, 1967. xviii+349pp.]

> Highly influential account by Olearius (or Oelschlager) (1603-71), the scholarly German secretary to successive embassies sent by Duke of Holstein to the tsar of Russia and the shah of Persia to negotiate trade agreements. The first embassy travelled from Lübeck via Riga to Moscow in 1633 and returned in April 1635 (pp. 1-32). The second in 1636 went via Moscow to Astrakhan and on to Persia from where it returned in 1639 (Muscovy, pp. 3-170). First published in Schleswig in 1647, the work went into numerous editions. Most translations including the English were from the second expanded edition of 1656.

A5) Paul of Aleppo, *The travels of Macarius, patriarch of Antioch*. Written by his attendant archdeacon, Paul of Aleppo, in Arabic. Translated by F.C. Belfour. London: printed for the Oriental Translation Committee and sold by John Murray, 1829-36. 2 vols.

> Paul (ff.1654-66) accompanied his father on extensive travels that began in Aleppo in July 1652 and took them through Ukraine before arriving in Moscow in January 1655. They then journeyed to Novgorod in August

1655 before returning to Moscow in September. They finally left the Russian capital in May 1656, making their way via Kiev to Moldavia (vol. I, pp. 163-421; II, pp. 1-316).

A6) [Collins, Samuel], *The present state of Russia, in a letter to a friend at London; written by an eminent person residing at the great Tzars court at Mosco for the space of nine years.* London: Dorman Newman, 1671. xxii+144pp.

> Dr Collins (1619-70), Essex-born and educated in Cambridge and Padua, served in 1660-69 as physician to Tsar Aleksei Mikhailovich. His posthumously published book was seemingly composed of letters (rather than a single letter) he sent from Moscow to the eminent scientist Robert Boyle.

A7) Gordon, Patrick, *Passages from the diary of General Patrick Gordon of Auchleuchries, A.D 1635-A.D. 1699.* Edited by Joseph Robertson. Aberdeen: the Spalding Club, 1859. xxxvi+244pp.

> The Scottish mercenary Gordon (1635-99) served in the Swedish and Polish armies before entering Russian service in 1661 and, despite periodic attempts to resign, remained until his death, rising to the rank of general. Introduced to Peter I in 1686, he became a close friend and confidant of the tsar and was responsible for suppressing the Streltsy revolt during Peter's absence in Europe (pp. 40-193).

A8) Gordon, Patrick, *Diary of General Patrick Gordon of Auchleuchries, 1635-1699.* Edited by Dmitry Fedosov. Aberdeen: AHRC Centre for Irish and Scottish Studies, 2009-. Vol. II: 1659-1667 (2010).

> The second volume of this on-going transcription of Gordon's extensive diaries that are preserved in the State Archive of Military History in Moscow covers the period 1659-67 that includes the first seven years of his Russian service (pp. 134-281).

A9) Miège, Guy, *A relation of three embassies from his Sacred Majestie Charles II, to the Great Duke of Muscovie, the King of Sweden, and the King of Denmark. Performed by the right ho^{ble} Earl of Carlisle, in the years 1663 & 1664. Written by an attendant on the embassies and published with his L^{ps} approbation.* London: John Starkey, 1669. 461pp.

> Introduction signed "G.M." Miège (1644-1718), Swiss-born attendant to Charles Howard, Earl of Carlisle, on his embassy to Russia, Sweden and Denmark to negotiate trade agreements. The embassy (including as the

earl's private secretary the poet Andrew Marvell) left England on 22 July 1663 and arrived in Archangel on 19 August, then proceeded via Vologda to Moscow. They departed the following year, travelling via Novgorod to Riga, where they arrived on 3 August 1664 (pp. 23-330).

A10) Struys, Jan Janszoon, *The voiages and travels of John Struys through Italy, Greece, Muscovy, Tartary, Media, Persia, East. India, Japan and other countries in Europe, Africa, and Asia.* London: Abel Swalle, 1684. xix+387pp.

> The last of the three voyages of the Dutch adventurer (d. 1694), described in the preface as "this accurate and painfull traveller", took him in September 1668 as a sailmaker on an expedition from Holland to Riga and then to Moscow via Novgorod, before departing down the Volga to Astrakhan and a meeting with Stenka Razin in September 1669 (pp. 113-206). The book ends with the narrative of the expedition's leader, **Captain David Butler**, from Ispahan, 6 March 1671 (pp. 364-78).

A11) 'English Factor', *A narrative of the greatest victory known in memory of man: being the total overthrow of the great rebel Stepan Radzin, with his army of one hundred thousand men, by the grand gzar [sic] of Russia, and his renowned general Dolerucko. Written by an English factor, from the port of Moskow.* London: printed by J.C. for Nath. Crouch, 1671. 5pp.

> Dated Moscow 15 February 1670/71 and allegedly written by a factor or merchant's agent, it is a largely make-believe account of the defeat of Razin by the *voevoda* Iurii Dolgorukii on 13 February, but the first to be published in England.

A12) [Anon.], *A relation concerning the particulars of the rebellion lately raised in Muscovy by Stenko Razin; its rise, progress, and stop; together with the manner of taking that rebel, the sentence of death passed upon him, and the execution of the same.* London: printed by Tho. Newcomb, 1672. 30pp.

> Dated Archangel 13/23 September 1671 on board *Queen Esther*, this document, "published by authority", is considered to be have been composed by an eye witness of at least some of the events, including Razin's execution on 6 June 1671. There were German and Dutch versions published in 1671.

A13) La Martinière, Pierre Martin de, *A new voyage into the northern countries being a discription of the manners, customs, superstition, buildings, and habits of* *the Norwegians, Laponians, Kilops, Borandians, Siberians, Samojedes, Zemblans and Islanders.* London: John Starkey, 1674. viii+153pp.

> La Martinière (1634-90), a French employee of a Danish trading company, sailed c.1670 to Norway, before reaching the sea of Murmansk and travelling through the northern regions of Muscovy into Siberia (pp. 42-128).

A14) [La Martinière, Pierre Martin de], *A new voyage to the north: containing a full account of Norway; the Laplands, both Danish, Swedish and Muscovite; of Borandia, Siberia, Samojedia, Zembla and Iseland: with the description of the religion and customs of these several nations. To which is added, a particular relation of the court of the czar, of the religion and customs of the Muscovites; and a short history of Muscovy, as it was taken by a French gentleman who resided there many years.* Written by Monsieur ***, employ'd by the company of merchants, trading to the North from Copenhagen. Now done into English. London: Thomas Hodgson and Anthony Barker, 1706. xiv+258pp.

> A new translation of La Martinière's superficial observations, greatly enlarged by much better written but extraneous material (pp. 97-201), allegedly supplied by one of the foreign exiles he had met in Siberia (pp. 22-258).

A15) Chardin, John, *The travels of Sir John Chardin into Persia and the East Indies. The first volume, containing the author's voyage from Paris to Ispahan. To which is added, the coronation of this present king of Persia, Solyman the Third.* London: Moses Pitt, 1686. xiv+417+ix+154pp.

> The Huguenot jeweller Sir John (Jean) Chardin (1643-1713), born in France but dying in London, left Paris on 17 August 1671 on a journey to Persia that ended in June 1673 and took him across the Caucasus to Tiflis in Georgia and thence to Erevan in Armenia (Georgia, pp. 165-245). The translation from his French original (also published in 1686) was done under his close scrutiny.

A16) Spathary, Nikolai Gavrilovich, 'Mission to China'. In John F. Baddeley, *Russia, Mongolia, China, being some record of the relations between them from the beginning of the XVth century to the death of Tsar Alexei Mikhailovich A.D. 1602-1676, rendered mainly in the form of narratives dictated or written by the envoys sent by the Russian tsars, or their voevodas in Siberia to the Kalmuck and Mongol khans & princes; and to the emperors of China; with introductions, historical and geographical, also a series of maps, showing the progress of geographical knowledge* *in regard to northern Asia during the XVIth, XVIIth, & early XVIIIth centuries, the texts taken more especially from manuscripts in the Moscow Foreign Office archives*. London: Macmillan and Co., 1919. 2 vols.

> Spathary (Nicolae Milescu, 1638-1708), a Moldavian scholar, arrived at the court of Aleksei in 1671 and worked as an interpreter in the *Posolskii prikaz* (Foreign Office). He was appointed chief of a mission to China that left Moscow on 3 March 1675 and travelled through Siberia. They reached the Chinese border in January 1676 and were to remain in Pekin until September. They arrived back in Moscow in the summer of 1677 after a long stay in Selenginsk. There are considerable gaps in Spathary's account, which begins in Tobolsk and ends in Selenginsk (vol. II, pp. 237-84, 420-22).

Fig. 32 Peter the Great (1698), by Godfrey Kneller. Oil on canvas. Royal Collection.

Fig. 33. Catherine I (1717), by Jean-Marc Nattier. Oil on canvas. Hermitage Museum, St Petersburg.

2. REIGNS OF PETER I (1682-1725), including joint reign with IVAN V (1682-1696) and regency of SOPHIA (1686-1689), and CATHERINE I (1725-1727)

See also: A7

B1) Avril, Philippe, *Travels into divers parts of Europe and Asia, undertaken by the French king's order to discover a new way by land into China, containing many curious remarks in natural philosophy, geography, hydrography, and history. Together with a description of Great Tartary, and of the different people who inhabit there.* Done out of French. London: Tim. Goodwin, 1693. 2 vols.

> The Jesuit missionary Avril (1654-98) with his companion Father Barbary, "disguis'd as Georgians", left Erevan on 23 April 1686 and travelled from Astrakhan up the Volga to Saratov and then to Moscow. They were in Warsaw early in 1687 but were once again in Moscow at the time of Peter I's first wedding (January 1689). Gathering information about trade routes to China, they seem to have travelled as far as the Chinese border. The account, designed to provide useful information for Jesuit missionaries, is divided into five "books", Armenia, (vol. I, pp. 1-63) Tartary (I, pp. 65-136), routes through Siberia to China (I, pp. 137-91), Muscovy (II, pp. 1-80) and Moldavia (II, pp. 81-132).

B2) C., T., *The new atlas, or, travels and voyages in Europe, Asia, Africa and America, thro' the most renowned parts of the world, viz. from England to the Dardanelles, thence to Constantinople, Egypt, Palestine, or the Holy Land, Syria, Mesopotamia, Chaldea, Persia, East-India, China, Tartary, Muscovy, and by Poland, the German empire, Flanders and Holland, to Spain and the West-Indies; with a brief account of Ethiopia, and the pilgrimage to Mecha and Medina in Arabia, containing what is rare and worthy of remarks in those vast countries;*

relating to buildings, antiquities, religion, manners, customs, princes, courts, or affairs, military and civil, or whatever else of any kind is worthy of note. Performed by an English gentleman, in nine years travel and voyages, more exact than ever. London: J. Cleave and A. Roper, 1698. viii+236pp.

> The author, signing himself "T.C" in a preface in which he mentions the recently completed embassy of Peter I, left London on 30 April 1684 for Constantinople. After travelling extensively through Egypt, Persia, India, China, and Tartary, he eventually (c.1687 or later) reached Astrakhan, which he describes in some detail. He then travelled up the Volga via Nizhnii Novgorod to Moscow, where he remained for some time, before visiting Novgorod, Vologda, Vladimir and Rostov, and departing via Poland (pp. 168-86).

B3) Gerbillon, Jean François, 'Travels into Tartary by P. Gerbillon, Jesuit, and French missionary in China'. In Jean-Baptiste Du Halde, *A description of the empire of China and Chinese-Tartary, together with the kingdoms of Korea, and Tibet: containing the geography and history (natural as well as civil) of those countries.* From the French [by Richard Brookes]. London: printed by T. Gardner for Edward Cave, 1738-41. 2 vols. [vol. II: printed by Edward Cave.]

> Father Gerbillon, a French Jesuit missionary at the Chinese court, undertook eight journeys into Tartary between 1688 and 1698, the last six in the retinue of the emperor. It is, however, the first two journeys (May 1688-June 1689 and June 1689-May 1690) that are of particular Russian interest, when he accompanied as interpreter the Chinese ambassadors sent to negotiate the treaty of Nerchinsk (1689). In 1688 he visited the border town of Selinginsk and reached Lake Baikal (vol. II, pp. 273-333). The French original, *Description geographique, historique...,* was published in Paris in 1735.

B4) La Neuville, Foy de, *An account of Muscovy, as it was in the year 1689. In which the troubles that happen'd in that empire from the present Czar Peter's election to the throne, to his being firmly settled in it, are particularly related. With a character of him, and his people.* London: Edward Castle, 1699. 119pp.

> La Neuville left Warsaw on 19 July 1689 as Polish envoy extraordinary but had returned by the beginning of 1690, having failed to secure an audience with the Tsars Ivan and Peter in Moscow (pp. 1-19). The rest of the book is devoted to events that had happened before his visit, e.g. the regency of Sophia, the Crimean campaign, as well as an essay on the Muscovites, "barbarians, suspicious and mistrustful, cruel, sodomites, gluttons, covetous, beggars and cowards".

B5) La Neuville, Foy de, *A curious and new account of Muscovy in the year 1689.* Edited and introduced by Lindsey Hughes. Translated from the French by J.A. Cutshall. London: School of Slavonic and East European Studies, 1994. xxxvi+78pp.

> A carefully edited and newly translated version of the Paris edition of 1698, *Relation curieuse et nouvelle de Moscovie* (pp. 1-72).

B6) Ides, Evert Ysbrants, *Three years travels from Moscow over-land to China: through Great Ustiga, Sirinia, Permia, Siberia, Daour, Great Tartary, &c. to Peking. Containing an exact and particular description of the extent and limit of those countries, and the customs of the barbarous inhabitants, with reference to their religion, government, marriages, daily imployments, habits, habitations, diet, death, funerals, &c. Written by his excellency E. Ysbrants Ides, ambassador from the Czar of Muscovy to the Emperor of China.* London: printed for W. Freeman, J. Walthoe, T. Newborough, J. Nicholson, and R. Parker, 1706. x+210pp.

> The embassy, headed by Ides, an experienced Danish diplomat, left Moscow on 14 March 1692 and arrived at the Chinese border on 11 September 1693 (pp. 1-51). It began its return journey on 19 February 1694 and reached Moscow on 1 January 1695 (pp. 81-107). Pp. 11-210 are devoted to 'a short description of China by a Chinese'.

B7) Brand, Adam, *A journal of an embassy from their majesties John and Peter Alexievitz, emperors of Muscovy, &c. over land into China through the provinces of Ustiugha, Siberia, Dauri, and the Great Tartary, to Peking, the capital city of the Chinese Empire. By Everard Isbrand, their ambassador in the years 1693, 1694, and 1695.* Written by Adam Brand, secretary of the embassy. Translated from the original in High-Dutch, printed at Hamburgh, 1698. *To which is added, Curious observations concerning the products of Russia,* by **H[einrich] W[ilhelm] Ludolf.** London: D. Brown, T. Goodwin, 1698. 134pp.

> The account of the Dutch secretary to Ides's embassy appeared in English eight years before the ambassador's. The interesting addition (pp. 119-34), given a separate title-page, is from the Latin of Ludolf (1655-1710), author of the *Grammatica russica*, published in Oxford in 1696, and is based on his own experiences in Russia as well as his reading.

B8) Allison, Thomas, *An account of a voyage from Archangel in Russia, in the year 1697. Of the ship and company wintering near the North Cape in the latitude of 71. Their manner of living, and what they suffered by the extream cold. Also remarkable observations of the climate, country and inhabitants. Together with a* *chart, describing the place where they lay, land in view, soundings, &c.* London: printed for D. Brown and R. Parker, 1699. 112pp.

> The ship's log of Allison, master of the *Ann of Yarmouth*, sailing from Archangel on 8 October 1697 and reaching Gravesend on 24 April 1698. Dedicated to the governor and consuls of the Russia Company, the book is trailed by the booksellers for its simple truth and "watry language" (a mariner's technical term)!

B9) Deane, John, *A letter from Moscow to the Marquess of Carmarthen, relating to the Czar of Muscovy's forwardness in his great navy &c. since his return home.* London: published by his lordship's permission, 1699. Single folio sheet.

> Son of Sir Anthony Deane, Charles II's eminent shipbuilder, John Deane (d. 1699) was recruited by Peter I during his visit to London. His letter, dated 8 March 1698/99, to Carmarthen, who had recommended him to the tsar, describes the state of the Russian navy after a visit to Voronezh.

B10) Perry, John, *The state of Russia, under the present czar. In relation to the several great and remarkable things he has done, as to his naval preparations, the regulating his army, the reforming his people, and improvement of his countrey. Particularly those works on which the author was employ'd, with the reasons of his quitting the czar's service, after having been fourteen years in that countrey.* London: Benjamin Tooke, 1716. vi+280pp.

> Captain Perry (1670-1732) was recruited during Peter I's visit to London in 1698 on a ten-year contract as a hydraulic engineer. He worked on various canal projects to link the Volga and the Don and Petersburg and the Volga. He returned to England in 1712, securing his release only with the greatest difficulty. The account of his experiences in Russia combines a fervent admiration of the tsar with strong condemnation of reactionary factions working against him. His book was one of the most influential of the period.

B11) Korb, Johann Georg, *Diary of an Austrian secretary of legation at the court of Czar Peter the Great.* Translated from the original Latin and edited by the Count Mac Donnell. London: Bradbury & Evans, 1863. 2 vols.

> Korb (1670-1741) accompanied the embassy of the Austrian ambassador Ignaz von Guarient und Rall that set out from Vienna on 10 January 1699, reaching Smolensk on 9 April and Moscow on 29 April. They left Moscow on the return journey on 23 July (vol. I, pp. 51-299; II, pp. 1-53). Notable for the "compendious description" of the revolt and suppression of the Streltsy (vol. II, pp. 69-121). The rare Latin original, *Diarium itineris in Moscoviam* was published in Vienna in 1700.

B12) 'Gentleman of Germany', 'A letter, from a certain gentleman of Germany, written from Musco concerning the siege of Asoph, and Kasikermeen, and the other warlike exploits of the Muscovites in that war, with some political remarks upon the most remarkable passages that have happened of late in the Muscovite empire, translated from the low Dutch.' In John Harris, *Navigantium atque itinerantium bibliotheca: or, a compleat collection of voyages and travels*. London: printed for Thomas Bennet, John Nicholson, and Daniel Midwinter, 1705. 2 vols.

> An intriguing piece which is tacked on to the account of the unnamed Foy de la Neuville and is possibly by "the sieur Newstad" whose promised offering on "the present state of Muscovy" is otherwise not included. It indeed describes the state of Muscovy from the time of Alexis, then Peter's campaign at Azov, before switching to the Grand Embassy, of which he says he was an eye-witness, and the destruction of the Streltsy (vol. II, pp. 223-28).

B13) Bruyn, Cornelis de, *Travels into Muscovy, Persia, and part of the East Indies Containing, An accurate description of whatever is most remarkable in those countries. And embellished with above 320 copper plates, representing the finest prospects, and most considerable cities in those parts; the different habits of the people; the singular and extraordinary birds, fishes, and plants which are there to be found: As likewise the antiquities of those countries, and particularly the noble ruins of the famous palace of Persepolis, called Chelminar by the Persians. The whole being delineated on the spot, from the respective objects. By M. Cornelius Le Bruyn. To which is added, an account of the journey of Mr. Isbrants, ambassador from Muscovy, through Russia and Tartary, to China; together with remarks on the travels of Sir John Chardin, and Mr Kempfer, and a letter written to the author on that subject*. London: A. Bettesworth and C. Hitch, S.Birt, C. Davis, J. Clarke, S. Harding, D. Browne, A. Millar, J. Shukburgh, and T. Osborne, 1737. 2 vols.

> The Dutch painter de Bruyn (otherwise de Bruijn, Le Brun, 1652-1727) left The Hague on 8 July 1701 and arrived in Archangel on 30 August. Gives detailed descriptions of the Samoeds and of Archangel and towns on the way to Moscow, where he arrived on 4 January 1702. Accompanied Peter to Voronezh, then returned to Moscow before eventually leaving Russia from Astrakhan in July 1703 en route to Paris (vol. I, pp. 1-95). On 4 July 1707 he again visited Astrakhan and travelled up the Volga to Moscow, where he met the tsar. He departed from Archangel on 23 August 1708 (vol. II, pp. 166-94). Translated from the French translation of the Dutch original.

B14) Chancel, A.D., *A new journey over Europe; from France thro' Savoy, Switzerland, Germany, Flanders, Holland, Denmark, Swedland, Muscovy, Poland, Hungary, Styria, Carinthia, the Venetian Territories, Italy, Naples, Sicily, Genoa, Spain, Portugal, France, Great Britain, and Ireland; with several observations on the laws, religion, and government, &c. of each. Together with an account of the births and marriages of all the kings and princes of Europe from the year 1650.* By a late traveller A.D. Chancel, M.A. London: for John Harding, 1714. xvi+264pp.

> The Frenchman Chancel relates "nothing but what I have seen, or taken out from approved Travellers", and it is from outdated accounts of others that he describes Muscovy, or rather, simply Moscow (pp. 62-4). He lists Peter's half-sister Sophia, "of a masculine body and temper", as still living (p. 250).

B15) Whitworth, Charles, ['Dispatches']. In *Sbornik russkogo imperatorskogo istoricheskogo obshchestva*, vols. XXXIX, L, LXI. St Petersburg: Academy of Sciences, 1884, 1886, 1888. viii+496pp; xii+558pp; xi+610pp.

> Whitworth, later Baron Whitworth (1675-1725) arrived in Moscow on 11 March 1705 as envoy extraordinary to offer apologies for the treatment of the Russian ambassador in London, A.A. Matveev, who had been thrown into a debtors' prison. He was made ambassador extraordinary in 1709 and left for England on 4 April 1710. After attending the tsar at Carlsbad in October 1711 he returned to St Petersburg on 31 January 1712, leaving finally at the end of June. During Whitworth's absence in 1710-12 dispatches were sent to London by his secretary **Ludwig Christoph Weisbrod**, acting as British *chargé d'affaires* (vol. L, pp. 351-427; LXI, pp. 40-41, 102-05, 108-28).

B16) Whitworth, Charles, *An account of Russia as it was in the year 1710.* Twickenham: Strawberry Hill, 1758. xxiv+158pp.

> On his return to England in April 1710 Whitworth wrote his account essentially as a government briefing document, giving particular attention to naval matters. It was only published nearly fifty years later by Horace Walpole at his famed press at Strawberry Hill and was often used as evidence of the state of contemporary, i.e. late Elizabethan, Russia (see D3).

B17) Strahlenberg, Philipp Johann von, *An historico-geographical description of the north and eastern parts of Europe and Asia; but more particularly of Russia, Siberia, and Great Tartary; both in their ancient and modern state: together with an entire new polyglot-table of the dialects of 32 Tartarian nations: and a vocabulary* *of the Kalmuck-Mungalian tongue. As also, a large and accurate map of those countries; and variety of cuts, representing Asiatik-Scythian antiquities.* Written originally in High German by Mr. Philip John von Strahlenberg, a Swedish officer, thirteen years captive in those parts. Now faithfully translated into English. London: printed for W. Innys and R. Manby, 1738. xiv+463pp.

> Captured at the battle of Poltava in 1709, the Swedish captain Strahlenberg (1676-1747) spent some thirteen years in Russia, principally in Siberia. His book, which first appeared in German in Stockholm in 1730, contains valuable geographical, ethnographical, and linguistic information about a vast region barely known in Europe and also an extensive chapter (pp. 233-72) on Peter I and his reign.

B18) La Motraye, Aubry de, *Travels through Europe, Asia, and into part of Africa; with proper cutts and maps. Containing a great variety of geographical, topographical, and political observations on those parts of the world; especially on Italy, Turky, Greece, Crim and Noghaian Tartaries, Circassia, Sweden, and Lapland. A curious collection of things particularly rare, both in nature and antiquity; such as remains of antient cities and colonies, inscriptions, idols, medals, minerals, &c.* London: for the author, 1723. 2 vols.

> La Mortraye (1674-1747) was in London during Peter's visit but never entered Russian territory during the tsar's lifetime. He sailed from London in November 1698 for Constantinople where he stayed for a number of years. After the outbreak of the Russo-Turkish war he paid his visit to the Crimea in 1711, visiting Ochakov, Bakhchiserai and Kaffa, and into Circassia and to the Volga estuary (vol. II, pp. 21-85).

B19) Bruce, Peter Henry, *Memoirs of Peter Henry Bruce, esq., a military officer, in the services of Prussia, Russia, and Great Britain. Containing an account of his travels in Germany, Russia, Tartary, Turkey, the West Indies, &c., as also, several very interesting private anecdotes of the Czar, Peter I, of Russia.* London: Printed for the author's widow, by T. Payne and Son, 1782. 446pp.

> A Scottish soldier-of-fortune, Bruce (1692-1757) served in the Russian army from 1711 to 1724, was sent on an embassy to Constantinople and took part in the Derbent expedition (pp. 33-374). Before his death in Scotland he translated his diary from German (his first language) into English.

B20) Mackenzie, George, and Jefferyes, James, ['Dispatches']. In *Sbornik russkogo imperatorskogo istoricheskogo obshchestva*, vol. LXI. St Petersburg: Academy of Sciences, 1888. xi+610pp.

78   In the Lands of the Romanovs

In the years following Whitworth's departure and the rupture in diplomatic relations in 1719, British representatives were given the rank of minister resident but resided for very short periods, if at all (James Haldane, for instance, appointed in September in 1716). Mackenzie arrived in St Petersburg on 28 September 1714 but left on 2 May 1715, whereas Captain Jefferyes, arriving on 12 January 1719, was obliged to retire to Dantzig on 15 October, after the tsar gave "me and the rest of the british nation sensible marks of his displeasure". He left at the same time as the Hanoverian resident, F.C. Weber (see B22). Mackenzie's dispatches are on pp. 258-380 and Jefferyes's on pp. 451-590.

B21) [Deane, John], *History of the Russian fleet during the reign of Peter the Great by a contemporary Englishman (1724).* Edited by Vice-Admiral Cyprian A.G. Bridge. London: for the Navy Records Society, 1899. xxvi+161pp.

Captain Deane (1680?-1761), who served in the Russian navy from 1712 until his dismissal in 1722, produced what is essentially a log of the movements of the Russian Baltic fleet until 1724. His identity was established on the basis of a signed copy of his manuscript, dedicated to George I, which contains further pages continuing his account up to 1725 (not included in 1899 edition). He had been sent back to Russia in June 1725 as British consul-general but was apprehended at Cronstadt and forced to return to England.

B22) [Weber, Friedrich Christian], *The present state of Russia. Being an account of the government of that country, both civil and ecclesiastical; of the Czar's forces by sea and land, the regulation of his finances, the several methods he made use of to civilize his people and improve the country, his transactions with several eastern princes, and what happened most remarkable at his court, particularly in relation to the last Czarewitz, from the year 1714, to 1720. The whole being the journal of a foreign minister who resided in Russia at that time. With a description of Petersbourg and Cronslot, and several other pieces relating to the affairs of Russia.* Translated from the High-Dutch. London: printed for W. Taylor, W. and J. Innys, and J. Osborn, 1722-23. 2 vols. [vol. II: 1722; vol. I: 1723].

Weber arrived in St Petersburg in February 1714 with a mission from the elector of Hanover (who became George I of England in August that year) and remained for five years as resident. He presented his work as a diary, sometimes revised with hindsight. His important account of St Petersburg (vol. I, pp. 293-352) was adapted from a German original of a few years earlier. Vol. II (which appeared a year earlier) contains various pieces including **Lauren Lange**'s journal of a journey from Petersburg to Peking in 1715-17 (pp. 3-43), the Swedish captain **J.B. Müller**'s description of the

Ostiaks, written in Tobolsk in 1716 (pp. 37-92), and **Cornelis de Bruyn**'s 'observations on Russia', 1701-08 (pp. 371-432).

B23) Bell, John, *Travels from St. Petersburg in Russia, to diverse parts of Asia.* Glasgow: printed for the author by Robert and Andrew Foulis; sold by R. & A. Foulis and A. Stalker at Glasgow; Kincaid & Bell at Edinburgh; A. Miller, J. Nourse, T. Becket & P.A. de Hondt, and C. Henderson in London; J. Leake, and J. Frederick at Bath; and T. Cadell at Bristol, 1763. 2 vols.

> Bell (1691-1780) arrived in Russia in August 1714 and was soon enlisted as doctor to accompany an embassy to Persia, headed by A.P. Valenskii. It left St Petersburg in July 1715 and returned three years later (vol. I, pp. 1-154). In July 1719 he set off again with the embassy of L.V. Izmailov, which travelled through Siberia to arrive at the Chinese border at the end of September 1720 (vol. I, pp. 155-308). They left Pekin on the return journey in March 1721 and arrived in Moscow, where they reported to Peter (vol. II, pp. 124-68). A third journey was with the Russian army under Peter I to Derbent in Persia, May-December 1722 (vol. II, pp. 323-69). After a decade in Scotland Bell returned to St Petersburg to work for the British consul-general Rondeau (see C10) and was sent on a final mission to Constantinople, December 1737-May 1738 (vol. II, pp. 373-426).

B24) Bering, Vitus, 'An account of the travels of capt Beerings, into Siberia'. In Jean-Baptiste Du Halde, *A description of the empire of China and Chinese-Tartary, together with the kingdoms of Korea, and Tibet: containing the geography and history (natural as well as civil) of those countries.* From the French [by Richard Brookes]. London: printed by T. Gardner for Edward Cave, 1738-1741. 2 vols. [vol. II: printed by Edward Cave.]

> The first expedition by Bering (1681-1741), a Dane recruited into Russian service, set out in January 1725 and returned to St Petersburg in March 1730. Succinct account from unknown source (vol. II, pp. 382-84).

B25) La Motraye, Aubry de, *The voyages and travels of A. De la Mottraye, in several provinces and places of the kingdoms and dukedoms of Prussia, Russia, Poland, &c..* London: Symon, Newton, 1732. 3 vols.

> The Frenchman La Motraye (see B18) eventually visited Russia and spent a month in St Petersburg from September 1726, a year after the death of Peter I during the short reign of Catherine I. He spent many of his later years in London, where his account was published in not identical English and French versions (vol. III, pp. 54-224).

Fig. 34 Peter II (c. 1730), by Ioann Vedekind.

Fig. 35 Anna Ivanovna (c. 1730). Unknown Artist. Moscow State Historical Museum.

Fig. 36 Empress Elizabeth (n.d.), by Ivan Argunov. Tretiakov Gallery, Moscow.

3. REIGNS OF PETER II (1727-1730), ANNA (1730-1740), IVAN VI (1740-1741), and ELIZABETH (1741-1762)

See also: B23, B24

C1) Manstein, Cristof Hermann, *Memoirs, historical, political, and military, from the year MDCCXXVII, to MDCCXLIV: a period comprehending many remarkable events, in particular the wars of Russia with Turkey and Sweden with a supplement, containing a summary account of the state of the military, the marine, the commerce, &c. of that great empire.* [Translated from French. With an 'advertisement' by David Hume.] London: T. Beckett and P.A. de Hondt, 1770. viii+424pp. [See also revised edition: *Contemporary memoirs of Russia, from the year 1727 to 1744.* London: Longman, Brown, Green, and Longmans, 1856. xvi+416pp.]

> General Manstein (1711-57), son of a Baltic German nobleman, was born in St Petersburg but educated in Germany before entering the Russian army and serving under Anna and Elizabeth. He deserted Russian service in 1744, joined the Prussian army and was killed during the Seven Years' War. He combines a general chronological history that includes much on court life and its personalities with detailed descriptions of the campaigns in which he took part. The 1856 edition is based on the longer French edition published in Amsterdam in 1771.

C2) Ward, Thomas, and Rondeau, Claudius, ['Dispatches']. In *Sbornik imperatorskogo russkogo istoricheskogo obshchestva*, vol. LXVI. St Petersburg: Academy of Sciences, 1889. viii+681pp.

> Thomas Ward (d. 1731), the recently appointed British consul-general, arrived in St Petersburg at the end of July 1728 and was accompanied by

Claudius Rondeau (d. 1739) as his secretary. Their dispatches, printed here in the originals with Russian translations, cover the period from 7 August 1728 to 20 June 1733, and include replies and instructions from London. The dispatches were largely written by Rondeau – only eleven were signed by Ward, who had requested (10 July 1730) that Rondeau be appointed resident, while he continue as consul-general. Rondeau was duly appointed resident but only on 11 September, months after Ward's death on 4 February 1731.

C3) [Vigor, Jane], *Letters from a lady, who resided some years in Russia, to her friend in England, with historical notes.* London: J. Dodsley, 1775. viii+207pp.

Daughter of a Yorkshire clergyman, Jane Goodwin (1699-1783) went to Russia in 1728 as the wife of the British consul-general Ward (see C2) and after his death in February 1731 soon became the wife of Rondeau (see C2). Rondeau died in October 1739 and Jane returned to England, accompanied by a Quaker Russia merchant, William Vigor, whom she was soon to marry. Her lively and gossipy letters are a valuable source for court life under the Empress Anna.

C4) Vigor, Jane, *Eleven additional letters from Russia, in the reign of Peter II. By the late Mrs Vigor. Never before published: with a preface and notes.* [London: J. Dodsley, 1784.] 88pp.

Letters published soon after Mrs Vigor's death but pertaining to her first two years in Russia (1728-29), when she was still Mrs Ward and Peter II was the tsar, and thus antedating those in the earlier publication, several of which were wrongly dated. The letters were the same format as the earlier (two) editions to be bound as one.

C5) Forbes, George, and Rondeau, Claudius, ['Dispatches']. In *Sbornik imperatorskogo russkogo istoricheskogo obshchestva*, vol. LXXVI. St Petersburg: Academy of Sciences, 1891. xix+591pp.

The dispatches and replies from London cover the period from 27 June 1733 to 11 August 1736. On 20 June 1733 George Forbes, 3rd Earl of Granard (1685-1765), the experienced Anglo-Irish naval commander and diplomat, arrived in St Petersburg as British envoy extraordinary and minister plenipotentiary to negotiate the first Anglo-Russian commercial agreement that was signed on 13 December 1734. A few dispatches were signed by Forbes but most bear the joint signatures of Forbes and Rondeau up to Forbes's departure from St Petersburg on 18 May 1734; thereafter all the dispatches are Rondeau's.

C6) [Locatelli Lanzi, Francesco], *Lettres Moscovites: or, Muscovian letters: containing an account of the form of government, customs, and manners of that great empire.* Written by an Italian officer of distinction. Translated from the French original, printed at Paris, 1735, by William Musgrave. London: printed for [E. Curl], 1736. xii+190pp.

> The Italian nobleman Locatelli Lanzi (1687-1770) arrived in Russia in 1733, seeking a placement in the Russian army, but instead joined an expedition of the Academy of Sciences to Kamchatka. He was, however, arrested as a spy at Kazan and brought back to St Petersburg. He was imprisoned there between December 1733 and October 1734 before eventually being allowed to leave Russia for Holland in November 1734, where he soon published his denunciation of Russian despotism.

C7) Waxell, Sven, *The American expedition.* With an introduction and note by M.A. Michael. [Translated from the Danish by M.A. Michael.] London, Edinburgh, Glasgow: William Hodge and Co., 1952. 236pp.

> Waxell (1701-62), a Swede, was one of eight lieutenants on Bering's second expedition, which set out for Siberia and Kamchatka in the spring of 1733 and was to end only a decade later, although Waxell himself did not return to St Petersburg until January 1749. His account of the expedition, written in German and based on his and others' journals, was composed in the 1750s. Waxell concentrates on what he suggests was the expedition's main purpose: exploring the strait between Novaia zemlia and the mainland, and then other islands, including what became known as Bering's Island, and on to Alaska (pp. 37-212). English translation from Skalberg's twentieth-century Danish version.

C8) Justice, Elizabeth, *A voyage to Russia: describing the laws, manners, and customs, of that great empire, as govern'd, at this present, by that excellent princess, the czarina, shewing the beauty of her palace, the grandeur of her courtiers, the forms of building at Petersburgh, and other places: with several entertaining adventures, that happened in the passage by sea and land.* York: printed by Thomas Gent, 1739. xiv+59pp. [2nd edition: *to which is added, four letters, wrote by the author when at Russia to a gentleman in London.* London: printed by G. Smith for the author, 1746. xviii+63pp.]

> Mrs Justice's sojourn in Petersburg, where she was governess to the daughters of a British merchant, Hill Evans, lasted from her arrival at Cronstadt on 30 August 1734 until her departure from there on 12 August 1737. Her "performance", which contains many a perceptive and

informative comment, was published to help meet her debts and also to counter rumours that she had never been to Russia (pp. 1-46). Additional letters in the second edition, addressed to a Captain Conduit (pp. 53-63), highlight her loneliness and prejudices.

C9) Cook, John, *Voyages and travels through the Russian empire, Tartary, and part of the kingdom of Persia.* Edinburgh: for the author, 1770. 2 vols.

Cook (1712-90), a young Scottish physician from Hamilton, arrived at Cronstadt on 29 July 1736 and was to remain until 1751. During his fourteen-year sojourn, he worked in hospitals in St Petersburg and in Astrakhan, accompanied Prince Golitsyn's embassy to Persia, and finished serving in military hospitals in Riga. His memoirs are entertaining, informative and generally reliable.

C10) Rondeau, Claudius, and Bell, John, ['Dispatches']. In *Sbornik imperatorskogo russkogo istoricheskogo obshchestva*, vol. LXXX. St Petersburg: Academy of Sciences, 1892. xx+570pp.

The dispatches cover the period from 14 August 1736 to 9 January 1740. The last five are written by John Bell (see B23), who since 1737 had been acting as secretary to Rondeau, and, following whose death in October 1739, acted virtually as British *chargé d'affaires* until the arrival of Edward Finch as minister.

C11) Spilman, James, *A journey through Russia into Persia; by two English gentlemen, who went in the year 1739, from Petersburg, in order to make a discovery how the trade from Great Britain might be carried on from Astracan over the Caspian. To which is annexed, a summary account of the rise of the famous Kouli Kan, and his successes, till he seated himself on the Persian throne.* London: Dodsley, 1742. 70pp.

Spilman (1680-1763), prominent Russia Company merchant and F.R.S., who had himself traded in Russia during Peter I's reign and made a major contribution to the Anglo-Russian treaty of commerce (1734), describes the exploration of trading routes undertaken by the sea captain and merchant John Elton (d. 1751) and the merchant Mungo Graham (d. 1747?).

C12) Steller, Georg Wilhelm, 'Steller's journal of Beering's voyage of discovery from Kamtchatka to the coast of America, in 1741'. In William Coxe, *Account of the Russian discoveries between Asia and America.* 4th edition: London: Cadell and Davies, 1803. xx+375pp.

Steller (1709-46), the young German naturalist and adjunct professor of the Petersburg Academy of Sciences, accompanied Bering on his second expedition (see C7). He describes the voyages made from Kamchatka across the Bering Sea to many of the islands and to Alaska. Coxe translated and summarized the version of Steller's journal (1743) published by Peter Simon Pallas in 1793 (pp. 17-71).

C13) Steller, Georg Wilhelm, *Bering's voyages: an account of the efforts of the Russians to determine the relation of Asia and America. Steller's journal of the sea voyage from Kamchatka to America and return on the second expedition, 1741-1742.* Edited by F.A. Golder. New York: American Geographical Society, 1925. 249pp.

This represents the first complete English translation by Leonhard Stejneger of Steller's journal, based on Pallas's edition.

C14) Steller, Georg Wilhelm, *Journal of a voyage with Bering 1741-1742.* Edited and with an introduction by O.W. Frost. Translated by Margritt A. Engel and O.W. Frost. Stanford: Stanford University Press, 1988. 252pp.

Scholarly edition and first modernized English translation of the manuscript text, written in more than one hand and preserved in the archives of the Academy of Sciences in Petersburg (pp. 42-182).

C15) Algarotti, Francesco, *Letters from Count Algarotti to Lord Hervey and the Marquis Scipio Maffei, containing the state of the trade, marine, revenues, and forces of the Russian Empire: with the history of the late war between the Russians and the Turks, and observations on the Baltic and the Caspian Seas. To which is added a dissertation on the reigns of the seven kings of Rome, and a dissertation on the empire of the Incas.* Translated from the Italian. London: Johnson and Payne, 1769. 2 vols.

Count Algarotti (1712-64), Italian scholar and art connoisseur, friend of Voltaire and Frederick the Great, left Gravesend on 21 May 1738 and arrived at Revel on 15 June, before proceeding to Cronstadt. Arriving in St Petersburg on 21 June he began his "account of this new city, of this great window in the North, thro' which Russia looks into Europe". On 21 August he was on his return journey, having described in letters III-VI to John, Lord Hervey (1696-1743), what he had seen and what information he had gathered (vol. I, pp. 29-141). Later letters, written from Danzig and Hamburg, also treat of Russian military matters.

C16) Bell, John, and Finch, Edward, ['Dispatches']. In *Sbornik imperatorskogo russkogo istoricheskogo obshchestva*, vol. LXXXV. St Petersburg: Academy of Sciences, 1893. xii+540pp.

> Four further dispatches from Bell (see C10) precede the arrival in St Petersburg on 10 June 1740 of the envoy extraordinary and plenipotentiary Edward Finch (1697-1771), previously British ambassador to Sweden, whose dispatches in this volume cover the period up to 14 March 1741 and thus include the death of Anna Ivanovna and the reign of Ivan VI.

C17) Finch, Edward, and Wych, Cyril, ['Dispatches']. In *Sbornik imperatorskogo russkogo istoricheskogo obshchestva*, vol. XCI. St Petersburg: Academy of Sciences, 1896.

> The final dispatches from Finch, covering the period from 18 March 1741 to 17 February 1742, embrace the short reign of the infant Ivan VI under the regency of his mother Anna Leopoldovna and the coup that brought Elizabeth to the throne on 6 December 1741 (pp. 1-447). Finch departed in February 1742 and was succeeded by Sir Cyril Wych (1695-1756), who arrived on 7 April 1742 (pp. 447-514).

C18) Wych, Cyril, ['Dispatches']. In *Sbornik imperatorskogo russkogo istoricheskogo obshchestva*, vol. XCIX. St Petersburg: Academy of Sciences, 1897. xvi+507pp.

> Dispatches cover the period from 14 July 1742 to 18 April 1744, with Wych awaiting the arrival of his successor, the Earl of Tyrawley. Half way through his term, on 8 May 1743, Wich had written of Elizabeth that "Never a princess in Europe came to the throne with greater appearances of making a glorious figure in Europe […], but her attachment to her pleasures spoils all, and will, I am afraid, in the end, produce irreparable mischiefs" (pp. 333-34).

C19) Hanway, Jonas, *An historical account of the British trade over the Caspian Sea: with a journal of travels from England through Russia into Persia; and back again through Russia, Germany and Holland. To which are added, the revolutions of Persia during the present century, with the particular history of the great usurper Nadir Kouli.* London: sold by Mr. Dodsley, Mr. Nourse, Mr. Millar, Mr. Vaillant, and Mr. Patterson, Mr. Waugh, Mr. Willock, 1753. 4 vols.

> Hanway (1712-86), merchant, philanthropist and miscellaneous writer, was a member of the British Factory in St Petersburg between 1743 and 1750, hoping to develop trade with Persia via the Caspian. After a general

account of British trade with Persia that includes excerpts from the 1739 journal of **Captain John Elton** (see C11), he describes his own journey out to Russia in April 1743 and his subsequent travels to Persia, including excerpts from the journal of **Thomas Woodroofe**, captain of the *Empress of Russia* and associate of Elton. He left Astrakhan for Persia in November 1743, returning to Russia in September 1744 (vol. I, pp. 71-158; II, pp. 1-15). He eventually leaves St Petersburg for London in July 1750 (pp. 166-73). After his return to England he remained an influential member of the Russia Company, was much involved in good works, and is said to have introduced the umbrella to the streets of London.

C20) Tyrawly, James O'Hara, Baron, and Hyndford, John Carmichael, Earl of, ['Dispatches']. In *Sbornik imperatorskogo russkogo istoricheskogo obshchestva*, vol. CII. St Petersburg: Academy of Sciences, 1898. lv+532pp.

The Irish soldier and future governor of Gibraltar Lord Tyrawly (1682-1774) arrived in St Petersburg as ambassador extraordinary and plenipotentiary on 29 February 1744 but was replaced within a year by Lord Hyndford (1701-67). Tyrawly left St Petersburg on 8 March 1745 but Hyndford had been there since 17 December 1744, and was raised from minister plenipotentiary to ambassador extraordinary and plenipotentiary on Tyrawly's departure. Tyrawly's dispatches are found pp. 1-227, and end with his assessment of Hyndford that "his lordship has so good an opinion of his own penetration that he wants no light from any body". This was written on 6 March 1745, the date of Hyndford's first dispatches that continue in this volume until 18 May 1745 (pp. 227-432).

C21) Hyndford, John Carmichael, Earl of, ['Dispatches']. In *Sbornik imperatorskogo russkogo istoricheskogo obshchestva*, vol. CIII. St Petersburg: Academy of Sciences, 1897. xxii+607pp.

The continuation of Hyndford's voluminous dispatches cover the period from 15 January 1746 to 11 May 1748 and open with the words "The conduct of this court grows everyday more and more mysterious".

C22) Hyndford, John Carmichael, Earl of, and Dickens, Melchior Guy, ['Dispatches']. In *Sbornik imperatorskogo russkogo istoricheskogo obshchestva*, vol. CX. St Petersburg: Academy of Sciences, 1901. xxxviii+654pp.

Hyndford's virtual five-year term came to an end in November 1749, when he was replaced by the career diplomat Dickens (1696-1775), previously minister in Sweden. Hyndford's dispatchers cover the period from 18 May 1745 to 14 February 1749, when he was already in Hanover on his return journey. Hyndford was in Moscow from late January until the end of September 1749. The first dispatch from Dickens from St Petersburg is dated 25 November 1749.

C23) Dickens, Melchior Guy, ['Dispatches']. In *Sbornik imperatorskogo russkogo istoricheskogo obshchestva*, vol. CXLVIII. Petrograd: Academy of Sciences, 1916. xxxii+554pp.

> Although Dickens was to remain in post until July 1755, the publication of his dispatches by the Russian Historical Society begins with his dispatch of 8 February 1750 and ends with that of 31 December 1753.

C24) d'Éon, Charles-Geneviève-Louis-Auguste-André-Tomothée, *The memoirs of Chevalier d'Éon.* Translated by Antonia White. With an introduction by Robert Baldick. London: Anthony Blond, 1970. xxii+314pp.

> According to Frédéric Gaillardet, the "editor" of the memoirs, first published in 1836, but to a large degree their fabricator, the notorious transvestite the chevalier d'Éon (1728-1810) paid three visits to St Petersburg between 1755 and 1760 on secret diplomatic missions, initially dressed as a woman. Much that is related is pure fantasy, but in 1756 he was acting as secretary to the French ambassador, the marquis de l'Hospital (pp. 40-96).

C25) Hanbury-Williams, Charles, *The life of Sir Charles Hanbury-Williams, poet, wit, diplomatist.* By the Earl of Ilchester and Mrs Langford-Brooke. London: Thornton Butterworth, 1929. 447pp.

> Sir Charles (1709-59), replacing Dickens as ambassador and plenipotentiary, arrived in the Russian capital on 17 June 1755 and left finally on 19 October 1757. Excerpts from his letters and dispatches (pp. 309-420).

C26) Hanbury-Williams, Charles, *Correspondence of Catherine the Great when Grand Duchess, with Sir Charles Hanbury-Williams and letters from Count Poniatowski.* Edited and translated by the Earl of Ilchester and Mrs Langford-Brooke. London: Thornton Butterworth, 1928. 288pp.

> Sir Charles recognized very early that it was the young Grand Duchess Ekaterina Alekseevna, the future Catherine II, whose friendship he should cultivate. He also encouraged the liaison between Catherine and Count Stanislas-Augustus Poniatowski, who was acting as his secretary. The correspondence of course was conducted in French and conveyed through the agency of Samuel Swallow (1724-76), the merchant who subsequently became British consul-general.

C27) Chappe d'Auteroche, Jean-Baptiste, *A journey into Siberia, made by order of the King of France by M. l'abbé Chappe d'Auteroche, of the Royal Academy of Sciences at Paris, in 1761: containing an account of the manners and customs of the Russians, the present state of their empire; with the natural history, and geographical description of their country, and level of the road from Paris to Tobolsky.* Translated from the French, with a preface by the translator. London: T. Jefferys, 1770. xx+396pp.

> The French astronomer Chappe (1722-69) journeyed to Siberia to observe the transit of Venus over the sun, leaving Paris in November 1760 and, travelling through Poland, reached St Petersburg on 13 February 1761. He eventually arrived at Tobolsk on 10 April, observed the transit on 6 June, and started on the return journey on 28 August. Back in the Russian capital on 1 November, he arrived in Paris in August 1762 (pp. 21-117). Essays on various aspects of Russia occupy the remaining 250 pages. The translation is an abridgement and re-arrangement of the original, published in three volumes in Paris in 1768.

C28) Emin, Joseph, *The life and adventures of Joseph Émïn, an Armenian.* Written in English by himself. London: n.p., 1792. 640pp. [See also *Life and Adventures of Emin Joseph Emin 1726-1809 written by himself.* 2nd edition, with portrait, correspondence, reproductions of original letters and map. Edited by his great-great-granddaughter Amy Apcar. Calcutta: printed and published by the Baptist Mission press, 1918. 2 vols.]

> Emin (1726-1809), after living some ten years in England and serving in the army, left for Russia in October 1761 to agitate for Armenian independence from Persian and Turkish rule. He arrived in the Russian capital just weeks before the death of the Empress Elizabeth and spent the next few years mainly in Georgia, pursuing his impossible dream, before settling in Ispahan. His autobiography is related in the third person (pp. 196-541).

Fig. 37 Great Duke Peter Fedorovich, later Peter III (1758), by Fedor Rokotov. Oil on canvas. Tretiakov Gallery, Moscow.

Fig. 38 Catherine II the Legislatress in the Temple of the Goddess of Justice (1783), by Dmitrii Levitskii. Oil on canvas. Russian Museum, St Petersburg.

4. REIGNS OF PETER III (1762) and CATHERINE II (1762-1796)

See also: C27, C28

D1) Keith, Robert Murray, ['Dispatches']. In *Sbornik imperatorskogo russkogo istoricheskogo obshchestva*, vol. XII. St Petersburg: Academy of Sciences, 1873. xxvii+499pp.

> Keith (d. 1774) had arrived in St Petersburg in March 1754 and served during the last years of Elizabeth's reign and the short reign of Peter III. Shortly after Catherine II's accession, the Russian government requested that a nobleman should occupy the post of British ambassador and Keith was removed in October 1762. It is only his dispatches for the period from 12 July to 7 September (with a few lines from a dispatch of 30 January 1762) that are reproduced here (pp. 1-40), but they include his substantial account of the overthrow of Peter III, "this unhappy prince, who had many excellent qualities" (pp. 2-12).

D2) Rulhière, Claude Carolman de, *A history, or anecdotes of the revolution in Russia, in the year 1762*. Translated from the French of m. de Rulhière. London: printed for M. Beauvalet; and sold by Debrett, Clarke, and Boosey, 1797. xxvii+200pp.

> Rulhière (1735-91) describes himself as attached to the French minister in Russia, de Breteuil, over a period of fifteen months, encompassing the palace revolution that deposed Peter III and brought his wife Catherine to the Russian throne in June 1762. The dedication of the manuscript to the comtesse d'Egmont, dated February 1768 (pp. vii-xxvii) and the letter to her that concludes the book, dated 25 August 1773 (pp. 176-200) are a defence of the authenticity of his account, which was only published in Paris in 1797, long after his death and soon after Catherine's.

http://dx.doi.org/10.11647/OBP.0042.04

92   *In the Lands of the Romanovs*

D3) *Gilchrist, Paul, A genuine letter from Paul Gilchrist, esq; merchant at Petersburgh, to Mr. Saunders, in London: giving a particular and circumstantial account of the great revolution in Russia, and the death of Peter III the late emperor in which that very extraordinary affair is set in a true light: to which is added a short account of the government, religion, laws and inhabitants of that country.* London: printed for J. Williams, 1762. iv+27pp.

> Although dated "Petersburgh, August 5 1762", a genuine letter it certainly was not, being a compilation from newspaper reports. There was, however, a merchant in the Russian capital with the surname of Gilchrist at this period. The appendix (pp. 22-27) was lifted from Charles Whitworth's *Account of Russia as it was in the year 1710*, published for the first time only in 1758.

D4) Buckinghamshire, Hobart, John, Earl of, *The despatches and correspondence of John, Second Earl of Buckinghamshire, ambassador to the court of Catherine II of Russia, 1762-1765.* Edited, with introduction and notes by Adelaide D'Arcy Collyer. London: Longmans, Green, & Co., 1900-02. 2 vols.

> The first British ambassador received by Catherine, Buckinghamshire (1723-93) arrived on 23 September 1762 and remained until January 1765, during which time he wrote voluminous dispatches and memoranda. These volumes contain both outgoing and incoming dispatches (vol. I, pp. 71-238; II, pp. 1-278). Some of his dispatches are also found in *Sbornik imperatorskogo russkogo istoricheskogo obshchestva*, vol. XII (1873), pp. 16-193.

D5) Macartney, George, *An account of Russia MDCCLXVII.* London: privately printed, 1768. viii+230pp.

> Sir George, later Earl of Macartney (1737-1806), arrived in St Petersburg on 27 December 1764 as British envoy extraordinary and left at the end of May 1767, having re-negotiated the commercial agreement in 1766. The work he describes as "a Russian Almanack for the Year 1767" was printed for distribution among friends and government ministers. It consisted of twelve chapters and an appendix (pp. 183-230, not by Macartney but by **Rev. J.G. King**), covering such subjects as population, revenues, the armed forces, and the church.

D6) Macartney, George, *Some account of the public life, and a selection from the unpublished writings, of the Earl of Macartney.* Edited by John Barrow. London: Cadell & Davis, 1807. 2 vols.

> Letters from Macartney in St Petersburg (vol. I, pp. 413-27) and extracts from his *Account* of 1768 (including King's essay, attributed here to Macartney), printed as an appendix in vol. II, pp. 2-93.

D7) Macartney, George, ['Dispatches']. In *Sbornik imperatorskogo russkogo istoricheskogo obshchestva,* vol. XII. St Petersburg: Academy of Sciences, 1873. xxviii+499pp.

> Dispatches to and from Macartney during his embassy, 1765-67 (pp. 194-300).

D8) King, John Glen, *The rites and ceremonies of the Greek Church, in Russia; containing an account of its doctrine, worship, and discipline.* London: printed for W. Owen; J. Dodsley; J. Rivington; and T. Becket and P.A. de Hondt, 1772. xxii+483pp.

> Rev. King (1732-87) was appointed chaplain to the English Church in St Petersburg in 1763 and held the post for eleven years before his return to England in 1774. He indicates that he had been encouraged to study the Russian church by Macartney and his essay 'The present state of the church of Russia, 1767', signed "the Rev. Mr. K.", appeared as an appendix in Macartney's *Account*. His great opus appeared during a sojourn in England when he received his Oxford D.D.

D9) King, John Glen, *Letter to the right reverend the Lord Bishop of Durham, containing some observations on the climate of Russia, and the northern countries.* London: printed for J. Dodsley, 1778. 23pp.

> Most notable for the yard-long engraving of the so-called "flying mountains" that fascinated visitors to Russia, the essay is King's description of the way extreme cold affected everyday life in Russia.

D10) Casanova di Seingalt, Giacomo Girolamo, *The memoirs of Jacques Casanova, written by himself de Seingalt in London and Moscow.* Now for the first time completely translated into English by Arthur Machen. London: privately printed, 1894. 6 vols.

> After his meeting with Frederick II in Berlin, Casanova (1725-98) travelled through the Baltic provinces, staying two months early in 1765 in Riga before reaching St Petersburg. In the Russian capital he met many notable Russian aristocrats, bought a peasant mistress (purchased after his departure by the architect Rinaldi), paid a short visit to Moscow, and was introduced to the empress in the Winter Palace, before leaving for Warsaw in October (vol. V, pp. 491-560).

D11) Pallas, Peter Simon, *Travels into Siberia and Tartary, provinces of the Russian empire. By S. Pallas, M.D. professor of natural history, &C.; taken by* *order of the Empress of Russia, under the direction of the Imperial Academy of Sciences at Petersburg, in 1768, 1769, 1770, 1771, 1772, 1773, and 1774, and now first translated into English* [by the Rev. Dr John Trusler]. Included as vols. II-IV of *The habitable world described, or the present state of the people in all parts of the globe, from north to south; shewing the situation, extent, climate, productions, animals, &c. of the different kingdoms and states; including all the new discoveries...* By John Trusler. London: printed for the author at the literary press, London, 1788-89.

> Pallas (1741-1811) was appointed professor of natural history at the St Petersburg Academy of Sciences in 1767. In 1768 he set out on a six-year expedition that was to take him through Siberia to the frontiers of China, recording as he went many new flowers and birds. His epic journey ended on 30 July 1774 with his arrival back in St Petersburg. *Reise durch verschiendene Provinzen des Russischen Reichs* was published in St Petersburg in 1771-76 and the celebrated French translation began to appear in the same year as Trusler's generally overlooked, if somewhat truncated and edited version.

D12) Pallas, Peter Simon, *A naturalist in Russia: letters from Peter Simon Pallas to Thomas Pennant.* Edited by Carol Urness. Minneapolis: University of Minnesota Press, 1967. iv+189pp.

> The first letter in this collection dates from 1766, when Pallas was still in The Hague, where he had met the English naturalist Pennant (1726-98) the previous year. The remaining sixteen letters, written between 1777 and October 1781, were sent from St Petersburg, subsequent to Pallas's return from his Siberian expedition. The long letters are full of details about the expedition and its findings in response to questions in Pennant's non-extant letters (pp. 14-158).

D13) Cathcart, Charles, and Cathcart, Jane, *The beautiful Mrs. Graham and the Cathcart circle.* By E. Maxtone Graham. London: Nisbet & Co., 1927. x+322pp.

> The 9th Lord Cathcart (1721-76), British ambassador extraordinary, arrived in St Petersburg with his wife and numerous children on 14 August 1768. A further, ninth, child was born in 1770, but Lady Cathcart (née Hamilton, b. 1726) died on 12 November 1771. Lord Cathcart and his children returned to England in August of the following year. Includes letters from Lady Cathcart (pp. 8-15) and three dispatches from Lord Cathcart (pp. 16-18, 20-23), as well as his moving tribute to his wife, 'Particulars addrest to Lady Cathcart's friends' (St Petersburg, 1771) (pp. 24-28).

D14) Cathcart, Charles, ['Dispatches']. In *Sbornik imperatorskogo russkogo istoricheskogo obshchestva*, vols. XII, XIX. St Petersburg: Academy of Sciences, 1873, 1876. xxviii+499pp; xviii+547pp.

> Dispatches to and from Cathcart for the periods from 4 January 1769 to 22 December 1769 (vol. XII, pp. 333-487) and from 26 January 1770 to 19 June 1772 (vol. XIX, pp. 1-276). Also included are dispatches by **Henry Shirley**, who arrived a few months before Cathcart in May 1767 and remained as his secretary (pp. 300-43).

D15) Richardson, William, *Anecdotes of the Russian Empire: in a series of letters, written, a few years ago, from St. Petersburg*. London: printed for W. Strahan, and T. Cadell, 1784. xvi+478pp.

> Richardson (1743-1814), tutor to Cathcart's sons since 1766, travelled with them to St Petersburg in 1768. Soon after their return he became Professor of Humanity at Glasgow University. His fifty-six letters, revised before publication, cover the beginning of the outward voyage to the first days of the return journey as far as Copenhagen in August- September 1772. Includes poetry and other material written from, but of little relevance to, Russia, but also important descriptions of events in the Russian capital and its environs and essays on such topics as serfdom and national character.

D16) Tóth, Ferenc [Tott, François], *Memoirs of the Baron de Tott, on the Turks and the Tartars.* Translated from the French, by an English gentleman at Paris, under the immediate inspection of the Baron. London: Printed and sold by J. Jarvis; and also by J. Debrett; T. Becket; and J. Sewell, 1785. 2 vols. [2nd edition with different title and additional material, London: printed for G.G.J. and J. Robinson, 1786, 4 parts in 2 vols.]

> Baron de Tóth (1733-93) was a military adviser to the Turks during the Russo-Turkish war of 1768-74. Describes his visit to the Crimea and southern Ukraine (I, 288-532).

D17) Dimsdale, Thomas, *Tracts on inoculation, written and published at St Petersburg in the year 1768, by command of her Imperial Majesty, the Empress of All the Russias: with additional observations on epidemic small-pox, on the nature of that disease, and on the different success of the various modes of inoculation.* London: printed by James Phillips for W. Owen, 1781. x+249pp.

> Author of *Present method of inoculating for the smallpox* (1767), Dr Dimsdale (1712-1800) was invited the following year to St Petersburg to inoculate the Empress and her son, the Grand Duke Paul. The inoculation was a

complete success and Dimsdale and his accompanying son Nathaniel were made barons of the Russian empire and showered with gifts. He returned early in 1769 to England, where he was elected F.R.S. Chapter I, 'Some account of a journey to Russia, and of the introduction of inoculation into that country', describes their momentous journey (pp. 1-91).

D18) *Marshall, Joseph, *Travels through Holland, Flanders, Germany, Denmark, Sweden, Lapland, Russia, the Ukraine and Poland, in the years 1768, 1769, and 1770. In which is particularly minuted the present state of those countries, reflecting their agriculture, population, manufactures, commerce, the arts, and useful undertakings.* London: printed for J. Almon, 1773. 3 vols.

A product of an "armchair" traveller (cf. D19, D58, D60) Full of absurdities, the work nonetheless has much convincing detail and is often quoted as an authentic record. Marshall states he was in Russia in 1769-70 and left St Petersburg on 3 April 1770 (vol. III, pp. 105-233).

D19) *Richard, John, *A tour from London to Petersburgh, from thence to Moscow, and return to London by way of Courland, Poland, Germany and Holland.* London: printed for T. Evans, 1778. viii [7]+222pp.

Greeted as "a catchpenny performance" by Jeremy Bentham, the work provides no evidence, internal or external, that Richard ever visited Russia. His letters, said to have written several years earlier during his tour, are superficial in the extreme and seem to have been inspired by information he received from Russians in England (pp. 7-130).

D20) [Calvert, Frederick], *Gaudia poetica, Latina, Anglica, et Gallica composita a° 1769.* [Augsburg]: privately printed, 1770. [ii+] xcviii [+19]pp.

The eccentric 6th Lord Baltimore (1731-71) arrived in St Petersburg in July 1769 and left a few weeks later for Germany, where he arranged the publication of his book, a quarto volume, magnificently produced with high-quality engravings to frame his four long Latin poems, two of which are devoted to Peterhof and Tsarskoe selo. Their translation into English prose, "The pleasures of poetry", explains their inclusion (pp. lix-lxviii).

D21) Benyovszky, Móricz, *Memoirs and travels of Mauritius Augustus Count de Benyowsky, magnate of the kingdoms of Hungary and Poland, one of the chiefs of the Confederation of Poland, &c, &c: consisting of his military operations in Poland, his exile into Kamchatka, his escape and voyage from that peninsular through the northern Pacific Ocean, touching at Japan and Formosa, to Canton in*

China, with an account of the French settlement he was appointed to form upon the island, written by himself. Translated from the original [French] manuscript [by William Nicholson]. London: printed for G.G.J. and J. Robinson, 1790. 2 vols. [See also as edited by Captain Samuel Pasfield Oliver, London: T. Fisher Unwin, 1893.]

> The Hungarian soldier of fortune Count Benyovszky (1746-86), a considerable manipulator of dates and embroiderer of facts in his own biography, provides a journal of his adventures in Russia. Serving with the Polish forces, he was captured by the Russians and arriving in St Petersburg in November 1769, was sent into Siberian exile. In Kamchatka he instigated a revolt among the exiles and eventually sailed away from Kamchatka in May 1771 en route for Japan and China (vol. I, pp. 36-383).

D22) Williams, John, *The rise, progress, and present state of the northern governments; viz. The United Provinces, Denmark, Sweden, Russia, and Poland: or, observations on the nature, constitution, religion, law, policy, customs, and commerce of each country; the manners and dispositions of the people; their military forces by land and sea; the revenues and resources of each power; and on the circumstances and conjunctures which have contributed to produce the various revolutions which have happened to them: the whole digested from the most authentic records and histories, and from the reflections and remarks made during a tour of five years through these nations.* London: printed for T. Beckett, 1777. 2 vols.

> Williams, deriding Voltaire for describing a country he had never visited, seems to have been in Russia in 1770. He refers to his interviews in St Petersburg and Moscow, consulting manuscripts (in German) in the Kremlin, and travelling "1700 versts in the Russian dominions to form some idea of the character of the mass of the people in this state". He provides an overview of the geography and history of Russia, dwelling in particular on the reign of Peter I and the overthrow of Peter III. There is little evidence of his own observations, even when writing on "manners and customs" (vol. II, pp. 1-343).

D23) Gunning, Robert, ['Dispatches']. In *Sbornik imperatorskogo russkogo istoricheskogo obshchestva*, vol. XIX. St Petersburg: Academy of Sciences, 1876. xviii+547pp.

> Sir Robert (1731-1816) replaced Cathcart as envoy extraordinary and plenipotentiary in 1772, arriving in St Petersburg on 18 June and leaving after a stay of some three and a half years in February 1776. Gunning was to enjoy a friendly relationship with the empress, who, at the request

of George III, invested him with the order of the Bath on 9 July 1773. Dispatches to and from Gunning for the period 30 June 1772 to 12 January 1776 (pp. 276-510). Also included are dispatches by **Richard Oakes**, who acted as *chargé d'affaires* until the arrival of Sir James Harris, 16 February to 22 November 1776 (pp. 510-22).

D24) Fries, Hans Jakob, *A Siberian journey: the journal of Hans Jakob Fries, 1774-1776*. Translated from the German and edited with a bibliographical introduction by Walther Kirchner. London: Frank Cass, 1974. xii+183pp.

> The young Zurich-born Fries (1749-1801) had arrived in St Petersburg on 1 September 1770 and moved to Moscow, where he began his medical training. In 1773 he became an under-surgeon and the following year he was attached to a regiment of dragoons fighting the Turks. It is in a letter to his parents in August 1779, when he was working in the admiralty hospital in St Petersburg, that he describes his career in the intervening years that took him after the end of the Russo-Turkish war on a journey through south-eastern Russia to Siberia, accompanying a Major Riedel on a mission to find recruits for the Russian army. They travelled from Orenburg to Omsk and on to Irkutsk, crossed Lake Baikal and went as far as Kiakhta before returning by the same route.

D25) Wraxall, Nathaniel William, *Cursory remarks made in a tour through some of the northern parts of Europe, particularly Copenhagen, Stockholm and Petersburgh*. London: T. Cadell, 1775. [2nd corrected edition with title *A tour through some of the northern parts...*, 1775; 4th corrected and augmented edition with title *A tour round the Baltic, through the northern countries of Europe...*, 1807.]

> Sir Nathaniel (1751-1831) set out on his voyage to the north in April 1774 and arrived in St Petersburg in August, staying only a month. The first British "grand tourist" to publish his account of Catherine's Russia, he describes the city, a visit to Peterhof, where he saw the empress, and conversations with the sculptor Falconet at work on his equestrian statue of Peter (pp. 202-88).

D26) Henniker, John, *A visit to Petersburgh: extracts from a northern tour in the years 1775 & 1776 through Copenhagen and Petersburgh to the river Swir joining the lakes of Onega and Ladoga*. Cambridge: Morison Room of the University Library, 1991. 8pp.; *Expedition to the river Swir: in a series of letters*. Cambridge: Morison Room of the University Library, 1992. 8pp.; *I must, I* *will digress: further ramblings on the river Swir.* Cambridge: [Morison Room of the University Library], 1998. 8pp.

> These are extracts from the manuscript diary of the 2nd Lord Henniker (1752-1821), which is now held in Cambridge (U.L.C. MS. Add. 8720). Henniker, grandson of a Russia Company merchant, arrived at Cronstadt on 14 July 1775 and returned to Copenhagen six weeks later. After sightseeing in and around the capital, he accompanied a prominent Petersburg merchant Timothy Raikes on a trip up the Neva, across Ladoga, to the river Svir to inspect factories.

D27) Harris, James, *Diaries and correspondence of James Harris, first Earl of Malmesbury; containing an account of his missions to the courts of Madrid, Frederick the Great, Catherine the Second, and The Hague; and his special missions to Berlin, Brunswick, and the French Republic.* Edited by his grandson, the Third Earl [James Howard Harris]. London: Richard Bentley, 1844. 4 vols.

> Sir James, later 1st Earl of Malmesbury (1746-1820), arrived in St Petersburg on 2 January 1778 as British envoy extraordinary and plenipotentiary and left on 8 September 1783. He was knighted in 1779. He enjoyed the benevolence of Catherine and Potemkin during a difficult five-year period that covered the end of the American War of Independence and Russia's Declaration of Armed Neutrality in 1780 (vol. I, pp. 155-542; II, pp. 1-58).

D28) Coxe, William, *Travels into Poland, Russia, Sweden, and Denmark, interspersed with historical relations and political inquiries.* London: printed by J. Nichols for T. Cadell, 1784. 2 vols.

> Rev. Coxe (1747-1828), Fellow of King's College, Cambridge, was tutor to George, Lord Herbert, later 11th Earl of Pembroke (1759-1827) on an extensive Grand Tour that took them eventually via Poland to Moscow, where they arrived in August 1778. They left St Petersburg for Stockholm, via Vyborg, on 3 February 1779 (vol. I, pp 240-588; II, pp. 3-311). Coxe visited Russia again in 1784-85 as tutor to Samuel Whitbread Jr. (1764-1815), son of the famous brewer. The materials he garnered on this occasion were incorporated into a third volume in 1790, completing the first edition. The second and third editions had appeared in the meantime and it is the fourth and fifth editions (5 vols., 1792 and 1802) that offer expanded and re-arranged versions. A sumptuous three-volume set in fifty copies was published in 1803 as Coxe's final statement on Russia.

D29) Coxe, William, *Henry, Elizabeth and George (1734-80): letters and diaries of Henry, Tenth Earl of Pembroke and his circle.* Edited by Lord Herbert. London: Jonathan Cape, 1939. 576pp.

> Contains three letters from Coxe from Russia in 1778 to the 10th Earl and his wife (pp. 125-26, 137-38, 145-46).

D30) Coxe, William, *Account of the prisons and hospitals in Russia, Sweden, and Denmark: with occasional remarks on the different modes of punishments in those countries.* London: printed for T. Cadell, 1781. viii+55pp.

> Dedicated to the famed prison reformer and philanthropist John Howard (pp. v-vi), it supplies detailed descriptions of prisons and hospitals in Moscow, Tver, Vyshnii Volochek, St Petersburg and Cronstadt visited by Coxe in 1778-79 (pp.1-30).

D31) [Rickman, John], *Journal of Captain Cook's last voyage to the Pacific Ocean, on Discovery; performed in the years 1776, 1777, 1778, 1779.* London: Edward Newberry, 1781. xlvi+396pp.

> The first, anonymously published, account of Cook's fateful third and last voyage is now attributed to Rickman, who was a lieutenant on the *Discovery*. The *Discovery*, commanded by Captain Charles Clerke (1743-79), and Cook's *Resolution* set sail in July 1776 and passed through the Bering Strait past Kamchatka in the summer of 1778. After Cook's death in Hawaii in February 1779, the expedition, now under the command of Captain Clerke, returned to Kamchatka, where they spent two months from late April to June and a further six weeks from late August to early October, during which time Clerke died and was buried at Petropavlovsk (pp. 337-75).

D32) Ledyard, John, *A journal of Captain Cook's last voyage to the Pacific Ocean, and in quest of a north-west passage, between Asia & America; performed in the years 1776, 1777, 1778, and 1779.* Hartford, Conn.: Nathaniel Patten, 1783. 208pp. [See *John Ledyard's journal of Captain Cook's last voyage.* Edited by James Kenneth Munford. With an introduction by Sinclair H. Hitchings. Corvallis, Oregon: Oregon State University Press, 1963. l+264pp.]

> The American Ledyard (1751-89) joined Cook's ship, the *Resolution*, as corporal of marines in Plymouth in July 1776. When compiling his own account of the expedition, he was undoubtedly aware of Rickman and, indeed, the Kamchatka section reproduces Rickman's (pp. 163-91).

D33) Gilbert, George, *Captain Cook's final voyage: the journal of Midshipman George Gilbert.* Introduced and edited by Christine Holmes. Horsham, Sussex: Caliban Books, 1982. 158pp.

> Gilbert (d. 1783?) was a midshipman on the *Resolution*, transferring to the *Discovery* in August 1779. His journal contains interesting notes on their time in Kamchatka, April-October 1779 (pp. 129-49).

D34) Reineggs, Jacob, and Bieberstein, Friedrich August, *A general, historical, and topographical description of Mount Caucasus. With a catalogue of plants indigenous to the country.* Translated from the works of Dr Reineggs and Marshall Bieberstein by Charles Wilkinson. London: C. Taylor; W. Miller, A. Collins, Darton and Harvey, 1807. 2 vols.

> A curious compilation, said to be appropriate for the contemporary political situation following Tilsit, from *Allegemaine historische-topographische Beschreibung des Kaukasus* (1796-97) by Dr Reineggs (1744-93) and *Tableau des provinces situées sur la côte occidentale de la Mer Caspienne entre les fleuves Terek et Kour* (1798) by Bieberstein (1768-1826). The Saxon adventurer Reineggs, real name Ehlich, arrived in Georgia in 1779, in 1781 travelled to St Petersburg, and accompanied Potemkin to Moldavia in 1789. His narrative ends at vol. II, p. 62, when without any break, Bieberstein's, referring to 1795-99 when he was with the Russian army in the Caucasus, begins. The catalogue of plants is found in vol. II, pp. 175-240.

D35) Bentham, Samuel, and Bentham, Jeremy, *The works of Jeremy Bentham.* Published under the superintendence of his executor, John Bowring. Edinburgh: William Tait, and London: Simpkin, Marshall, & Co., 1843. 11 vols.

> Samuel (1757-1831), the younger brother of the more famous Jeremy (1748-1832), left London to seek his fortune in Russia in August 1779, travelling via Riga to Moscow and down to New Russia. Early in 1781 he undertook an ambitious itinerary through Russia, travelling to Archangelsk before crossing the Urals and travelling to the Chinese border at Kiakhta, before returning to St Petersburg in October 1782. In March 1784 he entered the service of Potemkin to organize a model farm, shipyard, etc. on the prince's estates at Krichev in Belorussia. He was joined there in February 1786 by Jeremy, who remained until November of the following year. Samuel subsequently took part in the Russo-Turkish war, travelled again to Siberia, before returning to the south. He left Jassy in January 1791, after eleven years in Russia. (See vol. X, pp. 147-79).

D36) Bentham, Samuel, and Bentham, Jeremy, *The correspondence of Jeremy Bentham.* Vol. III (January 1781 to October 1788). Edited by Ian R. Christie. London: University of London Athlone Press, 1971. xxxiv+647pp; vol. IV (October 1788 to December 1793). Edited by Alexander Taylor Milne. London: Athlone Press, 1981. xlii+506pp.

> These volumes contain long excerpts from Samuel's voluminous letters to his brother from Russia as well as Jeremy's letters from Ukraine (vol. III, and IV, pp. 1-223 *passim*). For Samuel's visit to Russia during Alexander I's reign see F10.

D37) Ligne, Charles Joseph, de, *The Prince de Ligne: his memoirs, letters, and miscellaneous papers.* Selected and translated by Katharine Prescott Wormeley. With introduction and preface by C.-A. Sainte-Beuve and Madame de Staël-Holstein. London: William Heinemann, 1899. 2 vols.

> The Prince de Ligne (1735-1814), born in Belgium and a subject of Austria, first visited Russia in the summer of 1780, when he met the empress. On his return to Vienna he began the correspondence with her that ended only with her death (vol. I, pp. 302-20). In Feb 1786 Ligne accepted Catherine's invitation to join her entourage on her famous visit to the Crimea and joined her in Kiev early the next year. He describes the journey in letters to the marquise de Coigny in Paris (vol. II, pp. 8-44). After their return to St Petersburg, Ligne soon departed for Russian army under Potemkin in November 1787 and fought against the Turks until December 1788, when he left to join the Austrian army at the siege of Belgrade (vol. II, pp. 46-98).

D38) Elliot, Gilbert, *Life and letters of Sir Gilbert Elliot First Earl of Minto, from 1751 to 1806, when his public life in Europe was closed by his appointment to the vice-royalty of India.* Edited by his great-niece the Countess of Minto. London: Longmans, Green & Co., 1874. 3 vols.

> Sir Gilbert (1751-1814) was Sir James Harris's brother-in-law and travelled out to St Petersburg in June 1781 in order to escort back to England his ailing sister Harriet, Lady Harris. They left for England in mid-August. Excerpts from letters (vol. I, pp. 62-66).

D39) Howard, John, *The State of prisons in England and Wales, with preliminary observations, and an account of some foreign prisons.* Warrington: printed by William Eyres for T. Cadell, J. Johnson, and C. Dilly. 3rd edition 1784. 510pp.

> The first edition of this celebrated work appeared in 1777 and a second edition in 1780. It was only in the third edition that Howard (1726-90)

was able to incorporate his impressions of the prisons and hospitals in St Petersburg, Cronstadt, Vyshnii Volochek, Tver and Moscow he had visited in the summer of 1781 (pp. 85-95).

D40) Dimsdale, Elizabeth, *An English lady at the court of Catherine the Great: the journal of Baroness Elizabeth Dimsdale, 1781.* Edited, with an introduction and notes, by A.G. Cross. Cambridge: Crest, 1989. viii+108pp.

> Some twelve years after his first highly successful and lauded visit to St Petersburg to inoculate the empress and her son Paul, Dimsdale was invited again, to inoculate the Grand Dukes Alexander and Constantine. On this occasion he was accompanied by his third wife Elizabeth (1732-1812), whom he had recently married. Travelling overland, they arrived in St Petersburg on 8 August (p. 39). Three weeks later they removed to Tsarskoe selo, where the inoculation was to take place on 7 September. 25 September marked the return to the capital and their departure for England followed on 15 October (pp. 39-87).

D41) Forster, George, *A journey from Bengal to England through the northern part of India, Kashmire, Afghanistan, and Persia and into Russia by the Caspian Sea.* London: R. Faulder, 1798. 2 vols.

> In 1782-84 Forster (1752?-91) of the Indian civil service, travelling from Calcutta, sailed up the Volga to Moscow and then proceeded to St Petersburg, before returning to England (vol. II, pp. 304-97).

D42) [Walker, James], *Paramythia or mental pastimes being original anecdotes, historical, descriptive, humourous, and witty collected chiefly during a long residence at the court of Russia, by the author.* London: printed for Lawler and Quick, 1821. viii+175pp. [reprinted in *Engraved in the memory: James Walker, engraver to the Empress Catherine the Great, and his Russian anecdotes.* Edited and introduced by Anthony Cross. Oxford: Berg, 1993, pp. 28-152.]

> Walker (1748-1822) went to Russia in 1784 with the position of "engraver to her imperial majesty" (which continued under Catherine's successors, Paul and Alexander). His anonymously published collection of anecdotes contains English as well as Russian material, the latter reflecting what he heard and saw during the eighteen years he spent in St Petersburg.

D43) Ségur, Louis-Philippe, de, *Memoirs and recollections of Count Segur, ambassador from France to the courts of Russia and Prussia, &c., &c. written by himself.* London: Henry Colburn, 1825. 3 vols.

Brilliant, witty, friend of the *philosophes*, the comte de Ségur (1753-1830) was in every way an ideal choice as French minister plenipotentiary to the court of Catherine. Appointed on 16 December 1784, he arrived in St Petersburg on 10 March 1785 and remained until October 1789. He accompanied the empress on her journey to the Crimea in 1787. Russia, vol. II, pp. 152-355; III, pp. 1-445.

D44) Sauer, Martin, *An account of a geographical and astronomical expedition to the northern parts of Russia, for ascertaining the degrees of latitude and longitude of the mouth of the river Kovima; of the whole coast of the Tshutski, to East Cape; and of the islands in the eastern ocean, stretching from there to the American coast; performed, by command of her imperial majesty Catherine the Second, empress of all the Russias, by Commodore Joseph Billings, in the years 1785, &c., to 1794; the whole narrated from the original papers, by Martin Sauer, secretary to the expedition.* London: printed by A. Strahan for T. Cadell Jun. and W. Davies, 1802. xxviii+332+58pp.

The expedition under Captain Joseph Billings (1761-1806) set out from St Petersburg on 25 October 1785, travelling via Moscow and Kazan and reaching Ekaterinburg by 17 January 1786. On 3 July they arrived at the sea at Okhotsk. After some six years of exploration and scientific experiments along the coast, including Kamchatka, they began their return journey in August 1793 and saw St Petersburg again on 10 March 1794. Of the expedition's secretary Sauer, who had been resident in St Petersburg from at least 1782, nothing more is known; Billings was transferred to the Black Sea fleet and served until his retirement in 1799 with the rank of captain-commander.

D45) [Masson, Charles-François-Philibert], *Secret memoirs of the court of Petersburg; particularly toward the end of the reign of Catherine II, and the commencement of that of Paul I, forming a description of the manners of Petersburg, at the close of the eighteenth century; and containing various anecdotes, collected during a residence of ten years in that capital; together with remarks on the education of the grand-dukes, the manners of the ladies, and the religion of the people; serving as a supplement to the life of Catherine II.* Translated from the French. London: printed by C. Whittingham for T.N. Longman and O. Rees, 1800. 2 vols.

Published anonymously, the work enjoyed a *succès de scandale* for its alleged revelations and was translated into many languages following its appearance in Paris in 1800. Masson (1762-1807) had gone to Russia in 1785 to join his elder brother and soon entered the engineer cadet corps. He enjoyed rapid promotion and became secretary to Grand Duke Alexander in 1796. Accused of sympathy for French victories at the beginning of Paul's reign, he and his brother were escorted to the Russo-Polish border.

D46) Miranda, Sebastián Francisco, de, *Fragments from an XVIIIth century diary: the travels and adventures of Don Francisco de Miranda, precursor of the independence of Spanish America, in Spain, Africa, North America, Europe and at the court of Catherine the Great of Russia, 1771-1789*. Compiled and translated by Jordan Herbert Stabler, with a preface by R.B. Cunninghame Graham. Caracas: Tipografía 'La nación', 1931. 196pp.

> The Venezuelan soldier Francisco de Miranda (1750-1816), during extensive European travels, arrived at Kherson from Turkey on 7 October 1786 and remained in Russia until 18 September of the following year. During this time he visited the Crimea and then proceeded to Kiev, where he was presented to Catherine II, and thence to Moscow and St Petersburg. A mere taster from a fascinating diary, the full Spanish text of which is found in *Archivo del general Miranda: Viajes*, vol. II (Caracas, 1929), pp. 190-470.

D47) [Ellis, George, attrib.], *Memoir of a map of the countries comprehended between the Black Sea and the Caspian; with an account of the Caucasian nations, and vocabularies of their languages.* London: printed for J. Edwards, 1788. 80pp.

> Ellis (1753-1815), F.S.A. and F.R.S., spent several months in St Petersburg in 1786 and may have travelled south. The memoir is an attempt to classify the inhabitants of the Caucasus according to information supplied by Professor Pallas. The specimens of the various languages were drawn from Pallas's universal comparative dictionary, compiled with the encouragement of the empress.

D48) Craven, Elizabeth, *A Journey through the Crimea to Constantinople. In a series of letters from the right honourable Elizabeth Lady Craven to his serene highness the Margrave of Brandebourg, Anspach, and Bareith. Written in the year MDCCLXXXVI.* London: for H. Chamberlaine, R. Montcrieffe, W. Colles, G. Burnet, W. Wilson, 1789. 8+327pp [With changed title: *Letters from the right honourable Lady Craven, to his serene highness the Margrave of Anspach, during her travels through France, Germany, & Russia in 1785 and 1786.* 2nd edition, including a variety of letters not before published. London: printed by A.J. Valpy, and sold by H. Colburn, 1814. viii+316pp. Her *Memoirs of the Margravine of Anspach, formerly Lady Craven. Written by herself.* Paris:

A. and W. Galignani, 1826. 2 vols. contain a succinct version of her travels (vol. I, pp. 97-107).]

> On a tour that had begun in Paris in mid-June 1785, the "beautiful" Lady Craven (née Berkeley, later Margravine of Anspach, 1750-1828) arrived via Italy, Vienna and Warsaw in February 1786 in St Petersburg, where she was presented to the empress. She soon travelled via Moscow and Ukraine to the Crimea, "a delicious country; and an acquisition to Russia which she should never relinquish". She stayed at Kherson for a month, before crossing to Constantinople (pp. 164-258).

D49) [Sinclair, John], *General observations regarding the present state of the Russian empire.* London: privately printed, 1787. 49pp.

> In 1786 Sir John (1754-1835) planned a tour of the northern capitals of Europe which would fit into the seven-month Parliamentary recess between June 1786 and January 1787. Arriving in St Petersburg from Riga in August, he travelled home via Moscow and Kiev to Warsaw. On his return he wrote *General observations* for circulation among friends.

D50) Sinclair, John, *The correspondence of the right honourable Sir John Sinclair, bart. with reminiscences of the most distinguished characters who have appeared in Great Britain, and in foreign countries, during the last fifty years.* London: Henry Colburn and Richard Bentley, 1831. 2 vols.

> Sir John included most of the material from *General observations* into Part XXI, 'Travels in Russia, and correspondence with the natives of that country', of his collected correspondence (vol. II, pp. 241-85), although somewhat edited to reflect his later mellowed attitude towards Russia. Elsewhere there is much that is new, such as his description of his audience by Catherine on 25 August 1786 and his visit to Grand Duke Paul at Pavlovsk on 31 August (vol. I, pp. 7-13). See also vol. I, pp. 149-52 (Princess Dashkova), 209-12 (Rumiantsev-Zadunaiskii).

D51) La Pérouse, Jean-François de Galaup, de, *The voyage of La Pérouse round the world in the years 1785, 1786, 1787, and 1788, by the 'Boussole' and 'Astrolabe', under the command of J.F.G. de la Pérouse.* Published by order of the National Assembly under the superintendence of L.A. Milet-Mureau. London: printed for J. Johnson, 1798. 3 vols.

> The circumnavigation, commanded by the comte de La Pérouse (1741-88), reached Kamchatka and the Sea of Okhotsk in September 1787 (vol. III, pp. 1-37).

D52) La Pérouse, Jean-François de Galaup, de, *The journal of Jean-François de Galaup de la Pérouse 1785-1788.* Translated and edited by John Dunmore. London: The Hakluyt Society, 1994. 2 vols.

> Based on the newly discovered journal of La Pérouse in the French national archives, this edition also includes letters sent from Petropavlovsk. On Sakhalin and Kamchatka, pp. 284-376; letters, pp. 510-34.

D53) Lesseps, Jean-Baptiste-Barthélemy, de, *Travels in Kamtschatka, during the years 1787 and 1788.* Translated from the French. London: J. Johnson, 1790. 2 vols. in 1.

> De Lesseps (1766-1834), a translator attached to La Pérouse's expedition, was dispatched on 7 October 1787 from Petropavlovsk to take news of what had been achieved back to France as swiftly as possible. Forced to spend the winter of 1787-88 in Kamchatka, which he describes in detail, he reached Okhotsk only in June 1788. He met Billings in Iakutsk (see D44) and returned via Tomsk, Tobolsk and Ekaterinburg to St Petersburg, where he arrived by the end of September, before proceeding to Versailles to present the papers to the king (vol. I, pp. 1-283; II, pp. 1-382). French original: *Journal historique du voyage de m. de Lesseps depuis l'instant où il a quitté les frégates françoises au Port Saint Pierre et Saint Paul du Kamtschatka jusqu'à son arrivée en France le 17 Octobre, 1788* (Paris, 1790). Lesseps was later to serve several terms as French consul in St Petersburg.

D54) Damas d'Antigney, Joseph Elizabeth Roger, *Memoirs of the comte Roger de Damas (1787-1806).* Edited and annotated by Jacques Rambaud. Translated by Mrs. Rodolph Stawell. London: Chapman and Hall, 1913. xxxiv+492pp.

> In January 1788 the comte de Damas (1765-1823) joined the Russian forces fighting against the Turks and distinguished himself at Ochakov and Izmail and was decorated by the empress. He left Russia in January 1791 at the end of the campaign (pp. 16-145). In the winter of 1792-93 Damas returned to Russia in the suite of the comte d'Artois (pp. 192-95).

D55) Jones, John Paul, *Memoirs of Rear-Admiral Paul Jones, chevalier of the military order of merit, and of the Russian order of St Anne, &c., &c., now first compiled from his original journals and correspondence: including an account of his service under Prince Potemkin, prepared for publication by himself.* Edinburgh: Oliver and Boyd; London: Simpkin & Marshall, 1830. 2 vols.

After playing a colourful part in the American War of Independence, Jones (1747-92) became a rear-Admiral in the Russian navy. He arrived in St Petersburg early in May 1788, met the empress, and was dispatched to the south to serve under Potemkin. He played a leading role in the battle of the Liman but subsequently offended Potemkin and was recalled to the capital towards the end of 1788 A scandal involving a young girl in St Petersburg led to his leaving Russia in September 1789 (vol. I, pp. 327-31; II, pp. 1-195).

D56) Ledyard, John, *John Ledyard's journey through Russia and Siberia 1787-1788: the journal and selected letters.* Edited by Stephen D. Watrous. Madison, Milwaukee and London: University of Wisconsin Press, 1966. xiv+293pp.

Eight years after his first visit to Kamchatka (see D32), Ledyard returned to Russia. He arrived in St Petersburg in March 1787 and two months later set out on his momentous journey with the intention of traversing the whole of Russia. Travelling through Siberia, he visited Tobolsk, Tomsk and Irkutsk but got only as far as Iakutsk, where he arrived in mid-September. It was there that Ledyard met Billings and Sauer, with whom he returned later to Irkutsk in January 1788, where he was immediately arrested on orders from Catherine (for reasons never satisfactorily explained) and taken back to Moscow and expelled from Russia via Poland in March (pp. 122-232).

D57) Trevenen, James, *A memoir of James Trevenen.* Edited by Christopher Lloyd and R.C. Anderson. London: for the Navy Records Society, 1959. xv+247pp.

Trevenen (1760-90), who had been a midshipman on Cook's last voyage, joined the Russian navy as a captain with a plan approved by the empress for discovery and trade in the North Pacific, but the outbreak of the Russo-Turkish war led to its postponement. He arrived in St Petersburg on 7 October 1787 and was soon involved in the naval war against Sweden, dying in the battle of Vyborg on 9 July 1790 (pp. 97-242).

D58) *[Chantreau, Pierre Nicholas], *Philosophical, political and literary travels in Russia during the years 1788 & 1789.* Perth: printed for R. Morison, Junior, for R. Morison and Son, Perth; and Vernor and Hood, London, 1794. 2 vols.

Chantreau (1741-1808), like Marshall and Richard before him and Thomson later, was only in Russia in his mind's eye and assimilated material from others, such as Coxe. He was "travelling" in Britain as precisely the same period, according to the title of another of his compilations.

D59) Swinton, Andrew, *Travels into Norway, Denmark, and Russia, in the years 1788, 1789, 1790, and 1791.* London: printed for G.G.J. and J. Robinson, 1792. xxvii+506pp.

> Reaching Riga in October 1788, the Scottish tourist Swinton heard of the recent death of his kinsman admiral Samuel Greig on board his flagship at Revel, which he then visited. Arriving in St Petersburg in November, he was to spend over two years in the Russian capital, describing his impressions in a series of sentimental letters, before departing in March 1791 (pp. 126-496).

D60) *[Thomson, William], *Letters from Scandinavia, on the past and present state of the northern nations of Europe.* London: printed for G.G. and J. Robinson, 1796. 2 vols.

> Published anonymously, but Thomson (1746-1817) is recognized as its author. It is, however, a work of plagiarism (principally from Swinton) by an able and prodigiously productive hack. Despite its title, it is presented as letters from and mainly about Russia allegedly written between 1789 and May 1792. Russia, vol. I, pp. 1-471; II, pp. 1-279.

D61) Howard, John, *An account of the principal lazarettos in Europe; with various papers relative to the plague: together with further observations on some foreign prisons and hospitals; and additional remarks on the present state of those in Great Britain and Ireland.* London: printed for J. Johnson, C. Dilly, and T. Cadell, 1791. 2nd edition, with additions. vii+272+32pp.

> Howard paid a second visit to Russia in 1789, re-visiting many of the institutions he had seen in 1781 (see D39). Interested in questions of quarantine and plague control, he decided to travel to the Crimea and observe "the sickly state of the Russian army on the confines of Turkey", but in Kherson he contracted fever and died on 20 January 1790. His monument was to be much visited by British travellers in the nineteenth century. The appendix to this posthumous second edition contains the update on prisons in Riga, Cronstadt, St Petersburg, and Moscow and his descriptions of the harrowing scenes he saw in the south, (Kherson, Bogoiavlensk and Nikolaev) (Appendix, pp. 12-218).

D62) Hawkins (Hawkins-Whitsted), James, *Charlotte Sophie Countess Bentinck: her life and times, 1715-1800.* By her descendant Mrs. Aubrey Le Blond. London: Hutchinson & Co., 1912. 2 vols.

Captain Hawkins, later Admiral Sir James (1762-1849), and his travelling companion Count William Bentinck (1764-1813), after visiting the latter's illustrious grandmother in Germany, spent three weeks in St Petersburg in October 1789 and in addition to the social whirl, interested themselves in naval matters at Cronstadt. Extracts from Hawkins's diary (vol. I, pp. 113-23).

D63) [Colmore, Lionel], *Letters from the Continent, describing the manners and customs of Germany, Poland, Russia, and Switzerland, in the years 1790, 1791, and 1792, to a friend residing in England.* London: J. Hatchard, 1812. iv+275pp.

The amusing, satirical letters of Colmore (1765-1807), another young gentry tourist, were published posthumously and describe his social life in the Russian capital between mid-October 1790 and the end of April 1791. Only two letters (nos. IX-X) are, however, extant from his sojourn in St Petersburg (pp. 88-117), the next being date-lined Warsaw, 24 August 1791.

D64) Storch, Heinrich Friedrich von, *The picture of Petersburg.* From the German of Henry Storch. [Translated by William Tooke.] London: printed for T.N. Longman & O. Rees, 1801. xviii+591pp.

The most comprehensive account of St Petersburg in the last years of Catherine's reign (the preface is dated 1792). *Gemälde von St Petersburg* originally appeared in two volumes in Riga in 1793-94. Heinrich Storch (in his Russian variant, Andrei Karlovich Shtorkh) (1766-1838) was professor of belles-lettres at the Imperial Cadet Corps and a member of the Free Economic Society. There are several passages on the British community inserted by the translator, who had spent many years in Russia (see D69).

D65) Leveson Gower, Granville, *Lord Granville Leveson Gower (First Earl Granville): private correspondence 1781 to 1821.* Edited by his daughter-in-law Castalia Countess Granville. London: John Murray, 1916. 2 vols.

Just down from Oxford, the young tourists Lord Granville, later 1st Earl Granville (1773-1846), and his friend Lord Boringdon arrived in St Petersburg in October 1792, visited Moscow in December, and left for England via Warsaw (vol. I, pp. 55-64). Twelve years later, still only thirty-one, he was back in the Russian capital as British ambassador in October 1804 and negotiated an Anglo-Russian convention, signed on 11 April 1805. He returned to England in August 1806. The following April he was re-appointed ambassador, but was in Russia merely a few months before the treaty of Tilsit and the ensuing Russian declaration of war on 31 October 1807 led to his departure from St Petersburg on 9 November. His correspondence, mainly with Lady Bessborough, during these two periods is memorable for his protracted on-off love affair with the "princesse nocturne", Princess Evdokiia Golitsyna (vol. I, pp. 485-510; II, pp. 1- 207, 263-312).

D66) Parkinson, John, *A tour of Russia, Siberia and the Crimea 1792-1794.* Edited with an introduction by William Collier. London: Frank Cass & Co., 1971. xx+280pp.

> Parkinson (1754-1840, Oxford don and travelling tutor *par excellence*, accompanied Edward Wilbraham-Bootle (1771-1853), later 1st Lord Skelmersdale, on a truly remarkable tour. After some weeks in Scandinavia, they arrived in St Petersburg on 4 November 1792 and stayed until the following March. From Moscow they headed for Kazan, but choosing not to follow the Volga down to Astrakhan, headed for Perm and on into Siberia as far as Tobolsk in mid-April 1793. Their route then took them south to join the Volga and to travel down to Sarepta and Astrakhan, before journeying to Georgievsk and to the Crimea by August. They returned to St Petersburg at the end of December, via Kiev and Moscow. Only in March 1794 did they set off for Warsaw. Edited from his extensive manuscript diaries. Russia, pp. 20-228.

D67) Pallas, Peter Simon, *Travels through the southern provinces of the Russian Empire, in the years 1793 and 1794.* Translated from the German, without abridgment [?by A.F.M. Willich and Steven Porter]. London: Longman and O. Rees, T. Cadell Jun. and W. Davies, John Murray and S. Highley, 1802-03. 2 vols.

> Accompanied by his wife and daughter as well as by the Leipzig artist C.G.H. Geissler, who was to illustrate his account, Pallas (see D11-12) left St Petersburg on 1 February 1793. They travelled down the Volga to Astrakhan and then through the Caucasus to the Crimea. He spent the winter of 1793-94 near Simferopol and began the return journey on 18 July 1794, arriving back in the capital on 14 September 1794.

D68) Kynnersley, Mary, *The Baroness de Bode 1775-1803.* By William S. Childe-Permberton. London: Longmans, Green, and Co., 1900. xx+296pp.

> Daughter of a Staffordshire squire, Mary (d. 1812) married Charles Auguste Louis Frederick, Baron de Bode (d. 1797) in 1775 and lived in Alsace, then Germany, and finally, fleeing the Revolution, found refuge in Russia, where Catherine granted the Bodes estates in New Russia. The Bodes arrived in St Petersburg in August 1794 and the baroness's letters to her English relatives chart their subsequent life in Russia until February

1803, when the correspondence abruptly ceased (pp. 182-271). Mary died in Moscow in 1812 and her children remained in Russia.

D69) Niemcewicz, Julian Ursyn, *Notes of my captivity in Russia, in the years 1794, 1795, and 1796.* Translated from the original [Polish], by Alexander Laski. Edinburgh: William Tait; London: Simpkin, Marshall, & co. 1844. xxiii+251pp.

> The renowned Polish politician and man-of-letters Niemcewicz (1757-1841) was captured, together with Kosciuzsko, at the battle of Macieiowice on 10 October 1794. He spent twenty-six months in captivity in St Petersburg's Peter and Paul fortress before being released by Paul I. He finished his account in May 1800, while in exile in America, and the Polish original was first published in 1843.

D70) Guthrie, Maria, *A tour, performed in the years 1795-6, through the Taurida, or Crimea, the antient kingdom of Bosphorus, the once-powerful republic of Tauric Cherson, and all the other countries on the north shore of the Euxine, ceded to Russia by the Peace of Kainardgi and Jassy;* by Mrs Maria Guthrie, formerly acting directress of the imperial convent for the education of the female nobility of Russia; described in a series of letters to her husband, the editor, Matthew Guthrie, M.D., F.R.S. and F.S.A. of London and Edinburgh, member of the philosophical society of Manchester, &c. &c., physician to the first and second imperial corps of noble cadets in St Petersburgh, and councillor of state to his imperial majesty of all the Russias; the whole illustrated by a map of the tour along the Euxine coast, from the Dniester to the Cuban; with engravings of a great number of ancient coins, medals, monuments, inscriptions, and other curious objects. London: T. Cadell Junior and W. Davies, 1802. xxiv+446pp.

> The ninety-three posthumously published letters that Marie Guthrie (née Romaud-Survesnes, d. 1800) sent to her husband Matthew (1743-1807) in St Petersburg (pp. 1-308), were not only translated from French but were swollen under his "editorship" into the major description of the Crimea, present and particularly past and replete with all manner of archaeological and historical material, that was available to British readers at the beginning of the nineteenth century.

D71) Tooke, William, *A view of the Russian empire during the reign of Catharine the Second and to the close of the eighteenth century.* London: printed for T.N. Longman and O. Rees, and J. Debrett, 1799. 3 vols.

Tooke (1744-1820) was appointed chaplain to the British Factory at Cronstadt in March 1771 and in 1774 succeeded King to the Petersburg chaplaincy, where he remained until his final return to England in 1792 and to unceasing literary endeavour over a further three decades. Fellow of the Royal Society and a corresponding member of the Russian Academy of Sciences, he published many works on Russia, but his 2,000-page *View*, despite its obvious compilatory nature (which he wore, incidentally, as a badge of honour), gives the fullest expression to his profound and personal knowledge of Catherine's Russia.

Fig. 39 Paul I (n.d.), by Vladimir Borovikovskii. Oil on canvas.

5. REIGN OF PAUL I (1796-1801)

See also D45

E1) [Brown, Thomas], *The reminiscences of an old traveller throughout different parts of Europe*. Edinburgh: John Anderson, Jr., 1834. viii+202pp. [2nd edition, greatly enlarged, Edinburgh, 1835. viii+301pp.]

> First edition published anonymously. Brown (1770-1857) was a merchant in St Petersburg for over twenty-five years, but he provides a mere traveller's account of a journey via Mittau and Riga to St Petersburg and out through Finland to Sweden (pp. 165-81).

E2) [Hyde, Catherine, Marquise de Govion Broglio Solari], *Private anecdotes of foreign courts, by the author of 'Memoirs of the Princesse de Lamballe'*. London: Colburn, 1827. 2 vols.

> Gossipy general history of Russian court by Englishwoman (1755-1844), said to have been in Russia after death of Catherine and departing before assassination of Paul (vol. I, pp. 1-112).

E3) Tweddell, John, *Remains of the late John Tweddell Fellow of Trinity College Cambridge being a selection of his letters written from various parts of the Continent together with a republication of his Prolusiones juveniles an appendix containing some account of the author's collections mss. drawings &c. and of their extraordinary disappearance*. London: J. Mawman, 1815. 479+179pp. [2nd edition, Aug., 1816.]

> Tweddell (1766-99), Fellow of Trinity College, Cambridge, set out in September 1795 on extensive travels that took him through Ukraine, where he met Suvorov, and Russia (Jan. 1797-Feb 1798, pp. 132-65, 179-218), en route to Constantinople and to his death in Athens.

http://dx.doi.org/10.11647/OBP.0042.05

E4) Clarke, Edward Daniel, *Travels in various countries of Europe Asia and Africa*. Part the First: *Russia Tartary and Turkey*. London: T. Cadell and W. Davies, 1810. xxviii+759pp. [2nd edition, 5 vols., 1811-19, and other eds. See also *Travels in Russia, Tartary and Turkey...; with a memoir of the author, and numerous additions and notes, prepared for the present edition*. Edinburgh: W. and R. Chambers, 1839. 140pp. (double columns).]

> Two years after becoming a Fellow of Jesus College, Cambridge, Clarke (1769-1822), who had already travelled extensively through Britain and on the Continent, set off on a northern tour with a pupil, John Marten Cripps. They arrived in St Petersburg in January 1800, travelled to Moscow, and then south to the Sea of Azov, on to the Crimea and Odessa, which they left at the end of October for Constantinople (pp. 3-654). Like subsequent lifetime editions of Coxe's travels, Clarke's are also interesting for the changes, corrections and additions he introduced. Clarke's highly critical account of his "severe penance" in Paul's Russia was highly influential in Britain throughout the decades up to the Crimean War.

E5) Clarke, Edward Daniel, *The life and remains of the Rev. Edward Daniel Clarke, LL.D. professor of mineralogy in the University of Cambridge*. [Edited by William Otter.] London: printed by J.F. Dove, 1824. xii+667pp.

> Includes his letters from Russia and the Crimea, 1800 (pp. 383-448).

E6) Kotzebue, August Friedrich Ferdinand von, *The most remarkable year in the life of Augustus von Kotzebue; containing an account of his exile into Siberia, and of the other extraordinary events which happened to him in Russia*. Written by himself. Translated from the German by the Rev. Benjamin Beresford. London: printed by T. Gillet for Richard Phillips, 1802. 3 vols.

> After several years in Russian service, Kotzebue (1761-1819), dramatist and novelist, had retired to Weimar in 1797 but returned to Russia with his Russian wife in the spring of 1800. He was arrested after crossing the border, accused of being a Jacobin, and exiled to Siberia. Author of a play that was flattering to Paul I, he was pardoned, given estates in Livonia, and made director of the German theatre in St Petersburg. Translation of *Das merkwürdigste Jahr meines Lebens* (Berlin, 1801). Vol. III ends with 'An examination of a work entitled *Secret memoirs of the court of Russia*' (pp. 132-216), Kotzebue's rebuttal of Masson's work (see D45).

E7) Hunter, William, *A Short view of the political situation of the northern powers: founded on observations made during a tour through Russia, Sweden,* *and Denmark, in the last seven months of the year 1800. With conjectures on the probable issue of the approaching conflict.* London: Stockdale, 1801. 111pp.

> Hunter, member of the Inner Temple and prolific publicist, arrived in St Petersburg on 21 June 1800, shortly after expulsion of British ambassador, and paints a very negative picture of Paul's Russia, before departing in December for Denmark (pp. 23-54).

Fig. 40 Alexander I (c.1814/1815), by François de Gérard.

6. REIGN OF ALEXANDER I (1801-1825)

See also D65

F1) Atkinson, John Augustus and Walker, James, *Picturesque representation of the manners, customs, and amusements of the Russians, in one hundred coloured plates; with an accurate explanation of each plate in English and French.* London: printed by W. Bulmer & Co. for the proprietors, 1803-04. 3 folio vols.

> Walker (see D42) had been accompanied to Russia in 1784 by his wife Mary and stepson John (1775-1829?), who revealed a precocious talent as an artist that blossomed during Paul's reign. Atkinson had been making very lively sketches of Russian scenes and types for over a decade before etching them for publication two years after their return from Russia. Walker provided the informed commentary to each plate.

F2) Robinson, Thomas Philip, Baron Grantham, *The Grand Tour 1801-1803, being letters from Lord Grantham to his mother, from Prussia, Saxony, Russia, Austria, Switzerland, Italy & France.* Penzance: Triton Press, 1979. x+105pp.

> A typical young aristocratic tourist, the 3rd Baron Grantham (1781-1859) departed for Europe soon after graduating from St John's College, Cambridge. He arrived in St Petersburg at the end of August 1801 and proceeded to Moscow for the coronation of Alexander I. He left St Petersburg for Berlin in mid-February 1802. Seventeen chatty letters to his mother were sent from Russia (pp. 16-50).

F3) Wilmot, Martha, and Wilmot, Catherine, *The Russian journals of Martha and Catherine Wilmot; being an account of two Irish ladies of their adventures in Russia as guests of the celebrated Princess Daschkaw, containing vivid descriptions of contemporary court life and society, and lively anecdotes of many interesting historical characters 1803-1808.* Edited, with an introduction and notes, by the Marchioness of Londonderry and H.M. Hyde. London: Macmillan, 1934. xxvi+423pp.

> Martha Wilmot (1775-1873) arrived in Russia in 20 July 1803 to become companion to the famous Princess Ekaterina Dashkova whom her father had met in England. In August 1805 she was joined by her eldest sister Catherine (1773-1824). Catherine returned in the summer of 1807 but Martha only at the end of the following year. Also included are two long letters by Catherine's maid, **Eleanor Cavanagh** (pp. 179-90).

F4) Reuilly, Jean, *Travels in the Crimea, and along the shores of the Black Sea, performed during the year 1803.* London: Richard Phillips, 1807. 84pp.

> Baron de Reuilly (1780-1810) accompanied the new governor of Taurida, the duc de Richelieu, to Odessa. Translation of *Voyage en Crimée et sur les bords de la mer Noire pendant l'année 1803* (Paris, 1806).

F5) Rochechouart, Louis Victor Léon, *Memoirs of the Count de Rochechouart, 1788-1822 in France, southern Russia, in the Napoleonic Wars, and as commandant of Paris.* Authorised translation [from the French] by Francis Jackson. London: John Murray, 1920. xv+329pp.

> The comte de Rochechouart (1788-1858) arrived in Russia in 1804 and became aide-de-camp to the new governor-general of New Russia, the duc de Richelieu, in 1806. He served with the Russian army in Circassia, before returning to St Petersburg (pp. 48-142). He was Alexander I's aide-de-camp in 1812-14, leaving Russia in April 1813 as the allies advanced towards Paris (pp. 143-73).

F6) Carr, John, *A northern summer; or, travels round the Baltic, through Denmark, Sweden, Russia, Prussia, and part of Germany, in the year 1804.* London: printed by T. Gillet for Richard Phillips, 1805. xii+480pp.

> Sir John (1772-1832), inveterate traveller and Byron's "Green Erin's knight and Europe's wandering star", undertook a conventional northern tour that brought him to St Petersburg in May-November 1804. Much given to anecdotes, he paints a very favourable picture of the emperor and of the delights of his capital and its environs (pp. 196-420).

F7) Seume, Johann Gottfried, *A tour through part of Germany, Poland, Russia, Sweden, Denmark, &c., during the summer of 1805.* Translated from the German. London: Richard Phillips, 1807. 104pp.

Seume (1763-1810), a German author, who had been an officer in Russian service in the 1790s in Warsaw, revisited Poland as part of a northern tour that took him to Russia in May 1805 and he visited St Petersburg and Moscow before leaving via Vyborg at the end of July (pp. 14-56). The German original, *Mein Sommer, 1805* appeared in 1806.

F8) Reinbeck, Georg, *Travels from St Petersburgh through Moscow, Grodno, Warsaw, Breslaw, etc., to Germany in the year 1805; in a series of letters.* Translated from the German. London: Richard Phillips, 1807. iv+160pp.

Reinbeck (1766-1849), dramatist and poet, who had been a teacher of English and German in St Petersburg since 1792, returned to Germany for reasons of health in 1805 (pp. 5-46). German original: *Flüchtige Ammerkungen auf einer Reise von St. Petersburg über Moskwa, Grodno, Warschau, Breslau nach Deutschland im Jahre 1805* (1806).

F9) MacGill, Thomas, *Travels in Turkey, Italy and Russia, during the years 1803, 1804, 1805, & 1806; with an account of some of the Greek islands.* London: John Murray, and Edinburgh: A. Constable, 1808. 2 vols.

The author, "engaged almost continuously in the pursuits of commerce", visited Taganrog and Odessa between the beginning of June and the end of July 1805 (letters XVI-XX, vol. I, pp. 194-243). Vol. II is devoted wholly to Turkey, but contains as an appendix an interesting 'Letter respecting Odessa', dated August 1804 and written by **John Henry Sievrac**, "traveller for the House of Boesner and Co. of Brody and Odessa" (vol. II, pp. 193-207).

F10) Bentham, Samuel, *The correspondence of Jeremy Bentham.* Vol. VII (January 1802-December 1808). Edited by J.R. Dinwiddy. Oxford: Clarendon Press, 1988. xxxii+599pp.

Bentham (see D35-36), sent on a government mission to arrange for warships to be built in Russian dockyards for the British navy, arrived with his family in St Petersburg in early September 1805 and returned to London in December 1807. Letters from Samuel and members of his family to Jeremy (pp. 338-447 *passim*).

F11) Heber, Reginald, *The life of Reginald Heber, D.D., lord bishop of Calcutta; with selections from his correspondence, unpublished poems and private papers; together with a journal of his tour in Norway, Sweden, Russia, Hungary and*

Germany, and a history of the Cossaks. By his widow [Amelia]. London: John Murray, 1830. 2 vols.

> Heber (1783-1826), Fellow of All Souls, Oxford, accompanied by his old school friend John Thornton, arrived in St Petersburg in October 1805, remaining for nearly three months. After six weeks in Moscow, they set out on 13 March 1806 for Taganrog, and then proceeded through the territories of the Don Cossacks, before visiting the Crimea and the towns of New Russia. They left Odessa for Poland in June 1806 (vol. I, pp. 95-278). The unfinished 'History of the Cossaks' (vol. I, pp. 563-684).

F12) Campenhausen, Leyon Pierce Balthasar, *Travels through several provinces of the Russian Empire; with an historical account of the Zaporog Cossacks, and of Bessarabia, Moldavia, Wallachia, and the Crimea.* London: Richard Phillips, 1808. 134pp.

> Baron Campenhausen (1746-1807), German author, who had been attached to Potemkin's staff in the 1780s and was later vice-governor of Livonia, records his journeys through the southern border regions of the Russian empire (pp. 1-60). German original, *Bemerkungen über Russland, nebst einer kurzgefassten Geschichte der Zaporoger Kosaken, Bessarabiens, der Moldau und der Krimm*, was published in Leipzig in 1807.

F13) Porter, Robert Ker, *Travelling sketches in Russia and Sweden, during the years 1805, 1806, 1807, 1808.* London: Richard Phillips, 1809. 2 vols.

> Invited to paint a series of historical canvases for the new Admiralty in St Petersburg, Sir Robert (1777-1842) arrived at Cronstadt on 12 September 1805. Based on some fifty letters sent to his late friend Captain Henry Caulfield and enhanced by his drawings of people and places, the printed volumes describe his life in St Petersburg and two long trips to Moscow (February-June 1805 and November 1806 to February 1807) before he was obliged to leave the Russian capital in December 1807, following the treaty of Tilsit (vol. I, pp. 15-303;II, pp. 1-81).

F14) Green, George, *An original journal from London to St. Petersburgh, by way of Sweden; and, proceeding from thence, to Moscow, Riga, Mittau, and Berlin; with a description of the post towns, and every thing interesting, in the Russian and Prussian capitals, &c.; to which are added, the names, distances, and price, of every post; and a vocabulary of the most useful terms in English and Russian.* London: T. Boosey and J. Hatchard, 1813. xii+224pp.

According to its editorial (pp. iii-vi), offered as a useful guide-book and based on travels in 1805-07 by Green, a merchant "many years resident in Russia". Cronstadt, St Petersburg and post roads to Novgorod, Tver and Moscow. Russia, pp. 1-159. Vocabulary, pp. 177-224.

F15) Salvo, Carlo, marchese di, *Travels in the year 1806, from Italy to England, through the Tyrol, Styria, Bohemia, Gallicia, Poland and Livonia: containing the particulars of the liberation of Mrs. Spencer Smith, from the hands of the French police, and of her subsequent flight, effected and written by the Marquis de Salvo.* [Translated from Italian by W. Fraser.] London: Richard Phillips, 1807. lx+236pp.

The young di Salvo (1787-1860) engineered the escape of Mrs Frances Anne Smith, wife of a British diplomat and best known for her brief affair with Byron in 1809, on a long journey that eventually took them through Russian Poland and to the port of Riga in Livonia, where they took boat for England at the end of August 1806 (pp. 207-36). Of marginal interest, apart from the remark that "the Livonians do not like to be mistaken for Russians, notwithstanding their attachment to the government".

F16) D'Wolf, John, *A voyage to the North Pacific and a journey through Siberia more than half a century ago.* Cambridge, Mass.: Welch, Bigelow, and Co., 1861. 147pp.

D'Wolf, sometimes De Wolf (1779-1842), a sea captain from Bristol, Rhode Island, considered himself, wrongly, as "probably the first American who passed through Siberia" and recounted "principally from memory" a trading voyage that began in America on 13 August 1804 and took him eventually to Petropavlovsk in Kamchatka on 22 September 1806. On 26 May 1807 he sailed for Okhotsk and on 3 July began the long journey overland through Siberia, arriving in Moscow on 8 October and St Petersburg on 21 October, just as war was declared between England and Russia (pp. 73-142).

F17) Royston, Philip Yorke, *The remains of the late Viscount Royston. With a memoir of his life by the Rev. Henry Pepys B.D., prebendary of Wells, and late Fellow of St John's College, Cambridge.* London: John Murray, 1838. 332pp.

Viscount Royston (1784-1808), heir to 3rd Earl of Hardwicke, made an extensive tour through Russia to the Caucasus and the Crimea, described in letters to his father and friends in 1806-07 (pp. 42-181). Died in shipwreck on return journey on 7 April 1808.

F18) Wilson, Robert Thomas, *Life of General Sir Robert Wilson, from autobiographical memoirs, journals, narratives, correspondence, &c.* Edited by his nephew and son-in-law, the Rev. Herbert Randolph. London: John Murray, 1862. 2 vols.

> The last of the three works edited by the Rev. Randolph about Sir Robert (1777-1849), but left unfinished. It, however, covers events up to the end of 1807 and thus includes Wilson's first visits to Russia in the second half of that year. Wilson, already a seasoned and much decorated officer and author of several military works, was a member of a secret mission to the Prussian court, headed by Lord Hutchinson, in November 1806 and met many prominent Russian officers, including Mikhail Vorontsov and Hetman Platov. He went on to St Petersburg, where he arrived in August 1807 but was soon obliged to depart for the injudicious circulation of a lampoon against the Russo-French alliance.

F19) Wilson, Robert Thomas, *Brief remarks on the character and composition of the Russian army; and a sketch of the campaigns in Poland in the years 1806 and 1807.* London: Printed by C. Roworth, and sold by T. Egerton, 1810. xxix+276pp.

> The fruit of Wilson's first experience of service with the Russian army in the months before the treaty of Tilsit. A Russian translation appeared in 1812.

F20) [Kelsall, Charles], *Horae viaticae.* By Mela Britannicus [pseud.] Clifton and Bristol: for the author, 1830. xii+412pp.

> Kelsall (1782-1857), a young Cambridge graduate, visited St Petersburg, Moscow and the Crimea in 1806-07. His *Journal of a tour from St Petersburgh to Vienna in the year 1807* appears on pp. 1-17. The more interesting account of his journey to the Crimea was published only in French in his *Esquisses de mes travaux, de mes voyages, et de mes opinions* (1830).

F21) Campbell, Archibald, *Voyage round the world, from 1806 to 1812, in which Japan, Kamschatka, the Aleutian Islands, and the Sandwich Islands were visited; including a narrative of the author's shipwreck on the Island of Sannack, and his subsequent wreck in the ship's long-boat;.with an account of the present state of the Sandwich Islands and a vocabulary of their language.* Edited by James Smith. Edinburgh: Archibald Constable & Co., 1816. 288pp.

> According to the editor, the work was based partly on documents but mainly on the oral narrative of Campbell (b. 1787), who returned from his

voyage with both feet amputated after frost-bite and eked out an existence as a street musician in Edinburgh. Sailed on the *Eclipse*, a ship belonging to the Russian American company, that took him to Kamchatka (between 6 July and 8 August 1807) before continuing to Aleutian Islands (pp. 33-41).

F22) Klaproth, Julius Heinrich von, *Travels in the Caucasus and Georgia, performed in the years 1807 and 1808, by command of the Russian government, by Julius von Klaproth.* Translated from the German by F. Shoberl. Henry Colburn, 1814. xv+421pp.

> Klaproth (1783-1835) was invited to St Petersburg in 1804 as an associate of the Academy of Sciences and took part in the Golovkin embassy to China. In 1807 he was a member of a new expedition to the Caucasus and studied Ossetian and other languages. He returned to St Petersburg the following year and in 1811 he left Russia for good.

F23) Caulaincourt, Armand-Augustin-Louis de, *Memoirs of general de Caulaincourt, duke of Vicenza.* Edited by Jean Hanoteau. Translated by Hamish Miles. London: Cassell & Co. 1935-38. 3 vols.

> Caulaincourt, duc de Vicence (1773-1827), Napoleon's Master of the Horse, arrived in St Petersburg on 17 December 1807 as ambassador extraordinary. He remained until May 1811 (vol. I, pp. 8-80). In 1812 he was in Russia again but this time with the Grande armée and served throughout the campaign, accompanying the fleeing Napoleon in his carriage to Paris (vol. I, pp. 123-417). French original: *Mémoires du général de Caulaincourt* (1933).

F24) Adams, John Quincy, *Memoirs of John Quincy Adams, comprising portions of his diary from 1795 to 1848.* Edited by Charles Francis Adams. Philadelphia: Lippincott, 1874. 2 vols.

> On 5 August 1809 Adams (1767-1848), who had visited St Petersburg for the first time in the winter of 1781-82, sailed from Boston as American minister plenipotentiary and arrived at Cronstadt on 22 October. He was to remain in St Petersburg until 20 May 1814 (vol. II, pp. 45-629).

F25) Everett, Alexander Hill, *Critical and miscellaneous essays to which are added a few poems.* Boston: James Munroe, 1845. 2 vols.

> The young Harvard graduate Everett (1792-1847) accompanied Adams to Russia in 1809 as (unpaid) secretary of legation. His stay and experiences in Russia mentioned only *passim*.

F26) Coggeshall, George, 'Second voyage in the schooner Eliza, from New York to Sweden and Russia, and back to New York in the years 1810 and 1811', in his *Second series of voyages to various parts of the world, made between the years 1802 and 1841, selected from his ms. journal of eighty voyages.* New York: D. Appleton & Co., 1852. 335pp.

> American sea captain left New York on 30 August 1810 with a valuable cargo of sugar, coffee, and other commodities. After visiting various ports in the Baltic he made the harbour of Riga on 20 November but because of the ice and Napoleon's blockade was obliged to remain there until 25 May 1811, when he began the return voyage with a new cargo of canvas and other cloths. Some interesting remarks on Riga and its social life (pp. 94-103).

F27) [Freygang, Wilhelm and Frederika von], *Letters from the Caucasus and Georgia; to which are added, the account of a journey into Persia in 1812, and an abridged history of Persia since the time of Nadir Shah.* Translated from the French. London: John Murray, 1823. xiv+414pp.

> In 1811 Freygang (1783-1835), born in St Petersburg to a German physician, together with his wife (née Kudriavskaia) and children, journeyed to Tiflis to serve under the governor-general, the marchese di Paulucci. His wife's letters describe the perilous outward journey from 1 September to 30 November 1811, their stay in Tiflis, and their return journey in 1812 which ends with their sight of a burnt Moscow on 16 January 1813 (pp. 3-258). Then follows her husband's description of his diplomatic mission from Tiflis to Persia between 28 April and the end of June 1812 (pp. 259-367).

F28) Choiseul-Gouffier, Sophie, de, *Historical memoirs of the Emperor Alexander I and the court of Russia.* Translated from the original French by Mary Berenice Patterson. Chicago: A.C. McClurg, 1900. 321pp.

> Born Sophie de Tisenhaus, the daughter of a Polish nobleman, she was the wife of the French aristocrat M. de Choiseul-Gouffier. She first met Alexander I on 27 April 1812 and her memoirs essentially chart their friendship until his death in 1825, a year after the author left Russia. The translation is from the first (longer) edition of 1862.

F29) Staël-Holstein, Germaine, de, *Ten years' exile; or, memoirs of that interesting period of the life of the Baroness de Staël-Holstein, written by herself.* Published by her son [Auguste de Staël-Holstein]. London: Treuttel and

Würtz, Treuttel jun. and Richter, 1821. xvi+434pp. [Facsimile edition, with introduction by Margaret Crosland, Fontwell, Sussex: Centaur Press, 1968.]

> The famous author of *Delphine, ou l'Italie* and *De l'Allemagne* and exiled from France by Napoleon, baronness de Staël-Holstein, née Necker (1766-1817), better known as Mme de Staël, arrived in Russia on 14 July 1812. She travelled from Poland to Kiev and on to Moscow, thence ultimately to St Petersburg. After only two months and in the wake of Napoleon's invasion, she left Russia for Finland (pp. 301-425).

F30) Dobell, Peter, *Travels in Kamtchatka and Siberia; with a narrative of a residence in China.* London: Henry Colburn and Richard Bentley, 1830. 2 vols.

> Dobell (1772-1852), who had previously spent many years in China, arrived in Kamchatka on 21 August 1812. He describes his travels in 1812-13 through Kamchatka and mainland Siberia (with much on towns such as Okhotsk, Iakutsk, Irkutsk, and Tomsk), ending his narrative when he reaches the Urals and "Russia" en route for St Petersburg, but he was to spend many years living in the region and adds observations of further residences and journeys up to the beginning of 1828 (vol. I, pp. 1-351; II, pp. 1-124). Two years after the appearance of his own travels, Dobell published, under the pseudonym "a friend to truth", his polemical pamphlet *Russia as it is, and not as it has been represented; together with observations and reflections on the pernicious and deceitful policy of the new school.*

F31) Bonaparte, Napoleon, *The Corsican: a diary of Napoleon's life in his own words.* With preface by R.M. Johnston. London: Grant Richards, 1911. vi+526pp.

> Relatively few words by the French Emperor (1769-1821) about the disastrous Russian campaign from July to December 1812, re-arranged from various sources in diary form (pp. 347-66).

F32) Ségur, Philippe-Paul, de, *History of the expedition to Russia, undertaken by the Emperor Napoleon in the year 1812.* By General, Count Philip de Ségur. London: H.L. Hunt and C.C. Clarke, 1825. 2 vols. [2nd edition, carefully revised and corrected, Treuttel and Wurtz, Treuttel jun., and Richter, 1825.]

> Comte de Ségur (1780-1873), the son of the former ambassador to Catherine's court, was a general attached to Napoleon's staff during the Russian campaign. The French original, *Napoléon et la grande armée pendant l'année 1812*, appeared in 1825, as did a third edition with the title *La campagne de Russie.*

F33) Labaume, Eugène. *A circumstantial narrative of the campaign in Russia, embellished with plans of the battles of the Moskwa and Malo-Jaroslavitz; containing a faithful description of the affecting and interesting scenes, of which the author was an eye-witness.* Translated from the French [by E. Boyce]. London: Samuel Leigh, 1814. xii+408pp. [2nd edition, 'considerably improved', 1815. viii+412pp.]

> Labaume (1783-1849), an engineer officer serving under Prince Eugene, provided an eye-witness account of Napoleon's Russian campaign.

F34) Marbot, Jean-Baptiste-Antoine-Marcelin, de, *The memoirs of Baron de Marbot late lieutenant-general in the French army.* Translated from the French by Arthur John Butler. London: Longmans, Green, & Co., 1892. 2 vols.

> Baron de Marbot (1782-1854), highly critical of the works of Labaume and Ségur, served throughout the Russian campaign as a major commanding the 23rd chasseurs (vol. II, pp. 498-600). *Mémoires* appeared in 3 vols. in Paris in 1891.

F35) [Vaudoncourt, Frédéric-François-Guillaume, de], *Critical situation of Bonaparte in his retreat out of Russia; or, a faithful narrative of the repassing of the Beresina by the French army in 1812.* By an eye witness. Translated from the French, with notes written by an officer who was with the Russian army at the same period. London: printed by Haines and Turner for J. Hatchard, 1815. vi+65pp.

> Translation of *Relation impartiale du passage de la Bérézina, par l'armée française en 1812* (1814), published anonymously by baron de Vaudoncourt (1772-1845), who was captured by the Russians at Vilna and was taken to Grand Duke Constantine's palace at Strelna to recover from typhus.

F36) Roeder, Franz, *The ordeal of Captain Roeder. From the diary of an officer in the first battalion of Hessian life-guards during the Moscow campaign of 1812-13.* Translated and edited by Helen Roeder from the original manuscript. London: Methuen, 1960. 248pp.

> Unusual perspective of the Russian campaign from a Prussian officer, Captain Roeder (1774-1840) of the tenth corps, including his imprisonment in Vilna (pp. 96-218)

F37) Fezensac, Raimond-Emery-Philipp-Josephe de Montesquiou, de, *A journal of the Russian campaign of 1812*. Translated from the French of lieut.-general de Fezensac, with an introductory note of some passages connected with the campaign by W. Knollys. London: Parker, Furnivall, and Parker, 1852. cxxi+192pp.

> Duc de Fezensac (1784-1867), of a distinguished noble family and career officer, served with the fourth regiment of infantry of the third corps under Marshal Ney throughout the Russian campaign. The French original appeared in 1849.

F38) Coignet, Jean-Roch, *The narrative of Captain Coignet soldier of the Empire 1776-1850*. Edited from the original manuscript by Lorédan Larchey and translated from the French by Mrs M. Carey. London: Chatto & Windus, 1897. 316pp.

> Coignet (1776-1858?), a veteran of some thirteen years' service, was promoted to lieutenant at the beginning of the Russian campaign (pp. 208-44).

F39) Bourgogne, Adrien-Jean-Baptiste-François, *Memoirs of Sergeant Bourgogne (1812-1813)*. Authorized translation from the French original. Edited by Paul Cottin and Maurice Hénault. London: William Heinemann, 1899. xvi+356pp.

> Bourgogne (1785-1867) was a sergeant of the *vélites* (skirmishers) at the beginning of the Russian campaign. His memoirs are linked with those of Coignet in conveying directly the horrors of the retreat from Moscow.

F40) Walter, Jakob, *A German conscript with Napoleon. Jakob Walter's recollections of the campaigns of 1806-1807, 1809, and 1812-1813. According to a manuscript found at Lecompton, Kansas*. Edited and translated by Otto Springer, with historical collaboration by Frank E. Melvin. Lawrence: University of Kansas, Department of Journalism Press, 1938. v+231pp. [See also *The diary of a Napoleonic foot soldier*. Edited and with an introduction by Marc Raeff, Moreton-in-Marsh: Windrush Press, 1991, xxx+170pp.]

> Often harrowing description of the march to Moscow and the retreat, June-December 1812 by Walter (1788-1864), a Westphalian stonemason (pp. 17-109). German and English texts on opposite pages. German original: *Denkwürdige Geschichtsschreibung über die erlebte Militärdienstzeit des Verfassers dieses Schreibens*.

F41) [Guillemard, Robert], *Adventures of a French serjeant during his campaigns in Italy, Spain, Germany, Russia, &c., from 1805 to 1823, written by himself.* [Translated from the French by his editors, Charles-Ozé Barbaroux and Joseph-Alexandre Lardier.] London: Henry Colburn, 1826. xvi+345pp.

> Allegedly the man who shot Nelson at Trafalgar, Guillemard (1792-1867) served in Russia and was made an officer by Napoleon after Borodino, but was soon taken prisoner and marched off to Nizhnii Tagil in Siberia with other French prisoners until 1814 (pp. 135-84).

F42) François, Charles, *From Valmy to Waterloo: extracts from the diary of Capt. Charles François, a soldier of the Revolution and the Empire.* Translated and edited by Robert B. Douglas. With a preface by Jules Claretie. London: Everett & Co., 1906. 332pp.

> François was seriously wounded in the leg in the assault on a redoubt near Moscow. Short on detail, except for the gore (pp. 231-69).

F43) Vossler, Heinrich August, *With Napoleon in Russia 1812: the diary of Lt. H.A. Vossler a soldier of the Grand Army 1812-1813.* Translated [from the German manuscript] by Walter Wallich. London: Folio Society, 1969. 176pp.

> Vossler (1791-1848) was an officer with the Württemberg contingent from south Germany. In Russia, pp. 44-93.

F44) Uxkull, Boris von, *Arms and the woman: the diaries of Baron Boris Uxkull 1812-1819.* Edited by Detlev von Uexküll. Translated by Joel Carmichael. London: Secker & Warburg, 1966. 319pp.

> Baron Uxkull (1793-1870), an Estonian nobleman attached to the Russian headquarters staff, was eighteen when the war against Napoleon began. He was involved in all the action of the Russian campaign (pp. 15-112).

F45) Wilson, Robert Thomas, *Narrative of events during the invasion of Russia by Napoleon Bonaparte, and the retreat of the French army, 1812.* Edited by the Rev. Herbert Randolph. London: John Murray, 1860. xxv+412pp.

> In 1812, after a gap of some four years, General Wilson was again in Russia and fighting with the Russian army.

F46) Wilson, Robert Thomas, *Private diary of travels, personal services, and public events, during mission and employment with the European armies in the* *campaigns of 1812, 1813, 1814: from the invasion of France to the capture of Paris*. Edited by his nephew and son-in-law, the Rev. Herbert Randolph. London: John Murray, 1861. 2 vols. [A skilfully edited abridgment by Antony Brett-James appeared in 1964 under the title *General Wilson's journal 1812-1814*, London: William Kimber, 240pp.]

> When war was declared between France and Russia in June 1812, Wilson was in Constantinople with the British ambassador Robert Liston, negotiating a peace between Turkey and Russia. Travelling via Bucharest, Kiev and Smolensk, he arrived on 27 August in St Petersburg, where he was warmly received by the tsar and members of the imperial family and court. On 15 September he left to join Kutuzov and the Russian army, which he was to accompany throughout the campaign as they advanced towards Paris (Russia, vol. I, pp. 142-246).

F47) Cathcart, George, *Commentaries on the war in Russia and Germany in 1812 and 1813*. London: John Murray, 1850. xvi+383pp.

> Colonel Carthcart (1794-1854), who was killed at Inkerman during the Crimean War, was aide-de-camp and private secretary to his father, Lord Cathcart, when the latter was both British ambassador to Russia and military commissioner with the Russian army from 1812 (pp. 33-109). He was present at all the major battles in 1813.

F48) Werry, Francis Peter, *Personal memoirs and letters of Francis Peter Werry, attaché to the British embassies at St. Petersburgh and Vienna in 1812-1815*. Edited by his daughter [Eliza F. Werry]. London: Charles J. Skeet, 1861. 298pp.

> Werry (1788-1859) accompanied Lord Cathcart to St Petersburg in October 1812 (pp. 125-84).

F49) Paterson, John, *The book for every land: reminiscences of labour and adventure in the work of Bible circulation in the north of Europe and in Russia*. Edited, with a prefatory memoir, by William Lindsay Alexander. London: John Snow, 1858. xxxv+412pp.

> Rev. Paterson (1784-1858) arrived in Russia for the first time in August 1812 after some years in Scandinavia and Finland to continue his missionary work for the British and Foreign Bible Society. He was to remain until May 1827, a period of fifteen years during which he travelled extensively throughout Russia on behalf of the Russian Bible Society, including the Caucasus, as well as visiting Scandinavia. He was witness to many of the

momentous events of the time – his first visit to Moscow was on the eve of the battle of Borodino and subsequent devastation of the city, he was in St Petersburg at the time of the great flood of 1824 and of the Decembrist uprising (pp. 165-412).

F50) Gallatin, James, *A great peace maker: the diary of James Gallatin secretary to Albert Gallatin U.S. envoy to France and Holland 1813-1827 and negotiator of the treaty of Ghent.* Edited by Count Gallatin with an introduction by Viscount Boyce. London: William Heinemann, 1914. xv+316pp.

> The envoy's eldest son, James (1796?-1876), accompanied his father on a mission to St Petersburg following the Russian offer to mediate a peace treaty between Britain and America. Brief extracts from his diary, 21 July 1813-26 January 1814 (pp. 4-13).

F51) Bayard, James Asheton, *Letters of James Asheton Bayard, 1802-1814.* Edited by Henry C. Conrad. Wilmington: Historical Society of Delaware, 1901. 44pp.

> Bayard (1767-1815) was a member of the three-man commission (the others were Adams and Albert Gallatin) appointed to negotiate peace with Britain. He arrived in St Petersburg with Gallatin on 21 July 1813. Two letters he sent from the Russian capital (pp. 31-34).

F52) Lyttelton, Sarah Spencer, *Correspondence of Sarah Spencer Lady Lyttelton 1787-1870.* Edited by her great-granddaughter the hon. Mrs Hugh Wyndham. London: John Murray, 1912. xxiii+444pp.

> Lady Sarah (1787-1870) and her husband William Lyttelton, later 3rd Baron Lyttelton, followed their marriage in March 1813 with extensive travels which took them to Sweden and to St Petersburg, where they arrived on 5 November 1813. Left Russia on 12 June 1814. Letters and extracts from Sarah's diary (pp. 166-90).

F53) [Kolbe, Eduard], *Recollections of Russia during thirty-three years' residence.* By a German nobleman. Revised and translated, with the author's sanction, by Lascelles Wraxall. Edinburgh: Thomas Constable and Co., and London: Hamilton, Adams, and Co., 1855. 328pp.

> The title would indicate that Kolbe's acquaintance with Russia dates back to the last years of Alexander I's reign, but the German original was published in 1846 and thus points to c.1813, although there are few dates in Kolbe's very negative portrayal of Russia from the day of his arrival at

the Russian frontier in Courland. He witnessed the great flood of 1824, but his references are in the main to Nicholas's reign and to the early 1840s.

F54) James, John Thomas, *Journal of a tour in Germany, Sweden, Russia, Poland, during the years 1813 and 1814*. London: John Murray, 1816. viii+527pp.

> James (1786-1828) and an Oxford friend William Macmichael visited Russia during their northern tour, arriving in St Petersburg from Finland in March 1814. After a stay of some two months in the capital, they left on 12 June for Moscow, describing the devastation they found there and visiting the battlefield at Borodino. They then journeyed to Smolensk and Kiev, before entering Poland on 22 July (pp. 222-481).

F55) James, John Thomas, *Views in Russia Sweden Poland and Germany, drawn by the Rev. J. T. James.* London: John Murray, 1826-27. 5 parts.

> Shortly before he left England to become bishop of Calcutta, James, who had studied painting in Italy subsequent to his Russian trip of 1814, decided to produce his own lithographs from twenty-one of his original sketches, fifteen of which are of Russian scenes. They have facing explanatory texts from the extended 1819 edition of James's *Journal*. An album containing 162 drawings by James, many of them with Russian subjects and never reproduced, is held in the Department of Drawings of the State Russian Museum in St Petersburg.

F56) Johnston, Robert, *Travels through part of the Russian empire and the country of Poland, along the southern shores of the Baltic*. London: J.J. Stockdale, 1815. vii, xiv+460pp.

> Johnston (1783-1839), an Oxford graduate, travelled through Germany to reach St Petersburg in July 1814. Detailed description of the towns and villages on the road from the capital to Moscow. In September he left Moscow for Poland via Smolensk and Borodino (pp. 79-374).

F57) Walpole, Horatio, *Records of stirring times based upon unpublished documents from 1726-1822*. By the authoress of 'Old days in diplomacy' [C.A.A. Disbrowe]. Edited by M. Montgomery-Campbell. London: William Heinemann, 1908. xii+323pp.

> Includes six letters written to Edward Disbrowe in 1814-15 from St Petersburg by Lord Walpole, 3rd Earl of Orford (1783-1858) who had arrived in St Petersburg with Lord Cathcart in October 1812 and was appointed British minister to Russia, *ad interim*, on 4 August 1814 (pp. 178-81, 192-97).

F58) [Prior, James], *A voyage to St Petersburg in 1814; with remarks on the imperial Russian navy.* By a surgeon in the British navy. London: Richard Phillips, 1820. 74pp.

> Prior (1790?-1869) was a surgeon and already author of accounts of earlier voyages with the British navy, when he was assigned to the Russian squadron under Admiral George Tate returning to Cronstadt from Sheerness in June 1814. He writes very interestingly about Cronstadt and St Petersburg and provides an extensive portrait of Alexander I (pp. 30-74). Prior rose to be deputy-inspector of hospitals and was knighted in 1858. He was the author of biographies of Burke and Goldsmith and other works.

F59) Holderness, Mary, *New Russia: journey from Riga to the Crimea, by way of Kiev; with some account of the colonisation, and the manners and customs of the colonists, of new Russia; to which are added, notes relating to the Crim Tatars.* London: Sherwood, Jones & Co., 1823. viii+316pp. [2nd edition in 1827 was entitled *A journey from Riga.*]

> Holderness recounts her family's arrival at Riga in November 1815 and travel through Ukraine to Odessa and to the Crimea, also adding observations made on the return journey in 1820. Her notes on 'the Crim Tartars', revised and enlarged (pp. 208-316), were reprinted from her preceding book (see F60).

F60) Holderness, Mary, *Notes relating to the manners and customs of the Crim Tatars; written during a four years' residence among that people.* London: John Warren, 1821. vi+168pp.

> Holderness with her husband and three children lived in the village of Karagos in the Crimea from early 1816 until March 1820 (although it is nowhere specified what they did). Her sketches were well received and incorporated in *New Russia*.

F61) Lyall, Robert, *The character of the Russians, and a detailed history of Moscow; illustrated with numerous engravings; with a dissertation on the Russian language; and an appendix, containing tables, political, statistical, and historical; an account of the Imperial Agricultural Society of Moscow; a catalogue of plants found in and near Moscow; an essay on the origin and progress of architecture in Russia, &c. &c.* London: T. Cadell, and Edinburgh: W. Blackwood, 1823. cliv+639pp.

> Dr Lyall (1789-1831) left Scotland for St Petersburg in 1815 and became house physician for four years on the estate of Countess Orlova-Chesmenskaia.

He then married and moved, again as house physician, to an estate near Moscow. His book, which was to incur the wrath of the Russian authorities for its critique of the nobility and serfdom, was published soon after his final return from Russia in August 1823.

F62) Henderson, Ebenezer, and Paterson, John, *Extracts of letters from the Rev. John Paterson, and the Rev. Ebenezer Henderson, during their respective tours through the East Sea provinces of Russia, Sweden, Denmark, Jutland, Holstein, Swedish Pomerania, &c. to promote the object of the British and Foreign Bible Society.* London: Tilling and Hughes for the Society; Edinburgh: Oliphant, Waugh and Innes, 1817. 58pp.

> The Revs Henderson (1784-1858) and Paterson (see F49) were agents of the British and Foreign Bible Society. Extracts from letters by Paterson from 27 April 1816 to 26 January 1817 from St Petersburg and the Baltic Provinces (pp. 1-28) and by Henderson, arriving in St Petersburg at the end of December 1816 (pp. 52-58).

F63) Henderson, Ebenezer, *Biblical researches and travels in Russia; including a tour in the Crimea; and the passage of the Caucasus: with observations on the state of the Rabbinical and Karaite Jews, and the Mohammedan and pagan tribes, inhabiting the southern provinces of the Russian Empire.* London: James Nisbet, 1826. xii+538pp.

> Henderson's first visit to St Petersburg in 1816-17 was followed by an extensive stay from 1819 to 1825, during which time he also travelled to Kharkov, Odessa, Taganrog, Astrakhan and Tiflis.

F64) Henderson, Ebenezer, *Memoir of the Rev. Ebenezer Henderson, D.D., Ph.D., including his labours in Denmark, Iceland, Russia, etc. etc.* By Thulia Susannah Henderson [his daughter]. London: Knight & Son; Hamilton, Adams & Co., 1859. viii+476pp.

> Compiled by Henderson's daughter, Thulia Susannah Henderson (afterwards Engall), this extensive memoir includes material on Russia, previously found in his earlier publications (see F62-63) (pp. 207-22, 243-97).

F65) Pinkerton, Robert, *Extracts of letters from the Rev. Robert Pinkerton, on his late tour in Russia, Poland, and Germany to promote the object of the British and Foreign Bible Society; together with a letter from Prince Alexander Galitzin to Lord Teignmouth ('Regarding the cause of the Bible Society in*

Russia'). London: printed by Tilling and Hughes for British and Foreign Bible Society, 1817. 67pp.

> In 1812 the Rev. Pinkerton (d. 1855), who had originally been sent by the Edinburgh Missionary Society to its mission at Karass in the North Caucasus in 1805, joined the Revs John Paterson and Ebenezer Henderson in St Petersburg to promote the work of the British and Foreign Bible Society. On 22 March 1816 he undertook a tour of some seven thousand miles that took him to Tver, Moscow, Tula, Voronezh, Novocherkask, Taganrog and through the Crimea and on to Odessa by the end of July (pp. 1-27), before he crossed into Poland and on to Vienna and Berlin. He was back in Russia by the end of October and reached St Petersburg on 2 December 1816 (pp. 53-62).

F66) Pinkerton, Robert, *Russia; or, miscellaneous observations on the past and present state of that country and its inhabitants; compiled from notes made on the spot, during travels, at different times, in the service of the Bible Society, and a residence of many years in that country.* London: Seeley & Sons, 1833. viii+486pp.

> Pinkerton, who had left Russia for the last time in 1825, produced what he called a work of "miscellaneous character", mixing excerpts from travel diaries and journals of various years, notably his journey south to Odessa in 1819, with information derived from Russian sources to illustrate Russia's ecclesiastical and social history as well as its literature, folklore and proverbs.

F67) Venning, John, *Memorials of John Venning, esq. (formerly of St. Petersburgh, and late of Norwich), with numerous notices from his manuscripts relative to the imperial family of Russia.* By Thulia Susannah Henderson. London: Knight & Son, and Hamilton, Adams & Co., 1862. 320pp.

> Venning (1776-1858), prison reformer, curator of lunatic asylum in St Petersburg and well-known to members of the imperial family, returned to England in 1830 after nearly forty years in Russia (pp. 9-304). Mrs Henderson follows her memoir of her father (F64) with a similarly substantial account of Venning who arrived in St Petersburg in 1793 and established himself as a prominent merchant but after some years in London returned to devote himself to philanthropic causes in Russia (pp. 23-34).

F68) Venning, Walter, *Memoir of the life and character of Walter Venning, esq. A member of the committee of the London society for the improvement of prison discipline, &c. who died at St. Petersburgh, January 10th, 1821, from a fever contracted in visiting one of the gaols of that city.* By Richard Knill. With a preface by Robert Winter, D.D. London: printed by J. Haddon, sold by J. and A. Arch, 1822. 102pp.

> Contains extracts from letters and memoranda written by Venning (1781-1821) from 1817, when he returned to Russia (he had been there previously between 1799 and 1807) and helped create the Russian society for prisons. (For the Rev. Richard Knill in St Petersburg, see F87.)

F69) Macmichael, William, *Journey from Moscow to Constantinople, in the years 1817, 1818.* London: John Murray, 1819. vii+272pp.

> Dr Macmichael F.R.S. (1784-1839), who had first visited in Russia in 1814 with the Rev. J.T. James (see F53), returned at the very end of 1817 with a Mr Legh, "one of the most enterprising travellers of the present age", to see how Moscow was recovering from the disastrous fire of 1812. After a stay of nearly two weeks (4-16 December), they travelled south to Kiev and then into Moldavia and Bulgaria on their way to Constantinople. In his preface Macmichael suggested that the rapidity of the trip excused "the very imperfect observations contained in its recital" (pp. 1-71).

F70) Wheeler, Daniel, *Memoirs of the life and gospel labors of the late Daniel Wheeler, a minister of the Society of Friends.* [Edited by his son Daniel Wheeler]. London: Harvey and Darton; Charles Gilpin, 1842. xxviii+793pp.

> The eminent Quaker Wheeler (1771-1840) was invited to supervise agricultural improvements at Okhta near St Petersburg. He paid a preliminary visit in June 1817 (pp. 58-64) and returned to England. He set out again with family and assistants (20 people in all) in June 1818 and apart from visit to England in late 1830-June 1831, remained until he resigned in July 1832 (pp. 69-162, 179-95). He returned for a last time in March 1833.

F71) Benson, Jane, *From the Lune to the Neva sixty years ago; with Ackworth and 'Quaker' life by the way.* By J.B. London: Saml Harris & Co., 1879. 115pp.

> Mrs Benson, née Edmondson (1823-1906) tells the story of her father George Edmondson (1798-1863), who as a young man followed Wheeler to Russia in 1818 and remained until illness forced him to return in 1825 with his wife and infant daughter (pp. 72-115). Mrs Benson based her account on family documents but changed the names of people involved.

F72) Benson, Jane, *Quaker pioneers in Russia.* London: Headley Bros., 1902. 120pp.

> Mrs Benson refers briefly to her earlier book (F71) but re-tells the story of her parents in more detail and quoting from their letters in the general context of the experiences of Wheeler and Thomas Shillitoe (pp. 32-98).

F73) Gordon, Peter, *Fragment of the journal of a tour through Persia, in 1820.* London: K.J. Ford, 1833. 126pp.

> Curious compilation of various, mainly Russian journeys by land and sea by Captain Gordon, who lamented the loss of his other travel journals. As captain of the schooner *Brothers* he sailed from Calcutta to Okhotsk, where he arrived on 27 September 1817 and departed on 19 October (pp. 2-11). Then follows 'Extracts from the journal of a traveller through Siberia, on his route from Ochotsk to India', when he left Okhotsk in September 1819, sailed across Baikal and reached the edge of Siberia in January 1820 (pp. 11-42). The tour through Persia of the title begins in fact in Astrakhan in March 1820 and he travelled through the Caucasus to Tiflis and arrived in Persian territory only in mid-April (pp. 43-60).

F74) Wilson, Robert Thomas, *A sketch of the military and political power of Russia, in the year 1817.* London: James Ridgway, 1817. xv+208pp.

> Wilson's final work on Russia and the Russian army, from which he had been transferred on 7 September 1813 to become British commissioner with the Austrian army (see F18, F19, F46). Wilson never visited Russia again, but remained keenly interested in its past, present and future role in the European balance of power (pp. 1-158).

F75) Johnson, John, *A journey from India to England, through Persia, Georgia, Russia, Poland, and Prussia, in the year 1817.* London: Longman, Hurst, Rees, Orme, and Brown, 1818. x+376pp.

> Johnson, a lieutenant-colonel returning to England in 1817 after service in India, visited the Caucasus and Ukraine, including Kiev, and meeting the renowned General Ermolov, before leaving for Poland (pp. 236-349).

F76) Porter, Robert Ker, *Travels in Georgia, Persia, Armenia, ancient Babylonia, &c., &c., during the years 1817, 1818, 1819, and 1820.* London: Longman, Hurst, Rees, Orme, and Brown, 1821-82. 2 vols.

> Porter (see F13), called back to Russia by Alexander I in 1811 and soon afterwards marrying his Russian princess, embarked on extensive travels in August 1817 that took him south from St Petersburg into Georgia (including a memorable meeting with Hetman Platov in Novocherkask) and through the Caucasus to Persia and beyond (vol. I, pp. 1-170). He was to return to St Petersburg on 14 March 1820 after three years of travel.

F77) Taitbout de Marigny, Edouard, *Three voyages in the Black Sea to the coast of Circassia: including descriptions of the ports, and the importance of their trade; with sketches of the manners, customs, religion, &c., &c., of the Circassians.* Translated from the French. London: John Murray, 1837. xvi+303pp.

> Le chevalier Edouard Taitbout was appointed Dutch vice-consul for the ports of the Black Sea on 9 January 1821 and the last two voyages he describes were to Anapa in north Circassia in 1823 and 1824 (pp. 141-261). He had been in the region, however, since at least 1813, seeking commercial ties with Circassia, and he provides the journal of a voyage he made in May-July 1818 from Kerch to various ports (pp. 13-141). British interest in his work was stimulated by the ongoing Russian expansion in the Caucasus. During the Crimean War Taitbout's detailed surveys of the Black Sea, such as *The Black Sea pilot* (1855), were much reprinted and used.

F78) Grellet du Mabillier, Etienne de, *Memoirs of the life and gospel labours of Stephen Grellet.* Edited by Benjamin Seebohm. London: A.W. Bennett, 1860. 2 vols.

> Born into a French noble family, Grellet (1773-1855), assuming the English form of his name on becoming a Quaker in 1795, left on missionary work in northern Europe in the summer of 1818, arriving in the Russian capital in November. From St Petersburg he and William Allen travelled to Moscow and then south to the Crimea. They sailed from Odessa for Constantinople on 8 July 1819 (vol. I, pp. 343-426).

F79) Allen, William, *Life of William Allen, with selections from his correspondence.* London: Charles Gilpin, 1846. 3 vols.

> Allen (1770-1843) accompanied his fellow Quaker Grellet on missionary travels to St Petersburg and thence to the Crimea and Odessa between November 1818 and February 1819 (vol. I, pp. 420-68; II, pp. 1-93).

F80) Ramble, Rayford, *Travelling opinions and sketches, in Russia and Poland.* London: John Macrone, and Smith, Elder & Co., and Dublin: John Cumming, 1836. 226pp.

> Ramble sailed from London to Cronstadt in the early summer of 1819, although his account was written up only in 1835-36. From St Petersburg he went by boat via Lake Ladoga and eventually to Nizhnii Novgorod, returning to Moscow via Iaroslavl, "a town of no interest". Left Moscow at end of September for Poland and Germany (pp. 9-178).

F81) Bowring, John, *Autobiographical recollections of Sir John Bowring.* With a brief memoir by Lewin B. Bowring. London: Henry S. King & Co., 1877. viii+404pp.

> Sir John (1792-1872), later editor of the *Westminister Review*, travelled from Hamburg overland to St Petersburg, where he spent the winter of 1819-20, making the acquaintance of leading literary figures and collecting materials for his renowned *Specimens of the Russian poets* (pp. 117-25).

F82) Cochrane, John Dundas, *Narrative of a pedestrian journey through Russia and Siberian Tartary, from the frontiers of China to the Frozen Sea and Kamstchatka, performed during the years 1820, 1821, 1822, and 1823.* London: John Murray, 1824. xvi+564pp. [Three further editions were followed by a new edition with a necessary change in the title: *A pedestrian journey through Russia and Siberian Tartary, to the frontiers of China, the Frozen Sea, and Kamchatka*, London: Hurst, Chance & Co., and Edinburgh: Constable, 1829. 2 vols. See also the abridged Folio Society edition of 1983, edited and with an introduction by Mervyn Horder, 217pp.]

> Cochrane (1780-1825), a Royal Navy captain, had already earned a reputation as the "pedestrian traveller" before he embarked on his ambitious plan to travel round the world, on foot where possible. He reached St Petersburg on 30 April 1820 and set out on 24 May, walking, but using any form of transport when the opportunity arose. Reaching Okhotsk in June 1821, he proceeded to Kamchatka, where he married a local woman. Abandoning his original itinerary, they eventually arrived back in St Petersburg in May 1823, having met in Moscow the blind Holman (see F89), about to embark on his travels to Siberia (pp. 41-564).

F83) Reichard, Heinrich August Ottokar, *An itinerary of Denmark, Sweden, Norway & Russia, being a complete guide to travellers through those countries; containing a minute description of the post and cross roads, cities, towns, rivers, canals, inns, coins, modes and price of travelling; also a concise account of soil, produce, manufactures, population, naval and military forces and curiosities of each country.* London: printed for Samuel Leigh by G. Schulze, 1820. lxvii+220pp.

> An early and useful guide, said by the translator to be even more useful in English than in the original German, by Reichard (1751-1828). Information on Russia, pp. xlvii-lxiv, 117-220.

F84) Halen, Juan van, *Narrative of Don Juan van Halen's imprisonment in the dungeons of the Inquisition at Madrid, and his escape in 1817 and 1818; to which are added, his journey to Russia, his campaign with the army of the Caucasus, and his return to Spain in 1821.* Edited from the original Spanish manuscript by the author of 'Don Esteban' and 'Sandoval' [Valentin Llanos Guttiérez]. London: Henry Colburn, 1827. 2 vols.

> Spanish soldier-of-fortune, van Halen, Count de Perecamps, joined Russian service in 1819 and was assigned to the army in the Caucasus under General Ermolov. Allegedly expelled from Russia at the end of 1820 on the orders of the emperor, he returned to Spain via Austria and Switzerland. Virtually the whole of vol. II (pp. 30-469) is devoted to Russia and particularly Georgia.

F85) Lumsden, Thomas, *A journey from Merut in India to London, through Arabia, Persia, Armenia, Georgia, Russia, Austria, Switzerland, and France, during the years 1819 and 1820.* London: Black, Kingsbury, Parberry, & Allen; Edinburgh: Oliver & Boyd, and Macredie, Skelly, & Co., 1822. vi+272+12pp.

> A long-serving lieutenant in the Bengal Horse Artillery, Lumsden requested leave in England and travelled there on a year-long journey. He left Merut on 3 October 1819 and travelled via Persia, Armenia, Georgia, reaching Odessa on 2 September 1820. Leaving Russian Poland on 15 September for Austria and France, he reached Dover on 30 October 1820. Georgia and Russia, pp. 151-214.

F86) Glen, William, *Journal of a tour from Astrachan to Karass, north of the mountains of the Caucasus; containing remarks on the general appearance of the country, manners of the inhabitants, &c.; with the substance of many conversations with effendis, mollas, and other Mohammedans, on the questions at issue between them and Christians.* Edinburgh: Printed [by David Jack] for David Brown, John Wardlaw & Co., Edinburgh; William Turbull & Co., Wardlaw and Cunninghame, & M. Ogle, Glasgow; J. Finlay, Newcastle; Ogle, Duncan & Co., & J. Nisbit, London, 1823. 227pp.

> Rev. Glen (1778-1849) was sent in 1818 by the Edinburgh Missionary Society to Astrakhan, where he and his wife were to live for some five years, during which time he acquired his mastery of Persian and other languages. He set out from the Astrakhan mission on 8 October 1820 on his journey to the mission at Karass, near Georgievsk, arriving on 19

October. Describes life in the mission and travels around the region until 9 November, when the account simply finishes.

F87) Knill, Richard, *The life of the Rev. Richard Knill, of St Petersburgh: being selections from his reminiscences, journals, and correspondence, with a review of his character, by the late Rev. John Angell James.* By Charles M. Birrell. London: James Nisbett, 1860. viii+268pp.

> Knill (1787-1857) arrived in St Petersburg in November 1820 to promote the work of the Bible Society and met up with the Revs Paterson and Henderson. He finally left Russia in January 1833 (pp. 89-190). Includes his description of the Petersburg flood of 1824.

F88) Brooke, Arthur de Capell, *A winter in Lapland and Sweden, with various observations relating to Finmark and its inhabitants, made during a residency at Hammerfest, near the North Cape.* London: John Murray, 1827. xvi+612pp.

> In the delayed sequel to his *Travels through Sweden, Norway, and Finmark* (1823), Sir Arthur (1791-1858), a half-pay officer who had left England in May 1820, describes his remarkable travels into Russian Finmark or Lapland in December 1820 (pp. 504-60). He returned to England in February 1821. He also published in 1827 his *Winter sketches in Lapland, or illustrations of a journey from Alten, on the shores of the Polar Sea*, a series of twenty-four folio-size drawings on stone by D. Dighton and J.D. Harding from sketches by Brooke, including four specifically of Russian Lapland scenes.

F89) Holman, James, *Travels through Russia, Siberia, Poland, Austria, Saxony, Prussia, Hanover, etc., etc., undertaken during the years 1822, 1823, and 1824, while suffering from total blindness, and comprising an account of the author being conducted a state prisoner from the eastern parts of Siberia.* London: G.B. Whittaker, 1825. 2 vols.

> Holman (1786-1857), the famed blind traveller, followed his earlier European travels with more ambitious plans to circuit the world. He arrived in St Petersburg in 1822 and travelled through Siberia as far as Irkutsk, but was then arrested on suspicion of being a spy for the Russian American Company. He was conducted back forcibly to the frontier with Poland and expelled. Holman's correspondence with Cochrane (see F82), who doubted his claims, is included as an appendix.

F90) Lyall, Robert, *Travels in Russia, the Krimea, the Caucasus, and Georgia.* London: printed for T. Cadell, in the Strand, and Edinburgh: William Blackwood, 1825. 2 vols.

> Dr Lyall (see F61) acted as guide and physician to the Marquis Pucci, Count Salazar and Edward Penrhyn on travels from Moscow to southern Russia that took place between April and August 1822. The detailed itinerary is in vol. II, pp. 530-34. A work overloaded with references and quotations from the works of other travellers.

F91) Jones, George Matthew, *Travels in Norway, Sweden, Finland, Russia, and Turkey; also on the coasts of the Sea of Azof and of the Black Sea; with a review of the trade in those seas and of the systems adopted to man the fleets of the different powers of Europe, compared with that of England.* London: John Murray, 1827. 2 vols.

> Jones, a long-serving captain in the Royal Navy and meticulous diarist, followed earlier European tours with extensive travels that took him to St Petersburg at the end of September 1822. He spent some four months in the capital with an excursion to Revel before, following in the footsteps of his admired E.D. Clarke, he travelled to Moscow and then south, visiting Tula, Taganrog, Azov, and the Crimea, before arriving in Odessa, whence he sailed for Constantinople on 12 June 1823 (vol. I, pp. 283-582; II, pp. 1-390).

F92) Zwick, Heinrich August, *Calmuc Tartary; or, a journey from Sarepta to several Calmuc hordes of the Astracan government; from May 26 to August 21, 1823, undertaken, on behalf of the Russian Bible Society, by Henry Augustus Zwick and John Golfried Schill, and described by the former.* London: Holdsworth and Ball, 1831. iv+262pp.

> In 1818 Zwick (1796-1855), admitted into the Moravian Brotherhood in 1809, arrived in Sarepta on the Volga (the town founded by the Brotherhood in 1765) and made several missionary journeys among the Kalmyks prior to the journey recorded in this work. At the request of the Russian Bible Society, Zwick and his fellow missionary Schill were to distribute copies of a Kalmyk translation of the Matthew Gospel and other tracts among the five native hordes. They arrived back just days after the great fire that had devastated Sarepta (pp. 25-262). (German original: *Reise von Sarepta…* (Leipzig, 1827)). Zwick's pioneering linguistic studies were reflected in his West-Mongolian (Kalmyk) grammar of 1851.

F93) Clairmont, Claire, *The journals of Claire Clairmont 1814-1827.* Edited by Marion Kingston Stocking, with the assistance of David Mackenzie Stocking. Cambridge, Mass.: Harvard University Press, 1968. xxii+571pp.

> Clara Mary Jane (Claire) Clairmont (1798-1879), mistress of Byron and mother of his daughter Augusta, arrived in Moscow in late 1823 as governess to daughters of a Countess Zotova, before moving to a similar position in the Posnikov family. She left Russia in May 1828. Incomplete journals cover period from May 1825 to January 1827 (pp. 305-411).

F94) Clairmont, Claire, *The Clairmont correspondence: letters of Claire Clairmont, Charles Clairmont, and Fanny Imlay Godwin.* Edited by Marion Kingston Stocking. Baltimore and London: John Hopkins University Press, 1995. 2 vols.

> Letters from Moscow to Jane Williams and Mary Shelley, September 1824– July 1827 (vol. I, pp. 211-50).

F95) Hutchinson, William, 'Letter from Belaia tserkov', 13 September 1824', in *Autobiography of A. B. Granville, M.D., F.R.S.: being eighty-eight years of the life of a physician who practised his profession in Italy, Greece, Turkey, Spain, Portugal, the West Indies, Russia, Germany, France, and England.* Edited, with a brief account of the last years of his life, by his youngest daughter, Paulina B. Granville. London: Henry S. King & Co., 1874. 2 vols.

> Dr Hutchinson (1793-1850), editor of the *London medical and physical journal*, was briefly physician to Count and Countess Vorontsov in Odessa in the early months of 1824, suffered ill health, and was replaced by Dr Robert Lee (vol. II, pp. 228-30). Alexander Pushkin, who met Hutchinson in Odessa, dubbed him "the deaf philospher, the only intelligent atheist I have as yet met".

F96) Wilson, William Rae, *Travels in Russia.* London: Longman, Rees, Orme, Brown, and Green, 1828. 2 vols.

> Fellow of the Society of Arts and author of other books of travel, Wilson travelled through Germany to reach the Russian frontier on 6 June 1824 (despite his asserting that his tour was "during the summer of 1825" (vol. I, p. 2)) and spent the rest of the summer in St Petersburg and Moscow. He returned to the capital and left for Finland at the end of September. He is increasingly vague about dates, which allows him to add information about events that happened long after his departure, such as the death of Alexander and the Decembrist revolt (vol. I, pp. 162-383; II, pp. 1-144).

F97) Keppel, George Thomas, *Personal narrative of a journey from India to England, by Bussorah, Bagdad, the ruins of Babylon, Curdistan, the court of Persia, the western shore of the Caspian Sea, Astrakhan, Nishney Novogorod, Moscow, and St. Petersburgh, in the year 1824.* London: Henry Colburn, 1827. xii+338pp.

> Captain, later General Keppel (1799-1891), who became 6th Earl of Albemarle in 1849, left India in January 1824, entering Russian territory on 23 June and following the Volga from Astrakhan to Moscow. He then travelled to St Petersburg, where he arrived on 31 August but of which he left no description, and was home in early November (pp. 276-338).

F98) Keppel, George Thomas, *Fifty years of my life.* London: Macmillan and Co, 1876. 2 vols.

> A shortened version of his account of 1827, but with the added information about his three-week stay in St Petersburg and intriguing encounters with the Sablukovs, General Jomini and Sir Robert Ker Porter (vol. II, pp. 200-17).

F99) Prince, Nancy Gardner, *A narrative of the life and travels of Mrs Nancy Price.* Boston: for the author, 1850. 87pp. [Re-issued as *A black woman's odyssey through Russia and Jamaica: the narrative of Nancy Prince.* Introduction by Ronald G. Waters. New York: Markus Wiener, 1990.]

> The extraordinary autobiography of an African-American woman, known only through her own account of her life. Née Nancy Gardner (1799-c.1856), she married Nero Prince, who had arrived in Massachusetts from Russia, and in April 1824 she accompanied him to St Petersburg, where he was employed at the court. She witnessed the flood of November 1824, the Decembrist uprising, and the first years of Nicholas's reign, before her departure from St Petersburg on 14 August 1833.

F100) Moore, John, *A journey from London to Odessa, with notices of New Russia, etc.* London: for the author, 1833. vii+320pp.

> Eleven letters from the author to his friend C****, as he travelled from Calais through Poland to Odessa, "that remarkable city", where he spent three months from 19 August 1824. He returned by the same route (pp. 77-215).

F101) Shillitoe, Thomas, *Journal of the life, labours, and travels of Thomas Shillitoe, in the service of the gospel of Jesus Christ.* London: Harvey and Darton, 1839. 2 vols.

Shillitoe (1754-1836), a Quaker since 1778, arrived in St Petersburg from Denmark in early September 1824, was witness to the great flood in November, and remained in the city until 9 February 1825, when he left with Daniel Wheeler by sled for Riga (vol. II, pp. 69-117).

F102) Wassenaer, Marie Cornélie de, *A visit to St Petersburg 1824-1825.* Translated by Igor Vinogradoff [from the French manuscript]. Norwich: Michael Russell, 1994. 160pp.

The immensely rich young Dutchwoman, Cornélie Wassenaer (1799-1850) left Brussels on 8 September 1824 in her capacity as maid of honour to the Princess of Orange-Nassau (Anna, youngest daughter of Paul I) and spent a month at Gatchina before the royal party was installed in the Winter Palace on 17 November (two days before the great flood). They began their return journey on 28 July of the following year.

F103) Schnitzler, Jean Henri, *Secret history of the court and government of Russia under the emperors Alexander and Nicholas.* London: Richard Bentley, 1847. 2 vols.

Born in Strasbourg, Schnitzler (1802-71) spent four years between 1824 and 1828 in Russia, as a private tutor. He was an eye-witness to the events of 14 December 1825 and was present in Moscow for the coronation of Nicholas I. He was to write at least five books on Russian history and economic development, although his *Histoire intime de la Russie* (1847), in which he analyses the causes and effects of the Decembrist revolt, was the only one to appear in English.

F104) Disbrowe, Edward Cromwell, and Disbrowe, Anne, *Original letters from Russia, 1825-1828.* Edited by C[harlotte] A[nne] A[lbinia] D[isbrowe]. London: printed for private circulation at the Ladies' Printing Press, 1878. 296pp. [Later partially incorporated into *Old days in diplomacy: recollections of a closed century.* By the eldest daughter of the late Sir Edward Cromwell Disbrowe, G.C.G. With a preface by M. Montgomery-Campbell. London: Jarrold & Sons, 1903. 327pp. (Russian letters, pp. 73-165).]

Disbrowe (1790-1851) arrived in St Petersburg on 7 April 1825 as British minister plenipotentiary and was soon joined by his wife, her father, and her brother, John Kennedy (who was also to work in the embassy). Extracts of letters, written mainly by Mrs Disbrowe (1795-1855), are found in both editions, covering the death of Alexander I and the Decembrist revolt. The Disbrowes left the Russian capital on 23 February 1828.

F105) Bloomfield, Benjamin, *Memoir of Benjamin, Lord Bloomfield G.C.B., G.C.H.* Edited by Georgiana Lady Bloomfield. London: Chapman and Hall, 1884. 2 vols.

> Lord Bloomfield (1768-1846), British envoy extraordinary and minister plenipotentiary to Sweden from 1822 to 1832, made a ten-week tour of Russia in the summer of 1825 (29 June-7 September), visiting St Petersburg, Moscow, Nizhnii Novgorod and Kazan (vol. II, pp. 1-101).

F106) Lee, Robert, *The last days of Alexander, and the first days of Nicholas (emperors of Russia).* London: Richard Bentley, 1854. 210pp.

> Dr Lee (1793-1877), appointed personal physician to Count Mikhail Vorontsov, arrived in Odessa (via Poland) on 8 January 1825 and remained almost two years until November 1826, when he returned to London with the Vorontsovs. He provides a detailed account of the last illness and death of Alexander I, to whom he had been presented a few days earlier. There is also much on the Decembrist revolt.

F107) Wolff, Joseph, *Missionary journal and memoir of the Rev. Joseph Wolff, missionary to the Jews.* Written by himself. Revised and edited by John Bayford. London: Printed for the editor by James Duncan and I.B. Seeley & Son, 1827-29. 3 vols.

> Dubbed "the eccentric missionary" and best known for his journey to Bokhara in 1843 to seek the British officers Stoddart and Conolly (already executed), Rev. Wolff (1795-1862), born in Bavaria, was involved in the work of the London Society for Promoting Christianity among the Jews from 1819 and travelled extensively on its behalf. On 19 June 1825 he entered Georgia and over the next eight months travelled and preached in many towns and settlements, including the German colonies, in Georgia and the Crimea. Arriving in Taganrog, he received an invitation to meet the tsar, who was to die before they met. Wolff left Odessa for Constantinople on 8 February 1826 (vol. III (1829), pp. 189-288).

F108) Wolff, Joseph, *Travels and adventures of the Rev. Joseph Wolff, D.D., LL.D.* London: Saunders, Otley, and Co., 1860-61. 2 vols.

> Dictated and in the third person, Wolff's memoirs published shortly before his death include a brief account of his one excursion into Russian territory in 1825-26 (vol. II, pp. 363-69).

Fig. 41 Nicholas I (1856), by Vladimir Dmitrievich Sverchkov. Oil on canvas. Hermitage Museum, St Petersburg.

7. REIGN OF NICHOLAS I (1825-1855)

See also F67, F70, F87, F93, F94, F96, F99, F103, F104, F106, F107, F108, H21

G1) Walsh, Robert, 'Reminiscences of Russia', in *The Amulet*. Edited by S.C. Hall. London: Frederick Westley and A.H. Davis, 1835. Vol. X, 286pp.

> A member of the British and Foreign Bible Society, Rev. Walsh (1772-1852) visited St Petersburg in 1826. He comments on the sorry fate of the Russian Bible Society, on the assassination of Paul, but is silent about the Decembrists (pp. 145-76).

G2) Beechey, Frederick William, *Narrative of a voyage to the Pacific and Beering's Strait, to co-operate with the polar expeditions: performed in His Majesty's Ship Blossom, under the command of Captain F.W. Beechey, R.N., in the years 1825, 26, 27, 28.* London: Henry Colburn and Richard Bentley, 1831. 2 vols.

> Captain, later Rear-Admiral, Beechey (1796-1856) left England on 25 May 1825 for the Bering Strait to meet up with two earlier expeditions under Captains Parry and Franklin. A year later, on 28 July 1826, the *Blossom* arrived at Petropavlovsk in Kamchatka. It remained in the area until the end of October, when not having made contact with Franklin, it sailed for San Francisco (vol. I, pp. 324-471). On 3 July 1827 Beechey and his crew were back at Petropavlovsk, remaining until the end of September (vol. II, pp. 241-95).

G3) Peard, George, *To the Pacific with Beechey: the journal of Lieutenant George Peard of H.M.S. 'Blossom' 1825-1828.* Edited by Barry M. Gough. Cambridge: Cambridge University Press, 1973. x+272pp.

> Beechey's first lieutenant, Peard (1783-1837) noted in his journal, "on the 28th [July 1826] the fog cleared up and we saw to the NW. the mountainous coast of Kamptchatska streaked with snow and presenting a most dreary

http://dx.doi.org/10.11647/OBP.0042.07

appearance". His previously unpublished journal complements Beechey's more detailed account of their two visits to Kamchatka and the Bering Strait (pp. 139-72, 219-43).

G4) Erman, Georg Adolph, *Travels in Siberia: including excursions northwards, down the Obi, to the Polar Circle, and southwards, to the Chinese frontier.* Translated from the German by William Desborough Cooley. London: Longman, Brown, Green, and Longmans, 1848. 2 vols. [Vols. II-III of Cooley's *The world surveyed in the XIXth century; or, recent narratives of scientific and exploratory expeditions.*]

> The German scientist (1806-77) left Berlin on 25 April 1827 to participate in Professor Christoph Hansteen's expedition to Siberia seeking to test his theory of terrestrial magnetism. It was in May of the following year that Erman reached Okhotsk after extensive travels through Siberia that included side expeditions from Ekaterinburg to the silver mines in the Urals, from Tobolsk down the Ob, and across Baikal to Selenginsk. He provides in diary form a mass of information, not only of scientific interest but also on the lives of local peoples and of the exiles. An abridged version, particularly in its pre-Siberian part, of *Reise um die Erde durch Nord-Asien und die beiden Oceane* (1833-48).

G5) Granville, Augustus Bozzi, *St Petersburgh: a journal of travels to and from that capital; through Flanders, the Rhenish Provinces, Prussia, Russia, Poland, Silesia, Saxony, the Federated States of Germany, and France.* London: Henry Colburn, 1828. 2 vols. [2nd edition, carefully revised, and with considerable additions, 1829]

> Dr Granville (1783-1872) left England on 20 September 1827 as body physician to Count and Countess Mikhail Vorontsov and seventeen weeks later had returned. His brief stay in St Petersburg from 27 October to 10 December gave rise to the monumental description of all aspects of life in the capital (vol. I, pp. 414-577; II, pp. 1-524), such that a third edition of 1835 bore the title *Guide to St Petersburgh: a journal of travels.*

G6) Granville, Augustus Bozzi, *Autobiography of A. B. Granville, M.D., F.R.S.: being eighty-eight years of the life of a physician who practised his profession in Italy, Greece, Turkey, Spain, Portugal, the West Indies, Russia, Germany, France, and England.* Edited, with a brief account of the last years of his life, by his youngest daughter, Paulina B. Granville. London: Henry S. King & Co., 1874. 2 vols.

Granville recalls his first sojourn in Russia in 1827, referring readers to his book, but adds pages on his own health and reaction to Russian tea! (vol. II, pp. 238-50). In the spring of 1849 he went again to Russia to attend the pregnant Countess Chernysheva, wife of the minister of war, arriving at Cronstadt on 17 May and departing on 14 July. Towards the end of his stay he spent a few days in Moscow and was contemplating a work to be called *The two capitals, or sketches of the present state of St Petersburg and Moscow* that was never completed (pp. 386-408).

G7) Webster, James, *Travels through the Crimea, Turkey, and Egypt, performed during the years 1825-1828; including particulars of the last illness and death of the Emperor Alexander, and of the Russian conspiracy of 1825.* London: Henry Colburn and Richard Bentley, 1830. 2 vols.

> Published posthumously. The young Scot Webster (1802-28) of the Inner Temple died in Cairo after travelling with companion W.H. Newnham from Poland down to Odessa in 1827 (Russia: vol. I, pp. 32-101; II, pp. 333-39).

G8) Westminster, Elizabeth Mary Leveson Gower, Marchioness of, *Diary of a tour in Sweden, Norway, and Russia, in 1827, with letters.* London: Hurst and Blackett, 1879. 297pp.

> The Belgraves, as Elizabeth (1797-1891) and her husband Richard (1795-1869) were known from their marriage in 1819 until 1831 during the lifetime of his father, Earl Grosvenor, arrived in St Petersburg on 26 July 1827. They left for Moscow on 29 August, en route for the fair at Nizhnii Novgorod. They spent a week in Moscow on the return journey and a further week in St Petersburg before leaving on 20 August (pp. 136-250).

G9) Morton, Edward, *Travels in Russia, and a residence at St Petersburg and Odessa, in the years 1827-1829; intended to give some account of Russia as it is, and not as it is represented to be, &c. &c.* London: Longman, Rees, Orme, Brown, and Green, 1830. xix+486pp.

> Dr Morton followed Lee and Granville as physician to Count Mikhail Vorontsov and his family. He arrived at Cronstadt on 21 October 1827 and left St Petersburg with the Vorontsovs on 10 February 1828, travelling to Odessa, where he was to remain from March 1828 until June of the following year. He provides a substantial history of the city (pp. 175-330) and of the imperial visit in 1828 (pp. 367-85).

G10) [Lefevre, George William], *The life of a travelling physician, from his first introduction to practice; including twenty years' wanderings through the greater part of Europe.* London: Longman, Brown, Green and Longmans, 1843. 3 vols.

> Sir George (1798-1846) spent fifteen years in Russia, practising first and briefly in Odessa, before moving to St Petersburg. He returned to England in 1842. His very generalized Russian memoirs occupy all of vol. II (304pp.) and the beginning of vol. III (pp. 1-96). He was also author of *Observations on the nature and treatment of the cholera morbus, now prevailing epidemically in St Petersburg* (London, 1831). He was knighted in 1832 for his services as physician to the British embassy in St Petersburg.

G11) Alcock, Thomas, *Travels in Russia, Persia, Turkey, and Greece, in 1828-9.* London: Privately printed by E. Clarke and Son, 1831. viii+227pp.

> Alcock (1801-66), M.P. for the rotten borough of Newton in Lancashire in 1826-30, travelled to the seat of the conflict between Turkey and Russia to observe "the sort of warfare carried on against, as well as by, the Turks". He went by way of Vienna to Odessa, where he arrived in August 1828. He then toured the Crimea, before making his way to Tiflis, then Erevan, and into Persia. His comments are of a very general nature, not least on military operations, on which he writes "with great diffidence" (pp. 5-55).

G12) Armstrong, T.B., *Journal of travels in the seat of war, during the last two campaigns of Russia and Turkey; intended as an itinerary through the south of Russia, the Crimea, Georgia, and through Persia, Koordistan, and Asia Minor, to Constantinople.* London: A. Seguin, 1831. xvi+242pp. [Reissued: London: D. Dodson, 1838, as *Travels in Russia and Turkey...*]

> Two weeks after Alcock (see G11), Armstrong and his two companions arrived in Odessa on 2 September 1828, having also travelled via Vienna. There they saw the tsar but little else before they were on their way through the Crimea and Georgia to Tiflis, Erevan, and Tabriz in Persia, where they arrived in time to enjoy Christmas dinner at the British embassy (pp. 13-108).

G13) Parrot, Jacob Friedrich Wilhelm, *Journey to Ararat.* Translated by W.D. Cooley. London: Longman, Brown, Green, and Longmans, 1845. xii+375pp. [Vol. I of Cooley's *The world surveyed in the XIXth century; or, recent narratives of scientific and exploratory expeditions.*]

The Baltic German naturalist and traveller (1792-1841) left Dorpat, where he was the university's professor of natural philosophy, on 11 April 1829 and led a small expedition south through Russia to Tiflis. He was conducting experiments on terrestrial magnetism, but his travels were most notable for his successful ascent, at the third attempt, of Mt. Ararat on 9 October (p. 178). He arrived back in Dorpat on 30 March 1830. German original: *Reise zum Ararat* (Berlin, 1834).

G14) Alexander, James Edward, *Travels to the seat of war in the East, through Russia and the Crimea, in 1829; with sketches of the imperial fleet and army, personal adventures, and characteristic anecdotes.* London: Henry Colburn and Richard Bentley, 1830. 2 vols.

Captain, later, General Sir James (1803-85), left England in early May 1829 and reached St Petersburg by way of Revel and Cronstadt. He provides a detailed account of his journey from the capital to Nikolaev via Moscow and Kharkov. The second volume is devoted to his cruise with the Russian navy on the Black Sea and his general account of the hostilities between Russia and Turkey, which ends with his arrest as a spy and his being escorted back to St Petersburg, where he met the tsar, was exonerated, and left for England via Sweden at the beginning of 1830.

G15) Montieth, William, *Kars and Erzeroum: with the campaigns of Prince Paskiewitch in 1828 and 1829; and an account of Russia beyond the Caucasus, from the time of Peter the Great to the treaty of Turcoman and Adrianople.* London: Longman, Brown, Green, and Longmans, 1856. xvi+332pp.

It was only after the conclusion of the Crimean War that Monteith (1790-1864), by then a lt-general and F.R.S., thought it appropriate to publish materials he had gathered, from research and personal observation, during his twenty-year stint attached to the British mission in Persia. He came in close contact with General Paskevich in Tiflis and elsewhere and was involved in the settlement of the Russo-Persian boundary in 1829, at which time he left Persia to return to India.

G16) Groves, Anthony Norris, *Journal of Mr. Anthony N. Groves, missionary, during a journey from London to Bagdad, through Russia, Georgia, and Persia: also, a journal of some months' residence at Bagdad.* London: James Nisbet, 1831. xi+215pp.

Groves and his family sailed from Gravesend on 11 June 1829, arriving in Cronstadt on 3 July. Travelled south to Astrakhan, visiting Sarepta and

Karass en route, then through the Caucasus to Tiflis, before crossing into Persia and arriving in Baghdad on 6 December 1829 (pp. 1-130).

G17) Conolly, Arthur, *Journey to the north of India, overland from England, through Russia, Persia, and Affghaunistaun.* London: Richard Bentley, 1834. 2 vols.

> Lt. Conolly (1807-42) of the Bengal Light Cavalry describes a long journey "by a new route, through very interesting countries", that began in England on 10 August 1829 and finished in India in January 1831. He and two brother officers spent a month in St Petersburg before departing on 8 October for Moscow and travelling down to Tiflis and into Persia, where they arrived at the end of December, described succinctly in the opening chapter of his book (vol. I, pp. 1-12). Conolly, who is credited with coining the phrase "The Great Game", was to achieve melancholy fame when he and another British officer were executed in June 1842 by the emir of Bokhara on charges of spying.

G18) Rennie, John, *Autobiography of Sir John Rennie, F.R.S., past president of the Institution of Civil Engineers, comprising the history of his professional life, together with reminiscences dating from the commencement of the century to the present times.* London: E. & F.N. Spon, 1875. viii+464pp.

> The famous engineer Sir John Rennie (1794-1874) travelled out to St Petersburg on the same steamer as Lieutenant Conolly at the end of August 1829 and during his stay in the Russian capital spent much time with the Scottish engineers General Alexander Wilson and Charles Baird, before travelling to Moscow and leaving via Warsaw (pp. 252-62). In the spring of 1859 he was invited to Odessa to produce a plan for the paving of the streets and introducing a complete system of sewers (pp. 377-81).

G19) Slade, Adolphus, *Records of travels in Turkey, Greece, etc., and of a cruise in the Black Sea with the Capitan Pasha, in the years 1829, 1830, and 1831.* London: Saunders and Otley, 1832. 2 vols.

> Sir Adolphus (1804-77), a British admiral who in 1849 became also an admiral in the Turkish navy with the title of Mushaver Pasha, had been present, when still a half-pay lieutenant in the Royal Navy, at the battle of Navarino, and from 1828 to 1831 travelled extensively on both sides of the Bosphorus. He reached Constantinople in 1829, where he became friendly with Capitan Pasha, head of the Turkish navy, who invited him on a tour of the Black Sea. Turkey was at this time at war with Russia and Slade's comments are a unique British source (Russia, vol. I, pp. 485-519).

G20) Mignan, Robert, *A winter journey through Russia, the Caucasian Alps, and Georgia; thence across Mount Zagros, by the Pass of Xenophon and the Ten Thousand Greeks, into Koordistaun.* London: Richard Bentley, 1839. 2 vols.

> A captain in the Indian army, Mignan (d. 1852) arrived with his family from England in St Petersburg on 21 October 1829. They were to join the Persian envoy extraordinary, returning to Persia after conveying regrets at the recent murder of the Russian diplomat and dramatist Griboedov in Teheran. Their journey south in the severe winter of 1829 via Novocherkask and through the Caucasus to Tiflis was hazardous. They left Tiflis on 31 January 1830 on their way to the Persian border (pp. 1-112).

G21) Raikes, Thomas, *A visit to St Petersburg, in the winter of 1829-30.* London: Richard Bentley, 1838. xii+383pp.

> Presented as a series of twenty-six letters Raikes (1777-1848) addressed to an unknown friend between 8 November 1829 (at sea) and 25 March 1830 (leaving St Petersburg), the book was published years later allegedly to offer not only a picture of manners and mores in the capital but also an understanding of the development of Russian "power", threatening British interests (there is an appendix, dated 3 October 1837). Most notable for the description of his meeting with Pushkin on 23 December 1829 and for his letter (no. xvi) devoted to the Decembrists.

G22) Randolph, John, *John Randolph of Roanoke, 1773-1833: a biography based largely on new material.* New York and London: G.P. Putnam's Sons, 1922. 2 vols.

> Virginia planter and congressman, Randolph (1773-1833), appointed American envoy extraordinary and minister plenipotentiary to Russia by President Jackson in May 1830, landed in St Petersburg on 10 August. He was to serve only until 19 September, a matter of forty days, before leaving for London for reasons of ill-health and seeking permission to retire the following April (vol. I, pp. 634-61).

G23) Clay, John Randolph, *John Randolph Clay, America's first career diplomat.* By George Irvin Oeste. Philadelphia: University of Pennsylvania Press, 1966. 602pp.

> Clay (1808-85), Randolph's protégé, was appointed secretary of legation in St Petersburg at the age of twenty-one but just over a month after his arrival in St Petersburg found himself *chargé d'affaires* and presented to the tsar in December. He remained in Russia for seven years until 5 August

1837, serving as secretary of legation under ambassadors Buchanan and Wilkins. Brief extracts from his diary and letters (pp. 69-165). In July 1845 Clay returned to St Petersburg as *chargé d'affaires* and remained until 27 May 1847 (pp. 257-73).

G24) Barrow, John, Jr., *Excursions in the north of Europe, through parts of Russia, Finland, Sweden, Denmark, and Norway, in the years 1830 and 1833.* London: John Murray, 1834. ix+380pp.

Arriving by boat at Cronstadt on 4 July 1830, Barrow (1808-98) and his companion John Rouse left for Sweden at the end of September after a typical tour of the sights of St Petersburg and Moscow (pp. 39-139).

G25) Elliott, Charles Boileau, *Letters from the north of Europe; or, a journal of travels in Holland, Denmark, Norway, Sweden, Finland, Russia, Prussia, and Saxony.* London: Henry Colburn and Richard Bentley, 1832. xxiv+475pp.

Formerly of the Bengal civil service, member of R.G.S. and of Queens' College, Cambridge, Elliott (1803-75) left England on 23 June 1830 and after extensive travels through Scandinavia, crossed the Russian border from Finland on 14 September. Offered as revised and expanded letters to friends, they form the journal of a typical, if intelligent, tourist, who records the sights of St Petersburg and Moscow, but who suggests, with reason, that his opinions on national character are "first impressions". He left for Poland and Berlin at the end of September (pp. 266-423).

G26) Frankland, Charles Colville, *Narrative of a visit to the courts of Russia and Sweden, in the years 1830 and 1831.* London: Henry Colburn and Richard Bentley, 1832. 2 vols.

A commander in the Royal Navy, later admiral, Frankland (1797-1876) arrived in St Petersburg by way of Scandinavia on 27 September 1830 and left Cronstadt on 2 July 1831, having visited only Moscow and towns between the two capitals. He kept a diary that not only details what he did but also gives a plethora of names of people, Russian and British, whom he encountered (Pushkin included), fulfilling his promise to provide "a general idea of the society of the North, and of the sort of life a well-introduced stranger leads at Petersburgh and Moscow". He was there at the time of the Polish uprising and of the cholera outbreak in 1831 (vol. I, pp. 116-382; II, pp. 1-447).

G27) Holland, Henry, *Recollections of past life.* London: printed for the author by Spottiswoode & Co., 1870. 284pp.

> Sir Henry (1788-1893), F.R.S., physician extraordinary to Queen Victoria, narrates for the benefit of his children events of his long life, during which he visited Russia on two occasions, in the autumn of 1830 and in the autumn of 1852. Apart from conveying his impressions of the tsar, he is unfortunately reticent about his visits (pp. 146-47).

G28) [Haight, Sarah], *Letters from the Old World.* By a lady of New York. New York: Harper, 1839. 2 vols.

> Recently married Mrs Haight, née Rogers (1808-81), and her husband Richard sailed from Odessa for Constantinople in the late summer of 1830 (?), having evidently travelled across Russia from St Petersburg. The first letter is concerned almost entirely with the plague quarantine (vol. I, pp. 13-22).

G29) Stocqueler, Joachim Hayward, *Fifteen months' pilgrimage through untrodden tracts of Khazistan and Persia, in a journey from India to England, through parts of Turkish Arabia, Persia, Armenia, Russia, and Germany. Performed in the years 1831 and 1832.* London: Saundes and Otley, 1832. 2 vols.

> Stocqueler (1800-85) left India in February 1831 and eventually arrived in England on 3 May 1832. He sailed across the Black Sea to Odessa, where he arrived in November 1831 (vol. II, pp. 21-37). He travelled on through Poland and Germany. There is a further appendix on Odessa, pp. 226-28.

G30) Russell, William and Barry, D., *Official reports made to government by Drs. Russell & Barry, on the disease called cholera spasmodica, as observed during their mission to Russia in 1831; with an appendix, and other papers, extracts of letters, reports, and communications received from the Continent, relating to that disease.* London: Winchester and Varnham; Simpkin and Marshall; Hatchard and son, 1832. iv+147pp.

> Sent out to St Petersburg by the British government to investigate the outbreak of cholera, Drs Russell and Barry arrived at the beginning of July 1831. Over the next few weeks they sent back detailed reports, describing the situation at various factories and institutions. They left Russia on 10 October 1831.

G31) Birrell, Charles Mitchell, 'Recollections of St. Petersburg'. In *Evening recollections; or, samples from the lecture room.* Edited by John Hampden Gurney. London: Longman, Brown, Green, and Longmans, 1856. xvi+267pp.

> One of eight lecturers speaking on very varied topics at the Mechanics' Institute in Marylebone at the invitation of the editor, Rev. Gurney, Rev. Birrell (1811-80), pastor of Pembroke Baptist chapel in Liverpool, recalls his visit to the Russian capital "a considerable time ago", staying for seven months, from autumn to spring 1831-32. After a tourist's view of "this undoubtedly magnificent city", he touches on the ills of serfdom, discusses Nicholas I, whom he saw at the funeral of Constantine's wife in November 1831, before addressing "moral influences" and the work of the Bible Society (pp. 28-66).

G32) Buchanan, James, *The works of James Buchanan, comprising his speeches, state papers, and private correspondence.* Edited and collected by John Bassett Moore. Philadelphia and London: J.B. Lippincott Co., 1908-11. 12 vols.

> In March 1832 Buchanan (1791-1868), later 15th president of the United States, left "the most free and happy country on earth for a despotism more severe than any which exists in Europe", arriving in St Petersburg on 2 June as American envoy extraordinary and minister plenipotentiary. He departed on 12 August 1833, having concluded a commercial treaty and being more kindly disposed to the tsar and the country. Most of his correspondence is concerned with official matters but his letters to his brother contain a little about his social life and a visit to Moscow (vol. II (1908), pp. 193-382).

G33) Borrow, George Henry, *Letters of George Borrow to the British and Foreign Bible Society published by direction of the committee.* Edited by T.H. Darlow. London, New York and Toronto: Hodder and Stoughton, 1911. xviii+471pp.

> Borrow (1803-81) sailed from London for St Petersburg on 31 July 1833 as agent of the Bible Society to supervise the translation of the New Testament into Manchu. His twenty letters from St Petersburg to officers of the Society cover the period from August 1833 until August 1835. A report to the Society presented after his return from Russia in September 1835 contains vivid details of a visit to Moscow (pp. 21-96).

G34) Tietz, Friedrich von, *St. Petersburgh, Constantinople, and Napoli di Romania, in 1833 and 1834: a characteristic picture, drawn during a residence* *there.* Translated from the German by J.D. Haas. London: Adolphus Richter and Co.; Edinburgh: T. Clark; Dublin: Millikin and Son, 1836. 2 vols.

> Von Tietz, a counsellor at the Prussian legation in St Petersburg, who had first visited the Russian capital in 1832, describes his longer sojourn the following year and his great admiration for Nicholas I (vol. I, pp. 1-190). Translated from *Legationsrath, Errinnerungs-Skizzen aus Russland, der Türkei und Griechenland* (Coburg and Leipzig, 1836).

G35) Revere, Joseph Warren, *Keel and saddle: a retrospect of forty years of military and naval service.* Boston: James R. Osgood and Co., 1872. xiv+360pp.

> Early in his long and colourful career as sailor and soldier of distinction, Paul Revere's grandson (1812-80) served on a merchant ship that took him in the mid-1830s on a trip up the Baltic to Cronstadt and St Petersburg. There he allegedly saw Nicholas I make an incognito visit to inspect the ship and he also tells the story of a Polish fugitive describing the horrors of Siberian exile for his fellow countrymen (pp. 17-26).

G36) Ritchie, Leitch, *A journey to St. Petersburg and Moscow through Courland and Livonia.* (Heath's *Picturesque annual for 1836.*) London: Longman, Rees, Orme, Brown, Green, and Longman, 1836. 256pp.

> Reliable account by professional travel-writer enhanced by twenty-five engravings from original drawing by Alfred George Vickers. Stay in St Petersburg from April 1835 followed by six-week visit to Moscow.

G37) Coghlan, Francis, *A guide to St. Petersburg & Moscow, by Hamburg, Lubeck, Travemunde, and by steam-packet, across the Baltic to Cronstadt; fully detailing every form and expense from London-Bridge to St. Petersburg: from an actual visit in the autumn of 1835.* Illustrated with plans of St Petersburg, Moscow, Hamburg, and proposed railroad between Hamburg and Lubeck. London: Published for the author by C. Prout, and St Petersburg: L. Dixon, 1836. 269pp.

> A useful pocket guide to Cronstadt, St Petersburg and Moscow, antedating the first "Murray" by a few years (pp. 72-266).

G38) [Anon.], *Guide to Moscow, containing a description of the public edifices, historical notices, useful statistics, and an itinerary of the road from St. Petersburgh, to which is added a vocabulary of useful words and phrases.* London: Leigh and Son, 1835. viii+240pp.

A well-compiled and informative guide (part of Leigh's Guides for travellers on the continent), providing in pocket format what it promises in its title, and written by an unknown English author. He quotes as his authorities his own on-the-spot notes, the contribution of a long-time resident, and Lavaux's guide of 1824. There is an excellent large-scale plan of the city.

G39) Durham, John George Lambton, Earl of, *Life and letters of the First Earl of Durham 1792-1840.* By Stuart Johnson Reid. London: Longmans, Green, and Co., 1906. 2 vols.

Lambton, 1st Earl of Durham (1792-1840), was appointed ambassador and extraordinary and plenipotentiary on 8 July 1835. He set out for Russia on 26 July and, travelling via Constantinople, arrived in Odessa on 18 September. He reached St Petersburg in mid-November and was to remain until 10 June 1837. Reid's biography sadly gives only excerpts from his unpublished "private journal", his letters and dispatches, and little more from his extensive 'Report on the state of Russia' (vol. II, pp. 13-69, 125-26).

G40) De Ros, William Lennox Lascelles Fitzgerald, *Journal of a tour in the principalities, Crimea, and countries adjacent to the Black Sea, in the years 1835-36.* London: John W. Parker & Son, 1855. iv+164pp.

De Ros, 22nd Baron (1797-1874), who was to be quartermaster-general of the British army during the Crimean War, accompanied the Earl of Durham on his journey from London to Russia, with a brief to check "unusual preparations" for fortresses, ports, etc. in the Black Sea area. He travelled extensively in the Crimea but also journeyed with Durham to Kiev, where they met the tsar on 23 October. Eventually left Russian territory on 27 November, travelling overland to Vienna (pp. 61-125).

G41) Stephens, John Lloyd, *Incidents of travel, in Greece, Turkey, Russia and Poland.* London: Walker & Co., 1838. 596pp.

American lawyer (1805-52) arrived in Odessa from Turkey in 1835 and travelled via Kiev to Moscow and St Petersburg (pp. 265-510). Surprisingly popular work with several distinct British editions, some with variations in title.

G42) Paul, Robert Bateman, *Journal of a tour to Moscow in the summer of 1836.* London: Simpkin-Marshall & Co., and Whittaker & Co., 1836. xvii+238pp.

Rev. Paul (1798-1877), former Fellow of Exeter College, Oxford, and domestic chaplain to the Earl of Falmouth, accompanied the son of a friend on a summer excursion that took them by boat from Lübeck to Cronstadt on 29 June 1836. After two weeks in St Petersburg they travelled to Moscow, where they spent less than a week before heading back to the capital, which they left by carriage for Finland and Sweden on 28 July (pp. 6-163).

G43) Spencer, Edmund, *Travels in Circassia, Krim-Tartary, &c., including a steam voyage down the Danube, from Vienna to Constantinople and round the Black Sea, in 1836.* London: Henry Colburn, 1837. 2 vols. [3rd "cheap and revised" edition, 1839.]

> A journey begun in Vienna in April 1836 took Captain Spencer, despite his original plans, to Odessa and quarantine, and thence to the Crimea. He was then invited by Count Mikhail Vorontsov, Governor-General of New Russia, to join his party sailing along the coast of Circassia, before returning to explore again the Crimea (vol. I, pp. 210-338; II, pp. 1-186). He embarked from Odessa for Trebizond, from where he began his extensive travels into the interior of Circassia (II, pp. 208-425).

G44) Spencer, Edmund, *Travels in the western Caucasus, including a tour through Imeritia, Mingrelia, Turkey, Moldavia, Galicia, Silesia, and Moravia, in 1836.* London: Henry Colburn, 1838. 2 vols.

> The continuation of Spencer's travels through Circassia and his return home to England, no longer offered as letters sent en route but as chapters. After detailing his travels through parts of Circassia, threatened by Russia (vol. I, pp. 1-358; II, pp. 1-70), he crosses into Turkey and returns via Moldavia and Austria.

G45) Londonderry, Frances Anne Emily, *Russian journal of Lady Londonderry 1836-7.* Edited by W.A.L. Seaman and J.R. Sewell. London: John Murray, 1973. 185pp.

> Frances Anne (née Vane-Tempest, 1800-65) and her husband Charles Stewart, 3rd Marquis of Londonderry (1776-1854), and their eldest son Viscount Seaham left England on a northern tour on 3 August 1836 and arrived on 17 September in St Petersburg, where they stayed until 9 February 1837, except for a fortnight's excursion to Moscow (pp. 44-133).

G46) Londonderry, Charles William Stewart, *Recollections of a tour in the north of Europe in 1836-1837.* London: Richard Bentley, 1838. 2 vols.

> Unlike his wife's journal which remained in manuscript, Londonderry's drearier account appeared within a year of their return to England. It is

supplemented by a series of twenty-five essays, translated by an English friend in St Petersburg, on such topics as the trade of Odessa, a town they were dissuaded from travelling to see in 1837 (vol. I, pp. 80-275; II, pp. 1-31).

G47) Bremner, Robert, *Excursions in the interior of Russia; including sketches of the character and policy of the Emperor Nicholas, scenes in St. Petersburgh, &c. &c.* London: Henry Colburn, 1839. 2 vols.

> Bremner arrived at Cronstadt in July 1836 and devotes, despite his title, virtually the whole of his first volume to "that marvellous city" St Petersburg and to the emperor (pp. 20-500). The second volume details his journey to and stay in Moscow, before he embarks on his "excursion in the interior" that takes him via Vladimir to Nizhnii Novgorod and then south through Ukraine to the Black Sea and his final destination, Odessa. Some interesting observations and much information on the British in Russia.

G48) Bell, James Stanislaus, *Journal of a residence in Circassia during the years 1837, 1838 and 1839.* London: Edward Moxon, 1840. 2 vols.

> The Scottish adventurer Bell (1797-1858) fused his journal and letters sent to friends into a sequence of thirty-three letters, covering what was his second sojourn in Circassia from 14 April 1837 (sailing from Constantinople) to 12 February 1840, when he was back in Turkey prior to his return to London in May. His motives for going to Circassia were commercial, the desire (unfulfilled) to see the establishing of direct trade with Britain, but he gained instead "a thorough acquaintance with the habits, manners, and general character of the natives, and of their political and civil institutions". His narrative is enlivened by coloured lithographs from his own drawings.

G49) Turnerelli, Edward Tracy, *What I know of the late Emperor Nicholas and his family.* London: Edward Churton, 1855. ix+164pp.

> Turnerelli (1813-96), son of a sculptor and himself a sculptor and artist, went to Russia in 1836. He met the tsar for the first time on 10 June 1837 and was encouraged to "delineate" the ancient sites and buildings of Russia. His book charts his many meetings with members of the imperial family up to his departure in August 1854 and is a defence of the late tsar in the context of the anti-Russian feelings during the Crimean War.

G50) Turnerelli, Edward Tracy, *Russia on the borders of Asia: Kazan, the ancient capital of the Tartar Khans; with an account of the province to which it* *belongs, the tribes and races which form its population, etc.* London: Richard Bentley, 1854. 2 vols.

> Turnerelli arrived in Kazan on 20 July 1837 and became instructor in English and Latin at the university. His book, part history, part travel guide, reflects his extensive travels through the region and his detailed study of ancient monuments, many of which he drew for his earlier album, *Views of Kasan*, published in London in 1840.

G51) Turnerelli, Edward Tracy, *Memories of a life of toil: the autobiography of Tracy Turnerelli, 'the old conservative'; a record of work artistic, literary, and political, from 1835 to 1884*. London: Field and Tuer; Leadenhall Press; Simpkin, Marshall & Co.; and Hamilton, Adams & Co., 1884. 251pp.

> Much on his time in Russia, supplementing his earlier works (pp. 37-73), and on his continuing pro-Russian activities after his return to England.

G52) Samuel, Jacob, *The remnant found; or, the place of Israel's hiding discovered. Being a summary of proofs, showing that the Jews of Daghistan in the Caspian Sea are the remnant of the ten tribes, the result of personal investigation during a missionary tour of eight months in Georgia, by permission of the Russian government in the years 1837 and 1838.* London: J. Hatchard, 1841. xxx+133pp.

> Rev. Samuel, senior missionary to the Jews for India, Persia, and Arabia, travelled from Persia to Tiflis, where he stayed for five months from May 1837, and pursued his researches in Daghestan (pp. 37-47).

G53) Venables, Richard Lister, *Domestic scenes in Russia: in a series of letters describing a year's residence in that country, chiefly in the interior*. London: John Murray, 1839. xii+348pp. [2nd revised edition,1856. xviii+229pp.]

> Rev. Venables (1809-94), Cambridge M.A. and with a living at Whitney in Herefordshire, accompanying his Russian wife Mary (née Poltoratskaia) on a visit to see her brother, describes their year-long sojourn in Russia, beginning with their arrival at Cronstadt in mid-June 1837. After a week in St Petersburg, they travelled to Iaroslavl and on to Moscow. They spent many months in Tambov, before returning to St Petersburg at the end of March 1838. Venables was particularly interested in serfdom and conscription and depicting provincial life. He brought out a second edition at the end of the Crimean War, believing that what he described was still of relevance and interest to a British public.

G54) Dallas, George Mifflin, *Diary of George Mifflin Dallas while United States minister to Russia 1837 to 1839, and to England 1856 to 1861.* Edited by Susan Dallas. Philadelphia: J.B. Lippincott Co., 1892. 443pp.

> The diary of the American envoy extraordinary and minister plenipotentiary (1792-1864) supplemented by extracts from letters, begins on 29 July 1837, as the ship on which he was sailing approached Cronstadt, and finishes with his departure on 24 July 1839. It is full of fascinating details, diplomatic and social, but also contains descriptions of such events as the burning of the Winter Palace in December 1837 and its "Reoccupation" in April 1839 (pp. 7-214).

G55) Demidoff, Anatole de, *Travels in southern Russia and the Crimea: through Hungary, Wallachia, & Moldavia, during the year 1837.* London: John Mitchell, 1853. 2 vols.

> Anatolii Nikolaevich Demidov, principe di San Donato (1813-70) set out from Paris on 14 June 1837 on an expedition, comprising mainly French engineers and scientists, especially the mineralogist Jean Jacques Huot (1790-1845) and the artist Denis Raffet (1804-60), to explore the mineral and other resources of Russia's new southern provinces. They crossed the Russo-Moldavian border on 3 August and made Odessa their headquarters, from which they explored surrounding areas, particularly the Crimea. An outbreak of plague forced them to return home by boat, leaving Odessa on 3 November for Constantinople (vol. I, pp. 289-370; II, pp. 1-311).

G56) Wilbraham, Richard, *Travels in the Trans-Caucasian provinces of Russia, and along the southern shore of the lakes of Van and Urumiah, in the autumn and winter of 1837.* London: John Murray, 1839. xvii+477pp.

> Captain Wilbraham (1811-1900), a British officer attached to the Persian army, travelled extensively in countries between the Caspian and the Black Sea, visiting Georgia and the Caucasus in September and October 1837 (pp. 112-282).

G57) Du Boulay, John Houssemayne, *Travels through Spitzbergen, Siberia, Russia, &c., and round the Seven Churches in Asia Minor, more than half a century ago.* Privately printed, c.1890. 62pp.

> Many years after the event, Du Boulay (1811-95), styling himself J.P. and of Donhead Hall in Wiltshire, recalls a visit he paid in 1837.

G58) Elliott, Charles Boileau, *Travels in the three great empires of Austria, Russia and Turkey.* London: Richard Bentley, 1838. 2 vols.

> Now styling himself vicar of Godalming and F.R.S., Elliott, who in the summer of 1830 had visited northern Russia (see G25), undertook a journey to more southern climes for reasons of health in 1837. Travelling from Vienna down the Danube, he eventually reached the Russian frontier with Moldavia and proceeded to Odessa. After a tour of the Crimea, boringly described and true to the words of the preface that the author offers "little that is new or erudite", he sails for Constantinople (vol. I, pp. 219-343).

G59) St John, Ferdinand, *Rambles in Germany, France, Italy and Russia, in search of sport.* London: Longman, Brown, Green, and Longmans, 1853. xix+233pp.

> St John (1804-65), son of 3rd Viscount Bolinbroke, spending the season with his family in Baden, was invited by Prince D* to accompany him on a short visit to Russia in August 1838 – the year established by the reference to the funeral of General Bistrom in St Petersburg. After a few days in Moscow, he stayed at Chemetewo (Sheremetevo) to shoot snipe, before proceeding to St Petersburg and then back to Baden (pp. 205-33).

G60) Slade, Adolphus, *Travels in Germany and Russia: including a steam voyage by the Danube and the Euxine from Vienna to Constantinople, in 1838-39.* London: Longman, Orme, Brown, Green, and Longmans, 1840. viii+512pp.

> Sir Adolphus (see G19) left England on 1 August 1838 and having descended the Danube to the Black Sea, sailed to Constantinople, whence he had cruised a decade earlier with the Turkish fleet. On this occasion he left by Russian steamer for Odessa and quarantine on 20 November. He was to remain there, seemingly doing very little and noting less, until the beginning of April 1839, when he left for the Austrian border (pp. 299-458).

G61) Layard, Austen Henry, *Autobiography and letters from his childhood until his appointment as H.M. ambassador at Madrid.* Edited by the hon. William N. Bruce, with a chapter on his parliamentary career by the rt. hon. Sir Arthur Otway. London: John Murray, 1903. 2 vols.

> Sir Austen (1817-94), the famed traveller, archaeologist, excavator of the Assyrian ruins of Nineveh, art historian, and diplomat, recalls a journey he made as a twenty-one-year old to Denmark, Sweden, Finland, and Russia

in the autumn of 1838. After a stay of some weeks in St Petersburg, he returned to London by steamship (vol. I, pp. 96-97). He was in the Crimea with the historian A.W. Kinglake in 1854. His Crimean journal, covering the period 8 September-6 November 1854, and a letter from Balaklava, are printed as appendices to vol. II, pp. 271-94.

G62) [Whatley, Thomas Denman and Layard, Austen Henry], *A handbook for travellers in Denmark, Norway, Sweden and Russia: being a guide to the principal routes in those countries with a minute description of Copenhagen, Stockholm, St Petersburg and Moscow.* London: John Murray, 1839. xi+276pp.

> An early example of Murray's famous *Handbooks for travellers* (begun in 1836) was edited by Whatley (1809-53?), Cambridge graduate and London barrister, signing the preface "T.D.W" and enlisting contributions from Layard, signed "H.L.", which included materials gathered on his visit to Scandinavia and Russia in 1838. Whatley seems to have been in Russia at the same period and they possibly travelled together.

G63) [Rigby, Elizabeth, Lady Eastlake], *A residence on the shores of the Baltic; described in a series of letters.* London: John Murray, 1841. 2 vols. [2nd edition with change of title: *Letters from the shores of the Baltic.* 1842.]

> Miss Rigby (1809-93), Lady Eastlake, after her marriage to Sir Charles Eastlake, president of the Royal Academy, set out to visit her married sister in Revel in October 1838 but first spent much time in the Russian capital (vol. I, pp. 31-116). She then went to Estonia (vol. I, pp. 117-293; II, pp. 1-182). She passed a further period in St Petersburg (vol. II, pp. 183-286), before returning to England in the spring of 1840.

G64) Eastlake, Elizabeth, *Journals and correspondence of Lady Eastlake.* Edited by her nephew, Charles Eastlake Smith. London: John Murray, 1895. 2 vols.

> In addition to the journey of 1838-40, described in her *Residence on the shores of the Baltic* (mentioned here vol. I, pp. 9-11), Elizabeth, now Lady Eastlake, paid two further visits to relatives in Estonia, in 1848 (vol. I, pp. 129-41) and in July-October 1878 (vol. II, pp. 257-63).

G65) Longworth, John Augustus, *A year among the Circassians.* London: Henry Colburn, 1840. 2 vols.

> Longworth (d. 1875), who for the last fifteen years of his life was the British consul-general to Serbia, recounts his adventures from April 1838, when

he sailed from Constantinople to Circassia and his return on 30 June 1839. Highly sympathetic to the tribesmen in their struggle against the Russians, he was (over-) optimistic about their future. During his stay he submitted reports to *The Times*, but unlike Bell (see G48), with whom he was much in contact, he wrote his account after his return.

G66) Custine, Astolphe-Louis-Léonard, de, *The empire of the Czar; or, observations on the social, political, and religious state and prospects of Russia, made during a journey through that empire*. Translated from the French. London: Longman, Brown, Green and Longmans, 1843. 3 vols.

The marquis de Custine (1790-1857) arrived at Cronstadt on 10 July 1839 and just over two months later, on 26 September, he left Russia with a great sense of relief. Apart from St Petersburg, he had seen briefly Moscow, Iaroslavl and Nizhnii Novgorod. *La Russie en 1839* (1843) was a damning critique of Nicholas I and his Russia. The English translation was republished several times during the Crimean War; retranslated as *Journey for our time* during the Cold War; republished in 1989 as *Empire of the czar: a journey through eternal Russia*, foreword by Daniel J. Boorstin, introduction by George F. Kennan.

G67) Cameron, George Poulett, *Personal adventures and excursions in Georgia, Circassia, and Russia.* London: Henry Colburn, 1845. 2 vols.

Lt-colonel Cameron (1805-82), who points out in his introduction that he had been in Russia at the same time as Custine and had returned to an England where Russophobia was the order of the day, presents his "some few light sketches of personal, or military narrative" in "the spirit of fair play". Beginning his return journey from Persia on 15 April 1838, he travelled to Tiflis and through the Caucasus to Vladikavkaz (vol. I). In vol. II, he describes his route via Kharkov and Tula to Moscow and St Petersburg, assessing the strengths of the Russian army and navy and mentioning in particular the hospitality he everywhere enjoyed.

G68) Jesse, William, *Notes of a half-pay in search of health; or, Russia, Circassia, and the Crimea, in 1839-40.* London: James Madden and Co., 1841. 2 vols.

Jesse (1809-71), a captain in the 75th Foot (Gordon Highlanders), was obliged by ill-health to become a half-pay officer in 1838. Recuperating in Italy, he met some Russian tourists who persuaded him to undertake travels in Russia. He arrived at Odessa from Constantinople on 21 June 1839 and remained there, with an excursion to the Crimea, until May of the following year before proceeding to Moscow and St Petersburg. He left the capital for Stockholm, "without regret, glad to escape from 'a land of tyrants and a den of slaves'". Most of vol. II is devoted to a series of essays on the Russian army, police, history, education, serfdom etc. (vol. I, pp. 53-298; II, pp. 1-308).

G69) Abbott, James, *Narrative of a journey from Heraut to Khiva, Moscow, and St Petersburgh, during the late Russian invasion of Khiva; with some account of the court of Khiva and the kingdom of Khaurism.* London: William H. Allen and Co., 1843. 2 vols. [2nd edition, with considerable additions, London: James Madden, 1856. 2 vols.]

Captain, later General Sir James (1807-96), of the Bengal artillery, was sent to Khiva in December 1839, to persuade the khan to release Russian prisoners. He proceeded to Russia to attempt, without success, mediation between Khiva and Russia. He reached Russian territory on the Caspian and travelled via Orenburg and Samara to Moscow and on to St Petersburg, where he was treated with suspicion. He left the Russian capital in August 1840 for London, where he had not been since 1823 (Russia, vol. II, pp. 67-227).

G70) Murchison, Roderick Impey, Verneuil, Edouard de, and Keyserling, Alexander von, *The geology of Russia in Europe and the Ural Mountains.* London: John Murray, 1845. 2 vols.

The fruit of three visits paid to Russia in the early 1840s by Murchison (1792-1871), F.R.S. and soon to be knighted and become long-time president of the Royal Geographical Society. He was accompanied on the first two visits of 1840 and 1841 by the French naturalist and paleontologist de Verneuil (1805-73), who was responsible for the second, French, volume, while von Keyserling (1815-91) was with him on the second and third (1843) journeys. Although an immense work of scientific exposition, many passages and footnotes make specific reference to places and events during Murchison's travels.

G71) Palmer, William, *Notes of a visit to the Russian Church in the years 1840, 1841.* Selected and arranged by John Henry, Cardinal Newman. London: Kegan Paul, Trench & Co., 1882. xxiv+572pp.

Rev. Palmer (1811-79), Fellow of Magdalen College, Oxford, arrived at Cronstadt on 19 August 1840, in order, as he explained in a letter he wrote to the tsar, "with the help and in the society of ecclesiastics, [to] learn the Russian language, and study the doctrines, discipline, and ritual of the Church" and so promote his vision of Anglo-Catholicism, "the reunion of the whole body in mutual love". His diaries record in great detail his meetings, conversations and visits in St Petersburg and Moscow with representatives of the church and government, with Princesses Meshcherskaia and Sofia Galitsyna, and many others, up to his departure from Cronstadt on 24 July 1841.

G72) Nolte, Vincent, *Fifty years in both hemispheres; or, reminiscences of a merchant's life.* Translated from the German. London: Trübner & Co., 1854. xii+473pp.

> Born in Italy to German parents, Nolte (b. 1779), a man of many parts and enterprises, was already an American citizen by the time he paid a short visit to Odessa in the autumn of 1840. He was engaged by a commercial house in Trieste to pursue debtors in the Russian town, where he made the acquaintance of Prince Mikhail Vorontsov (pp. 438-47).

G73) Cottrell, Charles Herbert, *Recollections of Siberia in the years 1840 and 1841.* London: John W. Parker, 1842. xii+410pp.

> Cottrell (d. 1860), Cambridge graduate, barrister and an accomplished scholar of German and Italian, begins his account in Moscow, whence he embarks in the late summer of 1840 for Siberia, travelling via Simbirsk and Orenburg. He journeyed as far as Irkutsk and Baikal before returning to St Petersburg some six months later in time to witness the marriage of the tsarevich to Princess Marie of Hesse on 28 April 1841. Very critical of existing English accounts (e.g. Dobell, Holman, Jesse), Cottrell offers his own considered views on the exile system, commerce, climate, resources, etc.

G74) *Stephens, W., *Travels through Russia and Poland in the Years 1840-41-42, illustrative of the manners and customs of the inhabitants of these countries.* London: Macrone, and Smith, Elder and Co, Cornhill, 1843. 226pp.

> A mysterious volume in that it reproduces line for line the account by Rayford Ramble (F80), published in 1836 by the same publisher, Macrone (who had died in 1837). It would seem to be an act of literary piracy. In addition it appears to be an extremely rare book: the only copy located is in the National Library of Ireland in Dublin and nothing is known about its alleged author.

G75) Köhl Johann Georg, *Russia: St. Petersburg, Moscow, Kharkoff, Riga, Odessa, the German provinces on the Baltic, the steppes, the Crimea, and the interior of the Empire.* London: Chapman and Hall, 1842. iv+530pp.

On the basis of his extensive travels through Russia in 1836-38, Köhl (1808-78) published in 1841 no less than nine volumes devoted to St Petersburg and various regions. This is a skilful condensation with particular emphasis on the capital (pp. 1-211).

G76) Köhl, Johann Georg, *Russia and the Russians, in 1842*. London: Henry Colburn, 1842-43. 2 vols.

A different translation, appearing in the same year, of Köhl's work on St Petersburg: vol. I is specifically subtitled 'Petersburg', while vol. II, without subtitle, is in fact a continuation of the same. It is in many ways an updating (and more reliable) of Granville's 1828 guide to the capital and the publishers use many of the same illustrations.

G77) Köhl, Johann Georg, *Panorama of St Petersburg*. London: Sims and Macintyre McIntyre, 1852. 224pp.

Yet another translation, but appearing under Kohl's original title and issued as vol. II in Sims and McIntyre's 'Bookcase' series.

G78) Todd, Charles Stewart, *Memoir of Col. Chas. S. Todd*. By G.W. Griffin. Philadelphia: Claxton, Remsen & Haffelfinger, 1873. 174pp.

Col. Todd (1791-1871), lawyer and briefly U.S. secretary of state (1816), arrived in St Petersburg in the summer of 1841 to begin a four-year stint as minister to Russia. This fulsome biography nevertheless includes texts of an address and a letter as well as a lecture, entitled 'Russia, her resources, religion, literature, &c.', he delivered in Kentucky in 1849 (pp. 78-112).

G79) Motley, John Lothrop, *The correspondence of John Lothrop Mottley*. Edited by George William Curtis. London: John Murray, 1889. 2 vols.

Mottley (1813-77) arrived in St Petersburg on 17 November 1841 as secretary of legation to the American mission headed by Colonel Charles Todd (see G78) Letters to his wife and mother (pp. 72-99) and extracts from his diary (pp. 108-21). Left early February 1842.

G80) Simpson, George, *Narrative of a journey round the world, during the years 1841 and 1842*. London: Henry Colburn, 1847. 2 vols.

Sir George (1787-1860), governor-in-chief of the Hudson's Bay Company's territories in North America since 1821, sailed from Sitka in Russian Alaska for Okhotsk in early June 1842. He was to travel from Okhotsk across Russia via Iakutsk, Irkutsk, Ekaterinburg, Kazan, and Moscow to St Petersburg, a journey that took ninety-one days and covered some 7,000 miles (vol. II, pp. 215-469).

G81) Hommaire de Hell, Xavier, *Travels in the steppes of the Caspian Sea, the Crimea, the Caucasus, &c.* With additions from various sources. London: Chapman and Hall, 1847. viii+436pp.

> Although nominally written by Xavier (1812-48), "all the descriptive part of this book of travels" (Preface) was written by his wife, **Adèle** (1815?-83). Translated from the three-volume French original of 1843-45.

G82) Wagner, Moritz, *Travels in Persia, Georgia and Koordistan; with sketches of the Cossacks and the Caucasus.* From the German of Dr Moritz Wagner. London: Hurst and Blackett, 1856. 3 vols.

> A version of three books by the German explorer and naturalist (1813-87), who spent much of 1843 in the Caucasus and Trans-Caucasia: *Der Kaukasus und das Land der Kosaken* (1848); *Reise nach Kolchis* (1851); *Reise nach Persien und dem Lande dar Kurden* (1851). In Part I he describes his travels from Kerch to Tiflis in February-March and his research during August in the mountains. There is an interesting chapter on Prince Mikhail Vorontsov whom Wagner met in the Crimea (vol. I; vol. II, pp. 1-105). Part II is devoted to his travels in the Colchis area of southern Georgia in the later spring of 1843 (vol. II, pp. 106-265). The remainder of the work concerns Wagner's time in Persia and Kurdistan.

G83) Haxthausen-Abbenburg, August Franz Ludwig Maria, von, *The Russian empire: its people, institutions, and resources.* Translated by Robert Farie, Esq. London: Chapman and Hall, 1856. 2 vols.

> Translated and abridged with the author's approval from the German original, *Studien über die innern Zustände, das Volksleben; und die ländlichen Einrichtungen Russlands* (1847-52). Haxthausen (1792-1866), arriving in St Petersburg in the spring of 1843, embarked on extensive travels throughout Russia that took him, first, to Moscow and then north to Iaroslavl and Vologda, before he followed the Volga down to Kazan and Saratov. He travelled south to Ekaterinoslav and entered the Crimea from Kerch. From Odessa he travelled back via Kiev to Moscow, where he arrived in November. His travels (vol. I, pp. 1-432; II, pp. 1-182) are followed by essays on various social and economic subjects.

G84) Haxthausen-Abbenburg, August Franz Ludwig Maria, von, *Transcaucasia: sketches of the nations and races between the Black Sea and the Caspian.* [Translated from the German by J.E. Taylor.] London: Chapman and Hall, 1854. xxiii+448pp.

> From Kerch, Haxthausen had travelled into the southern countries of the Caucasus.

G85) Haxthausen-Abbenburg, August Franz Ludwig Maria, von, *The tribes of the Caucasus; with an account of Schamyl and the Murids.* [Translated from the German by J.E. Taylor.] London: Chapman and Hall, 1855. viii+130pp.

> Ethnological and historical work on the tribes of the Caucasus written by the influential German agricultural scientist and writer. The work was based on his journey to the Caucasus region in the late summer and early autumn of 1843 as part of a wider commission by Tsar Nicholas I to undertake a study of land tenure and peasant conditions in the Russian interior and was a supplementary volume to his larger study *The Russian Empire*. Though the details derive from his personal observations, Haxthausen does not refer to his actual journey or give any personal details. The latter chapters focus on the Murids and the Imam Schamyl.

G86) [McCoy, Rebecca], *The Englishwoman in Russia: impressions of the society and manners of the Russians at home.* By a lady, ten years resident in that country. London: John Murray, 1855. xv+350pp.

> McCoy (1818-63) arrived in August 1843 in Archangel, where she received her diploma to teach English as a domestic tutor in 1845. She moved to St Petersburg, leaving Russia in April 1854. Her book in which she described life in the Russian provinces as well as in St Petersburg and Moscow appeared in fact in October 1854, when it was warmly reviewed by Charles Dickens in *Household Words*.

G87) Whistler, Anna Mathilda, *The life of James McNeill Whistler.* By Elizabeth Robins Pennell and Joseph Pennell. London: William Heinemann, 1908. 2 vols.

> Mrs Whistler (née McNeill, d. 1881) was the wife of the American railway engineer Major George Washington Whistler (1800-49), who had gone to Russia in 1842 to work on the Petersburg-Moscow railway, and "mother" of the noted painter (1834-1903). In September 1843 she and her sons joined her husband in St Petersburg. The Pennells made limited (and often inaccurate) use of her detailed diaries of their life in Russia, mainly concerned with family matters. The young painter left Russia in 1848 and his mother in 1849, following her husband's death (vol. II, pp. 11-23).

G88) Harrison, Joseph, Jr., *The iron worker and King Solomon: with a memoir and an appendix.* Philadelphia: J.B. Lippincott & Co., 1868. 60pp.

> Harrison (1810-74), American inventor of a new locomotive, received a contract in 1843 to supply locomotives and rolling stock for the new Petersburg-Moscow railway that made him very rich. He also assisted in the construction of the Blagoveshchenskii bridge (the first) across the Neva. In

this curious compilation, dedicated to his wife, children and grandchildren, Harrison included verses by himself and others, as well as a memoir, seemingly not written by himself, but of interest "to all those who are so near to me as yourselves", which tells of his years in Russia (pp. 29-35).

G89) Nasmyth, James, *James Nasmyth engineer: an autobiography.* Edited by Samuel Smiles. London: John Murray, 1883. xviii+456pp.

> The Scottish engineer and inventor of the steam hammer Nasmyth (1808-90) recounts his visit to St Petersburg in 1843 to try for a contract to supply locomotives for the Petersburg-Moscow line. He failed but received orders for boilers and machine parts. Met several of his fellow countrymen in Russian service such as General Alexander Wilson and Frances Baird (pp. 288-95).

G90) [Henningsen, Charles Frederick], *Revelations of Russia; or, the Emperor Nicholas and his empire, in 1844.* By one who has seen and describes. London: Henry Colburn, 1844. 2 vols. [With title *Revelations of Russia in 1846*. By an English Resident. 3rd edition. Revised and corrected by the author, with additional notes, and brought down to the present time. London: Henry Colburn, 1846. 2 vols.]

> Of Henningsen no biographical details are known nor are the dates of the stay of the self-styled eye-witness and "English resident" in Russia. Offers a critique of Nicholas I's despotic rule in the spirit of Custine to whom he frequently refers. Discusses the Decembrist uprising.

G91) [Henningsen, Charles Frederick], *Eastern Europe and the Emperor Nicholas.* By the author of 'Revelations of Russia'; 'The white slave'. London: Thomas Cautley Newby, 1846. 3 vols.

> Continues his attacks on Russian despotism with much on the fate of Poland. Volume II is devoted to Polish and Finnish literature but with an interesting chapter on Russian literature (pp. 116-53) with particular emphasis on the life and work of Pushkin, for which he uses an account by the French traveller Marmier and the writings and translations of Thomas Shaw. Vol. III, which opens with the words "Russia is not a country commonly visited by tourists", looks at the tsar's Russian advisers, but also has interesting pages on the role of British ambassadors (pp. 1-148).

G92) Koch, Karl Heinrich Emil, *The Crimea and Odessa: journal of a tour, with an account of the climate and vegetation.* Translated [from the German] by Joanna B. Horner. John Murray, 1855. xii+323pp. [Also published as:

The Crimea; with a visit to Odessa; including a chapter on the climate, soil and vegetation of the Crimean south coast, and southern Russia. London: George Routledge, 1855.]

> The German botanist professor Koch (1809-79) travelled through the Caucasus and Crimea in the autumn of 1844. He approached the Crimea via Kerch and in the space of the next few weeks (September-October) systematically explored the peninsular, paying particular attention to the flora but also providing very detailed descriptions of, e.g., Bakhchisarai and Alupka, before proceeding to Kherson, Nikolaev, and Odessa (which he had first visited in 1838).

G93) Seymour, Henry Danby, *Russia on the Black Sea and Sea of Azof: being a narrative of travels in the Crimea and bordering provinces; with notices of the naval, military, and commercial resources of those countries.* London: John Murray, 1855. xxiv+362pp.

> Based partly on the travels to the Crimea and southern Russia in 1844 and 1846 by Seymour (1820-77), M.P. for Poole since 1850, and partly on the travel accounts, histories and geographies of others, this was yet another book published to meet the interest aroused by the Crimean War.

G94) Harrison, Robert, *Notes of a nine years' residence in Russia, from 1844 to 1853; with notices of the Tzars Nicholas I and Alexander II.* London: T. Cautley Newby, 1855. xii+310pp.

> The first part of the work is devoted to Harrison's stay in St Petersburg, his various (undated) travels to Moscow and Simbirsk (pp. 1-93); the second part is essentially a series of essays on such topics as the peasantry, clergy, landowners, and military (pp. 94-310).

G95) Kinglake, Alexander William, *A summer in Russia.* Reprinted from the *New Monthly Magazine.* London, 1846. 114pp.

> Kinglake (1809-91), celebrated author of *Eothen* (1844), spent several weeks in the Russian capital in the late summer of 1845, much of the time as guest of the imperial family. Appeared originally in *New Monthly Magazine and Humorist* (Summer 1846), pp. 273-85, 409-19, 26-39.

G96) Bourke, Richard Southwell, *St. Petersburg and Moscow: a visit to the court of the czar.* London: Henry Colburn, 1846. 2 vols.

> At the time of his visit to Russia in June-August 1845 styled Lord Naas and later 6th Earl of Mayo, Bourke (1822-67) offered as "his first attempt in letters" a plain and frankly dull description of "a galloping and steaming

tour of eleven weeks" that took him to Moscow and home via Revel and Finland.

G97) [Bourne, Charlotte], *Russian chit chat; or, sketches of a residence in Russia*. By a lady. Edited by her sister. London: Longman, Brown, Green and Longmans; Coventry: George G. Pegg, 1856. iv+255pp.

> Charlotte was a governess to a daughter of the Dolgorukii family between 1845 and 1848 at Krasnoe, their estate near Tula, and in Moscow. Her book is full of fascinating information, particularly about the contemporary Russian literary scene.

G98) Bloomfield, Georgiana, *Reminiscences of court and diplomatic life*. London: Kegan Paul, Trench & Co., 1883. 403pp.

> Lady Georgiana, née Liddell (1822-1905), married John Arthur Douglas, 2nd Baron Bloomfield (1802-79), in September 1845, a year after his appointment as British envoy extraordinary and minister plenipotentiary in St Petersburg. They remained in Russia until 1851 (pp. 82-199).

G99) Montefiore, Moses Haim, *Diaries of Sir Moses and Lady Montefiore, comprising their life and work as recorded in their diaries from 1812 to 1883. With the addresses and speeches of Sir Moses; his correspondence with ministers, ambassadors, and representatives of public bodies; personal narratives of his missions in the cause of humanity; firmans and edicts of eastern monarchs; his opinions on financial, political, and religious subjects, and anecdotes and incidents referring to men of his time, as related by himself*. Edited by L[ouis] Loewe. London: Griffith, Farran, Okeden, & Welsh, 1890. 2 vols.

> The renowned Jewish banker and philanthropist Sir Moses (1784-1885) in his capacity as president of the Board of Deputies of British Jews was first invited to Russia in 1842 by Count Uvarov, but it was only four years later, on 1 April 1846, that he, accompanied by his wife, his secretary Louis Loewe, and a large retinue, arrived in St Petersburg. He was received by the tsar on 9 April and presented him with a memorial, pleading the cause of the Russian Jews. He then visited several towns where the Russian Jews were concentrated on his way to Warsaw (vol. I, pp. 330-58). In 1872 he went again to Russia to see Alexander II (vol. II, pp. 247-54) (see I106).

G100) Berlioz, Louis-Hector, *Autobiography of Hector Berlioz member of the Institute of France, from 1803 to 1865: comprising his travels in Italy, Germany, Russia, and England*. Translated by Rachel Scott Russell Holmes and Eleanor Holmes. London: Macmillan & Co., 1884. 2 vols. [cf. *The memoirs of Hector*

Berlioz. Translated and edited by David Cairns. London: Gollancz, 1969. 636pp.]

> Berlioz (1803-69) left Paris on 14 February 1847 and, fourteen days later, having taken a sledge at the Russian border, arrived in St Petersburg. He gave two profitable concerts in the capital, then departed for three weeks in Moscow, where he saw nothing other than a performance of Glinka's *Life for the tsar*. On his return to St Petersburg he gave a performance of *Romeo and Juliet*, before leaving "after Lent" for Riga and an unexpected, if less profitable concert (vol. I, pp. 259-91).

G101) Burrows, Silas Enoch, *America and Russia: correspondence, 1818 to 1848.* Edited by Mrs E.S. Mathews and R. Earl Burrows. Hartford, Conn.: privately printed, 1863. 167pp.

> The Connecticut ship-owner and merchant Burrows (1794-1870) visited St Petersburg with his wife and son in June-July 1847, intending to establish a magnetic telegraph.

G102) Thompson, Edward Pett, *Life in Russia; or, the discipline of despotism.* London: Smith, Elder, & Co., 1848. xiv+344pp.

> Wine merchant and former mayor of Dover as well as author of the *Notebook of a naturalist* (1845), Thompson (1802-70) suggests several earlier visits to Russia prior to that in 1847, described in a series of letters and offered as a key to the little-known Russians, mediated through his authorities Custine and Schnitzler. He arrived by boat from Lübeck, spent most of his time in St Petersburg before travelling to Moscow, and leaving by Revel en route to Stockholm (pp. 1-310). Lithographs by the "railway" artist John Cooke Bourne (1814-96), who had been in Kiev in 1847 with the engineer Charles Vignoles (1793-1875), who had been commissioned to construct the road bridge over the Dnieper.

G103) Maxwell, John S., *The czar, his court and people: including a tour in Norway and Sweden.* London: Richard Bentley, 1848. xii+243pp.

> American tourist, after visiting Norway and Sweden, sails to Cronstadt in July 1847 and embarks on a tour that takes him from St Petersburg to Moscow, Vladimir, Nizhnii Novgorod and Kazan. He returns by the same route, before leaving in late November for Warsaw and Vienna. Against despotism but very sympathetic towards Nicholas I (a "remarkable personage"), and very attentive to American presence and expertise (e.g. the railway engineers) (pp. 47-211).

G104) Hill, Samuel Smith, *Travels in Siberia.* London: Longman, Brown, Green and Longmans, 1854. 2 vols.

> Hill and his companion, a Mr Marshall, left Moscow on 29 July 1847 and headed for Nizhnii Novgorod and Kazan before crossing the Urals into Siberia, visiting Ekaterinburg, Omsk, Tomsk, Irkutsk, Iakutsk and so to Okhotsk. They sailed from Okhotsk to Kamchatka and finally left Petropavlovsk by sea on 15 November 1848.

G105) Cobden, Richard, *The life of Richard Cobden.* By John Morley. London: Chapman and Hall, 1881. 2 vols.

> Cobden (1804-65), M.P. and the "Manchester manufacturer", wrote much about Russia both before and after his only visit. Coming from Germany, he crossed the Russian border on 13 August 1847. He visited St Petersburg, Nizhnii Novgorod and Moscow, before leaving from Cronstadt on 26 September. Only brief extracts from his diary, which is in the British Library, are included (vol. I, pp. 450-61).

G106) Atkinson, Thomas Witlam, *Oriental and western Siberia: a narrative of seven years' explorations and adventures in Siberia, Mongolia, the Kirghis steppes, Chinese Tartary, and part of central Asia.* London: Hurst and Blackett, 1858. viii+611pp.

> Architect and painter, Atkinson (1799-1861), F.R.G.S., left Petersburg in early 1847 on extensive travels which took him as far as Irkutsk and the Chinese border. He returned to the capital in December 1853.

G107) Atkinson, Thomas Witlam, *Travels in the regions of the upper and lower Amoor, and the Russian acquisitions on the confines of India and China; with adventures among the mountain Kirghis; and the Manjours, Manyargs, Toungouz, Touzemtz, Goldi, and Gelyaks: the hunting and pastoral tribes.* London: Hurst and Blackett, 1860. xiii+570pp.

> A continuation of his travels, although it is probable that he did not travel as extensively by the Amur as he alleged but "borrowed" his material from other sources. Like his earlier book, this was also lavishly illustrated with his own watercolours.

G108) Atkinson, Lucy, *Recollections of Tartar steppes and their inhabitants.* London: John Murray, 1863. xvi+351pp.

Not once in nearly 1200 pages did Atkinson mention that he had a wife, whom he married (bigamously) in Moscow in February 1848 and took (and soon their son) with him on his subsequent years of travel. Lucy Sherrard Finley (1817-93), previously a governess in St Petersburg for some eight years, published her far more appealing and truthful account after her husband's death. It includes meetings with Decembrists in Siberian exile.

G109) Ditson, George Leighton, *Circassia; or, a tour to the Caucasus.* London: T.C Newby; New York: Stringer & Townsend, 1850. 455pp.

Massachusetts lawyer (1812-94) on extensive world travels begins his journal from his departure from Genoa on 23 September 1847 for Odessa. He visits the Crimea and reaches Circassia (part I); he then travels to Tiflis and on to Vladikavkaz but returning via Tiflis to Constantinople in early February 1848. Makes much of his friendship with Prince Vorontsov (to whom he dedicates his book) and claims to be the first American to visit and describe the region.

G110) Hooper, William Hulme, *Ten months among the tents of the Tuski; with incidents of an Arctic boat expedition in search of Sir John Franklin, as far as the Mackenzie River, and Cape Bathurst.* London: John Murray, 1853. xv+417pp.

Hooper (1827-54), lieutenant in the Royal Navy, sailed from Plymouth on H.M.S. *Plover* on 30 January 1848 in search of the ill-fated Franklin expedition. They reached the Bering Straits and Aleutian Islands and had their first encounter with the Chukchi (Tchutski, or, as Hooper insists, the Tuski) on 15 October and departed towards Russian America in July 1849 (pp. 6-212).

G111) Pfeiffer, Ida Laura, *A woman's journey round the world from Vienna to Brazil, Chili, Tahiti, China, Hindostan, Persia, and Asia Minor.* An unabridged translation from the German. London: National Illustrated Library, 1851. xvi+338pp.

The travel account of this intrepid middle-aged Austrian lady, Mrs Pfeiffer (née Reyer) (1797-1858) proved extremely popular in Britain with numerous editions under various titles in the 1850s. She left Vienna on 1 May 1846 and entered Russian territory on 12 August 1848, travelling from Persia. She visited Armenia and Georgia before sailing to the Crimea. She left Odessa for Constantinople on 2 October (pp. 300-28).

G112) Vassar, John Guy, Jr., *Twenty years around the world.* New York: Rudd & Carleton, 1881. 598pp.

> Nephew of the founder of Vassar College and himself a noted philanthropist, Vassar (1811-88) was an obsessive traveller, who included Russia in his itineraries on two occasions. In September 1848 he arrived in St Petersburg via Scandinavia, went on to Moscow before leaving for Warsaw (pp. 179-89). Ten years later, in May-early July 1858, he paid a much longer, more interesting and exacting visit to south Russia, arriving in Odessa from Constantinople and then spending much time in the Crimea, visiting the battle sites. He travelled on to Tiflis and through the Caucasus to Piatigorsk, before arriving in Taganrog and taking the boat back to Odessa (pp. 498-525).

G113) [Smith, Mary Ann Pellew], *Six years' travels in Russia.* By an English Lady. London: Hurst and Blackett, 1859. 2 vols.

> The exact years of Mrs Smith's sojourn (as governess or companion?) in Russia, like so much else that is vaguely dated and situated or marked with initials only, would seem to be 1848-54, ending with the death of Nicholas I. Most of the first volume is devoted to life in St Petersburg, following her arrival at Cronstadt, then come Novgorod and Moscow and a long stay at the estate of Krasnoe selo (vol. II, pp. 124-276), before a return to the capital.

G114) Scott, Charles Henry, *The Baltic, Black Sea, and the Crimea: comprising travels in Russia, a voyage down the Volga to Astrachan, and a tour through Crim Tartary.* London: Richard Bentley, 1854. xii+346pp.

> Leaving Stockholm by boat on 2 July 1850 for "a long tour in the Russian dominions", Scott and his friend, a Mr Gordon, travel from Moscow to Nizhnii and then down the Volga to Kazan and Astrakhan, a route he surprisingly believed "had never before been accomplished in the same manner" (by boat!). After visiting the Crimea, they left Odessa for Constantinople on 22 October.

G115) Lyons, Amelia (attrib.), *At home with the gentry: a Victorian English lady's diary of Russian country life.* Edited by John McNair. Nottingham: Bramcote Press, 1998. xxii+131pp.

> The original manuscript, entitled *A Russian boyard's home in 1851* and convincingly attributed to Amelia Lyons (1820-98), a governess to a Russian gentry family on its estate in Tambov province from 1851, covers the period from her arrival in Russia in late 1849 to her departure in July 1854.

G116) Ireland, John Busteed, *Wall-Street to Cashmere: a journal of five years in Asia, Africa, and Europe; comprising visits, during 1851, 2, 3, 4, 5, 6, to the Danemora iron mines, the "Seven Churches", plains of Troy, Palmyra, Jerusalem, Petra, Seringpatam, Surat; with scenes of the recent mutinies (Benares, Agra, Cawnpore, Luchnow, Delhi, etc., etc.), Cashmere, the Khyber Pass to Afghanistan, Java, China, and Mauritius.* London: Sampson Low, Son & Co., 1859. 531pp.

> New York lawyer (1823-1913), after visiting the Great Exhibition in London, arrives in St Petersburg on 4 August 1851 and after nearly three weeks, journeys to Moscow. He then heads south, travelling via Tula, Kursk and Kharkov to reach Odessa. He takes the boat to Constantinople on 10 September. India was his true objective and he offers only "a very brief abstract" of adventures en route (pp. 29-55).

G117) Spencer, Edmund, *Turkey, Russia, the Black Sea, and Circassia.* London: George Routledge, 1854. xii+412pp.

> Some twenty years after his previous tour of the region (see G43, G44), Spencer, who in the interim had published *The prophet of the Caucasus* (1840), a three-decker novel pervaded with his pro-Circassian sentiments, was again by the Black Sea. It would seem that in 1851, he had travelled through Hungary and Moldavia on his way to Constantinople, but there is no real evidence, apart from an alleged meeting with the tsar at Alupka, that he went again to Russia. The pages devoted to the Crimea and Circassia would seem to be a re-jigging of material from his earlier travels updated with contemporary political commentary (pp. 211-404).

G118) Vitzhum von Eckstädt, Karl Friedrich, *St. Petersburg and London in the years 1852-1864: reminiscences of Count Charles Frederick Vitzthum von Eckstaedt, late Saxon minister to the court of St. James'.* Translated from the German by Edward Fairfax Taylor. Edited with preface by Henry Reeve. London: Longmans, Green & Co., 1887. 2 vols.

> Von Eckstädt (1819-95) arrived in St Petersburg on 4 June 1852 and remained for a year as *chargé d'affaires* to the Saxon legation (vol. I, pp. 1-51).

G119) Channing, Walter, *A physician's vacation; or, a summer in Europe.* Boston: Ticknor and Fields, 1856. 564pp.

> Boston's leading obstetrician (1786-1876) and Harvard's first professor of midwifery, Dr Channing (1786-1876) included Russia in his summer tour, sailing from Stettin to Cronstadt, where he arrived on 15 June 1852. He kept a very detailed journal of what he saw and whom he met, especially doctors. Visited Moscow and left St Petersburg for Denmark on 1 July (pp. 158-292).

G120) MacGavock, Randal William, *A Tennessean abroad; or, letters from Europe, Africa, and Asia.* New York: Redfield, 1854. 398pp.

> Harvard-trained lawyer (1826-63), who died fighting for the Confederate army, spent eighteen months abroad between May 1851 and September 1852. Towards the end of his tour, c.July 1852, he visited Russia, sailing from Stettin to St Petersburg and visiting Moscow, before sailing to Sweden (pp. 354-82). Much of his book was based on letters he sent home to the *Daily Nashville Union*.

G121) Carr, James, *Russia as it is at the present time; in a series of letters.* By James Carr, a working man, lately returned from the interior of that empire to England. 2nd edition, revised and corrected, London: Whittaker & Co., and Manchester: James Galt & Co., 1855. 74pp.

> The first and quickly exhausted edition was for local circulation in Blackburn (not seen), the hometown to which Carr returned after some years as overseer at an unspecified cotton mill a day's journey from Moscow. His observations on Russian customs, habits, religion and amusements in a series of twenty-seven (undated) letters, written by "a plain working-man […] to amuse or instruct the class to which he belongs", but distinguished by "Truth", are frequently far more entertaining and perceptive than those of his "betters".

G122) Oliphant, Laurence, *The Russian shores of the Black Sea in the autumn of 1852; with a voyage down the Volga, and a tour through the country of the Don Cossacks.* Edinburgh and London: William Blackwood and Sons, 1853. xiv+366pp.

> Arriving in St Petersburg in August 1852, Oliphant (1829-88) and his companion Oswald Smith were thwarted in their attempt to go fishing in the White Sea and resolved to head south. From Moscow they travelled to Nizhnii Novgorod and there took the steamer *Samson* down the Volga to Astrakhan. They then made their way by land to Taganrog and thence by boat to Kerch and on the Crimea and Odessa. An additional chapter with his later reflections on the eve of war was written for the revised 2nd, 3rd and 4th editions, all appearing in 1854.

G123) Oliphant, Laurence, *Episodes of a life of adventure or moss from a rolling stone.* Edinburgh and London: William Blackwood and Sons, 1887. vi+420pp.

> His various adventures and travels in Russia and the Crimea in 1852 and during the Crimean War in the Crimea and Circassia in 1855 are succinctly retold (pp. 40-43, 79-106).

G124) Oliphant, Laurence, *Memoir of the life of Laurence Oliphant, and of Alice Oliphant, his wife.* By Mrs Margaret Oliphant Wilson Oliphant. Edinburgh and London: William Blackwood & Sons, 1891. 2 vols.

> Oliphant's cousin in her dutiful memoir includes letters he wrote to his mother from Russia in 1852 (vol. I, pp. 80-99) and from his second visit to Circassia in 1855 (vol. I, pp. 162-86).

G125) Hill, Samuel Smith, *Travels on the shores of the Baltic; extended to Moscow.* London: Arthur Hall, Virtue & Co., 1854. 302pp.

> Hill (see G103) returned to Moscow for a second time in the summer of 1853 (Russia, pp. 117-286).

G126) Choules, John Overton, *The cruise of the steam yacht North Star: to England, Russia, Denmark, France, Spain, Italy, Malta, Turkey, Madeira, etc.* London: James Blackwood, 1854. xviii+330pp.

> Dr Choules (1801-56), a New England clergyman, joined the Vanderbilts on a four-month cruise on their newly built yacht that took them on 21 June 1853 to Cronstadt. They spent much time at Peterhof and did the sights of the capital before sailing off for Denmark on 29 June (pp. 94-130).

G127) Brooks, Charles William Shirley, *The Russians of the south.* London: Longman, Brown, Green and Longmans, 1854. 147pp.

> Brooks (1816-74), special correspondent of the *Morning Chronicle*, travelled to Odessa from Vienna via Moldavia in the summer of 1853. Following a detailed description of Odessa (pp. 18-34), the work is devoted to essays on agriculture and serfdom and ends with a chapter on Bessarabia.

G128) Yeardley, John, *Memoir and diary of John Yeardley, minister of the gospel.* Edited by Charles Tylor. London: A.W. Bennett, 1859. viii+456pp.

> Yorkshire-born Yeardley (1786-1858), who joined the Society of Friends in May 1806, undertook no less than eight journeys through Europe to spread the gospel, the visit to Russia being the seventh, fulfilling his long-held wish to visit the German colonists in south Russia. He and his companion William Rasche arrived in St Petersburg by steam-packet from Hull on 9 July 1853 and then travelled south via Moscow, Orel, Kursk and Kharkov to Ekaterinoslav. Over the next month they visited several villages of the colonists as well as of the Molokans, travelling into the Crimea. They finally left by boat for Constantinople from Odessa on 9 September (pp. 399-417).

G129) Charleton, Robert Mason, *Memoir of Robert Charleton, compiled mainly from his letters.* Edited by his sister-in-law, Anna F. Fox. London: Samuel Harris & Co., 1873. viii+302pp.

> Charleton (1809-72) was one of the three Friends entrusted by the body called "Meetings for sufferings" to present an address to Nicholas I on the impending war. They arrived in Riga on 28 January 1854, were received in St Petersburg by the tsar, and departed 14 February. Charleton's letters, pp. 64-82.

G130) Sturge, Joseph, *Memoirs of Joseph Sturge.* By Henry Richard. London: S.W. Partridge & A.W. Bennett, 1864. xix+622pp.

> Sturge (1793-1859) accompanied Charleton and Robert Pease (1807-81) to present the address to Nicholas, the text of which is on pp. 474-75. For Sturge's letters, and some of Charleton's, pp. 464-82.

G131) Charleton, Robert Mason, Pease, Henry, and Sturge, Joseph, *Sleigh ride to Russia: an account of the Quaker Mission to St Petersburg by Robert Charleton, Henry Pease and Joseph Sturge in 1854 to present an address to Czar Nicholas from Meeting for Sufferings to try to avert the outbreak of the Crimean War.* Edited by Griselda Fox. York: William Sessions, 1985. x+120pp.

> An account of the 1854 Quaker mission written by Charleton's great-great-niece. It includes full transcripts of their letters, the first from Russian soil being from Pease to his son following the mission's arrival in St Petersburg. The bulk of and the bulkiest letters come from Charleton and Pease. Their letters contain descriptions of a guided tour around the Hermitage, Russian and English émigré attitudes towards peace, the sights of the city, interaction with Russian officials and their meeting with the tsar on 10 February (pp. 39-87).

Fig. 42 *Charge of the Light Cavalry Brigade, 25th Oct. 1854, under Major General the Earl of Cardigan*, print by William Simpson (1 March 1855).

8. THE CRIMEAN WAR (28 March 1854- 27 April 1856), with entries relating to the mid-September 1854 landings listed alphabetically

See also G61, G122, G124

H1) Royer, Alfred, *The English prisoners in Russia: a personal narrative of the first lieutenant of H.M.S. Tiger; together with an account of his journey in Russia, and his interview with the Emperor Nicholas and the principal persons in the empire.* London: Chapman and Hall, 1854. xii+195pp.

> After taking part in the bombardment of Odessa, HMS *Tiger* ran aground on 12 May 1854 and Royer and other officers and crew were captured by the Russians. Royer's account, however, is highly sympathetic to his "captors" in Odessa and elsewhere during his journey through Ukraine to Moscow and, by rail, to St Petersburg, where he was received by the tsar at Peterhof and freed to return to England at the end of June 1854. More of a tourist's guide than a war journal, it was published in September 1854 and went into six editions by the end of the year.

H2) [Barker, William Burckhardt], *Odessa and its inhabitants*. By an English prisoner in Russia. London: Thomas Bosworth, 1855. xii+174pp.

> Barker, born in Taganrog to German parents who were naturalized British citizens, joined the Royal Navy in 1847 as a midshipman on H.M.S. *Tiger*, which sailed to the Crimea in 1854 and took part in the bombardment of Odessa. Barker was among those subsequently captured. His book is thereafter essentially a very sympathetic account of the few weeks he spent in "captivity", befriended by the Potocki family and enjoying the social life of Odessa. He also published under his own name *A short historical account of the Crimea, from the earliest ages and during the Russian occupation, compiled from the best authorities* (1855).

http://dx.doi.org/10.11647/OBP.0042.08

H3) Montagu, Victor Alexander, *A middy's recollections, 1853-60.* London: Adam and Charles Black, 1898. xii+206pp.

> Rear-Admiral Montagu (1841-1915) recalls his time as a midshipman during the 1850s, including service in the Crimean War. A first section describes his service with the Baltic Fleet in 1854, remaining in the Baltic Sea until October (pp. 26-32). He re-enters the war in early 1855, when he sailed to Balaklava. Though he largely remained at sea, he made excursions to the battle sites of Balaklava and Inkerman. He details his average day as a midshipman, his involvement in the capture of Kerch on 25 May 1855 and of the successful assault on Kinburn on 17 October 1855. He sailed for home in late October 1855 (pp. 39-76).

H4) Montagu, Victor Alexander, *Reminiscences of Admiral Montagu.* London: Edward Arnold, 1910. viii+311pp.

> Montagu offers briefer descriptions of his time as a midshipman during the Crimean War and his occasional trips to the mainland to observe scenes of recent fighting (pp. 25-27), as well as his recollections of Sir Edmund Lyons (pp. 57-63).

H5) Napier, Charles, Dundas, James, et al, *Russian war 1854-55, Baltic and Black Sea: official correspondence.* Edited by David Bonner-Smith and Alfred Charles Dewar. London: Publications of the Navy Record Society, 1943-45. 3 vols.

> An expertly edited collection that contains the Admiralty correspondence with Vice-Admirals Sir Charles Napier (1786-1860) and Sir James Dundas (1785-1862) and Rear-Admirals Sir Richard Dundas (1802-61) and Sir Edmund Lyons (1790-1858) throughout the Crimean War. Vol. I relates to the Royal Navy's campaigns in the Baltic and the Black Sea in 1854, vol. II, to the Baltic campaign in 1855, and vol. III, to the Black Sea campaign in 1855. The majority of letters were written from on board ship, although there is the occasional letter written when ashore on Russian territory.

H6) Napier, Charles, *The history of the Baltic campaign of 1854.* Edited by George Butler Earp. London: Richard Bentley, 1857. xlviii+622pp.

> Vice-Admiral Napier (1786-1860) was in command of the Baltic fleet until he was made a scapegoat for the failure of British strategy in the Baltic in the autumn of 1854 and removed from office in October. He never set foot on Russian soil until he paid a visit to Cronstadt in late July 1856 and left a description of the fortress (pp. 592-97).

H7) Sulivan, Bartholomew James, *Life and letters of the late Admiral Sir Bartholomew James Sulivan, K.C.B. 1810-1890.* Edited by Henry Norton Sulivan. Introduction by Admiral Sir G.H. Richards. London: John Murray, 1896. xxii+442pp.

> Sir Bartholomew (1810-1910), naval surveyor and hydrographer, was detailed to assist first Sir Charles Napier and then Sir Richard Dundas during the British campaign in the Baltic. Commanding the paddle steamer HMS *Lightning*, he conducted many invaluable surveys of the shallow waters around the islands, leading to successful actions against fortresses, before he returned to England in the autumn of 1855. Most of the letters were written while on board various vessels and describe the on-going naval campaigning as well as numerous visits he made to islands off the Estonian coast (pp. 118-374).

H8) Romaine, William Govett, *Romaine's Crimean War: the letters and journal of William Govett Romaine: Deputy Judge-Advocate to the Army of the East 1854-56.* Edited by Colin Robins. Stroud: Sutton Publishing Limited, 2005. xxvii+315pp.

> As deputy judge-advocate to the British army in the Crimea Romaine (1816-93) was the most senior civilian working at Raglan's HQ. His detailed letters (beginning on 21 February 1854) and journal (from 21 February 1855) range wide over military, legal, logistical, and social matters (until 23 March 1856). The first of two appendices includes the proceedings of the Court of Inquiry, held on 9 November 1854, into the maltreatment of Russian prisoners following the battle of Inkerman, with related correspondence (9 November 1854 to 21 June 1855). The second contains letters, dating 26 January-8 February 1855, between Romaine, appointed to oversee the project, and the engineers constructing the Balaklava railway.

H9) Heath, Leopold George *Letters from the Black Sea during the Crimean War, 1854-1855.* London: Richard Bentley & Son, 1897. xx+246pp.

> Forty-six letters, dating from 10 April 1854 to 14 September 1855, were sent by Admiral Sir Leopold (1817-1907), serving in the Black Sea, initially as captain of HMS *Niger*, and, after a period ashore at Balaklava (27 October-8 November 1854), as captain of HMS *Sanspareil*. Away from the Crimea between 3 February and 12 March 1855, he returned as agent of transports, before leaving for England in November.

H10) Stothert, Samuel Kelson, *From the fleet in the fifties, a history of the Crimean War with which is incorporated letters written in 1854-56 by the Reverend*

S. Kelson Stothert. By Mrs Tom Kelly. Preface by Rear Admiral [Armand Temple] Powlett. London: Hurst and Blackett Ltd, 1902. xxviii+460pp.

> Mrs Tom Kelly, the declared author of this work, built her diplomatic and military history of the Crimean War around the numerous detailed letters to family members from Rev. Dr Stothert (1827-97), chaplain to the Naval Brigade. Stothert was in Crimean waters between April 1854 and early January 1855, and between mid-April and early October 1855, much of the time on board HMS *Queen*. However, he also describes visits to Balaklava and the British camp, and then to Sevastopol in mid-September 1855.

H11) [Anon.], *Cronstat and the Russian fleet.* London: John W. Parker and Son, 1854. 20pp.

> Written by a British resident "for some time past" in Russia and reprinted from *Fraser's Magazine* for May 1854, the essay offers a detailed description of the approach from the Baltic to Cronstadt and of its fortifications and naval strength.

[Mid-September 1854 landings]

H12) Adye, John Miller, *A review of the Crimean War, to the winter of 1854-55.* London: Hurst and Blackett, 1860. x+203pp.

> In May 1854, on the outbreak of the Crimean War, General Sir John (1819-1900) went to Turkey as brigade major of artillery. He was promoted to brevet major on 22 September and became adjutant-general of artillery. He arrived in the Crimea on 14 September 1854 and was present with the headquarters staff at the Alma, Balaklava, and Inkerman, serving throughout the siege of Sevastopol, and remaining until June 1856.

H13) Adye, John Miller, *Recollections of a military life.* London: Smith, Elder & Co., 1895. x+382pp.

> Sir John merged his personal experiences of the Crimean campaign with a general account of military strategies, achievements and failures (pp. 15-120). Between 29 August and 9 September 1872 he was again in the Crimea, accompanied by Colonel Charles Gordon, to inspect the state of the British war cemeteries (pp. 273-83).

H14) Allan, William, *My early soldiering days including the Crimean campaign.* Edinburgh: The Edinburgh Press, 1897. xii+189pp. [See also William Allan,

*Crimean letters: from the 41*st *(The Welch) Regiment 1854-6*. Edited by W. Alister Williams. Wrexham: Bridge Books, 2011. 224pp.]

> As a young ensign in the 41st Foot, the Welch Regiment, Major-General Allan (1832-1918) served throughout the Crimean War. He was present at the Alma on 20 September 1854, at Inkerman on 5 November and the following year, in the failed assaults on the Malakov and Redan in June and September. Between early December 1855 and February 1856 Allan was back in England, but returned to the Crimea in early March 1856 to describe events following the Treaty of Paris (pp. 46-174). His letters to his parents were edited for publication by his wife Jane Husey Allan. In an 'Epilogue' she describes a two-week trip with her husband to the Crimea in May 1893 and their visiting many of the battle sites (pp. 184-89).

H15) Andrews, Mottram, *A series of views in Turkey and the Crimea; from the embarkation at Gallipoli to the fall of Sebastopol.* London: T. McLean, 1856. 37pp.

> Lieutenant-Colonel Andrews (d. 1895) of the 28th Regiment was present at the siege of Sevastopol in 1854-55. His on-the-spot drawings of the town and other places such as the harbour at Balaklava were the basis for the lithographs with accompanying descriptions for the folio volume soon produced for military and aristocratic subscribers.

H16) [Anon.], *Manna in the camp; or, selections from the letters of a medical officer to his wife, during the eastern campaign in 1854-55.* Dublin: George Herbert; London: Hamilton Adams and Co., James Nisbet and Co.; Edinburgh: W.P. Kennedy and Shepherd & Elliot, 1858. 167pp.

> An unidentified Irish doctor sailed with the 9th Regiment of Foot from Dublin in March 1854 for Malta and on to Scutari. He landed at Kalamita Bay on 14 September (pp. 111-42). He accompanied wounded to Scutari on 8 December and returned to camp before Sevastopol on 4 January 1855, fell ill, and was evacuated to Scutari in early February and returned to England at the end of March (pp. 148-52). The eighty letters to his wife are more religious than medical or military in content.

H17) B., H[arry], *Letters from the Crimea, during the years 1854 and 1855.* London: Emily Faithfull, 1863. vii+151pp.

> The letters sent to his parents by an anonymous soldier in the 2nd Rifle Brigade cover the period from 14 September 1854, the day of the landing, until 24 September 1855, shortly before his death during the second British

assault on the Redan in early September 1855. He fought at the Alma, Balaklava and in the failed assault on the Redan on 18 June 1855.

H18) Barnston, William, and Barnston, Roger, *Letters from the Crimea and India.* Edited by Michael Trevor-Barnston. Farndon: M. Trevor-Barnston, 1998. xviii+270pp.

> The Barnston brothers, William (1832-72) and Roger (1826-57), served in different regiments during the war: William in the 55th Regiment that landed in Evpatoriia Bay on 14 September 1854; Roger in the 90th Regiment, arriving at Balaklava on 6 December 1854. William's letters describing the Crimea run from 17 September 1854 until 14 November 1854. Wounded at Inkerman, he was then invalided to Scutari. He was back in the Crimea from 1 March until his departure for Malta on 5 May 1856 (pp. 1-10, 17-26). Roger's more extensive letters run from 6 December 1854 until his departure on 30 June 1856. Subsequent to his promotion to deputy assistant quartermaster general on 16 January 1855, his letters describe his surveying duties. Later letters reflect his passion for photography. From May 1856 onwards he was involved in organising the embarkation of the British army from the Crimea (pp. 33-170).

H19) Bell, George, *Rough notes by an old soldier, during fifty years' service.* London: Day & Son, Limited, 1867. 2 vols.

> Major-General Sir George (1794-1877) commanded (as a lieutenant-colonel) the 1st Battalion Royal Regiment in the Crimea from 14 September 1854 to 16 March 1855. He writes critically of the privations and difficulties of camp life due to lack of supplies and provisions during the biting winter of 1854-55 and includes the text of a letter he sent to the *Times*, written on 12 December 1854, describing the *real* condition of the camp and state of the British campaign in contrast to the deceptions he believed were fed to the British public (vol. II, pp. 173-263).

H20) Bostock, John Aston, *Letters from India and the Crimea: selected from the correspondence of the late Deputy Surgeon-General Bostock.* London: George Bell & Sons, 1896. xx+270pp.

> Bostock (1815-95), who later became the deputy surgeon-general and honorary surgeon to Queen Victoria, was attached to the Scots Guards during the Crimean War. Letters detailing his experience in the Crimea run from 27 September 1854 until he leaves for Malta to recuperate on 30 March 1855. While rarely alluding to his work as a surgeon, they describe, often angrily, the deteriorating condition of the army, the limited and

inadequate supplies, the severe weather conditions, and the spread of cholera with occasional notices on the recent events of the campaign (pp. 198-250).

H21) Burgoyne, John Fox, *Life and correspondence of Field Marshal Sir John Burgoyne, bart.* Edited by Lieutenant-Colonel the Hon. George Wrottesley. London: Richard Bentley and Son, 1873. 2 vols.

> A lengthy section relates to Sir John's (1782-1871) service in the Crimea as lieutenant general in the British army between 17 September 1854 and 20 March 1855. A principal strategist during the first months of the war, he was made a scapegoat for the initial limited progress of the siege of Sevastopol and recalled by Secretary of State for War, Lord Panmure on 24 February 1855. There is extensive discussion of strategic planning at key moments during the campaign, disputes between the British and French military staffs, descriptions of the conduct of the siege, and angry letters ridiculing the British press's charges of incompetence; the last items reveal his reaction to his recall (vol. II, pp. 85-279).

H22) [Calthorpe, Somerset John Gough], *Letters from head-quarters; or, the realities of the war in the Crimea.* By an officer on the staff. London: John Murray, 1856. 2 vols.

> Lt.-Col. Calthorpe, later 7th baron Calthorpe (1831-1912), edited and published anonymously letters he had sent to friends from the Crimea, where he served as aide-de-camp to his uncle, Lord Raglan, whose reputation he stoutly defended. The letters run from 18 September 1854 until 30 June 1855 when, following Raglan's death on 28 June, Calthorpe returned to Britain. In addition to the detailed account of military actions, Calthorpe mentions his participation in a decoy mission by ship to Yalta in late May 1855 and recalls a pleasure trip he had made to the southern Crimean coast in the summer of 1851.

H23) [Cardigan, James Thomas Brudenell, Earl of], *Eight months on active service; or, a diary of a general officer of cavalry in 1854.* London: William Clowes and Sons, [1855]. 122pp.

> Cardigan (1797-1868), commander of the Light Brigade, kept a diary during 1854 in which the most notable entry not surprisingly relates his leading of the first line of the charge at Balaklava on 25 October 1854. Ill in November-early December, he was invalided to Constantinople on 6 December 1854.

H24) Chodasiewicz, Robert Adolf, *A voice from within the walls of Sebastopol: a narrative of the campaign in the Crimea, and of the events of the siege.* By Captain R. Hodasevich. London: John Murray, 1856. xii+252pp.

> A captain in the Tarutin regiment of chasseurs, Chodasiewicz (1832-96) arrived in the Crimea on 13 September 1854 and served at Alma and Balaklava and during the siege of Sevastopol. On 5 February 1855, he and a fellow Pole, having heard of the possible formation of a Polish legion to fight against the Russians and "throwing off the yoke of tyranny", deserted to the English lines near Balaklava and spent the rest of the war helping with intelligence and maps (several of which form an appendix).

H25) [Cler, Jean Joseph Gustave], *Reminiscences of an officer of zouaves.* Translated from the French. New York: D. Appleton and Co., 1860. 317pp.

> Colonel Cler (1814-59) commanded the 2nd Regiment of zouaves during the Crimean War, from their landing on 14 September 1854 until after the battle of the Malakov on 23 February 1855, when he was promoted to general and took command of the 62nd and 73rd infantry regiments. The zouaves set sail for Algeria in June 1856 (pp. 165-317). The French original, *Souvenirs d'un officier du 2me regiment de zouaves* had appeared in Paris in 1859, the year Cler was killed at the battle of Magenta.

H26) Clifford, Henry, *Henry Clifford V.C.: his letters and sketches from the Crimea.* Edited by Cuthbert Fitzherbert. Introduction by General Sir Bernard Paget. London: Joseph, 1956. 288pp.

> A collection of the letters of Sir Henry (1826-83) to family members, his detailed journal, and some thirty-three sketches and battlefield maps he produced in the Crimea during the period 18 September 1854-18 April 1856. An officer in the 1st Battalion of the Rifle Brigade, promoted to captain of the Light Division in December 1854 and brevet-major in July 1855, he was awarded the Victoria Cross for his actions at Inkerman on 5 November 1854. His letters and journal, mainly from the British camp before Sevastopol, offer an often detailed commentary on the siege, camp-life, and his opinions on the army leadership.

H27) Colebrooke, Thomas Edward, *Journal of two visits to the Crimea: in the autumns of 1854 & 1855: with remarks on the campaign.* London: Privately printed by T. & W. Boone for Dobell, 1856. viii+208pp.

> Liberal MP and later Dean of Faculties at the University of Glasgow, Sir Thomas (1813-90) belonged to the category of interested observer. Between 14 September and 3 November 1854 he was on board HMS *Britannia*,

witnessing the British landing at Kalamita Bay, visiting British camps at Evpatoriia and at Balaklava, recording his impressions and conversations with military personnel. On a second trip from 26 August until late October 1855, he notes how Balaklava had changed and offers a commentary on the British army's conduct of the siege of Sevastopol. In a third and final section Colebrooke offers his "remarks on the campaign".

H28) Dallas, George Frederick, *Eyewitness in the Crimea: the Crimean War letters (1854-1856) of Lt. Col. George Frederick Dallas.* Edited by Michael Hargreave Mawson. London: Greenhill Books, 2001. 320pp.

Company commander of the 46th Regiment of Foot, "Fred" Dallas (1827-88) wrote 137 letters to family and friends from the Crimea from 16 September 1854 to 10 July 1855. He writes of the harsh realities of camp life, but also of the developing friendships in his regiment and offers more cheerful anecdotes about camp life. He also writes critically of British strategy and the failures of the army's military leadership (pp. 32-255).

H29) Duberly, Frances Isabella, *Journal kept during the Russian war: from the departure of the army from England in April 1854, to the fall of Sebastopol.* London: Longman, Brown, Green and Longmans, 1855. 349pp.

Wife of the regimental paymaster of the 8th Hussars, Mrs Duberly, née Locke (1829-1903) loved above all else horses. She rode here, there and everywhere, witnessing the charge of the Light Brigade and entering Sevastopol soon after its fall in September 1855. By the time she and Captain Duberly returned to London, her journal was already published.

H30) Evelyn, George Palmer, *A diary of the Crimea.* Edited, with a preface, by Cyril Falls. London: Gerald Duckworth & Co., 1954. 148pp.

Evelyn (1823-89), a militia officer, set off from London for Constantinople on 13 December 1853, before the outbreak of war. In September 1854 he became one of the British officers officially attached to the staff of the Turkish army and joined the allied forces proceeding to the Crimea. He left the Crimea on 5 January 1855.

H31) Ewart, John Alexander, *The story of a soldier's life; or, peace, war, and mutiny.* London: Sampson Low, Marston, Searle, & Rivington, 1881. 2 vols.

General Sir John (1821-1904) served with the 93rd Sutherland Highlanders during the Crimean War from 14 September 1854 to 23 June 1856. He was promoted to deputy assistant quartermaster general in late September 1854 and to regimental major in mid-January 1855. He offers not only detailed accounts of the battles in which his regiment was involved but also of various reconnaissance and surveying missions. Following the armistice he describes socializing with the Russians, race meetings, and excursions to such sights as the Inkerman caves and Bakhchisarai (vol. I, pp. 171-446).

H32) [Fannan, David], *A burglar's life story in Glasgow, Edinburgh, London, Crimea, &c.* Glasgow: David Bryce and Son, 1897. 150pp.

The sprightly told "confession" of an ultimately reformed Scottish burglar, who in order to avoid arrest enlisted in the 79th Highlanders and served throughout the Crimean campaign, taking part in all the battles from Alma to the fall of Sevastopol with the exception of Balaklava before returning to his family in Glasgow and resuming his old life (pp. 23-42).

H33) [Farquharson, Robert Stuart], *Reminiscences of Crimean campaigning and Russian imprisonment. By one of 'the six hundred'.* Edinburgh: privately printed by Thomas Allan, [1883]. 107pp. [Published as *Crimean campaigning and Russian imprisonment*. Dundee: W. and D.C. Thomson, 1889. iv+140pp.]

A private in the 4th Light Dragoons, Farquharson (b. 1831) arrived in the Crimea on 18 September 1854, took part in the battle of the Alma on 20 September and, memorably, was in the second line of the charge of the Light Brigade under Paget's command, when he was captured by Cossacks. He was initially maltreated but subsequently received better treatment from Russian officers. He describes his march into captivity at Voronezh, via Simferopol, Ekaterinoslav, Kharkov, his experiences of being billeted on local families, his relations with fellow prisoners, and the beating he received on reaching prison. In August 1855 he was sent to Odessa and returned eventually to Balaklava on 27 October 1855.

H34) Goodlake, Gerald Littlehales, *Sharpshooter in the Crimea: the letters of Captain Goodlake, VC.* Edited by Michael Springman. Barnsley: Pen & Sword Military, 2005. x+228pp.

A lieutenant in the Coldstream Guards, Goodlake (1832-90) commanded the Sharpshooters of the Guards Brigade in the Crimea between mid-October and November 1854. He had landed in the Crimea on 14 September 1854 and left on 16 Jun 1856 (his letters run from 6 November 1854 until the end of May 1856). He served in the trenches during the winter of 1854-55 before his appointment as deputy assistant quartermaster General of the 1st Division, based at Balaklava between March 1855 and June 1856. His letters detail the main battles of the campaign as well as living conditions and soldier grievances.

H35) [Gowing, Timothy], *A soldier's experience: things not generally known, showing the price of war in blood and treasure. The Christian heroes–four bright examples: Sir Henry Havelock... Major Charles Henry Malan... Captain Hedley [Shafto Johnstone] Vicars... and Colonel John Blackader... By one of the Royal Fusiliers.* Colchester: Benham & Co., 1883. vi+274pp. [See also *A soldier's experience; or, a voice from the ranks; showing the cost of war, in blood and treasure: a personal narrative of the Crimean campaign, from the standpoint of the ranks; the Indian mutiny, and some of its atrocities; the Afghan campaign of 1865; also sketches of the career of some of England's commanders ...together with some things not generally known.* Nottingham: printed for the author by Thomas Forman & Sons, 1885. 494pp.]

> Gowing (1834-1908) served throughout the Crimean campaign with the Royal Fusiliers and was promoted to sergeant (during the Indian Mutiny, to colour-sergeant). Letters from the Crimea to his parents were written "under difficulty in a bleak tent or hut with the thermometer far below freezing point, with wet rags frozen on my back" and describe his participation at the Alma, Inkerman and many other battles (pp. 23-54, 60-124).

H36) Graham, Gerald, *Life, letters, and diaries of Lieut.-General Sir Gerald Graham, V.C., G.C.B., R.E. with portraits, plans, and his principal despatches.* By Robert Hamilton Vetch. Edinburgh and London: William Blackwood and Sons, 1901. xxiv+492pp.

> Lt-General Sir Gerald (1831-99) served as a 2nd lieutenant in the Royal Engineers and then in the 11th Company of the Royal Sappers and Miners in the Crimea. He sent numerous letters to his family over the period 17 September 1854 to13 July 1856 that offer personal, opinionated and often touching descriptions of his service on both the left and right flanks during the British siege of Sevastopol (pp. 24-134).

H37) Guys, Constantin, *Crimean war drawings 1854-1856.* Edited and introduced by Karen W. Smith. Cleveland, Ohio: Cleveland Museum of Art, 1978. 84pp.

> The French artist Guys (1802-82) was sent by *The Illustrated London News* as their roving military artist to follow the British army from its departure for Turkey and on to the Crimea. Fifty of his water-colours and sketches were exhibited at Cleveland and reproduced in the catalogue, together with the often detailed inscriptions that accompanied them. Most memorable is his eye-witness drawing of the charge of the Light Brigade (no. 20), but he

captures the routines of camp life, military reviews and ceremonies and the occasional "excursions" of British officers.

H38) Hall, John, *The life and letters of Sir John Hall M.D., K.C.B., F.R.C.S.* By Siddha Mohana Mitra. Introduction by Rear-Admiral Sir R. Massie. London: Longmans, Green, and Co., 1911. xxvi+560pp.

> Sir John (1795-1866) was the principal medical officer of the Medical Department in the Crimea and the inspector-general of hospitals from 14 September 1854 to 3 July 1856. Hall's Indian biographer transcribes extracts from his letters and memoranda that include letters written to the *Times,* to various medical professions both within and outside the British government, and many written to and about Florence Nightingale (pp. 319-465).

H39) Hamley, Edward Bruce, *The story of the campaign of Sebastopol, written in the camp.* Edinburgh and London: William Blackwood & Sons, 1855. xv+339pp.

> General Sir Edward (1824-93) who illustrated his account with his own drawings, was aide-de-camp to Sir Richard Dacres, commanding the artillery, throughout the Crimean campaign. His account had previously appeared as contributions to *Blackwood's magazine.*

H40) Hamley, Edward Bruce, *The war in the Crimea.* London: Seeley and Co., 1891. vii+312pp.

> General Hamley's systematic history of the war drew on his own experiences as well as on many sources published in the thirty-five years since the end of hostilities. In the interim he had become the first professor of military history at the new staff college at Sandhurst, the author of several novels, and was currently an M.P.

H41) Higginson, George Wentworth Alexander, *Seventy-one years of a guardsman's life.* London: Smith, Elder & Co., 1916. xii+403pp.

> The memoirs of General Sir George (1826-1927) include an extensive account of his involvement in the Crimean War between 14 September 1854 and early June 1856, when he was adjutant of the 3rd Battalion of the Grenadier Guards and, latterly, brigade-major. He was present, as participant or observer, at the major battles of the campaign. His account fuses later narrative comment with extracts from contemporary letters and journals (pp. 143-320). In 1884, when he was major-general of the Grenadier Guards, he was invited by Alexander III to attend a review of

the Russian army. His diary entries, dating from 11 August to 8 September, refer to dinners with Russia's military leadership and to trips to Cronstadt, Ropsha, Moscow and Krasnoe selo (pp. 354-72).

H42) Hodge, Edward Cooper, *'Little Hodge', being extracts from the diaries and letters of Colonel Edward Cooper Hodge written during the Crimean War, 1854-1856.* Edited by the Marquess of Anglesey. London: Leo Cooper, 1971. xiv+166pp.

> Colonel Hodge (1810-94) commanded the 4th Dragoon Guards throughout the Crimean War and took part in the charge of the Heavy Brigade at Balaklava. His diary, which he kept assiduously, is supplemented by letters he wrote to his mother and also by letters from Hodge's second-in-command, Major William Forrest.

H43) Home, Anthony Dickson, *Service memories.* Edited by Charles H. Melville. London: Edward Arnold, 1912. viii+340pp.

> The Scottish surgeon general Sir Anthony Home (1826-1914) began his Crimean service as a humble assistant-surgeon with the 8th Light Dragoons on 15 August 1854 and was promoted to surgeon with the 13th Light Dragoons on 9 February 1855. He somewhat sketchily describes his medical duties and life at British headquarters and occasional participation in the fighting. After recovering from illness in Scutari in early November-late December 1854, he returned to Balaklava, and took part in the expedition to Evpatoriia in September 1855. He left finally for Scutari in December 1855 (pp. 19-82).

H44) Image, John George, *The Crimean journal of Lieutenant Image.* Edited by David Ross. Winnipeg: Manitoba Museum of Man and Nature, 1971. 44pp.

> Image (1835-70), an officer in the 21st Regiment, Royal North British Fusiliers landed on 14 September 1854, fought at the Alma and Inkerman and was wounded during the assault on the Redan on 18 June 1855. He was invalided out on 10 July 1855.

H45) Jocelyn, John Strange, *With the Guards we shall go: a guardsman's letters in the Crimea, 1854-55.* Edited by Mabell, Countess of Airlie. London: Hodder and Stoughton, 1933. 322pp.

> Captain, later lieutenant-colonel, in the 1st Battalion of the Coldstream Guards, Jocelyn (1823-97), later 5th Earl of Roden, arrived at Evpatoriia on

14 September 1854. His letters to his father, edited by his great-niece, cover the period from 16 September 1854 to 30 June 1855, during which time he spent a short period between late February and 27 April 1855 recuperating in Constantinople, before returning to Balaklava. Many of his letters describe in a moving and angry fashion the terrible conditions at Balaklava, the illness among the British soldiers, the shortages of equipment and provisions shortages, and the responsibility of the government for the situation. His last letters describe the failed assault on the Malakov on 18 June and the heavy losses incurred.

H46) Jowett, William, *Diary of Sergeant William Jowett, of the Seventh Fusiliers, written during the Crimean War.* London: W. Kent and Co., 1856. 80pp.

> Sergeant Jowett (1830-56) died from wounds received during the second assault on the Redan on 8 September 1856. He had landed on 14 September 1854 and was present at the battles of the Alma, Balaklava, Inkerman and the two British assaults on the Redan. In his diary, the last entry of which dates from 6 September 1856, he writes movingly of the sufferings of soldiers in the trenches during the winter of 1854-55. A final section of the work contains letters Jowett sent to his family describing the complications with his wound that were to lead to his death.

H47) Lawson, George, *Surgeon in the Crimea: the experiences of George Lawson recorded in letters to his family 1854-1855.* Edited, enlarged and explained by Victor Bonham-Carter assisted by Monica Lawson. London: Constable, 1968. xiv+209pp.

> Dr Lawson (1831-1903) joined up at the outbreak of war in March 1854 as a young assistant-surgeon and served until June 1855, when he was invalided out. He was at the landing at Kalamita Bay on 14 September, at Balaklava, and the beginning of the siege of Sevastopol throughout the first severe winter, but he fell ill in May 1855 with typhus (pp. 69-178).

H48) Loyd-Lindsay, Robert James, *Lord Wantage. V.C., K.C.B.: a memoir.* By his wife [Harriet Sarah Loyd-Lindsay]. London: Smith, Elder & Co., 1907. xii+474pp.

> Loyd-Lindsay, later 1st Baron Wantage (1832-1901), Conservative MP, and a founder of the Red Cross, received the Victoria Cross for his actions at the Alma, when he was a captain in the Scots Fusilier Guards. The memoir includes excerpts from his journals and letters to family and friends from the Crimea from 14 September 1854 until 11 June 1856 (pp. 24-134). In the autumn of 1888 he re-visited the Crimea with his wife (pp. 319-20).

H49) Lysons, Daniel, *The Crimean War from first to last.* London: John Murray, 1895. x+298pp.

> Sir Daniel (1816-98) was a major in the 23rd Royal Welch Fusiliers, part of the Light Division, and purportedly the first British soldier to land on Crimean soil on 14 September 1854. He was subsequently promoted to the 2nd Division as assistant adjutant general and then, following his promotion to lieutenant-colonel, moved back to the Light Division. His letters from the Crimea begin on 16 September 1854 and end on 19 May 1856, a month before his departure on 14 June. He describes his participation in various battles and engagements, including the second British assault on the Redan on 8 September 1855, when he was wounded. His letters, following the armistice and peace, describe the social events and fraternizing with the Russians, as well as the beauties of the Crimean countryside.

H50) McMillan, William, *The diary of Sgt. W. McMillan.* Edited by Keith Hingle. London: The Coldstream Guards, [1990]. 36pp.

> McMillan (1825-93) served as a corporal, then lance sergeant, in the 1st Battalion Coldstream Guards, landing at Kalamita Bay, north of Sevastopol, on 14 September 1854. The diary runs virtually without a break until 6 December 1854, then resumes on 11 April 1855, but less consistently and much shorter, until 25 August. Alongside day-to-day activities, McMillan writes of his participation in the battles of the Alma and Inkerman, and the following year, in the assault on the Malakov on 18 June 1855.

H51) Mends, William Roberts, *Life of Admiral Sir Wm. R. Mends, late Director of Transports.* By his son Bowen Stilon Mends. London: John Murray, 1899. xvi+380pp.

> Extensive extracts from the letters of Admiral Mends (1812-97), who was both flag captain and chief of staff of the Mediterranean Fleet during the Crimean War and was personally responsible for the landing of the British forces on 14 September 1854. His letters start from that date and run until his departure from the Black Sea on 9 December 1855. Most were written while Mends was anchored at sea, but occasionally he writes of trips ashore to visit areas of recent fighting. (pp. 131-304).

H52) Mitchell, Albert, *Recollections of one of the Light Brigade.* Canterbury: N. Ginder, [1885]. 130pp.

> A sergeant in the 13th Light Dragoons, Mitchell (1830/31-97), who was in the first line during the charge of the Light Brigade, movingly describes

the attack, the desperate retreat and the trauma of the aftermath. He had landed on 14 September and was to leave in November 1855 (pp. 39-130).

H53) Munro, William, *Reminiscences of military service with the 93rd Sutherland Highlanders*. London: Hurst and Blackett, 1883. xii+330pp.

Dr Munro (1823-96), appointed surgeon to the 93rd Sutherland Highlanders in 1854 prior to his departure with the regiment to the Crimea, based his memoir on journals and letters written during the period 14 September 1854 to June 1856. He describes in particular detail the battle of Balaklava during which the 93rd, despite having a line only two men deep (the 'Thin Red Line'), withstood a Russian cavalry charge. Interesting also for Munro's tourism (to Simferopol, Alupka), following the February armistice (pp. 7-110).

H54) Nolan, Louis Edward, *Expedition to the Crimea*. Edited by Alan J. Guy and Alastair Massie. London: National Army Museum, 2010. x+104pp.

Notorious for his role in the events that led to the disastrous charge of the Light Brigade on 25 October 1854, Captain Nolan (1818-54) of the 5th Hussars and ADC to General Airey, was the first man to be killed. His journal runs from 14 September until 12 October 1854 and contains detailed military notes on the disembarking of the British army, patrolling duties along the coast at Evpatoriia, the battle of the Alma and its aftermath, and the incident at Mackenzie's Farm (pp. 42-83).

H55) O'Flaherty, Philip, *The young soldier*. Edinburgh: John Shepherd; Belfast: Shepherd & Aitchison, [1854]. 31pp.

The first of two small collections of letters (see also H91) written from the Crimea by the Protestant Irishman O'Flaherty, a private, later corporal, in the 7th Royal Fusiliers, covers the first months of the invasion, the battle of the Alma and the early stages of the siege of Sevastopol (pp. 24-28). An anonymous author provides a sketch of O'Flaherty's upbringing and religious beliefs.

H56) Paget, George Augustus Frederick, *The light cavalry brigade in the Crimea: extracts from the letters and journal of the late Gen. Lord George Paget, K.C.B., during the Crimean War*. London: John Murray, 1881. xii+345pp.

General Lord Paget (1818-80), who went to the Crimea as brevet-colonel in command of the 4th Light Dragoons, led the third line in the charge of the Light Brigade and was among the last to leave the field. He had arrived in the Crimea on 16 September 1854, but left on 11 November on the death of his father; he returned on 23 February 1855 and was joined for some months by his wife, before he finally departed on 9 December 1855. Extracts from his journal (pp. 15-151) are followed by later written chapters defending his actions in various battles, as well as other appendices, most interestingly, the comments on Paget's account by **Lieutenant-Colonel John Douglas** (1810-71), who led the 11th Hussars during the charge of the Light Brigade.

H57) Peard, George Shuldham, *Narrative of a campaign in the Crimea; including an account of the battles of Alma, Balaklava, and Inkermann.* London: Richard Bentley, 1855. viii+248pp.

Peard (1829-1918), a lieutenant in the 20th Regiment of Foot, who had arrived at Evpatoriia on 14 September, was one of the first serving soldiers to publish an account of the war, after being invalided to Scutari on 12 December 1854 and returning soon afterwards to England (pp. 35-227).

H58) Pennington, William Henry, *Left of six hundred.* London: privately printed, 1887. 17pp.

Private Pennington (1883-1923) of the 11th Hussars arrived in the Crimea on 14 September 1854 and was to take part in the charge of the Light Brigade. He was wounded, hospitalized at Scutari, and invalided to England in 1856. His account was reprinted in Mrs Tom Kelly, *From the fleet in the fifties* (1902), pp. 117-25, 128-38 (see also H10).

H59) Percy, Henry Hugh Manvers, *A bearskin's Crimea: Colonel Henry Percy VC and his brother officers.* By Algernon Percy. Barnsley: Leo Cooper, 2005. xxxiv+238pp.

Lieutenant-General Lord Henry Percy (1817-77), while serving as a captain in the Grenadier Guards, was awarded the Victoria Cross for his bravery at the battle of Inkerman and soon afterwards promoted to lieutenant-colonel. His letters and papers, covering the period 21 September 1854 to 13 July 1855, provided the basic material for this wider study of the Grenadier Guards' role in the Crimea written by a distant relative (pp. 20-173).

H60) Powell, Harry, *Recollections of a young soldier during the Crimean War.* Oxford: privately printed by Upstone and Doe, 1876. 30pp.

Powell (1830-86) was a trumpeter in the 13th Light Dragoons and one of the "six hundred" of the Light Brigade. He landed at Evpatoriia in mid-September 1854 and describes, in brief and unclear detail, his experiences, most importantly, of the charge and its aftermath. He left the Crimea after the fall of Sevastopol (pp. 12-29).

H61) Rawlins, James, *One hussar.* Edited by Ken Horton. Stourton: privately printed, [1985?]. vi+78pp.

> A trooper in the 8th Hussars, Rawlins (1832-1907) landed at Evpatoriia Bay on 15 September 1854, when entries in his diary begin. He served as an officers' servant attached to the British HQ in the camp before Sevastopol. He was involved in a number of the major military events, but the entries do not describe these in much detail: rather, they describe the camp life of an average soldier. He departed on 25 April 1856 (pp. 11-22)

H62) Robinson, Frederick, *Diary of the Crimean War.* London: Richard Bentley, 1856. xiv+443pp.

> An assistant surgeon with the Scots Fusilier Guards in the 1st Division and landing at Kalamita Bay on 14 September 1854, Robinson (1826-1901) submitted his diaries for publication in 1855 while still on active service before Sevastopol. In April 1855 he was called to British Headquarters at Balaklava, where he recorded life in the camp and in the town. Following the fall of Sevastopol, Robinson visited the town and the Redan fortress and journeyed through the Crimean countryside (pp. 149-443).

H63) Russell, William Howard, *The war: from the landing at Gallipoli to the death of Lord Raglan.* London: George Routledge & Co., 1855. ii+507pp. [Continued as: *The war: from the death of Lord Raglan to the evacuation of the Crimea; with additions and corrections.* London: George Routledge & Co., 1856. 486pp.; revised, with numerous emendations and additions, under the title: *The British expedition to the Crimea,* 1858. 629pp.]

> The collected letters to *The Times* by its famous correspondent (1820-1907), covering the period from 6 March 1854 to 29 June 1856. Russell left with the troops from Southampton, witnessed the unopposed landing at Evpatoriia on 14 September 1854, and reported all subsequent events until the proclamation of peace, bringing home to the British public the horrors of the war, the military mismanagement and the heroism of the soldiers. Russell was knighted in 1895 for services to journalism and is described on his monument in St Paul's as "the first and greatest of war correspondents".

H64) Sayer, Frederick, and Jervis, Thomas Best, *Despatches and papers relative to the campaign in Turkey, Asia Minor, and the Crimea, during the war with Russia in 1854, 1855, 1856, illustrated with original plans and drawings, executed* *at the topographical branch of the War Department, under the superintendence of Colonel Jervis, Director.* London: Harrison, 1857. v+447pp.

> Sayer (1832-1868), deputy-assistant lieutenant-general of the Horse Guards and a favourite at the British Court, fought in the Crimea, was wounded at the Alma in September 1854 and, after a period of recuperation at Scutari, was sent home. This is not a personal account, however, but a collection of official despatches and army papers and orders, covering the period from September 1854 to July 1856 and written by both the British commanders in chief (Raglan, Simpson, Codrington) and divisional commanders and others. Col. Jervis is responsible for the statistics and detailed maps.

H65) Smith, George Loy, *A Victorian RSM: from India to the Crimea.* Tunbridge Wells: D.J. Costello, 1987. 245pp.

> Regimental Sergeant Major Smith (1817-88) of the 11th Hussars was in the Crimea from 16 September 1854 until 25 January 1856 (apart from a supplies-securing mission to Constantinople between mid-November 1854 and January 1855). He offers particular detailed descriptions of the hussars' role at the Alma, Balaklava and Inkerman, and his involvement in the charge of the Light Brigade (pp. 96-211).

H66) Steevens, Nathaniel, *The Crimea campaign with 'the Connaught Rangers' 1854-55-56.* London: Griffith and Farran, 1878. xviii+359pp.

> Lt.-Colonel Steevens (d. 1894), arriving as a young lieutenant with his regiment, the 88th Regiment of Foot, the Connaught Rangers, on 14 September 1854 and soon promoted to captain and then major, was an engineer who became particularly involved with Turkish troops employed on entrenchment works at Sevastopol (he was awarded the Turkish Crimean War medal in 1855). He provides a detailed narrative of his experiences, based primarily on his letters and journals, written between the September landing and his eventual departure on 9 June 1856. Like many other officers, he took the opportunity, following the peace in late March 1856, to explore the sights of the Crimea (pp. 76-333).

H67) Stephenson, Frederick Charles Arthur, *At home and on the battlefield: letters from the Crimea, China and Egypt, 1854-88.* Edited by Mrs Frank Pownall. London: John Murray, 1915. xviii+383pp.

> Lt.-Colonel, later Sir Frederick, Stephenson (1821-1911) served throughout the Crimean War with the Scots Guards as military secretary to General Sir James Simpson. His letters to his family from the Crimea run from 14 September 1854 until 18 April 1856, except for a period away due to illness

between 7 August and 16 November 1855. He was present at the Alma and Inkerman and throughout the siege of Sevastopol. In his later letters, following the armistice, he describes the social pursuits and intercourse with Russian troops (pp. 63-162).

H68) [Sterling, Anthony Coningham], *Letters from the army in the Crimea, written during the years 1854, 1855, & 1856, by a staff officer who was there.* London: privately printed by Robson, Levey and Franklyn, 1857. xlviii+496pp. [Later edition with Sterling as author: *The story of the Highland Brigade in the Crimea, founded on letters written during the years 1854, 1855, and 1856.* London: Remington & Co., J. Macqueen, 1895. xxii+393pp.]

> The Crimean letters of Sir Anthony (1805-71), who was a brigade major and then an assistant adjutant general to Sir Colin Campbell and the Highland Division, run from 18 September 1854 to 29 November 1855 and then from 17 February to 8 May 1856. The letters, which describe the main battles, are supplemented by contextualising information provided by Sterling in 1857 and with copies of official reports. Feeling dishonoured at having had a junior officer promoted over him, Sterling left the Crimea in November (pp. 81-463). He returned in mid-February 1856 to the camp at Kamara and took part in negotiations with the Russians, before leaving in May 1856 (pp. 467-96).

H69) Walker, Charles Pyndar Beauchamp, *Days of a soldier's life, being letters written during active service in the Crimean, Chinese, Austro-Prussian (66) and Franco-Prussian (70-71) wars.* London: Chapman and Hall, 1894. 411pp.

> General Sir Charles (1817-94), later long-serving military attaché in Berlin, was in the Crimea from 14 September to 29 November 1854. As aide-de-camp to Lord Lucan and officer in the 7th Dragoon Guards, he was present at the Alma, Balaklava and Inkerman and left a brief eye-witness account of the charge of the Light Brigade (pp. 101-53).

H70) Wellesley, Edward, *Letters of a Victorian army officer Edward Wellesley: major, 73rd Regiment of Foot 1840-1854.* Stroud: Alan Sutton for the Army Records Society, 1995. xiv+224pp.

> The collected letters of Major Edward Wellesley (1823-54) of the 73rd Foot Regiment, who served briefly in the Crimea as assistant quartermaster-general in Lord Raglan's staff, but died of cholera on 20 September 1854. A section entitled 'To the Crimea' contains his letters from 17 March 1854 to 14 September 1854, just prior to his landing at Evpatoriia, but there is

no material written by Wellesley from the war itself, though a list of his personal possessions at the time of his death is of note (pp. 192-95).

H71) Whelan, James, *A veteran's memoirs: being episodes of his life and experiences.* Manchester: W. Woodford, 1907. 55pp.

Whelan, who served in the Royal marines during the Crimean War, is frequently vague about dates and events but apparently disembarked on 14 September 1854. His account is mainly interesting for the little sketches of camp life, such as Christmas celebrations in camp and the green coffee rationed to the British soldiers. He also describes a flogging he received in February 1855 for accusing a superior of lying (pp. 12-40).

H72) *Wickenden, William S., *Adventures before Sebastopol.* London: Printed for the author by Arthur Hall, Virtue, & Co., 1855. 179pp.

Fact or fiction? Do we disbelieve a man of the cloth? Rev. Wickenden (1795-1864), Cambridge M.A., curate of Lassington, author of much doggerel and styling himself "the bard of the forest" as well as "the Anglo-Circassian" on account of his so-called *Adventures in Circassia* (1847) and *A sequel to the adventures in Circassia,* (1848) (not included in the bibliography), describes his alleged expedition to Sevastopol in 1854. His Flashman-like adventures included exchanging clothing with a serving soldier and spending a night in the trenches with heroic results. Illness compelled him to return to England on 6 July, before the fall of the city.

H73) [Wilbraham, Richard], *Scenes in the camp and field: being sketches of the war in the Crimea.* London: Society for Promoting Christian Knowledge, 1857-59. 3 vols.

This account of an anonymous regiment's experiences throughout the Crimean campaign is attributed to Wilbraham (1811-1900), author of an 1837 account of Circassia (see G56), who was a major in the 7th Regiment of Foot, then adjutant general of the 2nd Division, and promoted to colonel in August 1855. The first volume covers the period from the invasion of Crimea to the battle of Inkerman. (pp. 53-131); the second, experience of the winter of 1854-55 and the outbreak of disease, during the siege of Sevastopol (pp. 41-143); the third, from the fall of Sevastopol to the eventual departure from the Crimea in the summer of 1856 (pp. 39-141). The work provides a voice to women accompanying the regiment and also includes sections on Crimean housekeeping, local landmarks, and religious monasteries.

H74) [Wilson, Charles Townshend], *Our veterans of 1854: in camp, and before the enemy. By a regimental officer*. London: Charles J. Skeet, 1859. 351pp.

> An officer of the Household Brigade, Wilson attempts to tell the story of the "Rank and File", the "base, common, and popular", from the landing on 14 September 1854 at Old Fort, south of Evpatoriia, to the hurricane of 14 November, which he terms the end of the "second act of the Russian War, when "our aristocratic military system proved rotten to the core", but "the real value of the Private Soldier" was established (pp. 105-351).

H75) Windham, Charles Ash, *The Crimean diary and letters of Lieut.-General Sir Charles Ash Windham, K. C. B., 'Redan Windham'; with observations upon his services during the Indian mutiny*. Edited by Major Hugh Pearse. Introduction by Sir William Howard Russell. London: Kegan Paul, Trench, Trübner & Co., Ltd., 1897. xii+272pp.

> Sir Charles (1810-70) served as quartermaster general of the 4th Division in the Crimean War and his letters and diary run from 14 September 1854 until 15 October 1855. He describes the battles of the Alma and Inkerman, the hurricane of 14 November 1854, as well as the routines and tedium of camp life. He led the storming party of the 2nd Division during the second assault on the Redan on 8 September 1855 (pp. 22-214).

H76) Woods, Nicholas Augustus, *The past campaign: a sketch of the war in the East, from the departure of Lord Raglan to the capture of Sevastopol*. London: Longman, Brown, Green and Longmans, 1855. 2 vols.

> Woods (1813-1906), the war correspondent in the Crimea for the *Morning Herald*, landed at Kalamita Bay on 14 September 1854 and although incapacitated by illness from early May, remained until mid-July 1855. Heavily based on personal observations, but supplemented from official sources and the testimony and correspondence of others, his journalistic account follows the campaign until the fall of Sevastopol. Strongly critical of Westminster politicians, he emphasizes the hardships and horrors of war (vol. I, pp. 285-439; II, pp. 1-365).

H77) Wright, Henry Press, *Recollections of a Crimean chaplain; and the story of Prince Daniel and Montenegro*. London: Ward and Lock, 1857. 141pp.

> Wright (1816-92), who had arrived in the Crimea in mid-September 1854 as principal chaplain to the British Army in the East, delivered on his return to England a series of public lectures at Canterbury. He writes of the religiosity of Raglan, the relations between the British army and clergy,

his burial duties in the aftermath of battles and his explorations of the surrounding countryside (pp. 23-83).

H78) 68th Light Infantry, *"Well done the 68th": the story of a Regiment, told by the men of the 68th Light Infantry, during the Crimean and New Zealand wars, 1854 to 1866.* By John Bilcliffe. Chippenham: Picton Publishing, 1995. 347pp.

> The letters and journals of eleven officers and men of the 68th Regiment serving in the Crimea were used in Bilcliffe's regimental history. They describe the hardships of camp life, the siege of Sevastopol, the incompetence of military superiors. Of particular note are the accounts given of the battle of Balaklava, the changing arms and equipment situation, and the harsh winter of 1854-55 (pp. 4-78).

H79) [Anon.], *The war, or, voices from the ranks.* London: George Routledge & Co., 1855. 220pp.

> A narrative of the campaign from the declaration of war to the battle of Inkerman and the hurricane of 14 November 1854. Includes often long extracts from the letters of mainly unidentified soldiers and sailors and the reports of war correspondents.

[End of mid-September 1854 Landings]

H80) Godman, Richard Temple, *The fields of war: a young cavalryman's Crimea campaign.* Edited by Philip Warner. London: John Murray, 1977. viii+215pp.

> Between 1 October 1854 and his departure from Balaklava on 19 November 1855 Godman (1832-1912), who rose to the rank of major-general, served as a cornet with the 5th Dragoon Guards and took part in the charge of the Heavy Brigade during the battle of Balaklava on 25 October 1854. His detailed letters to his family describe other actions in which he was involved as well as everyday life in the camps, discuss British press reporting of events, the vexed question of promotion, and record the deaths of friends and horses from battle, disease, deprivation and lack of medicine. Godman, incidentally, took three horses to the Crimea and brought them home unscathed (pp. 60-191).

H81) Wood, Evelyn, *The Crimea in 1854, and 1894. With plans, and illustrations from sketches taken on the spot by Colonel the Hon. W. K. Colville, C. B.* London: Chapman & Hall, Ld, 1895. xii+400pp.

Sir Evelyn (1838-1919), who was later to switch from the navy to the army, receive the Victoria Cross during the Indian Mutiny, and finish his career as a field-marshal, served in the Crimean War as a midshipman on board HMS *Queen*. He went ashore as a member of the Naval Brigade on 2 October 1854 and was appointed acting aide-de-camp to Captain Peel on 1 January 1855. Wounded in the failed British assault on the Redan on 18 June 1855, he was soon repatriated. His book was based a collection of articles originally published in the *Fortnightly Review*, describing his re-visiting the Crimea in August 1894 and re-living his experiences forty years earlier.

H82) Wood, Evelyn, *From midshipman to field marshal*. London: Methuen & Co., 1906. 2 vols.

A succinct account of his service in the Crimea (vol. I, pp. 28-98).

H83) [Bushby, Henry Jeffreys], *A month in the camp before Sebastopol. By a non-combatant*. London: Longman, Brown, Green and Longmans, 1855. x+125pp.

A collection of ten letters written by a tourist keen to observe the first months of the campaign. He arrived at Evpatoriia Bay on 3 October 1854 and departed on 10 November after an "enjoyable" trip, during which he was in the camp at Balaklava, witnessed the initial bombardment of Sevastopol, and saw a little of the battles at the Alma and Inkerman.

H84) Fisher-Rowe, Edward Rowe, *Extracts from letters of E.R. Fisher-Rowe (late captain, 4th Dragoon Guards), during the Crimean War, 1854-55*. Edited by his son, Major L.R. Fisher-Rowe. [Godalming]: privately printed, 1907. 59pp.

Fisher (d. 1907), a cornet in Hodge's regiment, writes home from the Crimea from 8 October 1854 to 29 November 1855, apart from the short period from early December 1854 to 11 January 1855, when he was invalided to Constantinople (pp. 16-59).

H85) [Buchanan, George,] *Letters from an officer of the Scots Greys to his mother during the Crimean War*. London: printed for private circulation by Rivingtons, 1856. 47pp.

A number of the letters Buchanan (d. 1863), a captain in the Scots Greys, sent to his mother date from 16 October 1854 to 9 July 1855, when he was based at the camp near Balaclava. He describes recent battles and skirmishing, provides news of the fate of his brother officers. He visits French positions before Sevastopol and is struck by the cowardice, the zouaves apart, of the French soldiers (pp. 9-41).

H86) Taylor, George Cavendish, *Journal of adventures with the British army, from the commencement of the War to the taking of Sebastopol.* London: Hurst and Blackett, 1856. 2 vols.

In the course of some ten months, from 25 October 1854 until 9 September 1855, punctuated by brief visits to Constantinople, Taylor (1826-89), formerly of the 95th Regiment, described events in the Crimea witnessed not as a combatant but as an interested observer. After a period with the Second Division at Sevastopol, he was with the expeditions to Kerch in May 1855, later at Inkerman and Balaklava. He witnessed the attack on Taganrog in June 1855, described the assaults on the Malakov and Redan later that month, and in a final visit in September, visited the evacuated Sevastopol.

H87) Simpson, William, *The autobiography of William Simpson, R.I. (Crimean Simpson).* Edited by George Eyre-Todd. London: T. Fisher Unwin, 1903). xvi+351pp.

The "earliest of war artists", Simpson (1823-99) received his first and most memorable encounter with Russia in October 1854, when he was sent to the Crimea by Colnaghi's. Over the next few months he produced numerous sketches from the war zone, including one of Balaklava at the behest of Queen Victoria. In May 1855 he joined the second Kerch expedition before returning to the Crimean battlefields, where he remained until September, when he was invited by the Duke of Newcastle to accompany him to Circassia. He returned to England at the end of the year for the publication of the sketches that brought him fame (pp. 19-79). In April 1869 he returned to the Crimea, visiting Sevastopol and other battle and burial sites (pp. 216-23). His third and final visit was with his wife in May 1883, when he produced his sketches of Alexander III's coronation and of scenes in Moscow and, subsequently, St Petersburg (pp. 298-99).

H88) Simpson, William, and Brackenbury, George, *The campaign in the Crimea: an historical sketch.* Accompanied by eighty double tinted plates from drawings taken on the spot by William Simpson. London: Paul and Dominic Colnaghi and Co. and Longman, Brown, Green, and Longmans, 1855-6. First series (1855): viii+112pp. Second series (1856): vi+136pp.

Brackenbury, styling himself "late secretary at Kadikoi to the honorary agents of the Crimean Army fund", provides an introductory overview of events (vol. I, pp. 1-56; II, pp. 1-77) and detailed commentaries to Simpson's drawings. Brackenbury left the Crimea in May 1855 before the end of the siege of Sevastopol. In the first series his own observations are amplified by sources such as Russell's dispatches to *The Times*; the second series is wholly dependent on borrowed material that includes Simpson's own letters.

H89) Codman, John, *An American transport in the Crimean War.* Introduction by I.C. Roper. New York: Bonnell, Silver & Co., 1897. 198pp.

Codman (1814-1900) was the captain of the American transport *William Penn*, chartered by the French, and tells his story, as the introduction suggests, "with simplicity and naturalness […] combined with a genuine love of humor". The ship left Marseilles on 1 November 1854 with troops and ammunition for the Crimea and sailed between Turkey and the Crimea until the contract with the French expired, after which Codman served with the Turks until the end of the war.

H90) Newman, George, *The prisoners of Voronesh: the diary of Sergeant George Newman, 23rd Regiment of Foot, The Royal Welch Fusiliers, taken prisoner at Inkerman.* Edited by David Inglesant. Old Woking: The Trustees of the Regimental Museum, The Royal Welch Fusiliers, 1977. xiv+260pp.

Sergeant Newman (b. 1828) began his diary on 5 November 1854, the very day he was captured at the battle of Inkerman, and completed it on 26 October 1855. He describes the 550-mile march from Sevastopol to Voronezh, via Perekop, Zaporozhe, Dnepropetrovsk, Novomoskovsk and Kharkov, reaching his destination sometime in February 1855. Newman chronicles his and his fellow prisoners' daily routine, interactions with the local population and observations on Russian customs. Released in August 1855, he travelled for seven weeks back to Balaklava, via Poltava and Odessa.

H91) O'Flaherty, Philip, *Sketches of the war: being a second series of letters.* Edinburgh: Shepherd and Elliot; London: Hamilton, Adams, and Co.; Belfast: Shepherd and Aitchison, 1855. 45pp.

In this second collection of letters (see H55) from 6 November 1854 until 28 April 1855, O'Flaherty describes his regiment's action at the battle of Inkerman on 5 November 1854, the hurricane on 14 November 1854, camp privations during the winter, proselytising conversations with Turkish troops and his distribution of religious material amongst both the British and Turkish soldiers, and his work as an interpreter between British engineers and Turkish troops. The last letter describes a visit to the camp of the French zouaves.

H92) Campbell, Colin Frederick, *Letters from camp to his relatives during the siege of Sebastopol.* Edited by R.B. Mansfield. Preface by Field-Marshal [Garnet Joseph] Wolseley. London: Richard Bentley and Son, 1894. xx+411pp.

> Campbell (1823/24-68) was a captain in the 46th Foot Regiment, promoted to major in March 1855, then assistant engineer in May 1855 and finally lt-colonel in December 1855 during service in the Crimea. The letters from Russian soil, addressed to various family members, run from his landing on 8 November 1854 until 31 March 1856, broken up by a period of leave in January 1855. Campbell was fiercely critical of the British military leadership, lack of preparation and flawed strategy, constant themes even as the supply situation began to improve in the spring of 1855.

H93) Young, Adam Graham, *A story of active service in foreign lands. Extracts from letters sent home from the Crimea 1854-1856.* Edinburgh: William Blackwood and Sons, 1886. viii+262pp.

> Young (d. 1897) was an assistant surgeon in the 2nd Battalion Rifle Brigade and present throughout the siege of Sevastopol. On 20 September 1855 he assumed responsibility for the medical care of the staff of the Light Division. His letters chronicle his experiences in the Crimea between 13 November 1854, when he landed at Kamesh Bay the day before the great hurricane, and his departure on 22 June 1856 (pp. 29-257).

H94) [Lluellyn, Richard], *Murder of a regiment: winter sketches from the Crimea, 1854-1855.* Edited by Colin Robins. Bowdon: Withycut House, 1994. 53pp.

> An officer in the 46th Foot Regiment, Lluellyn was in the Crimea from early November 1854 until his departure on 9 March 1855. Entries in his diary describe the British camp at Balaklava and before Sevastopol, fighting at Inkerman, the 14 November 1854 storm and the weeks he spent on board a vessel in Balaklava harbour when ill from fever (pp. 7-26).

H95) Creagh, James, *Sparks from camp fires: an autobiography.* London: Chapman and Hall, 1901. vi+339pp.

> Creagh (b. 1836), an ensign in the 1st Foot, arrived at Balaklava in the winter of 1854 and served eight months in the trenches. He left the Crimea in July

1856. Short on detail but rich in unexpected anecdotes, his autobiography recounts the terrible conditions of the winter of 1854-55, his witnessing of the Allied attack on the White Works and Quarries on 8-9 June 1855, his participation in the plundering of Sevastopol and his subsequent social interaction with French and Russian colleagues (pp. 112-213).

H96) Dunscombe, Nicholas, *Captain Dunscombe's diary: the real Crimean War that the British infantry knew. The diary of Captain Nicholas Dunscombe, 46th (South Devonshire) Foot.* Transcribed, edited and annotated by Major Colin Robins. Bowdon: Withycut House, 2003. 243pp.

> Dunscombe (d. 1870), promoted to captain in October 1855, had arrived at Balaklava with his regiment in November 1854 and remained in the Crimea until 14 March 1856 (apart from a short visit to Constantinople in January-February 1855). His diary consists of short entries, with frequent comments on the weather, recent military developments, actions in which he was personally involved, and observations about the practicalities and hardships of camp life.

H97) Jervis-Waldy, William Thomas, *From eight to eighty: the life of a Crimean and Indian Mutiny veteran.* London: Harrison & Sons, 1914. viii+224pp.

> In his "gossipy recollections", originally intended for the edification and amusement of his family, Jervis-Waldy (b. 1831) recalls his service as a young officer in the Duke of Cornwall's Regiment in the Crimea in November-December 1854 and, following a period of recuperation in Scutari in the spring and summer of 1856, the post-Armistice period, when he describes fraternizing with the Russians and making trips to battlefields and Crimean towns (pp. 42-87).

H98) Macormick [McCormick], Richard Cunningham, Jr., *Two months in and about the camp before Sebastopol.* London: William Wesley, 1855. 172pp.

> The young McCormick (1832-1901), the future eminent American politician and journalist, was sent to Europe for reasons of health, but within months became a correspondent reporting on the Crimean War for a number of New York papers. His book, based partly on his "hurried letters", recounts movingly his experiences with the British forces from the end of December 1854 to February 1855. He combines on-the-spot observation with "tourist" information gleaned from printed sources (pp. 12-128). After six weeks he returned to Constantinople and visited the hospitals at Scutari. The American edition was entitled *A visit to the camp before Sevastopol* (1855) with the correct spelling of his surname!

H99) O'Malley, James, *The life of James O'Malley.* Montreal: Desaulnier's Printing Co., 1893. 192pp.

> One-time corporal in the 17th Leicester Royal Bengal Tigers, the Irishman O'Malley devotes much of his autobiography to the time he spent in the Crimea between 2 December 1854 and 10 May 1856. Initially at the British camp before Sevastopol, O'Malley subsequently took part in the expedition that travelled to Odessa and was present at the surrender of the fortress of Kinburn on 17 October 1855 (pp. 63-188).

H100) West, Algernon Edward, *Recollections 1832 to 1886.* London: Smith, Elder, & Co., 1899. 2 vols.

> Sir Algernon (1832-1921), who was later to achieve prominence as principal private secretary to Gladstone, was invited to join a friend who was being sent by the Submarine Telegraph Company to "establish communication from the seat of war by means of a submarine cable". His diary covers the period from 12 December 1854 to early February 1855 that includes some ten days of cold and disillusionment at "gross mismanagement" spent at Balaklava (vol. I, pp. 161-78). He had earlier included a moving account of the battle of Inkerman sent to him on 7 November 1854 by **Captain E.S. Burnaby** (vol. I, pp. 127-36).

H101) Faughnan, Thomas, *Stirring incidents in the life of a British soldier: an autobiography.* Toronto: Hunter, Ruse and Company, 1879. 336pp.

> Among the stirring incidents that Faughnan (d. 1883) recalled during his retirement in Canada was the period from 15 December 1854 to 10 May 1856 that he spent in the Crimea as a corporal in the 17th Regiment of Foot. He provides detailed and moving accounts of the two British assaults on the Redan on 18 June and 8 September 1855; wounded during the former, he was evacuated to the hospital in Scutari, returning to Sevastopol on 20 August 1855 (pp. 146-252).

H102) Palmer, Ellen, *Crimean courtship.* Edited by Betty Askwith. Wilton: Michael Russell, 1985. 144pp.

> "Courted" by Archibald Peel, brother of Capt. William Peel VC, the commander of HMS *Diamond* in Crimean waters, Miss Palmer (1830-63) remained mainly in Turkey but paid a visit to the Crimea to visit her brother Robert, who was in the 11th Hussars and took part in the charge of the Light Brigade. Entries in her diary from the Crimea from 26 December 1854 until 29 January 1855, although succinct, reveal her as an intrepid

young lady, visiting the Inkerman battlefield under shellfire and also to
the trenches themselves during the height of winter (pp. 63-91).

H103) Gordon, Charles George, *General Gordon's letters from the Crimea, the Danube, and Armenia, August 18, 1854, to November 17, 1858.* Edited by Demetrius Charles Boulger. London: Chapman and Hall, 1884. xvi+205pp.

> It was as a young officer in the 39th Regiment that General Gordon (1833-85) landed in the Crimea at the end of 1854 – his first letter from the camp at Balaklava dates from 3 January 1855. Upbeat in tone, his letters for the most part describe the idleness of camp life but he gives a detailed account of his part in the failed British assault on the Redan on 18 June 1855 and his search for war trophies in the evacuated Sevastopol fortress. He participated in the Allied expedition that captured Kinburn in mid-October 1855. His last letter from Crimean soil is dated 10 May 1856 (pp. 9-98). Subsequent letters describe his service with the Boundary Commission, fixing the new frontier between Russia and Moldavia and Wallachia and then in Armenia between Russia and Turkey. He weaves in and out of Russian territory, including Georgia, from the end of June 1857 until finally leaving for Constantinople in mid-November (pp. 147-205).

H104) Hawley, Robert Beaufoy, *The Hawley letters: the letters of Captain R.B. Hawley, 89th, from the Crimea, December 1854 to August 1856.* Aldershot: Printed for the Society for Army Historical Research by Gale & Polden, 1970. 115pp.

> Hawley (1821-98), a captain in the 89th Regiment who was promoted to brevet-major on 2 November 1855, arrived at Balaklava on 5 January 1855 and remained in the Crimea until 5 July 1856. He did not participate in any of the major military events of the campaign and his letters reflect rather the everyday tedium of life in camp (pp. 19-115).

H105) Burgoyne, John Fox, *The military opinions of General Sir John Fox Burgoyne, bart., G.C.B.* Edited by Lieutenant-Colonel the Hon. George Wrottesley. London: Richard Bentley, 1859. viii+479pp.

> Part II of this collection of essays on military topics contains items relating to the Crimea. They include observations on the circumstances of the allied armies before Sevastopol (15 January 1855), an essay on the Sevastopol fortress's defences (November 1855), as well as Burgoyne's response to the critical reports of the army's conduct of the siege by Sir John McNeill and Colonel Alexander Murray Tulloch (pp. 145-253).

H106) Kelly, Richard Denis, *An officer's letters to his wife during the Crimean war.* With an introductory memoir by Ellen Catherine Tait. London: Elliot Stock, 1902. x+452pp.

> Ceylon-born Irishman General Sir Richard (1815-96), promoted to lieutenant-colonel in the 34th Regiment in March 1855, wrote detailed and frank letters to his wife from 17 January 1855 until 24 March 1856, edited and introduced by his daughter. Within weeks, on 23 March, Kelly was captured by the Russians and he describes his experience as a prisoner of war as he journeys from Sevastopol, via Simferopol and Ekaterinoslav, to Riazan, where he arrives on 25 May 1855. On his release he travelled back to Balaklava via Kursk, Kharkov, Poltava, Odessa and Constantinople between 14 August and 14 September 1855. An appendix contains letters regarding his falsely reported death in the British press in mid-March 1855 and a letter describing his time as a Russian prisoner Kelly wrote in October 1868 to the historian A.W. Kinglake.

H107) Bazancourt, César Lecat, *The Crimean expedition, to the capture of Sebastopol: chronicles of the war in the East, from its commencement, to the signing of the treaty of peace.* Translated by Robert Howe Gould. London: S. Low, Son & Co, 1856. 2 vols.

> Baron Bazancourt (1810-65), director of the Library of Compiègne under Louis Philippe and subsequently appointed France's military historiographer by Napoleon III, was sent by the French government to chronicle the Crimean expedition. The resulting two-volume work offers an inevitably French account of the campaign, an exhaustive narrative prefaced and concluded by sections on the war's origins and outcomes. It is written as an official history, but includes to a degree the personal observations of Bazancourt, who was in the Crimea from January until the autumn of 1855, together with the testimony of others and the evidence of despatches and correspondence.

H108) Goodman, Margaret, *Experiences of an English Sister of Mercy.* London: Smith, Elder & Co., 1862. 234pp.

> Goodman was a Devonport Sister of Mercy, a member of the group travelling with Florence Nightingale to the hospital at Scutari, where they arrived on 4 November 1854. Although mostly concerned with her work at Scutari, her account describes her visit to Balaclava in January 1855 and her interaction with British soldiers. She left soon after the armistice (pp. 209-34).

H109) Pack, Arthur John Reynell, *Sebastopol trenches and five months in them.* London: Kerby and Endean, 1878. viii+212pp.

> This is the posthumous publication of detailed journal entries by Colonel Pack (1817-60), of the 7th Regiment of Foot, the Royal Fusiliers, during five months in the trenches before Sevastopol between January and June 1855. Contains sketches drawn on the spot by **Captain Michael Biddulph** (1823-1904) of the Royal Artillery.

H110) Porter, Whitworth, *Life in the trenches before Sebastopol.* London: Longman, Brown, Green, and Longmans, 1856. x+195pp.

> Porter (1827-92), a major in the Royal Engineers, offers an anaesthetized and uncritical account of his time in the Crimea between January and May 1855, when he was invalided to Scutari. Many of his descriptions of camp life and daily routines are rarely linked to specific dates or events, but he includes extracts from his diary from 3 March to 11 May 1855 (pp. 23-180).

H111) Davis, Elizabeth, *The autobiography of Elizabeth Davis, a Balaklava nurse, daughter of Dafydd Cadwaladyr.* Edited by Jane Williams. London: Hurst and Blackett, 1857. 2 vols.

> After an "incredibly" eventful life that took her from Wales to Waterloo (just after the battle), to the West Indies, Tasmania, and many other places, Betsy Davis (1789-1860) volunteered as a nurse when the Crimean War broke out, but finished up as a cook in the hospital at Balaklava and was highly critical of Miss Nightingale (vol. II, pp. 127-200).

H112) Reid, Douglas Arthur, *Memories of the Crimean War: January 1855 to June 1856.* London: The St Catherine Press, 1911. xiv+206pp. [See also *Soldier-surgeon: the Crimean War letters of Douglas A. Reid, 1855-1856.* Edited by Joseph O. Baylen and Alan Conway. Knoxville: University of Tennessee Press, 1968. viii+158pp.]

> Reid (1833-1924), an assistant surgeon in the 90th Light Infantry, provides an account based upon letters sent home during his service on Russian soil between 2 February 1855 and 14 June 1856 (except for a period between early August and early September 1855, when he was invalided to Scutari). After his return from Scutari, Reid describes the terrible losses amongst the British and French forces in the trenches due to their proximity to the Russian lines and how in the wake of the failed British assault on the Redan on 8 September, he worked non-stop for forty-eight hours. His final letters describe the festivities following the fall of Sevastopol and his visits to the Russian lines following the Treaty of Paris (pp. 4-175).

H113) [Sullivan, Edward Robert], *A trip to the trenches in February and March, 1855. By an amateur.* London: Saunders and Otley, 1855. 284pp.

> Sir Edward (1826-99), fifth baronet of Thames Ditton and author of several travel works, describes a stay in the Crimea between 2 February and 6 March 1855, undertaken to satisfy his curiosity about the war. He provides very detailed descriptions of the difficult conditions at the British camp at Balaklava and visits various battle sites, with particular attention to the site of the battle of Inkermann (pp. 86-263).

H114) Fenton, Roger, *Roger Fenton, photographer of the Crimean War.* With an essay on his life and work by Helmut and Alison Gernsheim. London: Secker & Warburg, 1954. 106pp.

> Fenton (1819-69) had visited and photographed in Russia in 1852 but it was his visit to the Crimea that ensured his reputation. Taking with him his "photographic van", a wine-merchant's carriage converted into a mobile darkroom, two assistants, and letters of introduction from Prince Albert, Fenton left England on 20 February 1855. Over the next few months he photographed military commanders, local figures, and studies of camp life, and wrote copious letters, mainly to his wife Grace and to Thomas Agnew & Sons, the sponsors of his trip. The Gernsheims include extracts from the surviving twenty-five letters, preserved in two letter-books, over the period 27 February to 25 June 1855.

H115) Fox Maule, 2nd Baron Panmure, *The Panmure papers: being a selection from the correspondence of Fox Maule, second Baron Panmure, afterward eleventh Earl of Dalhousie, K. T. G.C.B.* Edited by Sir George Brisbane Douglas and Sir George Dalhousie Ramsay. London: Hodder and Stoughton, 1908. 2 vols.

> Lord Panmure (1801-74) was both Secretary-at-War and Secretary of State for War between February 1855 and the fall of the Palmerston ministry in February 1858, having been appointed following the public censure of the Duke of Newcastle for the poor conditions and equipment of the British army besieging Sevastopol. His papers, arranged by month and containing correspondence with political, military, diplomatic and royal figures, contain many letters, often edited, received from military figures based in the Crimea. Letters from **Lord Raglan** at Sevastopol run from 27 February 1855 until his death on 28 June 1855; from **Admiral Houston Stewart**, on board HMS *Hannibal*, from 24 March 1855 until 17 July 1855; from **General James Simpson** at the British camp before Sevastopol from 16 April 1855 until 10 November 1855; and, the most numerous, from **Major General William Codrington**, from 10 November 1855 until 11 July 1856, when he left Balaklava (vol. I; vol. II, pp. 1-271).

H116) Seacole, Mary, *Wonderful adventures of Mrs Seacole in many lands.* Edited by W.J.S. With an introductory preface by W.H. Russell, Esq., the 'Times' correspondent in the Crimea. London: James Blackwood, 1857. xii+200pp.

> Daughter of Scottish seafarer and a Jamaican former slave, Mary (née Grant, 1805-81) was on her third visit to England when the Crimean War broke out. Disappointed in her attempt to be accepted as a nurse, she travelled independently to Scutari to provide provisions to the troops. She set up a hotel at Balaklava in February 1855, took a food trolley to the front lines, and nursed, until her return in 1856 to England and to (short-lived) acclaim.

H117) Frossard, Émilien, *The French pastor at the seat of the war: letters written from the East.* Translated from the French. London: James Nisbet and Co., 1856. 302pp.

> A pastor of the French Reformed Church, Frossard (1802-81) was sent to the Crimea to care for the needs of the Protestants within the French army. Although he remained mostly in Turkish territory, he was on Crimean soil between 8 March and 27 March 1855. His letters include descriptions of visits to camp hospitals, life in the French camp before Sevastopol, his interaction with Turkish soldiers, his religious duties, and the phenomenon of war tourism (pp. 137-99). Back in Constantinople, he received letters from other pastors still in the Crimea.

H118) [Anon.], *A visit to Schamyl.* Translated from the German, with notes. London: John W. Parker and Son, 1857. ii+34pp.

> The original letter was published in Berlin in 1855 by a Prussian officer serving in the Russian army in a regiment commanded by Prince Mikhail Vorontsov. It recounts a meeting in March 1855 with Shamyl (1797-1871), the "imam of Daghestan" and leader of the Circassian resistance to Russian occupation, to effect the exchange of the family of Prince Chavtchavadze, imprisoned since July 1854, for Shamyl's eldest son.

H119) Laurie, Peter George, *My recollections of the Crimea and the siege of Sebastopol, 1854-1855.* Brentwood: privately printed, 1900. 36pp.

> Laurie (1838-1912) visited the British camp before Sevastopol between spring 1855 and early spring 1856, describing the daily routines and noting the soldiers' adoption of "moustachios" (pp. 20-36).

H120) Douglas, William, *Soldiering in sunshine and storm.* Edinburgh: Adam and Charles Black, 1865. viii+322pp.

> A private in the 10th Royal Hussars promoted to a commissariat position in October 1855, Douglas (b. 1827) describes his service in the Crimea from his arrival at Balaklava on 15 April 1855 to his departure for winter quarters in Turkey on 13 November 1855 (pp. 158-277).

H121) Buzzard, Thomas, *With the Turkish army in the Crimea and Asia Minor.* London: John Murray, 1915. x+310pp.

> Buzzard (1831-1919) was a British doctor attached to the Ottoman headquarters under Omer Pasha in the Crimea and Transcaucasia. This account, written some sixty years after the events but including frequent transcriptions from Buzzard's diary, contains a section relating to the Crimea that runs from his landing at Balaklava on 18 April 1855 until his departure on 8 October 1855 (pp. 35-205).

H122) Greig, David, *Letters from the Crimea: writing home, a Dundee doctor.* Edited by Douglas Hill. Introduction by Trevor Royle. Dundee: Dundee University Press, 2010. xi+224pp.

> Recently qualified as a doctor at Edinburgh, Greig (1832-90) sailed from England on the same ship as Florence Nightingale and reached the British military hospital at Scutari on 4 November 1854. It was only on 18 April 1855 that he went to the Crimea. In October he was aboard HMS *Albert* during the attack on Kinburn, then returned to the camp at Sevastopol. He eventually left the Crimea for Constantinople at the end of June 1856 (pp. 73-203).

H123) Christie, Peter, *Facts relating to the late Captain P. Christie, R. N. while principal agent of transports in the Black Sea.* Aberdeen: printed by John Avery, [1856]. 97pp.

> An anonymous defence of Christie (d. 1855), the Royal Navy's principal agent of transports at Balaklava, who died in April 1855 while returning from the Crimea to England to face a court martial on charges of being unfit for duty made against him in the House of Commons due to his actions during the 14 November 1854 storm. The work includes letters and memoranda by Christie (as well as letters of support from colleagues in the Crimea).

H124) Nightingale, Florence, *'I have done my duty': Florence Nightingale and the Crimean War, 1854-56*. Edited by Sue Goldie. Manchester: Manchester University Press, 1987. 326pp.

> A selection of 100 out of the 300 letters written by Nightingale (1820-1910) during the Crimean War to a variety of addressees: potential recruits, family, friends, colleagues, and officials in the War Office. They detail her work, her attempts to inform and influence Sidney Herbert at the War Office and to gain recognition of the nursing establishment by the Medical Department. Her first letter from Crimean soil is dated 10 May 1855 from Balaklava (pp. 128-30). A second series of letters was written during a visit to the Castle Hospital in Balaklava, between 15 October and mid-November 1855 (pp. 159-79). On her third visit from 24 March until 27 June 1856, she was based at the General Hospital in Balaklava, when her letters reflect her on-going wrangling with Sir John Hall and of her efforts to run the hospital (pp. 235-77).

H125) Soyer, Alexis, *Soyer's culinary campaign. Being historical reminiscences of the late war. With the plain art of cookery for military and civil institutions, the army, navy, public, etc. etc.* London: G. Routledge & Co., 1857. x+597pp.

> In his autobiography the French chef and dietician Soyer (1810-58) describes the three visits he made to the Crimea in 1855-56 to reform the catering facilities and practices of the British and French camps, including the installation of new models of field stoves. From his base in Constantinople, Soyer, accompanied by Florence Nightingale, first visited the British, French, Ottoman and Sardinian camps and inspected the ovens at Balaklava between May and June 1855 (pp. 160-289). In August-September 1855 he oversaw the installation of the new ovens and described the actions at Chernaia, the Malakov and the Redan and a visit to the newly evacuated Sevastopol (pp. 328-89). During the third trip, between March 1856 and June 1856, he describes social engagements, fraternising between the British and Russian armies and the celebratory events in camp following the peace accord (pp. 400-83).

H126) Alexander, James Edward, *Passages in the life of a soldier, or, military service in the East and West.* London: Hurst and Blackett, 1857. 2 vols.

> Twenty-five years after his first unhappy visit to the Crimea (see G14), Alexander, knighted in 1838 and now a lt-colonel, left Canada to join his regiment, the 14th Foot, in May 1855, remaining until June of the following year. He describes the last year of the war and his meetings with many fellow countrymen, both soldiers and non-combatants, such as Florence Nightingale and William Russell (vol. II, pp. 1-284).

H127) Tronson, John M., *Personal narrative of a voyage to Japan, Kamtschatka, Siberia, Tartary, and various parts of coast of China; in H.M.S. Barracouta.* London: Smith, Elder, & Co., 1859. xvi+414pp.

> Tronson was an officer on the steam-sloop *Barracouta* that took part in various expeditions over the years 1854-56 during the Crimean War. It was part of a squadron that entered the harbour of Petropavlovsk in Kamchatka on 1 June 1855 and subsequently razed fortifications and captured a Russian whaler, before sailing for the mouth of the Amur river in Siberia (pp. 89-149). In the following year they twice patrolled in the sea of Okhotsk (pp. 266-93, 301-39).

H128) Buchanan, George, *Camp life, as seen by a civilian: a personal narrative.* Glasgow: Charles Maclehose, 1871. xii+298pp.

> Dr Buchanan (1827-1905), on his appointment as a surgeon at one of the military hospitals near Sevastopol, travelled first to Constantinople, where his account begins on 25 June 1855, and then proceeded to Scutari. Arriving at Balaklava on 4 July, he was only there for a week (pp. 55-96) before escorting wounded back to Scutari, where he met Florence Nightingale. He arrived back in the Crimea only on 15 September, when his real experience of camp life can be said to begin. He describes sightseeing in Sevastopol, racing, and other activities before sailing for home on 20 October (pp. 176-274).

H129) Clayton, John William, *'Ubique', or, English country quarters, and eastern bivouac.* London: Charles J. Skeet, 1857. 175pp.

> Clayton (1833-1913), a cornet, later captain, in the 13th Light Dragoons, arrived in the Crimea in July 1855 but illness forced him to leave for Constantinople in September on board the hospital ship HMS *Severn*. He describes camp life at Balaklava, visits the site of the charge of the Light Brigade, and gives an account of the battle of Chernaia in August 1855, but in general he offers more an indulgent tourist's journal than a soldier's memoirs, describing trips taken purely for amusement (pp. 87-137).

H130) Hall, Jasper, *Letters from the Crimea: Captain Jasper Hall of the 4th (King's Own) Regiment of Foot to his sister and father.* Lancaster: King's Own Royal Regiment Museum, 1977. 36pp.

> Lieutenant in the 4th Regiment, promoted to captain on 29 December 1854, Hall (d. 1856) was appointed aide-de-camp to General Codrington in December 1855. Four of the five letters are datelined from the Crimea between 19 July 1855 and 26 February 1856 and recount life in the trenches,

his participation in the 8 September assault on the Redan, his visits to the newly evacuated Sevastopol fortress, and his attendance at a military review in February 1856.

H131) Money, A. and Money, George Henry, *Sevastopol: our tent in the Crimea; and wanderings in Sevastopol by two brothers*. London: Richard Bentley, 1856. xiv+443pp.

> The detailed description of the month-long excursion to the Crimea of the Money brothers, self-styled "travelling gentlemen", between 11 August and mid-September 1855. The first part is written by "A" from their arrival until his departure due to dysentery on 1 September (pp. 62-144); the narrative is continued with much detail on the siege of Sevastopol by George, who leaves two weeks later (pp. 151-355).

H132) Vieth, Frederick Harris Dawes, *Recollections of the Crimean campaign and the expedition to Kinburn in 1855: including also sporting and dramatic incidents in connection with garrison life in the Canadian lower provinces*. Montreal: John Lovell and Son, Limited, 1907. xiv+309pp.

> The young Canadian Vieth (d. 1910), who became a lieutenant in the 63rd West Suffolk Regiment five months after enlisting, arrived in the Crimea on 26 August 1855, just before the first assault on the Redan, and remained until the spring of 1856. He recalls his part in the seaborne attack on Kinburn on 17 October 1855 and his raising of the Queen's Colour, "the first British flag on the soil of Russia proper" (pp. 27-103).

H133) [Anon.], *Inside Sebastopol and experiences in camp: being the narrative of a journey to the ruins of Sebastopol, by way of Gibraltar, Malta, and Constantinople and back by way of Turkey, Italy, and France; accomplished in the autumn and winter of 1855*. London: Chapman and Hall, 1856. vi+382pp.

> Another example of war tourism. The anonymous author describes his long journey to and from the Crimea, where he spent nine days between 10 and 18 September 1855. He made excursions to key military positions during the siege of Sevastopol and to the evacuated town itself. He records conversations with British military personnel and included what he alleged was the first truthful account of the failed British assault on the Redan on 8 September 1855 based on the testimony of an unnamed British officer (pp. 133-244).

H134) Skene, James Henry, *With Lord Stratford in the Crimean War*. London: Richard Bentley and Son, 1883. iv+352pp.

> The Scottish ethnologist and diplomat Sir James (1812-1886), who served as the British consul in Aleppo during the Crimean conflict, writes much about the words and actions of Stratford Cannon, 1st Viscount Stratford de Redcliffe (1786-1880), the British ambassador at Constantinople, but also provides a general narrative of the war. Skene himself made at least two visits to Sevastopol, the first following the Russian evacuation from the city on 10 September 1855 (pp. 317-22), the second a few months later, when he accompanied Lord Stratford (pp. 338-46).

H135) Money, Edward, *Twelve months with the Bashi-Bazouks*. London: Chapman and Hall, 1857. iv+220pp.

> Money, who later was a lieutenant-colonel in the Indian army, wrote an account of the year he served as a captain in the Ottoman Bashi-Bazouk regiment, during which he spent a short period of leave in Sevastopol in late September and early October 1855, before returning to Constantinople (pp. 110-19).

H136) Wraxall, Frederic Charles Lascelles, *Camp life; or, passages from the story of a contingent*. London: Charles J. Skeet, 1860. xii+307pp.

> Author of numerous works of military theory, history and fiction, Sir Frederic (1828-65) recounts the time he spent as an assistant-commissary of the Field Train with the Turkish Contingent at Kerch, where he seems to have been based between autumn 1855 and summer 1856. The tone of the chapters is journalistic and often light-hearted, as he describes camp life, including much on the quality of food, servants and quarters. His relations with the Turkish Contingent were often poor, but he includes descriptions of various interesting individuals he met, his relations with and his views on the French troops, the organization of horse racing following the armistice and excursions out into the countryside around Kerch (pp. 12-217).

H137) Beddoe, John, *Memories of eighty years*. Bristol: J.W. Arrowsmith; London: Simpkin, Marshall, Hamilton, Kent & Co., 1910. xii+322pp.

> Dr Beddoe (b. 1826), F.R.S., was a member of the "Civil Hospital Staff" dispatched to Turkey to serve in a new hospital near Renkioi in the winter of 1854. In October of the following year he and a friend made a short trip to the Crimea, visiting the battlefields of the Redan, Inkerman and Balaklava (pp. 80-86).

H138) Aloysius, Mary, *Memories of the Crimea.* London: Burns & Oates, 1897. 128pp.

> Sister Mary (b. 1821) was one of a group of Irish nuns who served in the hospitals at Scutari, Koulali, and Balaklava. She arrived in Scutari at the end of December 1854 and nursed the wounded throughout the cholera outbreak, but on 7 October 1855 she left for Balaklava, where she remained until 12 April of the following year (pp. 59-96). In 1897 Queen Victoria bestowed on her the order of the Royal Red Cross.

H139) Oliphant, Laurence, *The Trans-Caucasian campaign of the Turkish army under Omer Pasha: a personal narrative.* Edinburgh and London: William Blackwood and Sons, 1856. xxviii+234pp.

> After embarking on a diplomatic career in the USA and Canada, Oliphant (see G120-23) returned to England in January 1855, but was soon on his way to Turkey and the Crimea, hoping to fulfil his wish of meeting Shamyl, the Caucasian leader. Instead he became attached as a special correspondent of *The Times* to the Turkish troops under Omer or Umar Pasha (1806-71) in their brief campaign in Circassia, witnessing their engagement with the Russians at the Ingur river.

H140) Oliphant, Laurence, *Patriots and filibusters; or, incidents of political and exploratory travel.* Edinburgh and London: William Blackwood and Sons, 1860. viii+242pp.

> Oliphant's recycling of material from his visit to Circassia in the last months of 1855, more travelogue than war-reporting, and forming Part I under the title 'Patriots' (pp. 1-131), reprinting "with corrections and additions" articles that had appeared in the June-July 1856 issues of *Blackwood's Magazine.*

H141) Lake, Henry Atwell, *Kars and our captivity in Russia: with letters from Gen. Sir W.F. Williams, Bart. of Kars, K.C.B.; Major Teesdale, C.B.; and the late Captain Thompson, C.B.* London: Richard Bentley, 1856. xv+367pp.

> After the fall of Kars on 28 November 1855, Colonel Sir Henry (1811-81), who had been responsible for the city's fortifications, set out, together with Gen. Williams, the general's secretary Henry Churchill, Major Teesdale, and Capt. Thompson, on their march into Russian captivity. They were to travel to Tiflis, where they remained for a month, before Lake and Thompson were ordered in January 1856 to proceed to Penza. They journeyed through the Caucasus, reached the Don at the beginning of February and travelled via Tambov to Penza, everywhere treated with respect and hospitality. It was in Penza that they were freed from captivity

with the ending of the war, and they travelled home via Moscow and St Petersburg (pp. 246-337).

H142) [Anon.], *Observations on the Turkish Contingent.* By a field officer of the force. London: Printed by Smith, Elder and Co., 1856. 31pp.

> Written at Kerch, the pamphlet is a rebuttal of criticisms of the Turkish Contingent which was staffed by East India Company officers. The anonymous author refers to perceived outrages ranging from grave desecration, plundering of towns, and murder, although there are no specific references to places in the Crimea itself. He also addresses the issue of cultural tensions between the various ethnic groups among the Turkish conscripts and their Christian officers following a severe outbreak of cholera.

H143) *[Murray, Eustace Clare Grenville], *Pictures from the battle fields.* By 'the roving Englishman'. London: George Routledge & Co., 1855. xxviii+259pp.

> The illegitimate son of the 1st Duke of Buckingham, Murray (1823-81) was British consul in Odessa for some thirteen years from 1856 (see I92). Prior to that, he was in Bulgaria and it is difficult to establish if and when he visited the Crimea, specifically Balaklava and the heights above Sevastopol, and to distinguish fact from fiction in subsequent chapters with observations on Allied and Russian officers and soldiers (p. 91-112).

H144) Shaw-Lefevre, George, *Photographic views of Sebastopol taken immediately after the retreat of the Russians, September 5, 1855.* London: J. Hogarth, 1856. Folio.

> A series of twelve photographs, taken by Shaw-Lefevre, Baron Eversley (1832-1928): they include views of the Malakov and Redan and also of HMS *Leander* in Balaklava harbour.

H145) Smith, William Adams, *A last appeal! War-peace, or an armed truce: with some observations on the condition, conduct, and prospects of the British soldier.* Portsmouth: Henry Lewis, and London: Hamilton and Co., 1856. viii+30pp.

> Describing himself as "recently returned from the Crimea" and having "sojourned in different parts of Turkey and the Crimea for a period of fifteen months" before leaving in November 1855, Smith introduces personal encounters with British soldiers in his impassioned lecture against an ignoble peace.

Fig. 43 Alexander II (n.d.), photographer unknown.

9. REIGN OF ALEXANDER II (1855-1881)

See also G64, G99, G112, G123, G124, H13, H87, H103

I1) [Eckardt, Julius Wilhelm Albert von], *Russia before and after the war.* By the author of 'Society in St. Petersburg' &c. Translated from the German (with later additions by the author) by Edward Fairfax Taylor. London: Longmans, Green, and Co., 1880. xiv+436pp.

> The German historian, journalist, and diplomat Dr Eckardt (1836-1908), who had studied law at St Petersburg, Dorpat, and Berlin, produced a series of informed studies of nineteenth-century Russia, two of which, *Modern Russia: comprising, Russia under Alexander II; Russian communism; The Greek Orthodox Church and its sects; The Baltic provinces of Russia* (1870) and *Distinguished persons in Russian society* (1873), had previously appeared in English translation, the first under his name. In this work he injects a few pages of personal reminiscences of the eight months in 1855 (following Nicholas I's death) that he spent at St Petersburg University (pp. 204-15).

I2) Habersham, Alexander Wylly, *My last cruise; or, where we went and what we saw: being an account of visits to the Malay and Loo-Choo islands, the coasts of China, Formosa, Japan, Kamtschatka, Siberia, and the mouth of the Amoor river.* Philadelphia: J.B. Lippincott & Co., 1857. 507pp.

> U.S. navy lieutenant Habersham (1826-83) presents his "strictly matter-of-fact" account of his voyage as a member of the North Pacific surveying and exploring expedition that set out from America on 21 June 1853. It reached Kamchatka in July 1855 and left Russian waters for San Francisco two months later, having visited various settlements (pp. 317-496).

http://dx.doi.org/10.11647/OBP.0042.09

I3) Pulling, John, *A tour in Southern Europe and the Crimea.* London: James Nisbet and Co., 1858. viii+138pp.

> Rev. Pulling, minister of a chapel on High Street Deptford, and his companion John Martin travelled first to Spain at the end of August 1855 and then proceeded from Gibraltar to Constantinople. After visiting the hospital at Scutari, they sailed to the Crimea and visited Balaklava and other battle sites (pp. 88-113) before returning to England overland via Greece and Italy.

I4) Galt, Edwin, *The camp and the cutter; or, a cruise to the Crimea.* London: Thomas Hodgson, 1856. xii+240pp.

> Galt was yet another anxious to visit the sites and "sights" of the Crimea, as the conflict neared its end. He left London in October 1855 to Malta, where he joined his "cutter", which he was, however, obliged to leave for repairs in Constantinople, when he sailed to Balaklava in December. Over the next month he endured the severity of a Crimean winter as he visited the battlefields, before returning to Constantinople, which he left for home on 18 February (pp. 61-170).

I5) White, Andrew Dickson, *Autobiography of Andrew Dickson White.* London: Macmillan and Co., 1905. 2 vols.

> White (1832-1918) served seven months as an attaché in the U.S. legation in St Petersburg in 1855 (vol. I, pp. 38-39). In November 1892 he returned as U.S. minister until December 1894 (vol. II, pp. 5-116). He describes in detail his meetings with Pobedonostsev and his walks and talks with Tolstoi in March 1894. See also on visit to Moscow (vol. II, pp. 453-55).

I6) McPherson, Duncan, *Antiquities of Kertch, and researches into the Cimmerian Bosphorus: with remarks on the ethnological and physical history of the Crimea.* London: Smith, Elder & Co., 1857. xiv+130pp.

> An impressive folio volume with numerous plates and in-text wood engravings in which an historical introduction is followed by a "detailed account of the author's researches" (pp. 31-108). These were conducted in 1855-56 during Dr McPherson's "scanty leisure" from his major important role as inspector-general of hospitals to the Turkish forces during the Crimean War.

I7) Mahony, James, *The book of the Baltic: being the North of Europe Steam Company's route to Denmark, Sweden and Russia, Norway, Prussia and the*

Hanseatic ports. London: Effingham Wilson; Dublin: McGlashan & Gill, 1857. 160pp.

> Designed as a tourist's guide to the northern ports to which the company's steamers sailed and to the towns reached by the connecting railway routes, it is based on a journey made by Mahony in 1856. His lively and informed account is accompanied by many of his own drawings. Although most attention is given to St Petersburg, Revel, Narva and Cronstadt are described, as are Moscow and, briefly, Nizhnii Novgorod (pp. 42-103).

I8) Blackwood, Alicia, *A narrative of personal experiences & impressions during a residence on the Bosphorus throughout the Crimean War.* London: Hatchard, 1881. viii+318pp.

> Lady Blackwood, née Lambart (1818-1913) and her husband, Rev. James Blackwood (d. 1882), on hearing of the battle of Inkerman, decided to sail to Turkey in December 1854, she to help in the hospital at Scutari and he as chaplain to the forces. Shortly after the peace on 31 March 1856 they paid a visit to the Crimea before returning to England. They arrived at Balaklava on 21 April and visited Sevastopol, Inkerman, and other sites and made an excursion to Bakhchiserai before leaving on 23 May (pp. 242-306). Her own drawings illustrate her book.

I9) Train, George Francis, *Young America abroad in Europe, Asia, and Australia: a series of letters from Java, Singapore, China, Bengal, Egypt, the Holy Land, the Crimea and its battlefields, England, Melbourne, Sydney, etc. etc.* [Introduction by Freeman Hunt.] London: Sampson Low, Son & co., 1857. xxii+480pp.

> Train (1829-1904), American businessman and entrepreneur, visited the Crimea from 28 April to 4 May 1856, shortly after the end of the war, visiting Balaklava and Sevastopol (pp. 288-316).

I10) Sala, George Augustus Henry, *A journey due north; being notes of a residence in Russia, in the summer of 1856.* London: Richard Bentley, 1858. viii+311pp.

> Although Sala (1828-95) "put Russia down in my juvenile itinerary as a place to be visited", it was as a special correspondent for *Household Words* appointed by its editor Charles Dickens that he sailed into Cronstadt on 20 May 1856. He remained until December and seems to have spent almost all his time in St Petersburg, although there are references to Tver and the Volga and country estates in what is an infuriatingly jokey-whimsy self-indulgent set of impressions (pp. 45-311).

I11) Bunbury, Selina, *Russia after the war: the narrative of a visit to that country in 1856.* London: Hurst and Blackett, 1857. 2 vols.

> Miss Bunbury (1802-82), prolific authoress of novels and travel books, as well as a collection of anecdotes about Peter the Great (1850), arrived at Cronstadt in the summer of 1856 with her charge Harry, but ennui, the lack of good water, and heat soon drove them to an extended stay in Finland. They then proceeded to Moscow to witness the coronation, but on their return to the capital they decided not to winter there, but head for "the shores of old England. Hurra!"

I12) Murphy, John, *Russia at the time of the coronation of Alexander II: being a series of letters addressed from Moscow and St. Petersburg to the 'Daily News'.* London: Bradbury and Evans, 1856. viii+171pp.

> The letters were "addressed" by its special correspondent to the *Daily News* but not all were sent or published. In addition to his detailed record of the coronation and accompanying events, Murphy describes the sights in St Petersburg and Moscow, with interesting information on the British presence, in letters dated from 11 August to 3 October 1856.

I13) Moltke, Helmut Karl Bernhard, *Field-marshal Count Moltke's letters from Russia.* Translated from the German by Robina Napier. London: C. Kegan Paul & Co., 1878. xxxii+163pp.

> Count Moltke (1800-91), attending the coronation in his capacity as chief of the Prussian general staff, describes his stay in St Petersburg and Moscow (which he infinitely preferred to the capital) in a series of letters dated from 15 August to 8 September 1856.

I14) Spottiswoode, William, *A tarantasse journey through eastern Russia in the autumn of 1856.* London: Longman, Brown, Green, Longmans, & Roberts, 1857. xii+258pp.

> The mathematician and physicist (1825-83), Fellow of the Royal Society and later its president, begins his account with his departure from Moscow on 3 September 1856, having travelled from England via Berlin, Warsaw and St Petersburg. Suggests (erroneously) that his route had previously been accomplished "almost exclusively" by scientific expeditions and offers a "three-month tour" without exciting incidents and political allusions. He travelled east via Kazan to Perm, then down to Orenburg, then west to Samara and Saratov, following the Volga down to Astrakhan, and returning via Tambov to Moscow and was back in Warsaw by 3 November. Fourteen of his own drawings accompany the text.

I15) Collins, Perry McDonough, *A voyage down the Amoor: with a land journey through Siberia, and incidental notices of Manchooria, Kamschatka, and Japan.* New York and London: D. Appleton and Company, 1860. 390pp. [See also *Siberian journey down the Amur to the Pacific 1856-1857.* Edited with an introduction by Charles Vevier. Madison: University of Wisconsin Press, 1962]

> The New-Yorker Collins (1813-1900), appointed official American commercial agent to the Amur river, undertook to travel the whole length of the river "to ascertain its fitness for steamboat navigation" and left Moscow on 3 December 1856 by the post road for Irkutsk. His journey down the Amur ended with his arrival in Nikolaevsk at the river's mouth on 10 July 1857 and subsequent departure from Petropavlovsk in Kamchatka on 7 October for America.

I16) Train, George Francis, *My life in many states and in foreign lands. Dictated in my seventy-fourth year.* London: William Heinemann, 1902. xxi+348pp.

> The year after his visit to the Crimea (pp. 215-20) (see I9), Train went again to Russia in 1857, visiting St Petersburg, Moscow and Nizhnii Novgorod (pp. 249-58).

I17) Hume, George, *Thirty-five years in Russia.* London: Simpkin, Marshall, Hamilton, Kent & Co., 1914. xxiii+320pp.

> Hume (b. 1836) arrived in Russia for the first time in 1857 and remained there until 1892, when illness obliged him to return to England. He was involved in a succession of business concerns, mainly agricultural machinery, travelled extensively throughout Ukraine, but resided mostly in Kharkov with his family.

I18) Gadsby, John, *A trip to Sebastopol, out and home, by way of Vienna, the Danube, Odessa, Constantinople, and Athens; together with some account of Russia and the Russians, their manners and customs, particulars and incidents of the war, anecdotes, &c.* London: Gadsby, 1858. 182pp.

> Publisher and lecturer, Gadsby set out from London on 29 June 1857 with the specific intention to write of "Sebastopol as I found it after the war". He arrived at Odessa on 12 July and visited Sevastopol and many of the battle sites before sailing away on 2 August (pp. 27-167). He makes liberal use of published sources such as Kohl and Custine.

I19) Stanley, Arthur Penrhyn, *The life and correspondence of Arthur Penrhyn Stanley, D.D., late Dean of Westminster.* By Rowland E. Prothero, with the co-operation and sanction of the Very Rev. G.G. Bradley, D.D., Dean of Westminster. London: John Murray, 1893. 2 vols.

> Shortly after his appointment as Regius Professor of ecclesiastical history at Oxford, Stanley (1815-81) undertook his first journey to Russia to study the history of the Greek Church. He arrived in St Petersburg on 1 August 1857, went on to Moscow, Vladimir, and Nizhnii Novgorod, and was back in Oxford by mid-October (vol. I, pp. 515-34). He paid his second visit to Russia in 1874 at the request of Queen Victoria to conduct the Protestant ceremony at the marriage of the Duke of Edinburgh. He and his wife left England on 9 January 1874 and their experiences in Russia are conveyed in a series of letters to his sister Mary (vol. II, pp. 423-44).

I20) Stanley, Arthur Penrhyn, *Letters and verses of Arthur Penrhyn Stanley, D.D. between the years 1829 and 1881.* Edited by Rowland E. Prothero. London: John Murray, 1895. viii+454pp.

> Includes Stanley's letters to his mother and George Grove during his 1857 visit to Russia (pp. 271-82) and also his five detailed letters to Queen Victoria during his 1874 visit (pp. 383-99).

I21) Latrobe, John Hazelhurst, *John H B. Latrobe and his times, 1803-1891.* By John E. Semmes. Baltimore: The Norman, Remington Co., 1917. 601pp.

> The Philadelphia lawyer (1803-91) was requested by Winans of the firm of Winans, Harrison, and Winans, that had gained a contract to remount the railway from St Petersburg to Moscow, to accompany him to Russia to represent the firm's interests. He arrived in Russia on 29 September 1857 and spent five months there with a short visit to Moscow at the end of February 1858. Large extracts from Latrobe's diary and letters (pp. 473-528).

I22) Heywood, Robert, *A journey to Russia in 1858.* Manchester: privately printed, 1918. ii+41pp.

> Heywood and his wife visited Russia at the invitation of Count Aleksandr Adlerberg, arriving in St Petersburg on 24 June 1858. Five weeks of typical tourism in St Petersburg, Moscow and St Petersburg again followed. The text of a lecture printed fifty years after he had delivered it to the Bolton Mechanics' Institute (of which he was a member).

I23) [Pearson, Charles Henry], *Russia, by a recent traveller: a series of letters originally published in 'The Continental Review'.* Revised and illustrated. London: William Francis Graham, 1859. vii+167pp.

Pearson (1830-91), a lecturer in history at King's College, London, spent two months in Russia in the summer of 1858, and was joined after two weeks in St Petersburg by an Oxford friend, Rev. Henry Boyd. They travelled to Tver and down the Volga as far as Kazan and returned via Vladimir to Moscow. A book, Pearson was later to recall, that did not meet his expenses, but brought the favourable attention of Alexander Herzen.

I24) Pearson, Charles Henry, *Charles Henry Pearson, Fellow of Oriel and education minister in Victoria: memorials by himself, his wife, and his friends.* Edited by William Stebbing. London: Longmans, Green, and Co., 1900. xiv+320pp.

Contains a little further material from Pearson's 'Story of my life', most notably about his visit to Poland at the time of the insurrection of 1863 (pp. 99-100, 109-18).

I25) Taylor, James Bayard, *Travels in Greece and Russia, with an excursion to Crete.* London: Sampson Low, Son & Co., 1859. 426pp.

Taylor (1825-78), eminent American poet and travel writer, first visited Russia in the summer of 1858, visiting St Petersburg and Moscow (pp. 315-426).

I26) Dumas, Alexandre Davy de la Pailleterie, *Adventures in czarist Russia.* Translated and edited by A.E. Murch. London: Peter Owen, 1960. 194pp.

In June 1858 the popular French novelist (1802-70) accompanied to Russia an aristocratic Russian family (the Kuleshev-Bezborodkos) he had met in Paris. After six weeks in St Petersburg and a fortnight in Finland, he proceeded to Moscow, where he was a guest of the Naryshkins. In September he set off down the Volga to Astrakhan, where his account finishes (pp. 38-194). Condensed translation from Dumas' four-volume *En Russie* (1860).

I27) Dumas, Alexandre Davy de la Pailleterie, *Adventures in the Caucasus.* Translated and edited by A.E. Murch. London: Peter Owen, 1962. 205pp.

In the sequel to his earlier book, Dumas recounts his travels and adventures in the Caucasus during the period that Shamyl was still waging his campaign for independence against the Russians. After leaving Astrakhan on 2 November 1858, he and a friend, the artist Moynet, travelled from Kizliar to Derbent and Baku and then to Tiflis. He left for France from Poti in February 1859 (pp. 15-205). Condensed translation from Dumas's *En Caucase* (1859).

I28) Gautier, Théophile, *Travels in Russia.* In *The works of Théophile Gautier.* Translated and edited by F.C. de Sumichrast. London: George G. Harrap, 1900-03. 24 vols.

> The celebrated French poet and novelist (1811-72) sailed from Lübeck to St Petersburg in the autumn of 1858 and spent the next seven months in the capital and Moscow before returning overland to Paris. With a poet's eye and palette he provides a refreshing and often original view of familiar places and events in the two capitals (vol. XIII (1902), pp. 92-358; XIV, pp. 3-131). Back in Paris, he was obsessed with memories of Russia and determined to spend a summer there and specifically to visit Nizhnii Novgorod, drawn by "the demon of travel" and the melody of its name. Continuing his work on a projected but only half-completed 'Art treasures of ancient and modern Russia', he went first to Moscow, then to Tver and down the Volga to Nizhnii (vol. XIV, pp. 133-211). The first French edition in book form of *Voyages en Russie* appeared in 1866.

I29) Pepys, Charlotte Maria, *A journey on a plank from Kiev to Eaux-Bonnes, 1859.* London: Hurst and Blackett, 1860. 2 vols.

> Lady Pepys (1822-89), who dedicated her book to Russian friends "in memory of days spent with them; days much enjoyed, and lovingly remembered", left Kiev on 23 June 1859, as an invalid, "on a plank", and thus deprived of the normal opportunities for sight-seeing. She travelled to Warsaw on her slow progress to Eaux-Bonnes and Pau, where she finished her book in October 1859. A few observations on Kiev apart (vol. I, pp. 1-15), her work's Russian interest lies in an appendix containing her verses and translations from the Russian, principally Lermontov, under her pen name of Viola (vol. II, pp. 253-71). The following year, she published her novel *Domestic sketches in Russia.*

I30) Smyth, Charles Piazzi, *Three cities in Russia.* London: Lovell Reeve & Co., 1862. 2 vols.

> The three cities Smyth and his wife Jesse (née Duncan) visited between July and late October 1859 and described in two vast volumes, totalling a thousand pages, were St Petersburg, Moscow and, less predictably, Novgorod. Smyth (1819-1900), Scottish astronomer royal from 1846 and F.R.S., offers much of scientific interest but is intent on also providing a sympathetic insight into "the feelings, traditions, and moving impulses of Russians".

I31) Tilley, Henry Arthur, *Japan, the Amoor, and the Pacific; with notice of other places comprised in a voyage of circumnavigation in the imperial Russian corvette "Rynda", in 1858-1860.* London: Smith, Elder and Co., 1861. xii+405pp.

> Invited in September 1858, for reasons never explained, to join Commodore Popov on his ship sailing from Brest to Japan and across the Pacific, the Irish traveller Tilley reached Nikolaevsk on the Amur a year later and took the opportunity to explore briefly the hinterland (pp. 203-47).

I32) Tilley, Henry Arthur, *Eastern Europe and western Asia: political and social sketches on Russia, Greece, and Syria in 1861-2-3.* London: Longman, Green, Longman, Roberts, & Green, 1864. xii+374pp.

> Almost immediately on his return to England, Tilley accompanied Popov to St Petersburg in the autumn of 1860. In January 1861 he was already in Syria (see preface of earlier book), having travelled from Moscow via Kharkov and Rostov to Taganrog and by boat to Odessa, before boarding the Russian frigate *Admiral* in November 1860 and beginning his second cruise (pp. 5-226). His travel account is padded out with essays on, for example, Russo-Polish relations and the emancipation of the serfs.

I33) Thornbury, George Walter, *Criss-cross journeys.* London: Hurst and Blackett, 1873. 2 vols.

> "Written not very long before the abolition of serfdom", c.1860, the four chapters Thornbury (1828-76) devoted to his short stay in Moscow (vol. II, pp. 245-342) cover visits to a mosque, a gypsy concert, a prison, and the sight of prisoners destined for Siberia.

I34) Edwards, Henry Sutherland, *The Russians at home: unpolitical sketches, showing what newspapers they read; what theatres they frequent; and how they eat, drink, and enjoy themselves; with other matter relating chiefly to literature and music, and to places of historical and religious interest in and about Moscow.* London: W.H. Allen and Co., 1861. iv+447pp.

> The title says it all, or almost. Edwards (1828-1906), who had spent many years in Russia, provides a detailed and informed account about the personalities and issues of Russian contemporary literary, musical, and artistic life, totally unexpected in the context of existing English writing on Russia. There is much on the censorship, journals, the fables of Krylov, the poetry of Pushkin and others, on opera and music, as well as on burning questions of the support for, and opposition to, the emancipation of the serfs.

I35) **[Anderson, Robert]**, *Sketches of Russian life before and during the emancipation of the serfs*. Edited by Henry Morley, Professor of English literature in University College, London. London: Chapman and Hall, 1866. vi+298pp.

> The author, whose verbose writings Professor Morley had edited and published previously in *All the year round*, had "spent fifteen years of a long life among the Russians in active business of divers kinds", although the various incidents he records all date from the 1860s. (Andersons, incidentally, had been trading in Russia since the eighteenth century.) He travelled extensively through Russia, recalling incidents in, for instance, Tula, Serpukhov, Moscow, and St Petersburg, often to illustrate the effects of serfdom and emancipation. Much on the British in Russia, particularly at time of the Crimean War.

I36) **Browne, John Ross,** *The land of Thor*. New York: Harper & Bros., 1867. 542pp.

> Irish-born American writer, artist and traveller, Browne (1821-75) left his family in Germany to arrive in Russia in July 1861 "with a knapsack on my back and a hundred dollars in my pocket" to make an extensive tour "along the borders of the Arctic". Utterly lonely in St Petersburg, he fared better in Moscow. Impressed most by the Russians' love of vodka, he offers essays on the serfs and emancipation and Russian civilization, before departing from Cronstadt a few weeks later for Revel and Finland (pp. 9-223).

I37) **[Morgan, Henry Arthur]**, *The northern circuit or brief notes of Sweden, Finland, and Russia.* Cambridge and London: Macmillan and Co., 1862. viii+122pp.

> A Cambridge don, later Master of Jesus, Rev. Morgan (1830-1912) and two friends, whom he calls Tew and the Captain, travel by steamer from Hull to Sweden in the summer of 1861 and eventually on to St Petersburg and Moscow. Superficial notes of a tourist who recommends six weeks in the north, but infinitely prefers Sweden to Russia (pp. 80-122).

I38) **Laurie, William Ferguson Beatson,** *Northern Europe (Denmark, Sweden, Russia) local, social, and political, in 1861; with a succinct continuation down to May, 1862.* London: Saunders, Otley, and Co., 1862. xii+382pp.

> Captain Laurie (1819-91), fresh from service in India, undertook a northern tour with his father in the summer of 1861, setting out in early August for

Scandinavia and arriving at Cronstadt in November. After a short stay in St Petersburg, they left by train for Poland and Berlin (pp. 171-229).

I39) Clay, Cassius Marcellus, *The life of Cassius Marcellus Clay: memoirs, writings, and speeches, showing his conduct in the overthrow of American slavery, the salvation of the Union, and the restoration of the autonomy of the states.* Cincinnati, Ohio: J. Fletcher Brennan and Co., 1886. 2 vols.

> Clay (1810-1903) was twice appointed U.S. minister to the court of Russia, arriving for the first time and briefly in 1861-62 and returning the following year for an extended stay until 1869. Gruff and vain, he delighted in his ignorance of court etiquette and prided himself on the good impression he made on everyone, from the emperor down and including all the most beautiful ladies at court (vol. I, pp. 293-96, 326-450).

I40) Taylor, James Bayard, *By-ways of Europe.* London: Sampson Low, Son, & Marston, 1869. 2 vols.

> In May 1862 Taylor accompanied Senator Simon Cameron, the newly appointed American minister to Russia, as his secretary of legation. He remained until May the following year. The first three sketches in *By-ways* relate to this period. The first, 'A cruise on Lake Ladoga' (vol. I, pp. 21-66), describes to a trip in July 1862 by Taylor and two American friends, "the first of our countrymen to visit the northern portion of the lake"; the second, 'Between Europe and Asia' is the description of a visit with the minister and other members of the legation to the fair at Nizhnii Novgorod and to Moscow (pp. 69-100); and the third is devoted to 'Winter-life in St Petersburg' (pp. 103-36).

I41) Taylor, James Bayard, *Life and letters of Bayard Taylor.* Edited by Marie Hansen-Taylor and Horace E. Scudder. London: Elliot Stock, 1884. 2 vols.

> Contains letters to his mother, friends and government officials during his year in St Petersburg (vol. I, pp. 386-414).

I42) Taylor, Marie Hansen, *On two continents: memories of half a century.* With the co-operation of Lilian Bayard Taylor Kiliani. London: Smith, Elder, & Co., 1905. xii+309pp.

> The German-born Marie Hansen (1829-1925), whom Taylor had married in October 1857, did not accompany her husband on his first visit to Russia the following year, but in July 1862 she joined him in St Petersburg (pp. 120-44).

I43) Moor, Henry, *A visit to Russia in the autumn of 1862.* Chapman and Hall, 1863. vi+234pp.

> Moor was invited to visit Russian friends at their estate near Pskov, where he was particularly interested in the implications of the recent emancipation act of 1861. He then travelled to Novgorod and on to Moscow. He visited the fair at Nizhnii before travelling to St Petersburg and home via Warsaw. His account had appeared the previous year in *Bentley's Miscellany*.

I44) Graves, Samuel Roberts, *A yachting cruise in the Baltic.* London: Longman, Green, Longman and Roberts, 1863. xii+399pp.

> Graves (1818-73), chairman of Liverpool's local marine board and commodore of the Royal Mersey Yacht Club, embarked in July 1862 on a cruise of the Baltic on the yacht *Ierne* that he and his companions decided to extend to St Petersburg, coinciding with a visit by Queen Victoria's son Prince Alfred. They then went by train to Moscow and pronounced themselves very happy with all they had seen and done (pp. 174-313).

I45) Anderson, Fortescue Lennox Macdonald, *Seven months' residence in Russian Poland in 1863.* London and Cambridge: Macmillan and Co., 1864. xii+214pp.

> Rev. Fortescue (b. 1832), son of the English chaplain in Bonn, accompanied his friend, the Polish nobleman Count Alexander von Bisping-Galen, from Germany in February 1863 to stay on his estate near Grodno. He was to be caught up in the insurrection of 1863 and falsely accused, was imprisoned in Grodno, before he was eventually released in mid-September after the intervention of three Oxbridge dons.

I46) O'Brien, Augustin P., *Petersburg and Warsaw: scenes witnessed during a residence in Poland and Russia in 1863-4.* London: Richard Bentley, 1864. viii+248pp.

> O'Brien left St Petersburg for Poland in August 1863, deeply pro-Polish in the wake of the recent insurrection. Over the next few months he interviewed Russian and Polish officials and visited prisons and came to what he offered as a more balanced view of the motives and conduct of both Polish insurrectionists and Russian oppressors.

I47) Michie, Alexander, *The Siberian overland route from Peking to Petersburg, through the deserts and steppes of Mongolia, Tartary, etc.* London: John Murray, 1864. xiii+402pp.

Inspired by his compatriot John Bell's eighteenth-century account of his journey from St Petersburg to Pekin, Michie (1833-1902) journeyed westwards, leaving the Chinese capital on 14 August 1863. From the Russian border at Kiakhta, he travelled on through Siberia via Irkutsk and Tomsk to Ekaterinburg, and then to Kazan and Moscow. He left St Petersburg in January 1864 (pp. 203-356).

I48) Mitford, Algernon, 1st Baron Redesdale, *Memories.* London: Hutchinson & Co., 1915. 2 vols.

Mitford (1837-1916) arrived in St Petersburg on 30 November 1863 to serve for six months in the British embassy under Lord Napier. He recalls political and social events in the capital and a visit to Moscow in May 1864 (vol. I, pp. 204-306).

I49) Zychlinski, Ludwik, *The memoirs of Ludwik Zychlinski: reminiscences of the American civil war, Siberia, and Poland.* Translated by Eugene Podraza. Edited with an introduction by James S. Pula. New York: Columbia University Press, 1993. xviii+111pp.

After serving as a volunteer in the Union army, the Polish patriot Zychlinski (1837-91) hurried back from America to his homeland on hearing of the January 1863 uprising. Captured by the Russians in December 1863, he was sentenced to twenty years' exile in Siberia, where he was to take part in the Baikal uprising in 1865, but was released in 1868 and returned to Poland (pp. 91-108).

I50) Grant Duff, Mountstuart Elphinstone, *Notes from a diary 1851-1872.* London: John Murray, 1897. 2 vols.

Sir Mountstuart (1829-1906), a keen student of Russian affairs and close friend of the noted Russian exile Nikolai Turgenev, paid a brief visit to St Petersburg in December 1863 to attend the marriage of his brother to a Miss Morgan of the British community. He also went to Moscow and Sergiev Posad before departing for Poland on 31 December (vol. I, pp. 243-45).

I51) Curtin, Jeremiah, *Memoirs of Jeremiah Curtin.* Edited with notes and introduction by Joseph Schafer. Madison: State Historical Society of Wisconsin, 1940. x+925pp.

Renowned American anthropologist, linguist, translator, and traveller, Curtin (1835-1906) was secretary of legation of the United States in St

Petersburg from 1864 to 1870 (pp. 78-293). In this posthumously published autobiography he also describes his subsequent visits from Poland to Kiev and St Petersburg at the end of 1898 (pp. 674-81) and to St Petersburg in the summer of 1900, deciding to travel home via Siberia, but first diverting from Moscow to see Tolstoi at Iasnaia Poliana, and finally reaching Vladivostok in October (pp. 776-815). He paid further short visits to 1901 to St Petersburg and Moscow (pp. 848-52). and to St Petersburg in May 1902 and at the end of 1904 (pp. 870-71, 895-96). Curtin held "the conviction that sometime Russia and America will be the great powers of the world".

I52) Ussher, John, *A journey from London to Persepolis; including wanderings in Daghestan, Georgia, Armenia, Kurdistan, Mesopotamia, and Persia.* London: Hurst and Blackett, 1865. xvi+703pp.

Ussher, F.R.G.S., undertook with a friend his long journey in the summer of 1864 "solely for purposes of pleasure and amusement", although its chief object was to visit Daghestan, scene of the activities of Schamyl. They first entered Russia at Odessa, explored the Crimea, before travelling through Georgia to Vladikavkaz and into Daghestan. They went to Baku before returning to Tiflis in late September and preparing to proceed to Armenia and beyond (pp. 27-230).

I53) Forsyth, William, *The great fair of Nijni Novogorod, and how we got there.* London: privately printed by W. Clowes & Sons, 1865. 117pp.

Forsyth (1812-99), later Q.C. and commissary of Cambridge University, and his brother Douglas left London on 8 August 1864, travelling to St Petersburg via Berlin and Warsaw. Impressions of the capital and Moscow precede the visit to the fair at Nizhnii, which they found disappointing and stayed less than a day, although he opined there was "no pleasanter country in which to make an autumn tour than Russland" (pp. 42-117).

I54) St John, Frederick Robert, *Reminiscences of a retired diplomat.* London: Chapman and Hall, 1905. xviii+315pp.

Sir Frederick (1831-1923), while serving at the Pekin embassy, was persuaded by the Americans Raphael Pumpelly (see I55) and Thomas Walsh to travel with them in November 1864 through Mongolia across Siberia. After a month's stay at Troitskozavodsk, waiting for the ice on Baikal to thicken, they journeyed on by sledge in "such discomfort and fatigue", before parting company in Irkutsk. St John continued to Nizhnii Novgorod, before taking the train to St Petersburg and leaving for England early in 1865 (pp. 86-102).

I55) Pumpelly, Raphael, *Across America and Asia: notes of a five years' journey around the world and of residence in Arizona, Japan and China.* New York: Leypoldt & Holt, 1870. xvi+454pp.

> Pumpelly (1837-1923), American geologist and later Harvard professor, began his travels at the end of 1860 and, after long periods of residence in Japan and China, journeyed (with Walsh and St John) from Pekin through Mongolia to Kiakhta and into Siberia at the end of December 1864. He stayed for three weeks in Irkutsk, before travelling to Ekaterinburg, visiting the copper mines at Nizhnii Tagilsk, and then by train from Nizhnii Novgorod to St Petersburg (pp. 388-427).

I56) Michell, Thomas, *Handbook for travellers in Russia, Poland, and Finland.* New edition, revised by Thomas Michell. London: John Murray, 1865. v+282pp.

> Michell (1835-99), born in Cronstadt, returned to Russia as 1860 as translator and attaché in the British embassy. In 1866 he was second secretary and consul. He used his first-hand knowledge of the country to revise completely the earlier Murray handbook (1849 version) and update it in four subsequent editions (1875-93).

I57) Goldsmid, Frederic John, *Telegraph and travel: a narrative of the formation and development of telegraphic communication between England and India, under the orders of her majesty's government, with incidental notices of the countries traversed by the lines.* London: Macmillan and Co., 1874. xiv+673pp.

> Colonel Sir Frederic (1818-1908) was at Kerch in December 1855 during the Crimean War, but it is his travels in 1865 (and partially in 1870, 1871, and 1872) that are the substance of the second "travel" part of his book, when he was chief director of the government Indo-European telegraph. Leaving London on 23 June 1865 en route for Tehran, he stopped in St Petersburg to consult the director of the Imperial Russian Telegraph, before proceeding down the Volga to Astrakhan and reached Baku on 22 July. Interleaved are excerpts from his diary of 1865 and references to his 1870 visit (pp. 474-529).

I58) Bush, Richard J., *Reindeer, dogs, and snow-shoes: a journal of Siberian travel and explorations made in the years 1865, 1866, and 1867.* London: Sampson Low, Son, and Marston, 1871. 529pp.

> One of a group of four members (who included George Kennan (see I59)) of a Russo-American telegraph surveying expedition, Bush sailed from San Francisco on 3 July 1865 for Petropavlovsk in Kamchatka. His book

is a detailed record of "what the author himself saw, heard, and endured during his sojourn of nearly three years in those cold, desolate, and unwritten, yet interesting regions", that for him was sailing on by Sakhalin to the Amur at Nikolaevsk and more or less following a line inland of the Sea of Okhotsk to finish among the Chukchis to await the boat to take them home to "the world and civilization" in September 1867.

I59) Kennan, George, *Tent life in Siberia; and adventures among the Koraks and other tribes in Kamtchatka and northern Asia.* London: Sampson Low, Son, and Marston, 1871. ix+425pp.

The complementary account to Bush's, far better known, and written by the young Kennan (1845-1924), who was to become one of the most eminent and influential of America's commentators on Russia (see J36). Notable for his closely observed notes on the lives and languages of native tribes.

I60) Whymper, Frederick, *Travel and adventure in the territory of Alaska, formerly Russian America – now ceded to the United States – and in various other parts of the north Pacific.* London: John Murray, 1868. xviii+331pp.

Whymper (1838-1901), artist and explorer, brother of the famous alpinist, twice visited Petropavlovsk in Kamchatka, in the course of long sea voyages, firstly in September-October 1865 (pp. 84-104) and then in July-early August of 1866, before preceding to the Siberian mainland and trading with the Chukchis (pp. 106-24).

I61) Pollington, John Horace Savile, *Half round the old world, being some account of a tour in Russia, the Caucasus, Persia, and Turkey, 1865-66.* London: Edward Moxon & Co., 1867. ii+403pp.

A tour that began in London on 14 July 1865 took Viscount Pollington (b. 1843), F.R.G.S., to St Petersburg, where he met up with his future travelling companion, Captain W-. They soon travelled to Moscow and then took a steamer down the Volga to Astrakhan. By 9 October they had crossed the Caspian, passed through Georgia and left Erevan en route for Persia (pp. 4-174). "An exact transcription of a diary", nothing more offered or added.

I62) Mounsey, August Henry, *A journey through the Caucasus and the interior of Persia.* London: Smith, Elder & Co., 1872. xii+336pp.

Mounsey (d. 1882), F.R.G.S., arrived at the port of Poti at the end of December 1865, having travelled from London via Constantinople. He travelled on to Tiflis, which he left in mid-January 1866 for Erevan, travelling in atrocious conditions. He then proceeded to his ultimate destination, Persia (pp. 14-82). He began the return journey on 3 July, crossing the Caspian to Baku and eventually proceeding up the Volga to Nizhnii Novgorod and by railway from there to England (pp. 328-33).

I63) Knox, Thomas Wallace, *Overland through Asia: pictures of Siberian, Chinese, and Tartar life; travels and adventures in Kamchatka, Siberia, China, Mongolia, Chinese Tartary, and European Russia, with full accounts of the Siberian exiles, their treatment, condition, and mode of life, a description of the Amoor River, and the Siberian shores of the Frozen Ocean.* London: Trübner & Co., 1871. xviii+608pp.

> Knox (1835-96) undertook his long journey for pleasure, for journalism, and as a member of the Russo-American Telegraph Company's expedition surveying for a possible "electric connection between Europe and the United States by way of Asia and Bering's Straits". He sailed from New York on 21 March 1866 to San Francisco and then to Petropavlovsk in Kamchatka. He crossed the sea of Okhotsk to the mouth of the Amur to start his journey up the river and then across Siberia, where he writes much about the exiles, past and present, before he reached St Petersburg five months and 600 pages later.

I64) Loubat, Joseph Florimond, *Narrative of the mission to Russia, in 1866, of the hon. Gustavus Vasa Fox, assistant-secretary of the navy. From the journal and notes of J.F. Loubat.* Edited by John D. Champlin, Jr. New York: D. Appleton and Co., 1873. viii+444pp.

> Fox (1821-83) was sent by Congress to congratulate Alexander II on his escape from assassination and sailed on the monitor *Miantonomoh* to St Petersburg, where he arrived on 5 August 1866. Over the following weeks until their departure on 27 September the Americans were fêted wherever they went, which included Moscow and towns along the Volga (pp. 78-409). The visit was chronicled in minute and fascinating detail by Vasa's secretary (1831-1927) and the appendices included the score of the 'Miantonomoh galop', composed for the piano by Heinrich Fürstnow in Fox's honour (pp. 430-35).

I65) Appleton, Nathan, *Russian life and society. As seen in 1866-67 by Appleton and Longfellow, two young travelers from the United States of America, who had been officers in the Union Army, and a journey to Russia with General Banks in 1869.* Boston: Murray and Emery, 1904. 226pp.

Letters to his family from Harvard graduate and brevet captain Appleton (1843-1906), who with his companion Longfellow (1844-93), son of the American poet, travelled to St Petersburg and Moscow in 1866-67. Appleton draws many comparisons between the abolition of slavery in the USA and the emancipation of the serfs in Russia, and focuses on other recent reforms, to argue for Russia's modernization and its plausibility as an American ally. In 1869 Appleton returned to Russia with General Nathaniel Prentice Banks (1816-94).

I66) Dicey, Edward James Stephen, *A month in Russia during the marriage of the czarevich.* London: Macmillan and Co., 1867. viii+248pp.

Journalist, newspaper editor, and author of travel and historical works, Dicey (1832-1911) left England at the end of October 1866 to attend the wedding of Aleksandr Aleksandrovich, the future Alexander III, to Princess Dagmar of Denmark (Maria Fedorovna), which took place on 9 November. Dicey was the only British journalist to follow the Prince of Wales and his party throughout his visit. The wedding and accompanying events in St Petersburg and in Moscow are described in great detail, but there is also much of interest on the British community in St Petersburg, including a description of the British seamen's hospital in Cronstadt, and Dicey's "low-life" visits to a tavern and music hall.

I67) Héritte-Viardot, Louise, *Memories and adventures.* Translated from the German by E.S. Bucheim. London: Mills & Boon, 1913. xiv+271pp.

Appointed professor at the conservatoire on the recommendation of Anton Rubinstein, Héritte-Viardot (1841-1918) arrived in St Petersburg in 1867. She describes artistic life in the capital, as well as trip into central Russia with a friend. Subsequent sections record a visit to the Crimea in 1868 and a prolonged stay in Moscow. She left for Geneva in 1871 (pp. 142-216).

I68) Sheepshanks, John, *My life in Mongolia and Siberia: from the Great Wall of China to the Ural Mountains.* London: Society for Promoting Christian Knowledge, 1903. xii+175pp.

Sheepshanks (1834-1909), who became Bishop of Norwich in 1893, spent many years abroad after being ordained in 1857. In late June 1867, following his visit to China and Mongolia and interested in inspecting Russo-Greek church missions in Siberia, he entered Russia at Kiakhta and made his way to Irkutsk, which he left on 26 September en route for Moscow (pp. 115-75).

I69) **Sheepshanks, John,** *A bishop in the rough.* Edited by D[avis]. Wallace Duthie. With a preface by the right rev. the Lord Bishop of Norwich. London: Smith, Elder & Co., 1909. xxxviii+386pp.

> Sheepshanks' life as a missionary in Canada and his work and travels in Asia as recounted by a member of his clergy includes his journey from Mongolia through Siberia to England in 1867 (pp. 351-82).

I70) **Lowth, George T.,** *Around the Kremlin; or, pictures of life in Moscow.* London: Hurst and Blackett, 1868. viii+346pp.

> Author and traveller, Lowth offers, despite the theft of his "Murray", an undemanding tour of the sights of Moscow, punctuated by visits to the estate of a Count L*, to Sergiev Posad, and to Nizhnii Novgorod.

I71) **Twain, Mark (pseudonym of Clemens, Samuel Langhorne),** *The new pilgrim's progress: a book of travel in pursuit of pleasure: the journey home.* London: John Camden Hotten, 1871. 259pp.

> In 1867 Twain (1835-1910), as a roving correspondent for a number of American newspapers, accompanied a group of American tourists sailing on the *Quaker City* for the Holy Land but with numerous stops and excursions en route. One such side trip was from Constantinople to Sevastopol, "probably the worst battered town in Russia or anywhere else", then to Odessa, and back to Yalta, where they were received by the tsar and his family (pp. 39-57). The first edition was published in the U.S.A. in 1869 under the title *The innocents abroad*, which was adopted for the first half of the book published in England the previous year.

I72) **Carroll, Lewis (pseudonym of Dodgson, Charles Lutwidge),** 'Journal of a tour in Russia in 1867'. In *The works of Lewis Carroll.* Feltham, Middlesex: Spring Books, 1968. 1130pp.

> Three years after writing *Alice's adventures in wonderland*, Rev. Dodgson (1832-97), mathematical lecturer at Christ Church, Oxford, embarked on a European tour that took him and a friend to St Petersburg on 27 July 1867 from where they departed on 26 August after an excursion to Moscow and Nizhnii Novgorod. Interesting above all for the descriptions of visits to monasteries and churches and Dodgson's fascination with the peculiarities of the Russian language (pp. 965-1005). First full publication in England of the journal that had first appeared in an edition of sixty-six copies as *Tour in 1867. By C.L. Dodgson. From the original manuscript in the collection of M.L. Parrish.* Philadelphia: Privately Printed, 1928.

I73) Liddon, Henry Parry, *Life and letters.* By John Octavius Johnston. With a concluding chapter by the Lord Bishop of Oxford. London: Longmans, Green, and Co., 1904. xii+424pp.

> Excerpts from the letters of Dodgson's companion on his tour, Rev. Liddon (1829-90), also of Christ Church (pp. 100-09).

I74) Creagh, James, *A scamper to Sebastopol and Jerusalem in 1867.* London: Richard Bentley & Son, 1873. 429pp.

> Irish-born Creagh, who had served as a captain in the 1st Royals during the Crimean War and was subsequently the author of several travelogues to the near east, travelled through Russian Poland on his way to Jerusalem. He later travelled by steamer to Odessa and then on to the Crimea, visiting the battle sites at Sevastopol and Balaklava as well as making trips to Bakhchisarai and Yalta, before reaching Kerch. There he took a steamer to Novorossiisk and explored parts of Circassia, before sailing from Poti to Batumi and into Turkey (pp. 213-93).

I75) Coston, Martha Jay, *A signal success: the work and travels of Mrs Martha J. Coston: an autobiography.* Philadelphia: J.B. Lippincott Co., 1886. 333pp.

> Mrs Coston, née Hunt (1828-1904), was an American naval officer's widow, who perfected a system of marine signalling he had invented and created a successful business. She arrived in St Petersburg with her niece at the beginning of August 1867 with the idea of interesting the Russians in the system through the agency of Admiral Farragut (see I76), but the letter she sent him was not received and her plans came to nothing (pp. 196-203).

I76) Montgomery, James Eglinton, *Our admiral's flag abroad: the cruise of Admiral D.G. Farragut, commanding the European squadron in 1867-68, in the flag-ship Franklin.* New York: G.P. Putnam & Son, 1869. xvi+464pp.

> The *Franklin* arrived at Cronstadt on 10 August 1867 and left three weeks later. The admiral's secretary reaches for the superlatives to describe the reception given to the Americans during their visits to St Petersburg, Nizhnii Novgorod, and Moscow (pp. 47-84).

I77) Robson, Isaac and Harvey, Thomas W., *Narrative of the visit of Isaac Robson and Thomas Harvey to the south of Russia.* London: n.p., 1868. 39pp.

> In 1867 the two Quakers heard the call to visit Molokan settlements near the Sea of Azov and travelled to Odessa. They then sailed to Yalta and sought without success an audience with the tsar who was at Livadia. They subsequently visited Mennonite villages in the southern steppes before departing from Odessa.

I78) Schuyler, Eugene, *Selected essays.* With a memoir by Evelyn Schuyler Schaeffer. London: Sampson Low, Marston, & Co., 1901. 364pp.

> The eminent American historian and diplomat (1840-90), author of a life of Peter the Great and translator of Turgenev, was appointed American consul in Moscow in September 1867, became secretary of legation in St Petersburg in the autumn of 1869, travelled widely, including a tour of Russian Central Asia (see I109), and left for a new appointment in Constantinople in February 1876 (pp. 21-56). Schuyler's long essay (published in 1889) on Tolstoi, whom he first met in October 1868, is also included (pp. 207-99).

I79) Hodgetts, Edward Arthur Brayley, *Moss from a rolling stone.* London: J.M. Dent & Sons, 1924. viii+304pp.

> Born in Berlin to English parents, Hodgetts (1859-1932) as a young boy first went to Russia at the end of the 1860s and remained until 1879, working ultimately in a Moscow bank (pp. 65-89). A decade later he returned from England to Russia as resident Petersburg correspondent of the new *Daily Graphic* (pp. 162-85). After a spell in Berlin he was again in Russia, reporting for Reuters on the famine of 1891-92 and meeting Tolstoi (pp. 207-25) (see J113). It was for the *Daily Graphic* that he went in 1895 to Tiflis and Baku to report on the Armenian massacres (pp. 261-82) (see K6).

I80) Freshfield, Douglas William, *Travels in the central Caucasus and Bashan, including visits to Ararat and Tabreez and ascents of Kazbek and Elbruz.* London: Longmans, Green & Co., 1869. xiii+509pp.

> The distinguished geographer and mountaineer (1845-1934) first visited the Caucasus with three friends in 1868. He made the first ascents of a series of peaks including Kazbek and Elbrus (pp. 141-496).

I81) Kennedy, John Pendleton, *At home and abroad: including a journal in Europe, 1867-68.* New York: G.P. Putnam and Sons, 1872. 415pp.

> Kennedy (1795-1870) was a prominent politician, novelist, and secretary of the U.S. navy. This posthumous publication includes his journal of travels that took him to from London via Stockholm to St Petersburg, where he arrived on 10 July 1868. He visited cathedrals, palaces and libraries in the capital and Moscow before leaving from St Petersburg for Hamburg at the beginning of August (pp. 400-10).

I82) Lamont, James, *Yachting in the Arctic seas, or, notes of five voyages of sport and discovery in the neighbourhood of Spitzbergen and Novaya Zemlya.* London: Chatto and Windus, 1876. viii+387pp.

Sir James (1828-1913), F.R.G.S., describes his journey to the Kara Sea on his specially-built three-masted schooner, the *Diana*, between April and August 1869, observing and shooting walruses, deer, and much else (pp. 1-198).

I83) [Ely, Jane, Marchioness of], *Mafeesh, or, nothing new; the journal of a tour in Greece, Turkey, Egypt, the Sinai-desert, Petra, Palestine, Syria, and Russia.* London: printed [by William Clowes and Sons] for private circulation. 2 vols.

> The journal of the tour undertaken by a much-loved lady of the bedchamber to Queen Victoria, Jane Loftus (1821-90), Dowager Marchioness of Ely (née Hope-Vere), her son, the 4th Marquess, and friends begins with their departure from Trieste on 16 November 1868. They eventually reached Constantinople and sailed for Odessa on 15 June 1869. After exploring the Crimea they made their way to Moscow via Rostov, travelling up the Don and then the Volga. Their journey, and the journal, finished with a visit to St Petersburg, most notable for a description of the imperial review at Krasnoe selo. They left for home on 10 July (vol. II, pp. 135-237).

I84) Harvey, Annie J., *Turkish harems and Circassian homes.* London: Hurst & Blackett, 1871. x+307pp.

> Mrs Harvey of Ickwell Bury, as she styles herself on the title page, spent "a past summer" (1869 or 70), cruising with her husband on the schooner yacht *Claymore* on the Black Sea. After visiting Constantinople and the Turkish coast, they headed for the Crimea, landing first at Evpatoria before proceeding to Sevastopol, from where they made several excursions to the battle sites. Yalta provided another prolonged stop with a visit to the Vorontsov palace at Alupka, before they sailed on for Sukhumi and the delights of the Circassian coast (pp. 111-270).

I85) Grey, Theresa Georgina, *Journal of a visit to Egypt, Constantinople, the Crimea, Greece, &c. in the suite of the Prince and Princess of Wales.* London: Smith, Elder & Co., 1869. viii+302pp.

> Styling herself the hon. Mrs William Grey, Swedish-born Theresa (1837-1901) (née von Stedingk), lady-in-waiting to the Princess of Wales, describes the cruise of the yacht *Ariadne*, which they joined at Trieste on 27 January 1869 and left at Brindisi on 2 May. They reached the Crimea on 12 April and proceeded to visit the major battle sites of the war, then the palaces at Livadia and Alupka, before sailing from Yalta three days later (pp. 172-89).

I86) Whyte, William Athenry, *A land journey from Asia to Europe: being an account of a camel and sledge journey from Canton to St. Petersburg through the* *plains of Mongolia and Siberia.* London: Sampson Low, Son, and Marston, 1871. xvi+336pp.

> Whyte (b. 1838), F.R.G.S., left Canton on his return journey to England in September 1869, leaving Mongolia and camels to reach Kiakhta in late October. Although he writes that his journey through Siberia to St Petersburg, where he arrived at the beginning of January 1870, was "once in a lifetime [and] more than sufficient", his account is uneventful and boringly written (pp. 188-336).

I87) **Barry, Herbert,** *Russia in 1870.* London: Wyman & Sons, 1871. xii+418pp.

> Barry, author of a concise account of the Russian metallurgical industry (1870), made his first visit to Russia in 1858 and lived there permanently from 1866 to 1870, when he was the director of a group of iron works in Vladimir, Tambov and Nizhnii Novgorod *gubernii*. He attacks the misrepresentation of Russian life in Hepworth Dixon's *Free Russia* and offers his own "fair account of the existing state of affairs", believing in the great potential of Russia in the post-Emancipation era. Chapters on provincial towns and villages, sports and pastimes, manufacturing, as well as on Siberia and the fair at Nizhnii Novgorod.

I88) **Barry, Herbert,** *Ivan at home; or, pictures of Russian life.* London: The Publishing Company, 1872. xvi+322pp.

> Barry followed up the success of his earlier book with a series of sketches of Russian life, manners and customs – weddings, funerals, village notables, superstitions, even strikes. Dedicated to Alexander II, whom Barry greatly admired.

I89) **Dixon, William Hepworth,** *Free Russia.* London: Hurst and Blackett, 1870. 2 vols.

> Although he refers to two earlier journeys in Russia, Dixon (1821-79), traveller and author, had in February 1870 only recently returned from travelling from Archangel to the Urals and down to Ukraine, visiting the great religious shrines at Solovetsk, Kiev, Novgorod and Sergiev Posad and interesting himself in particular in the religious life of the people. His wish to paint "the Living People" in free, i.e. post-Emancipation, Russia was aspirational rather than realized.

I90) **Wallace, Donald Mackenzie,** *Russia.* London: Cassell, Petter & Galpin, 1877. 2 vols.

> The classic study of post-Emancipation Russia written by the scholarly Scot Sir Donald (1841-1919), who arrived in Russia in March 1870 and

remained until December 1875, spending the winters in St Petersburg, Moscow and Iaroslavl and the summers wandering the countryside, gathering the reliable and wide-ranging data that he constantly updated for further editions, particularly those of 1905 and 1912. In 1887-88 he was correspondent of *The Times* in St Petersburg.

I91) Atkinson, Joseph Beavington, *An art tour to northern capitals of Europe.* London: Macmillan & Co., 1873. xii+455pp.

Atkinson (1822-86) offers the first detailed English-language account of art treasures in Russia that he saw during his visits to St Petersburg, Moscow, and Kiev in the summer of 1870. He arrived from Sweden in mid-July and left via Odessa and Austrian Poland two months later (pp. 149-433). Much on the Hermitage, particularly its imported art works, but also detailed attention to Russian art, ancient and modern, although his verdict is that "in Russia genius is exceptional, while mediocrity is all but universal".

I92) [Murray, Eustace Clare Grenville], *The Russians of to-day.* By the author of 'The Member for Paris' &C. London: Smith, Elder, & Co., 1878. xxi+304pp.

Although it is highly dubious that Murray's *Pictures from the battle fields* (1855) was based on a visit to the Crimean battlefields (see H144), his service as British consul in Odessa during at least the first decade of Alexander II's reign provided the material for the wide-ranging, if flippant sketches that purported to show aspects of Russian life in Odessa and surrounding region in the 1870s. His characters include Prince Wiskoff, Tripoff and a Jewish merchant Simon Iscariotovitch, but he is interesting, for instance, on the English in Russia, the character of the tsar, and the popularity of Russian authors.

I93) Kennan, George, *Vagabond life: the Caucasus journals of George Kennan.* Edited, with an introduction and afterword, by Frith Maier, with contributions by Daniel C. Waugh. Seattle and London: University of Washington Press, 2003. xvi+266pp.

In 1870 Kennan (see I59) returned to Russia for a second time, arriving at Cronstadt on 6 July, and travelling from St Petersburg on 27 August to Moscow and down the Volga to Astrakhan. By the time he sailed from Poti for Constantinople on 28 November he had spent some ten weeks travelling through the Caucasus (pp. 59-219). Unpublished in his lifetime, his (skilfully edited) diaries recount his adventures in a region new to Americans.

194) Wilkinson, David, *Whaling in many seas and cast adrift in Siberia, with a description of the manners, customs, and heathen ceremonies of various (Tchuktches) tribes of North-Eastern Siberia.* London: Henry J. Drane, 1906. 296pp.

> New Zealand-based explorer and whale hunter Wilkinson, whilst on a whaling expedition in the Arctic Ocean, was shipwrecked on 9 October 1870 and washed ashore somewhere on the East Cape of Siberia. He reached an Eskimo village, where he remained until the end of March 1871. He then made the treacherously difficult journey by sledge to Plover Bay, where he was picked up by another whaling vessel and remained in the region until the end of the whaling season in late September 1871.

195) Cunynghame, Arthur Augustus Thurlow, *Travels in the eastern Caucasus, on the Caspian and Black Seas, especially in Daghestan, and on the frontiers of Persia and Turkey, during the summer of 1871.* London: John Murray, 1872. xvi+367pp.

> General Sir Arthur (1812-84), who had served with distinction in the Crimea in 1854-55, was also an energetic traveller and writer of various books that included his journey with his son Henry (who illustrated the volume) from Constantinople to Odessa and on to the Crimea and through Georgia to Persia from late July to late September 1871 (pp. 83-349).

196) Bax, Bonham Ward, *The eastern seas: being the narrative of the voyage of H.M.S. 'Dwarf' in China, Japan, and Formosa; with a description of the coast of Russian Tartary and eastern Siberia, from the Corea to the river Amur.* London: John Murray, 1875. xii+287pp.

> Suggesting that the British public knew much about Russian central Asia, Captain Bax of the Royal Navy offered his account of the Russian eastern ports as something new. The *Dwarf* left Hong Kong in July 1871 and reached Russian waters on 1 August. They remained in the area until 11 September, visiting settlements and harbours, such as Vladivostok, described in some detail, and Nikolaevsk, before passing Sakhalin on their way to Japan (pp. 157-82).

197) Proctor, Edna Dean, *A Russian journey.* Boston: Houghton, Mifflin and Co., 1871. iv+321pp.

> The American poet (1829-1923) travelled to Russia in 1871 as part of a European tour, journeying from St Petersburg to Moscow and then down the Volga. It was in the Crimea, at Yalta, that she saw the tsar, lauding him

in verse, as she had almost everything else on her journey through Russia, which she left via Kishinev. In 1890 she published a "revised edition with prelude" that expressed her regret that freedom for the peasantry had still not been achieved.

I98) Richardson-Gardner, Robert, *A trip to St. Petersburg.* Westminster: printed for the author by T. Brettell and Co., 1872. 91pp.

> The reprinting of a series of letters from the author to his brother John that had previously appeared in the *Windsor and Eton Herald* and described a trip "in the dead of winter" that he, his wife, and three army officers had made not only to St Petersburg but also to Moscow. They arrived in the capital at the end of December 1871, visited Moscow for a few days at the end of January, and departed from St Petersburg for Warsaw early in February 1872.

I99) Harvie-Brown, John Alexander, *Travels of a naturalist in northern Europe, Norway, 1871, Archangel, 1872, Petchora, 1875.* London: Fisher Unwin, 1905. 2 vols.

> The Scottish ornithologist and prolific author (1844-1916) travelled extensively and visited northern Russia, studying bird life by the White and Kara seas, in the early 1870s (vol. I, pp. 125-60, II, pp. 261-477).

I100) Gilmour, James, *Among the Mongols.* London: The Religious Tract Society, 1883. xiv+382pp.

> Rev. Gilmour (1843-91), perhaps the most famous of the missionaries of the London Missionary Society, first went out to China in 1870 and spent twenty years among the Chinese and Mongols of Inner Mongolia, adding Mongol and Buriat to his many languages. In March 1871 he visited the abandoned missionary post at Selenginsk, a Siberian garrison town not far from the border with Outer Mongolia, and crossed Baikal to Irkutsk (pp. 28-54).

I101) Wellesley, Frederick Arthur, *With the Russians in peace and war: recollections of a military attaché.* London: Eveleigh Nash, 1905. viii+324pp.

> Appointed military attaché to the British embassy in St Petersburg in 1871 while still an absurdly inexperienced junior officer in the Coldstream Guards, the hon. Frederick (1845-1931) remained for seven years and travelled widely through Russia as part of his official and non-official duties, including the Kirghiz steppe and the Crimea. He was with the Russian imperial headquarters throughout the Russo-Turkish war of 1877-78.

I102) **Wellesley, Frederick Arthur,** *Recollections of soldier-diplomat.* Edited by his son Sir Victor Wellesley. London: Hutchinson & Co., 1948. 171pp.

> Includes a succinct account of his Russian experiences, to which his son has added new information about the secret mission with which he was entrusted by Queen Victoria during his short visit to England in August 1877 (pp. 11-149).

I103) **Prime, Samuel Irenaeus,** *The Alhambra and the Kremlin: the south and the north of Europe.* New York: Anson D.F. Randolph & Co., 1873. xxiv+482pp.

> An unusual – in intention if not in execution – comparison of primarily Spain and Russia offered by an American clergyman during travels in 1872 that took him from Spain through Switzerland to German and Poland and to St Petersburg and Moscow before proceeding to Finland and Scandinavia (pp. 284-370).

I104) **Carrington, George,** *Behind the scenes in Russia.* London: George Bell and Sons, 1874. xvi+224pp.

> A minor writer of fiction and travel, Carrington (b. 1844) claims originality for forsaking "description and illustration", suggesting that "if not critical I will be nothing", although the end product, including his hostile view of the Orthodox Church and of almost everything else, is unremarkable, except for its arrogance ("there is no literature"!). He seems to have arrived by train from Berlin in July 1872 and remained, in St Petersburg, Moscow, and possibly Orel, until the late summer of the following year.

I105) **Brooks, Phillips,** *Letters of travels.* London: Macmillan and Co., 1893. vii+386pp.

> Letters to members of his family sent by the late Bishop of Massachusetts (1835-93) during his various travels, which included the summer of 1872 in northern Europe. He sailed to St Petersburg and then visited Moscow and Nizhnii Novgorod before departing for Warsaw. Two letters of 18 and 25 August cover his visit (pp. 166-69).

I106) **Montefiore, Moses Haim,** *Report presented by Sir Moses Montefiore, bart., president, to the London Committee of Deputies of the British Jews on his return from his mission to St. Petersburg, August, 5632-1872.* London: printed by Wertheimer, Lea and Co., 1872. 24pp.

> The account of the second Russian journey undertaken by Sir Moses (in his eighty-eighth year), accompanied by Dr Loewe, his secretary, and Dr Daniel, his personal physician (for first journey in 1846, see G99). They

arrived in St Petersburg on 19 July 1872 and were received by the tsar in the Winter Palace on 24 July, when Sir Moses presented the address from the Board of British Jews, offering congratulations on the 200th anniversary of the birth of Peter the Great. His report highlights "the marked improvements" that had taken place in all areas, including the position of the Jews, since his last visit in 1846. They left on 25 July, travelling via Königsberg and Berlin.

I107) Thielmann, Max Guido von, *Journey in the Caucasus, Persia, and Turkey in Asia.* Translated by Charles Heneage. London: John Murray, 1875. 2 vols.

A secretary at the German embassy in St Petersburg, Baron von Thielmann (1846-1929) resolved to meet up with friends in Odessa in August 1872. Their extensive travels would take them by sea to Poti, before they struck inland through Georgia down to Erevan and then back northwards to reach the Caspian at Petrovsk and thence by sea to Baku and into Persia by mid-October (vol. I, pp. 1-308; II, pp. 1-19).

I108) Ker, David, *On the road to Khiva.* London: Henry S. King & Co., 1874. xvi+359pp.

The *Daily Telegraph*'s special correspondent in Khiva and later noted as a prolific author of stories for boys (including *Cossack and czar*), Ker (1842-1914) left England in early March 1873 and travelled via St Petersburg to the Black Sea and on to Tiflis, whence "my real journey commences". It is this eventful journey from Orenburg via the border forts of Kazalinsk and Perovskii to Turkestan, Tashkent, and Samarkand that forms the substance of his book.

I109) Schuyler, Eugene, *Turkistan: notes of a journey in Russian Turkistan, Khokand, Bukhara, and Kuldja.* London: Sampson Low, Marston, Searle, & Rivington, 1876. 2 vols.

Taking leave of absence from his post in St Petersburg (see I78), Schuyler left on 23 March 1873 and visited Orenburg, Tashkent, Samarkand, and Bokhara, before returning on 15 November, having amassed much information on the newly annexed regions and on the conduct of Russian officialdom.

I110) Buckham, George, *Notes from the journal of a tourist.* New York: Gavin Houston, 1890. 2 vols.

The American tourist Buckham, accompanied by his wife, visited St Petersburg and Moscow between 21 July and 8 August 1873 and produced precisely what his title promised (vol. II, pp. 385-421).

I111) **Wells, Sarah Furnas,** *Ten years travel around the world, or, from land to land, isle to isle and sea to sea, embracing twenty tours in England, Scotland, Ireland, France, Prussia, Belgium, Denmark, Sweden, Poland, Switzerland, Austria, Italy, Greece, Russia, Turkey, Holy Land, Syria, Egypt, India, Singapore, Java, Australia, South America, Central America, Sandwich Islands and North America.* Introduction by Rev. E.J. Scott. West Milton, Ohio: Morning Star Publishing Co., 1885. xxiv+653pp.

> An indefatigable traveller, Mrs Wells (1834-1912) paid three visits to Russia. She spent three months in St Petersburg and Moscow in the summer of 1873 (pp. 58-62). The following year, a tour through the Mediterranean took her eventually to Odessa, where she spent the month of July 1874 before travelling to Kiev for a further extended stay before leaving for Warsaw (pp. 97-101). Finally, specifically "to see the czar [Alexander III] crowned", she sailed from New York in the spring of 1883 and after witnessing the event in Moscow, returned from St Petersburg on 17 June (pp. 593-603).

I112) **Knox, Thomas Wallace,** *Backsheesh; or life and adventures in the Orient, with descriptive and humorous sketches of sights and scenes over the Atlantic, down the Danube, through the Crimea, in Turkey, Greece, Asia-Minor, Syria, Palestine, and Egypt, up the Nile in Nubia, and Equatorial Africa, etc., etc.* Hartford, Conn.: A.D. Worthington & Co., 1875. 694pp.

> Some six years after his previous foray into Siberia (see I63), Knox went to the Crimea as part of "a peaceful crusade to the East, undertaken for purposes of pleasure and profit". Sailing down the Danube, he arrived in Odessa and left immediately for a tour of the Crimea, visiting the battlefields, before returning to Odessa and sailing to Constantinople in the summer of 1873 (pp. 93-116).

I113) **Guthrie, Katherine Blanche,** *Through Russia: from St. Petersburg to Astrakhan and the Crimea.* London: Hurst and Blackett, 1874. 2 vols.

> Mrs Guthrie and her daughter planned a tour of art collections in the museums of leading European cities, including St Petersburg and Moscow, but were so fascinated by their stay in Moscow that they decided to extend their tour (three months in all in the summer of 1873) by sailing down the Volga and then journeying on to the Crimea, where they visited all the battle sites, before leaving for Constantinople.

I114) **Baker, Valentine,** *Clouds in the east: travels and adventures on the Perso-Turkoman frontier.* London: Chatto and Windus, 1876. xii+376pp.

Colonel Baker (1827-87), late commander of the 10th Hussars, set out with two other officers from London on 20 April 1873 with the aim of travelling through Central Asia to gather "political, geographical, and strategical information that might be valuable". They travelled via Vienna to Constantinople and entered Russian territory at Poti, travelling to Tiflis and on into Persia (pp. 18-42). They left Persia at the end of November and returned to England via Rostov, Moscow, and St Petersburg (pp. 318-28).

I115) **MacGahan, Januarius Aloysius,** *Campaigning on the Oxus, and the fall of Khiva.* London: Sampson Low, Marston, Searle and Rivington, 1874. x+438pp.

The *New York Herald* and *Daily News* correspondent (1844-78) offered his book as "rather a record of travel and adventure than a regular history of a military campaign". It begins with his journey to the Aral Sea in April 1873, accompanied as far as Fort Perovskii by Eugene Schuyler, the American *chargé d'affaires* in Petersburg, and ends with his return in September, having witnessed the fall of Khiva on 9 June, after adventures that gave him legendary status in Russia.

I116) **Nasir al-Din Shah,** *The diary of H.M. the Shah of Persia, during his tour through Europe in A.D. 1873. A* verbatim translation by J.W. Redhouse. London: John Murray, 1874. xx+427pp.

The first of three European journeys by the shah (1831-96) brought him and his entourage by boat to Astrakhan on 14 May 1873. They sailed up the Volga to Tsaritsyn and then proceeded by rail to Moscow and arrived in St Petersburg on 22 May, where, after a week of official engagements, they proceeded to Berlin (pp. 22-67). After visiting most of the European capitals, including London, the shah on his return journey sailed from Constantinople to Poti, where he arrived on 28 August, and then proceeded to Tiflis (pp. 401-27).

I117) **Phelps, Charles Harris,** *A trip from Finland to Persia, Dahgestan, and Circassia, delivered before the American Geographical Society, April 30, 1876.* New York: n.p., 1876. 28pp.

Lecture by New York lawyer (b. 1845) of his journey from St Petersburg to Moscow and then down the Volga to Astrakhan in July 1873, illustrated by photographs that are part of the Phelps photographic collection left to the *National Geographic.*

I118) **Stanley, Augusta Elizabeth Frederica,** *Later letters of Lady Augusta Stanley, 1864-1876, including many unpublished letters to and from Queen*

Victoria and correspondence with Dean Stanley, Lady Frances Baillie, and others. Edited by the Dean of Windsor [Albert Victor Baillie] and Hector Bolitho. London: Jonathan Cape, 1929. 288pp.

> Lady Stanley, née Bruce (1822-76), long-time confidante of Queen Victoria and officially designated one of "the Queen's ladies", accompanied her husband Dean Stanley (see I19) to Russia in January 1874 to attend the wedding of the Duke of Edinburgh. She wrote detailed letters to her sister during the visit (pp. 199-239).

I119) Telfer, John Buchan, *The Crimea and Transcaucasia, being the narrative of a journey in the Kouban, in Gouria, Georgia, Armenia, Ossety, Imeritia, Swannety, and Mingrelia, and in the Tauric range.* London: Henry S. King & Co., 1876. 2 vols.

> Telfer (1831?-1907), R.N., F.S.A. and F.R.G.S., writes in his preface that the book was in fact the result of two journeys he and his Russian wife (Ekaterina Muraveva, referred to as "K") made to the region during the three years he lived in south Russia (1873-76), fashioned into a substantial and well-informed guide-book for a 92-day round trip from Odessa and supplying all the information a tourist might need from sights to supplies.

I120) Meignan, Victor, *From Paris to Pekin over Siberian snows: a narrative of a journey by sledge over the snows of European Russia and Siberia, by caravan through Mongolia, across the Gobi Desert and the Great Wall, and by mule palanquin through China to Pekin.* Edited from the French by William Conn, with supplementary notes not contained in the original edition. London: W. Swan Sonnenschein and Co., 1885. xx+428pp.

> The young Frenchman (b. 1846) left Paris on 25 October 1873 to realize his dream of travelling through Siberia "in its wondrous winter garb" and it was only when he exchanged train for sledge at Nizhnii Novgorod on 15 December that his real journey begins and is described in detail as he travelled to the Chinese border via Perm, Tiumen, Omsk, Tomsk, Irkutsk and Lake Baikal by March 1874 (pp. 1-284).

I121) Wiggins, Joseph, *The life and voyages of Joseph Wiggins, F.R.G.S., modern discoverer of the Kara Sea route to Siberia based on his journals & letters.* By Henry Johnson. London: John Murray, 1907. xxiv+396pp.

> Captain Wiggins (1832-1905), one of the most celebrated of late Victorian Arctic explorers, pioneered the route via the Kara Sea to the Enesei and up the river to Eneseisk, making several voyages between 1874 and 1896.

He paid a further brief visit to Russia in April 1905 on the invitation of the Russian government to help organize famine relief efforts (pp. 25-64, 85-188, 191-92, 202-19, 250-55, 268-300, 317-25).

I122) Wood, Herbert, *The shores of Lake Aral.* London: Smith, Elder & Co., 1876. xxviii+352pp.

A major in the Royal Engineers and F.R.G.S., Wood was invited to join the Russian Geographical Society's expedition to Lake Aral, beginning his well-informed and detailed account with his departure from Samara in the spring of 1874.

I123) Butler-Johnstone, Henry Alexander Munro, *A trip up the Volga to the fair of Nijni-Novgorod.* Oxford and London: James Parker & Co., 1875. viii+151pp.

Butler-Johnstone (1837-1902), M.P., travelled on board the steamer *Alexander II* from Astrakhan to Nizhnii Novgorod in the summer of 1874, first describing his trip through "the most interesting portion of the Russian Empire" in a series of letters to the *Daily News*. Due attention is given to the German colonies around Saratov, the koumiss-cure establishments near Samara, and the attractions of Kazan, but it is the annual fair at Nizhnii that is described in particular and interesting detail (pp. 68-151).

I124) Grove, Florence Crauford, *'The frosty Caucasus': an account of a walk through part of the range and of an ascent of Elbruz in the summer of 1874.* London: Longmans, Green, and Co., 1875. x+341pp.

A founder member of the London Alpine Club and later its president, Grove (1838-1902) and three fellow climbers arrived in Odessa on 23 June 1874 en route for Kutais and thence into the mountains of the Caucasus. They were to scale the western summit of Elbruz on 28 July (p. 238).

I125) Godfrey, W.H.K., *Three months on the continent; or, the record of a tour through Europe in 1874: supplemented by the journal of a trip to the Great Lakes of America, in 1873.* Waterbury, Conn.: American Print Co., 1875. vii+180pp.

"Originally a hastily written series of letters to the Waterbury American newspaper, and has been published in book form at the request of friends, mainly for private circulation." They describe a tour in the summer of 1874 that takes the author from England to France, Belgium, Germany, and on to Russia, where he celebrates 4 July in St Petersburg with Marshall Jewell, the American minister, before travelling to Moscow, exiting via Poland for Austria and Italy (pp. 60-96).

I126) Boulton, Samuel Bagster, *The Russian empire: its origin and development.* London, Paris & New York: Cassell & Co., 1882. 192pp.

> Sir Samuel (1830-1918), founder and chairman of the London Labour Conciliation Board, included in his potted history of Russia impressions from his first tourist visit with members of his family in August 1874, which are interesting solely for the trip to the estate of Count S- and his English wife on an estate some hours' journey from the capital (pp. 5-57).

I127) Rae, Edward, *The land of the north wind; or, travels among the Laplanders and the Samoyedes.* London: John Murray, 1875. xvi+352pp.

> Rae (b. 1847), F.R.G.S., and his companion Henry Brandeth paid two visits to the Arctic region in 1873-74. It was the second of these, begun on 18 June 1874, that was to take them directly by ship from the Firth of Forth to Archangel. They then travel inland to Pinega and on to Mezen, where they encounter the Samoeds, whose life and language they attempt to study. Rae proves an amusing raconteur (pp. 144-352).

I128) Rae, Edward, *Siberia in Europe: impressions of the Samoyedes and their country.* Chester: Chester Society of Natural Science, 1876. 46pp.

> Rae's lecture on "the least known people in the world", given in Chester a year after the appearance of his book.

I129) Seebohm, Henry, *Siberia in Europe: a visit to the valley of the Petchora, in north-east Russia; with descriptions of the natural history, migration of birds, etc.* London: John Murray, 1880. xvi+311pp.

> The ornithologist Seebohm (1832-1895), accompanied by the zoologist John Alexander Harvie-Brown (see I99), left London on 3 March 1875, travelling via St Petersburg and Archangel to reach the lower valley of the Pechora, where their bird-watching (and shooting) began in earnest. They set sail on 3 August for Elsinore.

I130) Reed, Edward James, *Letters from Russia in 1875.* London: John Murray, 1876. xvi+90pp.

> The letters, which were previously published in *The Times*, begin on 6 October 1875 from Nikolaev, the Black Sea port, where the eminent naval architect Sir James (1830-1906), M.P., F.R.S., had arrived the previous day, travelling via Vienna, Cracow and Odessa. In six lengthy letters, the first four from New Russia and the Crimea and the last two from Moscow and St Petersburg, towards the end of the month, he describes Russian naval matters, particularly the development of circular ironclads for the defence

of the Azov Sea. Otherwise notable for his highly positive assessment of the marine artist Aivazovskii (pp. 58-61).

I131) Boker, George Henry, ['Letter'], in Eugene Schuyler, *Selected essays*. London: Sampson Low, Marston, & Co., 1901. 364pp.

> Prolific American dramatist and poet, most noted for his romantic drama *Francesca da Rimini* (1856), Boker (1823-90) had a brief career as a diplomat in the 1870s. Following a spell in Turkey he was posted as minister in 1875-78 to St Petersburg, from where on 26 October 1876 he addressed his letter to Schuyler about the reception of his book on Central Asia (see I108) (pp. 83-85).

I132) Burnaby, Frederick Gustavus, *A ride to Khiva: travels and adventures in central Asia. With maps and an appendix, containing, amongst other information, a series of march-routes, translated from several Russian works*. London: Cassell, Petter & Galpin, 1876. xviii+487pp.

> A captain in the Royal Horse Guards, Burnaby (1842-85), who had visited Russia for the first time in 1870, decided to use a period of leave to journey through Russia to Khiva to investigate the dangers for Britain of Russian expansionism. He set out from England on 30 November 1875 and, despite the hostile winter conditions, reached his goal in January 1876 and was received by the khan. He was back to England in March and was lionized for his exploits.

I133) Phillipps-Wolley, Clive, *Sport in the Crimea and Caucasus*. London: Richard Bentley & Son, 1881. x+370pp.

> British vice-consul in Kerch, Sir Clive (1853-1918), who first visited the Caucasus in February 1876, describes in detail several hunting expeditions he made in the area until his return to England in 1880. The book includes, incidentally, his first (unremarked) translation from Pushkin (pp. 359-61).

I134) Brehm, Alfred Edmund, *From North Pole to Equator: studies of wild life and scenes in many lands*. Translated from the German by Margaret R. Thomson. Edited by J. Arthur Thomson. London, Glasgow, Edinburgh, and Dublin: Blackie & Son, 1896. 592pp.

> The German naturalist Brehm (1829-84) travelled extensively through Siberia in 1876. After his death his son published his lectures and papers, which include several devoted to the animal, bird, and human (exiles as well as native peoples) life in Siberia and the Kirghiz steppe (pp. 86-168, 416-540). One entitled 'A journey in Siberia' details his itinerary from St Petersburg in March 1876 via Omsk, Semipalatinsk, Tashkent, across the

Kirgkiz steppe to the Altai mountains, then again into Siberia to the Urals and north to the tundra to visit the Ostiaks (pp. 390-415).

I135) Upton, Emory, *The armies of Europe & Asia: embracing official reports on the armies of Japan, China, India, Persia, Italy, Russia, Austria, Germany, France, and England; accompanied by letters descriptive of a journey from Japan to the Caucasus.* Portsmouth: Griffin & Co., 1878. x+446pp.

> Commandant of cadets at West Point from 1870 to 1875, Major-General Upton (1839-81) began in July 1875 a two-year world tour under instructions from the U.S. Secretary of War "to examine and report upon the organization, tactics, discipline, and the manoeuvres" of the various armies. His route took him on 6 April 1876 from Persia into Russia, and he traveled to Tiflis, then across the Caucasus to Rostov and to Sevastopol, where he arrived on 23 April. In addition to the information on the Russian army (pp. 146-60), there are two letters describing the Caucasus part of his journey (pp. 434-40).

I136) Eyre, Selwyn, *Sketches of Russian life and customs, made during a visit in 1876-7.* London: Remington and Co., 1878. ii+337pp.

> Eyre reaches Moscow via Warsaw in late July 1876. He remained there until the end of August 1877, penning the series of effusive letters that comprise his book. The impending Russo-Turkish war is a constant theme in his undemanding parade of "facts and pictures as they have been presented to my view".

I137) Bryce, James, *Transcaucasia and Ararat, being notes of a vacation tour in the autumn of 1876.* London: Macmillan and Co., 1877. x+420pp. [4th edition, with added chapter on Armenian question, 1896. x+526pp.]

> British jurist, historian and politician James Bryce, 1st Viscount Bryce of Dechmont (1838-1922), begins his account with his departure from Nizhnii Novgorod on 24 August 1876. He travels via Voronezh to Taganrog before journeying through the Caucasus to Tiflis. He leaves Tiflis on 6 September for Armenia, visiting Erevan and ascending Ararat, before retracing his steps via Tiflis to Poti on the Black Sea, whence he sails to Constantinople.

I138) Ainslie, Ainslie Douglas, *Russia: a lecture delivered at Fraserburgh and Petershead on the 10th and 11th January 1877.* Banff: printed at the Banffshire Journal Office, 1880. 42pp. [Included as 'Russia as I found it' (pp. 37-102), in his *Glances over past and present.* Edinburgh: David Douglas, 1913, viii+327pp.]

The text of a long, long lecture delivered by the poet and translator (1839-1929), following a recent visit to Russia in the summer of 1876. The first half was devoted to an overview of Russian history and literature (with interesting lines on Pushkin); the second, with the help of a magic lantern, to his tour of St Petersburg.

I139) Long, James, *A visit to Russia in 1876.* London: printed by R. Clay, Sons, and Taylor, 1876. 11pp.

Rev. Long (1814-87), eminent Anglo-Indian translator of Krylov's fables (1869) and commentator on both Russian and Indian affairs (see his *Village communities in India and Russia* (1870)), had visited Russia on two previous occasions, in 1863 and 1872-73, as he frequently recalls in his brief account of his third and final visit in the autumn of 1876. He visited clerics in St Petersburg and Moscow, discussing ecclesiastical matters and recommending greater understanding and intercourse between the Anglican and Russian churches.

I140) Roth, Henry Ling, *A sketch of the agriculture and peasantry of eastern Russia.* London: Baillière, Tindall, & Cox, 1878. viii+110pp.

After studies in London and Germany, the young Roth (1854-1925), future anthropologist and museum curator, went to Russia in 1876-77 to work in "practical farming" at Timashevo, a village near Samara. He travelled extensively throughout the Volga region, visiting the German and Swiss colonies, and studying agricultural practices and the life and customs of the peasants.

I141) Roth, Henry Ling, *Sketches and reminiscences from Queensland, Russia, and elsewhere... Reprinted from the "Halifax Courier", Sept., 1915 to May, 1916.* Halifax, 1916. 39pp.

Roth recalls his stay in Russia in 1876-77 and in Australia in 1878-84 in articles written for his local paper in Halifax, where he had settled in 1888.

I142) Burnaby, Frederick Gustavus, *On horseback through Asia Minor.* London: Cassell, Petter and Galpin, 1877. 2 vols.

Burnaby (see I132) used his next spell of extended leave to see the region from the Turkish side and travelled to Constantinople and thence to Kars and Batumi in the winter of 1876-77. It was a visit that increased his pro-Turkish stance and fears of the Russian threat to India.

I143) Baedeker, Friedrich Wilhelm, *Dr. Baedeker: and his apostolic work in Russia.* By Robert Sloan Latimer. With introductory notes by Princess

Nathalie Lieven and Lord Radstock. London: Morgan and Scott, 1907. 223pp.

> Dr Baedeker (1823-1906), German by birth but a British citizen, marrying and dying in England, was after his conversion in 1866 a tireless evangelist with the Russian empire as the particular centre of his activities. He first went to Russia in 1877 and in the course of the next three decades travelled throughout the empire from the Baltic provinces to Siberia and Sakhalin, and to the Caucasus and the Caspian. Long extracts from his diaries and letters (pp. 29-207).

I144) **Hoffman, Wickham,** *Leisure hours in Russia*. London: George Bell & Sons, 1883. 184pp.

> Secretary of the American legation in St Petersburg in the years 1877-82, Hoffman (1821-1900) spent most of his leisure hours translating poems from the Swedish of the Finnish poet Runeberg, but also wrote an essay on St Petersburg and another on Russian superstitions that first appeared in *Penn's monthly magazine* (pp. 1-29).

I145) **Seebohm, Henry,** *Siberia in Asia: a visit to the valley of the Yenesay in east Siberia; with descriptions of the natural history, migration of birds, etc.* London: John Murray, 1882. xviii+304pp.

> In early March 1877 Seebohm set out with the Arctic explorer Joseph Wiggins (see I120) on a journey to more distant parts of Siberia, travelling initially by train to Nizhnii Novgorod and then onwards by sledge. On 23 April they reached Wiggins's ship the *Thames*, on which they were to sail along the Enisei until it was wrecked early in July. Seebohm was obliged to return overland, reaching St Petersburg on 23 September and England on 10 October. After his death Seebohm's two books were published together as *Birds of Siberia* (1901).

I146) **Whishaw, James,** *The memoirs of James Whishaw*. Edited by Maxwell S. Leigh. London: Methuen, 1935. viii+303pp.

> Born in Archangel, Whishaw (1853-1933), scion of a British family resident in Russia since the reign of Catherine II, was taken at the age of six months to England, where he was brought up and educated. His real memoirs of Russia begin on his return to pursue a business career in 1877. He took Russian citizenship in 1884 and later become British vice-consul and a highly respected figure in St Petersburg. He left with his family in October 1917 and eventually regained British citizenship. His memoirs are invaluable for descriptions of the life of the British colony in St Petersburg, and in particular, its sporting pursuits (pp. 17-25, 58-205, 219-88).

I147) Whishaw, Frederick James (Fred), *Out of doors in Tsarland: a record of the seeings and doings of a wanderer in Russia.* London: Longmans, Green & Co., 1893. vii+380pp.

> Fred Whishaw (1854-1934) was born into a family of British merchants established in Russia since the late eighteenth century. He joined the family firm, but enjoyed hunting and fishing more. He returned soon after his marriage in 1880 to England, where he wrote over thirty novels for boys, most with a Russian setting.

I148) Whishaw, Frederick James (Fred), *The romance of the woods.* London: Longmans, Green & Co., 1895. 298pp.

> Series of essays and sketches on hunting and folk-lore, such as 'After ducks on Ladoga' and 'The folk-lore of the moujik'. No dates.

I149) Daily News, *The war correspondence of the 'Daily News', 1877, with a connecting narrative forming a continuous history of the war between Russia and Turkey to the fall of Kars, including the letters of Mr Archibald Forbes, Mr J[anuarius] A[loysius] Macgahan and many other special correspondents in Europe and Asia.* London: Macmillan & Co., 1877. 627pp. [2nd edition, 1878: *The war correspondence...; containing a full description of the taking of Kars.* 643pp.] — *The war correspondence of the 'Daily News', 1877-8, continued from the fall of Kars to the signature of the preliminaries of peace; with a connecting narrative forming a continuous history of the war between Russia and Turkey.* London: Macmillan & Co., 1878. xvi+599pp.

> The re-publishing of the reports, "hastily written in the bivouac, on the field of victory, or in some hovel on the line of retreat", filed by no less than seventeen international correspondents during the Russo-Turkish conflict of 1877-78, some of whom, such as Forbes and MacGahan, were to publish their own reports and reminiscences.

I150) Greene, Francis Vinton, *The Russian army and its campaigns in Turkey in 1877-1878.* London: W.H. Allen & Co., 1879. xv+459pp.

> Military attaché to the American legation in St Petersburg (1877-79) and a lieutenant in the engineers, but later achieving the rank of major general, Greene (1850-1921) attempts to provide a professional assessment of the Russian army and to narrate the events of the Russo-Turkish war which he had been sent from America to observe.

I151) Greene, Francis Vinton, *Sketches of army life in Russia*. London: W.H. Allen & Co., 1881. 326pp.

> Greene's follow-up to his previous book is his attempt to provide for a wider readership an insight into the life and mentality of the Russian soldier. It is also notable for chapters on the American and British reporters of the Russo-Turkish war, particularly MacGahan and Forbes, and on St Petersburg.

I152) Forbes, Archibald, *Souvenirs of some continents*. London: Macmillan & Co., 1885. 332pp.

> Correspondent of the *Daily News* during the Russo-Turkish war of 1877-78, Forbes (1838-1900) includes chapters relating to that period – on General Skobelev (pp. 1-46), his American colleague MacGahan (pp. 120-40), and his interview of Alexander II during the war (pp. 199-204). Later included in his *Memories and studies of war and peace* (1895), pp. 14-37, 361-66.

I153) [Herbert, Frederick William von], *The defence of Plevna, 1877*. Written by one who took part in it. London: Longmans, Green & Co., 1895. xvii+488pp. [2nd condensed edition with an introduction by General Sir John French, London: Smith, Elder & Co., 1911.]

> Captain Herbert, a British citizen of Anglo-German descent, joined the Turkish army in February 1877 as a seventeen-year-old lieutenant. He provides a vivid account of the battles in which he took part until his capture by the Russians at the fall of Plevna on 10 December 1877.

I154) Macpherson, R.B., *Under the red crescent: or, ambulance adventures in the Russo-Turkish war of 1877-78*. London: Hamilton, Adams & Co.; Edinburgh and Glasgow: John Menzies & Co., 1885. 213pp.

> Like the preceding work by Herbert, this account by a Scottish surgeon with the Turkish army is obviously not russocentric but included to give a more rounded picture of British involvement in the conflict.

I155) Stanley, Francis, *St. Petersburg to Plevna: containing interviews with leading Russian statesmen and generals*. London: Richard Bentley and Son, 1878. vi+246pp.

> Appointed special war correspondent of the *Manchester Guardian*, Stanley left England on 16 May 1877 to conduct his first interviews with, among others, Prince Petr Shuvalov and Admiral Greig in St Petersburg before proceeding to Bucharest to join the Russian army and numerous other

correspondents, to whose published accounts of the campaign and the fall of Plevna his provides an interesting and often divergent variant.

I156) McCosh, John, *Grand tours in many lands: a poem in ten cantos.* London: Remington and Co., 1881. xii+292pp.

An eccentric poetic addition to commentaries on the Russo-Turkish war, the fall of Plevna and capture of Kars by a Scottish doctor and noted amateur photographer (1805-85), who had been in the Indian medical service (1831-56) and travelled extensively around the Mediterranean. 'The war of the czar' occupies cantos VI-X (pp. 155-290).

I157) Dillon, Emile Joseph, *Russia today & yesterday.* London & Toronto: J.M. Dent and sons, 1929. xii+338pp.

The lapsed Irish Catholic Dr Dillon (1854-1933) arrived in Russia in 1877 and remained virtually throughout the whole of the reigns of Alexander III and Nicholas II. In the opening chapters of this book, describing his first visit to the Soviet Union in 1928, he recalls his early career in Russia, graduating from Petersburg university, becoming professor of comparative philology at the university of Kharkov, and editing an Odessa newspaper (pp. 1-36) (see also J89, K5)

I158) Young, John Russell, *Around the world with General Grant: a narrative of the visit of General U.S. Grant, ex-president of the United States to various countries in Europe, Asia, and Africa in 1877, 1878, 1879. To which are added certain conversations with General Grant on questions connected with American politics and history.* New York: American News Co., 1879. 734pp.

Young (1832-1901), a journalist for the New York *Herald* and later Librarian of Congress, acted as secretary to former president Ulysses S. Grant (1822-85) on a world tour that took them to St Petersburg and Moscow in July-August 1878 (pp. 464-94).

I159) Nordenskiöld, Adolf Erik, *The voyage of the Vega round Asia and Europe, with a historical review of previous journeys along the north coast of the Old World.* Translated [from the Swedish] by Alexander Leslie. London: Macmillan & Co., 1881. 2 vols.

The Swedish explorer (1832-1901), who had travelled as far as the Enisei in 1875 and 1876, interleaves the account of his new expedition with much material on earlier exploration from the sixteenth century onwards. The *Vega* left Tromsö on 21 July 1878, sailed across the Murman and Kara seas to the Enisei; they wintered among the Chukchis, until, released from the ice on 18 July 1878, they passed through the Bering Strait en route to Japan, where they arrived on 2 September 1879 (vol. I, pp. 1-524; II, pp. 1-295).

I160) Christie, James, *Men and things Russian; or, holiday travels in the lands of the czar*. Edinburgh: Andrew Elliot, Carlisle: Charles Thurnam & Sons, and London: Hamilton, 1879. viii+216pp.

> Acting chaplain to H.M. Forces and minister of the Presbyterian Church, Fisher Street, Carlisle, Rev. Christie spent the month of August 1878 on a holiday tour that took him from St Petersburg to Moscow, Nizhnii Novgorod, Kazan, Kiev and on to Warsaw.

I161) Nasir al-Din Shah, *A diary kept by His Majesty the Shah of Persia, during his journey to Europe in 1878*. From the Persian by Albert Houtum Schindler and Baron Louis de Norman. London: Richard Bentley & Son, 1879. 306pp.

> The second European tour by the shah (see I116) took him from Teheran to the Russian border, where he was met by Prince Menshikov on 4 July 1878. He travelled to St Petersburg via Erevan, Tiflis, Vladikavkaz, Ukraine and Moscow. He left for Berlin via Warsaw. As on his previous journey, the shah was particularly taken with theatrical and variety performances (pp. 51-122). On his return journey, he crossed from Austria into Russian territory beyond Brody and travelled extensively through the Caucasus and Daghestan, visiting the house in Taganrog where Alexander I died (pp. 275-306).

I162) Edwards, Henry Sutherland, *The Russians at home and the Russians abroad: sketches, unpolitical and political, of Russian life under Alexander II*. London: Wm. H. Allen & Co., 1879. 2 vols.

> Eighteen years after publishing *The Russians at home* (see I34), Edwards re-issued it in an abridged version as a first volume followed by a second, devoted explicitly to "political" matters. In a series of chapters based largely on articles he had written for newspapers in earlier years, he examines such questions as nihilism, panslavism, and Russian attitudes and policy towards Poland, Central Asia, and India.

I163) Swaine, Leopold Victor, *Camp and chancery in a soldier's life*. London: John Murray, 1926. xii+262pp.

> Major-General Sir Leopold (b. 1840), when a colonel, was sent to the St Petersburg embassy as military attaché at the very beginning of 1879, but remained less than five months before he returned to London and was soon transferred to Constantinople. His memories of those months are confined to embassy and court anecdotes (pp. 89-105).

I164) Dufferin and Ava, Frederick Temple Hamilton-Temple-Blackwood, 1st Marquis of, *The life of the marquis of Dufferin and Ava.* By Sir Alfred Lyall. London: John Murray, 1905. 2 vols.

> Petersburg was Lord Dufferin's (1826-1902) first ambassadorship and he served there from February 1879 until April 1881. This authorized biography contains extracts from his letters and diaries during this period, including, most vividly, his account of the assassination of the tsar (vol. I, pp. 288-324). Also included are 'Some recollections of service with Lord Dufferin at the St Petersburg embassy' by one of the attachés, **R.J. Kennedy** (vol. I, pp. 325-58).

I165) Dufferin and Ava, Hariot, *My Russian and Turkish journals.* London: John Murray, 1916. 350pp.

> The delightful diaries of Lady Dufferin, née Hamilton (1843-1916), contain all the minutiae of embassy and Petersburg social life lacking in her husband's (published) diaries (pp. 1-123).

I166) O'Donovan, Edmond, *The Merv oasis: travels and adventures east of the Caspian during the years 1879-80-81, including five months' residence among the Tekkés of Merv.* London: Smith, Elder, & Co., 1882. 2 vols.

> Special correspondent for the *Daily News*, O'Donovan (1844-83) offered his two large volumes as "a simple record of my wanderings around and beyond the Caspian", which began on 6 February 1879 with his arrival in Batumi and led to Tiflis and Baku, across the Caspian to Krasnovodsk, and on into Persia (vol. I, pp. 1-142).

I167) [Hamilton, Frederic], *The vanished pomps of yesterday, being some random reminiscences of a British diplomat.* London: Hodder and Stoughton, 1919. 375pp.

> Lord Hamilton (1865-1956), a career diplomat, was transferred from Potsdam to Petersburg in 1880, serving under Dufferin and his successor Sir Edward Thornton until his transfer to Portugal in 1883. His lively memoirs contain much on the social life in the capital and his prowess as a hunter, as well as marking events such as the assassination of Alexander II (pp. 83-217). Hamilton paid two subsequent short visits to Petersburg in 1910 and 1912, which he recalls briefly in a few nostalgic pages (pp. 354-64).

I168) Hamilton, Frederic, *The days before yesterday.* London: Hodder and Stoughton, 1920. 320pp.

> In his second volume of memoirs, now appearing under his name, Hamilton recalls his enthusiasm for amateur theatricals cultivated in diplomatic circles in St Petersburg (pp. 213-19). He also describes seeing Alexander II's assassins on their way to execution (pp. 226-27).

I169) Hamilton, Frederic, *Here, there and everywhere.* London: Hodder and Stoughton, 1921. xiv+304pp.

> In his third and final volume of memoirs, bearing the collective title of *My yesterdays,* Hamilton describes his trip down the Volga in 1881, accompanied by the French academician, the vicomte de Vogue, author of the influential *Le roman russe* (pp. 55-59). He also recalls the splendour and costs of the "bals des palmiers" in the Winter Palace (pp. 230-33).

I170) Baddeley, John Frederick, *Russia in the 'eighties': sport and politics.* London: Longmans, Green and Co., 1921. xvi+466pp.

> Baddeley (1854-1940), special correspondent of the London *Standard* throughout the 1880s, paid his first visit to Russia in February 1879 at the invitation of Count Petr Shuvalov, the Russian ambassador in London. True to its sub-title, the book mixes detailed reporting of the politics, both internal and international, of the period with much on the author's passion for hunting, shooting and fishing with both Russian friends and members of the British community.

I171) Lansdell, Henry, *Through Siberia.* London: Sampson Low, Marston, Searle, and Rivington, 1882. 2 vols.

> On 3 May 1879 Rev. Lansdell (1841-1919), intrepid traveller and would-be prison reformer, arrived in St Petersburg, bent on his mission to distribute religious tracts and bibles, particularly in Siberia. Over the next five months he travelled extensively, visiting all the principal towns and commenting not unfavourably on the penal system. He reached Kamchatka and eventually sailed from Vladivostok for San Francisco in September 1879.

I172) Sutherland-Leveson-Gower, Ronald Charles, *My reminiscences.* London: Kegan Paul, Trench, & Co., 1883. 2 vols.

Sculptor and art connoisseur, Lord Gower (1845-1916) arrived in St Petersburg on 2 July 1879 as part of a tour that had begun in Spain. His declared objective was "to see the gallery of paintings in the Winter Palace", which he did, enthusing over its "chief glory", the Rembrandts. On 6 July he left for Moscow, which greatly under-impressed him, and back in St Petersburg, he visited Tsarskoe selo, before departing for Berlin on 5 July (vol. II, pp. 294-301).

I173) Selfridge, Thomas Oliver, Jr., *Memoirs of Thomas O. Selfridge, jr., rear admiral, U.S.N.* New York and London: G.P. Putnam's Sons, 1924. xii+288pp.

Selfridge (1836-1924) first visited Russia in 1879, arriving on 15 July at Cronstadt as commander of the *Enterprise*. He paid a visit to Grand Duke Constantine, the then head of the Russian navy, and received Alexander II on board his ship on the tsar's birthday on 30 July (pp. 229-33). In 1896, now a rear-admiral and commanding the *Minneapolis*, he arrived at Cronstadt on 13 May to represent the American navy at the coronation of Nicholas II, of which he provides a detailed description as well as of the Khodynka stampede of 30 May (pp. 251-74).

I174) Cushman, Mary Ames, *She wrote it all down.* New York and London: Charles Scribner's Sons, 1936. xi+226pp.

Mrs Cushman (1864-1943) recalls her visit to St Petersburg as a young girl with her family in the winter of 1879 from her travel journals of 1876-80 (pp. 62-68).

I175) Wood, Charles, *Saunterings in Europe.* With an introductory note by W.M. Taylor, D.D. New York: Anson D.F. Randolph & Co., 1882. xiv+346pp.

A young New York pastor (1851-1936) spent three years studying at Berlin University, broken by travels to other parts of Europe. He left Berlin for Moscow in December 1879 and spent time in St Petersburg, enjoying above all the ice-hills (pp. 204-39).

I176) Kendig, John A.J., *Sketches of travel: the East, the Far East, and some of the by-paths thither.* Chicago: Chicago Legal News Co., 1882. 279pp.

An Illinois lawyer (1834-96) included a few weeks in Russia in January 1880 as part of a conventional round-the-world tour. From Russian Finland he travelled to St Petersburg via Cronstadt and then proceeded to Moscow, which he hailed as the most beautiful city in Europe, and Nizhnii Novgorod (pp. 40-42, 49-57).

I177) **Stoddard, John Lawson,** *Red-letter days abroad.* Boston: James R. Osgood and Co., 1884. xvi+202pp.

> Popular author-lecturer (1850-1931) describes, with numerous engravings, "the cities of the czar", St Petersburg and Moscow, during a visit in 1880 (pp. 105-202). The Russian material was later incorporated into his *John L. Stoddard's lectures,* VI (1900), p. 227-336.

I178) **Rae, Edward,** *The White Sea peninsula: a journey in Russian Lapland and Karelia.* London: John Murray, 1881. xviii+347pp.

> Rae, once again accompanied by H.P. Brandeth (see I127), sailed from England on 31 May 1880, aiming to reach Kola in Russian Lapland, from where they would travel down to Kem. They visited the Solovetskii monastery and sailed across the White Sea, following the coast around the peninsular. It was at Kola that Rae organized a most extraordinary "international" cricket match (pp. 292-96).

I179) **'Wanderer' (pseudonym of D'Avigdor, Elim Henry),** *Notes on the Caucasus.* London: Macmillan & Co., 1883. viii+280pp.

> Although frequently specific about time of day or day of the month, there are no indications of years in this account of journeys through the Caucasus. D'Avigdor (1841-95), of mixed Italian and Anglo-Jewish parentage and an engineer by profession, but a prolific writer on varied subjects in his later years, writes of "having passed upwards of a year in Circassia" and having "myself travelled, often quite alone, all over the Western Caucasus and the southern provinces, also in Circassia, and have been twice to the Caspian"

I180) **Foster, John Watson,** *Diplomatic memoirs.* London: Constable & Co., 1910. 2 vols.

> Indiana lawyer Foster (1836-1917) presented his credentials as American envoy extraordinary and minister plenipotentiary to Alexander II on 10 June 1880. He was in St Petersburg during the trials of the nihilists that began in November and at the time of the tsar's assassination in March 1881. He presented his new credentials to Alexander III in May 1881, but resigned from the diplomatic service for family reasons in November (pp. 146-215). He was, however, persuaded to undertake a second special mission to Russia in May 1897 as ambassador extraordinary and plenipotentiary to carry to represent the American case in the dispute with Britain over the protection of fur-seals in the Bering Sea. During his two-week stay he had two audiences with Nicholas II and met Witte (pp. 216-34).

Fig. 44 Alexander III (n.d.), photograph by Félix Nadar.

10. REIGN OF ALEXANDER III (1881-1894)

See also H13, H41, H48, H81, H87, I5, I79, I90, I111, I180

J1) Cox, Samuel S., *Arctic sunbeams: or from Broadway to the Bosphorus by way of the North Cape.* New York: G.P. Putnam's Sons, 1882. 347pp.

> Offered as the product of "the simple and harmless egotism of the author, and not the pretension of an archaeologist or discoverer", it is the record of eight months' travel round the world that takes the American tourist via Scandinavia into Russia in August 1881. Cox enlists as his guide a veteran English resident, a Mr Pilley (see J57), who shows him the sights in the capital and in Moscow, where Cox takes the train south to Odessa en route to Constantinople (pp. 216-337).

J2) Macpherson, Georgina E., *Upheaval!: reminiscences of Russia before and after the revolution.* Cowley: for the author, n.d. 72pp.

> Writing primarily to inform her family of their Russian ties, Georgina (b. c.1871), one of fifteen children born to Scottish parents in St Petersburg, where her father had founded the Baltic Iron Works and Shipbuilding Yard in the reign of Nicholas I, covers various aspects of Russian life and customs, but without any specific dates (pp. 7-40). Then follows the text of a lecture she used to give about her vicissitudes during the revolutions of 1917 and a long stay in the Kuban, first under Bolshevik, then White rule, before she eventually managed to get to Britain in 1920.

J3) Newcomb, Raymond Lee, *Our lost explorers: the narrative of the Jeannette Arctic expedition as related by the survivors, and in the records and last journals of Lieutenant De Long with graphic descriptions of Arctic Siberia, the Lena and its Delta, the native and exiled inhabitants of the country, etc.; and Mr. Newcomb's narrative of a winter overland journey from the Arctic Ocean to St. Petersburg.* Compiled by Richard W. Bliss and revised by Raymond Lee Newcomb.

http://dx.doi.org/10.11647/OBP.0042.10

With an introduction by Rev. W.L. Gage. Hartford, Conn.: American Publishing Co.; San Francisco: A.L. Bancroft & Co., 1882. 479pp.

> The ill-fated U.S.S. *Jeannette*, funded by the owner of the New York *Herald* to explore northwest of the Bering Strait, left San Francisco on 8 July 1879 and became entrapped in ice which crushed and sank it on 12 June 1881. This publication brings together various documents and journals by members of the expedition, some of which subsequently appeared separately. Newcomb (1849-1918), who collaborated on this composite publication, was the ship's naturalist and astronomer and included his own journal of events up to and including his journey back across Siberia to St Petersburg, where he arrived on 1 May 1882, meeting the tsar at Gatchina (pp. 277-365).

J4) De Long, George Washington, *The voyage of the Jeannette: the ship and ice journals of George W. De Long, lieutenant-commander U.S.N., and commander of the Polar expedition of 1879-1881.* Edited by his wife, Emma De Long. Boston and New York: Houghton, Mifflin and Co., 1883. 2 vols.

> The logs of the commander of the expedition (1844-81) whose conduct during and after the voyage was the subject of a posthumous enquiry and who was fully vindicated. Only two of the men in his boat that made land in Siberia survived, De Long dying of starvation. For Siberia, see [vol. II, continuous pagination] pp. 725-862.

J5) Melville, George Wallace, *In the Lena delta: a narrative of the search for Lieutenant-Commander De Long and his companions; followed by an account of the Greely relief expedition and a proposed method of reaching the North Pole.* Edited by Melville Philips. London: Longmans & Co., 1885. 510pp.

> Melville (1841-1912), who rose to be a rear-admiral, was the *Jeannette*'s chief engineer during its fateful expedition and in charge of the only one of the three small boats to make the Lena delta and safety on 17 September 1881. He then travelled back over a thousand miles in search of De Long and his men only to find them dead but retrieved the expedition's records. He received the Congressional gold medal for his bravery.

J6) Danenhower, John Wilson, *Lieutenant Danenhower's narrative of the "Jeannette".* Boston: James R. Osgood and Co., 1882. xii+102pp.

> The expedition's executive officer, Lt. Danenhower (1849-87) was in Melville's boat that reached the Lena delta. Virtually blind from an eye infection, he arrived back in the United States on 28 May 1882. This is a revised version of the account he had dictated in Irkutsk to John Jackson, special correspondent of the New York *Herald*, where it first appeared.

J7) Ambler, James Markham, *The private journal of James Markham Ambler, M.D., passed assistant surgeon United States navy and medical officer of the Arctic exploring steamer "Jeannette".* Introductory note by J.S. Gatewood. Washington, D.C.: US Government Printing Office, 1917. 38pp.

> Markham (1848-81), the ship's doctor, remained on the ship tending the sick and wounded and died there.

J8) Muir, John, *The cruise of the Corwin: journal of the Arctic expedition of 1881 in search of De Long and the Jeannette.* Edited [with an introduction] by William Frederic Badè. Boston and New York: Houghton Mifflin Co., 1917. xxxi+278pp.

> The revered Scottish-born American naturalist and advocate of wilderness (1838-1914) joined the *USS Corwin*, sent in early May 1881 to find the *Jeannette* and two missing whaling ships, to pursue his interests in botany and glaciation. He spent much time ashore among the Chukchis in June-July 1881 and was in the landing party that claimed Wrangel Island for America on 12 August 1881. The book was pieced together from Muir's newspaper correspondence, scientific articles and unpublished journals by his literary executor.

J9) Gilder, William Henry, *Ice-pack and tundra: an account of the search for the 'Jeannette' on a sledge journey through Siberia.* London: Sampson L, Marston, Searle, & Rivington, 1883. xii+344pp.

> Gilder (1838-1900), explorer and correspondent of the New York *Herald*, sailed on the *Rodgers* in the search for the *Jeannette* between July 1881 and August of the following year. When his ship burnt down, he travelled nearly 2,000 miles across Siberia to telegraph news of the disaster to the American government.

J10) Gallenga, Antonio Carlo Napoleone, *A summer tour in Russia.* London: Chapman and Hall, 1882. xii+426pp.

> Gallenga (1810-95) arrived in St Petersburg on 1 July 1881. Four months later, he returned home via Kiev and Warsaw, having travelled from Moscow down the Volga to Astrakhan and then through Georgia to Batumi and on to the Crimea and Odessa. Inspired by Mackenzie Wallace's *Russia*, he offers a sympathetic update, despite his suspicions of "a corrupt and tyrannical priesthood".

J11) Huntly, Charles Gordon, 11th Marquis of, *Travels, sport, and politics in the east of Europe.* London: Chapman and Hall, 1887. xii+311pp.

> Huntly (1847-1937), accompanied by his wife, reached Sevastopol on 14 July 1881 after a gentle journey down the Danube and on to Constantinople. They visited the battle sites before sailing from Yalta to Feodosia and then on to Batumi and Poti before taking the train to Tiflis and on to Vladikazkaz. They then proceeded to Taganrog and sailed to Kerch and, finally on their Russian leg, to Odessa, which they reached in October 1881(pp. 46-207).

J12) Scheutze, William Henry, *William Henry Scheutze.* Edited by Charles Deering. Chicago: R.R. Donnelly & Sons, 1903. [For private circulation.] x+165pp.

> Scheutze (1853-1902), a lieutenant-commander in the U.S. navy, was sent in 1882 to recover the bodies of victims on the *Jeannette*. He describes his journey in letters to his mother as well as a return visit in 1885, with gifts for the Russians who had helped the survivors.

J13) Phillipps-Wolley, Clive, *Savage Svanêtia.* London: Richard Bentley & Son, 1883. 2 vols.

> Two years after returning from the Crimea, Sir Clive (see I133) was tempted back to one of "the least known corners of the Caucasus", a region far inland from the Black Sea coast. He and a friend set out from London in the summer of 1882, travelling to Odessa and thence to Poti, before they went in search of game to shoot and scenery to admire among the mountains around Elbruz.

J14) Lansdell, Henry, *Russian central Asia: including Kuldja, Bokhara, Khiva, and Merv; with appendices on the fauna and flora of Russian Turkestan, and a bibliography of Russian central Asia, including 700 titles, chronologically and topically arranged.* London: Sampson Low, Marston, Searle and Rivington, 1885. 2 vols. [Revised and abridged version: *Through central Asia; with a map and appendix on the diplomacy and delimitation of the Russo-Afghan frontier* (1887).]

> Rev. Lansdell's second venture into the Russian empire (see I171), taking him and his tracts on this occasion by rail, water, carriage, horse and, indeed, camel some 12,000 miles into Siberia as far as Omsk. He then turned south towards Tashkent, Samarkand, and Baku, whence to Tiflis and eventually to Odessa, leaving London on 26 June and returning on 21 December 1882.

J15) Guillemard, Francis Henry Hill, *The cruise of the 'Marchesa' to Kamschatka & New Guinea with notices of Formosa, Liu-Kiu, and various islands of the Malay archipelago.* London: John Murray, 1886. 2 vols.

> Cambridge naturalist and F.R.G.S., Dr Guillemard (1852-1933) set sail from England on the newly commissioned schooner yacht on 8 January 1882 and, sailing from Japan, reached Kamchatka, its furthest destination, on 13 August. Until 27 September they explored the eastern side of the peninsular, recording the flora and fauna of the area (vol. I, pp. 66-228). There is an appendix on the birds of Kamchatka (vol. I, pp. 274-78).

J16) Noble, Edmund, *The Russian revolt: its causes, condition, and prospects.* London: Longmans, Green & Co., 1885. 269pp.

> Glasgow-born, Noble (1853-1937) emigrated to America in 1872, but it was as correspondent for the London *Daily News* that he twice visited Russia in 1882-84. Noble was later to write *Russia and the Russians* (1900), based almost exclusively on secondary sources and not revealing any personal experiences.

J17) Vogüé, Marie Eugène Melchior de, and Child, Theodore, *The tsar and his people or social life in Russia.* New York: Harper & Brothers, 1891. 435pp.

> A very interesting collection of nine essays without any editorial introduction or precise dating. The first two, 'Social life in Russia' (pp. 1-98) and 'Through the Caucasus' (pp. 101-47), were written by the vicomte de Vogüé (1848-1910), diplomat, writer, and member of the Académie française, and reflect his own experiences and travels, when he was attached to the French embassy in St Petersburg from October 1776 to 1882. The next five, 'Palatial Petersburg' (pp. 151-97), 'The fair of Nijnii-Novgorod' (pp. 201-42), 'Holy Moscow' (pp. 245-88), 'The Kremlin and Russian art' (291-337), and 'Modern Russian art' (pp. 341-90), were the work of the American traveller and artist Child (1846-92), that equally reflect his visits to Russia and his wide knowledge of Russian art. The first of the remaining two essays, 'Russian bronzes' (pp. 393-414) by Clarence Cook, deals with Russian exhibits at the Philadelphia Centennial Exhibition of 1876, while 'A Russian village' (pp. 417-35) was the contribution of the Russian artist Vasilii Vereshchagin.

J18) Vogüé, Marie Eugène Melchior de, *Russian portraits.* Translated by Elisabeth L. Cary. New York and London: G.P. Putnam's Sons (The Knickerbocker Press), 1895. xii+143pp.

Famed above all for his *Roman russe* (1886), Vogüé also published after his return from Russia *Histoires d'hiver*, which formed the basis for this translation of five sketches that reflect his sympathies for the Russian peasantry.

J19) Buel, James William, *Russian nihilism and exile life in Siberia: a graphic and chronological history of Russia's bloody nemesis, and a description of exile life in all its true but horrifying phases, being the results of a tour through Russia and Siberia made by the author, who carried with him letters of commendation from both the American and Russian governments.* San Francisco: A.L. Bancroft & Co., 1883. 547pp. [Re-issued as *A nemesis of misgovernment* ... Philadelphia: Historical Publishing Company, 1899.]

> A prolific author and journalist, Illinois-born Buel (1849-1920) left America on 24 June 1882, reaching Cronstadt via Hull. The first third of his book is devoted to a potted history of Russia with much detail on the nihilists (pp. 51-236). He then embarks on his travels through Siberia to inspect the exile system and take issue with the "Munchausen stories" of Lansdell (pp. 237-452). His impressions of life in St Petersburg (pp. 452-92) are followed by a visit to Warsaw and a general indictment of Russia's treatment of the Jews (pp. 492-535).

J20) Brown, John Croumbie, *Finland: its forest and forest management.* Edinburgh: Oliver and Boyd; London: Simpkin, Marshall, & Co. and William Rider & Son; Montreal: Dawson Bros., 1883. xvi+290pp.

> Rev. Dr Brown (1808-95), F.R.G.S., was pastor to the British and American church in St Petersburg between 1833 and 1839, but returned, after many years in Cape Province as Colonial Botanist, as summer locum for the then incumbents in the 1870s, visits that also allowed him to travel widely in Russia in pursuit of his interests in forestry and conservation. In connection with moves to establish a national school of forestry in Scotland from 1883, he embarked on a series of books on forestry throughout Europe that included four titles on Russia. In this, the first to be published, he begins with a description of a trip in June 1882 from St Petersburg to Kuopia, on the Saima See and to the Imatra Falls (pp. 3-30), before embarking on forestry matters.

J21) Brown, John Croumbie, *Forests and forestry in northern Russia and lands beyond.* Edinburgh: Oliver and Boyd; London: Simpkin, Marshall, & Co. and William Rider & Son; Montreal: Dawson Bros., 1884. viii+279pp.

Brown refers to a specific trip in the summer of 1882 to the provinces of Olonets, Vologda and Archangel to gather material for this, the second of his Russian works, as well as following his customary practice of quoting extensively from other printed accounts.

J22) Brown, John Croumbie, *Forests and forestry in Poland, Lithuania, the Ukraine, and the Baltic provinces of Russia, with notices of the export of timber from Memel, Dantzig, and Riga.* Edinburgh: Oliver and Boyd; London: Simpkin, Marshall, & Co. and William Rider & Son; Montreal: Dawson Bros., 1885. viii+276pp.

Brown published as his third contribution *Forestry in the mining districts of the Ural Mountains in Eastern Russia* (1884), but, as he admits, he did not travel to the Urals and relied on other sources for his information. His fourth volume, however, is based on frequent travels through western Russia and Poland, recalling specifically visits in 1836, 1873 and "my last", in 1878, that provide the personal element to his studies.

J23) Waddington, Mary King, *Letters of a diplomat's wife 1883-1900.* London: Smith, Elder & Co., 1903. vii+417pp.

American-born wife of a French citizen, Mme Waddington, née King (1845-1923), accompanied her husband to Moscow in May 1883 on his appointment as French ambassador extraordinary to attend the coronation of Alexander III. They left for home from St Petersburg on 21 June (pp. 26-127).

J24) Little, Anna P., *The world as we saw it.* By Mrs Amos R. Little. Boston: Cupples, 1887. 476pp.

Account of a family's world tour, east to west, in 1883. They reached Moscow via Poland and left from St Petersburg for Finland, eventually returning home via England.

J25) Wolseley, Garnet Joseph, *The letters of Lord and Lady Wolseley.* Edited by Sir George Arthur. London: William Heinemann, 1923. x+464pp.

Field-marshal Viscount Wolseley (1833-1913) was invited in May 1883 to accompany as general officer the Duke and Duchess of Edinburgh to Moscow to attend the coronation of Alexander III. In a series of letters to his wife he describes their arrival in Moscow on 21 May and the various events they attended before returning to England via St Petersburg (pp. 95-106).

J26) Marvin, Charles, *The region of eternal fire: an account of the petroleum region of the Caspian in 1883.* London: W.H. Allen & Co., 1884. viii+413pp. [Popular edition of 1888 revised with additional chapter.]

> One of the most prolific authors on questions of Russian expansionism in central Asia during the 1880s, Marvin (1854-90) after attending Alexander III's coronation in Moscow, decided to investigate the petroleum industry at Baku. His book is both a travelogue and a history of Baku and the region.

J27) Hunt, William Henry, *The life of William H. Hunt, by his son Thomas Hunt.* Brattleboro, Vermont: for the author, 1922. 360pp.

> Hunt (1823-84), formerly U. S. secretary of the navy, was appointed ambassador to Russia on 7 April 1882 and attended the coronation of Alexander III in May 1883. He died in St Petersburg on 27 February of the following year. The biography includes the text of a letter he sent on 6 November 1883 with his assessment of the relationship between autocracy and the people (pp. 271-83). See also the letters of Hunt's wife to her sister about their life in St Petersburg (pp. 284-355).

J28) Wells, Sara Furnas, *Ten years' travel around the world, or, from land to land, isle to isle and sea to sea, embracing twenty tours in England, Scotland, Ireland, France, Prussia, Belgium, Denmark, Sweden, Poland, Switzerland, Austria, Italy, Greece, Russia, Turkey, Holy Land, Syria, Egypt, India, Singapore, Java, Australia, South America, Central America, Sandwich Islands and North America.* Introduction by Rev. E.J. Scott. West Milton, Ohio: Morning Star Publishing Co., 1885. xxiv+653pp.

> Her eighteenth tour took Mrs Wells, M.D., formerly of the Women's Medical College in New York, from Finland to St Petersburg and on to Moscow in May 1883 for the coronation of the tsar, then back to the capital. She sailed from Cronstadt for England on 17 June (pp. 593-609).

J29) Raum, George Edward, *A tour round the world, being a brief sketch of the most interesting sights seen in Europe, Africa, Asia, and America, while on a two years' ramble.* New York: William S. Gottsberger, 1886. ii+430pp.

> What is very much a matter-of-fact guidebook to the sights, although apparently based on letters to his mother, suddenly is personalized with the description of the coronation of Alexander III in May 1883 that the artist and traveller Raum (1846-1935) and his wife Mary (1856-1947) witnessed during their stay in Moscow. They had travelled from St Petersburg and would seem to have gone on to the Crimea (pp. 74-96).

J30) [McCagg, Ezra Butler], *Six weeks of vacation in 1883*. Chicago: McDonnell Brothers, 1884. 152pp.

> A Chicago lawyer (1825-1908), identifying himself only by the initials E.B.McC. in his preface, travels from Moscow in the summer of 1883 down the Volga to the Caspian and on to the Caucasus and Constantinople before returning to Sistova (pp. 5-113).

J31) Sessions, Francis Charles, *From the land of the midnight sun to the Volga.* New York: Welch, Fracker Co., 1890. 167+xi pp.

> President of the Ohio Historical and Archaeological Society (1820-92) and his wife were members of a tourist group, who, having "done" Scandinavia, were shown the sights of St Petersburg, Moscow and Nizhnii Novgorod in August 1883 (pp. 98-167 + appendix).

J32) Taft, Alphonso, *Life of Alphonso Taft.* By Alexander Leonard Lewis. New York: Hawke Publishing Co., 1920. 307pp.

> American attorney-general under Ulysses S. Grant, Taft (1810-91) was appointed ambassador in St Petersburg by President Arthur in July 1884 and left a year later. His brief impressions of the imperial family and life in the Russian capital were originally given in an interview to a reporter from the *Tribune* (pp. 183-88).

J33) Hare, Augustus John Cuthbert, *Studies in Russia.* London: Smith, Elder & Co., 1885. x+504pp.

> When Hare (1834-1903) visited Russia in the summer of 1884, he was already the author of numerous biographies and travel books. He followed his usual practice of incorporating large doses of texts from other travellers' works as he visited – and sketched – St Petersburg, Novgorod, Moscow and Kiev, travelling home via Poland.

J34) Buckley, James Monroe, *The midnight sun: the tsar and the nihilist; adventures and observations in Norway, Sweden and Russia.* Boston: D. Lothrop and Co., 1886. xi+376pp.

> The American clergyman Dr Buckley (1836-1920), his eighteen-year old son, and a family friend set sail from New York on 19 June 1884 on a grand tour of northern Europe that would take them by the end of the summer from Scandinavia to St Petersburg, Moscow, and Nizhnii Novgorod and home via Poland. Committed to "an animated narrative", Buckley ends his

account with a series of essays, including one on nihilism, "the controlling cause of my visit to Russia" (pp. 149-376).

J35) Ninde, Mary Louise, *We two alone in Europe.* Chicago: Nansen, McClurg, & Co., 1886. 348pp.

Young Miss Ninde (1858-1947) and her friend "L.R.P." spent a year (1884-85?) on a grand tour that took them beyond Europe to Egypt and Turkey. To go to Russia was a spur-of-the-moment decision and they sailed from Sweden to see the sights of St Petersburg and Moscow before proceeding to Paris via Warsaw (pp. 169-200).

J36) Kennan, George, *Siberia and the exile system.* London: J.R. Osgood, McIlvaine & Co., 1891. 2 vols.

Sponsored by the *Century* magazine and accompanied by the Boston artist and photographer George Frost, Kennan (see I59, I93) arrived in Russia for his fourth visit in May 1885. He came prepared to give a favourable assessment of the penal system in Siberia, but subsequent meetings and events in Siberia radically changed his views and, through his subsequent book and lectures, those of America. In the course of eight months, between June 1885 and March of the following year, they covered some 8,000 miles within Siberia.

J37) Reynoso, Francisco de, *Reminiscences of a Spanish diplomat.* Recorded by Alice Pentlarge Kleeman. London: Hutchinson & Co., 1933. 287pp.

Reynoso (b. 1856), diplomat and one time ambassador to the Quirinal, was second secretary in the Spanish Legation in St Petersburg between June 1885 and sometime in 1886, when he was transferred to London. He describes diplomatic and high society life in the Russian capital (pp. 105-15).

J38) Leland, Lilian, *Travelling alone: a woman's journey around the world.* New York: American News Company, 1890. viii+358pp.

A young American woman (b. 1859) travelled alone on a journey of some 60,000 miles around the globe, begun in February 1884 and lasting over two years. She arrived in St Petersburg on 13 July 1885, did the sights, and then went to Moscow before departing a week later for Warsaw (pp. 269-77).

J39) Lothrop, Almira, *The court of Alexander III: letters of Mrs. Lothrop, wife of the late honorable George Van Ness Lothrop former minister plenipotentiary and* *envoy extraordinary of the United States to Russia.* Edited by William Prall. Philadelphia: John C. Winston Company, 1910. vi+208pp.

> Mrs Lothrop, née Strong (d. 1894), her husband, and daughters arrived in St Petersburg at the end of July 1885 and were to remain, long vacations in Italy, Paris, Berlin, and London apart, until 11 August 1888. Posthumously published letters to members of the family, full of social chit-chat with occasional interesting pen pictures of notable Russians.

J40) Ponafidine, Emma Cochran, *Russia – my home: an intimate record of personal experiences before, during and after the Bolshevist revolution.* Preface by William Lyon Phelps. Indianapolis: Bobbs-Merrill Co., 1931. 312pp.

> Daughter of an American missionary in Persia, Emma Cochran (1863-1958) married the Russian consul general in Tabriz, Petr Ponafidin (d. 1919) in 1885 and soon afterwards paid her first visit to Russia and the family estate of Bortniki on the shores of Lake Seliger near Ostashkov. Although they returned many times in subsequent years it was only after her husband's retirement in 1912 that they resided permanently in Russia and were to live through WWI and the revolutions of 1917 (pp. 17-88). The larger part of the book is devoted to the Soviet period up to 1921, when Emma and two sons escaped from Petrograd into Finland and on to New York.

J41) Yate, Arthur Campbell, *England and Russia face to face in Asia: travels with the Afghhan Boundary Commission.* Edinburgh and London: William Blackwood & Sons, 1887. viii+481pp.

> Lt. Yate (b. 1853) of the Bombay staff corps also acted as special correspondent of the *Daily Telegraph* and other papers and his book included virtually unrevised the articles already published. It was intended to be not only a record of the movements of the Afghan Boundary Commission, but also a description of travels through country that is "practically unknown to the civilized world". After leaving the Commission, he travelled from Herat to the Black Sea. Period covered 31 August 1885 to June 1886.

J42) Yate, Charles Edward, *Northern Afghanistan; or, letters from the Afghan Boundary Commission.* Edinburgh and London: William Blackwood & Sons, 1888. viii+430pp. [See also *North Afghanistan by Major C.E. Yate.* Introduction by Rudolph Abraham. London: Cambridge Scholars Press, 2000.]

> Colonel Sir Charles (1849-1940), elder brother of Lt. Yate, covers the period from the summer of 1885 until the return of the Commission to India in October 1886 and then follows the subsequent negotiations up to February

1888. He also recounts his return in February 1888 through Transcaspia to Ashkabad and by train to Tiflis and to the Black Sea (pp. 398-419).

J43) Hedin, Sven Anders von, *My life as an explorer*. [Translated from the Swedish by Alfhild Huebsch.] London: Cassell and Co., 1926. xii+498pp.

Famed Swedish geographer, photographer, polyglot, and travel writer (1865-1952) first went to Russia in 1885, travelling via St Petersburg through the Caucasus to Baku, where he spent seven months as a tutor (pp. 2-8). In 1890-91 he travelled through Transcaspia from Krasnovodsk and on to Bokhara and Samarkand before returning through European Russia to Stockholm (pp. 65-84). October 1893 saw him off again through Russia to Tashkent and then through Russian to Chinese Turkestan (pp. 85-110). He seems to have covered every blade of grass in Central Asia, Tibet, and Mongolia, before a comparatively sedate return home on the Trans-Siberian at the end of 1908 (pp. 476-77).

J44) Hedin, Sven Anders von, *From Pole to Pole: a book for young people*. London: Macmillan and Co., 1914. xvi+407pp.

An abridged translation of *Från Pol till Pol* that includes much from Hedin's numerous travels through the Russian empire: the Caucasus, 1885-86 (pp. 34-37), the Kirghiz steppe, 1893-95 (pp. 55-71), the Trans-Siberian and home via St Petersburg, 1908-09 (pp. 202-11).

J45) Spottiswoode, Robert Collinson D'Esterre, *Reminiscences*. Edinburgh and London: Edinburgh Press, for private circulaion, 1935. 158pp.

Career officer, born in India, Colonel Spottiswoode (b. 1841) decided soon after his marriage in 1885 to qualify as a Russian interpreter. He and his wife left for Moscow in early December. His "rough notes" touch on life in the English community and impressions of Moscow, "the queer eccentric looking town". Sending his wife home, he spent his last months with a Russian family in Khimki ("Heemká"), returned to London in April 1887 to pass his Russian examination, but instead of receiving a posting to Central Asia, spent the next forty-five years of his life in Ireland (pp. 119-35).

J46) Meriwether, Lee, *A tramp trip: how to see Europe on fifty cents a day*. New York and London: Harper and Bros., 1886. 276pp.

"Desirous of seeing something of low life", Meriwether (1862-1966) followed a year tramping from Gibraltar to the Bosphorus by sailing from Constantinople to Odessa early in 1886 and immediately pronounced "Russia is like a vast prison". He travelled via Kiev to Moscow and reached

St Petersburg, combining remarks on the way of life of the peasants with conventional tourist descriptions (pp. 203-30).

J47) Bateson, William, *Letters from the steppe written in the years 1886-1887.* Edited with an introduction by [his wife] Beatrice Bateson. London: Methuen & Co., 1928. xvi+222pp.

> Biologist and Cambridge don, Bateson (1861-1926) resolved to pursue his study of evolution and specifically of variation as observed at the Aral Sea and other salt lakes in the Kirghiz steppe. His letters, mainly to members of his family, begin in St Petersburg, where he arrived on 7 May 1886, and end in Petropavlovsk on 16 September 1887.

J48) Baddeley, Welbore St Clair, *Tchay and chianti; or, wanderings in Russia and Italy.* London: Sampson Low, Marston, Searle, and Rivington, 1887. xvi+260pp.

> Seeking no connection between Russia and Italy other than "merely aesthetic and naturalistic", Baddeley (1856-1945) visited St Petersburg in July 1886, made an excursion to the Imatra falls in Finland, before taking the train to Moscow and soon departing for Italy (pp. 1-112).

J49) Davis, Sarah Matilda Henry, *Norway nights and Russian days.* New York: Fords, Howard & Hulbert, 1887. 325pp.

> Mrs Davis visited St Petersburg and Moscow in the summer of 1886, sightseeing and shopping (pp. 213-325).

J50) Bouton, John Bell, *Roundabout to Moscow, an epicurean journey.* New York: D. Appleton and Co., 1887. xii+421pp.

> Bouton (1830-1902), American novelist and writer, visited Petersburg and Moscow in July 1886 (pp. 203-349, 419-21).

J51) Michell, Thomas, *Russian pictures: drawn with pen and pencil.* London: Religious Tract Society, 1889. 224pp.

> Michell (see I56) left Russia in 1874 after fourteen years in St Petersburg. For the present work, which was designed to give a succinct historical cum geographical overview of the vast Russian empire, he used some material from his Murray's *Handbook*. The chapter on the Crimea and the Caucasus was written by **Captain J. Buchan Telfer** (pp. 140-69). Many of the 124 illustrations are by Whymper.

J52) Wight, Orlando Williams, *People and countries visited in a winding journey around the world.* Detroit: Raynor and Taylor, 1888. xiv+518pp.

> Detroit physician and noted translator from French (particularly Balzac), Wight (1824-88) spent 1887 in extensive travels "to observe every country in which an Aryan people has established civil government. One looks in vain elsewhere for progress and liberty". In June-August he travelled from Batumi to Tiflis and through the Caucasus to Rostov, where he took the train to Moscow and on to St Petersburg. Adds long chapter on 'place of Russia in the European system', acknowledging Americans may feel he had "treated Russia too leniently". Impressed by the journalist Mikhail Katkov whom he met in Moscow a few days before his death (pp. 220-95).

J53) De Windt, Harry, *From Pekin to Calais by land.* London: Chapman and Hall, 1889. xii+656pp.

> The first of the several forays into the Russian empire by De Windt (1856-1933) (see J54, J98, J129, J134, J135, K91, K162, K377). The journey from Pekin, which he and his companion Lancaster left in May 1887, through Siberia, which they reached on 10 August, and ending in Paris in late October 1888, he described as "sadly devoid of interest" (Irkutsk excepted). (Russia, pp. 322-647).

J54) De Windt, Harry, *My restless life.* London: Grant Richards, 1909. 366pp.

> De Windt's relaxed autobiography includes his first journey across Siberia in 1887 (pp. 137-44), and his subsequent return in 1890 on the prompting of Mme Olga Novikova to inspect Russian prisons (see I94) (pp. 174-88). Finally, invited by the Prison Department at St Petersburg to resume his investigations in Siberia, he went for a third time, proceeding to Sakhalin, in late 1893 (see I131) (pp. 207-25).

J55) Ballou, Maturin Murray, *Due north, or glimpses of Scandinavia and Russia.* Boston: Ticknor & Co., 1887. xii+373pp.

> The Boston publisher, journalist, and author Ballou (1820-95), having "done" due south and due west, crossed the Atlantic in the summer of 1886 to start his northern tour in Copenhagen and proceeded via Norway and Sweden to St Petersburg. Moscow and Nizhnii Novgorod followed and he exited to Warsaw (pp. 201-352).

J56) Ballou, Maturin Murray, *Footprints of travel; or, journeyings in many lands*. Boston: Ginn, 1889. 360pp.

> Written for young readers, this round-the-world trip contains material from his various travels, including his 1886 visit to Russia (pp. 279-303).

J57) Guild, Curtis, *Britons and Muscovites, or, traits of two empires*. Boston: Lee and Shepard, 1888. xii+230pp.

> Editor of the Boston *Commercial Bulletin* and author of the travel accounts *Over the ocean* and *Abroad again*, Guild (1827-1911) travelled from London to Russia in 1886 and visited St Petersburg, Moscow and Nizhnii Novgorod, enlisting the help of James Pilley, a long-time British resident, as his guide and interpreter. Guild provides very much a tourist guide rather than a searching Anglo-Russian comparison (pp. 89-230).

J58) Stevens, Thomas, *Around the world on a bicycle: from Teheran to Yokohama*. London: Sampson Low, Marston & Co., 1888. xiv+477pp.

> This was in fact the second volume of the account of the monumental journey on a penny farthing by the American Stevens (b. 1855) that began on 22 April 1884 in San Francisco and ended on 17 December 1886 in Yokohama. His only time in Russia was bike-less, when he left Persia on a Russian steamer for Baku on 3 June 1886, then took the train to Tiflis and on to Batumi, before taking a steamer to Constantinople (pp. 250-64).

J59) Richardson, David N., *A girdle round the earth: home letters from foreign lands*. Chicago: McClurg and Co., 1888. xii+449pp.

> Owner of the *Iowa State Democrat* and an accomplished writer, Richardson (1832-98) set out from San Francisco on 18 August 1886, heading for China and Japan. He eventually got to Russia in the summer of the following year, reaching Moscow via Berlin and Warsaw and ending in St Petersburg, "the Chicago of northwestern Europe", before departing for Finland (pp. 380-405).

J60) Barnes, Demas, *In search of summer breezes in northern Europe. Revised letters to the "Brooklyn Eagle"*. New York: Charles F. Bloom, 1887. 141pp.

> Journalist and U.S. congressman, Barnes (1827-88) after spending the early summer of 1886 in England departed on a tour that took him from Finland to Russia, "fortified on all sides, not alone by fortresses and guns, but by a secret espionage". Travels from St Petersburg to Moscow and

visits Smolensk on his way to Poland. Writes less about sights than about general historical and social problems (pp. 47-102).

J61) Harrison, Jane Ellen, *Reminiscences of a student's life.* London: Hogarth Press, 1925. 90pp.

Classical scholar, linguist, noted feminist, and Fellow of Newnham College, Cambridge, Harrison (1850-1928) provides a very brief account of her trip to St Petersburg in September 1886 to study at the Hermitage, but mainly chides herself for not having immersed herself in Russian culture and society while she had the chance (pp. 76-79).

J62) Gaussen, William Frederick Armytage, *Memorials of a short life: a biographical sketch of W.F.A. Gaussen with essays on Russian life and literature.* Edited by G.F. Browne, canon of St Paul's, bishop of Stepney. London: T. Fisher Unwin, 1895. 263pp.

Gaussen (1863-93), who was to achieve recognition in his short life for his translations from Potapenko, first went to Russia in September 1886 in pursuit of his scientific interests, visiting the oil-fields of Baku. He later delivered a lecture about his journey from St Petersburg to the Caspian (pp. 61-108). He returned to Russia in June 1890 to stay with a family in Moscow for ten months and study the Russian language. Letters from that visit are also included (pp. 181-216).

J63) Walker, Bettina, *My musical experiences.* London: Richard Bentley and Son, 1890. iv+330pp.

A young English pianoforte student travelled to Germany, Italy and Russia to study under eminent teachers in the 1880s. She was in particular influenced by the German composer and pianist Adolf Henselt (1814-89), who in 1861 had been given Russian citizenship and ennobled and who divided his time between Germany and Russia. Miss Walker seems to have studied in St Petersburg on three or four occasions from about 1886, on the first occasion under a Miss Henrickson, who taught Henselt's method for twenty-five years in imperial institutes. She is much more informative on the Henselts and their flat than she is about life in St Petersburg (pp. 226-52, 280-85, 289-306).

J64) Gowing, Lionel Francis, *Five thousand miles in a sledge: a mid-winter journey across Siberia.* London: Chatto and Windus, 1889. xix+257pp.

Gowing (b. 1859) offers "a truthful record of a journey in which no English author has preceded the present writer", at least in winter. Sides with

Kennan in the dispute with Lansdell over penal conditions, but is intent on recording the facts of a journey that took him and his companion, Charles Uren, from Shanghai to Vladivostok in early November 1886 and some 4600 miles by sledge to Tiumen, where they arrived on 18 February 1887.

J65) Wilkinson, T.E., *Twenty years of continental work and travel*. With a preface by Sir Edmund Monson. London: Longmans, Green, and Co., 1906. xxiv+438pp.

Anglican bishop for central and eastern Europe, the Right Reverend Wilkinson (d. 1914) relates his constant travels throughout Europe over the preceding twenty years. These included many visits to Russia (which he had first visited as a young man in 1859), mainly through the Baltic provinces to St Petersburg and Moscow, in 1887 (pp. 33-47), 1890 (pp. 127-47), 1893 (pp. 190-98), 1896 (pp. 238-61), 1900 (pp. 325-29), 1902 (pp. 338-47), and 1905 (pp. 396-417).

J66) Brandes, Georg Morris Cohen, *Impressions of Russia*. Translated from the Danish by Samuel C. Eastman. London: Walter Scott, 1889. x+353pp.

Brandes (1842-1927), a highly influential literary critic and professor at the university of Copenhagen, was invited to St Petersburg and Moscow to deliver a series of lectures. He stayed in Russia for three months during 1887, spending some time on an estate south of Moscow. His book is divided into two parts, the second of which is an informed assessment of Russian literature, and even in the first, literary and cultural matters dominate.

J67) Hapgood, Isabel Florence, *Russian rambles*. London: Longmans, Green and Co., 1895. xi+369pp.

Hapgood (1851-1928), a leading American translator and writer on Russian literature, visited Russia on several occasions between 1887 and 1889. She spent much time with Tolstoi in Moscow and Iasnaia Poliana (pp. 148-202), travelled down the Volga to Nizhnii Novgorod, and "much attached to the Russian Church", resided in the "holy city" of Kiev. Her book was offered as "a collection of detached pictures", offering a sympathetic account of ordinary Russians.

J68) Colbeck, Alfred, *A summer's cruise in the waters of Greece, Turkey, and Russia*. London: T. Fisher Unwin, 1887. xii+416pp.

A detailed account of a Cornishman's leisurely voyage on the *Treloske* from Newport in south Wales through the Mediterranean and Aegean to Constantinople and then through the Black Sea and the Sea of Azov, where he visited Taganrog and made an excursion by train to Rostov, in the summer of 1887. His Russian account is padded out by chapters on the church and nihilism. (Russia, pp. 221-354.)

J69) Curtis, William Eleroy, *The land of the nihilist: Russia; its people, its palaces, its politics.* Chicago: Belford, Clarke, 1888. 323pp.

> A correspondent for the Chicago *Daily News,* Curtis (1850-1911) and wife journey to St Petersburg and Moscow in 1887. (For his journey, twenty-three years later, to the Black Sea area, see K220-21.)

J70) Heath, Perry Sanford, *A hoosier in Russia: the only white tsar – his imperialism, country and people.* New York, Baltimore, Chicago: Lorborn Publishing Co., 1888. 152pp.

> Indiana editor and publisher (1857-1927) tells "in a natural way, what I saw in a summer's travel, through a remarkable country, among a strange and interesting people", including the "promiscuous osculations of the natives" (pp. 7-138). There is much in his account about nihilists and on leaving Russia in August 1887 he met Stepniak in London, whose views he counters with those of a pro-tsarist Russian in Washington (pp. 139-52).

J71) Aldrich, Herbert Lincoln, *Arctic Alaska and Siberia, or, eight months with the Arctic whalemen.* Chicago: Rand, McNally, 1889. 234pp.

> As part of his research into the New Bedford whaling industry, Aldrich (b. 1860) joined a fleet seeking whales off Cape Bering and spent a few days in June 1887 with Siberian native tribes (pp. 42-62).

J72) [Brown, Elizabeth], *In pursuit of a shadow.* By a lady astronomer. London: Trübner & Co., 1888). 129pp.

> Director of the Solar Section of the Liverpool Astronomical Society, Elizabeth Brown (1830-99) and her companion "L" travelled to Russia via Sweden "to see the great Solar eclipse of August 19" (1887). They arrived in St Petersburg on 28 July, saw the sights there and in Moscow, and reached Kineshma on the Volga on 13 August. They were to stay at Pogost, the nearby summer home of a leading Russian astronomer, Professor B[redikhin], where two British members of the Royal Astronomical Society, Dr. C[opeland] and Father P[erry] had also been invited to observe the eclipse, which duly took place, but in conditions that left them disconsolate. They journeyed home down the Volga to Nizhnii Novgorod and by train via Warsaw (pp. 39-125).

J73) Cutting, Charles F., *Glimpses of Scandinavia and Russia.* Boston: Thomas Groom & Co., 1887. 94pp.

> American tourist "glimpses" St Petersburg, Moscow, and Nizhnii Novgorod during "a rapid journey in the summer of 1887", arriving at Cronstadt on 31 July and departing a fortnight later (pp. 54-94). Privately printed in 100 copies.

J74) Wardrop, John Oliver, *The kingdom of Georgia: notes of travel in a land of women, wine and song; to which are appended historical, literary and political sketches, specimens of the national music, and a compendious bibliography.* London: Sampson Low, Marston, Searle and Rivington, 1888. ix+202pp.

> For many years British consul in Kerch and later consul-general in St Petersburg until his transfer to Bucharest and retirement in 1910, Sir Oliver (1864-1948) travelled extensively through Georgia in 1887. He subsequently devoted himself to the study and promotion of Georgian culture and was in 1919-21 the British Chief Commissioner of Transcaucasus in Tbilisi.

J75) Lansdell, Henry, *Chinese Central Asia: a ride to little Tibet.* London: Sampson Low, Marston, & Co., 1893. 2 vols.

> Lansdell's (see I171) last "ride" took him initially across Russia and Russian protectorates, mainly by rail, before he entered Chinese Mongolia on 20 June 1888. He left London on 17 February for St Petersburg, where he stayed for a week before resuming a journey that took him to Moscow (for tea with Tolstoi) and through Ukraine to Sevastopol, Batumi, Tiflis, and Baku, and then to Bokhara, Samarkand and Tashkent (vol. I, pp. 3-151).

J76) Waters, Wallscourt Hely-Hutchinson, *"Secret and confidential": the experiences of a military attaché.* London: John Murray, 1926. xiv+388pp.

> Brigadier-General Waters (b. 1855) as a young officer studied Russian with a family in St Petersburg for a few months in early 1888 (pp. 3-13) and returned for a further visit in 1892 to observe military manoeuvres at Krasnoe selo (pp. 40-51). In 1893 came his appointment as military attaché at the British embassy which lasted for five years during which he travelled widely through the empire, including Siberia and Turkestan (pp. 61-241). After duty in South Africa he was sent in 1904 as the War Office representative with the Russian army in Manchuria, travelling across Russia (pp. 256-91). His final visit before the October Revolution came in October 1916, when he had an audience of the tsar at his headquarters at Mogilev (pp. 318-61).

J77) Waters, Wallscourt Hely-Hutchinson, *Russia then and now.* London: John Murray, 1935. xvi+308pp.

> In 1934 Waters was granted a visa to visit Soviet Union. In this account of his reaction to Russia under the Soviets he recalls in the opening chapter his earlier encounters with imperial Russia (pp. 1-8).

J78) Stead, William Thomas, *Truth about Russia.* London: Cassell & Co., 1888. viii+464pp.

> Editor of *Pall Mall*, the journal in which much of his material appeared as articles, the campaigning "new journalist" Stead (1849-1812), anxious about the prospects of a general war, left England in the early spring of 1888 to visit Paris, Berlin, and St Petersburg. From Petersburg he went to Moscow and spent a week in early June at Iasnaia Poliana with Tolstoi, writing at the latter's desk the chapters of his own book entitled *War or peace?* (pp. 38-457).

J79) Dobson, George, *Russia's railway advance into Central Asia: notes of a journey from St. Petersburg to Samarkand.* London: W.H. Allen & Co., 1890. xxiv+436pp.

> The first eight chapters comprise re-written letters originally sent to *The Times* in the spring of 1888, when Dobson (1850-1938) attended the opening of the Transcaspian railway. The last seven new chapters carry his reflections up to the time of writing (preface dated St Petersburg April 1890).

J80) Harrison, Carter Henry, *A race with the sun; or, a sixteen month's tour from Chicago around the world through Manitoba and British Columbia by the Canadian Pacific, Oregon and Washington, Japan, China, Siam, Straits settlements, Burmah, India, Ceylon, Egypt, Greece, Turkey, Roumania, Hungary, Austria, Poland, Transcaucasia, the Caspian sea and the Volga river, Russia, Finland, Sweden, Norway, Denmark, Prussia, Paris, London and home.* New York: G.P. Putnam's Sons; Chicago: W.E. Dibble & Co., 1889. xiv+569pp.

> Five-times mayor of Chicago and assassinated in office, Harrison (1825-93) took his son and a friend on the tour described in the title. His book is based on the detailed letters he sent back to newspapers. They arrived in Moscow from Poland on 12 June 1888 and then proceeded via Voronezh and Rostov to Vladikavkaz and on to Tiflis and Baku. They ascended the Volga from Astrakhan as far as Rybynsk before taking the train to St Petersburg. After a week of sight-seeing they took the train to Vyborg on

26 July. Russia had been for Harrison "a revelation in many things" and his letters are intelligent and full of interesting observations (pp. 380-470).

J81) Abercromby, John, *A trip through the eastern Caucasus, with a chapter on the languages of the country.* London: Edward Stanford, 1889. xvi+376pp.

> Soldier and archaeologist Abercromby (1841-1924), later 5th Baron, styling himself a corresponding member of the Finno-Ugrian Society, retained "nothing but pleasant recollections" from a six-week tour that began in Tiflis at the end of June 1888. Tiflis was the starting point for a first expedition over little-known passes of the Caucasus (pp. 1-206). Back in Tiflis, he then made his way to Baku, whence he sailed to Derbent and made a journey into the interior to Kubaichi and back (pp. 207-96).

J82) Birkbeck, William John, *Birkbeck and the Russian church, containing essays and articles by the late W. J. Birkbeck, M.A., F.S.A., written in the years 1888-1915.* Collected and edited by his friend Athelstan Riley. London: published for the Anglican and Eastern Association by the Society for Promoting Christian Knowledge, 1917. xii+372pp.

> Birkbeck (1859-1916), the leading British authority on the Russian church and author of *Russia and the English church during the last fifty years* (1895), visited Russia on numerous occasions from 1888, when he went to Kiev for the 900th anniversary of Russia's conversion to Christianity, until just before his death. Many of the articles in this collection refer directly to his travels.

J83) Blackstock, Emma Moulton Frazer, *The land of the Viking and the empire of the tsar.* New York and London: G.P. Putnam's Sons (The Knickerbocker Press), 1889. 213pp.

> American wife (b. 1860) of a leading Canadian lawyer, Mrs Blackstock travelled in the summer of 1888 with a group of friends from Stockholm to St Petersburg and on to Moscow, before leaving for Paris via Poland and Germany. "Russia impressed me as too vast to comprehend" (pp. 27-209).

J84) Mummery, Alfred Frederick, *My climbs in the Alps and Caucasus.* London: T. Fisher Unwin, 1895. xii+360pp.

> The famous climber and political economist (1855-95) visited the Caucasus in 1888 and made the first ascent of Dych Tau, which brought his election to the Alpine Club (pp. 258-323).

J85) McConaughy, David, Jr., *Rambles through Russia and in Norway and Sweden.* Philadelphia: Lippincott, 1888. 128pp.

> McConaughy (b. 1860), who was soon afterwards to become the Y.M.C.A.'s first foreign secretary in India, attended the Y.M.C.A. congress in Stockholm in August 1888 and also visited St Petersburg and Moscow, described in three letters originally published in the *Lutheran Observer* of Philadelphia. His emphasis is on the splendours of the churches and the piety of the people (pp. 8-16).

J86) Curzon, George Nathaniel, *Russia in central Asia in 1889, and the Anglo-Russian question.* London: Longmans, Green & Co., 1889. xxiii+477pp.

> Soon after becoming an M.P., Curzon (1859-1925), later 1st Marquess Curzon of Kedleston and viceroy of India from 1899, left London at the beginning of September 1888 for St Petersburg and headed south to Tiflis in order to embark on "a journey, taken under circumstances of exceptional ease and advantage" along the newly-constructed Transcaspian railway and through Russian possessions in Central Asia. His aim was to provide an up-to-date and objective political assessment (i.e up to 1889), without undue attention to matters of history or scenery. His book was dedicated "to the great army of Russophobes who mislead others, and Russophiles whom others mislead".

J87) Maude, Aylmer, *Tolstoy and his problems.* London: Constable & Co., 1901. viii+220pp.

> Maude (1858-1938), manager of the Anglo-Russian carpet company in Moscow until 1897 but best known as the leading English translator of Tolstoi, recalls his first visit to Tolstoi in Moscow in 1888 and subsequent meetings in the 1890s in his essay 'Talks with Tolstoy' (pp. 188-213). See also his diatribe 'The tsar's coronation' (of Nicholas II, which he attended in Moscow in 1896) (pp. 109-25) (see K25).

J88) Stone, Melville Elijah, *Fifty years a journalist.* Garden City, New York: Country Life Press, 1921. xiv, 371pp.

> Founder of a number of newspapers and later general manager of the Associated Press, Stone (1848-1929) describes several visits he made to Russia, the first of which was part of an extended European tour in 1888-89. He travelled as far as Nizhnii Novgorod and was a guest of the tsar at a military review at Tsarskoe selo (pp. 183-94). During the winter of 1903-04 he was in St Petersburg, negotiating the abolition of censorship on American journalists based in Russia. He records his dealings with numerous key

figures within the Russian government and his frequent conversations with Nicholas II. In 1904-05 he was responsible for organizing American reporting of the Russo-Japanese War and he himself reported on the subsequent peace negotiations at the Portsmouth Conference (pp. 278-96).

J89) Lanin, E. B. [pseudonym of Dillon, Emile Joseph], *Russian characteristics reprinted, with revisions, from the "Fortnightly review"*. London: Chapman and Hall, 1892. x+604pp.

> Published under a pseudonym, this volume brought together a series of highly perceptive and wide-ranging articles written in the period September 1889 and October 1891 by Dr Dillon (1855-1933) (see also I157, K5), who had also been since 1886 Russian correspondent of the *Daily Telegraph*. Published in USA under the title *Russian traits and terrors: a faithful picture of Russia today*.

J90) Howard, Benjamin Douglas, *Life with trans-Siberian savages*. London: Longmans, Green & Co., 1893. x+209pp.

> English-born, but achieving his reputation as a surgeon in America, particularly during the Civil War, Dr Howard (1836-1900) left London in the autumn of 1889 on "leisurely meanderings" that took him to China, Tibet, and through Russia to Vladivostok, where he conceived his plan to visit Sakhalin and study the life of the aboriginal inhabitants of the island, the Ainus.

J91) Howard, Benjamin Douglas, *Prisoners of Russia: a personal study of convict life in Sakhalin and Siberia*. New York: Appleton & Co., 1902. xxx+389pp.

> In 1890 Howard returned to Sakhalin as a guest of its governor to research and write this posthumously published account of the Siberian penal system. His work is primarily a study of the prison camp at Korsakovsk on the island, in which he records his exchanges with prisoners, penal officials, exiles and their families. He describes in considerable detail the conditions, diets, physiology, punishment and occupations of the prisoners but also the socio-economic situation of Sakhalin.

J92) Cumberland, C.S., *Sport on the Pamirs and Turkistan steppes*. Edinburgh and London: William Blackwood and Sons, 1895. x+278pp.

> Major Cumberland published his diary of his 1889 journey immediately after his return in the journal *Land and Water,* but increased British and Russian interest in the area prompted him to turn it years later into a

book. He had travelled from India via Kashmir, Chinese Turkestan, the Pamirs, and Asia Minor, compiling his "descriptions of scenery and sport" and gathering specimens he had shot. Towards the end of his journey he crossed the Karaart Pass at 15,800 feet and entered into territory claimed by Russia. He eventually made his way via Samarkand, Baku, and Tiflis to Odessa, which he reached on 9 July (pp. 239-74).

J93) Newton, William Wilberforce, *A run through Russia: the story of a visit to Count Tolstoi.* Hartford: Student Publishing Co., 1894. 211pp.

Sitting in a Russian church in Dresden, Newton (1843-1914), episcopal clergyman and author of religious tracts, decided under "the true impulse of the tourist-fit" to visit Russia with two fellow Americans between 2 and 15 April 1889 and to seek out Tolstoi, whom they located on the estate of Count Urusov at Sergiev Posad outside Moscow (pp. 8-211).

J94) Birse, Arthur Herbert, *Memoirs of an interpreter.* Foreword by the Earl of Avon. London: Michael Joseph, 1967. 254pp.

Born to Scottish parents in St Petersburg, Birse (1889-1981) was educated in the Russian capital and joined the merchant bankers Baring Bros. in 1906. In the first part of his autobiography he describes his business and family life in Russia up to 1917, when he went to England to enlist in the British army (pp. 18-35). Birse ultimately became famous as Churchill's Russian-English interpreter during WWII.

J95) Cook, Charles, *The prisons of the world: with stories of crime, criminals, and convicts.* With an introduction by C.H. Spurgeon. London: Morgan and Scott, 1891. xii+195pp.

Hyde Park evangelist and lecturer Cook arrived in St Petersburg with two objectives – "to distribute the Word of God among the prisoners of Russia" and to investigate the abuses and cruelties of which he had heard. His first visit to St Petersburg and Moscow in 1890 (pp. 160-72) was followed by a second in 1892, when he was accompanied by his wife (pp. 190-05).

J96) Norman, Henry, *The peoples and politics of the Far East: travels and studies in the British, French, Spanish and Portuguese colonies, Siberia, China, Japan, Korea, Siam and Malaya.* London: T. Fisher Unwin, 1895. xvi+608pp.

Norman (1858-1939), journalist, later M.P. and knighted (see K76), set off in 1887 on a four-year tour on behalf of several newspapers that took him briefly in c.1890 from Japan to Vladivostok, where he reflected on its strategic importance and progress on the Trans-Siberian railway (pp. 141-66).

J97) Morris, Isabel, *A summer in Kieff: or sunny days in southern Russia.* London: Ward and Downey, 1891. 205pp.

> An intrepid Scottish lady's solo visit to Kiev in 1890, travelling by train via Vienna, and amusing herself by observing Russian mores in town and country. Generalized account, enlivened by the drawings of Cochrane Morris (pp. 26-191).

J98) De Windt, Harry, *Siberia as it is.* With an introduction by her excellency Madame Olga Novikoff ('O.K.'). London: Chapman & Hall, 1892. xxiv+504pp.

> De Windt (see J53-54), now sporting F.R.G.S., left England on 21 July 1890, bound for Siberia via St Petersburg and Moscow to inspect the prisons. His route took him to Tobolsk, Tomsk and, finally, Tiumen. His aim to show that Siberia was "not so black as it is painted", principally by the American George Kennan, was achieved, he believed, with facts and statements "made with the utmost caution and deliberation". He includes in appendices letters about the state of prisons by other travellers, most interestingly on prisons in Tashkent, Samarkand, and Tiflis, by **Captain E. St. C. Pemberton** of the Royal Engineers (pp. 498-504).

J99) Stevens, Thomas, *Through Russia on a mustang.* London, Paris & Melbourne: Cassell & Co., 1892. xiv+334pp.

> Commissioned by the New York *World* to write articles about European Russia, Stevens (see J58) bought a mustang from a "wild west" show performing in Moscow and set off with a young Russian student as interpreter to travel down to the Crimea (visiting Tolstoi en route) and returning via the Don and Volga to Nizhnii Novgorod in the summer of 1890.

J100) Stoddard, Charles Augustus, *Across Russia: from the Baltic to the Danube.* London: Chapman and Hall, 1892. xii+258pp.

> American clergyman's conventional travelogue of his journey from Paris via Sweden and Finland to St Petersburg, where he arrived in July 1890, Moscow, Nizhnii Novgorod, and out via Warsaw and on to Budapest (pp. 27-231).

J101) Price, Julius Mendes, *From the Arctic Ocean to the Yellow Sea: the narrative of a journey, in 1890 and 1891, across Siberia, Mongolia, the Gobi Desert, and north China.* London: Sampson Low & Co., 1892. xxiv+384pp.

Price (1857-1924), F.R.G.S. and special artist for the *Illustrated London News*, in which many of his drawings originally appeared, sailed the route via the Kara Sea to the Enisei river pioneered by Wiggins. He was invited to accompany members of the Anglo-Siberian Trading Syndicate (an enterprise made redundant by the Trans-Siberian railway, as he explains in the preface to the 1893 edition). They sailed from London in the *Biscaya* on 18 July 1890, went up the Enisei as far as Krasnoiarsk, before proceding to Irkutsk (much on prisoners), and thence in February 1891 into Mongolia and China (pp. 1-248).

J102) Marsden, Kate, *On sledge and horseback to outcast Siberian lepers.* London: Record Press, 1892. xv+243pp.

A trained nurse, Marsden (1859-1931) left England in September 1890, travelling via Constantinople and the Crimea to Moscow. In February 1891 she set out for Siberia and travelling via Omsk and Irkutsk, visited the leper colony at Viluisk and searched in vain for a herb reputed to cure the disease. Back in Moscow in December 1891, she eventually left St Petersburg for England in May 1892. The same year she was elected to the Royal Geographical Society in London, but met widespread scepticism about what she had accomplished.

J103) Biddulph, Cuthbert Edward, *Four months in Persia, and a visit to Trans-Caspia.* London: Kegan Paul, Trench, Trübner & Co., 1892. vi+137pp.

Biddulph (1850-99), F.R.G.S. and a member of the Indian civil service, visited Transcaspia in 1890 and contributed articles to Indian and British journals. His view of the region was sober, less enthusiastic about the splendours of Samarkand and Bokhara than other travellers, critical of the trustworthiness of e.g. Vambéry's observations, and prepared to give the Russians their due for "right good work" in the region.

J104) Biddulph, Cuthbert Edward, *From London to Samarcand.* Bombay: The Times of India Steam Press, 1892. 53pp.

Another version of his journey from London in September 1890, when he travelled by train to Odessa, by boat to Batumi, train to Tiflis and Baku, across the Caspian to Uzun Ada, in order finally to take the Transcaspian line to Bokhara and Samarkand and end in Merv.

J105) Hapgood, Isabel Florence, *The great streets of the world.* London: James R. Osgood, McIlvaine, & Co., 1892. xiv+253pp.

> Hapgood (see J66) was one of seven authors contributing to this collection (lead author Richard Harding Davis). Her article 'The Névsky Prospékt' (pp. 211-53), which was to re-appear in *Russian rambles*, is here illustrated by twelve drawings, dated 1891-92, by Il'ia Repin.

J106) Allen, Thomas Gaskell, Jr. and Sachtleben, William Lewis, *Across Asia on a bicycle: the journey of two American students from Constantinople to Peking.* London: T. Fisher Unwin, 1895. xvi+234pp.

> The two young graduates of Washington University in St Louis, Missouri set out in June 1890 to circle the globe. Their journey to Peking and return took three years and covered 15,000 miles, during which they took more than 2,500 photographs. They climbed Mount Ararat, and eventually entered Russian territory from Persia, reaching Samarkand on 6 November 1890, and exiting into China (pp. 111-44).

J107) Allen, Henry Tureman, 'Wolf-hunting in Russia', in *Hunting in many lands. The book of the Boone and Crockett club.* Edited by Theodore Roosevelt and George Grinnell. New York: Forest and Stream Publishing Co., 1900. 447pp.

> Allen (1859-1930), who was U.S. military attaché in Russia in 1890-95, contributes a chapter on his pursuit of the Russian wolf (pp. 151-86).

J108) Boddy, Alexander Alfred, *With Russian pilgrims: being an account of a sojourn in the White Sea Monastery and a journey by the old trade route from the Arctic Sea to Moscow; also an appendix, giving a full history of the Solovetsk obitel, by the Venerable Archimandrite Melétii.* London: Wells Gardner, Darton & Co., 1892. xiv+347pp.

> Boddy (1854-1930), vicar of All Saints', Monwearmouth, Sunderland, F.R.G.S., and one of the founders of Pentecostalism in England, begins his account with his departure from Lapland for the White Sea in mid-May 1891. From Archangel he travelled with Russian pilgrims by steamer to the Solovetskii monastery, where he learnt much about the British bombardment during the Crimean War. His return to England was by way of Velikii Ustiug, down the Sukhona to Vologda, and on to Iaroslavl and Moscow.

J109) Frederic, Harold, *The new exodus: a study of Israel in Russia.* London: William Heinemann, 1904. 304pp.

The American novelist and journalist Frederic (1856-98) visited Kiev and Odessa on a brief visit from 23 July to 14 August 1891 to investigate the persecution of the Jews. His articles under the title 'An indictment of Russia' began to appear in the *New York Times* on 5 September 1891. His sympathetic portrayal was questioned by Joseph Pennell (see J110-11).

J110) Pennell, Joseph, *The adventures of an illustrator, mostly in following his authors in America & Europe.* London: T. Fisher Unwin, 1925. xxii+372pp.

The noted illustrator and artist Pennell (1857-1926), born in America but living in London from 1881, visited Kiev and Berdichev in 1891 to draw and photograph the Jewish community, but was detained in Berdichev as a spy and soon escorted out of the country (pp. 222-36).

J111) Pennell, Joseph, *The Jew at home: impressions of a summer and autumn spent with him in Russia and Austria.* London: William Heinemann, 1892. 130pp.

First appeared as a series of controversial articles in the *Illustrated London News* in December 1891. Pennell in his preface protests that he was neither "a Jew hater nor a Jew lover", but "what I did see I have simply put down in black and white" (pp. 82-130).

J112) Steveni, James William Barnes, *Through famine-stricken Russia.* London: Sampson Low, Marston & Co., 1892. xi+183pp.

Steveni (1860-1944), professor of English at St Petersburg's college of Peter the Great since 1887, journeyed to the areas suffering from the great famine of 1891-92 as special correspondent of the *Daily Chronicle*.

J113) Hodgetts, Edward Arthur Brayley, *In the track of Russian famine: the personal narrative of a journey through the famine districts of Russia.* London: T. Fisher Unwin, 1892. viii+237pp.

Hodgetts (see I79, K6) reported for Reuters on the famine and met Tolstoi in Moscow.

J114) Stadling, Jonas Jonsson, *In the land of Tolstoi: experiences of famine and misrule in Russia.* Edited by Will Reason. London: James Clarke & Co., 1897. xiv+286pp.

The Swede Stadling (1847-1935) describes his first meeting with Tolstoi at Riazan in March 1892 and his work to alleviate the plight of the starving.

Stadling then travels down the Volga, visiting Samara and Saratov, describing the settlements of German colonists and of Russian religious sects. Adapted from the Swedish original *Från det Hungrande Ryssland*.

J115) Edgar, William Crowell, *The Russian famine of 1891 and 1892: some particulars of the relief sent to the destitute peasants by the millers of America in the steamship Missouri; a brief history of the movement, a description of the relief commission's visit to Russia, and a list of subscribers to the fund.* Minneapolis: Millers and Manufacturers Insurance Co., 1893. 74pp.

> Edgar (1856-1932), editor of the *Northwestern Miller* and organizer of the relief effort, met the *Missouri* at Libau at the beginning of April 1892 and personally supervised the unloading and distribution of the flour. He then journeyed to Moscow and on to see the famine-affected areas, before returning to St Petersburg and an audience with the future Nicholas II.

J116) Reeves, Francis Brewster, *Russia then and now, 1892-1917: my mission to Russia during the famine of 1891-1892 with data bearing upon Russia of today.* New York and London: C.P. Putnam's Sons, the Knickerbocker Press, 1917. xiv+186pp.

> Reeves (1836-1922), a commissioner of the Citizens' Russian Famine relief of Philadelphia, arrived in Riga on 12 May 1892 to meet the S.S. *Indiana* which had arrived from America with food supplies. He describes the junketings in Riga and St Petersburg and, eventually, the distribution of the supplies in fifteen districts, including Riazan, where he met Tolstoi (pp. 1-112). Also included are letters from another commissioner, **Rudolph Blenkenburg** (pp. 129-34), as well as a long description by the Rabbi **Joseph Krausdorf** of his visit to Tolstoi in July 1894 (pp. 83-95). Other material from various sources including Reeves himself, purporting to discuss subsequent events leading to the "triumph of democracy over aristocracy".

J117) Talmage, Thomas De Witt, *T. De Witt Talmage: his life and work: biographical edition.* Edited by Louis Albert Banks, in conjunction with Benjamin J. Fernie, and George H. Sandison. London: O.W. Binkerd, 1902. 501pp.

> In June 1892 Rev. Dr Talmage (1832-1902), one of America's most influential clerics and preachers of the late nineteenth century, sailed to St Petersburg with his colleague Dr Klopsch to meet the steamship *Leo*, chartered by the *Christian Herald*, of which he was the editor, and bringing a consignment of food for famine relief. They were to receive the freedom of the city of Moscow and to meet the tsar during their visit (pp. 199-224).

J118) Lent, William Bement, *Gypsying beyond the sea from English fields to Salerno shores.* New York: Anson D.F. Rendolph & Co., 1893. 2 vols.

> Lent (d. 1902), author of several chatty but informative guide books, presents the major sights of St Petersburg, where he arrived by train from Berlin, and Moscow, from where he returned to exit to Finland, during a recent visit, seemingly in the summer of 1892 (vol. II, pp. 4-118).

J119) Bigelow, Poultney, *The borderland of Czar and Kaiser: notes from both sides of the Russian frontier.* London: Osgood, McIlvaine & Co., 1895. vi+343pp.

> New York lawyer and author Bigelow (1855-1954) visited Russia in June 1892 with the artist Frederic Remington, who was to illustrate his book. They were apparently sent by the U.S. government to investigate how the Baltic coast was being protected from erosion, but were regarded with suspicion and ultimately expelled. The book is curiously structured with little connection between chapters (several of which had appeared in *Harper's* in 1892-93) and moves between Poland, Germany, the Baltic, and St Petersburg. It includes long chapters on religious persecution and russification in the Baltic provinces. The book is, incidentally, dedicated to George Kennan for his "truth without malice" (pp. 1-130, 237-343).

J120) Bigelow, Poultney, *Seventy summers.* London: Edward Arnold & Co., 1925. 2 vols.

> In his rambling autobiography Bigelow recalls his first trip to Russia with Remington in June 1892 (vol. I, pp. 320-32). In 1896 he visited the south of Russia, crossing from Romania and making his way to Odessa. More concerned with his difficulties with Russia passport control and praise for George Kennan's book about Russia than providing any geographical or chronological information (vol. II, pp. 100-07).

J121) Neave, Joseph James, *Leaves from the journal of Joseph James Neave.* Edited, with notes, by Joseph J. Green. London: Headley Bros., 1911. 228pp.

> In March 1890 the Quaker Neave (1836-1913) received the call "Thou must go to Russia" to plead for liberty of conscience. He travelled from Australia to London and set out on 12 October 1892 for St Petersburg with his companion John Bellows (see J122). They met Pobedonostsev and then journeyed to Moscow, where they met Tolstoi. They travelled on to Vladikavkaz, where they met persecuted Stundists, and on to Tiflis, visiting the exiled Tolstoyan Prince Khilkov, and beyond to Shusha, near

the Persian border, before returning to the capital, which they left on 28 March 1893 (pp. 113-51).

J122) Bellows, John, *John Bellows: letters and memoir.* Edited by his wife [Elizabeth]. London: Kegan Paul, Trench, Trübner & Co., 1904. vi+392pp.

> The letters of Bellows (1831-1902), printer, scholar, and compiler of a noted French-English dictionary, provide a much fuller picture of the itinerary of the two Friends in 1892-93 and of the people they encountered. After their return to St Petersburg, Bellows, without Neave, went again to Moscow to see Tolstoi (pp. 107-238). Bellows was to pay another visit to Russia in December 1899 with Edmund Brooks to petition the tsar to allow a group of Dukhobors, exiled to Siberia, to join the rest of their community in Canada. He travelled once again to Moscow to see Tolstoi (pp. 330-04).

J123) Dunmore, Charles Adolphus Murray, 7th Earl of, *The Pamirs: being a narrative of a year's expedition on horseback and on foot through Kashmir, western Tibet, Chinese Tartary, and Russian Central Asia.* London: John Murray, 1893. 2 vols.

> Dunmore (1841-1907) arrived in India on 12 February 1892 to begin a journey that would take him and his companion, a Major Roche, across the Pamirs as far as Kashgar, near the Russian-Chinese border. On 13 December, Roche having been refused entry into Russian territory, Dunmore departed alone on the last leg of his journey that took him through the Alai mountains to Khokhand, Tashkent, and Samarkand, where he arrived at the beginning of February 1893. He then went via Baku, Tiflis and Batumi to Constantinople (vol. II, pp. 236-340).

J124) Burton, Reginald George, *Tropics and snows: a record of travel and adventure.* Illustrated by Miss Clare Burton from photographs and from sketches by the author. London: Edward Arnold, 1898. 349pp.

> During a year's leave in England, Captain Burton (1864-1951) of the Indian Staff Corps and late of the 1st West India Regiment, decided to learn Russian as "an accomplishment of something interesting and useful" and was sent to Moscow, arriving via Odessa, in November 1892. In February 1893 he was invited to stay for a week on an estate near Vitebsk, before returning to his studies in Moscow, which included surprisingly wide reading in Russian literature. In August he paid a visit to Nizhnii Novgorod by train and down the Volga to Astrakhan (pp. 125-80). He added two further general chapters on superstition versus civilization (pp. 181-96) and on the fighting qualities of the Cossacks (pp. 196-211).

J125) Garnett, Constance, *Constance Garnett, a life.* By Richard Garnett. London: Sinclair-Stevenson, 1991. xiv+402pp.

> The most famous of English translators of Russian literature, Mrs Garnett, née Black (1861-1946), paid her first visit to Russia in January-February 1893, visiting St Petersburg, Moscow, where she met Tolstoi, and Nizhnii Novgorod. The account of her visit is reconstructed from her letters (she did not keep a diary) by her grandson (pp. 115-30).

J126) Wenyon, Charles, *Across Siberia on the great post-road.* London: Charles H. Kelly, 1896. xii+240pp.

> Wenyon (1848-1924), a doctor in practice in China, considered himself one of the last Englishmen to undertake the journey across Siberia "in the old-fashioned way", travelling in the spring of 1893 from Vladivostok by tarantass, steamer, and rail as far as the column in the Urals marking the division of Asia and Europe (pp. 8-230).

J127) Jackson, Frederick George, *The great frozen land (Bolshaia zemelskija tundra): narrative of a winter journey across the tundras and a sojourn among the Samoyeds.* Edited from his journals by Arthur Montefiore. London: Macmillan & Co., 1895. xviii+297pp.

> The arctic explorer (1860-1938), F.R.G.S., completed a sledge journey of 3,000 miles across the Siberian tundra between the rivers Ob and Pechora in 1893.

J128) Welzl, Jan, *Thirty years in the golden north.* Translated by Paul Selver. With a foreword by Karel Capek. London: G. Allen & Unwin, 1932. 336pp.

> The Moravian eccentric (1868-1948), "around whom questions hover like mosquitoes on a warm Yukon day", relates his colourful account of his life and Munchausen-like adventures, which included a period from 1893, working on the Trans-Siberian and travelling through Siberia, to two journalists Bedrich Golombek and Edvard Valenta (pp. 19-149).

J129) De Windt, Harry, *My note-book at home and abroad.* London: Chapman & Hall, 1923. 288pp.

> De Windt's final, haphazardly presented reminiscences from his adventure-filled life include a visit to Gatchina, c.1893, specially to present a copy of his second book on Siberia to Nicholas II (then still Tsarevich), an earlier meeting with Rasputin in Tomsk (pp. 78-87) and a voyage on a Russian prison ship from Odessa to Sakhalin (pp. 109-14).

J130) Peel, Agnes Helen, *Polar gleams: an account of a voyage on the yacht 'Blencathra'.* With a preface by the Marquess of Dufferin and Ava, and contributions by Joseph Wiggins and Frederick G[eorge] Jackson. London: Edward Arnold, 1894. xviii+211pp.

> Helen (Nellie) Peel (b. 1870), daughter of Sir Robert and a London débutante in the 1892 season, suddenly decided the following year to sail to Siberia. She and her companion, exhibiting "the audacity of our modern maidens" (Lord Dufferin), embarked at Appledore on 25 July 1893 and returned to Dundee on 7 November after an adventurous voyage that took them to the Kara Sea and the mouth of the River Enisei with various stops at Samoed settlements and on the return journey, at Archangel (pp. 1-143). Various appendices include (pp. 147-82) **Wiggins'** account of his homeward journey through Siberia after leaving the *Blencathra*.

J131) Butterfield, Daniel Adams, *A biographical memorial of General David Butterfield including many addresses and military writings.* Edited by [his wife] Julia Lorrilard Butterfield. New York: Grafton Press, 1904. xii+379pp.

> Union general in the Civil War, Butterfield (1831-1901) paid two visits to Russia in an unsuccessful attempt to secure a concession to build a railway in Siberia: the first took place in the late 1880s, when he was accompanied by his wife (pp. 17-19); the second in 1893, which gave him material for a lecture he delivered on 9 April 1894 in New York in which he expressed the view that "statements of Russian despotism and cruelty are wildly exaggerated" (pp. 294-301).

J132) Lynch, Henry Finnis Blosse, *Armenia: travels and studies.* London: Longmans, Green, and Co., 1901. 2 vols.

> The English (but with an Armenian maternal grandmother) traveller, Persia-based businessman, and, later, Liberal politician (1862-1913) mixes travel account with historical, archaeological, geographical and sympathetic political analysis of Armenia. The first volume focuses on a journey Lynch made through Russian Armenia between 14 August 1893, with his arrival in Batumi from Trebizond, and 23 October 1894, when he enters Turkish territory near Kagyzman. Notable are the account of his ascent of Mount Ararat on 20 September 1893 and his extensive description and numerous photographs of a trip to the abandoned medieval city of Ani, near Kars.

J133) Hedin, Sven Anders von. *Through Asia.* Translated from the Swedish by J.T. Bealby. London: Methuen & Co., 1898. 2 vols.

The great Swedish geographer and travel writer (1865-1952) offers "a plain account", but a very weighty one, of his travels in Asia between 1893 and 1897. He travels from St Petersburg to the Kirghiz steppe and to the Russian Pamirs – and beyond. (Russia, vol. I, pp. 1-201; II, pp. 653-704.)

J134) De Windt, Harry, *The prisons of Siberia: lecture delivered to the Foreign Press Association in London, March 5th, 1895.* London: T. Brettell & Co., 1895. 23pp.

De Windt continues his polemic with Kennan in a lecture which he divided into two. In the first part he spoke of the great Siberian road, the mines, and the forwarding prison at Tomsk, which he had visited in August 1890 to take issue specifically with the American; in the second he spoke of Sakhalin. His conclusion: that Kennan should re-visit and see the improvements made since 1885.

J135) De Windt, Harry, *The new Siberia: being an account of a visit to the penal island of Sakhalin, and political prison and mines of the Trans-Baikal district, eastern Siberia.* London: Chapman & Hall, 1896. xiv+324pp.

"The probability of the total abolition of exile to Siberia in favour of deportation by sea to the Island of Sakhalin has suggested the title of this work, which contains little more than a series of sketches illustrative of life and travel in the remoter regions of Asiatic Russia." De Windt travelled from Japan in April 1894 on a Scottish-built Russian convict ship with nearly 800 prisoners for Sakhalin. After exploring the island he moved to Vladivostok to visit Siberian prisons and mines.

J136) Shoemaker, Michael Myers, *Trans-Caspia: the sealed provinces of the czar.* Cincinnati: the Robert Clarke Co., 1895. viii+310pp.

Shoemaker (1853-1924) with his companion J. de Bylandt reached St Petersburg from Berlin in May 1894 and proceeded by rail to Vladikavkaz to begin their 10,000 mile tour that included a trip on the Transcaspian railway to Bokhara and Samarkand and a brief excursion into Chinese territory. Sailed from Batumi for Turkey at the end of July (pp. 1-287).

J137) Trevor-Battye, Aubyn Bernard Rochfort, *Ice-bound on Kolguev: a chapter in the exploration of Arctic Europe; to which is added a record of the natural history of the island.* Westminster: Archibald Constable & Co., 1895. xxviii+458pp.

The naturalist and traveller Trevor-Battye (1855-1922) and his assistant Thomas Hyland travelled to Kolguev Island in the Barents Sea to survey its flora and fauna in June 1894. They were marooned there until September, when Samoed reindeer herders aided their escape.

J138) Pray, Eleanor Lord, *Letters from Vladivostok, 1894-1930.* Edited with introduction and notes by Brigitta Ingemanson. Biographical sketch by Paricia D. Silver. Seattle and London: University of Washington Press, 2013. xxxi+276pp.

Eleanor "Roxy" Lord (1868-1954), soon after her marriage to Frederick Pray (d. 1923), left America and travelling via Japan, arrived in Vladivostok in late June 1894. She was to remain until December 1930, during which time she wrote some 2,000 letters to her family and friends. From this archive Prof Ingemanson has woven a rich tapestry, organized into three parts, each chronological and entitled 'The people', 'The city' and 'The history' (pp. 5-216).

J139) Crosby, Ernest Howard, *Tolstoy as a schoolmaster.* London: Arthur C. Fifield, 1904. 94pp.

The year after publishing *Tolstoy and his message*, the American educational reformer (1856-1907) describes the count's views on education and the teaching methods employed at the village school which he observed during his visit to Iasnaia Poliana in 1894.

J140) Trevor-Battye, Aubyn Bernard Rochfort, *A northern highway of the Tsar.* Illustrated by the author. Westminster: Archibald Constable & Co., 1898. xiv+256pp.

In this volume Trevor-Battye (J136) describes the escape from Kolguev and the hazardous 1,000-mile, five-week journey back to Archangel in September-October 1894, during the *rasputnia*, the season of impassable roads.

J141) 'Oriental Widow', *Light thrown on a hideous empire.* By an oriental widow. London: Neville Beeman, 1897. xii+154pp.

Internal evidence suggests that the author was an American, probably female, whose knowledge of Russia extended from the last years of Alexander III's reign to the early years of Nicholas II's. Preface speaks of "the compiler and associates" of what is termed an "exposé of a monstruous government" for which "the deluge" is imminent. Attacks on church, censorship, bureaucracy, followed by chapter on 'Trans-Kaukasia' (pp. 113-43) that is informed and remarkably temperate.

J142) Freshfield, Douglas William, *The exploration of the Caucasus.* London and New York: Edward Arnold, 1896. 2 vols.

> Two truly mountainous volumes offer the *état present* of climbing and exploration in the Caucasus, essentially taken up to the end of the reign of Alexander III. Freshfield draws heavily on his three journeys in 1868 (see I80), 1887, and 1889 for a systematic account of the various regions of the Caucasus, arranged not chronologically but geographically. He includes contributions by other climber-explorers – **J.G. Cockin**, (vol. II, pp. 38-58), **H.W. Holder** (vol. II, pp. 2-37), **Hermann Woolley** (vol. II, pp. 93-114), and **Maurice de Déchy** (vol. II, pp. 174-90), but the overall authorship and responsibility is his.

Fig. 45 Tsar Nicholas II (1898), photograph by A.A. Pasetti.

11. REIGN OF NICHOLAS II (1894-1917)

See also: I51, I79, I143, I146, I167, I173, I179, I180, J40, J43, J44, J65, J76, J77, J82, J87, J88, J94, J120, J122, J140

K1) 'Viator', *Overland to Persia.* London: John and Edward Bumpus, 1906. xii+169pp.

> Anonymous account of a journey undertaken during a summer sometime in the 1890s. In a breezy narrative the English author describes his journey by train from Warsaw to Odessa and his travels with a Russian companion through the Crimean peninsula and along the Black Sea coast. They take the train through Georgia to Tiflis and proceed by horse into Persian territory. The text is enlivened with illustrations by Ambrose Dudley from sketches by the author (pp. 1-105).

K2) Harris, Walter Burton, *From Batum to Baghdad via Tiflis, Tabriz, and Persian Kurdistan.* Edinburgh and London: William Blackwood and Sons, 1896. xii+335pp.

> Harris (1866-1933), F.R.G.S., *Times* correspondent and Moroccan specialist, who had been in Archangel some years earlier, sailed from Constantinople for Batumi in April 1895 and went by train first to Tiflis and then by carriage to Erevan, and on into Persia, without incident or much of note (pp. 25-84).

K3) Muir, Hal Moncreiff, *A tour in Russia.* Leith: printed for the author by Mackenzie and Storrie, 1898. 76pp.

> A "humble account of travel" by an Edinburgh Scot, author of similar efforts for Switzerland and the Pyrenees, who sailed with three friends from Grangemouth to Cronstadt "several years ago", presumably c.1895. A conventional description of the sights of Petersburg and its environs and of an excursion to Moscow suddenly changes tack and is followed by a string of "stories" illustrating Russian religious, social and village life (pp. 26-70).

http://dx.doi.org/10.11647/OBP.0042.11

K4) Perris, George Herbert, *Russia in revolution.* London: Chapman & Hall, 1905. xvi+359pp.

> Offered as "a review of the last thirty-five years of Russian public life" and making copious use of printed sources and the active contribution of many Russian revolutionaries in exile, this account, dated 15 April 1905 and thus published before the tragic end of that year, is suffused with Perris's own memories from numerous visits to Russia during the first decade of Nicholas's reign. Perris (1866-1920), who had published *Leo Tolstoy, the grand mujik* (1898), contributed articles while in Russia to various papers including the *Daily Chronicle*.

K5) Dillon, Emile Joseph, *The eclipse of Russia.* London & Toronto: J.M. Dent and Sons, 1918. viii+420pp.

> Dedicated to the Russian premier Count Witte for whom Dillon had worked as private adviser from 1903 to 1914, this work, representing Dillon's bleak view of Russia under Nicholas II, also includes a chapter entitled 'Some personal recollections' (pp. 61-82). (See also I157 and, under pseudonym of Lanin, J89.)

K6) Hodgetts, Edward Arthur Brayley, *Round about Armenia: the record of a journey across the Balkans through Turkey, the Caucasus and Persia, in 1895.* London: Sampson Low, Marston & Co., 1896. xii+296pp.

> Hodgetts (see I79, J113) was later to call this trip on behalf of the *Daily Graphic* to report on the Turkish massacres of Armenians "the most interesting of the many journeys I had ever undertaken". It took him to Tiflis and Baku and into both Russian and Turkish Armenia.

K7) Jefferson, Robert Louis, *Awheel to Moscow and back: the record of a record cycle ride.* With a preface by A.R. Savile. London: Sampson Low, Marston & Co., 1895. xii+172pp.

> Cycling enthusiast Jefferson's first venture into Russia, making a round trip from Warsaw to Moscow in fifty days in April-June 1895 (pp. 61-159). (See also K30, K48.)

K8) Pearson, Henry John, *"Beyond Petsora eastwards": two summer voyages to Novaya Zemlya and the islands of the Barents Sea.* With appendices on the botany and geology by Col. H.W. Feilden. London: R.H. Porter, 1899. xiv+335pp.

> The Nottingham foundry-owner and dedicated ornithologist (1850-1913), together with his brother Charles, the Rev. Slater, and Col. Feilden, sailed on

a small steamer, the *Saxon,* to Russian Lapland and the islands of Kolguev and Novaia Zemlia in the summer of 1895, recording and collecting birds and their eggs. In 1897, on a larger steamer, the *Laura,* he and Feilden went as far as the Kara Sea. Their observations were first published in *Ibis* in 1896 and 1897.

K9) Demidov, Elim Pavlovich, *Hunting trips in the Caucasus.* London: Rowland Ward, 1898. xvi+319pp.

The immensely rich Demidov (1868-1943), 3rd Prince of San Donato, born in Vienna and dying in Athens, provided a "faithful account of three shooting trips to three different parts of the Caucasus". The first took him to the Kuban in the autumn of 1895; the second along the Russo-Persian border in the summer of 1896; the third, again to the Kuban, in the autumn of 1896. The last two accounts were in fact written by **Dr H.D. Levick**, who accompanied Demidov. The book was dedicated to St. George Littledale, who was also on the third expedition and who had shot in the Caucasus several times in earlier years. (For further expeditions, see K31 and K69).

K10) Patterson, John Edward, *My vagabondage, being the intimate autobiography of a nature's nomad.* London: William Heinemann, 1911. xix+373pp.

Patterson (1866-1919), Yorkshire-born merchant seaman and later novelist, recounts his adventures at sea, including disastrous shore-leave in St Petersburg at the end of the nineteenth century (pp. 252-66).

K11) Kenworthy, John Coleman, *A pilgrimage to Tolstoy: being letters written from Russia, to the 'New Age', January 1896.* Croydon: Brotherhood Publishing Co., 1896. 45pp.

Kenworthy (1863-1946), leader of the Croydon Brotherhood Church, came under the spell of Tolstoi's writings in 1890 and soon thereafter began a correspondence that led to his visit to Moscow at the end of 1895 and early 1896. In between his meetings with Tolstoi he paid a visit to Kostroma to see the "real" Russia of the countryside.

K12) Palmer, Francis H.E., *Russian life in town & country.* London: George Newnes, 1901. xii+271pp.

Based on a residence of several years in Russia (the author mentions incidents in 1895 and 1900), Palmer's contribution to the Newnes's 'Our neighbours' series is a detailed, informed and sympathetic account of the social and domestic life of the Russians in town and village.

K13) Joubert, Carl, *Russia as it really is.* London: Eveleigh Nash, 1904. xii+300pp.

> Joubert (d. 1906), an Englishman of Huguenot descent, who claimed to have visited as a tramp (*brodiaga*) almost every part of Russia including Sakhalin during nine years from c.1881, travelled there several times thereafter. It is a journey in 1896 that he recalls in particular in this first of three books he wrote in the space of eighteen months, condemning tyranny, the penal system, and anti-semitism, and sensing revolution.

K14) Olufsen, Axel Frits Olaf Henrik, *Through the unknown Pamirs: the second Danish Pamir expedition 1898-99.* London: William Heinemann, 1904. xxii+238pp.

> Lt. Olufsen (1865-1929) of the Danish army led two expeditions to the Pamirs in the 1890s. The first left Copenhagen on 25 March 1896 and returned on 1 March of the following year, travelling from St Petersburg via Georgia to Baku, across the Caspian, and by the Transcaspian railway to Samarkand, thereafter by tarantas and horse into the Pamirs. This journey was seen as essentially one of reconnoitring for the second expedition that lasted from 23 March 1898 to 22 November 1899. It was this second expedition, following the same outward route as far as Osh and then proceeding deep into south Pamir that produced the material for the book.

K15) Olufsen, Axel Frits Olaf Henrik, *The emir of Bokhara and his country: journeys and studies in Bokhara (with a chapter on my voyage on the Amu Darya to Khiva).* London: William Heinemann, 1911. xii+599pp.

> In a complementary volume to his 1904 work, Olufsen, now retired from the army, a professor and secretary to the Royal Danish Geographical Society, concentrates on a comprehensive study of Bokhara, both before and after it became a vassal state of Russia. Both Danish expeditions spent extended stays as guests of the emir in Bokhara.

K16) Bigham, Clive, *A ride through Western Asia.* London: Macmillan and Co., 1897. xii+284pp.

> Anxious to get to Armenia, Bigham left England on 22 June 1895 by what seemed, given the political situation, the most difficult route via Constantinople. He traversed Persia and eventually entered Russian territory on 20 April 1896. He travelled through Russian Turkestan and visited Bokhara and Samarkand, briefly entered China, and then across the steppe to Omsk and homewards by the Trans-Siberian to St Petersburg,

which he reached on 26 June. He calculated that he had travelled in Asia over 8,000 miles, half of which were on horseback (pp. 205-69).

K17) Gordon, Samuel, *A handful of exotics: scenes and incidents, chiefly of Russo-Jewish life.* London: Methuen & Co., 1897. x+297pp.

In his preface, dated September 1896, Gordon offers, as an amateur ethnographer, a series of "light sketches endeavour[ing] to depict the Russian Jew in his native surroundings". Two of the ten tales are devoted to non-Jewish subjects, "illustrating the environments in which the Russian Jew moves".

K18) Malcolm, Ian Zachary, *Trodden ways 1895-1930.* London: Macmillan and Co., 1930. xii+288pp.

Sir Ian (1868-1944), 17th chieftain of the clan Malcolm and a M.P., was attached to the British embassy for three weeks at the time of the coronation of Nicholas II in May 1896 and he records his impressions in an essay entitled 'The last coronation' (pp. 44-68). In 1916 he returned to Russia as British Red Cross commissioner, mainly in Petrograd but also visiting Kiev. He includes a description of his audience with the tsar at Tsarskoe selo (pp. 69-92).

K19) Logan, John Alexander, Jr., *In joyful Russia.* London: C. Arthur Pearson, 1897. x+275pp.

The American army officer Logan (1865-99) records "a thoroughly delightful" trip and defends his "rose-coloured" view of a country "in holiday attire" for the coronation of Nicholas II in Moscow on 26 May 1896. He even plays down the tragedy at the festival at Khodynskoe pole on 30 May for "it is not best to let the unthinking brood too deeply over the irretrievable" and what happened only underlined the "sympathy" between the people and the throne. Logan, his mother, and his friend G left Moscow for St Petersburg on 7 June, where they enjoyed further delights before "departing the land of the Great White Tsar with regret".

K20) Grenfell, Francis Wallace, *Three weeks in Moscow.* London: for the author by Harrison and Sons, 1896. iv+152pp.

Lt-General Sir Francis (1841-1925), afterwards 1st Baron Grenfell, was in the suite accompanying the Duke and Duchess of Connaught to attend the coronation of Nicholas II. In a series of letters to E. (Evelyn, his first wife), he describes their departure from Sheerness on 11 May on board the *Victoria and Albert* and arrival a week later at the English Embankment in St

Petersburg, proceeding to Moscow by train. Five days after the coronation he was also present at the public festival at Khodynskoe pole and reports on the tragedy that ensued. They sailed from St Petersburg on 9 June (pp. 10-116).

K21) Grenfell, Francis Wallace, *Memoirs of Field Marshall Lord Grenfell.* London: Hodder & Stoughton, 1925. xv+236pp.

Grenfell recalls his visit in 1896 (pp. 127-42).

K22) Creighton, Mandell, *Life and letters.* By his wife [Louise Creighton]. London: Longmans, Green, & Co., 1904. 2 vols.

Creighton (1843-1901), Bishop of Peterborough, represented the Anglican church at the coronation, travelling with W.J. Birkbeck, the acknowledged British authority on the Russian church. He describes his visit in letters to his wife and in a notebook, detailing his meetings with, among others, the patriarch and Pobedonostsev (vol. II, pp. 148-64).

K23) Sykes, Arthur Alkin, *The coronation cruise of the 'Midnight Sun' to Russia, Whitsuntide, 1896: a record.* London: for the author, 1896. 118pp.

Sykes (1861-1939), contributor to *Punch* and translator of Gogol's *Revizor*, joined a three-week tour (11 May-6 June) of five northern capitals that was designed to coincide with Nicholas II's coronation. Grenfell (see K20) mentions the "cheering" British tourists (168 in fact) on board the *Midnight Sun*, who made their way to Moscow for the great event but left before the tragedy of Khodynka (pp. 49-82).

K24) Davis, Richard Harding, *A year from a correspondent's note-book.* New York and London: Harper & Brothers, 1898. x+305pp.

Journalist, novelist, playwright, and F.R.G.S., Davis (1864-1916), later renowned for his war reporting, describes his visit to Russia for the coronation in May 1896 in an article previously published in *Harper's Magazine*, but makes no mention of the Khodynka tragedy (pp. 3-65).

K25) [Maude, Aylmer], *The tsar's coronation as seen by "De Monte Alto" resident in Moscow.* London and Croydon: Brotherhood Publishing Co., 1896. 128pp.

A healthy counterblast to accounts that "present nothing but the conventional, superficial laudations of a spectacle which enlightened conscience and sober reason must see in a wholly different light". Maude (see J86), the "resident" concealing his identity, follows the preparations for the event , the pageant itself, and in graphic detail the "catastrophe" at Khodynka on 18 May 1896, before penning an epilogue, suffused with the teachings of Tolstoi and railing against the perils of ultra-patriotism that affects equally the British.

K26) Addams, Jane, *Twenty years at Hull-House, with autobiographical notes.* New York: Macmillan, 1910. 462pp.

> Social activist, founder of the U.S. Settlement House movement and recipient of the Nobel Peace Prize, Addams (1860-1935) travelled with wealthy debutante Mary Rozet Smith to Russia in July 1896. Addams was yet another enthusiast for Tolstoi's social writings, but her meeting with him proved awkward and confrontational (pp. 266-74).

K27) Simpson, James Young, *Side-lights on Siberia: some account of the great Siberian railroad, the prisons and the exile system.* Edinburgh and London: William Blackwood and Sons, 1898. xvi+383pp.

> A journey undertaken in the summer of 1896 that took Simpson (1873-1934), who had recently graduated from Edinburgh University, along the Trans-Siberian. Offering not so much a travelogue as an investigation into the potential of Siberia and much about the penal system, Simpson sought "the truth" mid-point between the views of Kennan and De Windt, but predicted that revolution was inevitable.

K28) Mavor, Sam, *Memories of people and places.* London, Edinburgh and Glasgow: William Hodge and Co., 1940. iv+327pp.

> Russia played a large role in the life of the electrical engineer and industrialist, whose memoirs, gathered together when he was seventy six, comprise mainly articles he had written at various times for his firm's *Apprentices magazine*. Mavor (b. 1863) first went to Russia in the summer of 1896 to inspect the installation of electric lighting at the Thornton woollen mills in St Petersburg (pp. 5-9). He also describes a momentous journey to deliver a Tyne-built steamer from Newcastle to St Petersburg and then by the waterways to Astrakhan (pp. 163-86). In 1899 he made a pilgrimage to Solovetsk from Norway (pp. 187-213). His final visit to St Petersburg was in 1912.

K29) Fraser, John Foster, *Round the world on a wheel: being the narrative of a bicycle ride of nineteen thousand two hundred and thirty-seven miles through* *seventeen countries and across three continents, by John Foster Fraser, S. Edward Lunn, and F.H. Lowe.* London: Methuen, 1899. xii+532pp.

> Cycling trip by three friends across the world that began on 17 July 1896 and took 774 days was chronicled by Sir John (1868-1936). They entered Russia from Romania in the autumn en route for Odessa and thereafter cycled through the Crimea to the Caucasus and through Georgia to Erevan. Passing Ararat, they left Armenia and entered Persia (pp. 28-90). (See also K88, K90, K301)

K30) Jefferson, Robert Louis, *Roughing it in Siberia; with some account of the Trans-Siberian railway, and the gold-mining industry of Asiatic Russia.* London: Sampson Low, Marston & Co., 1897. 252pp.

> Forsaking for once his bike for the railway, Jefferson (see K7) accompanies three business associates from Moscow to Krasnoiarsk, the then terminus of the railway, and then down the Enisei in January-April 1897. Visited gold-mines, interviewed owners and miners, gathered samples of ore.

K31) Demidov, Elim Pavlovich, *After wild sheep in the Altai and Mongolia.* London: Rowland Ward, 1900. xii+324pp.

> Demidov (see K9) travelled with his wife and the great travellers St. George Littledale (1851-1931) and his wife Teresa (1839-1928) from London in April 1897 to shoot the wild sheep (*ovis ammon*), and much else.

K32) Gillis, Charles J., *A summer vacation in Iceland, Norway, Sweden and Russia.* New York: Printed for private distribution, 1898. 55pp.

> Seasoned traveller and author of a number of privately printed travel accounts, Gillis joined a party sailing from New York on 26 June 1897 for Scandinavia and Russia. Very brief notes with photographs on their visit to St Petersburg, Moscow, and then Peterhof, before they sailed off for Southampton towards the end of August (pp. 36-52).

K33) Dana, Charles A., *Eastern journeys: some notes of travel in Russia, in the Caucasus, and to Jerusalem.* New York: D. Appleton and Co., 1898. iv+146pp.

> A three-month round trip from New York in the summer of 1897 that takes the American tourists Dana (1819-97) and his wife first to Odessa by boat from Marseilles and then on to Batumi, through Georgia to Rostov and the railway link to Nizhnii and Moscow (pp. 17-101).

K34) Symons, Arthur William, *Cities.* London: J.M. Dent & Co., 1903. xii+261pp.

> In this collection of essays, printed previously in journals, the prolific literary scholar and author Symons (1865-1945) included 'Moscow', which he visited in the hot summer of 1897 and which he "hated", as much as Naples, in contrast to St Petersburg, which had "nothing to say" to him (pp. 155-85).

K35) Ridley, James Cartmell, *Reminiscences of Russia: the Ural mountains and adjoining Siberian district in 1897.* Newcastle-upon-Tyne: A. Reid & Co., 1898. 100pp.

> Prior to attending the International Geological Congress, held in St Petersburg in August 1897, Ridley and another unnamed delegate from Newcastle embarked on a long journey that took them by train via Warsaw to Moscow, where they arrived on 27 July. They then travelled by various forms of transport via Samara as far as Ekaterinburg and looped back to Moscow via Perm and Kazan, before proceeding to the capital for the conference. Highly impressed by "a great country", they sailed for home on 6 September.

K36) Hayes, Matthew Horace, *Among horses in Russia.* London: R.A. Everett & Co., 1900. xiv+214pp.

> Capt Hayes, a leading authority and author on all things equine, paid four visits to Russia. The first in July-September 1897, at the invitation of the imperial guards stationed at Krasnoe selo outside St Petersburg, was quickly followed by a second in October with further horses and a visit to an imperial stud at Dubrovka in Ukraine. Two further visits followed in March and August 1898, during the second of which he was later joined by his wife, a formidable horsewoman. Much valuable information on the famous Orlov stud and Russian horse-breeding.

K37) Honeyman, Abraham Van Doren, and Mason, Abbie Ranlett, *From America to Russia in summer of 1897.* Edited by A.V.D. Honeyman. Plainfield, New Jersey: Honeyman & Co., 1897. 167pp.

> Two chapters in this third collection of travel accounts by members of Honeyman tourist groups from New York and New Jersey are devoted to their visit to Russia in early August 1897: Mason describes their arrival in St Petersburg from Finland, their tour of the city sights, and a visit to the military review at Krasnoe selo (pp. 88-97); Honeyman (1849-1936) recounts the party's less enjoyable trip to Moscow, where they note the

greater level of poverty and social disorder compared to St Petersburg (pp. 98-114).

K38) Miles, Nelson Appleton, *Military Europe: a narrative of personal observation and personal experience.* New York: Doubleday & McClure Co., 1898. 112pp.

> U.S. major-general (1839-1925), veteran of the Civil War and Indian wars, arrived in Russia on 15 August 1897, was received by the tsar at Peterhof, and observed the annual manoeuvres of the Russian army at Krasnoe selo, before proceeding to Germany and France (pp. 73-94).

K39) Renshaw, Charles Jeremiah, *Travels in Russia.* London: National Union Publishing Co., 1900. 32pp.

> Dr Renshaw of Ashton-on-Mersey travelled by train to Moscow with a party of thirty men and ten women to attend the 12th International Medical Congress in August 1897. He briefly describes their outward journey, their stay in Moscow, their visit to Petersburg and homewards via Finland.

K40) Kerr, John, *Leaves from an inspector's notebook.* London: Thomas Nelson & Sons, [1913]. 278pp.

> Kerr (1830-1916), senior chief inspector of schools in Scotland, travelled to St Petersburg via Sweden and Finland en route for Moscow, where he also attended the Medical Congress that opened on 19 August in the Bolshoi theatre. He also went to the fair at Nizhnii Novgorod (pp. 158-76).

K41) Miles, Nelson Appleton, *Military Europe: a narrative of personal observation and personal experience.* New York: Doubleday & McClure Co., 1898. x+112pp.

> Commanding general of the United States army since 1895, Miles (1839-1925) attended Russian military manoeuvres at Krasnoe selo and was received at Peterhof by the tsar in August 1897 (pp. 73-94).

K42) Flint, Josiah Frederick, *Tramping with tramps: studies and sketches of vagabond life.* With prefatory note by Hon. Andrew D. White. New York: The Century Co., 1899. xvi+398pp.

> In part II of his book in which he details his experiences with tramps in various parts of the world, Flint (b. 1850) includes 'With the Russian goriouns [unfortunates]', describing his visit to Russia in 1897, when he

not only went to see Tolstoi but also "tramped" for some days in Vitebsk district (pp. 200-28).

K43) Perowne, John Thomas Woolrych, *Russian hosts and English guests in Central Asia.* London: The Scientific Press, 1898. xvi+198pp.

> Perowne, Cambridge graduate and translator from French and German, does "nothing more than describe a journey, made in November and December last, over the Transcaspian Military Railway". One of a party of twenty-five English who left Constantinople on 6 November 1897, Perowne, styling himself "something of a Russophil", charts their progress to Batumi and on to Tiflis and Baku, where they take the steamer to Krasnovodsk. There they board the Transcaspian railway for a three-week journey to Samarkand with various stops en route, including a reception by Kuropatkin, the governor-general, on their return to Ashabad.

K44) Phibbs, Isabelle Mary, *A visit to the Russians in Central Asia.* London: Kegan Paul, Trench, Trübner & Co., Ltd., 1899. viii+238pp.

> Travel writer in the same party as Perowne, although neither names the other, offers her account of the "marvellously interesting journey", which for her was marred only by a bout of influenza that made the return by train "almost entirely a blank".

K45) Loch, Emily, *The memoirs of Emily Loch: discretion in waiting, Tsarina Alexandra and the Christian family.* Edited by Judith Poore. Kinloss: Librario, 2007. 394pp.

> Emily (d. 1932), lady-in-waiting to Helena, Princess Christian, accompanied Princess Helena, Princess Christian's eldest daughter, on visit to the Russian imperial family during the winter of 1897-98 (pp. 183-252).

K46) Cobbold, Ralph Patteson, *Innermost Asia: travel & sport in the Pamirs.* London: William Heinemann, 1900. xviii+354pp.

> With the modest aim of making his book "the standard work of reference on its subject", Cobbold charts his travels and hunting through the Pamirs in 1897-98. Coming from the Chinese side, he crossed the Russian border at the beginning of January 1898 and travelled to lake Balkash, where he shot his first tiger. He returned to Kashgar before receiving permission to travel in the Russian Pamirs. At one stage detained as a spy, Cobbold is ultimately glad to make his way to "freedom" in British Kashmir (pp. 92-210).

K47) Colquhoun, Archibald Ross, *The 'overland' to China.* London: Harper & Brothers, 1900. xii+465pp.

> Much travelled in China over the previous twenty years, Colquhoun, F.R.G.S., was convinced of the importance of the nearly completed Trans-Siberian railway beyond the boundaries of Russia itself and undertook a journey from St Petersburg in late 1898 that took him to the temporary terminus of the railway at Baikal before travelling through Mongolia to Pekin. An attempt at a serious historico-geographical assessment, based on his own observations and "original sources" (pp. 1-149).

K48) Jefferson, Robert Louis, *A new ride to Khiva.* London: Methuen & Co., 1899. xii+352pp.

> Intent on replicating Burnaby's famous 1875-76 ride to Central Asia but purely for sporting reasons, Jefferson (see K7, K30) set out from England on the six-thousand mile trek in April 1898, entering Russia via Galicia. He made his way to Moscow and accompanied by Russian cycling friends, went to Nizhnii Novgorod and followed the Volga and on across the Kirghiz steppe until his reception by the khan of Khiva. He returned to England by ship via Constantinople and by train from Marseille (pp. 71-312).

K49) Vanderlip, Washington Baker, *In search of a Siberian Klondike. As told to Homer B. Hulbert.* London: T. Fisher Unwin, 1906. 315pp.

> American prospector Vanderlip (1863-1949) seached for gold and copper deposits in Siberia, Kamchatka and Sakhalin in 1898-89 and again in 1900. He describes wildlife and the indigenous peoples and narrates his encounters with rival prospectors and foreign adventurers.

K50) Stadling, Jonas Jonsson, *Through Siberia.* Edited by F.H.H. Guillemard. London: Archibald Constable & Co., 1901. xvi+315pp.

> Stadling (see J113) set out from Stockholm on 20 April 1898 on an unsuccessful expedition to find the Swedish explorer Andrée lost in northern Siberia. They travelled deep into Siberia, reaching the Enisei, before turning back, arriving in Stockholm (after another visit to Iasnaia Poliana) at the end of December after a journey of 15,500 miles.

K51) Bookwalter, John Wesley, *Siberia and Central Asia.* New York: Frederick A. Stokes, 1899. xxxi+548pp.

> The American manufacturer (1837-1915) records in detail and in numerous photographs his extensive travels throughout Siberia, the Caucasus,

and Central Asia during the summer and autumn of 1898. He showed particular interest in the transport infrastructure in the regions he visited as well as in their industries and commercial potential.

K52) Russell-Cotes, Annie Nelson, *Letters from Russia.* London: for the author, 1899. iv+50pp.

> Undemanding tourist's letters sent by Lady Russell-Cotes, née Clark, to her daughter E., beginning in St Petersburg on 28 August 1898 and ending in Göteborg on 22 September. From the capital they journeyed to Moscow and then to Nizhnii Novgorod, returning to Moscow and back to Petersburg (pp. 1-39).

K53) Reid, Arnot, *From Peking to Petersburg.* London: Edward Arnold, 1899. viii+300pp.

> An unremarkable account of a journey on the Trans-Siberian by a traveller, an "average indoors-man", who having arrived in Singapore, wanted to travel home to England by a different route. Entered Siberia at Kiakhta on 21 September 1898 and reached St Petersburg exactly fifty days after leaving Pekin (pp. 131-274).

K54) Leroy-Beaulieu, Pierre Paul, *The awakening of the East: Siberia—Japan—China.* Translated from the French by Richard Davey. With a preface by [Sir] Henry Norman. William Heinemann, 1900. xxvii+298pp.

> French economist (1843-1916), after extensive travels in 1898-99 through Siberia, Japan and China, writes a comparative study, drawing particular attention to the significance of the almost completed Trans-Siberian railway (pp. 1-80).

K55) Hammond, John Hays, *The autobiography of John Hays Hammond.* New York: Farrar & Rinehart, 1935. 2 vols.

> American mining engineer and diplomat (1885-1936) records his experiences of three trading missions to Russia between 1898 and 1912. In 1898, invited by the Minister of Finance Witte and accompanied by the English financier L. Hirsch, he surveyed mines and mineral resources in the Ural and Altai Mountains. He went again in 1910, meeting the tsar at Tsarskoe selo and negotiating an agreement over the use of American capital to finance Russian industries (vol. II, pp. 454-78). During a third visit to St Petersburg and Moscow in mid-May 1912 Hammond held talks with the prime minister and Witte (pp. 603-06).

K56) Oudendyk, William J., *Ways and by-ways in diplomacy.* London: Peter Davies, 1939. xii+386pp.

> The Dutch diplomat Oudendyk (b. 1874) received his first posting to the Dutch legation in China at the age of nineteen and spent much of his first long spell of leave from late 1898 to early 1900 in Moscow, where he learnt Russian. He visited Kiev and St Petersburg before taking the Trans-Siberian to Irkutsk and then proceeding to Vladivostok (pp. 78-92). In the summer of 1907 he arrived in St Petersburg as head of the Dutch legation, remaining until May 1908, when he was again appointed to China (pp. 133-47). After further service in China and Persia, whence he visited Russian Turkestan (pp. 183-90), he was in Russia at least three times in 1914-16 (pp. 201-10), before returning to Petrograd as temporary minister in the spring of 1917 and remaining until the end of 1918 (pp. 212-312).

K57) Beeby-Thompson, Arthur, *Oil pioneer: selected experiences and incidents associated with sixty years of world-wide petroleum exploration and oilfield development.* With a foreword by Herbert Hoover. London: Sidgwick and Jackson, 1961. 544pp.

> Newly employed by the European Petroleum Company, Beeby-Thompson (b. 1872) travelled out to Baku in November 1898. He combines technical data with his impressions of life in the area, where he remained until 1903. He returned to London to begin his career as a consultant oil engineer, published in 1904 a solid tome entitled *The oil fields of Russia and the Russian petroleum industry*, and was to pay one further short visit to the oilfields in 1905, when he witnessed violence between Armenians and Tartars (pp. 52-76).

K58) Pares, Bernard, *My Russian memoirs.* London: Jonathan Cape, 1931. 623pp.

> Sir Bernard (1867-1949), the pioneer of Russian studies at the universities of Liverpool and London, first visited Russia in 1898-99, when he attended lectures at Moscow University, and thereafter visited the country in many guises and on many occasions through WWI and finally left from Siberia in 1919. (See also K59, K123, K124, K309.)

K59) Pares, Bernard, *A wandering student: the story of a purpose.* Utica, New York: Syracuse University Press, 1948. xv+448pp.

> In this version of his memoirs, completed in 1947, Pares includes and reworks material on Russia included in his earlier books.

K60) Eagar, M., *Six years at the Russian court.* London: Hurst and Blackett, 1906. xvi+283pp.

> Irish Miss Eagar arrived in Petersburg in February 1899 as governess to the infant Grand Duchesses Olga and Tatiana and remained with the imperial family until the end of 1904. Her "slight sketches of life in the Palaces", offered as "plain, unvarnished truth", are naïve and undemanding but nonetheless provide intimate and unusual glimpses of the family in its Petersburg palaces and on holiday in the Crimea.

K61) Ossendowski, Ferdynand Antoni, *Man and mystery in Asia.* In collaboration with Lewis Stanton Palen. London: Edward Arnold & Co., 1924. xii+295pp.

> The first forty years of the colourful and adventurous life of the Pole Ossendowski (1878-1945) were inextricably bound with the fortunes of Russia from his birth in Russian Poland, through his education in Petersburg, extensive travels throughout the empire, political activity, imprisonment, and much else. In a first volume *Beasts, men and gods* (1923), he wrote of his escape from the Bolsheviks into Mongolia; here he returns to his earlier adventures in Siberia as far as Sakhalin from about 1899.

K62) Ossendowski, Ferdynand Antoni, *The shadow of the gloomy East.* Translated [from the Polish] by F.B. Czarnomski. London: George Allen & Unwin, 1925. 223pp.

> His self-styled "sketches" represent an attempt "to lay bare before the civilised world the true face of the Russian people", interesting above all for his personal memories, his three meetings with Rasputin, and service with Kolchak.

K63) Morton, Rosalie Slaughter, *A woman surgeon: the life and work of Rosalie Slaughter Morton.* London: Robert Hale & Co., 1937. 355pp.

> Shortly after graduating from medical school, Dr Morton (1876-1968), who was to become one of the most distinguished female doctors in America, went abroad to continue her studies in Germany. She spent the Christmas vacation of 1899 in St Petersburg, appalled by the contrasts of wealth and degrading poverty and with hindsight concluding that "here was Red Russia in the making, her garments dyed in blood". She then travelled to Moscow, where she visited Tolstoi on three occasions at his home in Khamovniki, recording in detail their conversations (pp. 75-86).

K64) Müller, Max, *Reminiscences of a roving life.* Exeter: William Pollard & Co., 1906. xii+125pp.

> Müller, not the famous Prof. Müller of Oxford University as he points out in his preface, recounts "the life of a wanderer – a vagabond – and nothing more". He made many cruises on the s.y. *Argonaut*, one of which that took him in 1899 to St Petersburg, whence he travelled to Moscow and Nizhnii Novgorod, and a later one to the Crimea, but he says little of any interest (pp. 118-23).

K65) Pearson, Henry J., *Three summers among the birds of Russian Lapland, with history of Saint Triphon's monastery and appendices.* London: R.H. Porter, 1904. xvi+216pp.

> In his second book, Pearson (see K8) describes three visits to Russian Lapland in 1899, 1901, and 1901 to observe, record, and photograph bird life (pp. 1-169). There follows a translated version of a Russian history of the monastery by the Pechenga river.

K66) Curtin, Jeremiah, *A journey in southern Siberia: the Mongols, their religion and their myths.* Boston: Little, Brown, and Co., 1909. xiv+319p.

> Curtin (see I51) journeyed from Moscow into southern Siberia to study the language, religion, and customs of the Buriats, living around Lake Baikal and on the only island within it. The account of his travels, from his arrival in Irkutsk on 9 July 1900 to his departure on 15 September, occupies pp. 18-91.

K67) Hill, Elizabeth, *In the mind's eye: the memoirs of Dame Elizabeth Hill.* Edited by Jean Stafford Smith. Lewes: The Book Guild Ltd., 1999. viii+520pp.

> Dame Elizabeth (1900-96), first professor of Slavonic studies at the University of Cambridge from 1948 to 1968, recalls her upbringing in St Petersburg in an Anglo-German family before their departure for England at the end of 1917 (pp. 3-55).

K68) Kenworthy, John Coleman, *Tolstoy: his life and works.* London and Newcastle-on-Tyne: Walter Scott Publishing Co., 1902. 255pp.

> In 1900 Kenworthy (see K11) went to Russia for a second time to see Tolstoi at Prince Obolenskii's country house outside Moscow for five days before proceeding alone to Iasnaia Poliana to absorb the atmosphere (pp. 210-28). Also included is the previously published description of his 1895 visit (pp. 47-98).

K69) Demidov, Elim Pavlovich, *A shooting trip to Kamchatka.* London: Rowland Ward, 1904. xvi+304pp.

> Travelling again with his fellow passionate sportsman St George Littledale, Demidov (see K9 and K31) completed the round trip from London across Siberia to Vladivostok by train and by steamer to Kamchatka in April-September 1900, shooting whatever moved whenever the opportunity arose.

K70) Clark, Francis Edward, *A new way around an old world.* New York & London: Harper & Brothers, 1901. xiv+212pp. [also published as *The Great Siberian Railway: what I saw on my journey.* London: S.W. Partridge and Co., 1904.]

> President of the United Society of Christian Endeavor and the World's Christian Endeavor Union, Dr Clark (1851-1927), his wife, and son reached Vladivostok from Japan on 31 May 1900 and began the six-week journey by the newly opened Trans-Siberian and by steamer to Moscow and home via St Petersburg – the first Americans "to go around the world by the new route".

K71) Clark, Francis Edward, *Memories of many men in many lands.* Boston: United Society of Christian Endeavor, 1922. 704pp.

> Succinct description of his 1900 journey across Siberia to Moscow (pp. 239-56).

K72) Roberts, James Hudson, *A flight for life and an inside view of Mongolia.* Boston: Pilgrim, 1903. 402pp.

> A missionary for the American Board of Commissioners for Foreign Missions based in Tientsin, Roberts (1851-1945) describes his and his mission's escape from China during the Boxer Rebellion in the summer of 1900. Travelling through Mongolia, he arrives in Russia at Kiakhta on 13 August and makes his way to Irkutsk, where he boards the Trans-Siberian railway. He reaches St Petersburg in mid-September (pp. 279-331).

K73) Meakin, Annette M.B., *A ribbon of iron.* London: Archibald Constable & Co., 1901. 320pp.

> Anthropologist, biographer, translator, Meakin (1867-1959), F.R.G.S., travelled with her mother along the Trans-Siberian railway from Moscow to Vladivostok in 1900.

K74) Benn, Edith Annie Fraser Parker, *An overland trek from India by side-saddle, camel, and rail; the record of a journey from Baluchistan to Europe.* London: Longmans, Green and Co., 1909. 343pp.

> The Russian stage of her journey took Mrs Benn through the Caucasus mountains and on to Georgia during late 1900 and early 1901 (pp. 274-96).

K75) Thwing, Charles Franklin, *Universities of the world.* New York: Macmillan Co., 1911. xvi+284pp.

> The president of Western Reserve University (1853-1937) visited over "years not a few" nineteen of the twenty universities he featured in a series of essays, including the university of St Petersburg. The year of his visit is not specified but would seem to be from the turn of the century (pp. 167-78).

K76) Norman, Henry, *All the Russias: travels and studies in contemporary European Russia, Finland, Siberia, the Caucasus, & central Asia*: London: William Heinemann, 1902. xvi+476pp.

> Norman (see J95), recently elected to Parliament, nevertheless undertook four journeys throughout the Russia empire in 1900-01 "to present a picture of the aspects of contemporary Russia of most interest to foreign readers", including the almost obligatory visit to Tolstoi at Iasnaia Poliana (pp. 47-63).

K77) Holmes, Burton, *The Burton Holmes lectures. With illustrations from photographs by the author.* Battle Creek, Michigan: The Little-Preston Company, 1901. 10 vols.

> The famous and successful American traveller and innovative travel lecturer (1870-1958) visited St Petersburg for the first time in April 1901 and then moved on to Moscow in May, taking a trip to Iasnaia Poliana, where he met and filmed Tolstoi. On 19 June he began his nine-day journey on the Trans-Siberian to Irkutsk. Crossing Baikal by ferry, he proceeded by train to the Cossack settlement of Stretensk, arriving in early July (vol. VIII, pp. 1-336). He then undertook a hazardous and seemingly endless journey along the Amur from Stretensk to Khabarovsk, before finally reaching Vladivostok (vol. IX, pp. 3-112). In his later guide to the Soviet Union, *The traveler's Russia* (1934), Holmes was to recall his earlier visits, particularly the meeting with Tolstoi.

K78) Beveridge, Albert Jeremiah, *The Russian advance.* New York and London: Harper & Brothers, 1904. ix+486pp.

> American historian and senator for Indiana, Beveridge (1862-1927) travelled through Russian and Siberia in 1901, intent on assessing the changing role of Russia in international politics. Much of his material was published in the Philadelphia *Saturday Evening Post* in the same year.

K79) Baring, Maurice, *The puppet show of memory.* London: Heinemann, 1922. ix+457pp.

> Baring (1874-1945), poet, dramatist, novelist, and translator with a profound love of Russia and its people, went to Russia for the first time in July 1901 as guest of Count Konstantin Benkendorf at his Tambov estate of Sosnovka (pp. 219-24). Many further visits, as family guest and as newspaper correspondent, ensued, all described in his autobiography, which covers the period up the outbreak of WWI (pp. 260-390). (See also K134, K146, K174-75, K231, K274.)

K80) Morgan, Christopher A., *From China by rail: an account of a journey from Shanghai to London via the Trans-Siberian Railways.* Edinburgh: Ballantyne, Hanson and Co., 1902. 139pp.

> British tourist describes his journey on the Trans-Siberian between 19 June and 20 August 1901, concentrating on the section between Vladivostok and Irkutsk.

K81) Senn, Nicholas, *Around the world via Siberia.* Chicago: W.B. Conkey Co., 1902. 402pp.

> Articles originally published in the *Chicago Tribune* by the professor of surgery at Rush Medical College and surgeon-general of Illinois (1844-1908), some of which describe his journey from St Petersburg to Vladivostok between 19 July and 25 August 1901 (pp. 36-198).

K82) Landor, Arnold Henry Savage, *Across coveted lands; or, a journey from Flushing (Holland) to Calcutta, overland.* London: Macmillan, 1902. 2 vols.

> Grandson of the poet, Landor (1865-1924), painter, traveller, and author, travelled from Warsaw to Kiev in 1901 and then on to Rostov and Baku, where he embarked on the mail steamer for Persia (vol. I, pp. 1-28).

K83) Meakin, Annette M.B., *In Russian Turkestan: a garden of Asia and its people.* London: George Allen, 1903. 304pp.

> Meakin's (see K73) journey through Russian central Asia in 1901 before her return to England in March 1902 takes her from Krasnovodsk on the Caspian via Askhabad and Merv to Bokhara (which she had first visited in 1896), Samarkand and Tashkent.

K84) Hawes, Charles Henry, *In the uttermost East: being an account of investigations among the natives and Russian convicts of the island of Sakhalin, with notes of travel in Korea, Siberia, and Manchuria.* London: Harper, 1903. xxviii+478pp.

> British anthropologist and associate director of Boston museum of fine art, Hawes (1867-1943) sailed from Japan to Vladivostok in August 1901, travelled to Khabarovsk, then went by boat along the Amur to Nikolaevsk before crossing to Sakhalin, "the island of punishment", where he observed the lives of both native tribes and imperial prisoners. After fifty adventure-filled days on the island, he returned by boat to Vladivostok and thence by train to Moscow and on to London, which he reached at the end of the year (pp. 15-464). Hawes was later to write the *Handbooks* on Eastern Siberia and on Sakhalin for the Foreign Office and published in 1920.

K85) Gerrare, Wirt, [pseudonym of Greener, William Oliver], *Greater Russia. The continental empire of the old world.* London: Heinemann, 1903. 310pp.

> Greener (1862-1935), author of *The story of Moscow* (1900), uses two journeys east and west to see "greater" Russia, i.e. particularly the areas east of Baikal and Russia's "port-hole on to the Pacific", and also slips in disguise into Manchuria. (See also K136.)

K86) Adams, Henry, *The education of Henry Adams: an autobiography.* Cambridge, Mass.: Riverside Press, 1918. 519pp.

> Adams (1838-1918), American journalist and member of the famous Adams political family, visited St Petersburg and Moscow between 17 August and 7 September 1901 (pp. 406-10).

K87) Adams, Henry, *Letters of Henry Adams, 1892-1918.* Edited by Worthington Chauncey Ford. Boston: Houghton Mifflin, 1938. 2 vols.

> Letters Adams sent to his friends Elizabeth Cameron and John Hay, describing his trip to Russia in 1901 (vol. II, pp. 339-50).

K88) Fraser, John Foster, *The real Siberia; together with an account of a dash through Manchuria.* London: Cassell & Co., 1902. 279pp.

"A mission of curiosity" at the behest of the owner of the *Yorkshire Post* saw Fraser (see K29) leave Moscow on 22 August 1901 by train, but not the Trans-Siberian. He travelled as far as Stretensk, from where he sailed by steamer down the Shilka and Amur rivers to Blagoveshchensk and then on to Khabarovsk. After his "dash" into Manchuria (pp. 208-55), he returned to Irkutsk at the end of October and boarded the Trans-Siberian for Moscow.

K89) Palmer, Frederick, *With my own eyes: a personal story of battle years.* London: Jarrolds, 1934. 350p.

The experienced American war correspondent (1873-1958) travelled with senators Beveridge and Cabot Lodge from Tokyo to Moscow on the Trans-Siberian en route for London in 1901, noting in particular the threat the railway brought to Japan and China (pp. 188-93). Palmer, very sympathetic to the Japanese cause, was to publish in 1904 *With Kuroki in Manchuria.*

K90) Fraser, John Foster, *Life's contrasts.* London: Cassel & Co., 1908. 339pp.

There was inevitably much in Fraser's earlier works (K29, K87) about convicts and exiles in Siberia and in this book of essays he recounts an encounter at Irkutsk with a political prisoner 'Ivan Ivanovitch', returning to his native Moscow after fifteen years' exile (pp. 33-57). In another sketch on 'the cloaks of religion' he recalls his visit to Kiev and its cathedral (pp. 76-82).

K91) Morgan, Wilma, *Glimpses of four continents, being an account of the travels of Richard Cope Morgan.* London: Morgan & Scott, 1911. xii+388pp.

As the "constant companion during the last eleven years" of her husband (1827-1908), founder of *The Christian,* Mrs Morgan was able to supplement extracts from his diaries and writings with her own personal observations. Unlike Morgan, who was exclusively concerned with visiting missions, preaching, and writing, she remarks on the places and countryside they saw. In September 1901 they were persuaded by Dr Baedeker (see I143) to accompany him to Russia. They went first to Rostov-on-Don and travelled through Georgia and on to Baku, Batumi, and the Crimea, visiting prison and meeting believers of various sects (pp. 123-36).

K92) De Windt, Harry, *From Paris to New York by land.* London: George Newnes, 1904. 311pp.

After failing in 1896 to travel by land from New York to Paris, De Windt succeeded in the opposite direction, leaving Paris on 19 December 1901 and reaching New York on 25 August 1902. The primary aim of the expedition was to assess the possibility of a Paris-New York rail link, but De Windt's three-man expedition travelled by rail, sled and foot to reach the Bering Strait at the end of April 1902 (pp. 1-193).

K93) Swenson, Olaf, *Northwest of the world: forty years' trading and hunting in Northern Siberia.* London: Robert Hale, 1951. 221pp.

> Swenson (1883-1938), born in Michigan to Swedish parents, sailed from Alaska to Siberia for the first time in 1902 with a group of prospectors from the North-eastern Siberian Company and made many further trips as a trader from 1905 through the 1930s. He came to know and admire the native Chukchi.

K94) Shoemaker, Michael Myers, *The great Siberian railway from St. Petersburg to Pekin.* New York and London: G.P. Putnam's Sons (The Knickerbocker Press). 1903. x+243pp.

> The Kentucky traveller and author Shoemaker (1853-1924) left St Petersburg in April 1902 to travel the Trans-Siberian as far as Chita (pp. 1-121), before crossing into Manchuria and on to Pekin. His aim was to present a description of the railway and the country it passes through, without worrying about prisons or politics.

K95) Cary, Clarence, *The Trans-Siberian route or notes of a journey from Pekin to New York in 1902.* New York: Evening Post Job Printing House, 1902. 53pp.

> American journalist Cary provides a discursive commentary on a journey taken along the Chinese Eastern and then Trans-Siberian railways between 5 August and 18 August 1902, detailing his own experiences and offering tips for future travellers.

K96) Lynch, George, *The path of empire.* London: Duckworth & Co. 1903. xx+257pp.

> Journalist and explorer Lynch (1868-1928) evaluates the potential political and economic impact of the Trans-Siberian following a journey along it during late 1902. Two early chapters describe his travels around the commercial terminus at Dalnii and the military terminus at Port Arthur (pp. 50-74). After discussing his travels in China, he returns to his westwards journey on the railway to Moscow (pp. 152-257).

K97) Edwards, William Seymour, *Through Scandinavia to Moscow.* Cincinnati: Robert Clarke Co., 1906. xiv+237pp.

> The Virginia lawyer Edwards (1856-1915) and his wife visited Russia as part of their honeymoon trip, arriving in St Petersburg from Stockholm early in September 1902. In a series of letters to his father, beginning on 16 September, he describes their short stays in the capital and Moscow and their exit via Smolensk on 21 September. He was highly aware of the vast abyss between rich and poor, predicting "a saturnalia of blood and tears, a squaring of ten centuries' accounts, more fraught with human anguish and human joy than ever dreamed a Marat and a Robespierre" (pp. 136-213).

K98) Polhill[-Turner], Arthur Twistleton, *Across Siberia with a baby, & a visit to a Chinese prison.* Edited with a preface by Robert Skinner, D. D. Cambridge: Deighton, Bell & Co., 1904. xii+84pp.

> Rev. Polhill (1863-1935) was one of the "Cambridge Seven" missionaries who worked for the China Island Mission from 1885 until he fled during the Boxer Rebellion in 1900. In the autumn of 1902 he returned to China, travelling on the Trans-Siberian Railway from Moscow on 5 October and departing from Port Arthur on 29 October. His account is based on a series of letters he sent to his brother and fellow missionary Cecil (pp. 1-54).

K99) Shoemaker, Michael Myers, *The heart of the Orient: saunterings through Georgia, Armenia, Persia, Turkomania, and Turkestan, to the vale of Paradise.* New York and London: G.P. Putnam's Sons (The Knickerbocker Press). 1904. xiv+416pp.

> In the winter of 1902 Shoemaker (see K94) travelled from Constantinople to Georgia and on to Baku, before reaching Persia (pp. 14-89). Leaving Persia once more for Baku, he then travels through Russian Central Asia, visiting Bokhara and Samarkand (from where he travels by *tarantas*). Returning finally to Baku, he takes the train to Moscow and on to St Petersburg (pp. 211-409).

K100) Miles, Nelson Appleton, *Serving the republic: memoirs of the civil and military life of Nelson. A. Miles.* New York and London: Harper and Bros., 1911. x+340pp.

> Shortly before his retirement from the army, Miles (see K38) by then a lieutenant-general, paid an official visit to China and Japan at the end of 1902, visiting also Port Arthur, where he met General Alekseev, and travelling on the Trans-Siberian on his way home via Paris and London (pp. 308-09).

K101) Vay de Vaya and Luskod, Peter, *Empire and emperors of Russia, China, Korea, and Japan: notes and recollections.* Preface by John Murray. London: John Murray, 1906. xxxii+399pp.

> Hungarian aristocrat and later bishop, Count Vay (1863-1948) was sent by Pope Leo XIII to investigate Catholic institutions in the east and was received by the tsar and tsaritsa at Peterhof, prior to his departure from St Petersburg for Siberia, Manchuria and beyond in 1902 (pp. 1-62).

K102) Turner, Samuel, *Siberia: a record of travel, climbing, and exploration.* With an introduction by Baron Heyking. London: T. Fisher Unwin, 1905. 361pp.

> Turner (1869-1929), F.R.G.S., went to Siberia to assess the dairy industry, but then, an expert climber, he explored the Altai mountains and climbed Mount Belukha during a visit lasting from March to May 1903.

K103) Turner, Samuel, *My climbing adventures in four continents.* London: T. Fisher Unwin, 1911. 283pp.

> Turner recapitulates his climbing expedition of 1903, but now including "quite a lot of details" previously omitted (pp. 91-166).

K104) Overton, Kathleen (Toni), *An odious child? memories 1903-1932.* Edited by Catherine Archer. Hertford: privately printed, 2000. ii+75pp.

> Mrs Overton, née Ward (1903-98) was born to British parents in St Petersburg, where her father was an engineer. She describes her childhood years in the Russian capital which they quitted in October 1916 during WWI to move to England (pp. 3-19).

K105) Fell, Edward Nelson, *Russian and nomad: tales of the Kirghiz steppes.* London: Duckworth & Co., 1916. xviii+201pp.

> American director of a London mining company that acquired coal and copper mines in the midst of the steppes near the headwaters of the river Ishim, Fell (b. 1857) spent several years between 1903 and 1908 working and mixing on friendly terms with Russian and Kirghiz. One 'tale' and the concluding 'Eagle's song' were written by his young daughter **Marian** (pp. 155-69, 200-01).

K106) Ronaldshay, Dundas, Lawrence John Lumley, Earl of, *On the outskirts of empire in Asia.* Edinburgh and London: William Blackwood and Sons, 1905. xxii+408pp.

> Ronaldshay (1876-1961), later 2nd Marquess of Zetland, F.R.G.S., politician, and author, was aide-de-camp to Lord Curzon, viceroy of India, during the years he travelled extensively in Asia. In April 1903 his travels took him from Persia to Baku and then to Krasnovodsk and the Transcaspian railway by which he went to Bokhara and Samarkand. He travelled across Turkestan to shoot wild sheep in the Altai. He completed the Russian part of his travels on the Trans-Siberian and by steamer eastwards towards Kharbin, which he reached at the beginning of October (pp. 155-315).

K107) Ronaldshay, Dundas, Lawrence John Lumley, Earl of, *An eastern miscellany.* Edinburgh and London: William Blackwood and Sons, 1911. xiv+422pp.

> A collection of essays and speeches, mostly already published and concerned principally with India and Japan, contains 'A Siberian mystery', on a visit to Tomsk and the legend of Alexander I/Fedor Kuzmich (pp. 36-44), an essay on Baku in 1905 (pp. 73-88), and 'Notes on a journey across Asia', partly in Russia (pp. 143-63).

K108) Swayne, Harold George Carlos, *Through the highlands of Siberia.* London: Rowland Ward, 1904. xiv+259pp.

> A major in the Royal Engineers, F.R.G.S., and inveterate hunter and photographer, Swayne (b. 1860) used three months of a year's furlough from service in India to travel in June 1903 to St Petersburg and Moscow with his wife and then on with his companion Seton Karr to Siberia and the Altai mountains to shoot wild rams.

K109) Pumpelly, Raphael, Davis, William Morris, Pumpelly, Raphael Welles, and Huntington, Ellsworth, *Explorations in Turkestan with an account of the basin of Eastern Persia and Sistan: expedition of 1903, under the direction of Raphael Pumpelly.* Washington, D.C.: Carnegie Institution of Washington, 1905. xii+324pp.

> The volume consists of five contributions from the four members of the Carnegie-sponsored expedition that left America in the spring of 1903

with the aim of investigating "the past and present physico-geographical conditions and archaelogical remains" of Turkestan. The members pursued somewhat different itineraries and it is 'A journey across Turkestan', the extensive contribution of Davis (1850-1934), professor of geology at Harvard, whose travels extended into Siberia, that is of general interest (pp. 23-119).

K110) Cockerell, Sydney Carlyle, *Friends of a lifetime: letters to Sydney Carlyle Cockerell.* Edited by Viola Meynell. London: Jonathan Cape, 1940. 384pp.

In July 1903 Sir Sydney (1867-1962), then a process engraver in partnership with Emery Walker and later director of the Fitzwilliam Museum in Cambridge, paid a visit with two American friends to Tolstoi at Iasnaia Poliana (pp. 78-86).

K111) Thomas, Joseph B., Jr., *Observations on borzoi called in America Russian wolfhounds, in a series of letters to a friend.* Foreword by Henry T. Allen. Boston and New York: Houghton Mifflin Co., 1912. viii+123pp.

All one needs to know about the borzoi, as communicated in letters to Major Allen, who had been American military attaché in St Petersburg. In letters 4 and 5 Thomas, Boston architect and financier and wolfhound fanatic and breeder, recalls his visits to St Petersburg, Tula and Moscow in August 1903 and in 1904 to visit kennels and to hunt (pp. 39-70).

K112) Story, Douglas, *To-morrow in the East.* London: Chapman & Hall, 1907. x+267pp.

The Scottish journalist (1872-1921) offered his book as "the result of ten years" observation as war-correspondent and special correspondent in the countries of the East", but he also included a chapter devoted to the powerful tsarist minister Count Witte, whom he interviewed in St Petersburg in August 1903 (pp. 227-42). For Story's reporting of the Russo-Japanese war, see K133.

K112a) Grafton, Charles Chapman, *The works of the Rt. Rev. Charles C. Grafton, S.T.D., LL.D.* Edited by B. Talbot Rogers. New York and London: Longmans, Green, and Co., 1914. 8 vols.

The bishop of Fond du Lac, Wisconsin (1830-1912) left New York on 22 August 1903 and returned on 8 November after a brief visit to St Petersburg, Moscow and Sergiev posad to promote "fraternal relations between the Eastern Church in Russia and the Church in America" (vol. IV, pp. 252-70). He was accompanied by the English scholar W.J. Birkbeck (see J82). Original American edition *A journey Godward* (Milwaukee: Young Churchman Co., 1910).

K113) Spring-Rice, Cecil Arthur, *The letters and friendships of Sir Cecil Spring Rice: a record.* Edited by Stephen Gwynn. London: Constable & Co., 1929. 2 vols.

> A career diplomat, Sir Cecil (1859-1918) served in the British embassy in St Petersburg from September 1903 until April 1906, when he was appointed minister in Persia. He was in St Petersburg throughout the Russo-Japanese war and the revolutionary events of 1905. His letters provide an informed view of events, not least those addressed to his close friend Mrs Roosevelt, wife of the American president (vol. I, pp. 362-504, II, pp. 1-76).

K114) Weale, Bertram Lenox Putnam [pseudonym of Simpson, Bertram Lenox], *Manchu and Muscovite: being letters from Manchuria written during the autumn of 1903, with an historical sketch entitled 'Prologue to the crisis', giving a complete account of the Manchurian frontiers from the earliest days and the growth and final meeting of the Russian and Chinese empires in the Amur regions.* London: Macmillan and Co., 1904. xx+552pp.

> Commissioned to write a series of articles on Manchuria, Simpson (1877-1930) travelled extensively through the country from September to November 1903. He was highly critical of Russian presence in the area and dedicated his book to the "gallant Japanese nation". (see also K163.)

K115) Ready, Oliver George, *Through Siberia and Manchuria by rail.* London: Chapman & Hall, 1904. 26pp.

> Following the declaration of war between Russia and Japan, Ready (1864-1940), English travel writer and author of *Life and Sport in China,* decided to publish his travel diary that was originally intended for private circulation in typescript. He travelled from London to Shanghai via the Trans-Siberian, boarding the train in Moscow on 21 October 1903, and reaching Dalnii on 4 November, where he pronounced "the railway in its entirety is flimsy and liable to collapse almost everywhere".

K116) Onslow, Richard William Alan, *Sixty-three years: diplomacy, the Great War and politics, with notes on travel, sport and other things.* London: Hutchinson, 1944, 204pp.

> British diplomat and civil servant, Earl Onslow (1876-1945), then Viscount Cranley, arrived in Petersburg to become personal secretary to the

ambassador, Sir Charles Scott, and his immediate successors, Sir Charles Hardinge and Sir Arthur Nicolson, between January 1904 and January 1906 and between May and September 1906. His recollections cover social and diplomatic life in the capital, momentous events like the Bloody Sunday massacre and the Russo-Japanese war, and fond memories of hunting and fishing trips (pp. 88-132).

K117) Ganz, Hugo Markus, *The downfall of Russia: behind the scenes in the realm of the czar.* London: Hodder and Stoughton, 1904. 320pp. [In the same year there appeared another version: *The land of riddles: Russia of to-day.* Translated from the German by H. Rosenthal. New York and London: Harper & Brothers, 1904. 330pp.]

> The German-born journalist (1862-1922) travelled from Vienna via Warsaw to St Petersburg at the very beginning of 1904 and was present, for instance, at the funeral of Nikolai Mikhailovskii on 10 February 1904, before travelling on to Moscow (pp. 33-320). His book contains much of interest, not least an assessment of the work of Repin (pp. 147-62), and includes a long account of his visit to to see Tolstoi at Iasnaia Poliana (pp. 274-320). Translated from the German original *Vor der Katastrofe* (1904).

K117a) Maud, Renée Elton, *One year at the Russian court: 1904-1905.* London: John Lane, 1918. vii+222pp.

> In memoirs written in 1917 Mrs Maud (née Gaudin de Villaine) recalls her visit as a young woman to Russia from early summer 1904 to the summer of 1905. Through her French and Russian connections (her maternal grandmother was Baroness Nikolay) she frequented court and diplomatic circles in St Petersburg, visited the Nikolay estate of Monrepos near Vyborg and stayed in Tiflis with other relatives. Back in the capital, she was unsumpathetic to the events of Bloody Sunday. The fourth and final part of her book (pp. 1107ff.) is devoted to Rasputin, based on what she later heard and read.

K118) Villari, Luigi, *Russia under the great shadow.* London: T. Fisher Unwin, 1905. 330pp.

> The Italian historian, traveller and diplomat (1876-1959) offered in part a record of observations noted during travels in Russia in the summer and autumn of 1904, but in the main an impersonal analysis of the state of Russian government, society and economy during the Russo-Japanese War. Arriving in St Petersburg in July 1904, he travelled on to Moscow and the fair at Nizhnii Novgorod, before taking the steamer down the Volga to Saratov, proceeding overland through Ukraine to Odessa and back to Kiev.

K119) Harper, Samuel Northrup, *The Russia I believe in: the memoirs of Samuel N. Harper, 1902-1941.* Edited by Paul V. Harper with the assistance of Ronald Thompson. Chicago: University of Chicago Press, 1945. xiv+279pp.

> Harper (1882-1943), who was to become professor of Russian language and institutions at the University of Chicago, where he taught from 1912, and be recognized as the first American-born scholar to devote an academic career to the study of Russia, made eighteen trips to Russia between 1904 and 1939. In the opening chapters of his autobiography he describes his early studies at the University of Moscow, his observation of the working of the Dumas between 1906 and 1910, his extensive travels through Russia when he was a lecturer at the University of Liverpool (1910-12), and finally his experiences during WWI and the subsequent Revolution, initially as adviser to Ambassador Francis in 1916 and then in 1917 as adviser and interpreter to the Root Mission (pp. 1-108).

K120) Bryan, William Jennings, *Under other flags: travels, lectures, speeches.* Lincoln, Nebraska: Woodruff-Colliers Printing Co., 1904. 397pp.

> Three-times defeated Democrat candidate for the American presidency and speech-maker extraordinary, Bryan (1860-1925) and his wife took a European sabbatical that included a visit to Russia in 1904. They travelled from Warsaw to Moscow, from where they made a trip to Iasnaia Poliana to see Tolstoi, whose "colossal strength lies in his heart more than in his mind" (pp. 96-108). Proceeding to St Petersburg, they were taken to Tsarskoe selo by the American ambassador to meet the tsar (pp. 77-85).

K121) Garnett, David, *The golden echo.* London: Chatto and Windus, 1935. 272pp.

> Twelve-year old David (1892-1981) accompanied his mother, the famous translator Constance Garnett, on her second visit to Russia in the summer of 1904. Arriving in St Petersburg on 16 May they moved after two weeks to Moscow and thence to stay with the novelist and landowner Aleksandr Ertel at his estate in Tambov province. They travelled back to England overland and arrived on 13 August (pp. 74-93).

K122) Joubert, Carl, *The truth about the tsar and the present state of Russia.* London: Eveleigh Nash, 1905. 265pp.

> In his second book, finished in December 1904, Joubert (see K13) writes of the Russo-Japanese conflict, but also takes issue with British apologists of the tsar, whom he dubs with prescience "the last of the Romanoffs".

K123) Pares, Bernard, *Russia and reform.* London: Archibald Constable, 1907. xiv+576pp.

> Pares (see K58, K59, K124, K309) was in close and constant contact with key liberal figures in the Duma. In this study of Russia before the revolution of 1905 and its aftermath he offers an informed analysis events based on his studies and his diaries and notebooks.

K124) Pares, Bernard, *The fall of the Russian monarchy: a study of the evidence.* London: Jonathan Cape, 1939. 510pp.

> This is Pares's retrospective on the causes of the 1917 revolutions, based on both published evidence and on the numerous interviews with leading players that he conducted from 1904 to 1914.

K125) Meakin, Annette M.B., *Russia: travels and studies.* London: Hurst and Blackett, 1906. xx+450pp.

> The third and weightiest work by the Russian-speaking anthropologist (see K73, K83), based on her extensive travels in 1904 that took her from St Petersburg via Moscow and Kharkov to the Crimea, and then via Odessa and Kishinev and Kiev on to Georgia and the Caucasus. She was yet another visitor to Tolstoi.

K126) McCullagh, Francis, *With the Cossacks, being the story of an Irishman who rode with the Cossacks throughout the Russo-Japanese war.* London: Eveleigh Nash, 1906. xiv+392pp.

> In August 1903 McCullagh (1874-1956) gave up his job with the English-language *Japan Times* and moved to Port Arthur, staying briefly en route in the Russian port of Dalnii. He was working for the Russian paper *Novyi krai*, when the Russo-Japanese war broke out in February 1904, and became "embedded" with the Russian forces until he was captured by the Japanese during the retreat from Mukden in March 1905 and taken to Japan as a prisoner of war. He was in Moscow by the end of the year, editing his book, which was based on dispatches he had sent to the *New York Herald*. He returned to Russia in 1920 during the Intervention and was captured by the Reds.

K127) McCormick, Frederick, *The tragedy of Russia in Pacific Asia.* London: Grant Richards, 1909. 2 vols.

> American journalist McCormick (b. 1870) provides a comprehensive account of the key battles of the Russo-Japanese War, during which he was

stationed with the Russian forces. Interspersing descriptive narrative with personal experiences, he begins before the outbreak of war in Port Arthur in January 1904 and describes events and battles until the cessation of hostilities. The second half of vol. II provides an account of the psychology, abilities and material situation of the average Russian soldier.

K128) McCully, Newton Alexander, *The Russo-Japanese War.* Edited by Richard von Doenhoff. Annapolis, Maryland: Naval Institute Press, 1977. xiv+338pp.

> Report of US navy Lt-Commander McCully (1867-1951), written in late 1905 and based on a diary he kept while assistant naval attaché in St Petersburg and subsequently with the Russian forces in the Far East during the Russo-Japanese War. It contains detailed accounts of his travels between 15 March 1904 and 18 July 1905 and his observations on the places and peoples he witnessed in Siberia and Manchuria.

K129) McKenzie, Frederick Arthur, *From Tokyo to Tiflis: uncensored letters from the war.* London: Hurst and Blackett, 1905. x+340pp.

> Special correspondent of the *Daily Mail*, the Canadian McKenzie (1869-1931) was with the Japanese army, sending his dispatches from the battlefields of the Russo-Japanese war. He also reported from Warsaw and Tiflis on the strikes and unrest in 1905 (pp. 285-327). McKenzie was later to write two accounts (1923, 1930) of his visits to Soviet Moscow under NEP.

K130) Kennard, Howard Percy, *The Russian peasant.* London: T. Werner Laurie, 1907. xvi+302pp.

> Dr Kennard (d. 1915) wrote the preface to his book in May 1907 from Samara, where he was helping in famine relief, and his work reflects his deep sympathies for the Russian peasantry among whom he had lived in many parts of European Russia since the time of the Russo-Japanese war. The first part of his book offers a comprehensive anthropological description of village life, focusing on customs, beliefs, family relationships and ceremonies. The second part is an historical overview of pre- and post-serfdom Russia, while the third is a sustained critique of the impact of bureaucracy, policing, censorship and surveillance, and the Church on the lives of the Russian peasantry.

K131) Gilliard, Pierre, *Thirteen years at the Russian court (a personal record of the last years and death of the Czar Nicholas II and his family).* Translated from the French by F. Appleby Holt. London: Hutchinson & Co., 1921. 304pp.

Gilliard (1879-1962) arrived in the Crimea in the autumn of 1904 as French tutor to Duke Sergei of Leuchtenberg and a year later, he became tutor to the tsar's daughters Olga and Tatiana. He remained with the imperial family virtually until the end, following them into Siberia, but was himself separated from them at Tiumen on 22 May 1918. He eventually returned to France in September 1920.

K132) Wilton, Robert Archibald, *Russia's agony.* London: Edward Arnold, 1918. xii+356pp.

Although born in Norwich, Wilton (1868-1925) was the son of a British mining engineer working in Russia and he dates his personal experience of the country back "nearly half a century" in the preface to his book (13 January 1918). It is, however, the last fourteen years he had been *The Times*'s correspondent that provide the material for his tracing of Russia's destiny through revolution and war "without fear or favour". Subsequently Wilton went to Siberia, but following the fall of Kolchak, escaped to Paris.

K133) Story, Douglas, *The campaign with Kuropatkin.* London: T. Werner Laurie, 1904. xii+301pp.

Story (see K112) travelled from Hong Kong via Tokyo to Mukden, where he was received by the Russian viceroy Alekseev and became the first foreign correspondent formally accredited to the Russian army on 24 April 1904. He wrote positively of the Russian officer and particularly of the ordinary soldier 'Ivan Ivanovitch'. He travelled home via the Trans-Siberian and on to St Petersburg.

K134) Baring, Maurice, *With the Russians in Manchuria.* London: Methuen & Co., 1905. xv+205pp.

In April 1904 Baring (see K79) was appointed as the *Morning Post*'s correspondent to cover the Russo-Japanese war and his book comprises the dispatches he sent to the paper. He travelled from Moscow on the Trans-Siberian railway and arrived in Kharbin on 19 May. He travelled on to Mukden and then nearer to the battlefields. He left Mukden for England at the beginning of December 1904. In August 1905 he left St Petersburg once more en route for Manchuria, where he was to remain until October. His book was dedicated to Guy Brooke (see K135).

K135) Brooke, Leopold Guy Francis Maynard Greville, *An eye-witness in Manchuria.* London: Eveleigh Nash, 1905. viii+312pp.

Brooke (1882-1928), later 6th Earl of Warwick, the Reuter's special correspondent covering the Russo-Japanese war, travelled with Baring from Moscow to Kharbin in May 1904. He remained for nine months with the Russian army, for which he expressed great admiration, and returned to England via St Petersburg.

K136) Greener, William Oliver, *A secret agent in Port Arthur.* London: Archibald Constable & Co., 1905. viii+316pp.

Greener, writing under his real name (cf. Wirt Gerrare, see K85) was sent to Port Arthur to report events of the Russo-Japanese war. He describes his journey from Moscow by rail, the ferry across Baikal, and on to Vladivostok before entering Manchuria (pp. 18-38). "The status of a secret agent is that of a special correspondent travelling incognito" and he reported back to both *The Times* and the *China Times* on what he witnessed.

K137) Henry, James Dodds, *Baku: an eventful history.* Introductory note by Sir Boverton Redwood. London: Archibald Constable & Co., 1906. xviii+256pp.

Editor of the *Petroleum World*, Henry (b. 1864) returned from the oilfields of Baku in February 1905 and attempted in his book to provide an informed update on Marvin's work of 1884 (J26) and an objective assessment of the city and its industry's potential.

K138) Joubert, Carl, *The fall of tsardom.* London: Eveleigh Nash, 1905. 255pp.

Joubert (see K13, K122) welcomed the 1905 revolution and the inexorable progress, as he hoped, towards a constitution.

K139) Noble, Algernon, *Siberian days: an engineer's record of travel and adventure in the wilds of Siberia.* London: H.F. and G. Witherby, 1928. 223pp.

Noble (d. 1975) provides a non-chronological account of his involvement in copper and coal mining in the Kirghiz steppe and in prospecting for gold in Siberia from Tomsk to Baikal, between 1905 and 1914.

K140) Meyer, George von Lengerke, *George von Lengerke Meyer, his life and public services.* By Mark Antony DeWolfe Howe. New York: Dodd, Mead and Co., 1919. 556pp.

Meyer (1864-1960) was American ambassador to Russia from April 1905 to January 1907, arriving in the midst of the Russo-Japanese War. His biographer includes generous selections from his letters (to President Roosevelt, Senator Lodge and his wife) and diary entries, particularly for 1905, but more selectively for 1906-07, where the focus is on the Algericas Conference and the first meeting of the Russian Duma on 10 May 1906 (pp. 137-335).

K141) Anet, Claude [pseudonym of Schopher, Jean], *Through Persia in a motor-car by Russia and the Caucasus.* Translated by M. Beresford Ryley. London: Hodder & Stoughton, 1907. xvi+281pp.

> Arriving in Russia in April 1905, Schopher (1868-1931), a Swiss professional tennis player and successful writer, drove through Bessarabia, the Caucasus and the Crimea. In Yalta he met Maksim Gorkii. In Georgia he noted the social tensions, strikes, and civil unrest. He took the train from Tiflis to Baku and the boat from there for Persia at the end of April (pp. 1-83).

K142) Sarolea, Charles Louis-Camille, *Count L.N. Tolstoy, his life and work.* London: T. Nelson and Sons, 1912. viii+384pp.

> The Belgian scholar (1870-1953), later professor of French at Edinburgh University and author of several books on Russia, was another pilgrim to Iasnaia Poliana, visiting "the Master" in May 1905 (pp. 316-36).

K143) Sarolea, Charles Louis-Camille, *Europe's debt to Russia.* London: William Heinemann, 1916. x+251pp.

> "An attempt to give a systematic and co-ordinated survey of Russian history and policy", following his further visit in 1915, Sarolea's work includes, at the "insistence" of Tolstoi, his personal impressions of 1905 and "the tragic events of the Russian Annus Mirabilis" (pp. 188-228).

K144) Villari, Luigi, *Fire and sword in the Caucasus.* London: T. Fisher Unwin, 1906. 347pp.

> Villari (see K118) provides an account of political unrest, ethnic tensions and violence in the Caucasus region during a stay in August-October 1905. His extensive travels took him to Batumi, Tiflis, Baku, and Erevan and he was in Vladikavkaz on the day the October Manifesto was published.

K145) Winter, Nevin Otto, *The Russian Empire of to-day and yesterday. The country and its peoples, together with a brief review of its history, past and present,* *and a survey of its social, political, and economic conditions.* London: Simpkin, Marshall & Co., 1913. xvi+487pp.

> Ohio lawyer and author, Winter (1869-1936) offers an extensive descriptive account of the Russian Empire, based to a large degree on personal observations made during visits in the early 1905 and 1912. In the first half he covers a variety of topics, including St Petersburg and Moscow, the status of Jews, the Russian character and social customs and structure, the education system and Russian literature, while in the second he provides a historical survey.

K146) Baring, Maurice, *A year in Russia.* London: Methuen & Co., 1907. xx+319pp.

> The year he covered in more letters sent to the *Morning Post* was from 8 August 1905 to 6 August 1906. Begins with his departure again for Mongolia and return to Moscow by 3 November and then alternates between Moscow and St Petersburg. He was witness to the revolutionary events that unfolded in the old capital and attended meetings of the Duma in the Taurida Palace. His "collection of notes, a bundle of impressions" includes an item on the 25th anniversary of the death of Dostoevskii.

K147) Ular, Alexander, *Russia from within.* London: Heinemann, 1905. xii+290pp.

> Ular (b. 1876) provides an account of the causes of the 1905 revolution which lays the blame primarily in the hands of the Russian political leadership and the tsar. Ular was in Russia at the time (the preface is dated May 1905), but his account is presented as a description of the basic facts, supplemented by the occasional reference to personal experiences and interviews he has undertaken.

K148) Walling, William English, *Russia's message: the true world import of the revolution.* London: A.C. Fifield, 1909. xviii+476pp.

> The prominent American socialist (1877-1936), who believed that "official Russia is in a land of lies", arrived in Petersburg for the first time at the end of 1905. Over the next two years he spent many months there, latterly with his new wife Anna Strunskaia, sending back numerous articles to American papers and journals and intent on "gaining a rounded view". He met and interviewed countless prominent Russian officials, ministers, and intellectuals, including Tolstoi, and concluded that the Russian revolution (of 1905) offered a message of hope for a new world civilization.

K149) Nevinson, Henry Woodd, *The dawn in Russia or scenes in the Russian revolution*. London and New York: Harper & brothers, 1906. xiv+349pp.

> Nevinson (1856-1941), sent to Petersburg by the *Daily Chronicle* as its special correspondent, offered his book as a description of "scenes which I witnessed in Russia during the winter of 1905-1906", some published in the newspaper, but all re-arranged and re-structured to give a general view of events not only in the capital, but also in Tula, Moscow, Odessa and elsewhere.

K150) Nevinson, Henry Woodd, *More changes more chances*. London: Nisbet & Co., 1925. xviii+427pp.

> In the second volume of his autobiography Nevinson recounts events already included in his 1906 book but also adds his subsequent travels through Georgia and the Crimea in 1906-07 (pp. 98-211). Later included in his condensed autobiography, *Fire of life* (1935), pp. 181-209.

K151) Hedin, Sven, *Overland to India.* London: Macmillan and Co., 1910. 2 vols.

> On his way to India and sailing from Constantinople across the Black Sea, Hedin (see J132) is caught up with events of the 1905 revolution, when his ship puts into Batumi at the end of October 1905. He details strikes and unrest in Batumi and decides to travel to Poti and take the train to Tiflis, but is forced to turn back and sail to Trebizond (vol. I, pp. 1-21).

K152) Bullard, Arthur, *The Russian pendulum: autocracy-democracy-bolshevism.* New York: Macmillan, 1919. xvi+256pp.

> American journalist and noted socialist Bullard (1879-1929) recalls in the opening chapters his first visit to Russia in the years 1905-08, when he sent back numerous articles to American journals, mostly under the pseudonym of Albert Edwards. In July 1917 he returned to Petrograd as head of the Russian branch of the American government's Committee on Public Information. He left from Archangel in June 1918, but returned to Vladivostok until November.

K153) Henderson, Nevile Meyrick, *Water under the bridges.* London: Hodder & Stoughton, 1945. 221pp.

> In the course of a long diplomatic career, Sir Nevile (1882-1942) served on two occasions in the British embassy in St Petersburg. He arrived in December 1905 and remained until April 1909 (pp. 24-48). After a spell in

Tokyo, he left for St Petersburg again in January 1912, travelling via the Trans-Siberian. He served under Sir George Buchanan until April 1914 (pp. 61-68). His posthumously published memoir is predominantly concerned with the routines of embassy life.

K154) Washburn, Stanley, *The cable game: the adventures of an American press-boat in Turkish waters during the Russian revolution.* London: Andrew Melrose, 1912. 222pp.

> The Minneapolis lawyer-turned-journalist Washburn (1878-1950), having just covered the Russo-Japanese war for the Chicago *Daily News,* was sent to Russia to report on the final stages of the 1905 revolution. He arrived in Odessa in December 1905 and then travelled on to Sevastopol and Batumi in search of newsworthy incidents of unrest and violence.

K155) Preston, Thomas, *Before the curtain.* London: John Murray, 1950. iv+313pp.

> Preston (1886-1976), later Sir Thomas, 6th baronet, "lived in Russia, off and on, since 1905, in almost every corner of this vast continent and amongst the most varied communities". He first worked in Batumi and for a mining company at Dzhanzhul, prior to entering Cambridge University in 1907. He then returned to prospecting and mining in Siberia until his appointment in 1913 as British vice-consul, subsequently consul, at Ekaterinburg, where he was still in post at the time of the murder of the imperial family. He remained in Siberia under the Whites until October 1920, but was to return to Russia in 1922 and remained as British official agent in Leningrad until 1926 (pp. 14-230).

K156) Decle, Lionel, *The new Russia.* London: Eveleigh Nash, 1906. 279pp.

> Stirred by the events of 1905, the British author Decle (1859-1907) arrived in St Petersburg in January 1906 to interview ministers and high officials in order to provide "a general *aperçu* of the present system under which the administration, the law, education, taxation are organized". In his preface he prides himself that many of his predictions had been realized, although the final sentence of his book had suggested that "there is only one thing impossible in Russia, and that is to understand the Russians".

K157) Durland, Kellogg, *The red reign: the true story of an adventurous year in Russia.* London: Hodder & Stoughton, 1908. xxvi+533pp.

> American journalist and adventurer Kellogg (1881-1911) provides a detailed account of his extensive travels throughout Russia between

January and December 1906. His intention was to portray as accurately as possible a country *in* revolution and witnessed in different contexts and circumstances. Thus he travelled to the Caucasus with a group of Cossack officers; observed the effects of famine around Saratov; interviewed the "terrorist" Maria Spiridonova at Tambov; attended the opening session of the Duma in St Petersburg; was in Cronstadt during the August mutiny; visited the British-run model industrial town of Iuzovka, before travelling to see Tolstoi at Iasnaia Poliana. In December he left Odessa for Constantinople.

K158) Niedieck, Paul, *Cruises in the Bering Sea, being records of further sport and travel.* Translated from the German by R.A. Ploetz. London: Rowland Ward, 1909. xvi+252pp.

Leaving London in March 1906, Niedieck, indefatigable hunter and specimen-collector, arrived in Kamchatka, via the USA and Japan, in April, remaining until July. He describes in detail his hunting of bears and walruses, but also provides descriptions of the lives of the various tribes and nomadic people he encounters (pp. 3-107). German original *Kreutzfahrten in Beringmeer* (1907).

K159) Bouillane de Lacoste, E.A. Henri de, *Around Afghanistan.* London: Sir Isaac Pitman & Sons, 1909. Preface by M. Georges Leygues. Translated from the French by J.G. Anderson. xxxii+218pp.

Major Bouillane de Lacoste (1894-1937) journeyed around Afghanistan's perimeter in the summer of 1906, entering Russian territory at Gaudan on the Persian-Turkestan border on 18 May, travelling on to Askhabad, where he took the Transcaspian railway to Andijan. Accompanied by a Kirghiz family, he travelled through the Alai and Trans-Alai region, leaving Russian territory at the Beik Pass (pp. 34-75).

K160) Fraser, David, *The marches of Hindustan, the record of a journey in Thibet, Trans-Himalayan India, Chinese Turkestan, Russian Turkestan, and Persia.* Edinburgh and London: William Blackwood and Sons, 1907. xvi+521pp.

Setting out in January 1906 on a 5630-mile journey, Fraser entered Russian Turkestan in October. He travelled through the mountains to Osh and Tashkent, from where he took the railway to Askabad and then crossed into Persia. He provides a history of Russian penetration into the area and an assessment of its military strength (pp. 284-376).

K161) Fraser, John Foster, *Red Russia.* London: Cassell and Co., 1907. xii+288pp.

> Fraser (see K29, K88, K90, K301) travelled through large areas of the Russia empire throughout 1906, assessing the mood and situation after the revolutionary events of 1905. Various chapters reflect his visits to St Petersburg, Moscow, Nizhnii Novgorod, Samara, Kazan, Bessarabia, the Caucasus and the Crimea, as well as Warsaw and Finland.

K162) De Windt, Harry, *Through savage Europe; being the narrative of a journey (undertaken as special correspondent of the "Westminster gazette"), throughout the Balkan states and European Russia.* London: T. Fisher Unwin, 1907. 300pp.

> De Windt departed from Trieste in the summer of 1906 by boat on a journey that was to take him through Montenegro, Bosnia, Bulgaria, and Romania, and finally into Russia, "the land of mystery, gloom, and death", where the "red flag" flew after the events of 1905. He visited Odessa, Rostov, Vladikavkaz, and Baku (pp. 261-89).

K163) Weale, Bertram Lenox Putnam [pseudonym of Simpson, Bertram Lenox], *The coming struggle in eastern Asia.* London: Macmillan and Co., 1908. xiv+656pp.

> Simpson offers his volume as the fourth and final in a series of "political treatises", opened by *Manchu and Muscovite* (1904) (see K114), that sought to examine Russo-Japanese rivalry. In the autumn of 1906 he sailed from Korea to Vladivostok, of which he provides a detailed assessment, and devotes Part I of his book to 'Russia beyond Lake Baikal', including Russian Manchuria (pp. 1-322).

K164) Gerhardi[e], Walter, *Memoirs of a polyglot,* London: Duckworth, 1931. 381pp.

> Son of the British industrialist Charles Alfred Gerhardi, the novelist and critic (1895-1977) describes his upbringing and education in St Petersburg between 1906 and 1912. Having moved to England, he found himself back in wartime and revolutionary Petrograd attached to the British embassy between 1916 and 1918. He was subsequently with the British intervention forces in Siberia until 1920 (pp. 1-153).

K165) Barrett, R.J., *Russia's new era. Being notes, impressions and experiences – personal, political, commercial and financial – of an extended tour in the empire* *of the tsar. With statistical tables, portraits, snapshots and other illustrations.* London: The Financier and Bullionist, Ltd., 1908. 292pp.

> Barrett, F.R.G.S., travelled extensively through Russia in the spring and summer of 1907 and provided a detailed social and economic account of Russia, with the primary focus on the commercial and investment opportunities available to the British.

K166) Barzini, Luigi, *Pekin to Paris: an account of Prince Borghese's journey across two continents in a motor-car.* Translated by L.P. de Castelvecchio. London: E. Grant Richards, 1907. 645pp.

> In the summer of 1907 the Italian war correspondent Barzini (1874-1947) accompanied Prince Scipione Borghese (1871-1927) in a famous motor race from Pekin to Paris. They drove to victory an Itala car on a 10,000-mile journey that took them through China into Siberia. Entering Siberia from Mongolia on 25 June, they travelled via Irkutsk, Tomsk, Omsk and Nizhnii Novgorod to Moscow, and then to St Petersburg, which they left on 1 August for Poland (pp. 297-594). The book is illustrated with numerous unique photographs, showing memorable encounters and the many breakdowns of the car. The Italian original was entitled *La metà del mondo vista da un'automobile da Pechino a Parigi in sessanta giorni.*

K167) Barrows, Isabel Chapin, *A sunny life: the biography of Samuel June Barrows.* Boston: Little, Brown and Company, 1913. xii+323pp.

> In her biography of her husband (1845-1909), the American Republican congressman and prison reformer, Isabel (1845-1913) records the trip the couple made in the summer of 1907 to visit prisons in St Petersburg, Moscow, and Nizhnii Novgorod. They then went down the Volga to Samara to see the lingering effects of the famine, and on their return journey, visited Tolstoi at Iasnaia Poliana (pp. 192-96, 204-05). In the spring of 1909 Isabel went alone to St Petersburg in connection with the arrest of Ekaterina Bereshkovskaia (1844-1934), "the little grandmother of the Revolution" (pp. 240-41).

K168) Jackson, Abraham Valentine Williams, *From Constantinople to the home of Omar Khayyam: travels in Transcaucasia and Northern Persia for historic and literary research.* New York: Macmillan Co., 1911. xxxiv+317pp.

> Jackson (1862-1937), American traveller and professor of Indo-Iranian languages at Columbia University, provides a combination of archaeological and linguistic scholarship and travel account of trips made through the Caspian and Transcaspian regions in 1907, 1908 and 1910. It is

a synthesis of observations and experiences from numerous research trips, but presented as a geographically consistent travel narrative that takes him into Russia at Sevastopol, through the Crimea and by steamer to Batumi, then via Tiflis to Baku. A second section focuses on the city of Baku; a third on a research trip to the city of Derbent in 1910 (pp. 12-84).

K169) **Fischer, Emil Sigmund,** *Overland via the Trans-Siberian railway: description of a trip from the Far East to Europe and the United States of America.* Tientsin: Tientsin Press, 1908. ix+44pp.

Fischer (1865-1945), best known for his later travels and writings on China and Japan, describes his return home from China in the summer of 1907.

K170) **Foulke, William Dudley,** *A random record of travel during fifty years.* New York: Oxford University Press, 1925. 241pp.

Noted journalist, author, and reformer, and from 1903 president of the American Society of Friends of Russian Freedom, Foulke (1848-1935) visited Finland and Russia from Norway in 1907. Routine tourist impressions of St Petersburg and Moscow ("a far more interesting place") also include description of a visit to the Duma and meeting with Prof. Miliukov (pp. 94-111).

K171) **Young, Charles Christian,** *Abused Russia.* New York: Devin-Adair Co., 1915. 109pp.

Dr Young (b. 1875) travelled to Russia in 1907 and again between 1912 and 1914. He attempts in his book to refute some of the criticisms and misconceptions held by Americans with regard to Russian society and politics and to urge a renewal of close links with Russia. A final chapter deals with Young's experiences when travelling as a sheep salesman through Turkmenistan between 1912 and 1914 and his observations on the region and the city of Bokhara.

K172) **Lydekker, Richard,** *A trip to Pilawin, the deer-park of Count Joseph Potocki in Volhynia Russia.* With a preface by Count Joseph Potocki. London: Rowland Ward, 1908. xiv+115pp.

Naturalist, geologist, and cataloguer of the Natural History Museum's fossil mammals, birds, and reptiles, Lydekker (1849-1915) was invited to visit the Pilawin preserve near the Potocki palace of Antoniny in present-day Ukraine. Travelling from London with his daughter, he arrived on 22 August 1907 and left on 4 September. He describes in expert detail and with excellent photographs the animals in the extensive forest preserve.

352 *In the Lands of the Romanovs*

K173) Bayne, Samuel Gamble, *Quicksteps through Scandinavia, with a retreat from Moscow.* New York and London: Harper & Brothers, 1908. 64pp.

> Irish-born Bayne (1844-1924), having made his fortune in banking and oil in America, indulged a liking for travel and authorship, visiting St Petersburg and Moscow in the summer of 1907. His visit to the Russian capital coincided with the opening ceremony of the Church of the Resurrection of Christ ('On the blood') which he mistakenly calls of the Ascension (pp. 17-31).

K174) Baring, Maurice, *Russian essays and stories.* London: Methuen & Co., 1908. xvii+295pp.

> A collection of eleven essays and seven stories, mostly originally published in the *Morning Post,* which cover a wide range of non-political (Baring's description) topics – travels, conversations, incidents, many of them literary.

K175) Baring, Maurice, *What I saw in Russia.* London: Nelson, 1913. 381pp.

> A compilation of selected chapters from his first three books about Russia, covering the period 1904-1907. The final three chapters (from *Russian essays*) describe his journeys down the Volga in August-September 1907 and to Vologda in the north in November of the same year.

K176) Foulke, William Dudley, *A random record of travel during fifty years.* New York: Oxford University Press, 1925. viii+241pp.

> The American travel writer recounts his trip to Russia, arriving from Finland in 1907, intermixing descriptions of life as a tourist in St Petersburg and Moscow with an assessment of the political climate and an account of a visit to the Duma while in St Petersburg (pp. 98-111).

K177) Murray, Robert H., *Around the world with Taft: a book of travel, description, history.* Detroit, Michigan: F.B. Dickerson Company, 1909. 412pp.

> Associated Press correspondent Murray was attached to then American secretary of war William Taft during a diplomatic mission to the Philippines that involved the party circumnavigating the world. Sailing from Manila, the Taft party arrived in Vladivostok on 17 November 1907 to board the Trans-Siberian that took them to Moscow. In early December they were in St Petersburg, where Taft met the tsar at Tsarskoe selo and they attended a military review (pp. 325-76).

K178) Wood, John Nicholas Price, *Travel & sport in Turkestan.* London: Chapman & Hall, 1910. xx+201pp.

> Wood, a captain in the 12th Royal Lancers, travelled from India in May 1907 to indulge a long-held dream of shooting along the borders of Mongolia and to return to England through Russian Turkestan. He was allowed into Russia on 23 November and travelled by train via Orenburg and Samara to Moscow, which he left for London on 20 December (pp. 179-94).

K179) Nostitz-Azabal, Madeleine, *Romance and revolutions.* London: Hutchinson & Co., 1937. 258pp.

> Three-times-married Iowa-born actress Madeleine Bouton, also known as Lilie, moved from her first husband, the German Count Guido von Nimptsch, to become the wife of Count Grigorii Nostitz, who took her to Russia in 1907, first to the family estate in Ukraine and then to Petersburg (pp. 66-89). There followed five years at the Russian embassy in Paris before they returned to Russia in 1914 and eventually escaped via Kiev and the Crimea at the end of 1918 (pp. 131-238).

K180) Tracey, Margot, *Red rose.* London: Newton Abbot and London: David & Charles, 1978. 230pp.

> Mrs Tracey (b. 1907), née Girard, born in Moscow to a rich French industrialist and his Russian wife, recounts her childhood and her and her sister's harrowing experiences during the revolution and the first years of Soviet rule until their eventual departure for France in 1921 (pp. 11-131). The second part of the book is devoted to an account of her visit as a tourist to Moscow in 1970. The book's title refers to the Soviet name for her family's Moscow factory.

K181) Scott, A. MacCallum, *Through Finland to St. Petersburg.* London: Grant Richards, 1908. 291pp.

> Essentially a guide-book to "this enterprising little country", Finland, with three concluding chapters on St Petersburg, where "the English visitor may study institutions and ways of life so strangely different from those he knows at home".

K182) Reynolds, Rothay, *My Russian year.* London: Mills & Boon, 1913. xii+304pp.

> The year would seem, from vague internal evidence, to have been 1908, but there are references to 1905 and 1906. A fluent speaker of Russian, the

British traveller and correspondent of the *Daily News*, Reynolds offers a series of sketches of people and places, designed "to make the reader see Russia as I have seen it", i.e. in all its variety and contradictoriness, as "the land of ideals", "the home of melodrama", "the land of liberty undreamt of by the shackled West", and much else.

K183) Reynolds, Rothay, *My Slav friends.* London: Mills & Boon, 1916. vii+312pp.

A second volume, very much in the style and spirit of the first, without evidence of later visits. His aim was "to write of people I have met, of cities I have visited", etc., using secondary sources to bolster his narration wherever necessary. There is a greater emphasis on the desirability of Anglo-Russian friendship and understanding without betraying the "truth" that the British public deserves.

K184) Calina, Josephine, *Scenes of Russian life.* London: Constable and Co., 1918. 302pp.

Calina (c.1890-1962), born and bred in Poland, spent several years "walking in the small dirty villages of Russia" after release from a Russian prison c.1908 and offered her sketches of prison and peasant life as taken "from the very depth of Russian life with its sadness and its humour". About the time of the October revolution she sought refuge in England, where she was to marry the eminent Shakespearean scholar Allardyce Nicoll and herself write *Shakespeare in Poland* (1923).

K185) Farmborough, Florence, *Nurse at the Russian front: a diary 1914-18.* London: Constable, 1974. 422pp.

Florence (1887-1978) originally went to Russia in 1908 as a governess and teacher of English, first in Kiev and later in Moscow. She trained as a nurse with the outbreak of WWI and served almost continuously at the front until 1917. When her unit was disbanded, she made her way back to England via the Trans-Siberian railway and steamers.

K186) Farmborough, Florence, *Russian album 1908-1918.* Edited by John Joliffe. [Salisbury]: M. Russell, 1979. 96pp.

Stunning photographs, covering the whole of Florence's ten years in Russia.

K187) Zur Mühlen, Hermynia, *The end and the beginning: the book of my life.* Translated, annotated and with an introduction by Lionel Gossman. Cambridge: Open Book Publishers, 2010. 297pp.

> Countess Zur Mühlen (1883-1951), the Austrian translator and author, lived six unhappy years on her husband's estate of Eigstfer in Russian Estonia between 1908 and 1913. She paints a vivid picture of life among a prejudiced and intolerant German community and reveals her sympathies for the oppressed. She also spent a summer in Petersburg (pp. 98-150). The present translation is an improved version of the original by Frank Barnes that appeared under the title *The runaway countess* in New York in 1930.

K188) Craig-McKerrow, Margaret, *Distant journeys, 1908-1928.* London: Baylis & Son, 1930. 369pp.

> In the spring of 1908 the German Mrs Craig-McKerrow (née Reibold) travelled from Japan to Russia, first via boat to Vladivostok, and then by the Trans-Siberian to Moscow. She describes her train journey and stay in Moscow (pp. 15-37). She re-visited Russia in 1928 (pp. 349-69).

K189) Close, Etta, *Excursions and some adventures.* London: Constable, 1926. 296pp.

> In September 1908 Miss Close, F.R.G.S., and a companion after a short stay in St Petersburg proceded to Moscow, where they boarded the Trans-Siberian to Kharbin (pp. 220-37). Following visits to China, Japan and Korea, they returned by train across a now wintery Siberia (pp. 292-95)

K190) Gibbes, Charles Sydney, *Tutor to the tsarevich: an intimate portrait of the last days of the Russian imperial family compiled from the papers of Charles Sydney Gibbes now in the possession of George Gibbes.* By J.C. Trewin. London: Macmillan, 1975. 148pp.

> Cambridge-educated Gibbes (1876-1963) was English tutor to the tsarevich and teacher to the four grand duchesses from the autumn of 1908 virtually until the murder of the imperial family in July 1918 in Ekaterinburg. Trewin's narrative incorporates long extracts from notes and diaries kept by Gibbes during the period.

K191) Browning, Oscar, *Memories of later years.* London: T. Fisher Unwin, 1923. 223pp.

Browning (1837-1923), following his retirement as history don at King's Cambridge, was invited to lecture on English literature and education at Petersburg university in the autumn of 1908 (pp. 116-19).

K192) Austin, Herbert Henry, *A scamper through the Far East, including a visit to Manchurian battlefields.* London: Edward Arnold, 1909. xvi+336pp.

Major Austin (1868-1937), of the Indian army and author of several books of exploration and travel, returns from leave in London via the Trans-Siberian in September 1908 (pp. 1-27). He left the train at Kharbin in order to visit the Russo-Japanese battlefields (pp. 28-164).

K193) Graham, Stephen, *Part of the wonderful scene: an autobiography.* London: Collins, 1964. 320pp.

Graham (1884-1974), the most prolific and influential of British writers on Russia in the first decades of the twentieth century and proponent of Holy Russia, recalls his obsession with Russia, his first brief holiday in 1906, and his numerous visits from 1908 to 1917 to almost all of the regions of a vast country that spawned no less than nine books over the same period (pp. 14-149). (See K232-34, K247, K248, K276-77, K289, K352.)

K194) Bates, Lindon Wallace, Jr., *The Russian Road to China.* London, Constable and Co., 1910. 391pp.

An American engineer, who had first been to Russia in 1896, Bates (1883-1915) travels from Russia to China during 1909, first by the Trans-Siberian Railway and then by sledge through Transbaikalia (pp. 1-172). A subsequent chapter provides political and ethnological observations on Russia's status in the world (pp. 273-321).

K195) Taft, Marcus Lorenzo, *Strange Siberia along the Trans-Siberian railway: a journey from the Great Wall of China to the skyscrapers of Manhattan.* New York: Eaton & Mains, 1911. 260pp.

Following years as a missionary in China, Taft (1850-1936) describes a final journey on the Trans-Siberian with his wife and daughter in the spring of 1909. He draws attention to the large Lutheran communities encountered along the railroad and comments on such topics as the steppes, architecture, and differences in American and Russian entrepreneurs. Their journey ends with quarantine for cholera upon leaving St Petersburg on 19 June, and an apology regarding the removal by the censors of six pages on Russia's policy towards the Jews.

K196) Loew, Charles E., *Reminiscences of the Nordland, or, glimpses of Scandinavia, Russia, Germany and the Netherlands.* New York: D.T. Bass, 1910. 322pp.

Loew describes a tourist trip he and a group of friends made to Russia in August-September 1909 (?), visiting the sights of St Petersburg and Moscow, before moving on to Berlin (pp. 157-258).

K197) Aflalo, Frederick George, *An idler in the near East.* London: John Milne, 1910. xvi+279pp.

Angler and naturalist, Aflalo (1870-1918) took a cruise on the Black Sea in the summer of 1909 after a long stay in Turkey and the Holy Land. He disembarked at Batumi and went to Tiflis, which he regarded as "a wonderful monument of bluff" (pp. 241-60).

K198) Hubback, John, *Russian realities, being impressions gathered during some recent journeys in Russia.* London: John Lane, The Bodley Head, 1915. xvi+279pp.

Recollections of eleven short journeys to Russia undertaken by the author between 1909 and 1914, frequently accompanied by his wife. He travelled extensively through southern Russia – Ukraine, the Crimea, the Caucasus, and down the Volga.

K199) Hone, Joseph Maunsell and Dickinson, Page Lawrence, *Persia in revolution. With notes of travel in the Caucasus.* London: Fisher Unwin, 1910. xvi+218pp.

Account by Hone (1882-1959) and Dickinson (b. 1881) of their travels through Transcaucasia and Persia during 1909, largely written by the former. They describe their outward journey from Warsaw to Resht (pp. 1-13) and their return from Persia, reaching Baku by steamer from Enzeli, and travelling through western Georgia to Kutais and Batumi. They note in particular signs of political unrest and growing Georgian nationalism (pp. 144-218).

K200) Hoover, Herbert, *The memoirs of Herbert Hoover: years of adventure 1874-1920.* New York: The Macmillan Company, 1951. xii+496pp.

> Hoover (1874-1964), thirty-first President of the United States, recalls the short yearly visits he paid to Russia between 1909 and 1914, when as a freelance mining engineer he was involved in projects in the Urals and later Altai mountains (pp. 102-09).

K201) Ingham, Ernest Graham, *From Japan to Jerusalem.* London: Church Missionary Society, 1911. viii+232pp.

> Rt Rev. Ingham (1851-1926), secretary of the Church Missionary Society and formerly bishop of Sierra Leone, accompanied by his wife travelled from London via Berlin to Moscow, where they arrived on 23 August 1909 and joined the Trans-Siberian which took them to Vladivostok by 4 September (pp. 6-18). They were en route for Japan and China to visit church missions and then made their way to India and Ceylon before returning home via Palestine and Egypt.

K202) Sara, Muriel, *Russia remembered.* With a foreword by Cuthbert Bardsley. Hayle, Cornwall: for the author, 1971. 62pp.

> Wife of a geologist-consultant to an oil company, Mrs Sara, née Tiack (1885-1975) joined her husband in St Petersburg and travelled to the oil fields at an unspecified place in the Caucasus, where they remained until the outbreak of WWI. They left Russia via Scandinavia in the winter of 1915 (pp. 7-48).

K203) Dukes, Paul, *The unending quest: autobiographical sketches.* London: Cassell & Co., 1950. 260pp.

> Famed and knighted for his exploits as a British secret agent in Russia following the October Revolution, recounted in his *Story of "ST 25"* (1938), Sir Paul (1889-1967) had arrived in the Russia empire for the first time in the summer of 1909, teaching English in Riga, before moving to St Petersburg, where he studied music at the conservatoire and became immersed in the musical and artistic life of the capital. He studied piano under Professor Anna Esipova and became close to the Petersburg-born conductor Albert Coates, as well as dabbling in fashionable spiritualism and working during WWI in the British embassy under Ambassador Buchanan (pp. 17-115).

K204) Harrison, Ernest John, *Peace or war, east of Baikal.* Yokohama: Kelly & Walsh, 1910. 563pp.

> Leading English expert on judo and later author of anti-Soviet novels, Harrison (1873-1961) was sent to Russia as a special correspondent of the Yokohama *Japan Herald* in 1909 to investigate the likelihood of a future Russo-Japanese or American-Japanese conflict. He spent the month of September travelling through eastern Siberia from Chita to Khabarovsk, before returning to Japan from Vladivostok (pp. 63-211).

K205) Latimer, Robert Sloan, *With Christ in Russia.* London: Hodder and Stoughton, 1910. x+239pp.

> Latimer followed his books on Dr Baedeker (see I143) and *Under three tsars*, a study of religious movements in the post-Crimean war period, with his own experiences in Russia in 1909, although offering it principally as a biography of the Russian Stundist Dr Wilhelm Fetler, his close friend and companion. Probing the religious situation in contemporary Russia, Latimer travelled extensively, visiting not only St Petersburg and Moscow but also Kiev, Tiflis and Baku.

K206) Etherton, Percy Thomas, *Across the roof of the world: a record of sport and travel through Kashmir, Gilgit, Hunza, the Pamirs, Chinese Turkistan, Mongolia and Siberia.* London: Constable and Co., 1911. xvi+437pp.

> Lt. Etherton (b. 1879), Indian army and F.R.G.S., embarked on his four-thousand mile journey from Lansdowne in the Himalayas in the spring of 1909, drawn by the politics of the region but more by the opportunities of shooting the wild sheep that had attracted the guns of his compatriots for the past two decades. He eventually entered Russian territory from Mongolia, following the river Irtysh, early in January 1910. He proceeded across the steppes by sledge via Ustkamenogorsk towards Barnaul to join the Trans-Siberian at Novonikolaevsk on 17 February (pp. 395-429).

K207) Kemp, Emily Georgiana, *The face of Manchuria, Korea & Russian Turkestan.* London: Chatto & Windus, 1910. xvi+248pp.

> Miss Kemp (b. 1860), F.R.G.S. and author of a book on China, accompanied by a friend, Miss MacDougall, decided to observe the present state of Manchuria and Korea under the twin threats of Japan and Russia. They

travelled out on the Trans-Siberian on 1 February 1910 and back again four months later, when they decided to make a detour from Samara down to Turkestan, visiting Bokhara and Samarkand before travelling home across the Caspian to Baku and Tiflis and Vienna (pp. 151-240).

K208) Bax, Arnold, *Farewell, my youth.* London: Longmans, Green & Co. 1943. 112pp.

The visit of the famed English composer Sir Arnold (1883-1953) to Russia in the late spring and summer of 1910 was in pursuit of the daughter of a wealthy Ukrainian landowner, Liubov' (Liuba) Nikolaevna Korolenko, who sadly did not return his love. Arriving in Petersburg from Lausanne in April, he travelled on to Moscow and then to the Korolenko estate near Lubny in Ukraine (pp. 63-79).

K209) Goodrich, Joseph King, *Russia in Europe and Asia.* Chicago: A.C. McClurg & Co., 1912. x+302pp.

After several years teaching in the Imperial Government College, Kyoto, the American Goodrich (1850-1921), who seems to have visited Vladivostok for the first time in 1899, travelled from Japan in July 1910 and described in detail his fifteen-day journey on the Trans-Siberian to Moscow (pp. 112-29). His attempt at a comprehensive account of Russia is primarily based on secondary literature and discussions Goodrich had with Russians and those involved in Russian affairs while he was based in Japan.

K210) Hertz, Carl, *A modern mystery merchant: the trials, tricks and travels of Carl Hertz, the famous American illusionist.* London: Hutchinson & Co., 1924. 319pp.

Hertz (1859-1924), born in San Francisco to a Russian father and Polish mother, writes of his visit to Russia in the summer of 1910. The magician and his wife (stage name Emilie D'Alton) performed for two months at the *Iar* restaurant in Moscow, before visiting St Petersburg, where he apparently gave a command performance before the tsar and tsaritsa (pp. 227-31).

K211) Washington, Booker Taliaferro, *The man farthest down: a record of observation and study in Europe.* With the collaboration of Robert E. Park. London: T. Fisher Unwin, 1912. 390pp.

In a chapter entitled 'A Russian border village' the African-American political leader and author (1856-1915) on a European tour describes his brief visit in August 1910 to a village called Barany on the Russian side of the Austrian

Poland/Russian Poland border and compares the status of the Russian peasant with that of the Mississippi Afro-American farmer (pp. 276-95).

K212) Crawford, Laura MacPherson, *Dear family: the travel letters and reminiscences of Laura MacPherson Crawford.* Edited by Ruth Saunders. Claremont, California: privately printed, 1946. xx+360pp.

> Canadian society wife and later Red Cross worker Mrs Crawford describes in a letter home her and her husband's visit to St Petersburg and Moscow, as well as to the Ponafidin estate near Ostashkov (see J40) in May 1910 (pp. 107-16).

K213) Eddy, Sherwood, *A pilgrimage of ideas; or the re-education of Sherwood Eddy.* New York: Farrar & Reinhart Inc., 1934. xiv+336pp.

> Intellectual autobiography of the American Protestant missionary and prolific author (1871-1963), who visited Russia some ten times between 1910 and 1930 and had published an analytical work entitled *The challenge of Russia* in 1931. In the final chapter he briefly discusses his two visits to imperial Russia in 1910 and 1912, before turning to his experiences during the Soviet period. In 1912 he attended student meetings in Kiev, Moscow and St Petersburg, noting an epidemic of suicide (pp. 313-23).

K214) Wood, Ruth Kedzie, *Honeymooning in Russia.* London: T. Fisher Unwin, 1911. vi+341pp.

> The honeymoon in Russia of an American couple, Mr and Mrs Philip D. Houghton, in the summer of 1910, related as much in dialogue as in descriptive prose by Joyce, Mrs Houghton, the alter ego, one assumes, of Ruth Wood (1880-1950), the author. It is nonetheless an informed and detailed tourist's visit to the attractions of St Petersburg, Vologda, and Iaroslavl', where they take the steamer down the Volga to Nizhnii Novgorod. They travel to Moscow and from there, through Ukraine to the Crimea and Odessa. They then journey to Kiev and exit to Warsaw. Contains Wood's translations of poems by such as Krylov, Nikitin, Nekrasov, Lermontov, and Kozlov.

K215) Christie, Isabella [Ella] Robertson, *Through Khiva to golden Samarkand: the remarkable story of a woman's adventurous journey alone through the deserts of Central Asia to the heart of Turkestan.* London: Seeley, Service & Co., 1925. 280pp.

> Renowned Scottish traveller and gardener, Christie (1861-1949), F.R.G.S., describes on the basis of her diaries her two expeditions as sole female

traveller to Russian Turkestan in 1910 and 1912. Her first journey was from Constantinople to Andijan (pp. 1-217); and the second from St Petersburg to Khiva, which she was the first British woman ever to enter (pp. 218-63).

K216) McCaig, Archibald, *Wonders of grace in Russia.* Riga: The Revival Press, 1926. 251pp.

Dr McCaig, Principal of Spurgeon's College in London, went to Russia for the first time in June 1910, accompanying the evangelical pastor William Fetler (author of *The Stundist in Siberian exile and other poems*) whom he had initially met as a student at the college, to initiate the building of the missionary society's tabernacle in St Petersburg. He also visited Novgorod, Schüsselburg and Moscow. He returned to Russia for the opening of the tabernacle in 1912 and paid two further visits in June 1912 and 1913 (pp. 11-185). His book is largely based on articles he wrote for various church periodicals during this period.

K217) Dobson, George, *St. Petersburg.* London: Adam & Charles Black, 1910. xii+158pp.

The first of three Russian guides commissioned by the Blacks, all enhanced by the paintings of the Belgian artist F. de Haenen (see K246, K261). A lively contemporary account by the former long-time *Times* correspondent in St Petersburg (see J78).

K218) Garstin, Denis, *Friendly Russia.* With an introduction by H.G. Wells. London: T. Fisher Unwin, 1915. 248pp.

Garstin (1890-1918) first went out to Russia as a tutor in about 1910, after leaving Cambridge, and living initially, it would seem, in the Crimea (pp. 15-184). The final section of his book (based largely on articles he contributed in 1913-14 to newspapers such as the *Morning Post* and the *Daily News*) was entitled 'The Russians in war' (pp. 185-248). After service in WWI, Garstin returned to Russia with the British Propaganda unit (under Hugh Walpole) and lost his life in north Russia, fighting against the Bolsheviks.

K219) Price, Morgan Philips, *Siberia.* London: Methuen & Co., 1912. xviii+308pp.

Price (1885-1973), who was to write several books on Russia (see K322, K379-81), provides a description of life in western and central Siberia, based on a trip undertaken during the spring and summer of 1910. In the first half of the book Price uses his stay in a number of locations to explore the social, religious and economic aspects of Siberia: Krasnoiarsk inspires an account of municipal life in a growing commercial town; the provincial town of Minusink allows him to explore a life less affected by "Western commercialism"; and the frontier village of Kushabar, on the north side of the Mongolian frontier on the Upper Enisei presents the life of the frontier peasant.

K220) Curtis, William Eleroy, *Turkestan: "the heart of Asia".* London: Hodder & Stoughton, 1911. 344pp.

Curtis, who had first visited Russia in the reign of Alexander III (see J68), spent the spring and early summer of 1910 in Turkestan, writing a series of detailed descriptions of the region that were to appear first in the *Chicago Record-Herald*. The photographs were taken by John T. McCutcheon during his earlier visit to Turkestan in the summer of 1906.

K221) Curtis, William Eleroy, *Around the Black Sea, Asia Minor, Armenia, Caucasus, Circassia, Daghestan, the Crimea, Roumania.* London: Hodder & Stoughton, 1911. 456pp.

Essentially a sequel both in time and manner to his previous book and similarly composed from letters sent to a Chicago paper. Curtis spent the rest of the summer and the autumn of 1910, visiting countries adjacent to the Black Sea, including Georgia (pp. 85-128), Baku and Daghestan (pp. 214-51), Odessa and the Crimea (pp. 252-347).

K222) Simpson, Eugene E., *Eugene E. Simpson's Travels in Russia, 1910 and 1912.* Taylorville, Ill.: for the author, 1916. 126pp.

Based on articles Simpson (1871-1929) sent to the New York *Musical Courier* during visits down the Volga and to the Crimea in the two summers. Simpson was an enthusiast of Russian music, classical and folk, and an admirer of Tchaikovsky, whose home at Klin he visited.

K223) Lied, Jonas, *Return to happiness.* London: Macmillan, 1943. xii+318pp. [American edition entitled: *Prospector in Siberia: the autobiography of Jonas Lied.* New York: Oxford University Press, 1945.]

The Norwegian entrepreneur (1881-1969), inspired by the example of Captain Wiggins, paid his first of many visits to Russia in May 1910 to investigate trading possibilities in Siberia on behalf of a London firm. In 1913 he sailed to the Kara Sea with Nansen. Thereafter he made frequent trips both to St Petersburg and Siberia, meeting important Russian businessmen, political figures, and the tsar. The October revolution brought his highly successful shipping and trading business to an end, but he continued to visit and live in the Soviet Union until 1931 (pp. 52-293).

K224) Lied, Jonas, *Siberian Arctic: the story of the Siberian Company.* London: Methuen, 1960. 217pp.

> Lied's history of the Siberian Company, which he helped found, repeats much of what appears in his autobiography but expectedly provides less detail about his own actions (pp. 50-111).

K225) Buchanan, George, *My mission to Russia and other diplomatic memories.* London: Cassell & Co., 1923. 2 vols.

> After relating his career as a diplomat from 1876, Sir George (1854-1924) describes in detail his long years as British ambassador in Petersburg from September 1910 to January 1918 (vol. I, pp. 91-253; II, pp. 1-248).

K226) Buchanan, Meriel, *Diplomacy and foreign courts.* With an introduction by Sir Bernard Pares. London: Hutchinson & Co., 1928. 288pp.

> A devoted daughter's parallel account of her father's postings and a vigorous defence of his character and actions during WWI and the revolutionary events of 1917. Meriel (1886-1959), from 1925 Mrs Knowling, also provides descriptions of the social life of high society in St Petersburg and her own experiences of the effects of war and revolution (pp. 133-243).

K227) Buchanan, Meriel, *Ambassador's daughter.* With a foreword by Sir Robert Bruce Lockhart. London: Cassell & Co., 1958. ix+239pp.

> In the last of the books she devoted to Russia and published in the year before her death, Meriel returns to her defence of her father's conduct, reworking much already familiar material (pp. 89-194).

K228) Buchanan, Meriel, *Recollections of imperial Russia.* London: Hutchinson & Co., 1923. vii+277pp.

> Essentially a re-hash of previous books which soon goes beyond personal memories of her arrival and early years in Petersburg to unoriginal histories of eighteenth-century rulers and spun-out descriptions of places with minimal personal input.

K229) Buchanan, Meriel, *The dissolution of an empire.* London: John Murray, 1932. 304pp.

> Meriel herself acknowledges that she might be "accused by some people of repeating myself to a monotonous degree", and this book, tracing her family's stay in Russia from 1910 to 1918 with added material for the following years, was not to be the last example.

K230) Buchanan, Meriel, *Victorian gallery.* London: Cassell & Co., 1956. x+219pp.

> Includes chapters devoted to people, Russian and British, whom she knew in Russia, such as Princess Zinaida Iusupova and Sir Henry Wilson (pp. 28-67, 103-95).

K231) Baring, Maurice, *The Russian people.* London: Methuen & Co., 1911. xix+366pp.

> A history and geography of Russia, based on the reading of many secondary sources, but also a summation of Baring's years of studying the Russian people in situ and constantly illuminated by his own anecdotes and observations. His intention was "to supply the average reader with an introduction to the course of Russian affairs".

K232) Graham, Stephen, *A vagabond in the Caucasus. With some notes of his experiences among the Russians.* London: John Lane, 1911. vii+311pp.

> Graham's long years "tramping" throughout Russia (and later America) began with his travels through the Caucasus in 1910. After spending a long winter in Kharkov, he remained in Moscow until Easter (to p. 116). The rest of the book concerns his time in the Caucasus as he moved from Vladikavkaz through the Gorge of Dariel to reach, months later, Tiflis. Amusingly, his book finishes with "a chapter for prospective tourists" (pp. 301-08).

K233) Graham, Stephen, *A tramp's sketches.* London: Macmillan, 1912. xiii+339pp.

> "Not so much a book about Russia as about the tramp", it is a paean to the joys of unfettered wanderings through the south of Russia, by the Black Sea, into Georgia, in the Crimea, and accompanying peasant pilgrims to Jerusalem (see K247).

K234) Graham, Stephen, *Undiscovered Russia.* London: John Lane, 1912. xvi+337pp.

> The particular area of Russia Graham was "discovering" for his readers was the north to which he had travelled from the Caucasus by way of Moscow in 1911. From Archangel he made long expeditions along the courses of the rivers Pinega and Dvina. When he finally left Archangel he returned to Moscow via Vologda and Kostroma, finishing his tramping at Vetluga, before making a detour to Rostov.

K235) Donner, Kai [Karl] Reinhold, *Among the Samoyed in Siberia.* Translated by Rinchart Kyler. Edited by Genevieve A. Highland. New Haven: Human Relations Area Files, 1954. xx+176pp.

> The Finnish linguist, ethnographer, and pioneer of Finno-Ugrian studies (1888-1935) describes two trips he made to Siberia, the first from August 1911 to June 1913 and the second in June-October 1914, illustrated by scores of his own photographs. He first travelled along the upper reaches of the Ob and the Enisei, describing the life of the Samoed peoples with whom he lived; and on his second journey he reached the northern slopes of the Saian mountains of south-eastern Siberia. The original account, *Bland Samojeder i Sibirien åren 1911-1913, 1914* was first published in 1915.

K236) Digby, George Bassett, *Tigers, gold, and witch-doctors.* London: John Lane, (The Bodley Head), 1928. 341pp.

> Digby (1888-1962), F.R.G.S., offered an account of "things that I found out in the course of my wanderings in Siberia", including not only those in his title, but also bears, wolves, mammoths, and much else. Well-read in earlier accounts of Siberia, he offers a lively narrative of several undated journeys in the years before WWI.

K237) Wright, Richardson Little, and Digby, George Bassett, *Through Siberia: an empire in the making.* London: Hurst and Blackett, 1913. viii+260pp.

> American journalist Wright (1887-1961) and British prospector Digby decided to travel "with the Russians" by third-class slow train from Moscow to Siberia in the spring of 1911. They went on to Kharbin and into Japanese Manchuria. In many ways a familiar route, but with some unusual encounters and interesting detail.

K238) Herbert, Agnes, *Casuals in the Caucasus: the diary of a sporting holiday.* London: John Lane, 1912. xii+331pp.

Accompanied by her cousins Cecily Windus and Kenneth Baird (of the Petersburg Bairds), Miss Herbert sailed from Gibraltar to Batumi to "shoot a little, climb a little" during the summer of 1911 in the Caucasus. A frothy, gossipy travelogue from an author who had already shot her way around Somaliland and Alaska (pp. 27-331).

K239) Phelps, William Lyon, *Autobiography with letters*. London: Oxford University Press, 1939. xxiii+986pp.

Phelps (1865-1943), Yale professor and author of *Essays on Russian novelists* (1917), paid his first and only visit to Russia with his wife in September 1911. They visited St Petersburg and Moscow, but only Nevskii Prospekt seems to have impressed him (pp. 522-28).

K240) Perry-Ayscough, Henry George Charles, and Otter-Barry, Robert Bruère, *With the Russians in Mongolia*. With a preface by Sir Claude Macdonald. London: John Lane, The Bodley Head, 1914. xxiv+344pp.

Perry-Ayscough of the Chinese Postal Service, F.R.G.S., and Captain Otter-Barry (b. 1879) of the Royal Sussex regiment, F.R.G.S., travelled through Mongolia at different times, the latter, in 1911, just before the Chinese Revolution, the former, in 1913, when Mongolia was already under Russian protection. Collaborating on the general chapters devoted to Mongolian history and Russo-Mongolian relations, the authors provide independent accounts of their travels through Mongolia and parts of Siberia. Only the final pages of Otter-Barry's contribution concern Siberia as he passes through the border town of Kiakhta to Verkhne-Udinsk to meet his wife from the Trans-Siberian on 12 July 1911 (pp. 175-84). In February 1913 Perry-Ayscough travelled from China through Manchuria and went by train to Verkhne-Udinsk on his way to the Mongolian capital (pp. 189-94). In April, leaving for England, he crossed into Siberia at Kosh Agach, proceeded to Biisk, and from there by steamer to Novonikolaevsk to catch the Trans-Siberian (pp. 241-94).

K241) Shaft, Arthur, *My Russian and English connections*. Broadstone: for the author, 1993. xiii+154pp.

Shaft (b. 1911), the youngest son of Anglo-French parents, both of whom had also been born in Russia, remembers his happy early years in Moscow and on an estate near Rzhev and then the increasingly difficult times under Soviet rule until the family was allowed to depart for England via Finland in the spring of 1920 (pp. 1-61).

K242) Lockhart, Robert Hamilton Bruce, *Memoirs of a secret agent, being an account of the author's early life in many lands and of his official mission in 1918.* London and New York: Putnam, 1931. xii+355pp.

> Lockhart (1887-1970) arrived in Moscow in January 1912 as British vice-consul, but was to serve throughout WWI as acting consul-general. His narrative of his life, or lives, "Russian and unofficial" and "official and mainly English", over the next five years is anecdotal, often amusing, and informative. In early September 1917 he was recalled to London (pp. 53-192). The second half of the book is devoted to his more "famous" exploits after his return to Soviet Moscow in January 1918, his arrest in September for involvement in the alleged anti-Bolshevik "Lockhart plot", and expulsion in early October.

K243) Lockhart, Robert Hamilton Bruce, *My Europe.* London: Putnam, 1952. x+273pp.

> In the opening two chapters, 'Moscow before the wars' and 'Prelude to revolution', Lockhart recalls his Moscow years from 1912 to 1917 (pp. 3-28).

K244) Lockhart, Robert Hamilton Bruce, *Giants cast long shadows.* London: Putnam, 1960. 253pp.

> In his collection of essays devoted to distinguished people in all walks of life is 'Missionaries of sport', in which Lockhart recalls Lancashire-born Clem Charnock, credited with introducing soccer into Russia in 1887 and members of the Charnock clan with whom he played for the "Morozovtsy" in Moscow in 1912 (pp. 172-80).

K245) Young, Ernest, *From Russia to Siam, with a voyage down the Danube: sketches of travel in many lands.* London: Max Goschen, 1914. xii+328pp.

> Young (1869-1952), travel writer, published a book on Finland in 1912. It was during his sojourn that he sailed from Sortovala (then in the Grand Duchy) to visit the Russian Orthodox monastery on the island of Walamo/Valaam in Lake Ladoga. He spent five days in a guest cell, interviewing the monks and observing their way of life (pp. 3-35).

K246) Grove, Henry Montgomery, *Moscow.* London: Adam and Charles Black, 1912. viii+142pp.

> The companion to Dobson's book on St Petersburg (see K217), Grove's follows the same mixture of historical and contemporary commentary to

accompany de Haenen's paintings. (see also K261). Grove was the long-serving British consul-general in Moscow.

K247) Graham, Stephen, *With the Russian pilgrims to Jerusalem.* London: Macmillan and Co., 1913. x+306 pp.

> It was in Constantinople in 1912 that Graham joined the boat containing some 500 Russian peasant pilgrims bound for Jaffa and then travelling on to Jerusalem but it was as if he found himself "in a populous Russian village on a market day". Thus not strictly a travelogue through Russia, it merits inclusion for its vivid evocation of Russian peasants and their stories. He returned to Odessa after Easter to begin more solitary tramping.

K248) Graham, Stephen, *Changing Russia.* London: John Lane, 1913. ix+309pp.

> "The journal of a tramp" through southern parts of Russia in 1912, mainly to Batumi via such resorts as Sochi and Sukhumi, and, later, through the Crimea. Written, allegedly, "with an eye to the ways and thoughts of the Intelligentsia" during a period of rapid change.

K249) Cripps, Frederick Heyworth, *Life's a gamble.* With a foreword by Lord Burnham. London: Odhams Press, 1957. 208pp.

> The hon. Fred Cripps, later 3rd Lord Parmoor (1885-1977), went to Russia in about 1912 as a merchant banker and he remained until the summer of 1914, when he returned to England to join the army. Although his office was in Peterburg, he travelled to other parts of Russia, including the Urals. Among his close friends was Shaliapin (pp. 81-97). In 1919 he went to Soviet Moscow and over the next five or six years was engaged in an astonishing variety of business and leisure activities, including organizing his own ballet company (pp. 127-55).

K250) Lee, Helena Crumett, *Across Siberian alone: an American woman's adventures.* London: John Lane, Bodley Press, 1914. 220pp.

> After attending her daughter's wedding in Shanghai, Mrs Lee sails to Dalnii in September 1912 to begin her long lone train journey to Moscow, where her account ends. Boarding the Trans-Siberian Railway (or the Chinese Eastern Railway extension) at Chang Chung, she travels to Irkutsk, where she breaks her journey and dines with exiles and discusses the Siberian prison system. She then makes a detour to Tomsk and visits the university. Her declared aim was to spread knowledge in America of Siberia (pp. 40-220).

K251) Fraser, Eugenie, *A house by the Dvina: a Russian childhood.* Edinburgh: Mainstream Publishing Co., 1984. ii+281pp.

> Daughter of a Russian father and a Scottish mother, Eugenie, née Sholts (1905-2002) was brought up in Archangel. She relates her family story from 1912 to 1920, when she and her mother escaped to Scotland. She and her husband visited the family home in 1972, described in *The Dvina remains* (1996).

K252) Bury, Herbert, *Russian life to-day.* London, A.R. Mowbray & Co., 1915. vii+270pp.

> Bury (1853-1933), Anglican bishop of Northern and Central Europe, travelled extensively throughout Russia in 1912-14, visiting Anglican congregations in western Russia and beyond the Urals as far as Petropavlovsk, and into the Kirghiz steppe. Offers his book as an "impressionistic description of Russian life" and includes a very respectful audience with the tsar at Tsarskoe selo.

K253) Wood, Ruth Kedzie, *The tourist's Russia.* London: Andrew Melrose, 1912. viii+253pp.

> The first of several contributions by Wood (see K214) to the 'Tourist's' series (Spain, California, etc.), adapted for both American and British publics. It is her substitute for an English-language Baedeker, the lack of which she regretted in her earlier book but which was to appear in 1914 (see K271).

K254) Steveni, William Barnes, *Things seen in Russia.* Seeley, Service & Co., 1913. 260pp.

> A contribution to the popular small-format 'Things seen' series that includes the statutory, but delightful, fifty illustrations, written by a long-time British resident of St Petersburg (see J111, K266), who concentrates mainly on the capital, Moscow and Kiev.

K255) Forse, Edward John George, *From Warsaw to Moscow: from the travel diaries of Edward J.G. Forse.* Southbourne: for the author. xvipp.

> Rev. Forse (1877-1942), F.R.G.S., vicar of Southbourne, Bournemouth and author of several books of travel and art history, describes in some detail his train journey, begun in Warsaw on 3 September 1913, to the old Russian capital. He explores the streets and famous, mainly religious, buildings of

Moscow, which he leaves on 8 September, at which point his narrative comes to an abrupt end.

K256) Ransome, Arthur, *The autobiography of Arthur Ransome.* Edited, with prologue and epilogue, by Rupert Hart-Davis. London: Jonathan Cape, 1976. 368pp.

>Author and journalist Ransome (1884-1967) first went to Russia in June-September 1913 to study the language and folklore and returned in May-August of the following year to write a guide to St Petersburg (pp. 159-70). On 30 December 1914 he was back in newly-named Petrograd and thereafter in and out of Russia (and later the Baltic states) until 1924, reporting war and revolution, writing, fishing, and wooing Trotskii's secretary (pp. 159-319).

K257) Le Blond, Elizabeth, *Day in, day out.* [With a foreword by E.F. Benson.] London: John Lane, 1928. 264pp.

>The three-times married Mrs Le Blond, née Hawkins-Whitsted (1861-1934), the greatest lady mountaineer of the age, not to mention her prowess as cyclist and car driver, accompanied her husband on a tour that took them to China and Korea in 1912 and then by the Trans-Siberian railway to Moscow in June 1913. Her husband obliged to return to England, she remained sightseeing in Moscow and then St Petersburg (pp. 165-77).

K258) Wheeler, William Webb, *The other side of the earth.* St. Joseph, Missouri: privately printed, 1913. 208pp.

>American merchant and author of various travel accounts, Wheeler (1845-1925) passed from Manchuria into Russia in June 1913 and travelled east on the Trans-Siberian. He proceeded to St Petersburg and then travelled to Moscow, noting the usual sights (pp. 169-201).

K259) Shelley, Gerard, *The blue steppes: adventures among Russians.* London: John Hamilton, 1925. 268pp.

>Shelley (b. 1892) produced two versions of his memoirs of his years in Russia from 1913, when he was invited by Count and Countess Torlov to stay on their estate near Kharkov, to 1920, when he escaped from Petrograd to Finland. He spent time in Petrograd and Moscow and also visited the Crimea before the revolution. A linguist who quickly acquired Russian and worked for some time as an interpreter for the Russians during WWI, Shelley also translated the Russian poets, including Pushkin, Lermontov, and Blok.

K260) Shelley, Gerard, *The speckled domes: episodes of an Englishman's life in Russia.* Duckworth, 1925. 256pp.

> A less sprightly version of Shelley's adventures, but also different in other respects, not least in the manner of his ultimate escape, here disguised as a woman! In both accounts there is much on his acquaintance with Rasputin, whom he met for the first time in April 1915 and whom he defended.

K261) Stewart, Hugh, *Provincial Russia.* London: Adam and Charles Black, 1913. viii+173pp.

> The final volume in a series that was re-issued in the same year as a single volume under the title *Russia,* displaying to the full the talent of the painter de Haenen (see K217, K246). Stewart (1884-1934) who had travelled widely through Russia from about 1906, provided a succinct account of the various regions.

K262) Johnson, William Eugene, *The liquor problem in Russia.* Westerville, Ohio: American Issue Publishing Co., 1915. 230pp.

> The American social reformer and prohibition campaigner Johnson (1862-1945) travelled to Russia in 1913 to do "some muckraking in connection with the vodka monopoly", but found a welcome change in government attitudes towards alcohol production.

K263) Bruce, Henry James, *Silken Dalliance.* London: Constable, 1946. viii+183pp.

> After service in Vienna and Berlin Bruce (1880-1951) was posted as Head of Chancery to the British embassy in Petersburg at the end of August 1913 and remained there for five momentous years, before he and his wife, the ballerina Tamara Karsavina, whom he married in the Russian capital in 1915, finally left from Murmansk in July 1918. His memoirs are a curious mixture of personal adventures and observation and potted eighteenth-century Russian history (pp. 135-75).

K264) Bruce, Henry James, *Thirty-dozen moons.* London: Constable and Co., 1949. 189pp.

> In his second book of memoirs Bruce describes his courting of Diagilev's prima ballerina Karsavina from autumn 1913 to the following summer (pp. 1-10).

K265) Vecchi, Joseph, *"The tavern is my drum": my autobiography.* Preface by Negley Farson. London: Odhams Press, 1948. 224pp.

> The Italian restaurateur (d. 1961) moved from *Claridge*'s in London to the *Kaiserhof* in Berlin, and in September 1913, on to the newly-opened hotel *Astoria* in St Petersburg, where he managed the French restaurant until the hotel was requisitioned in April 1916. He then worked at the *Felicien* and the *Bear*, before going to Kiev's *Grand Hotel*. He returned to Petrograd in March 1917 and a final venture, *The Little Palace*. At the end of 1917 he left his "beloved" Russia via Murmansk, eventually settling in London (pp. 29-152).

K266) Steveni, William Barnes, *The Russian army from within.* London: Hodder & Stoughton, 1914. 184pp.

> Steveni (see J112, K254) travelled from the capital to the Caucasus in 1913 to report on the state of the Russian army at the behest of London newspapers.

K267) Mears, John Henry, and Collyer, Charles B.D., *Racing the moon (and winning): being the story of the swiftest journey ever made, a circumnavigation of the globe by airplane and steamship in 23 days, 15 hours, 21 minutes and 3 seconds by two men and a dog.* New York: Rae D. Henkle Co., 1928. 320pp.

> It is not the journey of 1928, when Broadway producer Mears regained the world record, but his original journey in 1913 to gain the record for the first time that is relevant. Mears (1878-1956) left New York on 2 July 1913 and returned thirty-five days, twenty-one hours, thirty-five minutes, eighteen and four-fifths seconds later. In the course of that journey, by steamship and train, he passed, twelve days on, through St Petersburg and took the Trans-Siberian in Moscow to Omsk, then went into China (pp. 245-85).

K268) Nansen, Fridtjof Wedel-Jarlsberg, *Through Siberia, the land of the future.* Translated from the Norwegian by Arthur G. Chater. London: William Heinemann, 1914. xvi+478pp.

> The Norwegian scientist and explorer Nansen (1861-1930), who was to win the Nobel Peace Prize in 1922, set out from Norway in August 1913 with, among others, Jonas Lied (see K223) to attempt "to open up a regular trade connexion with the interior of Siberia, via the Kara Sea and the mouth of the Yenisei". They arrived back in Petrograd after penetrating as far as the Manchurian border, at the very end of October.

K269) Dickinson, Duncan, *Through Spain: the record of journey from St. Petersburg to Tangier, by way of Paris, Madrid, Cordova, Seville and Cadiz; and thence to Gibraltar, Ronda and Granada.* London: Methuen & Co., 1914. xxiv+197pp.

> The author, it would seem, was born or raised in Russia ("home") and thus in the summer of 1913 begins his long train journey to Spain at the Warsaw station in Petersburg, briefly describing the scenery on his way to the border (pp. 1-4).

K270) Bryce, James, *Memories of travel.* London: Macmillan, 1923. 300pp.

> Posthumously published collection of travel sketches includes Lord Bryce's recollections, written in 1922, of a journey on the Trans-Siberian in August-September 1913 with an excursion via Tomsk to the Altai mountains (pp. 254-95). Bryce had previously visited Russia in 1876 (see I137).

K271) Baedeker, Karl, *Russia with Teheran, Port Arthur, and Peking: handbook for travellers.* London: George Allen & Unwin, 1914. lxiv+590.

> Published on the eve of WWI, the travellers' indispensable *vade mecum*, prepared with meticulous detail and accuracy by the "Baedeker" editor and his associates, "who have repeatedly explored the country with a view to procuring the latest possible information". It was so soon to become a historical document.

K272) Keller, Otto, *St. Petersburg and its environs, Finland, Moscow, Kiev, Odessa, Warsaw, Riga, a tour on the Volga, the Crimea and the Caucasus, with plans of St. Petersburg and of the environs of St. Petersburg, railway map of Russia, sketches of the Hermitage and the museum of Alexander III.* London: Siegle, Hill & Co., 1914. ii+168pp.

> Keller (1838-1927) had been in resident in St Petersburg for ten years at the time of writing and the guide book is based on his personal experiences and specifically slanted for the English visitor.

K273) Williams, Harold Whitmore, *Russia of the Russians.* London: Sir Isaac Pitman & Sons, 1914. x+430pp.

> Although specifically written for the series 'Countries and peoples' and suppressing the personal element, it reflects the deep knowledge and love of pre-WWI Russia of the astonishing New-Zealand linguist and esteemed newspaper correspondent. Hugely informative about all

aspects of contemporary Russia, particularly the arts, it is especially notable for the chapter (pp. 389-424) on St Petersburg, where Williams (1876-1928) arrived for the first time in December 1904 and left finally in March 1918.

K274) Baring, Maurice, *The Mainsprings of Russia.* London: Thomas Nelson and Sons, 1914. xi+328pp.

> An attempt to provide "a single idea of the more important factors in Russian life" based on Baring's personal observations and travels over many years. The book is dedicated to H.G. Wells, recalling the time they spent together in St Petersburg in 1914.

K275) Byford, Charles Thomas, *The soul of Russia.* London: Kingsgate Press, 1914. 396pp.

> Based on his extensive travels through Russia, including the Baltic States and the Crimea during presumably the early years of the century, Byford's study aimed to present "a concise view of the spiritual and religious forces at work" in contemporary Russia, with an overarching theme of the growth in religious liberty in the Russian Empire. Each chapter, devoted to the Orthodox church and to sects such as the Dukhobors and Molokans, is prefaced by a list of secondary sources he has consulted.

K276) Graham, Stephen, *The way of Martha and the way of Mary.* London: Macmillan, 1915. xii+291pp.

> In his quest for the essence of Eastern Christianity Graham travelled from Paris to Kiev in January 1914 and then to Moscow, where he completed his book in September of the following year. He visited the Convent of Martha and Mary in Moscow to see Nesterov's painting of the saints, who embodied for him the paths of faith and service. In the third and final section he describes his journey in May 1915 to Egypt to visit monasteries and shrines and thence "to make a journey to Russia the way Christianity came to her".

K277) Graham, Stephen, *The death of yesterday.* London: Ernest Benn, 1930. iii+179pp.

> In the essay 'At the Moscow Art Theatre: 1914', Graham recalls his visits to see performances of *Hamlet*, Chekhov's *The cherry orchard* and Andreev's *Anathema* (pp. 129-46).

K278) Keeling, H.V., *Bolshevism: Mr. Keeling's five years in Russia.* Edited by E.H. Haywood. London: Hodder & Stoughton, 1919. 212pp.

> Keeling was sent to Russia in February 1914 to assist in the setting up of a patent photo-litho process in St Petersburg and to train Russian workers. He stayed on for five years, working as a jobbing mechanic in the capital and other towns, before escaping via Finland. The editor contributed both preface and final chapter entitled 'The theory of Bolshevism' (pp. 199-212).

K279) Bartlett, Robert A., *The last voyage of the 'Karluk', flagship of Vilhjalmar Stefannson's Canadian Arctic expedition of 1913-1916.* As related by her master Robert A. Bartlett, and here set down by Ralph T. Hale. Boston: Small, Maynard and Co., 1916. vi+329pp.

> The Canadian captain "Bob" Bartlett (1875-1946) recounts the ill-fated last voyage of the *Karluk*, which was crushed by ice and sank on 11 January 1914. In their overland trek to safety, Bartlett and others reached Wrangell Island on 12 March 1914, but only he and one companion then proceeded to cross over to the north-east Siberian mainland, which they reached on 4 April and encountered a settlement of Chukchis. After many further exploits and surprising meetings, he finally stepped on American soil on 28 May (pp. 161-281).

K280) Bartlett, Robert A., *The log of Bob Bartlett: the true story of forty years of seafaring and exploration.* New York and London: G.P. Putnam's Sons, 1928. xii+252pp.

> Includes a succinct account of the *Karluk* expedition (pp. 254-79).

K281) Moore, Benjamin Burges, *From Moscow to the Persian Gulf, being the journal of a disenchanted traveller in Turkestan and Persia.* New York and London: G.P. Putnam's Sons, 1915. xx+450pp.

> The journal of an American traveller, reflecting his non-definitive "unfavourable opinion of Persia and her people". He begins his journey from Moscow on 8 February 1914, en route for Samarkand and Bokhara in Russian Turkestan, before he crosses into Persia on 20 February (pp. 3-70).

K282) Dawe, Rosamond E., *A memoir of an English governess in Russia, 1914-1917.* Chichester: Bishop Otter College, 1973. vi+26pp. [Revised edition, Woking: Unwin Brothers, 1976. x+45pp.]

The eighteen-year-old Rosamond (1896-1990) left Norwich in May 1914 to teach English to the three eldest Naumov daughters on the family estate near Samara on the Volga. Two years later, she moved to the Tolstoi family at Tsarskoe selo and, finally, held a position with the Miklashevskii family, taking her to Kislovodsk before returning to Petrograd, where she witnessed the aftermath of the February revolution. She returned to England in June 1917 via Scandinavia.

K283) Wardell, John Wilford, *In the Kirghiz Steppes*. London: Gallery Press, 1961. 190pp.

Wardell, a draughtsman and engineer with the London firm of Walter Perkins, was sent on a three-year contract to work for the British-owned Spasskii Copper Mine Ltd in southern Siberia. He left England on 16 May 1914 but it was the end of September 1919 before he and his wife Lily (who had joined him in July 1914) and other British, caught by war and revolution, were able to leave from Vladivostok for China and home. Unusual and fascinating account of life and work among the Kazaks.

K284) Czaplicka, Marya Antonina, *My Siberian year*. London: Mills & Boon, 1916. 306pp.

The Polish-born Oxford anthropologist (1884-1921), already author of *Aboriginal Siberia* (1914), based on printed sources, spent a year of fieldwork between May 1914 and the spring of the following year in the northern tundra by the Enisei, accompanied by the American anthropologist Hubert Hall.

K285) Anderson, Herbert Foster, *Borderline Russia.* London: Cresset Press, 1942. 238pp.

Recently graduated, Anderson (b. 1890) accepted a position as manager of an estate in Tambov *guberniia*, where he remained from June 1914 to the summer of the following year, when he sought to return to England on hearing of the declaration of war (pp. 1-29).

K286) Levings, Grace M., *Travel sketches of Norway, Sweden, Russia, Austria, Belgium and Holland*. Boston: Richard G. Badger; Toronto: Copp Clark Co., 1916. 168pp.

A European tour by an American couple – Mrs Levings refers to her husband throughout as "Doctor" – that took them from Stockholm by boat to Petrograd. Routine tourist notes of the sights of Petrograd and Moscow, before they move on to Vienna (pp. 64-103). No dates and no mention of the war, but use of Petrograd, if not afterthought, suggests possibly summer of 1914.

K287) Boultbee, Rosamond, *Pilgrimages and personalities.* London: Hutchinson & Co., 1924. 328pp.

The Canadian journalist (1878-1957) paid a first brief visit to Russia in early 1914 to visit friends in Kiev (pp. 64-66). She returned for a second time in July 1915, spending two months in Petrograd, before leaving in September for Kiev. After a lengthy stay in Kiev, she moved to Odessa, where she was to remain for three months, before departing for Romania via Kishinev in the spring of 1916. In April she returned to Odessa and then visited Moscow, which delighted her and where she stayed until July (pp. 96-148, 176-89).

K288) Graham, Stephen, *Through Russian Central Asia.* London, New York: Cassell and Co., 1916. xii+279pp.

In the early summer of 1914 Graham left Vladikavkaz by train for Bokhara and Tashkent. A little beyond Tashkent he began his travels on foot, by cart, and horse and eventually crossed into Siberia and reached Semipalatinsk, the place of Dostoevskii's exile. His articles to the *Times* chronicled his progress at the time, but he delayed publication of the book until after its successor (K289).

K289) Graham, Stephen, *Russia and the world. A study of the war and a statement of the world-problems that now confront Russia and Great Britain.* London: Cassell and Co., 1915. xi+259pp. [Revised and enlarged edition, 1917. 301pp.]

Graham was in the Altai mountains by the Mongolian frontier when news of the outbreak of WWI reached him in July 1914. He travelled to Moscow in September (pp. 3-32). The rest of the book is devoted to general essays and memorable meetings, before he made his first ever visit to St Petersburg/Petrograd on his way home to England (pp. 243-46).

K290) Haviland, Maud Doria, *A summer on the Yenisei (1914).* London: Edward Arnold, 1915. xii+328pp.

The ornithologist Miss Haviland, inspired by the writings of Seebohm, joined the expedition to the Enisei, organized by Marya Czaplicka and Hubert Hall. She and the artist Dora Curtis reached Golchika on the Enesei on 29 June 1914 and remained there for two months, observing and registering birds. Leaving their other two companions, they returned to a Britain at war, via Norway, on 9 October.

K291) Nicholas, Prince of Greece, *Political memoirs 1914-1917: pages from my diary.* London: Hutchinson & Co., 1928. 319pp.

In July 1914 Prince Nicholas (b. 1872) and his family travelled from Athens to pay their yearly visit to his mother-in-law Grand Duchess Vladimir and, two days before the declaration of war, reached Tsarskoe selo, where they met the tsar (pp. 18-22). In July 1916 he was sent to Russia on an unsuccessful mission from the Greek government to explain Greek neutrality in the war. He was received by the tsar at Mogilev, before he proceeded to Petrograd, where he had meetings with Russian ministers and foreign ambassadors. He left in October (pp. 133-80).

K292) Lethbridge, Alan Bourchier, *The new Russia: from the White Sea to the Siberian steppe.* London: Mills and Boon, 1915. xvi+314pp.

Lethbridge had been in Russia several times, including Siberia in 1907, before he resolved to undertake his northern journey in 1914, inspired by a reading of Kliuchevskii "to whet the appetite for a first-hand experience of that wonderful North that is so bound up with the creation of the modern Russian Empire". He and his wife Marjorie followed a route that took them from Archangel to Solovets and via Velikii Ustiug and Viatka to Perm and across the Urals to Ekaterinburg. They went as far as Tiumen and Omsk, before returning to Petrograd by train, but, because of the war, were obliged to return to England from Archangel.

K293) Lethbridge, Marjorie Colt and Lethbridge, Alan Bourchier, *The soul of the Russian.* London: John Lane, 1916. xii+238pp.

A collection of twenty-eight sketches, ten written by Marjorie (b. 1882), who also published semi-fictional tales under the title *Russian chaps* (1916), and eighteen by Alan, on a wide variety of subjects, historical, cultural, geographical, and social, appearing originally in London newspapers and journals in 1914-15.

K294) Merry, Walter Mansell, *Two months in Russia July-September, 1914.* Oxford: B.H. Blackwell, 1916. iv+202pp.

Invited to St Petersburg to be the temporary chaplain to the British community, Rev. Merry, vicar of St Michael's, Oxford, arrived in the Russian capital on 13 July 1914 and left with considerably more difficulty on 3 September for Sweden. Offers selections from his journal without additions other than the division into three parts: before the war; the beginning of the war, when he undertook a journey to Odessa in the vain hope of leaving via the Black Sea; and wartime Petrograd and ultimate departure (pp. 8-172).

K295) Scudder, Jared Waterbury, *Russia in the summer of 1914, with discussion of her pressing problems.* Boston: Richard G. Badger, 1920. 193pp.

> American theologian and missionary, best known for his Latin textbooks, Scudder (1863-1934) arrived at Cronstadt from Stockholm on 23 July 1914. After a few days of sightseeing in St Petersburg, he was in Moscow when war was declared, witnessed anti-German riots, and hurried back to the capital, eventually managing to leave for Finland on 11 August.

K296) Gaunt, Mary, *A broken journey; wanderings from the Hoang-Ho to the island of Saghalien and the upper reaches of the Amur River.* London: Werner Laurie, 1919. 295pp.

> Tourist travelling from China to Russia, partly via train, partly via steamer along the Amur River, found herself in the Russian far east in July 1914, just as war is declared. Describes her long, arduous return journey to St Petersburg and then the difficulty in getting from Russia to Finland (pp. 157-268).

K297) Paléologue, Maurice, *An ambassador's memoirs.* Translated from the French by F.A. Holt. London: Hutchinson & Co., 1924-25. 3 vols.

> France's last ambassador to imperial Russia, Paléologue (1859-1944) kept meticulous diaries of his four-year sojourn in St Petersburg, beginning with the entry for 20 July 1914, marking the visit of President Poincaré, and ending with 17 May 1917, when he was already in Finland.

K298) Kroeger, Theodor, *The forgotten village: four years in Siberia.* London: Hutchinson & Co., 1936. 320pp.

> Russian-born and educated, but a German national, Kroeger (1891-1958) recalls twenty years after the events his experiences as a POW during WWI. He had attempted to flee to Germany following the declaration of war in August 1914, but was arrested on suspicion of being a spy and sent first to Schlüsselberg, then to a camp near Baikal. Charges against him were dropped in March 1916, but he had married and continued to live in Siberia until his eventual departure for Germany after the death of his wife in late 1919.

K299) Fortescue, Granville Roland, *Russia, the Balkans and the Dardanelles.* London: Andrew Melrose, 1915. 285pp.

> Fortescue (1875-1952), American soldier and military attaché during the Russo-Japanese war, was the special correspondent of the *Daily Telegraph* with the Russian army in Poland in 1914-15, before illness forced him to leave for England. He considered "the campaigns I had witnessed there will rank among the greatest military events in history" and believed "the Russian infantryman one of the finest soldiers in the world" (pp. 15-139).

K300) Morse, John, *An Englishman in the Russian ranks.* London: Duckworth & Co., 1915. vi+337pp.

> When WWI began, Morse, an English businessman, was in Germany and to avoid internment he crossed over into Russian Poland on 2 August 1914. Intent on returning home, in the event he stayed and fought for nine months with the Russian army, until he was captured by the Germans. He was to escape and make his way to the Russian lines. He eventually reached Riga, which he left on 20 May 1915 for Sweden and England.

K301) Fraser, John Foster, *Russia of today.* London: Cassell and Co., 1915. viii+289pp.

> Fraser (see also K29, K88, K90, K161) had first visited Russia in 1896 and his 'Russia of today' was the Petrograd and Moscow with its "happy British colony" that he visited in 1914 at the beginning of WWI. He ends with guarded optimism for the changed Russia that will emerge after the war!

K302) West, Julius, *Soldiers of the tsar and other sketches and studies of the Russia of to-day.* London: The Iris Publishing Co., 1915. xvi+167pp.

> West (1891-1918), born in Russia but leaving when two months old with his journalist father Semen Rappoport, returned during the first months of WWI. He offers an attractive collection of sketches based on "long chats with Russians of all classes", alongside articles on Petrograd, Moscow and Warsaw in wartime, and on the vogue for translations from Russian literature (several of which – from Andreev and Chekhov – he himself made).

K303) Brändström, Elsa, *Among prisoners of war in Russia and Siberia.* Translated from the German by C. Mabel Rickmers. With a preface by Nathan Söderblom. London: Hutchinson & Co., 1929. 284pp.

Daughter of the Swedish ambassador to Russia and living in St Petersburg since 1908, Brändström (1888-1948) describes her activities and experiences as an official Swedish Red Cross delegate from winter 1914 until summer 1920, during which time she travelled to all the concentration centres for prisoners of war in European Russia and in Siberia as far as Vladivostok, her work bringing her in touch with an estimated 700,000 POWs. The German original was entitled *Unter Kriegsgefangenen in Rußland und Sibirien, 1914–1920* (Leipzig, 1927).

K304) Gibson, William J., *Wild career: my crowded years of adventure in Russia and the Near East.* London: George G. Harrap, 1935. 288pp.

Born in Canada, but brought up in St Petersburg, Gibson volunteered for the Russian army in the summer of 1914. He subsequently worked for the Russian secret service in Central Asia. He was in Petrograd, working as a newspaper correspondent, during the February Revolution and witnessed Lenin's arrival at the Finland Station. After a spell as a Soviet commissar, he eventually left Petrograd at the end of 1918 (pp. 1-200).

K305) Buchanan, Meriel, *Petrograd the city of trouble, 1914-1918.* [With a foreword by Hugh Walpole.] London: W. Collins & Sons, 1918. 262pp.

The first published of Meriel's books on Russia, it describes in detail her experiences of life in Petrograd from the declaration of war through to the rise and succession to power of the Bolsheviks.

K306) Bauermeister, Alexander ('Agricola'), *Spies break through: memoirs of a German secret service officer.* Translated [from the German] and introduced by Hector C. Bywater. London: Constable and Co., 1934. 185pp.

The leading German spymaster on the Eastern Front in WWI, Lt. Bauermeister (1899-1940), was born in St Petersburg, which he left in 1914 and was based in Königsberg, decoding Russian communiqués. He assumed a prominent role in the Russo-German armistice negotiations in November 1917.

K307) Dietrich, Johann, *Tovarish; the odyssey of a Siberian exile.* Narrated by Paul Cölestin Ettighoffer. Translated from the German by M.H. Jerome. London: Hutchinson & Co., 1935. 288pp.

The account of an escape from Siberia by the German telepathist and hypnotist Johann Dietrich (b. 1885), as told to the novelist Ettighoffer (1896-1975). Dietrich, in St Petersburg on business just as WWI began, sought to flee Russian territory, but was arrested at Orenburg and exiled in early

1915. In 1917 he escaped to Irkutsk, where he developed his telepathic skills, and left Russia via Vladivostok in the autumn.

K308) Arbenina, Stella, *Through terror to freedom: the dramatic story of an Englishwoman's life and adventures in Russia before, during & after the Revolution.* London: Hutchinson & Co., 1930. 288pp.

> Née Whishaw, member of a British family that had been in Russia since the eighteenth century, Stella (1885-1976) was the wife of Baron Pavel Meyendorf at the time of the October revolution. She relates in somewhat chaotic fashion her early life, her passion for acting, and her experiences during and after the revolution, before they escaped initially to Revel (pp. 9-273). It was in Berlin in 1921 that she assumed the stage name of Arbenina, which she retained in England, where she arrived in June 1923.

K309) Pares, Bernard, *Day by day with the Russian army, 1914-1915.* London: Constable & Co., 1915. xi+287pp.

> Pares (see K58, K59, K123, K124) left England in August 1914, spent six weeks in newly-named Petrograd, and begins his day-by-day account on 8 October from Vilna and ends on 19 June 1915, when he left the front. The book finishes with the diary of an Austrian officer serving in Galicia, March-May 1915 (pp. 261-82).

K310) Hanbury-Williams, John, *The Emperor Nicholas II as I knew him.* London: Arthur L. Humphreys, 1922. xii+271pp.

> Major-General Sir John (1859-1946) was chief of the British Military Mission in Russia between August 1914 and April 1917. He was attached to the G.H.Q. of the Russian armies at Mogilev and had a unique opportunity to observe and converse with the tsar. His book consists principally of diary entries, followed by sketches of the emperor, the tsarevich, Grand Duke Nikolai Nikolaevich and General Alekseev (pp. 217-64).

K311) Knox, Alfred William Fortescue, *With the Russian army 1914-1917, being chiefly extracts from the diary of a military attaché.* London: Hutchinson & Co., 1921. 2 vols.

> Military attaché at the Petersburg embassy from 1911 and a fluent Russian speaker, Major-General Sir Alfred (1870-1964), later a Conservative politician, was appointed liaison officer to the Russian army in 1914-17 and kept the detailed diaries which form the substance of these volumes, augmented by additional later comment and analysis. The first volume describes warfare on the eastern front, particularly in Poland, between

September 1914 and September 1915; the second continues with an account of the fighting during 1916, particularly the Brusilov Offensive. The later chapters describe Knox's observations of growing political unrest within the Russian army and an eye-witness account of the February Revolution, subsequent rapid decline of order within the army, the failed Kerenskii offensive and the October Revolution. He left Russia on 8 January 1918.

K312) Blair, Dorian, *Russian hazard: the adventures of a British secret agent in Russia.* Edited (?) by C.H. Dand. London: Robert Hale & Co., 1937. 288pp.

Allegedly born in St Petersburg c.1893 to Scoto-Russian parents, Blair returned to Russia in August 1914 to embark on a succession of increasingly implausible undercover adventures that involved burning the body of Rasputin, plotting to kidnap the tsar, and later, Trotskii and Lenin, at the instigation of Kerenskii. (pp. 13-147). The "scarlet pimpernel", as he styles himself, was captured by the Cheka on 31 December 1917, but survived to be involved in even more unlikely exploits before escaping to England in 1920.

K313) Washburn, Stanley, *Field notes from the Russian front.* London: Andrew Melrose, 1915. 291pp.

Washburn, who had covered the Russo-Japanese war (see K154), returned to Russia in 1914 as the special war correspondent of *The Times* with the Russian armies. The dispatches, which were largely published in *The Times* and American newspapers, begin with his report from Petrograd on 10 September 1914 and continue from the Polish front, from where his final report is datelined 15 January 1915. This became the first volume of a trilogy of dispatches (see K340, K363). The book is also notable for the photographs by the *Daily Mirror*'s George Mewes, the only "official" English photographer with the Russian armies.

K314) Britnieva, Mary, *One woman's story.* London: Arthur Barker, 1934. 287pp.

Born to Anglo-Russian parents in Russia, Mary (maiden name unknown) begins her "story" on 29 September 1914, the day she, a new Red Cross nurse, was to leave with her field hospital for the eastern front. She recounts her experiences in East Prussia, on the Warsaw front, and in Warsaw itself up to the beginning of the great retreat in July 1915. During a period of leave in April 1916 she visited her mother's estate at Chistopol in Kazan province (pp. 9-64). The rest of the book is devoted to her life from the beginning of 1918, when she married Aleksandr Britnev, the head doctor, her departure for England in 1922, her subsequent return visits, and final farewell in 1930.

K315) Walpole, Hugh, *Hugh Walpole: a biography.* By Rupert Hart-Davis. London: Macmillan & Co., 1952. xiv+503pp.

The prolific and once-popular novelist (1884-1941) arrived in Russia at the end of September 1914 as a correspondent for the *Daily Mail* and *Saturday Review*. He also found material and inspiration for his two Russia-centred novels *The dark forest* (1916) and *The secret city* (1919). He joined a Russian Red Cross unit in the Carpathians, before leaving for England in October 1915. He returned in February 1916 as head of a new British propaganda unit in Petrograd. He left finally for home on 8 November 1917, the morning after the start of the October Revolution. Excerpts from his journal and his letters, especially to Henry James (pp. 123-64). The text of the long memorandum on the February Revolution that he composed at the request of the British ambassador is on pp. 449-69.

K316) Marye, George Thomas, *Nearing the end in imperial Russia.* London: Selwyn & Blount, 1929. 479pp.

Lawyer and banker Marye (1849-1933) arrived in Petrograd on 24 October 1914 as the American ambassador to Russia. He remained until mid-March 1916. Although his title was obviously influenced by later events, Marye stresses that he was publishing his "notes and jottings" with their "first impressions of events" just as they were written.

K317) Thurstan, Violetta, *Field hospital and flying column, being the journal of an English nursing sister in Belgium & Russia.* London and New York: G.P. Putnam's Sons, 1915. viii+184pp.

Red Cross nurse Thurstan (1879-1978), after service in Belgium, volunteered for the Russian Red Cross. She left Copenhagen on 24 October 1914 for Petrograd via Lapland and Finland and was sent to Warsaw and the eastern front. Wounded by shrapnel and ill with pleurisy, she convalesced in Petrograd, where she finished her journal of an eventful 1914 (pp. 106-78).

K318) Roberts, Carl Eric Bechhofer, *Russia at the cross roads.* With an introduction by A.H. Murray. London: Kegan Paul, Trench, Trübner & Co, 1916. viii+201pp.

The work arose from a year-long stay in Russia from late 1914 by Roberts (1894-1949), styling himself at that period Bechhofer, and offers in ten chapters his thoughts on the Russian character and society, developments in literature and ideas, and musings on Russia's future.

K319) Roberts, Carl Eric Bechhofer, *A wanderer's log: being some memories of travel in India, the Far East, Russia, the Mediterranean & elsewhere.* London: Mills & Boon, 1922. 246pp.

In late 1914 Bechhofer, wanting to learn Russian, took a post as a tutor with a Ukrainian family, before leaving it to go to Kiev, and then to Batumi. Back in Petrograd, he recalls his visit to the literary cabaret, 'The Stray Dog', and his encounter with Rasputin (pp. 127-54). A further chapter describes his experiences with Denikin's army around Moscow in 1919 and a final trip to Moscow and around the Volga as a newspaper correspondent in the autumn of 1921, the subjects of subsequent books (pp. 155-82).

K320) Farson, Negley, *The way of a transgressor.* London: Victor Gollancz, 1935. 640pp.

In his lively autobiography, the American adventurer (1890-1960) recounts his first visit to Russia in the winter of 1914 to sell munitions to the Russian military authorities. He also visited Archangel, Moscow and the Crimea until illness forced him to return to America (pp. 126-226). He returned in 1916 to a Petrograd inexorably moving towards revolution and describes in detail events of "the Kerensky revolution" and its aftermath before he left to join the American air force (pp. 252-316). In 1928-29 he was in Soviet Russia with his wife for an extensive tour (pp. 542-81).

K321) Krist, Gustav, *Prisoner in the forbidden land.* Translated from the German by E[mily] O[verend] Lorimer. London: Faber & Faber, 1938. 344pp.

"Gurk" Krist (1894-1937), an Austrian POW, captured by the Russians on the eastern front in November 1914, describes his long years of captivity in Turkestan, first at Katta-Kurgan, near Samarkand, from which he escaped into Persia, but was re-captured and remained in camps into the Soviet period. He was finally repatriated in late 1921. German original entitled *Pascholl plenny!* (Vienna, 1936).

K322) Price, Morgan Philips, *War and revolution in Asiatic Russia.* London: Allen & Unwin, 1918. 296pp.

Price (see K219, K379-81) returned to Russia in November 1914 as special correspondent for the *Manchester Guardian*. Frustrated in his attempt to report from the eastern front, he made his way to the less controlled Caucasus, where he spent much of 1915 and all of 1916. His book, written in Tiflis and completed in Petrograd in 1916-17, provides an overview of the Caucasus campaign, followed by an account of Price's activities as journalist and relief worker in the region, and finishes with his analysis of Russian involvement in Central Asia and the impact of the February revolution.

K323) Cantacuzène, Julia, *My life here and there.* New York: Charles Scribner's Sons, 1921. 322pp.

> Princess Cantacuzène, née Grant, also styled Countess Speranskaia (1876-1975), the granddaughter of U.S. president Ulysses Grant, married the Russian diplomat Prince Mikhail Cantacuzène (Kantakuzen) in 1899 and moved to Russia, where she was to remain until 1917. In this, the last of her three books to be published, she recalls her first years in Russia.

K324) Cantacuzène, Julia, *Revolutionary days: recollections of Romanoffs and Bolsheviki 1914-1917.* London: Chapman & Hall, 1920. vi+411pp. [See *Revolutionary days, including passages from My life here and there 1876-1917.* Edited by Terence Emmons. Chicago: R.R. Donnelly & Sons, 1999. lx+442pp.]

> Princess Cantacuzène in the first of her three books to be published traces her family's fortunes from the beginning of WWI, in Petrograd, Kiev and the Crimea, to their escape to Finland in 1917.

K325) Cantacuzène, Julia, *Russian people: revolutionary recollections.* New York: Charles Scribner's Sons, 1920. 358pp.

> Chapters on Kolchak and Denikin as well as vignettes of Russian life, first published in the *Saturday Evening Post.*

K326) Urch, Reginald Oliver Gilling, *"We generally shoot Englishmen": an English schoolmaster's five years of mild adventure in Moscow (1915-1920).* London: Allen & Unwin, 1936. 300pp.

> "Five years in Russia of a rather ordinary English family not connected with any official missions, consulates, or services, but sharing the lot of average families then living in Russia." The Urches, husband, wife, and two children had apparently been for some time in Riga before being forced by war events to move to Moscow in the autumn of 1915. There Urch began to teach at the re-established Riga Polytechnic as lecturer in commerce and his wife established an English kindergarten until the Bolsheviks won the battle for Moscow (pp. 19-93). Thereafter it is a tale of Urch's vicissitudes under the Soviets, including imprisonment in the Butyrskii prison.

K327) Price, Hereward Thimbleby, *Boche and Bolshevik: experiences of an Englishman in the German army and in Russian prisons.* London: John Murray, 1919. viii+247pp.

> Son of a missionary, Madagascar-born, Oxford-educated, Price (1880-1964), later professor of English at University of Michigan, was drafted into the German army while lecturing at Bonn in 1915. Captured by the Russians on the eastern front, he was marched to a POW camp near Stretensk in Siberia. Released following the February Revolution, he moved to Irkutsk, working as a tutor in a Russian family until he escaped in 1918 with the help of the British consul (pp. 94-243). His book consists of a series of articles he contributed to the *China Illustrated Weekly* between November 1918 and February 1919.

K328) Fyfe, Henry Hamilton, *My seven selves.* London: George Allen & Unwin, 1935. 320pp.

> The renowned Scottish newspaper editor and war correspondent (1869-1951) was sent from the Western front to Russia in 1915, and was eventually allowed to the Galician front the following year. In August 1916 he was ordered to Bucharest, from where he returned in December, reaching Petrograd on the 30th, the day after the murder of Rasputin, which he was the first British journalist to report (pp. 191-202, 210-13). Many of his (censored) articles from Russia appeared in such publications as the *War Illustrated*, but, sadly, his war articles and "a vast quantity of matter that could not be printed" have never been collected.

K329) Pierce, Ruth, *Trapped in "Black Russia": letters June-November 1915.* Boston and New York: Houghton Mifflin Company, 1918. 150pp.

> A series of letters that the American traveller Mrs Pierce sent to her parents from Kiev, where she stayed between 30 June and early November 1915. For six weeks in August-September she was under house arrest for alleged espionage. She witnessed the transportation of Galician Jews through Kiev to Siberia, visited a Jewish detention camp, and recorded scenes in the city as the Germans approached after the fall of Warsaw.

K330) Cresson, William Penn, *The Cossacks: their history and country.* New York: Brentano's, 1919. x+239pp.

> One-time captain in the American Expeditionary Force and formerly secretary at the American embassy in Petrograd, Cresson (1873-1932) attempts to produce a "comprehensive study of Cossack life and history", based in part on his travels through Cossack regions between 1915 and 1917 (see particularly pp. 196-239).

K331) Pollock, John, *War and revolution in Russia: sketches and studies.* London: Constable & Co., 1918. xviii+280pp.

> Sir John (1878-1963), 4th Baronet of Haddon and a former Fellow of Trinity College, Cambridge, went to Poland in 1915 as a representative of the Great Britain to Poland Committee, set up to aid refugees during WWI. He subsequently became an International Commissioner with the Russian Red Cross. He was in Petrograd during both revolutions and visited Kiev, Saratov, Voronezh, and Ekaterinodar. He also acted as correspondent for the *Manchester Guardian* and other English newspapers and his book, completed in Russia in September 1917, largely comprises articles he sent to them.

K332) Pollock, John, *Time's chariot.* London: John Murray, 1950. xii+280pp.

> In his memoirs Sir John recalls succinctly (pp. 213-35) the four years he spent in Russia from March 1915 to May 1919, the "red" months of which he described in his *Bolshevik adventure* (1919).

K333) Sykes, Ella Constance, and Sykes, Percy, *Through deserts and oases of Central Asia.* London: Macmillan, 1920. xii+340pp.

> In March 1915 Miss Sykes (d. 1939) accompanied her brother, Brigadier-General Sir Percy (1867-1945), to Kashgar in Chinese Turkestan, where he was to deputise for the British consul-general. They were obliged to travel via Scandinavia to Petrograd and then they took the train to Tashkent and proceeded by carriage to their destination (pp. 7-35). They later set out on a tour to the Russian Pamirs and the "roof of the world", crossing into Russian territory on 18 June and returning in mid-July (pp. 129-47). Miss Sykes wrote all the initial chapters of travel and adventure which form part I; her brother contributed the (non-Russian) material on Chinese Turkestan in part II.

K334) Dwinger, Edwin Erich, *The army behind barbed wire: a Siberian diary.* Translated by Ian F. D. Morrow. London: George Allen & Unwin Ltd, 1930. 341pp.

> German soldier, nationalist, and prolific author Dwinger (1898-1981) relates experiences as POW in Siberia between 1915 and 1918 and his enduring relationships and friendships with fellow POWs. Taken prisoner at Windau in Latvia, Dwinger spent much of 1915 recuperating in a Moscow hospital, before being sent in 1916 to Siberia, imprisoned in various camps until his eventual release and departure from Russia in late 1918.

K335) Liddell, Robert Scotland, *On the Russian front.* London: Simpkin, Marshall, Hamilton, Kent, 1916. x+273pp.

> Liddell (b. 1885) arrived in Petrograd in the spring of 1915 and soon moved to Warsaw, where he served as a member of the Group of Polish Red Cross Volunteers with the Russian army. He also contributed articles to the *Sphere* as its special correspondent, writing "nearly every line to the accompaniment of guns". He describes the Russian retreat through Poland in May-August, evincing great admiration for the ordinary Russian soldier. Preface dated March 1916 "with the active Russian army".

K336) Liddell, Robert Scotland, *Actions and reactions in Russia.* London: Chapman and Hall, 1917. viii+227pp.

> "Russia to-day is not the Russia of two years ago. Russia has changed miraculously", Liddell wrote in his sequel to *On the Russian front*. He had in the interim been to Romania and to the Caucasian front and became, he claimed, the only British subject in command of a Russian army unit. His narrative ranges widely over Russia, from Odessa and the Crimea to Georgia and Minsk.

K337) Liddell, Robert Scotland, *"Sestra" (Sister): sketches from the Russian front.* London: Hodder and Stoughton, 1917. viii+244pp.

> The final contribution to an impressive trilogy. Fourteen sketches, several of which, including the title sketch, have as their heroines nurses who figured prominently in his earlier accounts.

K338) Steveni, William Barnes, *Petrograd past and present.* London: Grant Richards, 1915. viii+319pp.

> Steveni (see J111, K254, K266), who arrived as a boy of sixteen at the end of the reign of Alexander II and lived seven years in Cronstadt before moving to the capital, produced one of the best, if little-known, books on the Russian capital with a particular emphasis on British presence and influence and a happy mixture of history, anecdote, and personal observation.

K339) Templeton, Isabel Molison, *The old lady in room 2.* Bearsted, Kent: for the author, 1976. ii+184pp.

> Mrs Templeton, née Young (1886-1976) sailed out to Archangel in January 1915 to join her husband, a Scottish engineer working for the Maikop Pipeline & Transport Co. in Ekaterinodar in the Kuban, where they were to live until April 1917, when worsening conditions forced them to leave,

although her husband was subsequently detained in Russia until May 1918 (pp. 1-9, 47-97).

K340) Washburn, Stanley, *The Russian campaign. April to August, 1915, being the second volume of "Field notes from the Russian front."* London: Andrew Melrose, 1916. 348pp.

> Washburn (see K154, K313, K362) details fighting between the Russian and Austro-German armies in the early summer of 1915 and the decline in Russian fortunes. The dispatches alternate between the Warsaw and Galician fronts and include chapters on Eugene Hurd (an American doctor working for the Russian Red Cross), the German gas attacks, meetings with the Russian generals Ivanov and Brusilov.

K341) Kohn, Hans, *Living in a world revolution: my encounters with history.* New York: Simon and Schuster, 1964. xxii+211pp.

> The Czech Jewish philosopher and historian (1891-1971) recalls the years he spent as a POW in Russia during and after WWI. Taken prisoner on 21 March 1915 during the Carpathian campaign, he was to remain in Russia until 12 January 1920. Initially marched off to Lemberg, he was then sent to a camp in Samarkand, from which he escaped in February 1916. Recaptured a month later, he was moved to camps in Siberia, where he learnt Russian and came to admire his captors, before being freed in 1918 and starting his slow exit from Russia (pp. 88-99).

K342) McCormick, Robert Rutherford, *With the Russian army, being the experiences of a national guardsman.* London: Macmillan, 1915. xvi+306pp.

> Son of a former ambassador to Russia and a major in the First Cavalry of the Illinois National Guards, McCormick (1880-1955) arrived in Petrograd in April 1915 as foreign correspondent of *Chicago Tribune*, interviewing the tsar and foreign minister Sazonov, before leaving for Warsaw and the eastern front.

K343) Balch, Emily G., *Women at The Hague: the International Congress of Women and its results. By three delegates to the Congress from the United States [Jane Addams, Emily G. Balch, Alice Hamilton].* New York: Macmillan Co., 1915. 171pp.

> Wellesley professor Balch (1867-1961) was a member of a delegation from the Congress assigned to Scandinavia and Russia. She arrived in Petrograd

on 10 June 1915, interviewing during her two-week stay the Minister of Foreign Affairs Sazonov (pp. 103-04).

K344) Simpson, James Young, *The self-discovery of Russia.* London: Constable and Company, 1916. viii+227pp.

Young, who had first visited Russia in 1896 (K27) and was by now professor of natural science at his *alma mater* Edinburgh, offers his views on a number of topics, including the prohibition of vodka, conditions on the Galician front, and religion, based on his observations and conversations with Russians in the summer of 1915.

K345) Coxwell, Charles Fillingham, *Through Russia in war-time.* London: T.F. Unwin, 1917. 311pp.

Thwarted by the sinking of the *Lusitania* from sailing from New York to London, Coxwell (b. 1856) was redirected to Archangel in June 1915 and decided to seize the opportunity to tour Russia, visiting many towns and provinces in the south west Russia over the following eleven weeks. Returning to Petrograd in mid-August 1915, Coxwell, in later years a prolific translator from Russian literature, made an excursion into Lapland on his journey back to England.

K346) [Stopford, Albert Henry], *The Russian diary of an Englishman: Petrograd, 1915-1917.* London: William Heinemann, 1919. xiv+228pp.

A member of the Irish aristocracy, Stopford had previously visited Petrograd in March 1914, but his book, comprising extracts from his diary and letters, covers the period from 18 July 1915 to 26 September 1917. His exact role and the nature of his "affairs" are unclear, although he was uncommonly well connected with the Russian elite, including the emperor, but particularly with the Grand Duchess Vladimir, and with the British embassy. He returned briefly to England in October 1916, but he travelled fairly extensively in Russia, visiting Mogilev, Moscow, the Crimea, and the Caucasus.

K347) Grow, Malcolm Cummings, *Surgeon Grow: an American in the Russian fighting.* New York: Frederick A. Stokes Co., 1918. xvi+304pp.

Grow (1887-1960) was a lieutenant-colonel in the Imperial Russian Army Medical Corps during WWI and finished his career as the first surgeon-general of the U.S. air force. Arriving in Petrograd in September 1915, he was soon sent to the front. In his book he describes his activities at the front during two periods: September 1915 to Easter 1916 and June 1916 to March 1917. He met the tsar at a staff dinner and he was awarded the cross of St George. He was in Petrograd in mid-1917, noting the increasing poverty and unrest, and left Russia after the October revolution to join the American army.

K348) Thurstan, Violetta, *The people who run, being the tragedy of the refugees in Russia.* London and New York: G. P. Putnam's Sons, 1916. x+175p.

In her second book Thurstan (see K317) describes the demographics, conditions, and first-hand experiences of Polish, Baltic, Rumanian, and Russian refugees fleeing the eastern front during the summer and autumn of 1915. Arriving in Petrograd from Newcastle in December 1915, she spent Christmas with refugee children in Gatchina and Petrograd before travelling to Moscow. She went on to Kiev and Kazan to observe, and report in glowing terms, the government response to the refugee problem.

K349) Gorer, Geoffrey, and Rickman, John, *The people of Great Russia: a psychological study.* London: Cresset Press, 1949. iv+236pp.

An attempt to understand the people of Russia in terms of their "principal motives" and "typical behaviour". It is Rickman, a country doctor with the Friends' War Victims Relief Unit between 1916 and 1918, who provided the on-the-spot experience of life in Russian villages in his 'Russian Camera Obscura. Ten Sketches of Russian Peasant Life (1916-1918)' (pp. 23-89).

K350) Bury, Herbert, *Here and there in the war area.* London: A.R. Mowbray & Co., 1916. xii+325pp.

Bishop Bury (see K252) paid "a particularly inspiring visit to Russia" in the first months of 1916, arriving from Scandinavia. He was mainly in St Petersburg and in Moscow, travelling there with Sir George Buchanan, who was to receive the freedom of the city, and everywhere records Russian enthusiasm for Britain (pp. 238-325). Bury was later to make and describe visits to Soviet Russia in the 1920s in his *Russia from within* (1927).

K351) Hoare, Samuel John Gurney, *The fourth seal: the end of a Russian chapter.* London: William Heinemann, 1930. iii+377pp.

Sir Samuel, Viscount Templeton (1880-1959), having learnt Russian, was sent to Petrograd by British intelligence in March 1916 to work with the Russian general staff. He eventually became head of the British military mission and remained, together with his wife Lady Maud Lygon, in Russia until March 1917 when his services were required in Rome. Interesting pen-portraits of many prominent Russian and British figures in the Russian capital (pp. 34-359).

K352) Graham, Stephen, *Russia in 1916.* London: Cassell & Co., 1917. vii+179pp.

Graham's last book on pre-Revolutionary Russia is essentially a series of essays, reflecting his journey to Ekaterina and Archangel and on to Moscow, followed by travels into central Russia down as far as the Caucasus and return to England in October 1916 via Petrograd. A reprise of his old themes, offered as "my little book of the hour" to keep in touch with our allies.

K353) Francis, David Rowland, *Russia from the American embassy, April, 1916 – November, 1918.* New York: Charles Scribner, 1922. xiii+349pp.

Appointed American ambassador to Russia by President Woodrow Wilson, the democrat politician Francis (1850-1927) was in Petrograd throughout the revolutionary period and provides a chronological account of events, based on his letters, diary, and official papers.

K354) Francis, David Rowland, *Dollars and diplomacy: ambassador David Rowland Francis and the fall of tsarism, 1916-1917.* Edited by Jamie H. Cockfield. Durham, N.C.: Duke University Press, 1981. x+149pp.

Eighty-one of Francis's letters to friends and family from April 1916 to March 1917. See also the microfilmed *Russia in transition: the diplomatic papers of David. R. Francis, U.S. ambassador to Russia, 1916-1918.* Edited by Robert Chadwell Williams and Robert Lester. Frederick, Maryland: University Publications of America, 1986.

K355) Ruhl, Arthur, *White nights and other Russian impressions: With illustrations from photographs.* New York: Charles Scribner's Sons, 1917. x+248pp.

American journalist and travel writer (b. 1876) spent the summer of 1916 in Russia, visiting Petrograd and Kiev, then the front near Minsk, before travelling down the Volga to Astrakhan. An interesting chapter is devoted to his attending a performance of Chekhov's *Three Sisters* at the Moscow Art Theatre that gave him insight into the Russian character.

K356) Barber, Margaret H., *A British nurse in Bolshevik Russia.* London: A.C. Fifield, 1920. 64pp.

Daughter of an Anglican clergyman, Barber came to Russia as a Red Cross nurse during WWI and lived and worked in hospitals in a number of Russian cities from Petrograd to Astrakhan between April 1916 and December 1919.

K357) Power, Rhoda, *Under Cossack and Bolshevik.* London: Methuen & Co., 1919. iv+279pp.

Power (1890-1957), later known as a broadcaster and children's author, sailed from Newcastle for Petrograd via Scandinavia in 1916 to work as governess to the daughter of a Russian businessman in Rostov-on-Don. She describes life there and a trip in autumn 1917 to Odessa, where hostile attitudes towards her employers induced them to flee, leaving Rhoda behind. She witnessed fighting between the Red Guards and Cossack forces, the subsequent Cossack victory and life under their rule during the winter of 1917-18, the following Bolshevik victory in the spring of 1918, and their subsequent retreat in the face of advancing White Army. Power finally flees to Murmansk and leaves for England on a refugee boat.

K358) Child, Richard Washburn, *Potential Russia.* London: T. Fisher Unwin, 1916. vi+221pp.

Massachusetts lawyer and journalist, later U.S. ambassador to Italy and apologist of fascism, Child (1881-1935) was sent to Russia early in 1916 by *Collier's Weekly*, in which and in other journals he first published many of the sketches gathered together for his book. He sought to assess the effect of the war on the Russian people and the economy and he ended by calling for greater American investment in "an empire of contradictions" but of great potential.

K359) Beable, William Henry, *Commercial Russia.* London: Constable, 1918. 263pp.

Beable organized and led the Anglo-Russian Trade Commission, visiting Russia between April and October 1916 and during the spring of 1917. He travelled widely throughout western Russia, seeking to demonstrate the potential opportunities available to English manufacturers in Russia.

K360) Stanford Doreen, *Sun and snow: a Siberian adventure.* London: Longmans, 1963. 158pp.

In May 1916 the twenty-year-old Doreen left England to join her parents in Siberia, where her father, a mining engineer, had worked for the previous eight years. Met in Petrograd by her parents, she travelled with them by train to Krasnoiarsk, by steamer along the Enisei, then by *tarantas* to their final destination of Ulen and its copper mine. A year later, they were forced to move and her father found employment until June 1919 at a gold mine in Olkhovskii beyond Minusinsk. They were eventually able to escape from Vladivostok in May 1920.

K361) Heald, Edward Thornton, *Witness to revolution: letters from Russia 1916-1919.* Edited by James B. Gidney. Kent, Ohio: Kent State University Press, 1972. xx+367pp.

Informal family letters and diary entries written by Heald (1885-1967), who arrived in Petrograd in late September 1916 as field secretary of the American YMCA for its prisoner of war relief programme. He remained in Petrograd until July 1917, when he was assigned to the Russian army in Minsk, which the German advance forced him to leave for Kiev in September. He witnessed the February revolution in Petrograd and the October in Kiev, where he described the battles between Ukrainian nationalists and Bolsheviks for control of the city. He was in Siberia during the first few months of the Russian Civil War and was in Vladivostok when the American Expeditionary Force landed.

K362) Washburn, Stanley, *The Russian offensive. Being the third volume of "Field notes from the Russian front," embracing the period from June 15 to September 1, 1916.* London: Constable, 1917. 193pp.

In his final volume (see K313, K340) Washburn covers the successful Russian offensive that culminated in the taking of the town of Brody during the summer of 1916.

K363) Boleslavski, Richard, and Woodward, Helen, *Way of the Lancer.* Indianapolis: Bobbs-Merrill, 1932. 316pp.

Autobiographical account of Boleslavski's (1887-1937) experience fighting with a Polish volunteer lancer regiment within the Russian army. The account describes his experiences of life on the eastern front from autumn 1916 onwards, and charts the breakdown of discipline within the Russian army following the February Revolution. Following Nicholas II's abdication, Boleslavski's regiment withdraws from the Russian army and attempts to make its way back to Poland.

K364) Inglis, Elsie Maud, *Dr Elsie Inglis*. By Lady Frances Balfour: London: Hodder and Stoughton, 1918. x+253pp.

> The famed Scottish suffragette and doctor (1864-1917), after serving in Serbia during the first years of WWI, left with her seventy-six-strong nursing unit of the Scottish Women's Hospitals for Russia in September 1916. From Archangel they travelled via Moscow south to Odessa, where they were to remain until the following October. They left Archangel on the return journey on 18 November 1917; but Dr Inglis died on 27 November, the day after the ship reached Newcastle. Letters to her family and friends (pp. 197-233).

K365) Inglis, Elsie Maud, *Between the lines: letters and diaries from Elsie Inglis's Russian unit*. Arranged and edited by Audrey Fawcett Cahill. Edinburgh: Pentland Press, 1999. x+372pp.

> The "choral narrative" the editor promised in her earlier book.

K366) Fawcett, Margaret, *The First World War papers of Margaret Fawcett: letters and diaries from Russia and Roumania 1916-1917.* Edited and with an introduction by Audrey Fawcett Cahill. Pietermaritzburg: Wyllie Desktop Publishing, 1993. viii+144pp.

> The specific Russian element in the two diaries and a letter-book of Margaret Fawcett (b. 1892), an orderly in Dr Inglis's unit, is the initial journey from Archangel to Odessa in September 1916 and the return journey a year later (pp. 28-32, 38-40, 52-55, 62-67, 78-80, 104-08, 121-22).

K367) Colquhoun, James, *Adventures in red Russia from the Black Sea to the White Sea.* London: John Murray, 1926. viii+193pp. [Printed for private circulation.]

> Chairman of the Caucasus Copper Company and with previous visits to Russia, the Scottish engineer (b. c.1858) arrived in Petrograd on 13 October 1916 en route for Tiflis. His final destination was Borchka near the Turkish border, where he was to supervise the reconstruction of the metallurgical plant, damaged by Turkish forces. He was subsequently caught up in the revolutionary events of 1917 and continuing incursions by the Turks. He eventually made his escape through Georgia and reached Tsaritsyn, whence he went by steamer to Nizhnii Novgorod. He made his way to Murmansk and sailed for England on 16 June 1918.

K368) Austin, Walter, *A war zone gadabout: being an authentic account of four trips to the fighting nations during 1914, '15, '16.* Boston: R.H. Hinkley Co., 1917. 161pp.

> A "mere gadabout tourist" and correspondent for the Massachusetts weekly *Dedham Transcript,* Austin arrived in Petrograd on 11 November 1916, leaving three weeks later on 1 December after a round trip to Moscow. He attended a meeting of the Duma and heard Sturmer and Miliukov speak (pp. 112-54).

K369) Dosch-Fleurot, Arno Walter, *Through war to revolution, being the experiences of a newspaper correspondent in war and revolution, 1914-1920.* London: John Lane, 1931. xii+242pp.

> Dosch-Fleurot (1879-1951), correspondent of the New York *World,* was sent from the western front to Petrograd in November 1916 and was soon caught up by the revolutionary events of 1917. He was to remain until the end of 1918, when he escaped via Finland (pp. 97-215).

K370) Harper, Florence MacLeod, *Runaway Russia.* New York: Century Co., 1918. ix+321pp.

> Harper left Vancouver in December 1916 to spend nine months in Russia as staff war correspondent of *Leslie's Weekly,* reaching Petrograd via the Trans-Siberian from Kharbin. Working with the magazine's photographer Donald Thompson (see K372), she was witness to the street violence during the February Revolution. In April she travelled to the eastern front to work as a surgical nurse at a Red Cross field hospital. Back in the capital in June 1917, she met members of the Women's Battalion of Death and visited Cronstadt, before departing for Finland in early September.

K371) Thompson, Donald C., *Donald Thompson in Russia.* New York: Century Co., 1918. xix+353pp.

> American photographer Donald Thompson (b. 1895), who had previously been in Russia in March-May 1915, returned to work with Florence Harper for *Leslie's Weekly,* arriving via the Trans-Siberian in Petrograd on 17 February 1917. In a series of letters to his wife and in photographs, he captured the events through the spring and summer of 1917 not only in the capital but also at the Galician front and in Moscow, before leaving in August 1917 via the Manchurian border.

K372) Thompson, Donald C. and Harper, Florence Macleod, *From Czar to Kaiser: the betrayal of Russia.* Garden City, New York: Doubleday, Page & Co., 1918. viii+200pp.

> The work is a collection of extraordinary photographs taken by Thompson and arranged thematically: before the revolution, during the February revolution in Petrograd, the May parades and labour riots in Petrograd, hospital conditions on the eastern front, the women's battalion, the July riots in Petrograd, from the front line and riots by the Bolsheviks during the autumn. Harper provides brief descriptions of each photograph.

K373) Petersson, C.E.W., *How to do business with Russia: hints and advice to business men dealing with Russia.* With notes and additional chapters by W. Barnes Steveni and a foreword by Charles E. Musgrave. London: Sir Isaac Pitman & Sons., 1917. xviii+202pp.

> Designed as a sort of businessman's *Baedeker* to encourage trade with Russia and written by an experienced merchant operating in Riga and St Petersburg, it fell foul of revolutionary events immediately on publication. The preface by the secretary of the London chamber of commerce is dated February 1917 and the preface written by long-standing Petersburg resident Steveni is dated April 1917, acknowledging that the February revolution would modify "mostly for the best" conditions – but October rendered it an historical document with fascinating information about what was.

K374) Souiny-Seydlitz, Leonie Ida Philipovna, *Russia of yesterday and to-morrow.* New York: The Century Co., 1917. 382pp.

> Following her marriage to Baron Seidlits, the Czech-born author (b. 1865) moved to Russia, where she lived for many years until emigrating to the USA in 1914. The most interesting chapters in her attempt to give a wide-reaching survey are her comparison of Russia and America (pp. 220-55) and 'Russian art, dramatic literature and music', where she discusses, among other topics, the Moscow Arts Theatre and Stanislaslavskii (pp. 256-85). Published in June 1917, the book finishes with guarded optimism after the events of February.

K375) Wilson, Henry Hughes, *Field-Marshall Sir Henry Wilson: his life and diaries.* By Major-General Sir C.E. Callwell. With a preface by Marshal Foch. London: Cassell and Co., 1927. 2 vols.

> Wilson (1864-1922), director of British military operations since 1910, after visiting Paris and Berlin, paid a brief first visit to St Petersburg, Moscow,

and Kiev in September 1912 (vol. I, p. 117). In January 1917 he headed the joint allied mission to Russia (a party of some fifty British, French and Italian representatives) that sailed on the *Kildonan Castle* for the White Sea. He arrived in Petrograd on 29 January, proceeded to the front at Pskov on 8 February, and journeyed on to Moscow via Riga and Minsk. After further talks in Petrograd, he sailed from Russia on 25 February (vol. I, pp. 312-22).

K376) De Windt, Harry, *Russia as I know it.* London: Chapman and Hall, 1917. xii+232pp.

De Windt's final summing-up of his experiences of Russia, where he covered some 50,000 miles and spent some four years between 1887 and the time of writing (preface dated April 1917). Includes more on European Russia than previously (including Petrograd, which he disliked) but also covers Finland, Ukraine, the Crimea, the Caucasus, Siberia and central Asia. (See J53 for full listing of other entries.)

K377) Hall, Bert, *One man's war: the story of the Lafayette escadrille.* Edited by John Jacob Niles. London: John Hamilton, 1829. 352pp.

Hall, a "seasoned Soldier of Fortune", was a member of an American volunteer squadron within the French air service that arrived in Russia on 12 January 1917 to aid the Russian air service. He witnessed the major events of the revolutions before escaping via the Trans-Siberian to China at the end of the year (pp. 226-76).

K378) Houghteling, James Lawrence, Jr., *A diary of the Russian revolution.* New York: Dodd, Mead & Co., 1918. xxii+195pp.

Houghteling (1883-1937), an attaché in the American embassy in Petrograd from 19 January 1917, provides a diary of events leading up to and during the February revolution in the capital and in Moscow. He left Petrograd for Siberia on 3 April.

K379) Price, Morgan Philips, *My reminiscences of the Russian revolution.* London: George Allen & Unwin, 1921. 402pp.

Price's third book (see K219, K322, K380-81) was dedicated to those in Britain who, like himself, "defended the Soviet republic of Russia against the onslaughts of the international bondholders". He offers "a consecutive account", relying on his own experiences and diaries for the first one and a half years of the revolution and devoting only the last two chapters to developments in the period after he left Russia in 1919.

K380) Price, Morgan Philips, *My three revolutions.* London: George Allen & Unwin, 1969. 310pp.

> The three revolutions were the Russian, the German, and the British, and of these the Russian had a major impact "in the most critical period of my life" and "greatly influenced my critical thinking for a time". Writing in his eighties, Price reviews all his visits to Russia between 1908 and 1917 (pp. 21-94).

K381) Price, Morgan Philips, *Dispatches from the revolution: Russia 1916-18.* Edited by Tania Rose. Foreword by Eric Hobsbawn. London: Pluto Press, 1997. xiv+181pp.

> A skilfully edited "selection of Price's unpublished memoranda, letters to his family, and some of his published articles [from the *Manchester Guardian*] with a bearing on the revolutions which reflect not only the events as they unfolded but also his own reactions to them" represents a significant addition to Price's four other published books on Russia. The letters and articles were written from Tiflis, Kutais, Rostov-on-Don, Samara, Petrograd, and Moscow (pp. 18-154).

K382) Brennan, Hugh, *Sidelights on Russia.* London: David Nutt, 1918. 112pp.

> Lecturer in Russian at the University of Glasgow, Brennan refers to an earlier visit to the south of Russia c.1908. It is, however, the events of 1917 (pre-October), when he was in Petrograd, that are the centre of attention as he assesses the British – and British colony's – position in the light of revolutionary events, stressing the need to study the language and seize business opportunities in the context of persisting hopes for the emergence of "a new, great, and democratic Russia".

K383) Jones, Stinton, *Russia in revolution, being the experiences of an Englishman in Petrograd during the upheaval.* London: Herbert Jenkins, 1917. xvi+279pp.

> The British engineer arrived in Moscow for the first time in November 1905, but remained for twelve years, married a Russian, travelled extensively throughout Russia, and viewed the February revolution from his office on Nevskii Prospect and on the streets. He provides a graphic account of the five days from 10 to 14 March.

K384) Pollock, John, *The Bolshevik adventure.* London: Constable & Co., 1919. 276pp.

> The second instalment of Pollock's adventures in Russia (see K331, K332), here specifically the period of the February and October revolutions and ending with his escape.

K385) Rivet, Charles, *The last of the Romanovs.* Translated, with an introduction by Hardress O'Grady. London: Constable and Company, 1918. 246pp.

> Rivet (b. 1881), who had been in Russia since 1901, firstly as a university teacher and then as Petrograd correspondent of the Paris *Le Temps,* provides a sympathetic analysis of the February revolution, presented in three parts 'Unknown Russia', 'The Revolution' and 'France and Germany'.

K386) Maugham, William Somerset, *A writer's notebook.* London: William Heinemann, 1949. xvi+349pp.

> Maugham (1874-1965) was in Petrograd between the February and October revolutions, operating as a British "secret agent", such as he was later mockingly to portray in his novel *Ashenden* (1928). Under the heading '1917' his notebook contains his jottings on Russian literature and Dostoevskii in particular, on the Russian character and such personalities as Kerenskii and Savinkov, and on Nevskii Prospekt and the Alexander Nevskii lavra (pp. 139-79).

K387) De Robien, Louis, *The diary of a diplomat in Russia, 1917-1918.* Translated from the French by Camilla Sykes. London: Michael Joseph, 1969. 319pp.

> Comte Louis (1888-1958) was attached to the French embassy in St Petersburg from 1914 but it was only at the beginning of March 1917 that he began to record daily events in the capital. His diary is a fascinating and opinionated record of events and personalities not only in the capital but also, from March 1918, in Helsingfors and Vologda, to where the embassy was relocated, and from Archangel, whence he and his wife left in December 1919 for Paris.

K388) Anet, Claude [pseudonym of Schopher, Jean], *Through the Russian revolution: notes of an eye-witness, from 12th March-30th May.* London: Hutchinson, 1917. 253pp. illus.

Schopher (see K141) returned to Russia as the correspondent of the *Petit Parisien* and sent off to Paris vivid daily accounts of the events he witnessed in Petrograd over a twelve-week period, beginning in fact on 7 March 1917. This is a translation of the first of the four volumes of the French original, covering a longer period.

Bibliography of Bibliographies

Adelung, Friedrich von, *Kritisch-literärische Übersicht der Reisenden in Russland bis 1700, deren Berichte bekannt sind*. St Petersburg: Eggers, 1846. 2 vols.

Babey, Anna Maria, *Americans in Russia, 1776-1917: a study of the American travelers in Russia from the American Revolution to the Russian Revolution*. New York: The Comet Press, 1938.

Beard, Michael, 'European travelers in the Trans-Caspian before 1917', *Cahiers du monde russe et soviétique*, vol. XIII (1972), pp. 590-96.

Bibliothèque impériale publique de St.-Pétersbourg, *Catalogue de la section des Russica ou écrits sur la Russie en langues étrangères*. St Petersburg, 1873; reprint: Amsterdam: P. Schippers, 1964. 2 vols.

Cliff, David, *A Crimean War bibliography in two parts*. N.p: Crimean Research Society, n.d.

Cox, Edward Godfrey, *A reference guide to the literature of travel, including voyages, geographical descriptions, adventures, shipwrecks and expeditions*. Seattle: University of Washington, 1935. Vol. I 'The old world'.

Crowther, Peter A., *A bibliography of works in English on early Russian history to 1800*. Oxford: Basil Blackwell, 1969.

Egan, David R. and Egan, Melinda A., *Russian autocrats from Ivan the Great to the fall of the Romanov dynasty: an annotated bibliography of English language sources to 1985*. Metuchen, N.J. & London: The Scarecrow Press, 1987.

Howego, Raymond John, *Encyclopedia of exploration to 1800*. Potts Point, Aus: Hardern House, 2003.

Iakovleva, I.G., *Dorevoliutsionnye izdaniia po istorii SSSR v inostrannom fonde GPB: sistematicheskii ukazatel'*. Leningrad: State Public Library, 1986.

Nerhood, Harry, *To Russia and return: an annotated bibliography of travelers' English-language accounts of Russia from the ninth century to the present*. Columbus, Ohio: Ohio State University Press, 1968.

Poe, Marshall, *Foreign descriptions of Muscovy: an analytic bibliography of primary and secondary sources*. Columbus, Ohio: Slavica Publishers, 1965.

Smele, Jonathan D., *The Russian Revolution and Civil War 1917-1921: an annotated bibliography*. London: Continuum International Publishing Group, 2002.

Smith, Harold Frederick, *American travelers abroad: bibliography of accounts published before 1900*. Carbondale: South Illinois University Press, 1969.

Speake, Jennifer (ed.), *Literature of travel and exploration: an encyclopedia*. New York & London: Fitzroy Dearborn, 2003. 3 vols.

Waddington, Patrick, *A bibliography of English-language books and pamphlets relating to Russia and things Russian, printed in the United Kingdom in the nineteenth century (1801-1900)*. Upper Hutt, N.Z.: Whirinaki Press, 2001.

Index of Authors

68th Light Infantry, H78
Abbott, James, G69
Abercromby, John, J81
Adams, Henry, K86, K87
Adams, John Quincy, F24
Addams, Jane, K26
Adye, John Miller, H12, H13
Aflalo, Frederick George, K197
Ainslie, Ainslie Douglas, I138
Alcock, Thomas, G11
Aldrich, Herbert Lincoln, J71
Alexander, James Edward, G14, H126
Algarotti, Francesco, C15
Allan, William, H14
Allen, Henry Tureman, J107
Allen, Thomas Gaskell, Jr., J106
Allen, William, F79
Allison, Thomas, B8
Aloysius, Mary, H138
Ambler, James Markham, J7
Anderson, Fortescue Lennox Macdonald, I45
Anderson, Herbert Foster, K285
Anderson, Robert, I35
Andrews, Mottram, H15
Anet, Claude [pseudonym]; see Schopher, Jean
Anon., A11, A12, B12, G38, H11, H16, H79, H118, H133, H142
Appleton, Nathan, I65
Arbenina, Stella, K308
Armstrong, T.B., G12
Atkinson, John Augustus, F1
Atkinson, Joseph Beavington, I91
Atkinson, Lucy, G108
Atkinson, Thomas Witlam, G106, G107

Austin, Herbert Henry, K192
Austin, Walter, K368
Avril, Philippe, B1

B., Harry, H17
Baddeley, John Frederick, I170
Baddeley, Welbore St Clair, J48
Baedeker, Friedrich Wilhelm, I143
Baedeker, Karl, K271
Baker, Valentine, I114
Balch, Emily G., K343
Ballou, Maturin Murray, J55, J56
Barber, Margaret H., K356
Baring, Maurice, K79, K134, K146, K174, K175, K231, K274
Barker, William Burckhardt, H2
Barnes, Demas, J60
Barnston, Roger, H18
Barnston, William, H18
Barrett, R. J., K165
Barrow, John, jr., G24
Barrows, Isabel Chapin, K167
Barry, D., G30
Barry, Herbert, I87, I88
Bartlett, Robert A., K279, K280
Barzini, Luigi, K166
Bates, Lindon Wallace, jr., K194
Bateson, William, J47
Bauermeister, Alexander ('Agricola'), K306
Bax, Arnold, K208
Bax, Bonham Ward, I96
Bayard, James Asheton, F51
Bayne, Samuel Gamble, K173
Bazancourt, César Lecat, H107
Beable, William Henry, K359

Beauplan, Guillaume Le Vasseur, de, A3
Beddoe, John, H137
Beeby-Thompson, Arthur, K57
Beechey, Frederick William, G2
Bell, George, H19
Bell, James Stanislaus, G48
Bell, John, B23, C10, C16
Bellows, John, J122
Benn, Edith Annie Fraser Parker, K74
Benson, Jane, F71, F72
Bentham, Jeremy, D35, D36
Bentham, Samuel, D35, D36, F10
Benyovszky, Móricz, D21
Bering, Vitus, B24
Berlioz, Louis-Hector, G100
Beveridge, Albert Jeremiah, K78
Biddulph, Cuthbert Edward, J103, J104
Biddulph, Michael, H109
Bieberstein, Friedrich August, D34
Bigelow, Poultney, J119, J120
Bigham, Clive, K16
Birkbeck, William John, J82
Birrell, Charles Mitchell, G31
Birse, Arthur Herbert, J94
Blackstock, Emma Moulton Frazer, J83
Blackwood, Alicia, I8
Blair, Dorian, K312
Bleckenburg, Rudolph, J116
Bloomfield, Benjamin, F105
Bloomfield, Georgiana, G98
Boddy, Alexander Alfred, J108
Boker, George Henry, I131
Boleslavski, Richard, K363
Bonaparte, Napoleon, F31
Bookwalter, John Wesley, K51
Borrow, George Henry, G33
Bostock, John Aston, H20
Bouillane de Lacoste, E.A. Henri de, K159
Boultbee, Rosamond, K287
Boulton, Samuel Bagster, I126
Bourgogne, Adrien-Jean-Baptiste-François, F39
Bourke, Richard Southwell, G96
Bourne, Charlotte, G97
Bouton, John Bell, J50
Bowring, John, F81
Brackenbury, George, H88
Brand, Adam, B7
Brandes, Georg Morris Cohen, J66

Brändström, Elsa, K303
Brehm, Alfred Edmund, I134
Bremner, Robert, G47
Brennan, Hugh, K382
Britnieva, Mary, K314
Brooke, Arthur de Capell, F88
Brooke, Leopold Guy Francis Maynard Greville, K135
Brooks, Charles William Shirley, G127
Brooks, Phillips, I109
Brown, Elizabeth, J72
Brown, John Croumbie, J20, J21, J22
Brown, Thomas, E1
Browne, John Ross, I36
Browning, Oscar, K191
Bruce, Henry James, K263, K264
Bruce, Peter Henry, B19
Bruyn, Cornelis de, B13, B22
Bryan, William Jennings, K120
Bryce, James, I137, K270
Buchanan, George, H128, H85, K225
Buchanan, James, G32
Buchanan, Meriel, K226, K227, K228, K229, K230, K305
Buckham, George, I110
Buckinghamshire, Hobart, John, Earl of, D4
Buckley, James Monroe, J34
Buel, James William, J19
Bullard, Arthur, K152
Bunbury, Selina, I11
Burgoyne, John Fox, H105, H21
Burnaby, E.S., H100
Burnaby, Frederick Gustavus, I132, I142
Burrows, Silas Enoch, G101
Burton, Reginald George, J124
Bury, Herbert, K252, K350
Bush, Richard J., I58
Bushby, Henry Jeffreys, H83
Butler, David, A10
Butler-Johnstone, Henry Alexander Munro, I123
Butterfield, Daniel Adams, J131
Buzzard, Thomas, H121
Byford, Charles Thomas, K275

C., T., B2
Calina, Josephine, K184
Calthorpe, Somerset John Gough, H22

Calvert, Frederick, D20
Cameron, George Poulett, G67
Campbell, Archibald, F21
Campbell, Colin Frederick, H92
Campenhausen, Leyon Pierce Balthasar, F12
Cantacuzène, Julia, K323, K324, K325
Cardigan, James Thomas Brudenell, Earl of, H23
Carr, James, G121
Carr, John, F6
Carrington, George, I104
Carroll, Lewis [pseudonym]; see Dodgson, Charles Lutwidge
Cary, Clarence, K95
Casanova di Seingalt, Giacomo Girolamo, D10
Cathcart, Charles, D13, D14
Cathcart, George, F47
Cathcart, Jane, D13
Caulaincourt, Armand-Augustin-Louis de, F23
Cavanagh, Eleanor, F3
Chancel, A.D., B14
Channing, Walter, G119
Chantreau, Pierre Nicholas, D58
Chappe d'Auteroche, Jean-Baptiste, C27
Chardin, John, A15
Charleton, Robert Mason, G129, G131
Child, Richard Washburn, K358
Child, Theodore, J17
Chodasiewicz, Robert Adolf, H24
Choiseul-Gouffier, Sophie, de, F28
Choules, John Overton, G126
Christie, Isabella (Ella) Robertson, K215
Christie, James, I160
Christie, Peter, H123
Clairmont, Claire, F93, F94
Clark, Francis Edward, K70, K71
Clarke, Edward Daniel, E4, E5
Clay, Cassius Marcellus, I39
Clay, John Randolph, G23
Clayton, John William, H129
Clemens, Samuel Langhorne, I71
Cler, Jean Joseph Gustave, H25
Clifford, Henry, H26
Close, Etta, K189
Cobbold, Ralph Patteson, K46
Cobden, Richard, G105

Cochrane, John Dundas, F82
Cockerell, Sydney Carlyle, K110
Cockin, J.G., J141
Codman, John, H89
Codrington, William, H115
Coggeshall, George, F26
Coghlan, Francis, G37
Coignet, Jean-Roch, F38
Colbeck, Alfred, J68
Colebrooke, Thomas Edward, H27
Collins, Perry McDonough, I15
Collins, Samuel, A6
Collyer, Charles B.D., K267
Colmore, Lionel, D63
Colquhoun, Archibald Ross, K47
Colquhoun, James, K367
Conolly, Arthur, G17
Cook, Charles, J95
Cook, John, C9
Coston, Martha Jay, I75
Cottrell, Charles Herbert, G73
Cox, Samuel S., J1
Coxe, William, C12, D28, D29, D30
Coxwell, Charles Fillingham, K345
Craig-McKerrow, Margaret, K188
Craven, Elizabeth, D48
Crawford, Laura MacPherson, K212
Creagh, James, H95, I74
Creighton, Mandell, K22
Cresson, William Penn, K330
Cripps, Frederick Heyworth, K249
Crosby, Ernest Howard, J139
Cumberland, C.S., J92
Cunynghame, Arthur Augustus Thurlow, I95
Curtin, Jeremiah, I51, K66
Curtis, William Eleroy, J69, K220, K221
Curzon, George Nathaniel, J86
Cushman, Mary Ames, I174
Custine, Astolphe-Louis-Léonard, de, G66
Cutting, Charles F., J73
Czaplicka, Marya Antonina, K284

D'Avigdor, Elim Henry, I179
D'Éon, Charles-Geneviève-Louis-Auguste-André-Tomothée, C24
D'Wolf, John, F16
Daily News, I149

Dallas, George Frederick, H28
Dallas, George Mifflin, G54
Damas d'Antigney, Joseph Elizabeth Roger, D54
Dana, Charles A., K33
Danenhower, John Wilson, J6
Davis, Elizabeth, H111
Davis, Richard Harding, K24
Davis, Sarah Matilda Henry, J49
Davis, William Morris, K109
Dawe, Rosamond E., K282
De Déchy, Maurice, J141
De Long, George Washington, J4
De Robien, Louis, K387
De Ros, William Lennox Lascelles Fitzgerald, G40
De Windt, Harry, J53, J54, J98, J129, J134, J135, K92, K162, K376
Deane, John (d. 1699), B9
Deane, John (d. 1761), B21
Decle, Lionel, K156
Demidoff, Anatole de, G55
Demidov, Elim Pavlovich, K9, K31, K69
Dicey, Edward James Stephen, I66
Dickens, Melchior Guy, C22, C23
Dickinson, Duncan, K269
Dickinson, Page Lawrence, K199
Dietrich, Johann, K307
Digby, George Bassett, K236, K237
Dillon, Emile Joseph, I157, J89, K5
Dimsdale, Elizabeth, D40
Dimsdale, Thomas, D17
Disbrowe, Anne, F104
Disbrowe, Edward Cromwell, F104
Ditson, George Leighton, G109
Dixon, William Hepworth, I89
Dobell, Peter, F30
Dobson, George, J79, K217, K338
Dodgson, Charles Lutwidge, I72
Donner, Kai (Karl) Reinhold, K235
Dosch-Fleurot, Arno Walter, K369
Douglas, John, H56
Douglas, William, H120
Du Boulay, John Houssemayne, G57
Duberly, Frances Isabella, H29
Dufferin and Ava, Frederick Temple Hamilton-Temple-Blackwood, 1st Marquis of, I164
Dufferin and Ava, Hariot, I165

Dukes, Paul, K203
Dumas, Alexandre Davy de la Pailleterie, I26, I27
Dundas, James, H5
Dunmore, Charles Adolphus Murray, 7th Earl of, J123
Dunscombe, Nicholas, H96
Durham, John George Lambton, Earl of, G39
Durland, Kellogg, K157
Dwinger, Edwin Erich, K334

Eagar, M., K60
Eastlake, Elizabeth, G63, G64
Eckardt, Julius Wilhelm Albert von, I1
Eddy, Sherwood, K213
Edgar, William Crowell, J115
Edwards, Henry Sutherland, I34, I162
Edwards, William Seymour, K97
Elliot, Gilbert, D38
Elliott, Charles Boileau, G25, G58
Ellis, George, D47
Elton, John, C19
Ely, Jane, Marchioness of, I83
Emin, Joseph, C28
English Factor, A11
Erman, Georg Adolph, G4
Etherton, Percy Thomas, K206
Evelyn, George Palmer, H30
Everett, Alexander Hill, F25
Ewart, John Alexander, H31
Eyre, Selwyn, I136

Fannan, David, H32
Farmborough, Florence, K185, K186
Farquharson, Robert Stuart, H33
Farson, Negley, K320
Faughnan, Thomas, H101
Fawcett, Margaret, K366
Fell, Edward Nelson, K105
Fell, Marian, K105
Fezensac, Raimond-Emery-Philipp-Josephe de Montesquiou, de, F37
Finch, Edward, C16, C17
Fischer, Emil Sigmund, K169
Fisher-Rowe, Edward Rowe, H84
Flint, Josiah Frederick, K42
Forbes, Archibald, I152
Forbes, George, C5

Forse, Edward John George, K255
Forster, George, D41
Forsyth, William, I53
Fortescue, Granville Roland, K299
Foster, John Watson, I180
Foulke, William Dudley, K170, K176
Fox Maule, 2nd Baron Panmure, H115
Francis, David Rowland, K353, K354
François, Charles, F42
Frankland, Charles Colville, G26
Fraser, David, K160
Fraser, Eugenie, K251
Fraser, John Foster, K29, K88, K90, K161, K301
Frederic, Harold, J109
Freshfield, Douglas William, I80, J142
Freygang, Frederika von, F27
Freygang, Wilhelm von, F27
Fries, Hans Jakob, D24
Frossard, Émilien, H117
Fyfe, Henry Hamilton, K328

Gadsby, John, I18
Gallatin, James, F50
Gallenga, Antonio Carlo Napoleone, J10
Galt, Edwin, I4
Ganz, Hugo Markus, K117
Garnett, Constance, J125
Garnett, David, K121
Garstin, Denis, K218
Gaunt, Mary, K296
Gaussen, William Frederick Armytage, J62
Gautier, Théophile, I28
'Gentleman of Germany', B12
Gerbillon, Jean François, B3
Gerhardi(e), Walter, K164
Gerrare, Wirt [pseudonym]; see Greener, William Oliver
Gibbes, Charles Sydney, K190
Gibson, William J., K304
Gilbert, George, D33
Gilchrist, Paul, D3
Gilder, William Henry, J9
Gilliard, Pierre, K131
Gillis, Charles J., K32
Gilmour, James, I100
Glen, William, F86
Godfrey, W.H.K., I125

Godman, Richard Temple, H80
Goldsmid, Frederic John, I57
Goodlake, Gerald Littlehales, H34
Goodman, Margaret, H108
Goodrich, Joseph King, K209
Gordon, Charles George, H103
Gordon, Patrick, A7, A8
Gordon, Peter, F73
Gordon, Samuel, K17
Gorer, Geoffrey, K349
Gourdon, William, A1
Gowing, Lionel Francis, J64
Gowing, Timothy, H35
Grafton, Charles Chapman, K112a
Graham, Gerald, H36
Graham, Stephen, K193, K232, K233, K234, K247, K248, K276, K277, K288, K289, K352
Grant Duff, Mountstuart Elphinstone, I50
Granville, Augustus Bozzi, G5, G6
Graves, Samuel Roberts, I44
Green, George, F14
Greene, Francis Vinton, I150, I151
Greener, William Oliver, K85, K136
Greig, David, H122
Grellet du Mabillier, Etienne de, F78
Grenfell, Francis Wallace, K20, K21
Grey, Theresa Georgina, I85
Grove, Florence Crauford, I124
Grove, Henry Montgomery, K246
Groves, Anthony Norris, G16
Grow, Malcolm Cummings, K347
Guild, Curtis, J57
Guillemard, Francis Henry Hill, J15
Guillemard, Robert, F41
Gunning, Robert, D23
Guthrie, Katherine Blanche, I113
Guthrie, Maria, D70
Guys, Constantin, H37

Habersham, Alexander Wylly, I2
Haight, Sarah, G28
Halen, Juan van, F84
Hall, Bert, K377
Hall, Jasper, H130
Hall, John, H38
Hamilton, Frederic, I167, I168, I169
Hamley, Edward Bruce, H39, H40

Hammond, John Hays, K55
Hanbury-Williams, Charles, C25, C26
Hanbury-Williams, John, K310
Hanway, Jonas, C19
Hapgood, Isabel Florence, J67, J105
Hare, Augustus John Cuthbert, J33
Harper, Florence MacLeod, K370, K372
Harper, Samuel Northrup, K119
Harris, James, D27
Harris, Walter Burton, K2
Harrison, Carter Henry, J80
Harrison, Ernest John, K204
Harrison, Jane Ellen, J61
Harrison, Joseph, Jr., G88
Harrison, Robert, G94
Harvey, Annie J., I84
Harvey, Thomas W., I77
Harvie-Brown, John Alexander, I99
Haviland, Maud Doria, K290
Hawes, Charles Henry, K84
Hawkins (Hawkins-Whitsted), James, D62
Hawley, Robert Beaufoy, H104
Haxthausen-Abbenburg, August Franz Ludwig Maria, von, G83, G84, G85
Hayes, Matthew Horace, K36
Heald, Edward Thornton, K361
Heath, Leopold George, H9
Heath, Perry Sanford, J70
Heber, Reginald, F11
Hedin, Sven Anders von, J43, J44, J133, K151
Henderson, Ebenezer, F62, F63, F64
Henderson, Nevile Meyrick, K153
Henniker, John, D26
Henningsen, Charles Frederick, G90, G91
Henry, James Dodds, K137
Herbert, Agnes, K238
Herbert, Frederick William von, I153
Héritte-Viardot, Louise, I67
Hertz, Carl, K210
Heywood, Robert, I22
Higginson, George Wentworth Alexander, H41
Hill, Elizabeth, K67
Hill, Samuel Smith, G104, G125
Hoare, Samuel John Gurney, K351
Hodge, Edward Cooper, H42

Hodgetts, Edward Arthur Brayley, I79, J113, K6
Hoffman, Wickham, I144
Holder, H.W., J141
Holderness, Mary, F59, F60
Holland, Henry, G27
Holman, James, F89
Holmes, Burton, K77
Home, Anthony Dickson, H43
Hommaire de Hell, Adèle, G81
Hommaire de Hell, Xavier, G81
Hone, Joseph Maunsell, K199
Honeyman, Abraham Van Doren, K37
Hooper, William Hulme, G110
Hoover, Herbert, K200
Houghteling, James Lawrence, Jr., K378
Howard, Benjamin Douglas, J90, J91
Howard, John, D39, D61
Hubback, John, K198
Hume, George, I17
Hunt, William Henry, J27
Hunter, William, E7
Huntington, Ellsworth, K109
Huntly, Charles Gordon, 11th Marquis of, J11
Hutchinson, William, F95
Hyde, Catherine, Marquise de Govion Broglio Solari, E2
Hyndford, John Carmichael, Earl of, C20, C21, C22

Ides, Evert Ysbrants, B6
Image, John George, H44
Ingham, Ernest Graham, K201
Inglis, Elsie Maud, K364, K365
Ireland, John Busteed, G116

Jackson, Abraham Valentine Williams, K168
Jackson, Frederick George, J127
James, John Thomas, F54, F55
Jefferson, Robert Louis, K7, K30, K48
Jefferyes, James, B20
Jervis, Thomas Best, H64
Jervis-Waldy, William Thomas, H97
Jesse, William, G68
Jocelyn, John Strange, H45
Johnson, John, F75
Johnson, William Eugene, K262

Johnston, Robert, F56
Jones, George Matthew, F91
Jones, John Paul, D55
Jones, Stinton, K383
Joubert, Carl, K13, K122, K138
Jowett, William, H46
Justice, Elizabeth, C8

Keeling, H.V., K278
Keith, Robert Murray, D1
Keller, Otto, K272
Kelly, Richard Denis, H106
Kelsall, Charles, F20
Kemp, Emily Georgiana, K207
Kendig, John A.J., I176
Kennan, George, I59, I93, J36
Kennard, Howard Percy, K130
Kennedy, John Pendleton, I81
Kennedy, R.J., I164
Kenworthy, John Coleman, K11, K68
Keppel, George Thomas, F97, F98
Ker, David, I108
Kerr, John, K40
Keyserling, Alexander von, G70
King, John Glen, D5, D8, D9
Kinglake, Alexander William, G95
Klaproth, Julius Heinrich von, F22
Knill, Richard, F87
Knox, Alfred William Fortescue, K311
Knox, Thomas Wallace, I63, I112
Koch, Karl Heinrich Emil, G92
Köhl, Johann Georg, G75, G76, G77
Kohn, Hans, K341
Kolbe, Eduard, F53
Korb, Johann Georg, B11
Kotzebue, August Friedrich Ferdinand von, E6
Krausdorf, Joseph, J116
Krist, Gustav, K321
Kroeger, Theodor, K298
Kynnersley, Mary, D68

La Martinière, Pierre Martin de, A13, A14
La Motraye, Aubry de, B18, B25
La Neuville, Foy de, B4, B5
La Pérouse, Jean-François de Galaup, de, D51, D52
Labaume, Eugène, F33

Lake, Henry Atwell, H141
Lamont, James, I82
Landor, Arnold Henry Savage, K82
Lange, Lauren, B22
Lanin, E.B. [pseudonym]; see Dillon, Emile Joseph
Lansdell, Henry, I171, J14, J75
Latimer, Robert Sloan, K205
Latrobe, John Hazelhurst, I21
Laurie, Peter George, H119
Laurie, William Ferguson Beatson, I38
Lawson, George, H47
Layard, Austen Henry, G61, G62
Le Blond, Elizabeth, K257
Le Brun, Cornelius; see Bruyn, Cornelis de
Ledyard, John, D32, D56
Lee, Helena Crumett, K250
Lee, Robert, F106
Lefevre, George William, G10
Leland, Lilian, J38
Lent, William Bement, J118
Leroy-Beaulieu, Pierre Paul, K54
Lesseps, Jean-Baptiste-Barthélemy, de, D53
Lethbridge, Alan Bourchier, K292, K293
Lethbridge, Marjorie Colt, K293
Leveson Gower, Granville, D65
Levings, Grace M., K286
Liddell, Robert Scotland, K335, K336, K337
Liddon, Henry Parry, I73
Lied, Jonas, K223, K224
Ligne, Charles Joseph, de, D37
Little, Anna P., J24
Lluellyn, Richard, H94
Locatelli Lanzi, Francesco, C6
Loch, Emily, K45
Lockhart, Robert Hamilton Bruce, K242, K243, K244
Loew, Charles E., K196
Logan, John Alexander, Jr., K19
Londonderry, Charles William Stewart, G46
Londonderry, Frances Anne Emily, G45
Long, James, I139
Longworth, John Augustus, G65
Lothrop, Almira, J39
Loubat, Joseph Florimond, I64
Lowth, George T., I70

Loyd-Lindsay, Robert James, H48
Ludolf, Heinrich Wilhelm, B7
Lumsden, Thomas, F85
Lyall, Robert, F61, F90
Lydekker, Richard, K172
Lynch, George, K96
Lynch, Henry Finnis Blosse, J132
Lyons, Amelia, G115
Lysons, Daniel, H49
Lyttelton, Sarah Spencer, F52

Macartney, George, D5, D6, D7
McCagg, Ezra Butler, J30
McCaig, Archibald, K216
McConaughy, David, Jr., J85
McCormick, Frederick, K127
McCormick, Robert Rutherford, K342
McCosh, John, I156
McCoy, Rebecca, G86
McCullagh, Francis, K126
McCully, Newton Alexander, K128
MacGahan, Januarius Aloysius, I115
MacGavock, Randal William, G120
MacGill, Thomas, F9
McKenzie, Frederick Arthur, K129
Mackenzie, George, B20
Macmichael, William, F69
McMillan, William, H50
Macormick (MacCormick), Richard Cunningham, Jr., H98
McPherson, Duncan, I6
Macpherson, Georgina E., J2
Macpherson, R.B., I154
Mahony, James, I7
Malcolm, Ian Zachary, K18
Manstein, Cristof Hermann, C1
Marbot, Jean-Baptiste-Antoine-Marcelin, de, F34
Marsden, Kate, J102
Marshall, Joseph, D18
Marvin, Charles, J26
Marye, George Thomas, K316
Mason, Abbie Ranlett, K37
Masson, Charles-François-Philibert, D45
Maud, Renée Elton, K117a
Maude, Aylmer, J87, K25
Maugham, William Somerset, K386
Mavor, Sam, K28

Maxwell, John S, G103
Meakin, Annette M.B., K73, K83, K125
Mears, John Henry, K267
Meignan, Victor, I120
Mela Britannicus [pseudonym]; see Kelsall, Charles
Melville, George Wallace, J5
Mends, William Roberts, H51
Meriwether, Lee, J46
Merry, Walter Mansell, K294
Meyer, George von Lengerke, K140
Michell, Thomas, I56, J51
Michie, Alexander, I47
Miège, Guy, A9
Mignan, Robert, G20
Miles, Nelson Appleton, K38, K41, K100
Miranda, Sebastián Francisco, de, D46
Mitchell, Albert, H52
Mitford, Algernon, 1st Baron Redesdale, I48
Moltke, Helmut Karl Bernhard, I13
Money, A., H131
Money, Edward, H135
Money, George Henry, H131
Montagu, Victor Alexander, H3, H4
Montefiore, Moses Haim, G99, I106
Montgomery, James Eglinton, I76
Montieth, William, G15
Moor, Henry, I43
Moore, Benjamin Burges, K281
Moore, John, F100
Morgan, Christopher A., K80
Morgan, Henry Arthur, I37
Morgan, Wilma, K91
Morris, Isabel, J97
Morse, John, K300
Morton, Edward, G9
Morton, Rosalie Slaughter, K63
Motley, John Lothrop, G79
Mounsey, August Henry, I62
Müller, J.B., B22
Müller, Max, K64
Muir, Hal Moncreiff, K3
Muir, John, J8
Mummery, Alfred Frederick, J84
Munro, William, H53
Murchison, Roderick Impey, G70
Murphy, John, I12

Murray, Eustace Clare Grenville, H143, I92
Murray, Robert H., K177

Nansen, Fridtjof Wedel-Jarlsberg, K268
Napier, Charles, H5, H6
Nasir al-Din Shah, I116, I161
Nasmyth, James, G89
Neave, Joseph James, J121
Nevinson, Henry Woodd, K149, K150
Newcomb, Raymond Lee, J3
Newman, George, H90
Newton, William Wilberforce, J93
Nicholas, Prince of Greece, K291
Niedieck, Paul, K158
Niemcewicz, Julian Ursyn, D69
Nightingale, Florence, H124
Ninde, Mary Louise, J35
Noble, Algernon, K139
Noble, Edmund, J16
Nolan, Louis Edward, H54
Nolte, Vincent, G72
Nordenskiöld, Adolf Erik, I159
Norman, Henry, J96, K76
Nostitz-Azabal, Madeleine, K179

O'Brien, Augustin P., I46
O'Donovan, Edmond, I166
O'Flaherty, Philip, H55, H91
O'Malley, James, H99
Oakes, Richard, D23
Olearius, Adam, A4
Oliphant, Laurence, G122, G123, G124, H139, H140
Olufsen, Axel Frits Olaf Henrik, K14, K15
Onslow, Richard William Alan, K116
'Oriental Widow', J141
Ossendowski, Ferdynand Antoni, K61, K62
Otter-Barry, Robert Bruère, K240
Oudendyk, William J., K56
Overton, Kathleen (Toni), K104

Pack, Arthur John Reynell, H109
Paget, George Augustus Frederick, H56
Paléologue, Maurice, K297
Pallas, Peter Simon, D11, D12, D67
Palmer, Ellen, H102

Palmer, Francis H. E., K12
Palmer, Frederick, K89
Palmer, William, G71
Pares, Bernard, K58, K59, K123, K124, K309
Parkinson, John, D66
Parrot, Jacob Friedrich Wilhelm, G13
Paterson, John, F49, F62
Patterson, John Edward, K10
Paul of Aleppo, A5
Paul, Robert Bateman, G42
Peard, George Shuldham, H57
Peard, George, G3
Pearson, Charles Henry, I23, I24
Pearson, Henry John., K8, K65
Pease, Henry, G131
Peel, Agnes Helen, J130
Pemberton, E. St. C., J98
Pennell, Joseph, J110, J111
Pennington, William Henry, H58
Pepys, Charlotte Maria, I29
Percy, Henry Hugh Manvers, H59
Perowne, John Thomas Woolrych, K43
Perris, George Herbert, K4
Perry, John, B10
Perry-Ayscough, Henry George Charles, K240
Petersson, C.E.W., K373
Pfeiffer, Ida Laura, G111
Phelps, Charles Harris, I117
Phelps, William Lyon, K239
Phibbs, Isabelle Mary, K44
Phillipps-Wolley, Clive, I133, J13
Pierce, Ruth, K329
Pinkerton, Robert, F65, F66
Polhill(-Turner), Arthur Twistleton, K98
Pollington, John Horace Savile, I61
Pollock, John, K331, K332, K384
Ponafidine, Emma Cochran, J40
Porter, Robert Ker, F13, F76
Porter, Whitworth, H110
Powell, Harry, H60
Power, Rhoda, K357
Pray, Eleanor Lord, J138
Preston, Thomas, K155
Price, Hereward Thimbleby, K327
Price, Julius Mendes, J101
Price, Morgan Philips, K219, K322, K379, K380, K381

Prime, Samuel Irenaeus, I103
Prince, Nancy Gardner, F99
Prior, James, F58
Proctor, Edna Dean, I97
Pulling, John, I3
Pumpelly, Raphael Welles, K109
Pumpelly, Raphael, I55, K109

Rae, Edward, I127, I128, I178
Raglan, Fitzroy James Henry Somerset, Lord, H115
Raikes, Thomas, G21
Ramble, Rayford, F80
Randolph, John, G22
Ransome, Arthur, K256
Raum, George Edward, J29
Rawlins, James, H61
Ready, Oliver George, K115
Reed, Edward James, I130
Reeves, Francis Brewster, J116
Reichard, Heinrich August Ottokar, F83
Reid, Arnot, K53
Reid, Douglas Arthur, H112
Reinbeck, Georg, F8
Reineggs, Jacob, D34
Rennie, John, G18
Renshaw, Charles Jeremiah, K39
Reuilly, Jean, F4
Revere, Joseph Warren, G35
Reynolds, Rothay, K182, K183
Reynoso, Francisco de, J37
Richard, John, D19
Richardson, David N., J59
Richardson, William, D15
Richardson-Gardner, Robert, I98
Rickman, John, D31, K350
Ridley, James Cartmell, K35
Rigby, Elizabeth; see Eastlake, Elizabeth
Ritchie, Leitch, G36
Rivet, Charles, K385
Roberts, Carl Eric Bechhofer, K318, K319
Roberts, James Hudson, K72
Robinson, Frederick, H62
Robinson, Thomas Philip, Baron Grantham, F2
Robson, Isaac, I77
Rochechouart, Louis Victor Léon, F5
Roeder, Franz, F36
Romaine, William Govett, H8

Ronaldshay, Dundas, Lawrence John Lumley, Earl of,, K106, K107
Rondeau, Claudius, C2, C5, C10
Roth, Henry Ling, I140, I141
Royer, Alfred, H1
Royston, Philip Yorke, F17
Ruhl, Arthur, K355
Rulhière, Claude Carolman de, D2
Russell, William Howard, H63
Russell, William, G30
Russell-Cotes, Annie Nelson, K52

Sachtleben, William Lewis, J106
Sala, George Augustus Henry, I10
Salvo, Carlo, marchese di, F15
Samuel, Jacob, G52
Sara, Muriel, K202
Sarolea, Charles Louis-Camille, K142, K143
Sauer, Martin, D44
Sayer, Frederick, H64
Scheutze, William Henry, J12
Schnitzler, Jean Henri, F103
Schopher, Jean, K141, K388
Schuyler, Eugene, I78, I109
Scott, A. MacCallum, K181
Scott, Charles Henry, G114
Scudder, Jared Waterbury, K295
Seacole, Mary, H116
Seebohm, Henry, I129, I145
Ségur, Louis-Philippe, de, D43
Ségur, Philippe-Paul, de, F32
Selfridge, Thomas Oliver, Jr., I173
Senn, Nicholas, K81
Sessions, Francis Charles, J31
Seume, Johann Gottfried, F7
Seymour, Henry Danby, G93
Shaft, Arthur, K241
Shaw-Lefevre, George, H144
Sheepshanks, John, I68, I69
Shelley, Gerard, K259, K260
Shillitoe, Thomas, F101
Shirley, Henry, D14
Shoemaker, Michael Myers, J136, K94, K99
Sievrac, John Henry, F9
Simpson, Bertram Lenox, K114, K163
Simpson, Eugene E., K222
Simpson, George, G80

Simpson, James Young, K27, K344
Simpson, James, H115
Simpson, William, H87, H88
Sinclair, John, D49, D50
Skene, James Henry, H134
Slade, Adolphus, G19, G60
Smith, George Loy, H65
Smith, Mary Ann Pellew, G113
Smith, William Adams, H145
Smyth, Charles Piazzi, I30
Souiny-Seydlitz, Leonie Ida Philipovna, K374
Soyer, Alexis, H125
Spathary, Nikolai Gavrilovich, A16
Spencer, Edmund, G43, G44, G117
Spilman, James, C11
Spottiswoode, Robert Collinson D'Esterre, J45
Spottiswoode, William, I14
Spring-Rice, Cecil Arthur, K113
St John, Ferdinand, G59
St John, Frederick Robert, I54
Stadling, Jonas Jonsson, J114, K50
Staël-Holstein, Germaine, de, F29
Stanford, Doreen, K360
Stanley, Arthur Penrhyn, I19, I20
Stanley, Augusta Elizabeth Frederica, I118
Stanley, Francis, I155
Stead, William Thomas, J78
Steevens, Nathaniel, H66
Steller, Georg Wilhelm, C12, C13, C14
Stephens, John Lloyd, G41
Stephens, W., G74
Stephenson, Frederick Charles Arthur, H67
Sterling, Anthony Coningham, H68
Steveni, James William Barnes, J112, K254, K266, K338
Stevens, Thomas, J58, J99
Stewart, Houston, H115
Stewart, Hugh, K261
Stocqueler, Joachim Hayward, G29
Stoddard, Charles Augustus, J100
Stoddard, John Lawson, I177
Stone, Melville Elijah, J88
Stopford, Albert Henry, K346
Storch, Heinrich Friedrich von, D64
Story, Douglas, K112, K133

Stothert, Samuel Kelson, H10
Strahlenberg, Philipp Johann von, B17
Struys, Jan Janszoon, A10
Sturge, Joseph, G130, G131
Sulivan, Bartholomew James, H7
Sullivan, Edward Robert, H114
Sutherland-Leveson-Gower, Ronald Charles, I172
Swaine, Leopold Victor, I163
Swayne, Harold George Carlos, K108
Swenson, Olaf, K93
Swinton, Andrew, D59
Sykes, Arthur Alkin, K23
Sykes, Ella Constance, K333
Sykes, Percy, K333
Symons, Arthur William, K34

Taft, Alphonso, J32
Taft, Marcus Lorenzo, K195
Taitbout de Marigny, Edouard, F77
Talmage, Thomas De Witt, J117
Taylor, George Cavendish, H86
Taylor, James Bayard, I25, I40, I41
Taylor, Marie Hansen, I42
Telfer, John Buchan, I119, J51
Templeton, Isabel Molison, K339
Thielmann, Max Guido von, I107
Thomas, Joseph B., Jr., K111
Thompson, Donald C., K371, K372
Thompson, Edward Pett, G102
Thomson, William, D60
Thornbury, George Walter, I33
Thurstan, Violetta, K317, K348
Thwing, Charles Franklin, K75
Tietz, Friedrich von, G34
Tilley, Henry Arthur, I31, I32
Todd, Charles Stewart, G78
Tooke, William, D71
Tóth, Ferenc, D16
Tott, François; see Tóth, Ferenc
Tracey, Margot, K180
Tradescant, John, A2
Train, George Francis, I9, I16
Trevenen, James, D57
Trevor-Battye, Aubyn Bernard Rochfort, J137, J140
Tronson, John M., H127
Turner, Samuel, K102, K103

Turnerelli, Edward Tracy, G49, G50, G51
Twain, Mark [pseudonym]; see Clement, Samuel Langhorne
Tweddell, John, E3
Tyrawly, James O'Hara, Baron, C20

Ular, Alexander, K147
Upton, Emory, I135
Urch, Reginald Oliver Gilling, K326
Ussher, John, I52
Uxkull, Boris von, F44

Vanderlip, Washington Baker, K49
Vassar, John Guy, Jr., G112
Vaudoncourt, Frédéric-François-Guillaume, de, F35
Vay de Vaya and Luskod, Peter, K101
Vecchi, Joseph, K265
Venables, Richard Lister, G53
Venning, John, F67
Venning, Walter, F68
Verneuil, Edouard de, G70
'Viator' [pseudonym], K1
Vieth, Frederick Harris Dawes, H132
Vigor, Jane, C3, C4
Villari, Luigi, K118, K144
Vitzhum von Eckstädt, Karl Friedrich, G118
Vogüé, Marie Eugène Melchior de, J17, J18
Vossler, Heinrich August, F43

Waddington, Mary King, J23
Wagner, Moritz, G82
Walker, Bettina, J63
Walker, Charles Pyndar Beauchamp, H69
Walker, James, D42, F1
Wallace, Donald Mackenzie, I90
Walling, William English, K148
Walpole, Horatio, F57
Walpole, Hugh, K315
Walsh, Robert, G1
Walter, Jakob, F40
'Wanderer' [pseudonym]; see D'Avigdor, Elim Henry
Ward, Thomas, C2
Wardell, John Wilford, K283

Wardrop, John Oliver, J74
Washburn, Stanley, K154, K313, K340, K362
Washington, Booker Taliaferro, K211
Wassenaer, Marie Cornélie de, F102
Waters, Wallscourt Hely-Hutchinson, J76, J77
Waxell, Sven, C7
Weale, Bertram Lenox Putnam [pseudonym]; see Simpson, Bertram Lenox
Weber, Friedrich Christian, B22
Webster, James, G7
Weisbrod, Ludwig Christoph, B15
Wellesley, Edward, H70
Wellesley, Frederick Arthur, I101, I102
Wells, Sarah Furnas, I111, J28
Welzl, Jan, J128
Wenyon, Charles, J126
Werry, Francis Peter, F48
West, Algernon Edward, H100
West, Julius, K302
Westminster, Elizabeth Mary Leveson Gower, Marchioness of, G8
Whatley, Thomas Denman, G62
Wheeler, Daniel, F70
Wheeler, William Webb, K258
Whelan, James, H71
Whishaw, Frederick James (Fred), I147, I148
Whishaw, James, I146
Whistler, Anna Mathilda, G87
White, Andrew Dickson, I5
Whitworth, Charles, B15, B16
Whymper, Frederick, I60
Whyte, William Athenry, I86
Wickenden, William S., H72
Wiggins, Joseph, I121, J130
Wight, Orlando Williams, J52
Wilbraham, Richard, G56, H73
Wilkinson, David, I94
Wilkinson, T.E., J65
Williams, Harold Whitmore, K273
Williams, John, D22
Wilmot Catherine, F3
Wilmot, Martha, F3
Wilson, Charles Townshend, H74
Wilson, Henry Hughes, K375

Wilson, Robert Thomas, F18, F19, F45, F46, F74
Wilson, William Rae, F96
Wilton, Robert Archibald, K132
Windham, Charles Ash, H75
Winter, Nevin Otto, K145
Wolff, Joseph, F107, F108
Wolseley, Garnet Joseph, J25
Wood, Charles, I175
Wood, Evelyn, H81, H82
Wood, Herbert, I122
Wood, John Nicholas Price, K178
Wood, Ruth Kedzie, K214, K253
Woodroofe, Thomas, C19
Woods, Nicholas Augustus, H76
Woodward, Helen, K364
Woolley, Hermann, J141

Wraxall, Frederic Charles Lascelles, H136
Wraxall, Nathaniel William, D25
Wright, Henry Press, H77
Wright, Richardson Little, K237
Wych, Cyril, C17, C18

Yate, Arthur Campbell, J41
Yate, Charles Edward, J42
Yeardley, John, G128
Young, Adam Graham, H93
Young, Charles Christian, K171
Young, Ernest, K245
Young, John Russell, I158

Zur Mühlen, Hermynia, K187
Zwick, Heinrich August, F92
Zychlinski, Ludwik, I49

This book does not end here...

At Open Book Publishers, we are changing the nature of the traditional academic book. The title you have just read will not be left on a library shelf, but will be accessed online by hundreds of readers each month across the globe. We make all our books free to read online so that students, researchers and members of the public who can't afford a printed edition can still have access to the same ideas as you.

Our digital publishing model also allows us to produce online supplementary material, including extra chapters, reviews, links and other digital resources. Find *In the Lands of the Romanovs* on our website to access its online extras. Please check this page regularly for ongoing updates, and join the conversation by leaving your own comments:

http://www.openbookpublishers.com/isbn/9781783740574

If you enjoyed this book, and feel that research like this should be available to all readers, regardless of their income, please think about donating to us. Our company is run entirely by academics, and our publishing decisions are based on intellectual merit and public value rather than on commercial viability. We do not operate for profit and all donations, as with all other revenue we generate, will be used to finance new Open Access publications.

For further information about what we do, how to donate to OBP, additional digital material related to our titles or to order our books, please visit our website.

Knowledge is for sharing

www.ingramcontent.com/pod-product-compliance
Lightning Source LLC
Chambersburg PA
CBHW051802230426
43672CB00012B/2606